September 19–21, 2012
Leuven, Belgium

Association for
Computing Machinery

Advancing Computing as a Science & Profession

PPDP'12

Proceedings of the 2012 ACM SIGPLAN

Principles and Practice of Declarative Programming

In cooperation with:

ACM SIGPLAN

Association for
Computing Machinery

Advancing Computing as a Science & Profession

The Association for Computing Machinery
2 Penn Plaza, Suite 701
New York, New York 10121-0701

Notice to Past Authors of ACM-Published Articles
ACM intends to create a complete electronic archive of all articles and/or other material previously published by ACM. If you have written a work that has been previously published by ACM in any journal or conference proceedings prior to 1978, or any SIG Newsletter at any time, and you do NOT want this work to appear in the ACM Digital Library, please inform permissions@acm.org, stating the title of the work, the author(s), and where and when published.

ISBN: 978-1-4503-1522-7

Additional copies may be ordered prepaid from:

ACM Order Department
PO Box 30777
New York, NY 10087-0777, USA

Phone: 1-800-342-6626 (USA and Canada)
+1-212-626-0500 (Global)
Fax: +1-212-944-1318
E-mail: acmhelp@acm.org
Hours of Operation: 8:30 am – 4:30 pm ET

Printed in the USA

Foreword

It is our great pleasure to welcome you to the *14th Symposium on Principles and Practice of Declarative Programming – PPDP'12.* This year's symposium continues its long tradition of bringing together researchers from the various declarative programming communities, including those working in the logic, constraint and functional programming paradigms. Our mission is to stimulate research in the use of logical formalisms and methods for specifying, performing, and share novel solutions for analysing computations, including mechanisms for mobility, modularity, concurrency, object-orientation, security, verification and static analysis.

The call for papers attracted 42 submissions from Australia, Austria, Belgium, Brazil, Canada, Colombia, Denmark, France, Germany, Italy, Netherlands, Portugal, Qatar, Reunion, Serbia, Singapore, Slovenia, Spain, Sweden, Turkey, the United Kingdom and the United States, although some authors withdrew their papers for various reasons. The Program Committee (PC) too had a very international feel, drawn from 16 different countries. The PC accepted 18 papers in all that cover a variety of topics, including the applications of declarative languages. All papers received at least 3 reviews; external reviewers contributed 38 of these reviews. In addition, the proceedings includes the invited paper, "Symbolic Evaluation Graphs and Term Rewriting — A General Methodology for Analyzing Logic Programs", kindly contributed by Jürgen Giesl and his colleagues, that supports the PPDP'12/LOPSTR'12 joint invited talk. We are delighted that Torben Schaub agreed to give the PPDP'12 invited talk on "Answer Set Solving in Practice". In addition, the program includes the invited talk, "Indexing Structures in Programming Language Semantics and Design" by Marcelo Fiore. This talk celebrates the paper "Semantic analysis of normalisation by evaluation for typed lambda calculus" by Marcelo that (at the time of writing) is the most highly cited paper from the PDPP'02 proceedings.

Putting together *PPDP'12* was a team effort. First of all, we would like to thank the authors and the invited speakers for providing the content of the program. We would like to express our gratitude to the program committee and external reviewers, who worked very hard in reviewing papers and providing suggestions for their improvements. We would also like to thank Dimitar Shterionov for maintaining the *PPDP'12* web site and Jon Sneyers for his effort in advertising the symposium.

We hope that you will find this program stimulating and thought provoking and that the symposium will provide you with a valuable opportunity to share ideas with other researchers and practitioners from institutions around the world.

Danny De Schreye and Gerda Janssens
PDPP'12 General Chairs
University of Leuven, Belgium

Andy King
PPDP'12 Program Chair
University of Kent, UK

Table of Contents

Concurrency

Session Chair: Hayo Thielecke *(University of Birmingham)*

Applications

Session Chair: Julio Mariño *(Universidad Politécnica de Madrid)*

2012 International Symposium on Principles and Practice of Declarative Programming

General Chairs: Danny De Schreye and Gerda Janssens *(University of Leuven, Belgium)*

Program Chair: Andy King *(University of Kent, UK)*

Publicity and Web Chairs: Jon Sneyers and Dimitar Shterionov *(University of Leuven, Belgium)*

Steering Committee Chair: Francisco J. Lopez Fraguas *(Complutense University, Spain)*

Steering Committee:
Michael Leuschel *(University of Düsseldorf, Germany)*
Andreas Podelski *(University of Freiburg, Germany)*
Elvira Albert *(Complutense University, Spain)*
Sergio Antoy *(Portland State University, USA)*
António Porto *(University of Porto, Portugal)*
Maribel Fernandez *(Kings College London, UK)*
Temur Kutsia *(University of Linz, Austria)*
Michael Hanus *(University of Kiel, Germany)*
Jeremy Gibbons *(University of Oxford, UK)*
Peter Schneider-Kamp *(University of Southern Denmark)*

Program Committee:
Slim Abdennadher *(German University in Cairo, Egypt)*
Puri Arenas *(Complutense University, Spain)*
Marcello Balduccini *(Kodak Research Labs, USA)*
Amir Ben-Amram *(Tel-Aviv Academic College, Israel)*
Philip Cox *(Dalhousie University, Canada)*
Marina De Vos *(University of Bath, UK)*
Martin Erwig *(Oregon State University, USA)*
Martin Gebser *(University of Potsdam, Germany)*
Jacob Howe *(City University London, UK)*
Joxan Jaffar *(National University of Singapore, Singapore)*
Gabriele Keller *(University of New South Wales, Australia)*
Julia Lawall *(INRIA Paris-Rocquencourt, France)*
Rita Loogen *(Philipps-Universität Marburg, Germany)*
Greg Michaelson *(Heriot-Watt University, UK)*
Matthew Might *(University of Utah, USA)*
Henrik Nilsson *(University of Nottingham, UK)*
Catuscia Palamidessi *(INRIA Saclay and École Polytechnique, France)*
Kostis Sagonas *(Uppsala University, Sweden and NTUA)*
Taisuke Sato *(Tokyo Institute of Technology, Japan)*
Peter Schneider-Kamp *(University of Southern Denmark, Denmark)*
Tom Schrijvers *(University of Ghent, Belgium)*
Terrance Swift *(Universidade Nova de Lisboa, Portugal and Johns Hopkins University, USA)*
Mirek Truszczynski *(University of Kentucky, USA)*
Stephanie Weirich *(University of Pennsylvania, USA)*

Additional reviewers:

Wyatt Allen
Benjamin Andres
Tim Bauer
Sheng Chen
Sandeep Chintabathina
Mike Codish
Jesús Correas Fernández
James Cussens
Ugo Dal Lago
Mischa Dieterle
Gregory Duck
Robby Findler
Sebastian Fischer
Marco Giunti
Thomas Horstmeyer
Neil Jones
Arne König
Lunjin Lu
Virgile Mogbil
Dimitris Mostrous
Lasse Nielsen
Nikolaos Papaspyrou
Adrian Riesco
Fernando Saenz-Perez
Andrew Santosa
Marius Schneider
Haifeng Shen
Chengzheng Sun
Doaitse Swierstra
Naoyuki Tamura
Kazunori Ueda
Razvan Voicu
Eric Walkingshaw
Roland Yap
Amiram Yehudai
Neng-Fa Zhou

In cooperation with: acm SIGPLAN

Symbolic Evaluation Graphs and Term Rewriting — A General Methodology for Analyzing Logic Programs *

Jürgen Giesl
LuFG Informatik 2, RWTH Aachen University, Germany
giesl@informatik.rwth-aachen.de

Thomas Ströder
LuFG Informatik 2, RWTH Aachen University, Germany
stroeder@informatik.rwth-aachen.de

Peter Schneider-Kamp
Dept. of Mathematics and Computer Science, University of Southern Denmark
petersk@imada.sdu.dk

Fabian Emmes
LuFG Informatik 2, RWTH Aachen University, Germany
emmes@informatik.rwth-aachen.de

Carsten Fuhs
Dept. of Computer Science, University College London, United Kingdom
c.fuhs@cs.ucl.ac.uk

Abstract

There exist many powerful techniques to analyze *termination* and *complexity* of *term rewrite systems* (TRSs). Our goal is to use these techniques for the analysis of other programming languages as well. For instance, approaches to prove termination of definite logic programs by a transformation to TRSs have been studied for decades. However, a challenge is to handle languages with more complex evaluation strategies (such as Prolog, where predicates like the *cut* influence the control flow). In this paper, we present a general methodology for the analysis of such programs. Here, the logic program is first transformed into a *symbolic evaluation graph* which represents all possible evaluations in a finite way. Afterwards, different analyses can be performed on these graphs. In particular, one can generate TRSs from such graphs and apply existing tools for termination or complexity analysis of TRSs to infer information on the termination or complexity of the original logic program.

Categories and Subject Descriptors D.1.6 [*Programming Techniques*]: Logic Programming; F.3.1 [*Logics and Meanings of Programs*]: Specifying and Verifying and Reasoning about Programs—Mechanical Verification; I.2.2 [*Artificial Intelligence*]: Automatic Programming—Automatic Analysis of Algorithms

General Terms Languages, Theory, Verification

Keywords Logic Programs, Prolog, Term Rewriting, Termination, Complexity, Determinacy

* Supported by the DFG under grant GI 274/5-3, the DFG Research Training Group 1298 (*AlgoSyn*), and the Danish Council for Independent Research, Natural Sciences.

PPDP'12, September 19–21, 2012, Leuven, Belgium.

1. Introduction

We are concerned with analyzing "semantical" properties of logic programs, like *termination*, *complexity*, and *determinacy* (i.e., the question whether all queries in a specific class succeed at most once). While there are techniques and tools that analyze logic programs *directly*, we present a general *transformational* methodology for such analyses. In this way, one can re-use existing powerful techniques and tools that have been developed for *term rewriting*.

For well-moded definite logic programs, there are several transformations to TRSs such that termination of the TRS implies termination of the original logic program [33]. We extended these transformations to arbitrary definite programs in [35].

However, Prolog programs typically use the *cut* predicate. To handle the non-trivial control flow induced by cuts, in [37] we introduced a pre-processing method where a Prolog program is first transformed into a *symbolic evaluation graph*. (These graphs were inspired by related approaches to program optimization [38] and were called "termination graphs" in [37].) Symbolic evaluation graphs also represent those aspects of the program that cannot easily be expressed in term rewriting. We also developed similar approaches for other programming languages like Java and Haskell [7–9, 17]. For Prolog, the transformation from the program to the symbolic evaluation graph relies on a new "linear" operational semantics which we presented in [41]. From the symbolic evaluation graph, one can then generate a simpler program (without cuts) whose termination implies termination of the original Prolog program. In [37] we generated definite logic programs from the graph (whose termination could then be analyzed by transforming them further to TRSs, for example). In [40], we presented a more powerful approach which generates so-called *dependency triples* [31, 36] from the graph.

In the current paper, we show that the symbolic evaluation graph cannot only be used for termination analysis, but it is also very suitable as the basis for several other analyses, such as complexity or determinacy analysis. So symbolic evaluation graphs and term rewriting can be seen as a general methodology for the analysis of programming languages like Prolog.[1]

[1] This methodology can also be used to analyze programs in other languages. For example, in [8] we used similar graphs not just for termination proofs, but also for disproving termination and for detecting `NullPointerExceptions` in Java programs.

After recapitulating the underlying operational semantics in Sect. 2, we introduce the symbolic evaluation graph in Sect. 3. To use this graph for different forms of program analysis, we present several new theorems which express the connection between the "abstract evaluations" represented in the graph and the "concrete evaluations" of actual queries.

In Sect. 4, we present a new improved approach for termination analysis of logic programs, where one directly generates *term rewrite systems* from the symbolic evaluation graph. This results in a substantially more powerful approach than [37]. Compared to [40], our new approach is considerably simpler and it allows us to apply *any* tool for termination of TRSs when analyzing the termination of logic programs. So one does not need tools that handle the (non-standard) notion of "dependency triples" anymore.

In Sect. 5 we show that symbolic evaluation graphs and the TRSs generated from the graphs can also be used in order to analyze the *complexity* of logic programs. Here, we rely on recent results which show how to adapt techniques for termination analysis of TRSs in order to prove asymptotic upper bounds for the runtime complexity of TRSs automatically.

Finally, Sect. 6 demonstrates that the symbolic evaluation graph can also be used to analyze whether a class of queries is *deterministic*. Besides being interesting on its own, such a determinacy analysis is also needed in our new approach for complexity analysis of logic programs in Sect. 5.

We implemented all our contributions in our automated termination tool AProVE [15] and performed extensive experiments to compare our approaches with existing analysis techniques which work directly on logic programs. It turned out that our approaches for termination and complexity clearly outperform related existing techniques. For determinacy analysis, our approach can handle many examples where existing methods fail, but there are also many examples where the existing techniques are superior. Thus, here it would be promising to couple our approach with existing ones. All proofs can be found in [18].

2. Preliminaries and Operational Semantics of Prolog

See, e.g., [2] for the basics of logic programming. We label individual cuts to make their scope explicit. Thus, we use a signature Σ containing $\{!_m/0 \mid m \in \mathbb{N}\}$ and all predicate and function symbols. As in the ISO standard for Prolog [23], we do not distinguish between predicate and function symbols and just consider *terms* $\mathcal{T}(\Sigma, \mathcal{V})$ and no atoms.

A *query* is a sequence of terms. Let $Query(\Sigma, \mathcal{V})$ denote the set of all queries, where $\square$ is the empty query. A *clause* is a pair h :- B where the *head* h is a term and the *body* B is a query. If B is empty, then we write just "h" instead of "h :- $\square$". A *logic program* $\mathcal{P}$ is a finite sequence of clauses.

We now briefly recapitulate our operational semantics from [41], which is equivalent to the ISO semantics in [23]. As shown in [41], both semantics yield the same answer substitutions, the same termination behavior, and the same complexity. The advantage of our semantics is that it is particularly suitable for an extension to *classes* of queries, i.e., for the symbolic evaluation of *abstract* states, cf. Sect. 3. This makes our semantics particularly well suited for analyzing logic programs.

Our semantics is given by a set of inference rules that operate on *states*. A *state* has the form $(G_1 \mid \ldots \mid G_n)$ where each G_i is a *goal*. Here, G_1 represents the current query and $(G_2 \mid \ldots \mid G_n)$ represents the queries that have to be considered next. This backtrack information is contained in the state in order to describe the effect of cuts. Since each state contains all backtracking goals, our semantics is *linear* (i.e., an *evaluation* with these rules is just a sequence of states and not a search tree as in the ISO semantics).

Essentially, a *goal* is just a query, i.e., a sequence of terms. But to compute answer substitutions, a goal is labeled by a substitution which collects the unifiers used up to now. So if $(t_1, \ldots, t_k)$ is a query, then a goal has the form $(t_1, \ldots, t_k)_\theta$ for a substitution θ. In addition, a goal can also be labeled by a clause c, where $(t_1, \ldots, t_k)^c_\theta$ means that the next resolution has to be performed with clause c. Moreover, a goal can also be a *scope marker* $?_m$ for $m \in \mathbb{N}$. This marker denotes the end of the scope of cuts $!_m$ labeled with m. Whenever a cut $!_m$ is reached, all goals preceding $?_m$ are discarded.

Def. 1 shows the inference rules for the part of Prolog defining definite logic programming and the cut. See [41] for the inference rules for full Prolog. Here, S and S' are states and the query Q may also be $\square$ (then "(t, Q)" is t).

DEFINITION 1 (Operational Semantics).

$$\frac{\square_\theta \mid S}{S}\ (\text{SUC}) \qquad \frac{(t, Q)^{h\,:-\,B}_\theta \mid S}{(B\sigma, Q\sigma)_{\theta\sigma} \mid S}\ (\text{EVAL})\ \textit{if } mgu(t,h) = \sigma$$

$$\frac{?_m \mid S}{S}\ (\text{FAIL}) \qquad \frac{(t, Q)^{h\,:-\,B}_\theta \mid S}{S}\ (\text{BACKTRACK})\ \textit{if } t \not\sim h$$

$$\frac{(t, Q)_\theta \mid S}{(t, Q)^{c_1[!/!_m]}_\theta \mid \ldots \mid (t, Q)^{c_a[!/!_m]}_\theta \mid ?_m \mid S}\ (\text{CASE})$$

where t is no cut or variable, m is fresh, and $Slice_{\mathcal{P}}(t) = (c_1, \ldots, c_a)$

$$\frac{(!_m, Q)_\theta \mid S \mid ?_m \mid S'}{Q_\theta \mid ?_m \mid S'}\ (\text{CUT})\ \textit{where } S \textit{ contains no } ?_m \qquad \frac{(!_m, Q)_\theta \mid S}{Q_\theta}\ (\text{CUT})\ \textit{where } S \textit{ contains no } ?_m$$

The SUC rule is applicable if the first goal of our sequence could be proved. Then we backtrack to the next goal in the sequence. FAIL means that for the current m-th case analysis, there are no further backtracking possibilities. But the whole evaluation does not have to fail, since the state S may still contain further alternative goals which have to be examined.

To make the backtracking possibilities explicit, the resolution of a program clause with the first atom t of the current goal is split into two operations. The CASE rule determines which clauses could be applied to t by slicing the program according to t's root symbol. Here, $Slice_{\mathcal{P}}(\mathsf{p}(t_1, \ldots, t_n))$ is the sequence of all program clauses "h :- B" from $\mathcal{P}$ where $root(h) = \mathsf{p}/n$. The variables in program clauses are renamed when this is necessary to ensure variable-disjointness with the states. Thus, CASE replaces the current goal $(t, Q)_\theta$ by a goal labeled with the first such clause and adds copies of $(t, Q)_\theta$ labeled by the other potentially applicable clauses as backtracking possibilities. Here, the top-down clause selection rule is taken into account. The cuts in these clauses are labeled by a fresh mark $m \in \mathbb{N}$ (i.e., $c[!/!_m]$ is the clause c where all cuts ! are replaced by $!_m$), and $?_m$ is added at the end of the new backtracking goals to denote their scope.

EXAMPLE 2. *Consider the following logic program.*

$$\mathsf{star}(XS, [\,]) \text{ :- } !. \qquad (1)$$

$$\mathsf{star}([\,], ZS) \text{ :- } !, \mathsf{eq}(ZS, [\,]). \qquad (2)$$

$$\mathsf{star}(XS, ZS) \text{ :- } \mathsf{app}(XS, YS, ZS), \mathsf{star}(XS, YS). \qquad (3)$$

$$\mathsf{app}([\,], YS, YS). \qquad (4)$$

$$\mathsf{app}([X \mid XS], YS, [X \mid ZS]) \text{ :- } \mathsf{app}(XS, YS, ZS). \qquad (5)$$

$$\mathsf{eq}(X, X). \qquad (6)$$

Here, $\mathsf{star}(t_1, t_2)$ *holds iff* t_2 *results from repeated concatenation of* t_1. *So we have* $\mathsf{star}([1,2], [\,])$, $\mathsf{star}([1,2], [1,2])$, $\mathsf{star}([1,2], [1, 2,$

1, 2]), *etc. The cut in rule (2) is needed for termination of queries of the form* star([ ], t). *For the query* star([1, 2], [ ]), *we obtain the following evaluation, where we omitted the labeling by substitutions for readability.*

$$\begin{array}{rl} \mathsf{star}([1,2],[\,]) & \vdash_{\text{CASE}} \\ \mathsf{star}([1,2],[\,])^{(1')} \mid \mathsf{star}([1,2],[\,])^{(2')} \mid \mathsf{star}([1,2],[\,])^{(3)} \mid ?_1 & \vdash_{\text{EVAL}} \\ !_1 \mid \mathsf{star}([1,2],[\,])^{(2')} \mid \mathsf{star}([1,2],[\,])^{(3)} \mid ?_1 & \vdash_{\text{CUT}} \\ \square \mid ?_1 & \vdash_{\text{SUC}} \\ ?_1 & \vdash_{\text{FAIL}} \varepsilon \end{array}$$

So the CASE *rule results in a state which represents a case analysis where we first try to apply the* star-*clause (1). The state also contains the next backtracking goals, since when backtracking later on, we would use clauses (2) and (3). Here,* $(1')$ *denotes* $(1)[!/!_1]$ *and* $(2')$ *denotes* $(2)[!/!_1]$.

For a goal $(t,Q)_\theta^{h\,:-\,B}$, if t unifies[2] with the head h of the program clause, we apply EVAL. This rule replaces t by the body B of the clause and applies the mgu σ to the result. Moreover, σ contributes to the answer substitution, i.e., we replace the label θ by $\theta\sigma$.

If t does not unify with h (denoted "$t \not\sim h$"), we apply the BACKTRACK rule. Then, h :- B cannot be used and we backtrack to the next goal in our backtracking sequence.

Finally, there are two CUT rules. The first rule removes all backtracking information on the level m where the cut was introduced. Since its scope is explicitly represented by $!_m$ and $?_m$, we have turned the cut into a *local* operation depending only on the current state. Note that $?_m$ must not be deleted as the current goal Q_θ could still lead to another cut $!_m$. The second CUT rule is used if $?_m$ is missing (e.g., if a cut $!_m$ is already in the initial query). We treat such states as if $?_m$ were added at the end of the state.

For each query Q, its corresponding *initial state* consists of just $(Q[!/!_1])_{id}$ (i.e., all cuts in Q are labeled by a fresh number like 1 and the goal is labeled by the identity substitution id). The query Q is *terminating* if all evaluations starting in its corresponding initial state are finite. Our inference rules can also be used to define *answer substitutions*.

DEFINITION 3 (Answer Substitution). *Let S be a state with a single goal Q_σ (which may additionally be labeled by a clause c). We say that θ is an* answer substitution *for S if there is an evaluation from S to a state $(\square_{\sigma\theta} \mid S_{suffix})$ for a (possibly empty) state S_{suffix} (i.e., $(\square_{\sigma\theta} \mid S_{suffix})$ is obtained by repeatedly applying rules from Def. 1 to S). Similarly, θ is an* answer substitution *for a query if it is an answer substitution for the query's initial state.*

3. From Prolog to Symbolic Evaluation Graphs

We now explain the construction of *symbolic evaluation graphs* which represent all evaluations of a logic program for a certain *class* of queries. While we already presented such graphs in [37], here we introduce a new formulation of the corresponding abstract inference rules which is suitable for generating TRSs afterwards. Moreover, we present new theorems (Thm. 5, 8, and 10) which express the exact connection between abstract and concrete evaluations. These theorems will be used to prove the soundness of our analyses later on.

We consider classes of atomic queries described by a $\mathsf{p}/n \in \Sigma$ and a *moding function* $m : \Sigma \times \mathbb{N} \to \{in, out\}$. So m determines which arguments of a symbol are "inputs". The corresponding class of queries is $\mathcal{Q}_m^{\mathsf{p}} = \{\mathsf{p}(t_1,\ldots,t_n) \mid \mathcal{V}(t_i) = \varnothing$ for all i with $m(\mathsf{p},i) = in\}$. Here, "$\mathcal{V}(t_i)$" denotes the set of all variables occurring in t_i. So for the program of Ex. 2, we might regard the class of queries $\mathcal{Q}_m^{\mathsf{star}}$ where $m(\mathsf{star},1) = m(\mathsf{star},2) = in$. Thus, $\mathcal{Q}_m^{\mathsf{star}} = \{\mathsf{star}(t_1,t_2) \mid t_1, t_2$ are ground$\}$.

To represent classes of queries, we regard *abstract* states that stand for sets of concrete states. Instead of "ordinary" variables $\mathcal{N}$, abstract states use abstract variables $\mathcal{A} = \{T_1, T_2, \ldots\}$ representing fixed, but arbitrary terms (i.e., $\mathcal{V} = \mathcal{N} \uplus \mathcal{A}$).

To obtain concrete states from an abstract one, we use *concretizations*. A concretization is a substitution γ which replaces all abstract variables by concrete terms, i.e., $Dom(\gamma) = \mathcal{A}$ and $\mathcal{V}(Range(\gamma)) \subseteq \mathcal{N}$. To determine by which terms an abstract variable may be instantiated, we add a knowledge base $KB = (\mathcal{G},\mathcal{U})$ to each state, where $\mathcal{G} \subseteq \mathcal{A}$ and $\mathcal{U} \subseteq \mathcal{T}(\Sigma,\mathcal{V}) \times \mathcal{T}(\Sigma,\mathcal{V})$. The variables in $\mathcal{G}$ may only be instantiated by ground terms, i.e., $\mathcal{V}(Range(\gamma|_\mathcal{G})) = \varnothing$. Here, "$\gamma|_\mathcal{G}$" denotes the restriction of γ to $\mathcal{G}$, i.e., $\gamma|_\mathcal{G}(X) = \gamma(X)$ for $X \in \mathcal{G}$ and $\gamma|_\mathcal{G}(X) = X$ for $X \in \mathcal{V} \setminus \mathcal{G}$. A pair $(t,t') \in \mathcal{U}$ means that we are restricted to concretizations γ where $t\gamma \not\sim t'\gamma$, i.e., t and t' must not be unifiable after γ is applied. Then we say that γ is a concretization *w.r.t.* KB.

Thus, an abstract state has the form $(S; KB)$. Here, S has the form $(G_1 \mid \ldots \mid G_n)$ where the G_i are goals over the signature Σ and the abstract variables $\mathcal{A}$ (i.e., they do not contain variables from $\mathcal{N}$). In contrast to [37], we again label all goals (except scope markers) by substitutions $\theta : \mathcal{V} \to \mathcal{T}(\Sigma,\mathcal{A})$ in order to store which substitutions were applied during an evaluation. These substitution labels will be necessary for the synthesis of TRSs in Sect. 4.

The notion of *concretization* can also be used for states. A (concrete) state S' is a concretization of $(S; KB)$ if there exists a concretization γ w.r.t. KB such that S' results from $S\gamma$ by replacing the substitution labels of its goals by arbitrary (possibly different) substitutions $\theta : \mathcal{N} \to \mathcal{T}(\Sigma,\mathcal{N})$. To ease readability, we often write "$S\gamma$" to denote an arbitrary concretization of $(S; KB)$. Let $\mathcal{CON}(S; KB)$ denote the set of all concretizations of an abstract state $(S; KB)$.

For a class $\mathcal{Q}_m^{\mathsf{p}}$ with p/n, now the *initial state* is $(\mathsf{p}(T_1,\ldots,T_n)_{id}, (\mathcal{G},\varnothing))$, where $\mathcal{G}$ contains all T_i with $m(\mathsf{p},i) = in$.

We now adapt the inference rules of Def. 1 to abstract states. The rules SUC, FAIL, CUT, and CASE do not change the knowledge base and are straightforward to adapt. In Def. 1, we determined which of the rules EVAL and BACKTRACK to apply by trying to unify the first term t with the head h of the corresponding clause. But in the abstract case we might need to apply EVAL for some concretizations and BACKTRACK for others. The abstract BACKTRACK rule in Def. 4 can be used if $t\gamma$ does not unify with h for *any* concretization γ. Otherwise, $t\gamma$ unifies with h for *some* concretizations γ, but possibly not for *others*. Thus, the abstract EVAL rule has two successor states to combine both the concrete EVAL and the concrete BACKTRACK rule. Consequently, we now obtain symbolic evaluation trees instead of sequences.

DEFINITION 4 (Abstract Inference Rules).

$$\frac{(\square_\theta \mid S); KB}{S; KB}\ (\text{SUC}) \qquad \frac{((!_m,Q)_\theta \mid S \mid ?_m \mid S'); KB}{(Q_\theta \mid ?_m \mid S'); KB}\ (\text{CUT})\ \textit{where } S \textit{ contains no } ?_m$$

$$\frac{(?_m \mid S); KB}{S; KB}\ (\text{FAIL}) \qquad \frac{((!_m,Q)_\theta \mid S); KB}{Q_\theta; KB}\ (\text{CUT})\ \textit{where } S \textit{ contains no } ?_m$$

$$\frac{((t,Q)_\theta \mid S); KB}{((t,Q)_\theta^{c_1[!/!_m]} \mid \ldots \mid (t,Q)_\theta^{c_a[!/!_m]} \mid ?_m \mid S); KB}\ (\text{CASE})$$

where t is no cut or variable, m is fresh, $Slice_\mathcal{P}(t) = (c_1,\ldots,c_a)$

[2] In this paper, we consider unification with occurs check. Our method could be extended to unification without occurs check, but we left this as future work since most programs do not rely on the absence or presence of the occurs check.

$$\frac{((t,Q)^{h\,:\text{-}\,B}_{\theta} \mid S); KB}{S; KB} \;(\textsc{Backtrack})\quad \begin{array}{l}\textit{if there is no concretiza-}\\ \textit{tion } \gamma \textit{ w.r.t. } KB \textit{ such that}\\ t\gamma \sim h.\end{array}$$

$$\frac{((t,Q)^{h\,:\text{-}\,B}_{\theta} \mid S); (\mathcal{G},\mathcal{U})}{((B\sigma,Q\sigma)_{\theta\sigma} \mid S'); (\mathcal{G}',\mathcal{U}\sigma|_{\mathcal{G}}) \qquad S; (\mathcal{G},\mathcal{U} \cup \{(t,h)\})} \;(\textsc{Eval})$$

if $mgu(t,h) = \sigma$*. W.l.o.g.,* $\mathcal{V}(Range(\sigma))$ *only contains fresh abstract variables and* $Dom(\sigma)$ *contains all previously occurring variables. Moreover,* $\mathcal{G}' = \mathcal{A}(Range(\sigma|_{\mathcal{G}}))$ *and* S' *results from* S *by applying the substitution* $\sigma|_{\mathcal{G}}$ *to its goals and by composing* $\sigma|_{\mathcal{G}}$ *with the substitution labels of its goals.*

To handle "sharing" effects correctly [37], w.l.o.g. we assume that $mgu(t,h) = \sigma$ renames all occurring variables to fresh abstract variables in EVAL. The knowledge base is updated differently for the successors corresponding to the concrete EVAL and BACKTRACK rule. For all concretizations corresponding to the second successor of EVAL, the concretization of t does not unify with h. Hence, here we add (t,h) to $\mathcal{U}$.

Now consider concretizations γ where $t\gamma$ and h unify, i.e., these concretizations γ correspond to the first successor of the EVAL rule. Then for any $T \in \mathcal{G}$, $T\gamma$ is a ground instance of $T\sigma$. Hence, we replace all $T \in \mathcal{G}$ by $T\sigma$, i.e., we apply $\sigma|_{\mathcal{G}}$ to S. The new set $\mathcal{G}'$ of variables that may only be instantiated by ground terms are the abstract variables occurring in $Range(\sigma|_{\mathcal{G}})$ (denoted "$\mathcal{A}(Range(\sigma|_{\mathcal{G}}))$"). As before, t is replaced by the instantiated clause body B and the previous substitution label θ is composed with the mgu σ (yielding $\theta\sigma$).

Thm. 5 states that any concrete evaluation with Def. 1 can also be simulated with the abstract rules of Def. 4.

THEOREM 5 (Soundness of Abstract Rules). *Let* $(S; KB)$ *be an abstract state with a concretization* $S\gamma \in \mathcal{CON}(S; KB)$*, and let* S_{next} *be the successor of* $S\gamma$ *according to the operational semantics in Def. 1. Then the abstract state* $(S; KB)$ *has a successor* $(S'; KB')$ *according to an inference rule from Def. 4 such that* $S_{next} \in \mathcal{CON}(S'; KB')$.

As an example, consider the program from Ex. 2 and the class of queries $\mathcal{Q}_m^{\mathsf{star}}$. The corresponding initial state is $(\mathsf{star}(T_1,T_2)_{id}; (\{T_1,T_2\},\varnothing))$. A *symbolic evaluation* starting with this state A is depicted in Fig. 6. The nodes of such a symbolic evaluation graph are states and each step from a node to its children is done by an inference rule. To save space, we omitted the knowledge base from the states $(S; (\mathcal{G},\mathcal{U}))$. Instead, we overlined all variables contained in $\mathcal{G}$ and labeled those edges where new information is added to $\mathcal{U}$.

The child of A is B with $(\mathsf{star}(\overline{T_1},\overline{T_2})^{(1')}_{id} \mid \mathsf{star}(\overline{T_1},\overline{T_2})^{(2')}_{id} \mid \mathsf{star}(\overline{T_1},\overline{T_2})^{(3)}_{id} \mid ?_1)$. In Fig. 6 we simplified the states by removing markers $?_m$ that occur at the end of a state. This is possible, since applying the first CUT rule to a state ending in $?_m$ corresponds to applying the second CUT rule to the same state without $?_m$. Moreover, $(1')$ and $(2')$ again abbreviate $(1)[!/!_1]$ and $(2)[!/!_1]$.

In B, $(1')$ is used for the next evaluation. EVAL yields two successors: In C, $\sigma_1 = mgu(\mathsf{star}(\overline{T_1},\overline{T_2}),\mathsf{star}(XS,[\,])) = \{\overline{T_1}/\overline{T_3}, XS/\overline{T_3}, \overline{T_2}/[\,]\}$ leads to $((!_1)_{\sigma_1} \mid \mathsf{star}(\overline{T_3},[\,])^{(2')}_{\sigma_2} \mid \mathsf{star}(\overline{T_3},[\,])^{(3)}_{\sigma_2})$. Here, $\sigma_2 = \sigma_1|_{\{\overline{T_1},\overline{T_2}\}}$. In the second successor D of B, we add the information $\mathsf{star}(\overline{T_1},\overline{T_2}) \not\sim \mathsf{star}(XS,[\,])$ to $\mathcal{U}$ (thus, we labeled the edge from B to D accordingly).

Unfortunately, even for terminating queries, in general the rules of Def. 4 yield an infinite tree. The reason is that there is no bound on the size of terms represented by the abstract variables and hence, the abstract EVAL rule can be applied infinitely often. To represent all possible evaluations in a finite way, we need additional inference rules to obtain finite symbolic evaluation graphs instead of infinite trees.

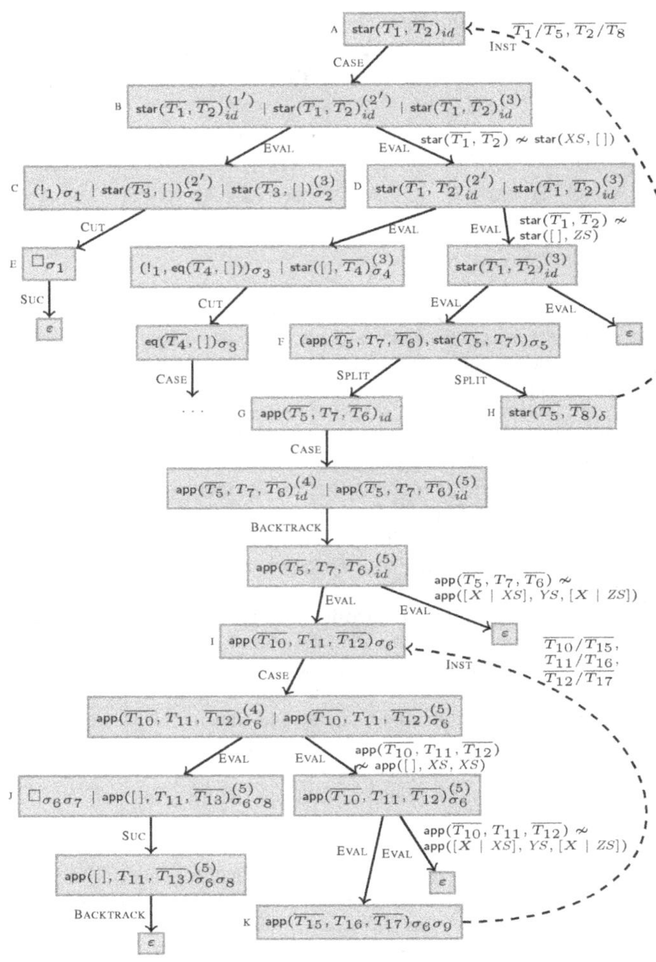

Figure 6. Symbolic Evaluation Graph for Ex. 2

To this end, we use an additional INST rule which allows us to connect the current state $(S; KB)$ with a previous state $(S'; KB')$, provided that the current state is an instance of the previous state. In other words, every concretization of $(S; KB)$ must be a concretization of $(S'; KB')$. More precisely, there must be a matching substitution μ such that $S'\mu = S$ up to the substitutions used for labeling goals in S' and S. These substitution labels do not have to be taken into account here, since we will not generate rewrite rules from paths that traverse INST edges in Sect. 4. Moreover, for $KB' = (\mathcal{G}',\mathcal{U}')$ and $KB = (\mathcal{G},\mathcal{U})$, $\mathcal{G}'$ and $\mathcal{G}$ must be the same (modulo μ) and all constraints from $\mathcal{U}'$ must occur in $\mathcal{U}$ (modulo μ). Then we say that μ is *associated* to $(S; KB)$ and label the resulting INST edge with μ. For example, in Fig. 6, $\mu = \{\overline{T_1}/\overline{T_5}, \overline{T_2}/\overline{T_8}\}$ is associated to H and the edge from H to A is labeled with μ. We only define the INST rule for states containing a single goal. As indicated by our experiments, this is no severe restriction in practice.[3]

[3] In [37] and in our implementation, we use an additional inference rule to split up sequences of goals, but we omitted it here for readability. Adding this rule allows us to construct a symbolic evaluation graph for each program and query.

DEFINITION 7 (Abstract Rules: INST).

$$\frac{S;(\mathcal{G},\mathcal{U})}{S';(\mathcal{G}',\mathcal{U}')}\ (\text{INST})$$ *if $S = Q_\theta$ and $S' = Q'_{\theta'}$ or $S = Q^c_\theta$ and $S' = Q'^c_{\theta'}$ for some non-empty queries Q and Q', such that there is a μ with $Dom(\mu) \subseteq \mathcal{A}$, $\mathcal{V}(Range(\mu)) \subseteq \mathcal{A}$, $Q = Q'\mu$, $\mathcal{G} = \bigcup_{T\in\mathcal{G}'} \mathcal{V}(T\mu)$, and $\mathcal{U}'\mu \subseteq \mathcal{U}$.*

Thm. 8 states that every concrete state represented by an INST node is also represented by its successor.

THEOREM 8 (Soundness of INST). *Let $(S; KB)$ be an abstract state, let $(S'; KB')$ be its successor according to the INST rule, and let μ be associated to $(S; KB)$. If $S\gamma \in \mathcal{CON}(S;KB)$, then for $\gamma'=\mu\gamma$ we have $S'\gamma' \in \mathcal{CON}(S';KB')$.*

Moreover, we also need a SPLIT inference rule to split a state $((t, Q)_\theta; KB)$ into $(t_{id}; KB)$ and $((Q\delta)_\delta; KB')$, where δ approximates the answer substitutions for t. Such a SPLIT is often needed to make the INST rule applicable. We say that δ is *associated* to $((t, Q)_\theta; KB)$. The previous substitution label θ does not have to be taken into account here, since we will not generate rewrite rules from paths that traverse SPLIT nodes in Sect. 4. Thus, we can reset the substitution label θ to id in the first successor of the SPLIT node and store the associated substitution δ in the substitution label of the second successor. Similar to the INST rule, we only define the SPLIT rule for states containing a single goal.

DEFINITION 9 (Abstract Rules: SPLIT).

$$\frac{(t,Q)_\theta;(\mathcal{G},\mathcal{U})}{t_{id};(\mathcal{G},\mathcal{U}) \quad (Q\delta)_\delta;(\mathcal{G}',\mathcal{U}\delta)}\ (\text{SPLIT})$$ *where δ replaces all previously occurring variables from $\mathcal{A}\setminus\mathcal{G}$ by fresh abstract variables and $\mathcal{G}' = \mathcal{G} \cup NextG(t,\mathcal{G})\delta$.*

Here, $NextG$ is defined as follows. We assume that we have a *groundness analysis* function $Ground_\mathcal{P} : \Sigma \times 2^\mathbb{N} \to 2^\mathbb{N}$, see, e.g., [22]. If $\mathsf{p}/n \in \Sigma$ and $\{i_1,\ldots,i_m\} \subseteq \{1,\ldots,n\}$, then $Ground_\mathcal{P}(\mathsf{p},\{i_1,\ldots,i_m\}) = \{j_1,\ldots,j_k\}$ means that any query $\mathsf{p}(t_1,\ldots,t_n) \in \mathcal{T}(\Sigma,\mathcal{N})$ where $t_{i_1},\ldots,t_{i_m}$ are ground only has answer substitutions θ where $t_{j_1}\theta,\ldots,t_{j_k}\theta$ are ground. So $Ground_\mathcal{P}$ approximates which positions of p will become ground if the "input" positions $i_1,\ldots,i_m$ are ground. Now if $t = \mathsf{p}(t_1,\ldots,t_n) \in \mathcal{T}(\Sigma,\mathcal{A})$ is an abstract term where $t_{i_1},\ldots,t_{i_m}$ become ground in every concretization (i.e., all their variables are from $\mathcal{G}$), then $NextG(t,\mathcal{G})$ returns all variables in t that will be made ground by every answer substitution for any concretization of t. Thus, $NextG(t,\mathcal{G})$ contains the variables of $t_{j_1},\ldots,t_{j_k}$. So formally

$$NextG(\mathsf{p}(t_1,\ldots,t_n),\mathcal{G}) = \bigcup_{j\in Ground_\mathcal{P}(\mathsf{p},\ \{i\mid\mathcal{V}(t_i)\subseteq\mathcal{G}\}\ )} \mathcal{V}(t_j).$$

Hence, in the second successor of the SPLIT rule, the variables in $NextG(t,\mathcal{G})$ can be added to the groundness set $\mathcal{G}$. Since these variables were renamed by δ, we extend $\mathcal{G}$ by $NextG(t,\mathcal{G})\delta$.

For instance, in Fig. 6, we split the query $\mathsf{app}(\overline{T_5},T_7,\overline{T_6})$, $\mathsf{star}(\overline{T_5},T_7)$ in state F. Thus, the first successor of F is $\mathsf{app}(\overline{T_5},T_7,\overline{T_6})$ in state G. By groundness analysis, we infer that every successful evaluation of $\mathsf{app}(\overline{T_5},T_7,\overline{T_6})$ instantiates T_7 by ground terms, i.e., $Ground_\mathcal{P}(\mathsf{app},\{1,3\}) = \{1,2,3\}$. Thus, for $\mathcal{G} = \{T_5,T_6\}$, we have $NextG(\mathsf{app}(T_5,T_7,T_6),\mathcal{G}) = \mathcal{V}(T_5)\cup\mathcal{V}(T_7)\cup\mathcal{V}(T_6) = \{T_5,T_7,T_6\}$. So in the second successor H of F, we use the substitution $\delta(T_7) = T_8$ and extend the groundness set $\mathcal{G}$ of F by $NextG(\mathsf{app}(T_5,T_7,T_6),\mathcal{G})\delta = \{T_5,T_8,T_6\}$. Thus, T_8 is also overlined in Fig. 6.

Thm. 10 shows the soundness of SPLIT. Suppose that we apply the SPLIT rule to $((t,Q)_\theta;KB)$, which yields $(t_{id};KB)$ and $((Q\delta)_\delta;KB')$. Any evaluation of a concrete state $(t\gamma,Q\gamma) \in \mathcal{CON}((t,Q)_\theta;KB)$ consists of parts where one evaluates $t\gamma$ (yielding some answer substitution θ') and of parts where one evaluates $Q\gamma\theta'$. Clearly, those parts which correspond to evaluations of $t\gamma$ can be simulated by the left successor of the SPLIT node (since $t\gamma \in \mathcal{CON}(t_{id};KB)$). Thm. 10 states that the parts of the overall evaluation which correspond to evaluations of $Q\gamma\theta'$ can be simulated by the right successor of the SPLIT node (i.e., $Q\gamma\theta' \in \mathcal{CON}((Q\delta)_\delta;KB')$).

THEOREM 10 (Soundness of SPLIT). *Let $((t,Q)_\theta;KB)$ be an abstract state and let $(t_{id};KB)$ and $((Q\delta)_\delta;KB')$ be its successors according to the SPLIT rule. Let $(t\gamma,Q\gamma) \in \mathcal{CON}((t,Q)_\theta;KB)$ and let θ' be an answer substitution of $(t\gamma)_{id}$. Then we have $Q\gamma\theta' \in \mathcal{CON}((Q\delta)_\delta;KB')$.*

We define *symbolic evaluation graphs* as a subclass of the graphs obtained by the rules of Def. 4, 7, and 9. They must not have any cycles consisting only of INST edges, as this would lead to trivially non-terminating TRSs. Moreover, their only leaves may be nodes where no inference rule is applicable anymore (i.e., the graphs must be "fully expanded"). The graph in Fig. 6 is indeed a symbolic evaluation graph.

DEFINITION 11 (Symbolic Evaluation Graph). *A finite graph built from an initial state using Def. 4, 7, and 9 is a* symbolic evaluation graph *(or "evaluation graph" for short) iff there is no cycle consisting only of* INST *edges and all leaves are of the form $(\varepsilon; KB)$.*[4]

4. From Symbolic Evaluation Graphs to TRSs – Termination Analysis

Now our goal is to show termination of all concrete states represented by the graph's initial state. To this end, we synthesize a TRS from the symbolic evaluation graph. This TRS has the following property: if there is an evaluation from a concretization of one state to a concretization of another state which may be crucial for termination, then there is a corresponding rewrite sequence w.r.t. the TRS. Then automated tools for termination analysis of TRSs can be used to show termination of the synthesized TRS and this implies termination of the original logic program. See, e.g., [13, 16, 43] for an overview of techniques for automatically proving termination of TRSs.

For the basics of term rewriting, we refer to [6]. A *term rewrite system* $\mathcal{R}$ is a finite set of rules $\ell \to r$ where $\ell \notin \mathcal{V}$ and $\mathcal{V}(r) \subseteq \mathcal{V}(\ell)$. The rewrite relation $t \to_\mathcal{R} t'$ for two terms t and t' holds iff there is an $\ell \to r \in \mathcal{R}$, a position pos, and a substitution σ such that $\ell\sigma = t|_{pos}$ and $t' = t[r\sigma]_{pos}$. Here, $t|_{pos}$ is the subterm of t at position pos and $t[r\sigma]_{pos}$ results from replacing the subterm $t|_{pos}$ at position pos in t by the term $r\sigma$. The rewrite step is *innermost* (denoted $t \xrightarrow{i}_\mathcal{R} t'$) iff no proper subterm of $\ell\sigma$ can be rewritten.

To obtain a TRS from an evaluation graph Gr, we encode the states as terms. For each state $s = (S;(\mathcal{G},\mathcal{U}))$, we use two fresh function symbols f^{in}_s and f^{out}_s. The arguments of f^{in}_s are the variables in $\mathcal{G}$ (which represent ground terms). The arguments of f^{out}_s are those remaining abstract variables which will be made ground by every answer substitution for any concretization of s. They are again determined by groundness analysis [22]. Formally, the encoding of states is done by two functions enc^{in} and enc^{out}.

For instance, for the state F in Fig. 6, we obtain $enc^{in}(\text{F}) = f^{in}_\text{F}(T_5,T_6)$ (as $\mathcal{G} = \{T_5,T_6\}$ in F) and $enc^{out}(\text{F}) = f^{out}_\text{F}(T_7)$. The reason is that if γ instantiates T_5 and T_6 by ground terms, then

[4] The application of inference rules to abstract states is not deterministic. In our prover AProVE, we implemented a heuristic [39] to generate symbolic evaluation graphs automatically which turned out to be very suitable for subsequent analyses in our empirical evaluations.

every answer substitution of $(\mathsf{app}(T_5, T_7, T_6)\gamma, \mathsf{star}(T_5, T_7)\gamma)$ instantiates $T_7\gamma$ to a ground term as well.

For an INST node like H with associated substitution μ we do not introduce fresh function symbols, but use the function symbol of its (more general) successor instead. So we take the terms resulting from its successor A and apply μ to them. In other words, $enc^{in}(\text{H}) = enc^{in}(\text{A})\,\mu = f^{in}_{\text{A}}(T_1, T_2)\,\mu = f^{in}_{\text{A}}(T_5, T_8)$ and $enc^{out}(\text{H}) = enc^{out}(\text{A})\,\mu = f^{out}_{\text{A}}\,\mu = f^{out}_{\text{A}}$.

In the following, for an evaluation graph Gr and an inference rule RULE, $Rule(Gr)$ denotes all nodes of Gr to which RULE was applied. Let $Succ_i(s)$ denote the i-th child of node s and $Succ_i(Rule(Gr))$ denotes the set of i-th children of all nodes from $Rule(Gr)$.

DEFINITION 12 (Encoding States as Terms). *Let s be an abstract state with a single goal (i.e., $s = ((t_1, \ldots, t_k)_\theta; (\mathcal{G}, \mathcal{U}))$), and let $\mathcal{V}(s) = \mathcal{V}(t_1) \cup \ldots \cup \mathcal{V}(t_k)$. We define*

$$enc^{in}(s) = \begin{cases} enc^{in}(Succ_1(s))\,\mu, & \text{if } s \in Inst(Gr) \text{ where } \mu \text{ is associated to } s \\ f^{in}_s(\mathcal{G}^{in}(s)), & \text{otherwise, where } \mathcal{G}^{in}(s) = \mathcal{G} \cap \mathcal{V}(s) \end{cases}$$

$$enc^{out}(s) = \begin{cases} enc^{out}(Succ_1(s))\,\mu, & \text{if } s \in Inst(Gr) \text{ where } \mu \text{ is associated to } s \\ f^{out}_s(\mathcal{G}^{out}(s)), & \text{otherwise, where } \mathcal{G}^{out}(s) = NextG((t_1, \ldots, t_k), \mathcal{G}) \setminus \mathcal{G} \end{cases}$$

Here, we extended $NextG$ to work also on queries:

$$NextG((t_1, \ldots, t_k), \mathcal{G}) = NextG(t_1, \mathcal{G}) \cup NextG(\,(t_2, \ldots, t_k),\ NextG(t_1, \mathcal{G})\,).$$

So to compute $NextG((t_1, \ldots, t_k), \mathcal{G})$ for a query $(t_1, \ldots, t_k)$, in the beginning we only know that the variables in $\mathcal{G}$ represent ground terms. Then we compute the variables $NextG(t_1, \mathcal{G})$ which are made ground by all answer substitutions for concretizations of t_1. Next, we compute $NextG(t_2, NextG(t_1, \mathcal{G}))$ which are made ground by all answer substitutions for concretizations of t_2, etc.

Now we encode the paths of Gr as rewrite rules. However, we only consider *connection paths* of Gr, which suffice to analyze termination. Connection paths are non-empty paths that start in the root node of the graph or in a successor of an INST or SPLIT node, provided that these states are not INST or SPLIT nodes themselves. So the start states in our example are A, G, and I. Moreover, connection paths end in an INST, SPLIT, or SUC node or in the successor of an INST node, while not traversing INST or SPLIT nodes or successors of INST nodes in between. So in our example, the end states are A, E, F, H, I, J, K, but apart from E and J, connection paths may not traverse any of these end nodes in between.

Thus, we have connection paths from A to E, A to F, G to I, I to J, and I to K. These paths cover all ways through the graph except for INST edges (which are covered by the encoding of states to terms), for SPLIT edges (which we consider later in Def. 15), and for graph parts without cycles or SUC nodes (which cannot cause non-termination).

DEFINITION 13 (Connection Path). *A path $\pi = s_1 \ldots s_k$ is a* connection path *of an evaluation graph Gr iff $k > 1$ and*

- $s_1 \in \{root(Gr)\} \cup Succ_1(Inst(Gr) \cup Split(Gr)) \cup Succ_2(Split(Gr))$
- $s_k \in Inst(Gr) \cup Split(Gr) \cup Suc(Gr) \cup Succ_1(Inst(Gr))$
- *for all* $1 \leq j < k$, $s_j \notin Inst(Gr) \cup Split(Gr)$
- *for all* $1 < j < k$, $s_j \notin Succ_1(Inst(Gr))$

For a connection path π, let σ_π represent the unifiers that were applied along the path. These unifiers can be determined by "comparing" the substitution labels of the first and the last state of the path (i.e., the goal in π's first state has a substitution label θ and the first goal of π's last state is labeled by $\theta\sigma_\pi$). So for the connection path π from A to F we have $\sigma_\pi = \sigma_5$, where $\sigma_5(\overline{T_1}) = \overline{T_5}$ and $\sigma_5(\overline{T_2}) = \overline{T_6}$. For this path, we generate rewrite rules which evaluate the instantiated input term $enc^{in}(\text{A})\,\sigma_\pi$ for the start node A to its output term $enc^{out}(\text{A})\,\sigma_\pi$ if the input term $enc^{in}(\text{F})$ for the end node can be evaluated to its output term $enc^{out}(\text{F})$. So we get $enc^{in}(\text{A})\,\sigma_\pi \to \mathsf{u}_{\text{A,F}}(\,enc^{in}(\text{F}), \mathcal{V}(enc^{in}(\text{A})\,\sigma_\pi)\,)$ and $\mathsf{u}_{\text{A,F}}(\,enc^{out}(\text{F}),\ \mathcal{V}(enc^{in}(\text{A})\,\sigma_\pi)\,) \to enc^{out}(\text{A})\,\sigma_\pi$ for a fresh function symbol $\mathsf{u}_{\text{A,F}}$. In our example, this yields

$$f^{in}_{\text{A}}(T_5, T_6) \to \mathsf{u}_{\text{A,F}}(f^{in}_{\text{F}}(T_5, T_6), T_5, T_6) \tag{7}$$

$$\mathsf{u}_{\text{A,F}}(f^{out}_{\text{F}}(T_7), T_5, T_6) \to f^{out}_{\text{A}} \tag{8}$$

However, for connection paths π' like the one from A to E which end in a SUC node, the resulting rewrite rule directly evaluates the instantiated input term $enc^{in}(\text{A})\,\sigma_{\pi'}$ for the start node A to its output term $enc^{out}(\text{A})\,\sigma_{\pi'}$. So we obtain

$$f^{in}_{\text{A}}(T_3, [\,]) \to f^{out}_{\text{A}} \tag{9}$$

DEFINITION 14 (Rules for Connection Paths). *Let π be a connection path $s_1 \ldots s_k$ in a symbolic evaluation graph. Let the (only) goal in s_1 be labeled by the substitution θ and let the first goal in s_k be labeled by the substitution $\theta\,\sigma_\pi$. If $s_k \in Suc(Gr)$, then we define $ConnectionRules(\pi) = \{enc^{in}(s_1)\sigma_\pi \to enc^{out}(s_1)\,\sigma_\pi\}$. Otherwise, $ConnectionRules(\pi) =$*

$$\{\, enc^{in}(s_1)\,\sigma_\pi \to \mathsf{u}_{s_1,s_k}(\,enc^{in}(s_k),\ \mathcal{V}(enc^{in}(s_1)\,\sigma_\pi)\,),\quad \mathsf{u}_{s_1,s_k}(\,enc^{out}(s_k),\ \mathcal{V}(enc^{in}(s_1)\,\sigma_\pi)\,) \to enc^{out}(s_1)\,\sigma_\pi \,\},$$

where u_{s_1,s_k} is a fresh function symbol.

In addition to the rules for connection paths, we also need rewrite rules to simulate the evaluation of SPLIT nodes like F. Let δ be the substitution associated to F (i.e., δ represents the answer substitution of F's first successor G). Then the SPLIT node F succeeds (i.e., $enc^{in}(\text{F})\,\delta$ can be evaluated to $enc^{out}(\text{F})\,\delta$) if both successors G and H succeed (i.e., $enc^{in}(\text{G})\,\delta$ can be evaluated to $enc^{out}(\text{G})\,\delta$ and $enc^{in}(\text{H})$ can be evaluated to $enc^{out}(\text{H})$). Note that $enc^{in}(\text{F})$ and $enc^{in}(\text{G})$ only contain "input" arguments (i.e., abstract variables from $\mathcal{G}$) and thus, δ does not modify them. Hence, $enc^{in}(\text{F})\,\delta = enc^{in}(\text{F})$ and $enc^{in}(\text{G})\,\delta = enc^{in}(\text{G})$. So we obtain

$$f^{in}_{\text{F}}(T_5, T_6) \to \mathsf{u}_{\text{F,G}}(f^{in}_{\text{G}}(T_5, T_6), T_5, T_6) \tag{10}$$

$$\mathsf{u}_{\text{F,G}}(f^{out}_{\text{G}}(T_8), T_5, T_6) \to \mathsf{u}_{\text{G,H}}(f^{in}_{\text{A}}(T_5, T_8), T_5, T_6, T_8) \tag{11}$$

$$\mathsf{u}_{\text{G,H}}(f^{out}_{\text{A}}, T_5, T_6, T_8) \to f^{out}_{\text{F}}(T_8) \tag{12}$$

DEFINITION 15 (Rules for Split, $\mathcal{R}(Gr)$). *Let $s \in Split(Gr)$, $s_1 = Succ_1(s)$, and $s_2 = Succ_2(s)$. Moreover, let δ be the substitution associated to s. Then $SplitRules(s) =$*

$$\{\, enc^{in}(s) \to \mathsf{u}_{s,s_1}(\,enc^{in}(s_1),\ \mathcal{V}(enc^{in}(s))\,),$$
$$\mathsf{u}_{s,s_1}(\,enc^{out}(s_1)\,\delta,\ \mathcal{V}(enc^{in}(s))\,) \to \mathsf{u}_{s_1,s_2}(\,enc^{in}(s_2),\ \mathcal{V}(enc^{in}(s)) \cup \mathcal{V}(enc^{out}(s_1)\delta)\,),$$
$$\mathsf{u}_{s_1,s_2}(enc^{out}(s_2), \mathcal{V}(enc^{in}(s)) \cup \mathcal{V}(enc^{out}(s_1)\,\delta)) \to enc^{out}(s)\delta \,\}$$

$\mathcal{R}(Gr)$ consists of $ConnectionRules(\pi)$ for all connection paths π and of $SplitRules(s)$ for all SPLIT *nodes s of Gr.*

For the graph Gr of Fig. 6, the resulting TRS $\mathcal{R}(Gr)$ consists of (7) – (12) and the connection rules (13), (14) for the path from G to I (where $\sigma_6(\overline{T_5}) = [\overline{T_9} \mid \overline{T_{10}}], \sigma_6(T_7) = T_{11}, \sigma_6(\overline{T_6}) = [\overline{T_9} \mid \overline{T_{12}}]$), the rules (15), (16) for I to K (where $\sigma_9(\overline{T_{10}}) = [\overline{T_{14}} \mid \overline{T_{15}}], \sigma_9(T_{11}) = T_{16}, \sigma_9(\overline{T_{12}}) = [\overline{T_{14}} \mid \overline{T_{17}}]$), and (17) for I to J (where $\sigma_8 = \sigma_7|_{\{\overline{T_{10}}, \overline{T_{12}}\}}$ with $\sigma_8(\overline{T_{10}}) = [\,], \sigma_8(\overline{T_{12}}) = \overline{T_{13}}$).

$$f_{\mathsf{G}}^{in}([T_9 \mid T_{10}], [T_9 \mid T_{12}]) \to \mathsf{u}_{\mathsf{G,I}}(f_{\mathsf{I}}^{in}(T_{10}, T_{12}), T_9, T_{10}, T_{12}) \quad (13)$$

$$\mathsf{u}_{\mathsf{G,I}}(f_{\mathsf{I}}^{out}(T_{11}), T_9, T_{10}, T_{12}) \to f_{\mathsf{G}}^{out}(T_{11}) \quad (14)$$

$$f_{\mathsf{I}}^{in}([T_{14} \mid T_{15}], [T_{14} \mid T_{17}]) \to \mathsf{u}_{\mathsf{I,K}}(f_{\mathsf{I}}^{in}(T_{15}, T_{17}), T_{14}, T_{15}, T_{17}) \quad (15)$$

$$\mathsf{u}_{\mathsf{I,K}}(f_{\mathsf{I}}^{out}(T_{16}), T_{14}, T_{15}, T_{17}) \to f_{\mathsf{I}}^{out}(T_{16}) \quad (16)$$

$$f_{\mathsf{I}}^{in}([\,], T_{13}) \to f_{\mathsf{I}}^{out}(T_{13}) \quad (17)$$

Thm. 16 states that the resulting TRS can simulate all successful evaluations represented in the graph, i.e., it simulates all computations of the logic program.

THEOREM 16 (TRS Simulates Semantics). *Let* $s = (S; KB)$ *be a start node of a connection path or a* SPLIT *node in a graph* Gr, $S\gamma \in \mathcal{CON}(s)$, *and let* θ *be an answer substitution for* $S\gamma$. *Then* $enc^{in}(s)\gamma \xrightarrow{i}^{+}_{\mathcal{R}(Gr)} enc^{out}(s)\gamma\theta$.

Virtually all modern TRS termination tools can prove that $\mathcal{R}(Gr)$ is terminating in our example. Thm. 17 shows that this implies termination of all queries corresponding to the root of Gr. Hence, by our approach, one can prove termination of non-definite logic programs like Ex. 2 automatically.

THEOREM 17 (Soundness of Termination Analysis). *Let* $\mathcal{P}$ *be a logic program,* $\mathsf{p} \in \Sigma$, m *a moding function, and let* Gr *be a symbolic evaluation graph for* $\mathcal{P}$ *whose root is the initial state corresponding to* $\mathcal{Q}_m^{\mathsf{p}}$. *If the TRS* $\mathcal{R}(Gr)$ *is innermost terminating, then there is no infinite evaluation starting with any query from* $\mathcal{Q}_m^{\mathsf{p}}$. *Thus, all these queries are terminating w.r.t. the program* $\mathcal{P}$.

We implemented our approach for termination analysis in the tool AProVE [15]. In addition to the cut, our implementation handles many further features of Prolog. For our experiments, AProVE ran on all 477 Prolog programs of the *Termination Problem Database* (TPDB, version 8.0.6), which is the collection of examples used in the annual *International Termination Competition*.[5] 300 of them are definite logic programs, whereas the remaining 177 programs contain advanced features like cuts. 37 of the 477 examples are known to be non-terminating. The experiments were run on 2.2 GHz Quad-Opteron 848 Linux machines with a timeout of 60 seconds per program. In the table, "**Yes**" indicates the number of examples where termination could be proved and "**RT**" is the average runtime (in seconds) per example.

	Yes	RT
AProVE-[35]	265	7.1
AProVE-[37]	287	7.6
AProVE-[40]	340	5.7
AProVE-New	342	6.5

All termination tools for logic programs except AProVE ignore cuts, i.e., they try to prove termination of the program that results from removing the cuts. This is sensible, since cuts are not always needed for termination. Indeed, the variant AProVE-[35] implements our technique from [35] which ignores cuts and directly translates logic programs to TRSs. Still, it proves termination of 31 of the 177 non-definite programs. Other existing termination tools would not yield better results, as AProVE-[35] is already the most powerful tool for definite logic programs (as shown by the experiments in [35]) and as most of the remaining non-definite examples do not terminate anymore if one removes cuts. AProVE-[37] implements our approach from [37] which introduced evaluation graphs, but transforms them to definite logic programs instead of TRSs. This approach is much more powerful than [35] on examples with cut, but it fails on many definite logic programs where [35] was successful. The approach of the current paper (implemented in AProVE-New)[6] considers other paths in the graph than [37]. Thus, it simulates the evaluations of the original logic program more concisely and results in a more powerful approach (both for definite and non-definite programs).

[40] improved upon [37] by generating "dependency triples" from evaluation graphs. Indeed, AProVE-New and AProVE-[40] have almost the same power. But while the back-end of [40] required a tool that can handle the (non-standard) notion of dependency triples, our new approach works with any tool for termination of TRSs. Moreover, the approach of the current paper has the advantage that the TRSs generated for termination analysis can also be used for analyzing other properties like complexity, as shown in Sect. 5.

5. From Symbolic Evaluation Graphs to TRSs – Complexity Analysis

We briefly recapitulate the required notions for complexity of TRSs. The *defined symbols* of a TRS $\mathcal{R}$ are $\Sigma_d = \{root(\ell) \mid \ell \to r \in \mathcal{R}\}$, i.e., these are the function symbols that can be "evaluated". So for $\mathcal{R}(Gr)$ from Sect. 4, we have $\Sigma_d = \{f_{\mathsf{A}}^{in}, \mathsf{u}_{\mathsf{A,F}}, f_{\mathsf{F}}^{in}, \mathsf{u}_{\mathsf{F,G}}, \mathsf{u}_{\mathsf{G,H}}, f_{\mathsf{G}}^{in}, \mathsf{u}_{\mathsf{G,I}}, f_{\mathsf{I}}^{in}, \mathsf{u}_{\mathsf{I,K}}\}$. Different notions of complexity have been proposed for TRSs. In this paper, we focus on *innermost runtime complexity* [21], which corresponds to the notion of complexity used for programming languages. Here, one only considers rewrite sequences starting with *basic* terms $\mathsf{f}(t_1, \ldots, t_n)$, where $\mathsf{f} \in \Sigma_d$ and $t_1, \ldots, t_n$ do not contain symbols from Σ_d. The *innermost runtime complexity function* $irc_{\mathcal{R}}$ maps any $n \in \mathbb{N}$ to the length of the longest sequence of $\xrightarrow{i}_{\mathcal{R}}$-steps starting with a basic term t where $|t| \leq n$. Here, $|t|$ is the number of variables and function symbols occurring in t. To measure the complexity of a TRS $\mathcal{R}$, we determine the asymptotic growth of $irc_{\mathcal{R}}$, i.e., we say that $\mathcal{R}$ has linear complexity iff $irc_{\mathcal{R}}(n) \in \mathcal{O}(n)$, quadratic complexity iff $irc_{\mathcal{R}}(n) \in \mathcal{O}(n^2)$, etc. Tools for automated complexity analysis of TRSs can automatically determine $irc_{\mathcal{R}(Gr)}(n) \in \mathcal{O}(n)$ for $\mathcal{R}(Gr) = \{(7) - (17)\}$ from Sect. 4.[7]

Moreover, we also have to define the notion of "complexity" for logic programs. For a logic program $\mathcal{P}$ and a query Q, we consider the length of the longest evaluation starting in the initial state for Q. As shown in [41], this length is equal to the number of unification attempts when traversing the whole SLD tree according to the ISO semantics [23], up to a constant factor.[8] For a moding function m, and any term $\mathsf{p}(t_1, \ldots, t_n)$, its *moded size* is $|\mathsf{p}(t_1, \ldots, t_n)|_m = 1 + \Sigma_{i \in \{i \,\mid\, 1 \leq i \leq n, m(\mathsf{p}, i) = in\}} |t_i|$. Thus, for a class of queries $\mathcal{Q}_m^{\mathsf{p}}$, the Prolog *runtime complexity function* $prc_{\mathcal{P}, \mathcal{Q}_m^{\mathsf{p}}}$ maps any $n \in \mathbb{N}$ to the length of the longest evaluation starting with the initial state for some query $Q \in \mathcal{Q}_m^{\mathsf{p}}$ with $|Q|_m \leq n$.

To analyze $prc_{\mathcal{P}, \mathcal{Q}_m^{\mathsf{p}}}(n)$, we generate an evaluation graph Gr for $\mathcal{Q}_m^{\mathsf{p}}$ as in Sect. 3 and obtain the TRS $\mathcal{R}(Gr)$ as in Sect. 4. At first sight, one might expect that asymptotically, $irc_{\mathcal{R}(Gr)}(n)$ is indeed an upper bound of $prc_{\mathcal{P}, \mathcal{Q}_m^{\mathsf{p}}}(n)$. This would allow us to use

[5] In these competitions, AProVE was the most powerful tool for termination of logic programs, see `http://termination-portal.org/wiki/Termination_Competition/`.

[6] To benefit from the full power of rewriting-based termination analysis, in our implementation we generate TRSs together with an *argument filtering*, as in [35]. In this way, one can also handle examples where ground information on the arguments of predicates is not sufficient.

[7] For example, this can be determined by the tool TCT [3]. While AProVE was the most powerful tool for innermost runtime complexity analysis in the recent termination competitions, here it only obtains $irc_{\mathcal{R}(Gr)}(n) \in \mathcal{O}(n^2)$.

[8] In contrast, other approaches like [10–12, 30] use the number of resolution steps to measure complexity. As long as one does not consider dynamic built-in predicates like assert/1, these measures are asymptotically equivalent, as the number of unification attempts at each resolution step is bounded by a constant (i.e., by the number of program clauses).

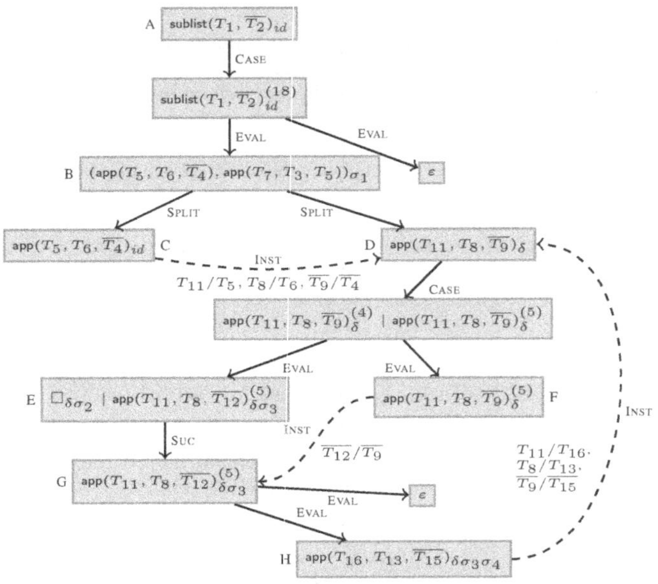

Figure 19. Symbolic Evaluation Graph for Ex. 18

existing methods for complexity analysis of TRSs in order to derive upper bounds on the runtime of logic programs.

In fact for Ex. 2, both $irc_{\mathcal{R}(Gr)}(n)$ and $prc_{\mathcal{P},\mathcal{Q}^{\mathsf{star}}_m}(n)$ are in $\mathcal{O}(n)$, i.e., the complexity of the logic program for $\mathcal{Q}^{\mathsf{star}}_m$ is also linear. But in general, $irc_{\mathcal{R}(Gr)}(n)$ is not necessarily an upper bound of $prc_{\mathcal{P},\mathcal{Q}^{\mathsf{p}}_m}(n)$. This can happen if Gr contains a SPLIT node whose first successor is *not deterministic*. A query Q is *deterministic* iff it generates at most one answer substitution at most once [25]. Similarly, we call an abstract state s *deterministic* iff each of its concretizations has at most one evaluation to a state of the form $(\square_\theta \mid S)$.

EXAMPLE 18. *To see the problems with* SPLIT *nodes whose first successor is not deterministic, consider the following program from the TPDB which consists of the clauses (4) and (5) for* app *and the following rule:*

$$\mathsf{sublist}(X,Y) \text{ :- } \mathsf{app}(P,U,Y),\ \mathsf{app}(V,X,P). \tag{18}$$

We regard the class of queries $\mathcal{Q}^{\mathsf{sublist}}_m$, *where* $m(\mathsf{sublist},1) = out$ *and* $m(\mathsf{sublist},2) = in$. *The program computes (by backtracking) all sublists of a given list. Its complexity is quadratic since the first* app*-call results in a linear evaluation with a linear number of solutions. The second* app*-call again needs linear time, but due to backtracking, it is called linearly often.*

We obtain the evaluation graph Gr *in Fig. 19. For readability, we omitted labels* $t \leadsto t'$ *on* EVAL*-edges. We have* $\sigma_1(T_1) = T_3, \sigma_1(\overline{T_2}) = \overline{T_4}$; $\sigma_2(T_8) = \overline{T_{12}}, \sigma_2(\overline{T_9}) = \overline{T_{12}}, \sigma_2(T_{11}) = []$; $\sigma_3(\overline{T_9}) = \overline{T_{12}}$; $\sigma_4(T_8) = T_{13}, \sigma_4(\overline{T_{12}}) = [\overline{T_{14}} \mid \overline{T_{15}}], \sigma_4(T_{11}) = [\overline{T_{14}} \mid T_{16}]$; *and* $\delta(T_3) = T_8, \delta(T_5) = \overline{T_9}, \delta(T_6) = \overline{T_{10}}, \delta(T_7) = T_{11}$.

This symbolic evaluation graph has connection paths from A *to* B, D *to* E, D *to* G, D *to* F, *and* G *to* H. *It gives rise to the following TRS* $\mathcal{R}(Gr)$.

$$f^{in}_{\mathsf{A}}(T_4) \to \mathsf{u}_{\mathsf{A,B}}(f^{in}_{\mathsf{B}}(T_4), T_4) \tag{19}$$

$$\mathsf{u}_{\mathsf{A,B}}(f^{out}_{\mathsf{B}}(T_5,T_6,T_7,T_3), T_4) \to f^{out}_{\mathsf{A}}(T_3) \tag{20}$$

$$f^{in}_{\mathsf{B}}(T_4) \to \mathsf{u}_{\mathsf{B,C}}(f^{in}_{\mathsf{D}}(T_4), T_4) \tag{21}$$

$$\mathsf{u}_{\mathsf{B,C}}(f^{out}_{\mathsf{D}}(T_9,T_{10}), T_4) \to \mathsf{u}_{\mathsf{C,D}}(f^{in}_{\mathsf{D}}(T_9), T_4, T_9, T_{10}) \tag{22}$$

$$\mathsf{u}_{\mathsf{C,D}}(f^{out}_{\mathsf{D}}(T_{11},T_8), T_4, T_9, T_{10}) \to f^{out}_{\mathsf{B}}(T_9,T_{10},T_{11},T_8) \tag{23}$$

$$f^{in}_{\mathsf{D}}(T_{12}) \to f^{out}_{\mathsf{D}}([], T_{12}) \tag{24}$$

$$f^{in}_{\mathsf{D}}(T_{12}) \to \mathsf{u}_{\mathsf{D,G}}(f^{in}_{\mathsf{G}}(T_{12}), T_{12}) \tag{25}$$

$$\mathsf{u}_{\mathsf{D,G}}(f^{out}_{\mathsf{G}}(T_{11},T_8), T_{12}) \to f^{out}_{\mathsf{D}}(T_{11},T_8) \tag{26}$$

$$f^{in}_{\mathsf{D}}(T_9) \to \mathsf{u}_{\mathsf{D,F}}(f^{in}_{\mathsf{G}}(T_9), T_9) \tag{27}$$

$$\mathsf{u}_{\mathsf{D,F}}(f^{out}_{\mathsf{G}}(T_{11},T_8), T_9) \to f^{out}_{\mathsf{D}}(T_{11},T_8) \tag{28}$$

$$f^{in}_{\mathsf{G}}([T_{14} \mid T_{15}]) \to \mathsf{u}_{\mathsf{G,H}}(f^{in}_{\mathsf{D}}(T_{15}), T_{14}, T_{15}) \tag{29}$$

$$\mathsf{u}_{\mathsf{G,H}}(f^{out}_{\mathsf{D}}(T_{16},T_{13}), T_{14}, T_{15}) \to f^{out}_{\mathsf{G}}([T_{14} \mid T_{16}], T_{13}) \tag{30}$$

Its termination is easy to prove by tools like AProVE, *which implies termination of the logic program by Thm. 17. However, this TRS cannot be used for complexity analysis, as* $irc_{\mathcal{R}(Gr)}$ *is linear whereas the runtime complexity of the original logic program is quadratic. For an analogous reason, complexity analysis of such examples is also not possible by transformations from logic programs to TRSs like [33, 35].*

For complexity analysis, we need a more sophisticated treatment of SPLIT *nodes than for termination analysis. For termination, we only have to approximate the form of the answer substitutions that are computed for the first successor of a* SPLIT *node. This suffices to analyze termination of the evaluations starting in the second successor. However for complexity analysis, we also need to know* how many *answer substitutions are computed for the first successor of a* SPLIT *node, since the evaluation of the second successor is repeated for each such answer substitution. If the first successor of a* SPLIT *node (i.e., a node like* C) *has* k *answer substitutions, then the evaluation of the second successor (i.e., of* D) *is repeated* k *times. This is not simulated by the TRS, which replaces backtracking by non-deterministic choice. So after applying rule (21), one has to perform a "first* f^{in}_{D}*-reduction" to evaluate the* f^{in}_{D}*-term in the right-hand side to a* f^{out}_{D}*-term. There exist several possibilities for this reduction (e.g., by using (24), (25), or (27)). So one chooses one such reduction non-deterministically. Afterwards, the remaining rewrite sequence continues with rule (22). However, the TRS does not reflect that in the logic program, one would backtrack afterwards and repeat this remaining rewrite sequence with rule (22), for* every possible *"first* f^{in}_{D}*-reduction" from* $f^{in}_{\mathsf{D}}(\ldots)$ *to* $f^{out}_{\mathsf{D}}(\ldots)$.

However, for the star-example of Ex. 2, the first successor G of the only SPLIT node F in the graph of Fig. 6 is deterministic. The reason is that there is at most one answer substitution for any query $\mathsf{app}(t_5, t_7, t_6)$, where t_5 and t_6 are ground terms. In Sect. 6, we will show how to use evaluation graphs in order to analyze determinacy automatically.

Nevertheless, even if all first successors of SPLIT nodes are deterministic, $irc_{\mathcal{R}(Gr)}$ is not necessarily an upper bound of $prc_{\mathcal{P},\mathcal{Q}^{\mathsf{p}}_m}$. This can happen if (i) a SPLIT node s can reach itself via a non-empty path, (ii) its first successor s' reaches a SUC node s'', and (iii) s'' reaches a cycle in the graph.

EXAMPLE 21. *Consider the following program* $\mathcal{P}$ *and the set of queries* $\mathcal{Q}^{\mathsf{a}}_m$ *where* $m(\mathsf{a},1) = in$.

$$\begin{aligned} \mathsf{a}(X) &\text{ :- } \mathsf{b}(X), \mathsf{q}(X).\\ \mathsf{b}(X)&.\\ \mathsf{b}(X) &\text{ :- } \mathsf{p}(X).\\ \mathsf{p}(\mathsf{s}(X)) &\text{ :- } \mathsf{p}(X).\\ \mathsf{q}(\mathsf{s}(X)) &\text{ :- } \mathsf{a}(X). \end{aligned}$$

In the corresponding symbolic evaluation graph in Fig. 20, dotted arrows abbreviate paths of several edges. We have $\sigma_1(\overline{T_1}) = \overline{T_2}$, $\sigma_2(\overline{T_2}) = \overline{T_3}$, $\sigma_3(\overline{T_3}) = \overline{T_4}$, $\sigma_4(\overline{T_4}) = \mathsf{s}(\overline{T_5})$, *and* $\sigma_5(\overline{T_2}) =$

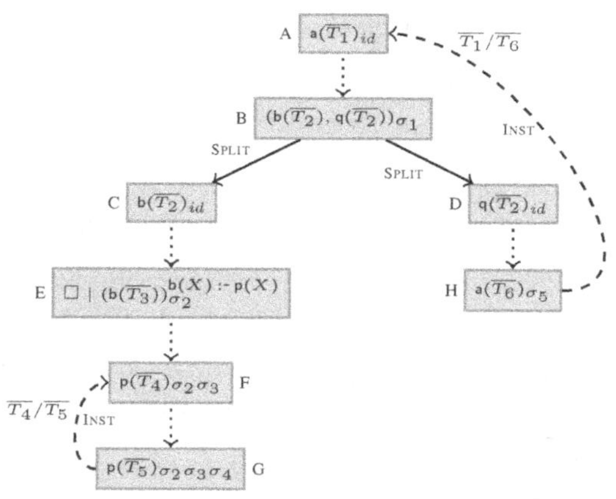

Figure 20. Symbolic Evaluation Graph for Ex. 21

$\mathsf{s}(\overline{T_6})$. *Here, (i) the* SPLIT *node* B *reaches itself via a non-empty path, (ii) its first successor* C *reaches a* SUC *node* E*, and (iii)* E *reaches another cycle (from* F *to* G*). The graph has connection paths from* A *to* B*,* C *to* E*,* C *to* F*,* F *to* G*, and* D *to* H*. It results in the following TRS.*

$$f^{in}_{\mathrm{A}}(T_2) \to \mathsf{u}_{\mathrm{A,B}}(f^{in}_{\mathrm{B}}(T_2), T_2) \quad (31)$$
$$\mathsf{u}_{\mathrm{A,B}}(f^{out}_{\mathrm{B}}, T_2) \to f^{out}_{\mathrm{A}} \quad (32)$$
$$f^{in}_{\mathrm{B}}(T_2) \to \mathsf{u}_{\mathrm{B,C}}(f^{in}_{\mathrm{C}}(T_2), T_2) \quad (33)$$
$$\mathsf{u}_{\mathrm{B,C}}(f^{out}_{\mathrm{C}}, T_2) \to \mathsf{u}_{\mathrm{C,D}}(f^{in}_{\mathrm{D}}(T_2), T_2) \quad (34)$$
$$\mathsf{u}_{\mathrm{C,D}}(f^{out}_{\mathrm{D}}, T_2) \to f^{out}_{\mathrm{B}} \quad (35)$$
$$f^{in}_{\mathrm{C}}(T_3) \to f^{out}_{\mathrm{C}} \quad (36)$$
$$f^{in}_{\mathrm{C}}(T_4) \to \mathsf{u}_{\mathrm{C,F}}(f^{in}_{\mathrm{F}}(T_4), T_4) \quad (37)$$
$$\mathsf{u}_{\mathrm{C,F}}(f^{out}_{\mathrm{F}}, T_4) \to f^{out}_{\mathrm{C}} \quad (38)$$
$$f^{in}_{\mathrm{F}}(\mathsf{s}(T_5)) \to \mathsf{u}_{\mathrm{F,G}}(f^{in}_{\mathrm{F}}(T_5), T_5) \quad (39)$$
$$\mathsf{u}_{\mathrm{F,G}}(f^{out}_{\mathrm{F}}, T_5) \to f^{out}_{\mathrm{F}} \quad (40)$$
$$f^{in}_{\mathrm{D}}(\mathsf{s}(T_6)) \to \mathsf{u}_{\mathrm{D,H}}(f^{in}_{\mathrm{A}}(T_6), T_6) \quad (41)$$
$$\mathsf{u}_{\mathrm{D,H}}(f^{out}_{\mathrm{A}}, T_6) \to f^{out}_{\mathrm{D}} \quad (42)$$

For the complexity $prc_{\mathcal{P},\mathcal{Q}^{\mathrm{a}}_m}$ *of this program, each call to* b *yields both a success (from* C *to* E *in constant time) and a failing further computation (by the cycle from* F *to* G *which takes linear time). Since* b *is called linearly often (by the cycle from* A *to* H*), we obtain a quadratic runtime in total.*

However, the resulting TRS only has linear complexity. Here, the backtracking after the SUC *node* E *is modeled by non-deterministic choice. So to evaluate an* f^{in}_{C}*-term, one* either *uses rule (36) which corresponds to the path from* C *to* E or *the rules (37), (38) which correspond to the path from* C *to* F, but not both. *The traversal of the cycle from* A *to* H *can only continue if one evaluates* f^{in}_{C} *by rule (36), which works in constant time. Only then can the right-hand side of (33) evaluate to the left-hand side of (34).*

Def. 22 captures when $irc_{\mathcal{R}(Gr)}$ is no upper bound of $prc_{\mathcal{P},\mathcal{Q}^{\mathsf{p}}_m}$.

DEFINITION 22 (Multiplicative SPLIT Nodes). *A* SPLIT *node s in a symbolic evaluation graph Gr is called* multiplicative *iff its first successor is not deterministic or if s satisfies the three conditions* (i) – (iii) *above. Let* $mults(Gr)$ *be the set of all multiplicative* SPLIT *nodes of Gr.*

The only SPLIT node F in the graph of Fig. 6 is indeed non-multiplicative. Its first successor G is deterministic and while F can reach itself via a non-empty path, the only SUC node reachable from its first successor G is J, but J cannot reach a cycle in Gr (i.e., (iii) does not hold).

Thm. 23 shows that if the symbolic evaluation graph only contains non-multiplicative SPLIT nodes, our approach can also be used for complexity analysis of logic programs. So the linear complexity of $\mathcal{R}(Gr)$ in our example indeed implies linear complexity of the original program from Ex. 2.

THEOREM 23 (Soundness of Complexity Analysis I). *Let* $\mathcal{P}$ *be a logic program,* $\mathsf{p} \in \Sigma$*,* m *a moding function, and let* Gr *be a symbolic evaluation graph for* $\mathcal{P}$ *whose root is the initial state corresponding to* $\mathcal{Q}^{\mathsf{p}}_m$*. If* Gr *has no multiplicative* SPLIT *nodes, then* $prc_{\mathcal{P},\mathcal{Q}^{\mathsf{p}}_m}(n) \in \mathcal{O}(irc_{\mathcal{R}(Gr)}(n))$.

We now extend our approach to also handle examples like Ex. 18 where the evaluation graph Gr contains multiplicative SPLIT nodes (i.e., here we have $mults(Gr) = \{\mathrm{B}\}$).

To this end, we generate two *separate* TRSs $\mathcal{R}(Gr_{\mathrm{C}})$ and $\mathcal{R}(Gr_{\mathrm{D}})$ for the subgraphs starting in the two successors C and D of a multiplicative SPLIT node like B in Ex. 18, and multiply their complexity functions $irc_{\mathcal{R}(Gr_{\mathrm{C}}),\mathcal{R}(Gr)}$ and $irc_{\mathcal{R}(Gr_{\mathrm{D}}),\mathcal{R}(Gr)}$. Here, $irc_{\mathcal{R}(Gr_{\mathrm{C}}),\mathcal{R}(Gr)}$ differs from the ordinary complexity function $irc_{\mathcal{R}(Gr)}$ by only counting those rewrite steps that are done with the sub-TRS $\mathcal{R}(Gr_{\mathrm{C}}) \subseteq \mathcal{R}(Gr)$.

In general, for any $\mathcal{R}' \subseteq \mathcal{R}$, the function $irc_{\mathcal{R}',\mathcal{R}}$ maps any $n \in \mathbb{N}$ to the maximal number of $\xrightarrow{\mathrm{i}}_{\mathcal{R}'}$-steps that occur in any sequence of $\xrightarrow{\mathrm{i}}_{\mathcal{R}}$-steps starting with a basic term t where $|t| \leq n$. Related notions of "relative" complexity for TRSs were used in, e.g., [4, 21, 32, 42]. Most existing automated complexity provers can also approximate $irc_{\mathcal{R}',\mathcal{R}}$ asymptotically.

The function $irc_{\mathcal{R}(Gr_{\mathrm{C}}),\mathcal{R}(Gr)}$ indeed also yields an upper bound on the number of answer substitutions for C, because the number of answer substitutions cannot be larger than the number of evaluation steps. In our example, both the runtime and the number of answer substitutions for the call $\mathsf{app}(T_5, T_6, \overline{T_4})$ in node C is linear in the size of $\overline{T_4}$'s concretization. Thus, the call $\mathsf{app}(T_{11}, T_8, \overline{T_9})$ in node D, which has linear runtime itself, needs to be repeated a linear number of times. Hence, by multiplying the linear runtime complexities of $irc_{\mathcal{R}(Gr_{\mathrm{C}}),\mathcal{R}(Gr)}$ and $irc_{\mathcal{R}(Gr_{\mathrm{D}}),\mathcal{R}(Gr)}$, we obtain the correct result that the runtime of the original logic program is (at most) quadratic.

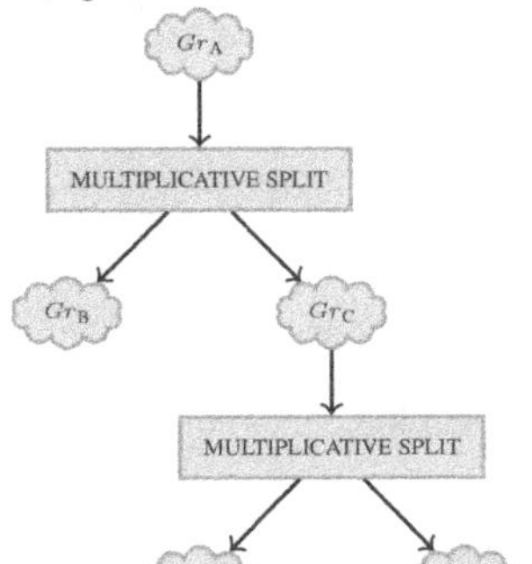

So we use the multiplicative SPLIT nodes of a symbolic evaluation graph Gr to decompose Gr into subgraphs, such that multiplicative SPLIT nodes only occur as the leaves of subgraphs. As an example, the symbolic evaluation graph on the side is decomposed into the subgraphs $Gr_{\mathrm{A}}, \ldots, Gr_{\mathrm{E}}$ (the subgraphs Gr_{A} and Gr_{C} include the respective multiplicative SPLIT node as a leaf). We now determine the runtime complexities $irc_{\mathcal{R}(Gr_{\mathrm{A}}),\mathcal{R}(Gr)}, \ldots, irc_{\mathcal{R}(Gr_{\mathrm{E}}),\mathcal{R}(Gr)}$ separately and combine them to obtain an upper bound for the runtime of the whole logic program. As discussed above, the runtime complexity functions resulting from subgraphs of a multiplicative SPLIT node have to be multiplied. In contrast, the runtimes for subgraphs above a multiplicative SPLIT node have to be added. So for the graph on the side, we obtain $irc_{\mathcal{R}(Gr_{\mathrm{A}}),\mathcal{R}(Gr)}(n) + irc_{\mathcal{R}(Gr_{\mathrm{B}}),\mathcal{R}(Gr)}(n) \cdot (irc_{\mathcal{R}(Gr_{\mathrm{C}}),\mathcal{R}(Gr)}(n) + irc_{\mathcal{R}(Gr_{\mathrm{D}}),\mathcal{R}(Gr)}(n) \cdot irc_{\mathcal{R}(Gr_{\mathrm{E}}),\mathcal{R}(Gr)}(n))$ as an approximation for the complexity of the logic program.

To ensure that the symbolic evaluation graph can indeed be decomposed into subgraphs as desired, we have to require that no multiplicative SPLIT node can reach itself again.

DEFINITION 24 (Decomposable Graphs). *A symbolic evaluation graph Gr is called* decomposable *iff there is no non-empty path from a node $s \in mults(Gr)$ to itself.*

The graph in Ex. 18 is decomposable. However, decomposability is a restriction and there are programs in the TPDB whose complexity we cannot analyze, because our graph construction yields a non-decomposable evaluation graph.[9] For instance, the graph in Ex. 21 is not decomposable.

For any node s, the *subgraph at node s* starts in s and stops when reaching multiplicative SPLIT nodes.

DEFINITION 25 (Subgraphs). *Let Gr be a decomposable evaluation graph with nodes V and edges E (i.e., $Gr = (V, E)$) and let $s \in V$. We define the* subgraph of Gr at node s *as the minimal graph $Gr_s = (V_s, E_s)$ with $s \in V_s$ that satisfies the following property: whenever $s_1 \in V_s \setminus mults(Gr)$ and $(s_1, s_2) \in E$, then $s_2 \in V_s$ and $(s_1, s_2) \in E_s$.*

Now we decompose the symbolic evaluation graph into the subgraph at the root node and into the subgraphs at all successors of multiplicative SPLIT nodes. So the graph in Ex. 18 is decomposed into Gr_{A}, Gr_{C}, and Gr_{D}, where Gr_{A} contains the 4 nodes from A to B and to ε, Gr_{C} contains all other nodes, and Gr_{D} contains all nodes of Gr_{C} except C.

$\mathcal{R}(Gr_{\text{A}}) = \{(19) - (23)\}$ consists of $ConnectionRules(\pi)$ for the connection path π from A to B and of $SplitRules(\text{B})$. For both Gr_{C} and Gr_{D}, we get the same TRS, because C is an instance of D, i.e., $\mathcal{R}(Gr_{\text{C}}) = \mathcal{R}(Gr_{\text{D}}) = \{(24) - (30)\}$.

For the complexity of the original logic program, we combine the complexities of the sub-TRSs as discussed before. So we multiply the complexities resulting from subgraphs of multiplicative SPLIT nodes, and add all other complexities. The function $cplx_s(n)$ approximates the runtime of the logic program represented by the subgraph of Gr at node s.

DEFINITION 26 (Complexity for Subgraphs). *Let $Gr = (V, E)$ be decomposable. For any $s \in V$ and $n \in \mathbb{N}$, let*

$$cplx_s(n) = \begin{cases} cplx_{Succ_1(s)}(n) \cdot cplx_{Succ_2(s)}(n), & \text{if } s \in mults(Gr) \\ irc_{\mathcal{R}(Gr_s), \mathcal{R}(Gr)}(n) + \\ \Sigma_{s' \in mults(Gr) \cap Gr_s}\ cplx_{s'}(n), & \text{otherwise} \end{cases}$$

So in Ex. 18, we obtain $cplx_{\text{A}}(n) =$

$$\begin{aligned} & irc_{\mathcal{R}(Gr_{\text{A}}), \mathcal{R}(Gr)}(n) + cplx_{\text{B}}(n) & = \\ & irc_{\mathcal{R}(Gr_{\text{A}}), \mathcal{R}(Gr)}(n) + cplx_{\text{C}}(n) \cdot cplx_{\text{D}}(n) & = \\ & irc_{\mathcal{R}(Gr_{\text{A}}), \mathcal{R}(Gr)}(n) + irc_{\mathcal{R}(Gr_{\text{C}}), \mathcal{R}(Gr)}(n) \cdot irc_{\mathcal{R}(Gr_{\text{D}}), \mathcal{R}(Gr)}(n) & \end{aligned}$$

Thm. 27 states that combining the complexities of the TRSs as in Def. 26 indeed yields an upper bound for the complexity of the original logic program.

THEOREM 27 (Soundness of Complexity Analysis II). *Let $\mathcal{P}$ be a logic program, $\mathsf{p} \in \Sigma$, m a moding function, and let Gr be a symbolic evaluation graph for $\mathcal{P}$ whose root is the initial state corresponding to $\mathcal{Q}_m^{\mathsf{p}}$. If Gr is decomposable, then we have $prc_{\mathcal{P}, \mathcal{Q}_m^{\mathsf{p}}}(n) \in \mathcal{O}(cplx_{root(Gr)}(n))$.*

For Ex. 18, tools for complexity analysis of TRSs like TCT and AProVE automatically prove $irc_{\mathcal{R}(Gr_{\text{A}}), \mathcal{R}(Gr)}(n) \in \mathcal{O}(n)$,[10] $irc_{\mathcal{R}(Gr_{\text{C}}), \mathcal{R}(Gr)}(n) \in \mathcal{O}(n)$, $irc_{\mathcal{R}(Gr_{\text{D}}), \mathcal{R}(Gr)}(n) \in \mathcal{O}(n)$. This implies $cplx_{\text{A}}(n) = irc_{\mathcal{R}(Gr_{\text{A}}), \mathcal{R}(Gr)}(n) + irc_{\mathcal{R}(Gr_{\text{C}}), \mathcal{R}(Gr)}(n) \cdot irc_{\mathcal{R}(Gr_{\text{D}}), \mathcal{R}(Gr)}(n) \in \mathcal{O}(n^2)$. Thus, also $prc_{\mathcal{P}, \mathcal{Q}_m^{\mathsf{sublist}}}(n) \in \mathcal{O}(n^2)$.

Note that Thm. 27 subsumes Thm. 23. Every evaluation graph Gr without multiplicative SPLIT nodes is decomposable and here we have $cplx_{root(Gr)}(n) = irc_{\mathcal{R}(Gr)}(n)$.

We also implemented our approach for complexity analysis in our tool AProVE [15]. Existing approaches for direct complexity analysis of logic programs (e.g., [10–12, 24, 30])[11] are restricted to well-moded logic programs. In contrast, our approach is applicable to a much wider class of logic programs (including non-well-moded and non-definite programs).[12] To compare their power, we evaluated AProVE against the Complexity Analysis System for LOGic (CASLOG) [11] and the Ciao Preprocessor (CiaoPP) [19, 20], which implements the approach of [30]. We ran the three tools on all 477 Prolog programs from the TPDB, again using 2.2 GHz Quad-Opteron 848 Linux machines with a timeout of 60 seconds per program. For CiaoPP we used both the original cost analysis (CiaoPP-o) and CiaoPP's new resource framework which allows to measure different forms of costs (CiaoPP-r). Here, we chose the cost measure "`res_steps`" which approximates the number of resolution steps needed in evaluations. Moreover, we also used CiaoPP to infer the mode and measure information required by CASLOG.

	$\mathcal{O}(1)$	$\mathcal{O}(n)$	$\mathcal{O}(n^2)$	$\mathcal{O}(n \cdot 2^n)$	bounds	RT
CASLOG	1	21	4	**3**	29	14.8
CiaoPP-o	3	19	4	**3**	29	11.7
CiaoPP-r	3	18	4	**3**	28	12.5
AProVE	**54**	**117**	**37**	0	**208**	**10.6**

In the above table, we used one row for each tool. The first four columns give the number of programs that could be shown to have a constant bound ($\mathcal{O}(1)$), a linear or quadratic polynomial bound ($\mathcal{O}(n)$ or $\mathcal{O}(n^2)$), or an exponential bound ($\mathcal{O}(n \cdot 2^n)$).[13] In column 5 and 6 we give the total number of upper bounds that could be found by the tool and its average runtime on each example. We highlight the best tool for each column using bold font.

The table shows that AProVE can find upper bounds for a much larger subset (42.8%) of the programs than any of the other tools (6.1%). Nevertheless, there are 6 examples where CASLOG or CiaoPP can prove constant (1), linear (1), quadratic (1), or exponential bounds (3), whereas AProVE fails. In summary, the experiments clearly demonstrate that our transformational approach for determining upper bounds advances the state of the art in automated complexity analysis of logic programs significantly.

[9] An extension of our method to examples with non-decomposable evaluation graphs would be an interesting topic for further work. However, even with the restriction to decomposable graphs, our approach is substantially more powerful than all previous techniques for automated complexity analysis of logic programs, cf. the end of this section. In our experiments, there were only 3 examples where other tools could prove an (exponential) upper bound while we failed because of non-decomposability.

[10] We even have $irc_{\mathcal{R}(Gr_{\text{A}}), \mathcal{R}(Gr)}(n) \in \mathcal{O}(1)$, i.e., as in Footnote 7, the bounds found by the tools are not always tight.

[11] Some approaches also deduce *lower* complexity bounds for logic programs [12, 24], while we only infer *upper* bounds.

[12] However, our implementation currently does not treat built-in integer arithmetic, while [10–12, 30] handle linear arithmetic constraints. But our approach could be extended by generating TRSs with built-in integers [14] from the evaluation graphs. This was also done in our approaches for termination analysis of Java via term rewriting [7, 9].

[13] The back-end of AProVE for complexity analysis of TRSs currently only implements techniques for detecting polynomial bounds. When extending the TRS back-end by other techniques like [5], we could also infer exponential bounds.

6. Symbolic Evaluation Graphs for Determinacy Analysis

Finally, after having shown how symbolic evaluation graphs can be used for termination and complexity analysis, we consider a third kind of analysis, viz. *determinacy analysis* (cf. the definition of "determinacy" before Ex. 18). Several approaches for determinacy analysis have been developed (e.g., [25–29, 34]). Moreover, determinacy analysis is also needed for complexity analysis to detect non-deterministic SPLIT nodes in Thm. 23 and 27.

Every successful evaluation corresponds to a path to a SUC node in the evaluation graph. Therefore, this graph is very well suited as a basis for determinacy analysis. A sufficient criterion for determinacy of a state s in the graph is if there is no path starting in s which traverses more than one SUC node. In other words, if s reaches a SUC node s', then there may be no further non-empty path from s' to a SUC node.

THEOREM 28 (Soundness of Determinacy Criterion). *Let $\mathcal{P}$ be a logic program and let Gr be a symbolic evaluation graph for $\mathcal{P}$. Let s be a node in Gr such that for all* SUC *nodes s' reachable from s, there is no non-empty path from s' to a* SUC *node. Then s is deterministic. Thus, if s is the initial state corresponding to $\mathcal{Q}_m^{\mathsf{p}}$ for a $\mathsf{p} \in \Sigma$ and a moding function m, then all queries in $\mathcal{Q}_m^{\mathsf{p}}$ are also deterministic.*

For example, all nodes in the evaluation graph of Fig. 6 satisfy the above determinacy criterion, since there are no non-empty paths from the two SUC nodes E or J to a SUC node again. So the first successor G of the SPLIT node F is deterministic and thus, F is not multiplicative.

In contrast, the node C of the graph in Ex. 18 does not satisfy the determinacy criterion, since it reaches E which has a non-empty cycle to itself. Indeed, C is not deterministic and the corresponding SPLIT node B is multiplicative.

Finally, the nodes in the evaluation graph of Ex. 21 are again deterministic, since the only SUC node E has no non-empty path to itself. But since the SPLIT node B satisfies the conditions (i) – (iii), it is nevertheless multiplicative.

Our experiments in Sect. 5 indicate that the criterion of Thm. 28 is strong enough to detect non-multiplicative SPLIT nodes for complexity analysis. But in general, this criterion only represents a first step towards determinacy analysis based on symbolic evaluation graphs and several additional sufficient criteria for determinacy would be possible.

This is also indicated by our experiments when comparing the implementation of our determinacy analysis in AProVE with the determinacy analysis implemented in CiaoPP [28].[14] We again tested both tools on all 477 logic programs from the TPDB. On definite programs, CiaoPP was clearly more powerful (it proved determinacy for 132 out of 300 programs, whereas AProVE only succeeded for 19 programs). But on non-definite programs, AProVE's determinacy analysis is stronger (here, AProVE showed determinacy of 75 out of 177 examples, whereas CiaoPP only succeeded for 61 programs). Altogether, our new determinacy criterion based on evaluation graphs is a substantial addition to existing determinacy analyses, since AProVE succeeded on 58 examples where CiaoPP failed. In other words, by coupling our new technique with existing ones, the power of determinacy analysis can be increased significantly.

[14] We did not compare with the determinacy analyzer spdet implemented in SICStus Prolog 4.2.1, since it reports both false positives and false negatives.

7. Conclusion

We presented the symbolic evaluation graph and the use of term rewriting as a general methodology for the analysis of logic programs. These graphs represent all evaluations of a (possibly non-definite) logic program in a finite way. Therefore, they can be used as the basis for many different kinds of analyses. In particular, one can translate their paths to rewrite rules and use existing techniques from term rewriting to analyze the termination and complexity of the original logic program. Moreover, one can also perform analyses directly on the evaluation graph (e.g., to examine determinacy).

The current paper does not only give an overview on our previous work on this topic, but it introduces numerous new results. In Sect. 3, we presented a new formulation of the abstract inference rules which is suitable for the subsequent generation of TRSs. Moreover, the theorems of this section (on the connection between concrete and abstract evaluation rules) are new contributions. The approach for termination analysis in Sect. 4 is also substantially different from our earlier approaches, because it directly generates TRSs from evaluation graphs. In particular, this allows us to use the same approach for both termination and complexity analysis. The contributions in Sect. 5 and Sect. 6 (on complexity and determinacy analysis) are completely new.

We implemented all our results in the tool AProVE. Our experiments show that our approaches to termination and complexity analysis are more powerful than previous ones and that our approach to determinacy analysis is a substantial addition to existing ones. See [1] for further details on the experiments and to run AProVE via a web interface.[15]

Acknowledgments

We thank M. Hermenegildo and P. López-García for their support. Without it, the experimental comparisons with CASLOG and CiaoPP would not have been possible. We also thank N.-W. Lin for agreeing to make the updated version of CASLOG (running under SICStus 4 or Ciao) available on [1].

References

[1] `http://aprove.informatik.rwth-aachen.de/eval/LPGraphs/`.

[2] K. R. Apt. *From Logic Programming to Prolog*. Prentice Hall, 1997.

[3] M. Avanzini, G. Moser, and A. Schnabl. Automated implicit computational complexity analysis. In *Proc. IJCAR '08*, LNAI 5195, pages 132–138, 2008.

[4] M. Avanzini and G. Moser. Dependency pairs and polynomial path orders. In *Proc. RTA '09*, LNCS 5595, pages 48–62, 2009.

[5] M. Avanzini, N. Eguchi, and G. Moser. A path order for rewrite systems that compute exponential time functions. In *Proc. RTA '11*, LIPIcs 10, pages 123–138, 2011.

[6] F. Baader and T. Nipkow. *Term Rewriting and All That*. Cambridge University Press, 1998.

[7] M. Brockschmidt, C. Otto, and J. Giesl. Modular termination proofs of recursive Java Bytecode programs by term rewriting. In *Proc. RTA '11*, LIPIcs 10, pages 155–170, 2011.

[8] M. Brockschmidt, T. Ströder, C. Otto, and J. Giesl. Automated detection of non-termination and `NullPointerExceptions` for Java Bytecode. In *Proc. FoVeOOS '11*, LNCS 7421, pages 123–141, 2012.

[9] M. Brockschmidt, R. Musiol, C. Otto, and J. Giesl. Automated termination proofs for Java programs with cyclic data. In *Proc. CAV '12*, LNCS 7358, pages 105–122, 2012.

[10] S. K. Debray, N.-W. Lin, and M. V. Hermenegildo. Task granularity analysis in logic programs. In *Proc. PLDI '90*, pages 174–188. ACM Press, 1990.

[15] [1] also contains a version of the paper with all proofs [18].

[11] S. K. Debray and N.-W. Lin. Cost analysis of logic programs. *ACM Transactions on Programming Languages and Systems*, 15:826–875, 1993.

[12] S. K. Debray, P. López-García, M. V. Hermenegildo, and N.-W. Lin. Lower bound cost estimation for logic programs. In *Proc. ILPS '97*, pages 291–305. MIT Press, 1997.

[13] N. Dershowitz. Termination of rewriting. *Journal of Symbolic Computation*, 3(1–2), pages 69–116, 1987.

[14] C. Fuhs, J. Giesl, M. Plücker, P. Schneider-Kamp, and S. Falke. Proving termination of integer term rewriting. In *Proc. RTA '09*, LNCS 5595, pages 32–47, 2009.

[15] J. Giesl, P. Schneider-Kamp, and R. Thiemann. AProVE 1.2: Automatic termination proofs in the dependency pair framework. In *Proc. IJCAR '06*, LNAI 4130, pages 281–286, 2006.

[16] J. Giesl, R. Thiemann, P. Schneider-Kamp, and S. Falke. Mechanizing and improving dependency pairs. *Journal of Automated Reasoning*, 37(3), pages 155–203, 2006.

[17] J. Giesl, M. Raffelsieper, P. Schneider-Kamp, S. Swiderski, and R. Thiemann. Automated termination proofs for Haskell by term rewriting. *ACM Transactions on Programming Languages and Systems*, 33(2), 2011.

[18] J. Giesl, T. Ströder, P. Schneider-Kamp, F. Emmes, and C. Fuhs. Symbolic evaluation graphs and term rewriting – a general methodology for analyzing logic programs. Technical Report AIB 2012-12, RWTH Aachen University, 2012. Available from `http://aib.informatik.rwth-aachen.de` and [1].

[19] M. V. Hermenegildo, G. Puebla, F. Bueno, and P. López-García. Integrated program debugging, verification, and optimization using abstract interpretation (and the Ciao system preprocessor). *Science of Computer Programming*, 58(1-2):115–140, 2005.

[20] M. V. Hermenegildo, F. Bueno, M. Carro, P. López-García, E. Mera, J. F. Morales, and G. Puebla. An overview of Ciao and its design philosophy. *Theory and Practice of Logic Programming*, 12:219–252, 2012.

[21] N. Hirokawa and G. Moser. Automated complexity analysis based on the dependency pair method. In *Proc. IJCAR '08*, LNAI 5195, pages 364–379, 2008.

[22] J. M. Howe and A. King. Efficient groundness analysis in Prolog. *Theory and Practice of Logic Programming*, 3(1):95–124, 2003.

[23] ISO/IEC 13211-1. *Information technology - Programming languages - Prolog*. 1995.

[24] A. King, K. Shen, and F. Benoy. Lower-bound time-complexity analysis of logic programs. In *Proc. ILPS '97*, pages 261–285. MIT Press, 1997.

[25] A. King, L. Lu, and S. Genaim. Detecting determinacy in Prolog programs. In *Proc. ICLP '06*, LNCS 4079, pages 132–147, 2006.

[26] J. Kriener and A. King. RedAlert: Determinacy inference for Prolog. In *Proc. ICLP '11, Theory and Practice of Logic Programming*, 11(4-5):537–553, 2011.

[27] J. Kriener and A. King. Mutual exclusion by interpolation. In *Proc. FLOPS '12*, LNCS 7294, pages 182–196, 2012.

[28] P. López-García, F. Bueno, and M. V. Hermenegildo. Automatic inference of determinacy and mutual exclusion for logic programs using mode and type analyses. *New Generation Computing*, 28(2):177–206, 2010.

[29] T. Mogensen. A semantics-based determinacy analysis for Prolog with cut. In *Proc. Ershov Memorial Conference '96*, LNCS 1181, pages 374–385, 1996.

[30] J. A. Navas, E. Mera, P. López-García, and M. V. Hermenegildo. User-definable resource bounds analysis for logic programs. In *Proc. ICLP '07*, LNCS 4670, pages 348–363, 2007.

[31] M. T. Nguyen, J. Giesl, and P. Schneider-Kamp. Termination analysis of logic programs based on dependency graphs. In *Proc. LOPSTR '07*, LNCS 4915, pages 8–22, 2008.

[32] L. Noschinski, F. Emmes, and J. Giesl. The dependency pair framework for automated complexity analysis of term rewrite systems. In *Proc. CADE '11*, LNAI 6803, pages 422–438, 2011.

[33] E. Ohlebusch. Termination of logic programs: Transformational methods revisited. *Applicable Algebra in Engineering, Communication and Computing*, 12(1-2):73–116, 2001.

[34] D. Sahlin. Determinacy analysis for full Prolog. In *Proc. PEPM '91*, pages 23–30. ACM Press, 1991.

[35] P. Schneider-Kamp, J. Giesl, A. Serebrenik, and R. Thiemann. Automated termination proofs for logic programs by term rewriting. *ACM Transactions on Computational Logic*, 11(1), 2009.

[36] P. Schneider-Kamp, J. Giesl, and M. T. Nguyen. The dependency triple framework for termination of logic programs. In *Proc. LOPSTR '09*, LNCS 6037, pages 37–51, 2010.

[37] P. Schneider-Kamp, J. Giesl, T. Ströder, A. Serebrenik, and R. Thiemann. Automated termination analysis for logic programs with cut. In *Proc. ICLP '10, Theory and Practice of Logic Programming*, 10(4-6):365–381, 2010.

[38] M. H. Sørensen and R. Glück. An algorithm of generalization in positive supercompilation. In *Proc. ILPS '95*, pages 465–479. MIT Press, 1995.

[39] T. Ströder. Towards termination analysis of real Prolog programs. Diploma Thesis, RWTH Aachen University, 2010. Available from [1].

[40] T. Ströder, P. Schneider-Kamp, and J. Giesl. Dependency triples for improving termination analysis of logic programs with cut. In *Proc. LOPSTR '10*, LNCS 6564, pages 184–199, 2011.

[41] T. Ströder, F. Emmes, P. Schneider-Kamp, J. Giesl, and C. Fuhs. A linear operational semantics for termination and complexity analysis of ISO Prolog. In *Proc. LOPSTR '11*, LNCS, 2012. To appear. Available from [1].

[42] H. Zankl and M. Korp. Modular complexity analysis via relative complexity. In *Proc. RTA '10*, LIPIcs 6, pages 385–400, 2010.

[43] H. Zantema. Termination. In Terese, editor, *Term Rewriting Systems*, pages 181–259. Cambridge University Press, 2003.

Matrix Code

M.H. van Emden

Department of Computer Science
University of Victoria, Victoria, Canada
vanemden@cs.uvic.ca

Abstract

Matrix Code gives imperative programming a mathematical semantics and heuristic power comparable in quality to functional and logic programming. A program in matrix code is developed incrementally from a specification in pre/post-condition form. The computations of a code matrix are characterized by powers of the matrix when it is interpreted as a transformation in a space of vectors of logical conditions. Correctness of a code matrix is expressed in terms of a fixpoint of the transformation.

Categories and Subject Descriptors D.1.4 [*Programming Techniques*]: Sequential Programming; D.2.4 [*Software/Program Verification*]: Correctness Proofs; D.3.3 [*Programming Languages*]: Language Constructs and Features—Control Structures; F.3.3 [*Studies of Program Constructs*]: Control Primitives

General Terms program verification, programming methodology

Keywords Floyd assertions, Hoare logic, verification-driven programming

1. Introduction

By *imperative programming* we will understand the writing of code in which the state of the computation is explicitly manipulated by assignments that change the value of a variable. As a programming paradigm, imperative programming should be compared, and contrasted, with functional and logic programming. Compared to these latter paradigms, imperative programming is in an unsatisfactory state. At least as a first approximation, a definition in functional or logic programming is both a specification and is executable. In imperative programming proving that a function body meets its specification is such a challenge that it is not considered part of a programmer's task. Another difference, probably related, is that functional and logic programming have an elegant mathematical semantics in which the behaviour of a definition is characterized as a fixpoint of the transformation associated with the definition.

This paper is a contribution to imperative programming in the form of a new language, called *Matrix Code*, in which programs take the form of a matrix with binary relations among states as entries. Matrix Code is distinguished by a development process that begins with a null code matrix, progresses with small, obvious steps, and ends with a matrix that is of a special form that is trivially translatable to a conventional language like Java or C. The result of the translation has the same behaviour as the one determined by the mathematical semantics of the code matrix. Therefore the latter can be said to be executable. As every stage in the development process is partially correct with respect to the specification (the correctness of the initial null code matrix is *very* partial) Matrix Code comes close to the ideal in which the code is itself a proof of partial correctness.

Plan of the paper In Section 2 we give a small example of the verification of imperative code by Hoare's method. We note certain features that point in the direction of Matrix Code. In Section 4 we define this language and show the same example translated to it. In Section 5 we explain how a code matrix is executed and we define its set of computations. In Section 6 we use the fact that a code matrix is not only an executable program but also a set of verification conditions to characterize partial correctness in terms of a fixpoint of the matrix. In Section 8 we solve the problem of Section 2 in the systematic manner that is unique to Matrix Code. The final two sections survey related work and draw conclusions.

2. Hoare's verification method

As an introduction to the verification method for imperative programming due to Hoare [10] we verify a Java version of the prime-number generating program developed by Dijkstra in [6]. The Java version of this program is shown in Figure 1.

We think of a computation as a sequence of *computation states* each of which consists of a *control state* (a code location) and a *data state* (a tuple of values of the variables)[1]. According to Hoare's method, conditions are attached to code locations. The conditions assert that certain relations between program variables hold at the code locations. When such a condition occurs in a loop, it is the familiar invariant of that loop. In Figure 1 we have indicated by the comments S, A, B, C, and H where these conditions have to be placed. Figure 2 contains the corresponding conditions.

The verification of the function as a whole relies on the verification of a number of implications defined in terms of conditions and program elements such as tests and statements. Consider Figure 1: because there is an execution path from A to B, one has to show the truth of

```
{A && k<N} j=p[k-1]+2; n=0; {B},
```

which has as meaning: if `A && k<N` (the *precondition*) is true and if

```
j=p[k-1]+2; n=0;
```

is executed, then `B` (the *postcondition*) is true. Because of the three elements: precondition, postcondition, and the item in between, this is called a *Hoare triple*. Figure 2 contains not only the conditions

[1] In this paper we consider only code that executes in a single activation record.

PPDP'12, September 19–21, 2012, Leuven, Belgium.

```
public static void primes(int[] p, int N) {
  // S
  int j,k,n;
  p[0] = 2; p[1] = 3; k = 2;
  // A
  while (k<N) {
    j = p[k-1]+2; n = 0;
    // B
    while (p[n]*p[n] <= j) {
      // C
      if (j%p[n+1] != 0) n++;
      else {j += 2; n = 0;}
    }
    p[k++] = j;
  }
  // H
}
```

Figure 1. A Java function for filling `p[0..N-1]` with the first `N` primes. At the points indicated by the comments S, A, B, C, H we need conditions to allow verification by Hoare's method. The identifiers and the structure are the same as in Dijkstra's example [6].

```
Conditions:
S: p[0..N-1] exists and N>1
H: p[0..N-1] are the first N primes
A: S && p[0..k-1] are the first k primes && k <= N
B: A && k<N && relB(p, k, n, j)
C: B && p[n]*p[n] <= j

relB(p,k,n,j)} means that there is no prime
between p[k-1] and j, and that j is not divided
by any prime in p[0..n], and that n<k.

Hoare triples:

{S} p[0]=2; p[1]=3; k=2; {A}
{A && k >= N}  {H}
{A && k < N} j=p[k-1]+2; n=0; {B}
{B && p[n]*p[n] <= j} {C}
{B && p[n]*p[n] > j} p[k++] = j {A}
{C && j%p[n+1] != 0} n++ {B}
{C && j%p[n+1] == 0} j += 2; n = 0 {B}
```

Figure 2. Conditions and Hoare triples for Figure 1. The meaning of a Hoare triple $\{$`A0`$\}$ `CODE` $\{$`A1`$\}$ is that if condition `A0` is true and if `CODE` is executed with termination, then condition `A1` is true.

for Figure 1, but also the set of verification conditions in the form of Hoare triples.

The term "condition" for the type of thing that occurs as precondition and postcondition in a Hoare triple is, in our view, rather compelling. However, it seems that in certain contexts "assertion" is a more natural alternative term. In this paper we will use both. At the same time, one should make a distinction between the condition as a linguistic expression and the set that is the meaning of that expression. We trust no confusion arises as we use "assertion" and "condition" interchangeably for both the expression and the meaning.

Figure 1 may seem to be the obvious, or even only, solution to the problem. But instructors in a beginners' programming course will see a wondrously creative variety of alternative solutions. Being solutions, they can all be verified by the same set of triples as in Figure 2. What all these solutions also have in common is the flow chart, and this flow chart is also verified by the same set of triples. In this sense the flowchart is a language-independent notation for an algorithm that also accommodates Hoare's verification method. In fact, the method originates with Floyd [8], who introduced it with flow charts. In spite of their merit of language-independence and verifiability we are not satisfied with flow charts because of their lack of heuristic power and because the lack of an attractive mathematical model. Flow charts are interesting because they are only a small step away from Matrix Code, which does have these two properties. We describe this step in the remainder of this section.

It would be tempting to say that, once we have a sufficient set of Hoare triples, we can forget the program in Figure 1: all information about it is in the Hoare triples of Figure 2. This may seem so because, for example, in

```
{A && k < N} j=p[k-1]+2; n=0; {B}
```

`A` stands for the condition defined earlier in that figure. What is missing is the fact that condition `A` is tied to code location `A`. We need the preconditions to be identified by a single letter that stands for a condition, so that all triples have the form {`P`}`S`{`Q`}.

We will show that an algorithm as set of triples of the form {`P`}`S`{`Q`} has an attractive mathematical model and has considerable heuristic power. Assuming then that all the information about an algorithm is in a set of items of the form {`P`}`S`{`Q`}, what is a convenient format for such a set? The most obvious seems a graph where the nodes represent conditions and where the directed edges are labeled with the middle items of the triples. Such a graph is also often used to represent a sparse matrix. A disadvantage of the matrix format is that it takes up an amount of space that is quadratic in the number of nodes. However the mathematical model that we propose for an algorithm as set of triples of the form {`P`}`S`{`Q`} is that of a transformation in a certain type of vector space of conditions. We are used to having such transformations represented by matrices rather than graphs. As in other uses of such transformations, matrix multiplication is a familiar and fundamental operation. For most people graph multiplication, though perfectly well defined, is not familiar. Hence we opt for the matrix representation and use Matrix Code as name for an algorithm as set of triples of the form {`P`}`S`{`Q`}.

But we are running ahead of the story: this is only relevant if we can get all triples in the form {`P`}`S`{`Q`}. We do this by generalizing the `S` from a statement to a binary relation between data states. Because of the essential role of binary relations we review and introduce the needed terminology and notation.

3. Preliminaries on binary relations

As binary relations are essential to Matrix Code we review notation and terminology. For the purposes of this paper, a binary relation R on a set D is a subset of the Cartesian product $D \times D$. If (s_0, s_1)

is in a binary relation, then we say that s_0 is an *input*; s_1 an *output* of the relation.

The null relation is the empty subset of $D \times D$. The identity relation I_D on D is $\{(s_0, s_1) \in D \times D : s_0 = s_1\}$. The union $R_0 \cup R_1$ of binary relations R_0 and R_1 is defined to be their union as subsets of $D \times D$. The composition $R_0; R_1$ of binary relations R_0 and R_1 is $\{(s_0, s_1) \in D \times D : \exists t \in D.\ (s_0, t) \in R_0 \wedge (t, s_1) \in R_1\}$. The inverse R^{-1} of a binary relation R is $\{(t, s) \in D \times D : (s, t) \in R\}$.

Let us call subsets of D *conditions*, anticipating their future use. The *left projection* of a binary relation R is defined as the condition $\{x \in D : \exists y \in D.\ (x, y) \in R\}$. Dually, the *right projection* of a binary relation R is defined as the condition $\{y \in D : \exists x \in D.\ (x, y) \in R\}$.

We generalize I_D to I_c, which means, for any condition $c \subseteq D$, by definition, $\{(x, x) \in D \times D : x \in c\}$. This induces a one-to-one relation between c and I_c:

$$x \in c \leftrightarrow (x, x) \in I_c.$$

Accordingly, at times we view a condition (alias assertion) as a subset of D; at times as a subset of I_D.

DEFINITION 1. *Given a condition $p \subseteq D$ and a binary relation $R \subseteq (D \times D)$, we write* {p}R *for the right projection of $I(p); R$, where $I(p)$ is the binary relation $\{(x, x) \in D \times D : x \in p\}$.*

Hoare triples were intended to be applied to program statements. However, they have a natural interpretation for binary relations, as follows.

DEFINITION 2. *The Hoare triple* {p}R{q} *holds iff*

$$\{p\}R \subseteq q.$$

DEFINITION 3. *A* trace *of a relation $R \subseteq (D \times D)$ is a possibly infinite sequence of elements of D such that for any pair $(s, s') \in (D \times D)$ such that s' follows s in the sequence we have that $(s, s') \in R$.*

A trace $s_0 \dots s_{n-1}$ is closed *iff there is no $d \in D$ such that $(s_{n-1}, d) \in R$.*

A segment *$[\alpha, \omega]$ of a trace is a contiguous subsequence of the trace; $\alpha \in D$ is the first, $\omega \in D$ is the last element in the segment.*

4. Matrix code

As a first step toward matrix code we modify the nature of the middle term of the Hoare triple {P}T{Q}. Conventionally T is a statement of a conventional language, typically changing the value of one or more variables.

Let us regard the collection of all variables accessible to the code as a tuple of the values indexed by the names of the variables. We call this tuple the *data state*. Thus, in Figure 1 the data state consists of the array p and the variables k, n, j.

The effect of a statement can be modeled as a binary relation on data states. Expressed in terms of sets, such a relation R is the set of pairs (x, y) such that $(x, y) \in R$ iff R's output y is a possible data state after executing the statement R, when R's input x is the data state before. This captures all terminating statements. In particular, an assignment statement v = E corresponds to the binary relation consisting of pairs (x, y) of data states where the v component of y is equal to the result of evaluating E, and all other components of y are equal to the corresponding ones in x.

We may have that R is not single-valued: there may exist x, y_0, and y_1 such that $(x, y_0) \in R$ and $(x, y_1) \in R$ and $y_0 \neq y_1$. That is, we admit nondeterministic statements, so y_0 is *a possible* output rather than *the* output. Modeling a statement as a relation R allows us to account for another computational phenomenon: it may be that for some x there is no y such that $(x, y) \in R$. This expresses the fact that for some data states as input the effect of the statement is not defined. For example, if the input data state x is such that in this data state $w = 0$, then for the relation modeling the statement $u := u/w$ there is no corresponding output y. But of course R can be a *function* on the set of data states so that it is defined for every state as input and that for each of these there is one and only one output.

We modeled the middle term T, which is conventionally a statement, in {P}T{Q} as a binary relation. We now generalize T by allowing it to be any binary relation over data states. We call this generalization of T a *transition*.

A transition may denote the empty relation. The identity relation on a set Δ of data states is $\{(s, s) : s \in \Delta\}$. A transition in the form of a boolean expression b denotes a subset of the identity relation. Such a transition we call a *guard*, following [7].

Thus guards can be composed with other transitions. If r_1 and r_2 are the meanings of transitions t_1 and t_2, then $r_1; r_2$ is the meaning of $t_1; t_2$, which is the transition consisting of the execution of t_1 followed by the execution of t_2. But either or both of t_1 and t_2 may be a guard, and then the effect of $t_1; t_2$ is equally well determined by the definition of composition of binary relations. The interpretation of transition elements allows the composition of a guard with any transition, whether that is a guard or not. For example, `v--; v > 0` and `v > 1; v--` are both well-defined transitions.

```
Conditions:
{S} p[0]=2; p[1]=3; k=2; {A}
{A} k >= N  {H}
{A} k < N; j=p[k-1]+2; n=0; {B}
{B} p[n]*p[n] <= j {C}
{B} p[n]*p[n] > j; p[k++] = j {A}
{C} j%p[n+1] != 0; n++ {B}
{C} j%p[n+1] == 0; j += 2; n = 0 {B}
```

Figure 3. Hoare triples for Figure 1. The middle terms in the verification conditions are transitions.

The purpose of the introduction of transitions is that we can write the verification conditions of Figure 2 as in Figure 3. We introduce a new programming language so that Figure 3 is itself a program and so that Figure 3 is also the verification of that program.

A natural notation of a set of items of the form {P}T{Q} is a matrix with rows and columns labeled by conditions. In this way the verification conditions of Figure 3 become the code matrix in Figure 12, a program in Matrix Code, the language. As we customarily do, the empty row of the start label and the empty column of the halt label have been omitted.

DEFINITION 4. *Given a set L of labels, a tuple of variables, boolean expressions testing a relation among the subset of these variables, and statements defined on a subset of these variables. A* code matrix *consists of an L-by-L matrix M, an L-indexed row vector of conditions preceding the sequence of rows of M, and an L-indexed column vector of conditions following the sequence of columns of M. For all i and j in L the element M_{ij} of column i and row j*[2] *is a* transition, *an expression denoting a binary relation. Among the labels there is one that labels an empty row; this is the* start label. *Among the labels there is one that labels an empty column; this is the* halt label.

[2] Note the transposition from the usual order. In this way the direction of execution is from i to j.

A code matrix is a way of writing a set of verification conditions, so has the status of a formula of logic. Yet it is also a program for a suitably defined abstract machine. This will be proved by defining the computations of a code matrix.

Matrix Code is a programming language that relies on an underlying base language in which to define the types of the variables and in which to write the statements and boolean expressions that make up the transitions. Matrix Code is defined informally, as done here. The fragments of base language that are needed are defined according to the standard of Java or C, as the case may be.

Some conventions for writing a code matrix: if a cell contains the null relation as a transition, then nothing is written in the cell; if a row or column is empty, it is omitted.

5. The computations of a code matrix

Section 4 gave a syntax of matrix code. We now define its operational semantics by defining execution of a code matrix.

DEFINITION 5. *A* computation state *is a pair (l, v) where l is a* control state *(in the form of a label) and v is a* data state *(in the form of a tuple of values of variables).*

Execution of a code matrix consists of the execution agent performing a sequence of cycles. The agent carries a computation state which is updated during a cycle. At the beginning of the cycle the agent carries state (l, v). It enters from the top of the matrix through the column labeled by l until it encounters a non-empty cell. Let r be the row in which this cell occurs and let R be the relation modeling the transition in this cell. If the data state v of the agent is such that there is a $(v, w) \in R$, then the agent exits to the right with computation state (r, w). This completes the cycle, and the agent begins a new cycle unless it exited through row `H`.

The agent may start a cycle in a column that does not contain a transition having its data state as input. In that case the agent does not complete the cycle.

Initially the agent carries the control state `S`. If and when the control state changes to `H`, execution halts with success.

DEFINITION 6. *The* binary relation associated with *a code matrix M with set Σ of computation states is the set of pairs $((l, v), (l', v')) \in \Sigma \times \Sigma$ such that $(v, v') \in M_{l,l'}$, the element in column l and row l' of M.*

A computation of *M is a trace of the binary relation associated with M.*

A computation is closed *if it is closed as a trace.*

See Figure 4 for an example of a computation.

```
N = 3

control | data
state   | state
        | k      j      n    p
  --------------------------------
      S | ?      ?      ?    {?,?,?}
      A | 2      ?      ?    {2,3,?}
      B | 2      5      0    {2,3,?}
      C | 2      5      0    {2,3,?}
      B | 2      5      1    {2,3,?}
      A | 3      5      1    {2,3,5}
      H | 3      5      1    {2,3,5}
```

Figure 4. Example of the trace for `N` equals 3 of the code matrix in Figure 12.

If a row is empty, then its label can only occur in the first state of any computation. Such a label is the start label. If a column is empty, then any computation state containing its label has to terminate the computation. Such a label is the halt label. In Figure 12, S is the start label and H is the halt label.

DEFINITION 7. *A computation is* successful *if it is closed and if its last computation state contains the halt label as control state; otherwise a closed computation is* failed.

DEFINITION 8. *Let M and N be code matrices with the same set L of labels and the same set Δ of data states. The* product MN *of M and N is a code matrix with L as set of labels and Δ as set of data states and with the cell $(MN)_{ik}$ in column i and row k containing $\bigcup_{j \in L} M_{ij}; N_{jk}$.*

Let I be the L-labeled matrix of binary relations over Δ that has the identity relation on Δ on the main diagonal and the empty relation elsewhere. Then we have $IM = MI = M$ with M any L-labeled matrix with binary relations over Δ as elements. We write M^n for $M^{n-1}M$ for a positive integer n while $M^0 = I$.

Matrix code can be viewed as a format for defining new binary relations in terms of the binary relations given by the statements and boolean expressions of the base language.

DEFINITION 9. *The* relation computed by *a code matrix M with start label S and halt label H is defined to be the set of (s, t) in $\Delta \times \Delta$ such that there exists a computation of M that starts with (S, s) and ends with (H, t).*

We characterize the relation computed by a code matrix in terms of its powers. First two lemmas concerning these powers.

LEMMA 1. *If a code matrix M has a computation containing a segment $[(l, s), (l', s')]$, then there exists an n such that $(s, s') \in (M^n)_{l,l'}$.*

Proof We proceed by induction on the segment length k. If $k = 1$ the computation has the form $(l, s), (l', s')$, so that (l', s') is the successor of (l, s). By Definition 6 we have $(s, s') \in M_{l,l'}$.

We assume the lemma true for k.

$(l, s), (l_1, s_1), \ldots, (l_{k-1}, s_{k-1}), (l', s')$ is a computation implies that there exists an n such that $(s, s_{k-1}) \in M^n_{l,l'}$ (by the induction hypothesis) and $(s_{k-1}, s') \in M_{l_{k-1},l'}$. By Definition 8 this implies that $(s, s') \in M^{n+1}_{l,l'}$.

LEMMA 2. *$(s, s') \in (M^n)_{l,l'}$ implies that there exists a segment $[(l, s), (l', s')]$ of a computation of M; this holds for all $n = 1, 2, \ldots$*

Proof We proceed by induction on n. $(s, s') \in M_{l,l'}$ implies that $[(l, s), (l', s')]$ is a segment. This takes care of the base case $n = 1$.

Assume the lemma for n.

$(s, s'') \in (M^{n+1})_{l,l''}$ implies that there exists an s' and an l' such that $(s, s') \in (M^n)_{l,l'}$ and $(s', s'') \in M_{l',l''}$ by Definition 8. Hence, by the induction assumption there exists a segment $[(l, s), (l', s')]$ and $(s', s'') \in M_{l',l''}$, which implies, by Definition 6, that there exists a segment $[(l, s), (l'', s'')]$ of a computation of M.

THEOREM 1. *Suppose that M is a code matrix with start state S and halt state H, with a finite set of labels, and a finite set of data states. Then the relation computed by M is $\bigcup_{i=0}^{\infty}(M^i)_{S,H}$.*

Proof Suppose that the pair (s, t) of data states is in the relation computation computed by M. By Definition 9 there exists a computation of M that begins with (S, s) and ends with (H, t).

According to Lemma 1 there is an n such that $(s,t) \in (M^n)_{S,H}$. Hence $(s,t) \in \bigcup_{n=0}^{\infty}(M^n)_{S,H}$.

Suppose that $(s,t) \in \bigcup_{n=0}^{\infty}(M^n)_{S,H}$. By the finiteness assumptions there exists an n such that $(s,t) \in (M^n)_{S,H}$. According to Lemma 2 this implies that there exists a computation of M that begins with (S,s) and ends with (H,t). Therefore (s,t) is in the relation computed by M, according to Definition 9.

6. Verification of matrix code

If the matrix in matrix code is in a certain relation with its row vector of preconditions and column vector of postconditions, then its computations are partially correct. In this section Theorem 2 makes this claim precise.

Conditions Transitions can be regarded as transformations of a single input to a single output. A transition can also be regarded as a *condition transformer*: transition T transforms condition p into the condition $\{\mathtt{p}\}\mathtt{T}$.

We characterize transitions by conditions of the form $\{\mathtt{p}\}\mathtt{T} \subseteq q$. According to Definition 2 this is written as $\{\mathtt{p}\}\mathtt{T}\{\mathtt{q}\}$. This notation was introduced with T as a binary relation in general. When T is the relation computed by a code matrix, this implies that condition p does not imply termination. Hence the correctness expressed by $\{\mathtt{p}\}\mathtt{T}\{\mathtt{q}\}$ is *partial* correctness.

In case the code matrix is nondeterministic there may be data states in p that begin computations that end in different data states; $\{\mathtt{p}\}\mathtt{T}\{\mathtt{q}\}$ implies that these final data states are all in q.

Condition vectors The transitions that are the elements of a code matrix define transformations on individual conditions. The matrix as a whole defines a transformation on condition *vectors*: vectors of conditions indexed by labels. The computations of a matrix have as elements computation states, which have the form (l,v), where l is a label and v is a data state. A set P of computation states defines a condition vector C by $C_l = \{v \in \Delta : (l,v) \in P\}$ for all $l \in L$. Conversely, C can be used to define $P = \bigcup_{l \in L}\{(l,v) : v \in C_l\}$. As the two correspondences are each others' inverse, condition vectors are isomorphic to sets of computation states.

DEFINITION 10. *The expression* $\{\mathtt{P}\}\mathtt{M}\{\mathtt{Q}\}$ *asserts that*

$$(\{\mathtt{P}\}\mathtt{M}) \subseteq Q,$$

where $\{\mathtt{P}\}\mathtt{M}$ *is the condition vector of which the i-th element is* $\bigcup_{j \in L} I(P_j); M_{ij}$*, for all* $i \in L$*. Here* $I(C)$ *is defined as the following subset of the identity relation on data states:* $\{(s,s) \in \Delta \times \Delta : C \textit{ is true in } s\}$.

THEOREM 2. *Given a code matrix* M *and a condition vector* V *satisfying* $\{\mathtt{V}\}\mathtt{M}\{\mathtt{V}\}$*. For any computation state* (l',s') *of any computation beginning with* (l,s) *such that* $s \in V_l$ *it is the case that* $s' \in V_{l'}$.

Proof
We proceed by induction on the length n of the computation. If $n = 1$ (one state in the computation) we have $(l',s') = (l,s)$. Assume the theorem true for computations of length n. Consider the computation

$$(l,s),(l_1,s_1),\ldots,(l_{n-1},s_{n-1}),(l',s').$$

By the induction assumption $s_{n-1} \in V_{l_{n-1}}$. By Definition 6 $(s_{n-1},s') \in M_{l_{n-1},l'}$. It is given that $\{\mathtt{V}\}\mathtt{M}\{\mathtt{V}\}$, hence in particular that $\{\mathtt{V}_{\mathtt{l}_{n-1}}\}\mathtt{M}_{\mathtt{l}_{n-1},\mathtt{l}'}\{\mathtt{V}_{\mathtt{l}'}\}$. It follows that $s' \in V_{l'}$, which establishes the theorem for the computation of length $n+1$.

7. Mathematical semantics

A condition vector F such that $\{\mathtt{F}\}\mathtt{M} = F$ is a fixpoint of M when M is regarded as a transformer of condition vectors. Typically F is such that it has a compact description by means of boolean expressions. This is so because it derives from a program specification. But there is no reason to believe that this holds for $\{\mathtt{F}\}\mathtt{M}$. What makes Floyd's method useful is that it does not require finding a fixpoint of M, but only requires a solution V of $\{\mathtt{V}\}\mathtt{M} \subseteq V$ such that V_S is the condition at the start node and V_H the one at the halt node.

The fact that M, a monotonic transformation, is guaranteed, by the Knaster/Tarski theorem, to have a fixpoint is of no practical significance for two reasons. In the first place, we are not interested in verifying a given code matrix: the reason for using matrix code is that it helps us discover a program satisfying the specification. In the second place, the iterative algorithm that proves the existence of a fixpoint is not practically executable. The resulting fixpoint (the least such) is unlikely to have an intelligible description.

Condition vectors are an example of a *semimodule*, a generalization of the familiar vector space. In a vector space the scalars are elements of a field (e.g. the reals). If the scalars are generalized to elements of a ring (e.g. the integers), the vector space becomes a module. The analog of addition of integers is union of binary relations. Union does not have an inverse, so that we find that binary relations over a given domain are a semiring. The corresponding generalization of a vector is a semimodule. Thus the mathematical model of imperative programming obtained by Matrix Code is given by the theory of semimodules.

Semimodules are important in pure mathematics. For their role in programming we refer to Parker's monograph [12]. Parker defines a general framework, partial-order programming, which captures numerical optimization problems as well as functional and logic programming. As Parker shows, partial-order programming can take as special form semilinear partial-order programming, where the partially-ordered spaces take the form of semimodules. Examples of problems that find a natural formulation as transformations in semimodules expressible by matrices are: path reliability, path connectivity, maximum capacity paths, k-shortest paths, regular expressions, word abbreviations, path and cutset enumeration, and certain scheduling problems. In this paper we show that Matrix Code is semilinear partial-order programming, thereby inheriting a rich theory and sharing algebraic properties with many important applications.

8. Systematic program development

Floyd's method is difficult to apply because it is difficult to find the required conditions even when the program is correct. Because of this Dijkstra [4, 5] advocated parallel development of code and proof. In this section we demonstrate parallel development of a code matrix for the sample problem solved in Figure 1: to fill an array with the first N prime numbers in increasing order.

Background on prime numbers Before we start, let us review what we need to know about prime numbers. The following list of facts is not intended as a complete or nonredundant set of axioms; they are a selection to guide us in the choice of conditions and transitions.

1. *A prime is a positive integer that has no divisors.* (We do not count 1 or the integer itself as divisors. Moreover, 1 is not a prime.)
2. *There are infinitely many primes*, so the problem can be solved for any n.
3. *2 and 3 are the first two primes.* So a way to get started is to accept these as given and place them in the beginning of the

table. This has the advantage that we always have the situation where the last prime in the table is odd and the next odd number is the first candidate to be tested for the next prime.

4. *If a number has a divisor, then it has a prime divisor.* This can be used to save effort: we only have to test for divisibility by smaller primes, and these are already in the table.
5. *If a number has a divisor, then it has a prime divisor less than or equal to its square root.* This implies that we do not have to test the candidate for the next prime for divisibility by all primes already in the table.
6. *The square of every prime is greater than the next prime.* The significance of this fact will become apparent as we proceed.

Deriving the code matrix The distinctive advantage of matrix code is that a matrix can be expanded from the specification in small steps using only the *logic* of the application without needing to attend to the *control* component of the algorithm. Thus matrix code is an example of Kowalski's principle "Algorithm = Logic + Control" [11].

We assume that the specification exists in the form of a precondition and a postcondition. This gives rise to code matrix with one row and one column; the one in Figure 5.

`S: p[0..N-1] exists & N>1`	
`/*which T?*/`	`H: p[0..N-1] contains the first N primes`

Figure 5. There is only an empty transition T such that {S}T{H}.

The one element of this matrix is the transition T such that {S}T{H} is true. That is, T has to be a simple combination of guards and assignment statements that places the N first primes in p, whatever N is. Absent such a T, we leave the matrix cell empty. The resulting code matrix satisfies {S}T{H}, which makes it partially correct, but *very* partially so: it has no successful computations. Although Figure 5 is the correct start of the development process, it is not the last step.

As it is too ambitious to place all primes in the array with a single transition, a reasonable thing to try is to fill it with the first k primes and then try to add the next prime after `p[k-1]`.

We need a condition A that is intermediate in the sense that {S}T1{A} and {A}T2{H} for simple T1 and T2. Such a condition is: the first k primes in increasing order are in `p[0..k-1]` with `1 < k <= N`.

Condition A is promising because it is easy to think of such a T1 and such a T2. The result is in Figure 6.

This again is a partially correct code matrix. It is a slight improvement in that it solves the problem if N happens to be one or two. In all other cases it leads to failed computations. The difficulty is that in column A we may have that `k < N`, so that we cannot make the transition to H. We need to find the next prime after `p[k-1]`. Let j be the current candidate for this next prime. That suggests for condition B: A is true and j is such that there is no prime greater than `p[k-1]` and less than j. Moreover, j is not divisible by any of `p[0..n]`. This condition is abbreviated to `relB(p,k,n,j)`. It is a useful condition, as there is a simple transition that makes this true.

In the new column B it is easy to detect whether n is large enough to conclude that j is the next prime after `p[k-1]`. We place the corresponding transition in column B and we have Figure 11.

`A:`	`S: p[0..N-1] exists & N>1`	
`k >= N`		`H: p[0..N-1] contains the first N primes`
	`p[0] = 2; p[1] = 3; k = 2`	`A: p[0..k-1] contains the first k primes & k <= N`

Figure 6. In column A the case `k < N` is missing.

There are still failed computations. (In fact, there is still no way to get beyond $N = 2$.) The way ahead is clear: a transition is missing in column B, for the situation where n is too small to conclude that j is the next prime. That in itself produces condition C and, with it, a new row and column.

In column C the missing information is whether j, the candidate for the next prime, is divisible by `p[n+1]`. If not, then n can be incremented, and condition B is verified. If so, then j is not a prime and the search for the next prime must be restarted with `j+2`. This determines a transition in column C that verifies condition C, so is placed in that row. See Figure 12.

Up till now we detected with every additional row and column that the new column lacked a transition. Not this time: none of the columns has a missing transition. The code matrix has no failed computations. So it gives the correct answer by exiting in row H, or it continues in an infinite computation. As we have only proved partial correctness, this latter alternative remains a possibility.

Termination For an infinite computation to arise, there must be at least one condition that is revisited an infinite number of times. For each condition we give a reason why it can only be revisited a finite number of times.

1. Condition A. For this condition to be returned to, k has to have increased.
2. Condition B. For this condition to be returned to, n or j has to have increased.
3. Condition C. For this condition to be returned to, n has to have increased.

The transitions have been chosen so that the corresponding revisiting condition is satisfied. As none of these conditions can be satisfied an infinite number of times, the code matrix has no infinite computation.

Running matrix code Running a code matrix in current practice requires translation to a currently available language. Our examples of matrix code have been constructed for ease of translation to languages like Java or C. This entails a drastic reduction in expressivity. Let us now demonstrate translation using Figure 12 as example.

As there is a similarity between the control states and the states of a finite-state automaton (FSA), a good starting point for systematic translation of a code matrix is the pattern according to which an FSA is implemented. This is usually done by introducing a constant for every state and to let a variable, say, `state` assume these constants as values. An infinite loop containing a `switch` controlled by `state` then contains a `case` statement for every control state. The fact that in a programming language the case statements are not restricted to input or output is the generalization that produces a code matrix from an FSA.

Each column of a code matrix translates to a `case` statement. The order in which the translations of the columns occur does not matter as long as `state` is initialized at S. Here we have arbitrarily chosen alphabetic order. In this way Figure 12 translates to the following.

```
public static void primesCM(int[] p, int N) {
  final int S=0, A=1, B=2, C=3, H=4;
  int state=S;      // control state
  int j=0, k=0, n=0; // data state
  while (true) {
    switch (state) {
      case A:
        if (k >= N) state = H;
        else {j = p[k-1]+2; n = 0; state = B;}
      break;
      case B: if (p[n]*p[n] > j) {
                p[k++] = j; state = A;
              } else state = C;
      break;
      case C:
        if (j%p[n+1] != 0) {n++; state = B;}
        else {j += 2; n = 0; state = C;}
      break;
      case H: return;
      case S: p[0] = 2; p[1] = 3; k = 2; state = A;
      break;
    }
  }
}
```

Figure 7. Translation of the code matrix in Figure 12 to Java.

A transition `b0;S0` in column X and row R_0 and transition `!b0;S1` in column X and row R_1 translate to `case X: if (b0) {S0; state = R0;} else {S1; state = R1} break;` in the above code.

9. Expressiveness of matrix code

The Java code obtained by translating a code matrix is quite different from what one conventionally would write: compare Figure 1 with Figure 7. In this example Matrix Code has the advantage of being a verification and of being easy to discover. But in the prime-number problem Matrix Code does not lead to a more efficient program: it has the same set of computations as the conventional one.

In this section we present an example where Matrix Code makes it easy to discover an algorithm that is more efficient than what is obtained via the conventional programming style. Consider the merging of two monotonically nondecreasing input streams into a single output stream. We have available the following C++ functions.

```
bool getL(int& x);  // output parameter x
bool getR(int& x);  // output parameter x
void putL();
void putR();
```

where `getL` (`getR`) tests the left (right) input stream for emptiness. In case of nonemptiness the output parameter `x` gets the value of the first element of the stream. Neither `getL` nor `getR` change any of the streams. This is only done by the functions `putL()` and `putR()` which transfer the first element of a nonempty left or right input stream to the output stream.

Figure 8 is a typical program for this situation. It typically acts in two stages. In the first stage both input streams are nonempty. In the second stage one of the input streams is empty so that all that remains to be done is to copy the other stream to the output.

```
void eMerge() {
  int u,v;
  while (getL(u) && getR(v))
    if (u <= v) putL();
    else        putR();
  while (getL(u)) putL();
  while (getR(v)) putR();
}
```

Figure 8. A structured program for merging two streams.

This algorithm performs unnecessary tests: in the first stage only one of the input streams is changed, so that only that one needs to be tested for emptiness; here both are tested[3]. It is superfluous tests like this that allow the algorithm to be as simple as it is.

Of course it is unlikely that it is important to save the kind of test just mentioned. But there are many types of merging situations and there may be some in which it does matter. An advantage of matrix code is that it does not bias the programmer towards including superfluous tests.

We proceed to develop a code matrix for merging. The assertions need to indicate whether it is known that an input stream is empty and, if not, what its first element is. If an input stream is possibly empty then we represent it by "?". We write "e" if an input stream is empty. Nonemptiness is indicated by writing "`x:?`", where `x` is the first element. We have to do this for each of the input streams; we write e.g. the assertion `(u:?,v:?)` to mean that both input streams are nonempty and have first elements `u` and `v`, respectively.

With these conventions we can state the program's specification as obtaining a transition from the state `S`, which is `?:?`, to the state `H`, which is `e:e`, while maintaining the invariant that the result of appending the output stream to the result of merging the input streams is constant. Accordingly, the development starts with Figure 9.

`S:(?,?)`	
`/*which T?*/`	`H:(e,e)`

Figure 9. Matrix code corresponding to specification of the merging program. But there is no `T` such that `{S}T{H}`. The conditions in this figure, as well as those in Figures 13 and 14 include the unstated conjunct that the result of appending the output stream to the merge of the input streams is equal to the merge of the input streams in the initial state.

As always with matrix code, we start with the conditions. Which do we need, in addition to the `(?,?)` and `(e,e)` given by the specification? For each of the input streams there are three states of information:

[3] With the one exception when the left input stream runs out at the same time as, or before, the right input stream.

* ?
* e
* x:? for some first element x

It is to be expected that the two input streams can assume each of the three information states independently, for a total of nine conditions.

It is desirable that the initial condition (?,?) of minimal information does not arise during a computation of the code matrix. Under the assumption that we can avoid this there will be only rows for the eight other conditions. By the time we will have populated the columns for these eight conditions we will see whether this assumption was justified.

This problem is easy because the conditions are determined by the nature of the problem. For each condition there is an obvious and easy-to-realize revisiting condition. If there is at least one unknown input stream at least one of them has to become known before revisiting. If both input streams are known, then at least one of them has to have its first element transferred to output before revisiting. See Figure 14, where the transitions have been chosen to conform to the revisiting requirements. As each column either has no guard or two complementary guards, no additional rows are needed.

The translation of this table to C++ is given below. As the order of the translations of the columns is immaterial, we have placed them in alphabetic order by label.

```
void mMerge() {
  int u,v;
  typedef enum{S,A,B,C,D,E,F,G,H} State;
  State state = S; // control state
  while(true) {
    switch(state) {
      case A: state = (getR(v))?C:D; break;
      case B: if (getR(v)) {putR(); state = B;}
         else state = H; break;
      case C: if (u <= v) {putL(); state = E;}
         else {putR(); state = A;} break;
      case D: putL(); state = F; break;
      case E: state = getL(u)?C:G; break;
      case F: state = getL(u)?D:H; break;
      case G: putR(); state = B; break;
      case H: return;
      case S: state = getL(u)?A:B; break;
    }
  }
}
```

Figure 10. A C++ function for merging two streams translated from Figure 14.

The reason for developing a code matrix for the merge problem was the desire to avoid the superfluous tests of a function like the `eMerge` listed in Figure 8. To see in how far `mMerge` improves in this respect we have run both functions on the same set of pairs of input streams and counted the calls executed in both merge functions.

Such comparisons are of course dependent on the nature of the input streams. For example, the more equal in length the input streams are, the more favourable for `mMerge`. Accordingly we have used a random-number generator to determine the lengths of the input streams. The input streams themselves are monotonically increasing with random increments.

	getL	getR	putL	putR
eMerge	1756	2691	871	1819
mMerge	872	1821	871	1819
eMerge	1067	830	655	410
mMerge	656	411	655	410
eMerge	3261	735	2894	365
mMerge	2895	366	2894	365
eMerge	1355	1024	844	509
mMerge	845	510	844	509

Each pair of successive lines gives the result of running `eMerge` and `mMerge` on the same pair of input streams. The lengths of the streams are not listed separately, as they are equal to the number of calls to `putL` and `putR` shown in the table.

A merge function needs to make at least one call to `getL` (`getR`) for every element of the left (right) input stream. It can be seen that `mMerge` remains close to this minimum, while `eMerge` does not.

This example is notable in that matrix code yields an unfamiliar, test-optimal algorithm by *default*. Structured programming tends to reduce the number of control states. Matrix code lacks this bias: in its use it is natural to introduce control states as needed to serve as memory for test outcomes.

10. Related work

The following comment has been made on Matrix Code: "*Although it reeks of flow charts, the proposal has some merit.*" The comment has some merit: flow charts are indeed closely related to Matrix Code. Flow charts were widely used as an informal programming notation from the early 1950s to 1970. Floyd [8] showed how assertions and verification conditions can prove a flow chart partially correct. Hoare [10] introduced the notation of triples for the verification conditions and cast Floyd's method in the form of inference rules for control structures such as `while ... do ...` and `if ... then ... else ...`

Dijkstra observed that verifying assertions are difficult to find for existing code, so that an attempt at verification is a costly undertaking with an uncertain outcome. He argued [4, 5] that code and correctness should be "developed in parallel". The proposal seems to have found no response, if only for the lack of specifics in the proposal. Given the fact that Dijkstra's proposal was considered unrealistically utopian, and still is, it is interesting to read what seems to be the first treatise [9] on programming in the modern sense, published in 1946. Here programs are expressed in the form of *flow diagrams*. At first sight one might think that these are flow charts under another name. This is not the case: flow diagrams consist of executable code integrated with assertions, with the understanding that a consistent flow diagram proves the correctness of the computations performed by it.

The imperative part of a flow diagram was translated to machine code (this was before the appearance of assemblers). I found no indication in [9] that it was even contemplated to split off the imperative part of the flow diagram. Thus we see that what was a vague proposal [4, 5], and regarded as unrealistically utopian in 1970, was fully worked out in 1946 and may have become a practical reality in 1951 when the IAS machine became operational.

By the time flow charts appeared, the proof part of flow diagrams had been dropped. And apparently forgotten, for Floyd's discovery was published in 1967 and universally acknowledged as such. Floyd's format is rather different, and, in our opinion, preferable to the flow diagrams of [9]. Matrix Code can be regarded as a simplification of Floyd's flow chart annotated with assertions, a simplification made possible by the use of transitions that provide a common generalization of statements and tests. Apt and Schaerf unify statements and tests in their nondeterministic control structures [1].

Code matrices can be regarded as generalized Finite-State Automata. The control states of code matrices are similar to the states in Finite-State Automata; the data states have no counterpart in FSAs. Data states can contain variables of widely varying types. These can include streams of characters, so that code matrices can simulate FSAs with input and/or output. This possibility makes Matrix Code reminiscent of Dana Scott's proposal [13] to put an end to the proliferation of new variations of FSA by replacing them by programs defined to run on suitably defined machines.

In spite of Scott's injunction, variants of FSA continued to appear. Of special interest in this context are *labeled transition systems* which are used to model and verify reactive systems [2]. Here the set of states is often not finite and there is typically no halt state. Such systems are specified by rules of the form $P \xrightarrow{A} Q$ to indicate the possibility of a transition from state P to state Q accompanied by action A. Mathematically the rules are viewed as a ternary relation containing triples consisting of P, A, and Q. This is of course unobjectionable, but the alternative view of the rules as constituting a matrix indexed by states, containing in this instance A as element indexed by P and Q has the advantage of connecting the theory to that of semilinear programming in the sense of Parker. Another variant of FSA are the *augmented transition networks* used in linguistics [15].

The property that a code matrix is both a set of logical formulas and an executable program is reminiscent of logic programming, especially its aspect of separating logic from control [11]. A special form of logic program corresponding to imperative programs was investigated in [3]. The modification of flow charts by means of binary relations was introduced in [14].

11. Conclusions

In this paper we write programs as matrices with binary relations as elements. These matrices can be regarded as transformations in a generalized vector space, where vectors have assertions about data states as elements. Computations of the programs are characterized by powers of the matrix and verified assertions show up as generalized eigenvectors of the matrix. Such results may be dismissed as frivolous theorizing. It seems to us that they are related to the following practical benefits.

Our motivation was to address the fact that imperative programming is in an unsatisfactory state compared to functional and logic programming. In the latter paradigms, implementation is, or is close to, specification. In imperative programming the relation between implementation and specification is the verification problem, a problem considered too hard for the practising programmer. We proposed Matrix Code as an imperative programming language where the same construct can be read as logical formula and can serve as basis for a routine translation to Java or `C`.

Another practical benefit is that it seems possible in some cases to develop algorithms incrementally by small, obvious steps from the specification. In this paper we go through such steps for an algorithm to fill a table with prime numbers using the method of trial division. Whether or not this success is an exceptional case, it seems certain that progress has been made in the direction of the old dream according to which the production of verified code is facilitated by developing proof and code in parallel.

Acknowledgments

Thanks to Paul McJones, Mantis Cheng, and the reviewers for their help in improving the paper. This research benefited from facilities provided by the University of Victoria and by the Natural Science and Engineering Research Council of Canada.

References

[1] K.R. Apt and A. Schaerf. Search and imperative programming. *POPL '97*, pages 67–79.

[2] C. Baier and J.P. Katoen. *Principles of Model Checking*. MIT Press, 2008.

[3] Keith L. Clark and M.H. van Emden. Consequence Verification of Flowcharts. *IEEE Transactions on Software Engineering*, SE-7:52–60, January 1981.

[4] E.W. Dijkstra. A constructive approach to the problem of program correctness. *BIT*, 8:174–186, 1968.

[5] Edsger W. Dijkstra. Concern for correctness as a guiding principle for program composition. In J.S.J. Hugo, editor, *The Fourth Generation*, pages 359–367. Infotech, Ltd, 1971.

[6] Edsger W. Dijkstra. Notes on structured programming. In O.-J. Dahl, E.W. Dijkstra, and C.A.R. Hoare, editors, *Structured Programming*, pages 1–72. Academic Press, 1972.

[7] E.W. Dijkstra. *A Discipline of Programming*. Prentice Hall, 1976.

[8] Robert W. Floyd. Assigning meanings to programs. In J.T. Schwartz, editor, *Proceedings Symposium in Applied Mathematics*, pages 19–32. American Mathematical Society, 1967.

[9] H.H. Goldstine and J. von Neumann. Planning and coding of problems for an electronic computing instrument. Part II, volume 1, 1946. Reprinted in: *John von Neumann: Collected Works*, Pages 80 - 151, volume V. A.H. Taub, editor. Pergamon Press, 1963.

[10] C.A.R. Hoare. An axiomatic basis for computer programming. *Communications of the ACM*, 12(10):576–583, 1969.

[11] R.A. Kowalski. Algorithm = Logic + Control. *Comm. ACM*, 22:424–436, 1979.

[12] D. Stott Parker. Partial order programming. Technical Report CSD-870067, Computer Science Department, University of California at Los Angeles, 1987.

[13] Dana Scott. Some definitional suggestions for automata theory. *Journal of Computer and Systems Sciences*, 1:187–212, 1967.

[14] M.H. van Emden. Programming with verification conditions. *IEEE Transactions on Software Engineering*, vol. 3(1979), pp 148–159.

[15] W.A. Woods. Transition network grammars. *Comm. ACM*, 13:591–606, 1970.

B:	A:	S: p[0..N-1] exists & N>1	
	k >= N		H: p[0..N-1] contains the first N primes
p[n]*p[n]>j; p[k++]=j		p[0] = 2; p[1] = 3; k = 2	A: p[0..k-1] contains the first k primes & k <= N
	k<N; j = p[k-1]+2; n=0		B: A & k<N & relB(p,k,n,j)

Figure 11. In column A we have added a transition in column A for the case that `k < N`. In that case we can start finding the next prime after `p[k-1]` because we know that there is enough space in `p` to store it. `relB(p,k,n,j)` means that there is no prime between the last prime found and `j` and that `n<k`, and that `j` is not divided by any prime in `p[0..n]`.

C:	B:	A:	S: p[0..N-1] exists & N>1	
		k >= N		H: p[0..N-1] contains the first N primes
	p[n]*p[n]>j; p[k++]=j		p[0] = 2; p[1] = 3; k = 2	A: p[0..k-1] contains the first k primes & k <= N
j%p[n+1]!=0; n++		k<N; j = p[k-1]+2; n=0		B: A & k<N & relB(p,k,n,j)
j%p[n+1]==0; j += 2; n=0	p[n]*p[n]<= j			C: B & p[n]*p[n] <= j

Figure 12. This figure is both a general example of a code matrix and the final stage of the development consisting of the sequence of Figures 5, 6, and 11. Change from Figure 11: row and column with label C are added. There are no incomplete columns. This, as well as each of the previous versions is partially correct, as implied by the validity of the verification condition for each of the null matrix elements. The absence of incomplete columns opens the possibility of total correctness, but does not prove it.

A	S:(?,?)	
		H:(e,e)
	getL(u)	A:(u:?,?)
	!getL(u)	B:(e,?)
getR(v)		C:(u:?,v:?)
!getR(v)		D:(u:?,e)

Figure 13. See Figure 9. An input stream needs to be tested; the left one is chosen arbitrarily. This gives rise to new conditions. Columns for these will cause addition of yet more conditions. See Figure 14.

G	F	E	D	C	B	A	S:(?,?)	
	!getL(u)				!getR(v)			H:(e,e)
				u>v; putR()			getL(u)	A:(u:?,?)
putR()					getR(v); putR()		!getL(u)	B:(e,?)
		getL(u)				getR(v)		C:(u:?,v:?)
	getL(u)					!getR(v)		D:(u:?,e)
				u <= v; putL()				E:(?,v:?)
			putL()					F:(?,e)
		!getL(u)						G:(e,v:?)

Figure 14. The complete code matrix for the merging problem, continuing Figures 9 and 13.

Automatic Synthesis of Specifications for First Order Curry Programs

Giovanni Bacci   Marco Comini
DIMI, University of Udine (Italy)
giovanni.bacci@uniud.it, marco.comini@uniud.it

Marco A. Feliú   Alicia Villanueva
DSIC, Universitat Politècnica de València (Spain)
mfeliu@dsic.upv.es, villanue@dsic.upv.es

Abstract

This paper presents a technique to automatically infer algebraic property-oriented specifications from first-order Curry programs. Curry is a lazy functional logic language and the interaction between laziness and logical variables raises some additional difficulties with respect to other proposals for functional languages. Our technique statically infers from the source code of a Curry program a specification which consists of a set of equations relating (nested) operation calls that have the same behavior. We propose a (glass-box) semantic-based inference method which relies on a fully-abstract (condensed) semantics for achieving, to some extent, the correctness of the inferred specification, differently from other (black-box) approaches based on testing techniques.

Categories and Subject Descriptors F.3.1 [*Logics and meaning of programs*]: Specifying and Verifying and Reasoning about programs—Specification techniques; D.3.2 [*Programming Languages*]: Constraint and logic languages

General Terms Documentation, Languages, Verification

Keywords Curry, property-oriented specifications, semantic-based inference methods

1. Introduction

Specifications have been widely used for several purposes: they can be used to aid (formal) verification, validation or testing, to instrument software development, as summaries in program understanding, as documentation of programs, to discover components in libraries or services in a network context, etc. [, , , , , , ,]. Depending on the context and the use of specifications, they can be defined, either manually or automatically, before coding (e.g. for validation purposes), during the program coding (e.g. for testing or understanding purposes), or after the code has been written (for verification or documentation). We can find several proposals of (automatic) inference of high-level specifications (from an executable or from the source code) of a system, like [, , ,], which have proven to be very helpful.

In the literature, specification formalisms have been classified through some common characteristics [ ]. It is frequent to distinguish between *property-oriented* specifications and *model-oriented* or *functional* specifications. It can be said that property-oriented specifications are at a higher description level than other kinds of specifications: they consist in an indirect definition of the system's behavior by means of stating a set of properties, usually in the form of axioms, that the system must satisfy [,]. In other words, a specification does not represent the functionality of the program (the output of the system) but its properties in terms of relations among the operations that can be invoked in the program (i.e., identifies different calls that have the same behavior when executed). This kind of specifications is particularly well suited for program understanding: the user can realize non-evident information about the behavior of a given function by observing its relation with other functions. Moreover, the inferred properties can manifest potential symptoms of program errors which can be used as input for (formal) validation and verification purposes.

Clearly, the task of automatically inferring program specifications is in general undecidable and, given the complexity of the problem, there exists a large number of different proposals which impose several restrictions. Many aspects vary from one solution to another: the kind of specifications that are computed (e.g., model-oriented vs. property-oriented specifications), the kind of programs considered, the correctness or completeness of the method, etc.

We can identify two mainstream approaches to perform the inference of specifications: glass-box and black-box. The glass-box approach [,] assumes that the source code of the program is available. In this context, the goal of inferring a specification is mainly applied to document the code, or to understand it [ ]. Therefore, the specification must be more succinct and comprehensible than the source code itself. The inferred specification can also be used to automatize the testing process of the program [ ] or to verify that a given property holds [ ]. The black-box approach [,] works only by running the executable. This means that the only information used during the inference process is the input-output behavior of the program. In this setting, the inferred specification is often used to discover the functionality of the system (or services in a network) [ ]. Although black-box approaches work without any restriction on the considered language –which is rarely the case in a glass-box approach– in general, they cannot *guarantee* the correctness of the results (whereas indeed semantics-based glass-box approaches can).

For this work, we took inspiration from QuickSpec [ ], which is an (almost) black-box inference approach for Haskell programs [ ] based on testing. QuickSpec automatically infers program specifications as sets of equations of the form $e_1 = e_2$, where e_1, e_2 are generic program expressions that (should) have the same computational behavior. This approach has two properties that we like:

PPDP'12, September 19–21, 2012, Leuven, Belgium.

it is completely automatic as it needs only the program to run, plus some indications on target functions and generic values to be employed in equations, and

the outcomes are very intuitive since they are expressed *only* in terms of the program components, so the user does not need any kind of extra knowledge to interpret the results.

However, our proposal ended up being radically different from QuickSpec:

- First, we aim to infer *correct* (algebraic) property-oriented specifications. To this end, instead of a testing-based approach, we propose a glass-box *semantic-based* approach.
- Second, we consider the functional logic language Curry [,]. Curry is a multi-paradigm programming language that combines in a seamless way features from functional programming (nested expressions, lazy evaluation, higher-order functions) and logic programming (logical variables, partial data structures, built-in search). Due to lazy evaluation in presence of (free) logical variables, the problem of inferring specifications for this kind of languages poses several additional problems w.r.t. other paradigms. We discuss these issues in Section 2.

In the rest of the paper, we first introduce the problem of generating useful specifications for the functional logic paradigm by discussing a simple, illustrative example. In Section 3, we define our notion of specification, which is composed of equations of different kinds. Thereafter, in Section 4, we explain how the specifications are computed in detail. In Section 5 we show some examples of specifications computed by the prototype implementing the technique. Finally, Section 6 discusses the most related work and Section 7 concludes.

2. Analysis of the issues posed by the logical features of Curry

Curry is a *lazy* functional *logic* language which admits free (logical) variables in expressions and whose program rules are evaluated non-deterministically. Differently from the functional case[1], due to the logical features, an equation $e_1 = e_2$ can be interpreted in many different ways. We will discuss the key points of the problem by means of a (very simple) illustrative example.

The syntax of Curry is very similar to that of Haskell. Variables and function names start with a character in lower case, whereas data constructors and type names start with a letter in upper case. For a complete description of the Curry language, the interested reader can consult [ ]. In this work, we assume that the reader is familiar with the syntax and basic semantic notions of Haskell.

EXAMPLE 2.1 (BOOLEAN LOGIC EXAMPLE)

Consider the definition of the boolean data type with values `True` and `False` and operations `and`, `or`, `not` and `imp`:

```
and True x = x
and False _ = False
or True _ = True
or False x = x
not True = False
not False = True
imp False x = True
imp True x = x
```

This is a pretty standard "short-cut" definition of boolean connectives. For example, the definition of `and` states that whenever the first argument is equal to `False`, the function returns the value `False`, regardless of the value of the second argument. Since the language is lazy, in this case the second argument will not be evaluated.

For this example, one could expect a (property-oriented) specification with equations like[2]

$$\texttt{imp x y} = \texttt{or (not x) y} \quad (2.1)$$

$$\texttt{not (or x y)} = \texttt{and (not x) (not y)} \quad (2.2)$$

$$\texttt{not (and x y)} = \texttt{or (not x) (not y)} \quad (2.3)$$

$$\texttt{not (not x)} = \texttt{x} \quad (2.4)$$

$$\texttt{and x (and y z)} = \texttt{and (and x y) z} \quad (2.5)$$

$$\texttt{and x y} = \texttt{and y x} \quad (2.6)$$

which are well-known laws among the (theoretical) boolean operators. This comprehensible specification aids the user to learn the properties of the program. In addition, the specification can be useful to detect bugs in the program by observing both, properties (equations) that occur in the specification but were not expected, and expected equations that are missing. These equations, of the form $e_1 = e_2$, can be read as

all possible outcomes for e_1 *are also outcomes for* e_2,
and vice versa. (2.7)

In the following, we call this notion of equivalence *computed result equivalence* and we denote it by $=_{CR}$.

Actually, Equations (2.1), (2.2), (2.3), (2.5) and (2.6) are *literally* valid in this sense since, in Curry, free variables are admitted in expressions, and the mentioned equations are valid *as they are*. This is quite different from the pure functional case where equations *have to be interpreted* as properties that hold for any *ground* instance of the variables occurring in the equation.

On the contrary, Equation (2.4) is not *literally* valid. Let us first introduce the notation for evaluations. The expression $\{\texttt{x/True}\} \cdot \texttt{True}$ denotes that the normal form `True` (at the right of the $\cdot$ symbol) has been reached with computed answer substitution $\{\texttt{x/True}\}$ (at the left of the $\cdot$ symbol). Now we are ready to discuss Equation (2.4). The goal on the left hand side of the equation `not (not x)` evaluates to two normal forms: $\{\texttt{x/True}\} \cdot \texttt{True}$ and $\{\texttt{x/False}\} \cdot \texttt{False}$, whereas the right hand side of the equation `x` evaluates just to $\{\} \cdot \texttt{x}$. Note however that any ground instance of the two goals evaluates to the same results, namely both `True` and `not (not True)` evaluate to $\{\} \cdot \texttt{True}$, and both `False` and `not (not False)` evaluate to $\{\} \cdot \texttt{False}$.

This fact motivates the use of an additional notion of equivalence, called *ground equivalence*, which can be helpful for the user since the equations that hold under this equivalence represent, in general, interesting properties of the program. We denote it by $=_G$. This notion coincides with the (only possible) equivalence notion used in the pure functional paradigm: two terms are ground equivalent if, for all ground instances, the outcomes of both terms coincide.

Because of the presence of logical variables, there is another very relevant difference w.r.t. the pure functional case, concerned with *contextual equivalence*: given a valid equation $e_1 = e_2$, is it true that, for any context C, the equation $C[e_1] = C[e_2]$ still holds? Curry is not referentially transparent[3] w.r.t. its operational behavior, i.e., an expression can produce different computed values

[1] Actually, different from a language without logical variables that may be instantiated during execution.

[2] In this section, our main goal is to give the intuition of the specification computed by our approach, thus we show just a subset of the equations satisfied by the program.

[3] The concept of referential transparency of a language can be stated in terms of a formal semantics as: the semantics equivalence of two expres-

when it is embedded in a context that binds its free variables (as shown by the following example), which makes the answer to the question posed above not straightforward.

EXAMPLE 2.2

Given a program with the following rules

```
g x = C (h x)
g' A = C A
h A = A
f (C x) B = B
```

the expressions `g x` and `g' x` compute the same result, namely $\{x/A\} \cdot$ `C A`. However, the expression `f (g x) x` computes one result, namely $\{x/B\} \cdot$ `B`, while expression `f (g' x) x` computes none.

Thus, in the Curry case, becomes mandatory to *additionally* ask in the equivalence notion of (2.7) that the outcomes must be equal also when the two terms are embedded within any context. We call this equivalence *contextual equivalence* and we denote it by $=_C$. Actually, Equations (2.1), (2.2), (2.3) and (2.5) are valid w.r.t. this equivalence notion.

We can see that $=_C$ is (obviously) stronger than $=_{CR}$, which is in turn stronger than $=_G$. As a conclusion, for our example we would get the following (partial) specification.[4]

`imp x y` $=_C$ `or (not x) y`

`not (or x y)` $=_C$ `and (not x) (not y)`

`not (and x y)` $=_C$ `or (not x) (not y)`

`and x (and y z)` $=_C$ `and (and x y) z`

`not (not x)` $=_G$ `x`

`and x y` $=_G$ `and y x`

This example has shown, first, the kind of property-oriented specifications that we want to compute from the program, and second, the need to consider different kinds of equalities between terms in order to get a useful specification. It is worth noticing that adopting *only* a notion of equivalence based on the referentially transparent semantics (the $=_C$ equivalence) can be too restrictive: we may lose important properties. However, by using the just the weaker notions we cannot know if two equivalent expression are also equivalent within any context.

The need of determining $=_C$ equalities can explain the reason because we believe that, in the case of Curry, the use of a semantics-based approach can be more suited than testing-based approaches. In a test-based approach expressions should have to be nested within some outer context in order to establish their $=_C$ equivalence. Since the number of needed terms to be evaluated grows exponentially w.r.t. the depth of nestings, the addition of a further outer context would dramatically alter the performance. Moreover, if we try to mitigate this problem by reducing the number of terms/tests to be checked, the quality of the produced equations degrades sensibly. On the contrary, a semantics-based approach, based on a fully abstract semantics, achieves the $=_C$ equivalence by construction.

3. Formalization of equivalence notions

In this section, we formally present all the kinds of term equivalence notions that are used to compute equations of the specification. We need first to introduce some basic formal notions that are used in the rest of the paper.

We say that a first order Curry program is a set of rules P built over a signature Σ which is partitioned in $\mathcal{C}$, the *constructor* symbols, and $\mathcal{D}$, the *defined* symbols. $\mathcal{V}$ denotes a (fixed) countably infinite set of variables and $\mathcal{T}(\Sigma, \mathcal{V})$ denotes the terms built over signature Σ and variables $\mathcal{V}$. A *fresh* variable is a variable that appears nowhere else.

The semantics. We evaluate first order Curry programs on the condensed, goal-independent semantics recently defined in [,] for functional logic programs. We preferred this semantics instead of the established (small-step) operational and I/O semantics [,] because they do not fulfill referential transparency, whereas the former does. This fact makes the (more elaborated) semantics of [,] an appropriate base semantics for computing specifications w.r.t. $=_C$. Moreover, this semantics has another property which is very important from a pragmatical point of view: it is condensed, meaning that denotations are the smallest possible (between all those semantics which are fully abstract). This is an almost essential feature in order to develop a semantic-based tool which has to *compute* the semantics. In particular, with this semantics it is reasonable to compute a finite number of iterations of the program's denotation itself, while the computation of the other mentioned semantics is not.

The denotation $\mathcal{F}[\![P]\!]$ of a program P is the least fixed-point of an immediate consequence operator $\mathcal{P}[\![P]\!]$. This operator is based on a term evaluation function $\mathcal{E}[\![t]\!]$ which, for any term $t \in \mathcal{T}(\Sigma, \mathcal{V})$, gives the semantics of t as $\mathcal{E}[\![t]\!]_{\mathcal{F}[\![P]\!]}$. Intuitively, the evaluation $\mathcal{E}[\![t]\!]_{\mathcal{F}[\![P]\!]}$ computes a tree-like structure collecting the "relevant history" of the computation of all computed results of t, abstracting from function calls and focusing only on the way in which the result is built. In particular, every leaf of the tree represents a normal form of the initial term. Nodes are pairs of the form $\sigma \cdot s$, where σ is a substitution (binding variables of the initial expression with linear constructor terms), and s is a partially computed value, that is, a term in $\mathcal{T}(\mathcal{C}, \mathcal{V} \cup \mathcal{V}_\varrho)$ that may contain special variables $\varrho_0, \varrho_1, \ldots \in \mathcal{V}_\varrho$ (a set disjoint from $\mathcal{V}$) indicating an unevaluated subterm. Leaves with no occurrences of special variables are computed results. We denote by $cr(T)$ the set of computed results of the semantic tree T.

Full-abstraction w.r.t. the behavior and referential transparency of the semantics are proven in [ ]. Thus, it holds that $cr(\mathcal{E}[\![t]\!]_{\mathcal{F}[\![P]\!]})$ corresponds to the set of computed outcomes of t using P. Moreover, given two terms e and e', and a generic context $C[\cdot]$, it holds that if $\mathcal{E}[\![e]\!]_{\mathcal{F}[\![P]\!]} = \mathcal{E}[\![e']\!]_{\mathcal{F}[\![P]\!]}$, then $\mathcal{E}[\![C[e]]\!]_{\mathcal{F}[\![P]\!]} = \mathcal{E}[\![C[e']]\!]_{\mathcal{F}[\![P]\!]}$.

The following states the correctness of the semantics.

THEOREM 3.1 ([ ]) *Let P be a first-order Curry program and t be a term in $\mathcal{T}(\Sigma, \mathcal{V})$. Then $cr(\mathcal{E}[\![t]\!]_{\mathcal{F}[\![P]\!]})$ corresponds to the set of computed outcomes of t using P.*

Moreover, $\mathcal{E}[\![\cdot]\!]_{\mathcal{F}[\![P]\!]}$ fulfills referential transparency:

THEOREM 3.2 *Let P be a first-order Curry program, e, e' terms in $\mathcal{T}(\Sigma, \mathcal{V})$, and $C[\cdot]$ be a context. If $\mathcal{E}[\![e]\!]_{\mathcal{F}[\![P]\!]} = \mathcal{E}[\![e']\!]_{\mathcal{F}[\![P]\!]}$, then $\mathcal{E}[\![C[e]]\!]_{\mathcal{F}[\![P]\!]} = \mathcal{E}[\![C[e']]\!]_{\mathcal{F}[\![P]\!]}$.*

EXAMPLE 3.3 (EXAMPLE 2.2 CONTINUED)

The computed semantics for the program P in Example 2.2 is the following:

$$\mathcal{F}[\![P]\!] = \begin{cases} \texttt{g x} \mapsto \varepsilon \cdot \varrho \xrightarrow{\varrho} \varepsilon \cdot \texttt{C}\ \varrho_1 \xrightarrow{\varrho_1} \{\texttt{x/A}\} \cdot \texttt{C A} \\ \texttt{g' x} \mapsto \varepsilon \cdot \varrho \xrightarrow{\varrho} \{\texttt{x/A}\} \cdot \texttt{C A} \\ \texttt{h x} \mapsto \varepsilon \cdot \varrho \xrightarrow{\varrho} \{\texttt{x/A}\} \cdot \texttt{A} \\ \texttt{f x y} \mapsto \varepsilon \cdot \varrho \xrightarrow{\varrho} \{\texttt{x/C x', y/B}\} \cdot \texttt{B} \end{cases}$$

---

sions e, e' implies the semantics equivalence of e and e' when used within any context $C[\cdot]$. Namely, $\forall e, e', C.\ [\![e]\!] = [\![e']\!] \implies [\![C[e]]\!] = [\![C[e']]\!]$.

[4] As we will show later, our technique computes a complete specification for a specific *size* of terms in equations.

The semantics of a program P is a family of semantic trees indexed by most general expressions (a function symbol applied to distinct variables). Edges in the semantic tree are labeled with the special variable that is instantiated with an expression (that may contain another special variable). Below we show the evaluation of the two expressions that lead to different computed results in the example:

$$\mathcal{E}[\![\texttt{f (g x) x}]\!]_{\mathcal{F}[\![P]\!]} = \varepsilon \cdot \varrho \xrightarrow{\varrho} \{\texttt{x/B}\} \cdot \texttt{B}$$
$$\mathcal{E}[\![\texttt{f (g' x) x}]\!]_{\mathcal{F}[\![P]\!]} = \varepsilon \cdot \varrho$$

Note that $\varepsilon \cdot \varrho$ is not a computed result due to the occurrence of the ϱ variable.

Even if this semantics is condensed, the trees in denotations can be infinite both in depth and in width, as we show with the following example.

EXAMPLE 3.4

Consider the classical append function:

```
append [] y = y
append (x:xs) y = x:(append xs y)
```

The semantics of the function append in $\mathcal{F}[\![P]\!]$ is

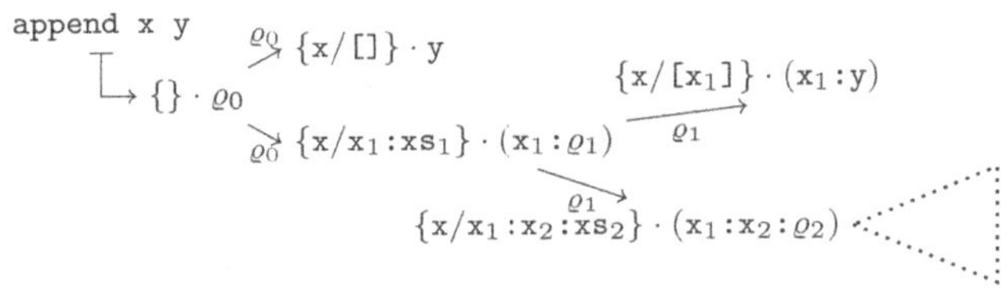

The dotted triangle in the figure denotes that the semantics has not been completely computed.

In order to deal with infinite trees, we need to use an approximated (abstract) semantics (obtained by abstract interpretation [,]) for the computation of our inference method (in Section 4). A discussion about effectiveness and precision regarding this issue is given in Section 4.1.

The specification. Formally, an algebraic specification $\mathcal{S}$ is a set of (sequences of) equations of the form $t_1 =_K t_2 =_K \ldots =_K t_n$, with $K \in \{C, CR, G\}$ and $t_1, t_2, \ldots, t_n \in \mathcal{T}(\Sigma, \mathcal{V})$. K distinguishes the kinds of computational equalities that we previously informally discussed, which we now present formally.

Contextual Equivalence $=_C$. This equivalence states that two terms t_1 and t_2 are equivalent if $C[t_1]$ and $C[t_2]$ have the same behavior for any context $C[\cdot]$. This is the most difficult equivalence to be established by testing approaches. However, by using the semantics $\mathcal{F}[\![P]\!]$ it is really easy because the semantics is fully abstract w.r.t. the contextual program behavior equivalence [ ]. Therefore, two terms t_1 and t_2 are related by the contextual relation $=_C$ if and only if their semantics coincide, namely

$$t_1 =_C t_2 \iff \mathcal{E}[\![t_1]\!]_{\mathcal{F}[\![P]\!]} = \mathcal{E}[\![t_2]\!]_{\mathcal{F}[\![P]\!]}$$

Intuitively, due to the definition of this semantics, this means that *all the ways* in which these two terms reach their normal forms coincide. Note that $=_C$ does not capture termination properties, which is out of our current scope. However, thanks to the abstraction of the semantics, the inference technique that we are now proposing can work even if we have a non-terminating function, a situation in which black-box approaches cannot work at all.

Computed-result equivalence $=_{CR}$. This notion of equivalence states that two terms are equivalent when the outcomes of their evaluation are the same. Therefore, the computed-result equivalence abstracts from the way in which the results evolve during computation.

It is important to note that we can determine $=_{CR}$ just by collecting the leaves of $\mathcal{E}[\![e]\!]_{\mathcal{F}[\![P]\!]}$. This means that if we define a function cr that, given a semantic tree computed by the evaluation function, collects the leaves of the tree, then it holds that

$$t_1 =_{CR} t_2 \iff cr(\mathcal{E}[\![t_1]\!]_{\mathcal{F}[\![P]\!]}) = cr(\mathcal{E}[\![t_2]\!]_{\mathcal{F}[\![P]\!]})$$

The $=_{CR}$ equivalence is coarser than $=_C$ ($=_C \subsetneq =_{CR}$) as shown by Example 2.2.

Ground Equivalence $=_G$. This equivalence states that two terms are equivalent if all their possible ground instances have the same outcomes. This equivalence can be obtained by generating all ground instances of the leaves of $\mathcal{E}[\![e]\!]_{\mathcal{F}[\![P]\!]}$. We will discuss on possible effective implementations of this notion further ahead.

Note that the ground equivalence $=_G$ is the only possible notion in the pure functional paradigm. This fact allows one to have an intuition of the reason why the problem of specification synthesis is more complex in the functional logic paradigm.

To summarize, by construction, we have that $=_C \subsetneq =_{CR} \subsetneq =_G$ and only $=_C$ is referentially transparent (i.e., a congruence w.r.t. contextual embedding).

4. Deriving Specifications from Programs

Now we are ready to describe the process of inferring specifications. The input of the process consists of the Curry program to be analyzed and two additional parameters: a *relevant* API, denoted Σ^r, and a maximum term size, max_size. The *relevant* API allows the user to choose the operations in the program that will be present in the inferred specification, whereas the maximum term size limits the size of the terms in the specification. As a consequence, these two parameters tune the granularity of the specification, both making the process terminating and allowing the user to keep the specification concise and easy to understand. The output consists of a set of equations represented by equivalence classes of terms. Note that inferred equations may differ for the same program depending on the considered API and on the maximum term size. Similarly to other property-oriented approaches like [ ], the computed specification is complete up to terms of size max_size, i.e., it includes all the properties (relations) that hold between the operations in the relevant API and that are expressible by terms of size less or equal than max_size.

The inference process consists of three phases, as depicted in Figure 1. First, (an approximation of) the semantics of the input program is computed. Second, a partition of terms, formed with functions from the relevant API of size less or equal to the provided maximum size is computed. In our implementation, the size of a term is determined by its depth; however, the inference process is parametric w.r.t. the *size* function, thus other notions for size are allowed (e.g., number of parameters, length, etc.). Each equivalence class of the partition contains terms that are equivalent w.r.t. the contextual equivalence $=_C$ defined in Section 3. Finally, the equations of the specification are generated: first, the equations of the contextual partition are computed, and then, the equations corresponding to the other two notions of equivalence are computed by transforming the semantics.

In the following, we explain in detail the phases of the computation process by referring to the pseudo-code given in Algorithm 1. For the sake of comprehension, we present an untyped version of the algorithm. The actual one is a straightforward modification conformant w.r.t. types.

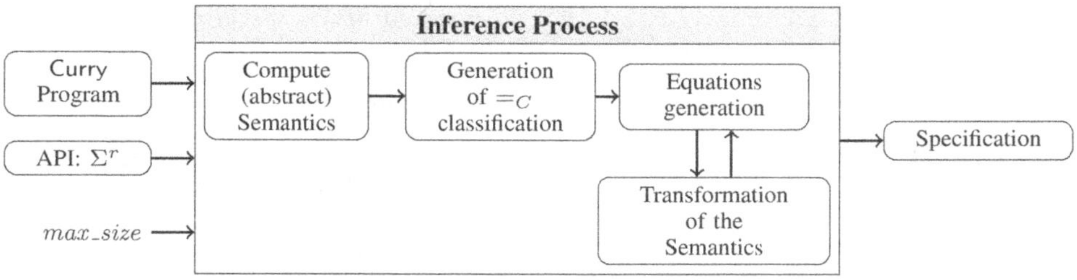

Figure 1. A general view of the inference process.

Algorithm 1 Inference of an algebraic specification

Require: Program P;
Program's *relevant* API Σ^r;
Maximum term size max_size
1. Compute $\mathcal{F}[\![P]\!]$: the (abstract) semantics of P
2. $part \leftarrow initial\_part(\mathcal{F}[\![P]\!])$
3. **repeat**
4. $part' \leftarrow part$
5. **for all** $f/n \in \Sigma^r$ **do**
6. **for all** $ec_1, \ldots, ec_n \in part$ such that at least one ec_i has been introduced in the previous iteration **do**
7. $t \leftarrow f(rep(ec_1), \ldots, rep(ec_n))$ where the $rep(ec_i)$ are renamed apart
8. **if** $t \notin part$ **and** $size(t) \leq max\_size$ **then**
9. $s \leftarrow \mathcal{E}[\![t]\!]_{\mathcal{F}[\![P]\!]}$: Compute the (abstract) semantics of term t
10. $add\_to\_partition(t, s, part')$
11. **end if**
12. **end for**
13. **end for**
14. **until** $part' = part$
15. $specification \leftarrow \emptyset$
16. $add\_equations(specification, part)$
17. **for all** $kind \in [CR, G]$ **do**
18. $part \leftarrow transform\_semantics(kind, part)$
19. $add\_equations(specification, part)$
20. **end for**
21. **return** $specification$

Computation of the abstract semantics (and initial classification). The first phase of the algorithm, Lines 1 to 2 (in Algorithm 1), is the computation of the initial classification that is needed to compute the classification w.r.t. $=_C$. It is based on the computation of an approximation of the semantics of the program (abstract semantics).

Terms are classified by their semantics into a data structure, which we call *partition*, consisting of a set of *equivalence classes* (ec) formed by

- $sem(ec)$: the semantics of (all) the terms in that class
- $rep(ec)$: the *representative term* of the class, which is defined as the smallest term in the class (w.r.t. the function *size*), and
- $terms(ec)$: the set of terms belonging to that equivalence class.

The *representative term* is used in order to avoid much redundancy in the generation of equations. The generation process is iterative, thus we generate first equations of smaller size, and then we increment the size until the size limit is reached. Instead of using every term of an equivalence class to build new terms of greater size, we just use the representative term.

With the program's semantics, the $initial\_part$ function builds the initial classification which contains:

- one class for a free (logical) variable $\langle \mathcal{E}[\![x]\!]_{\mathcal{F}[\![P]\!]},\, x,\, \{x\}\rangle$;[5]
- the classes for any built-in or user-defined constructor.

During the definition of the initial classification, it might occur that two terms, for instance $t_1 := f(x_1, \ldots, x_n)$ and $t_2 := g(y_1, \ldots, y_n)$, have the same semantics. If this happens, we don't generate two different classes, one for each term, but the second generated term is added to the class of the first one. For this particular example, we would have $\langle \mathcal{E}[\![t_1]\!]_{\mathcal{F}[\![P]\!]},\, t_1,\, \{t_1, t_2\}\rangle$.

Generation of $=_C$ classification. The second phase of the algorithm, Lines 3 to 14, is the (iterative) computation of the classification of terms w.r.t. $=_C$. As mentioned before, this classification is also the basis for the generation of the other kinds of equivalence classes.

We iteratively select all symbols f/n of the relevant API Σ^r (Line 5) [6] and n equivalence classes $ec_1, \ldots, ec_n$ from the current partition (Line 6) such that at least one ec_i was newly produced in the previous iteration. We build the term $t := f(t_1, \ldots, t_n)$, where each t_i is the representative term of ec_i, i.e., $t_i = rep(ec_i)$. In this way, by construction, the term t has surely not been considered yet; Then, we compute the semantics $s = \mathcal{E}[\![t]\!]_{\mathcal{F}[\![P]\!]}$ and update the current partition $part'$ by using the auxiliary method $add\_to\_partition(t, s, part')$ (Lines 7 to 11). Here, the compositionality of the semantics makes possible to compute the semantics of terms (Line 9) efficaciously: since the semantics $s_i = sem(ec_i)$ for each term t_i is already stored in ec_i, then the computation of the semantics of t can be done in an efficient way just by *nesting* the semantics s_i into the semantics of $f(x_1, \ldots, x_n)$. This semantics nesting operation is the core of the $\mathcal{E}$ operation.[7]

The $add\_to\_partition(t, s, part)$ function looks for an equivalence class ec in the current classification $part$ whose semantics coincides with s. If it is found, then the term t is added to the set of terms in ec. Otherwise, a new equivalence class $\langle s,\, t,\, \{t\}\rangle$ is created.

If the partition suffers any modification during the current iteration (i.e., any term is added to the partition), then the algorithm iterates. This phase terminates eventually because at each iteration we consider, by construction, terms which are different from those already existing in the partition and whose size is strictly greater than the size of its subterms (but the size is bounded by max_size).

The following example illustrates how the iterative process works:

[5] The typed version of the inference method uses one variable for each type.

[6] Following the standard notation f/n denotes a function f of arity n.

[7] The interested reader can see [ ] for the technical details about the semantic operators.

EXAMPLE 4.1

Let us recall the program of Example 2.1 and choose as relevant API the functions `and`, `or` and `not`. The following are the terms considered during the first iteration:

$$t_{1.1} := \texttt{not x}$$
$$t_{1.2} := \texttt{and x y}$$
$$t_{1.3} := \texttt{or x y}$$

Since the semantics of all these terms are different, three new classes are added to the initial partition. Thus, the partition at the end of the first iteration consists of four equivalence classes: the three corresponding to terms $t_{1.1}$, $t_{1.2}$ and $t_{1.3}$ and the equivalence class for the boolean free variable.

Then, during the second iteration, the following two terms (among others) are built

$$t_{2.1} := \texttt{and (not x) (not x')}$$
$$t_{2.2} := \texttt{not (or x y)}$$

More specifically, the term $t_{2.1}$ is built as the instantiation of $t_{1.2}$ with $t_{1.1}$ (in both arguments), and the term $t_{2.2}$ is the instantiation of $t_{1.1}$ with $t_{1.3}$. The semantics of these two terms is the same, but it is different from the semantics of the existing equivalence classes. Therefore, during this iteration (at least) a new class ec_1 for this new semantics is added, having as representative the term $t_{2.2}$ (i.e., $rep(ec_1) = t_{2.2}$).

From this point on, only the representative of the class will be used for constructing new terms. This means that terms like `not (and (not x) (not x'))`, which is the instantiation of $t_{1.1}$ with $t_{2.1}$, will never be built since only $t_{2.1}$ can be used.

We recall here that, thanks to the closedness w.r.t. context of the semantics, this strategy for generating terms is *safe*. In other words, when we avoid to build a term, it is because it is not able to produce a behavior different from the behaviors already included by the existing terms, thus we are not losing completeness.

Although the overall strategy has been organized in order to avoid much redundancy in equations, there is one additional issue that may introduce a little redundancy. In particular, it might occur that we generate and classify a term which introduces a property that can be deduced from other equations.

Let us discuss this with an artificial example that uses the terms in Example 4.1.

EXAMPLE 4.2

The two terms $t_{2.1}$ and $t_{2.2}$ belong to the same equivalence class, $t_{2.1}, t_{2.2} \in terms(ec_1)$, which means that, as we describe below, the equation `and (not x) (not y)` $=_C$ `not (or x y)` can be generated. Now, assume that there exists a second equivalence class, ec_2, that includes the terms `not (not x)` and `x`, thus allowing the generation of the equation `not (not x)` $=_C$ `x`.

Let us move to the following iteration and assume that $t_{2.1}$ is the representative of ec_1. Then, one of the built terms is `not (and (not x) (not y))`, which is the instantiation of `not x` with $t_{2.1}$. Let us suppose that the semantics of this term is the same as that of the term `or x y`, thus it is added to its equivalence class. This implies that the corresponding equation `not (and (not x) (not y))` $=_C$ `or x y` will be generated. However, this equation is redundant because it can be deduced from the other (smaller) two.

These redundant equations are not common. In fact, the example above is not a real one since in our example the generated equation is `and (not x) (not y)` $=_{CR}$ `not (or x y)`. Moreover, as we will illustrate later, the eventual presence of these redundant equations does not propagate to other equations.

Generation of the specification The third phase of the algorithm (Lines 15 to 20) constructs the specification for the provided Curry program. First, Line 16 computes the $=_C$ equations from the current partition. Since we have avoided much redundancy thanks to the strategy used to generate the equivalence classes, the $add\_equations$ function needs only to take each equivalence class with more than one term and generate equations for these terms.

This function generates also a side effect on the equivalence classes that is needed in the successive steps. Namely, it modifies the third component of the classes so that it replaces the (non-singleton) set of terms with a singleton set containing just the representative term.

Then, Lines 17 to 20 compute the equations corresponding to the other equivalence notions defined in Section 3. Let us explain in detail the case for the computed result equations (kind CR). As already noted, from the (tree) semantics T in the equivalence classes computed during the second phase of the algorithm, it is possible to construct (by losing the tree internal structure and collecting just the computed result leaves $cr(T)$) the semantics that models the computed result behavior. Therefore, we apply this transformation to the semantic values of each equivalence class. After the transformation, some of the equivalence classes which had different semantic values may now collapse into the same class. This transformation and reclassification is performed by the $transform\_semantics$ function. The resulting (coarser) partition is then used to produce the $=_{CR}$ equations by an application of $add\_equations$.

Thanks to the fact that $add\_equations$ ends with a partition made of just singleton term sets, we cannot generate (again) equations $t_1 =_{CR} t_2$ when an equation $t_1 =_C t_2$ had been already issued.

Let us clarify this phase by an example.

EXAMPLE 4.3

Assume we have a partition consisting of three equivalence classes with semantics s_1, s_2 and s_3 and representative terms t_{11}, t_{22} and t_{31}:

$$ec_1 = \langle s_1, t_{11}, \{t_{11}, t_{12}, t_{13}\}\rangle$$
$$ec_2 = \langle s_2, t_{22}, \{t_{21}, t_{22}\}\rangle$$
$$ec_3 = \langle s_3, t_{31}, \{t_{31}\}\rangle$$

The $add\_equations$ procedure generates the equations

$$\{t_{11} =_C t_{12} =_C t_{13},$$
$$t_{21} =_C t_{22}\}$$

and, as side effect, the partition becomes

$$ec_1 = \langle s_1, t_{11}, \{t_{11}\}\rangle$$
$$ec_2 = \langle s_2, t_{22}, \{t_{22}\}\rangle$$
$$ec_3 = \langle s_3, t_{31}, \{t_{31}\}\rangle$$

Now, assume that $cr(s_1) = x_0$ and $cr(s_2) = cr(s_3) = x_1$. Then, after applying $transform\_semantics$, we obtain the new partition

$$ec_4 = \langle x_0,\ t_{11},\ \{t_{11}\}\rangle$$
$$ec_5 = \langle x_1,\ t_{22},\ \{t_{22}, t_{31}\}\rangle$$

Hence, the only new equation is $t_{22} =_{CR} t_{31}$. Indeed, equation $t_{11} =_{CR} t_{12}$ is uninteresting, since we already know $t_{11} =_C t_{12}$ and equation $t_{21} =_{CR} t_{31}$ is redundant (because $t_{21} =_C t_{22}$ and $t_{22} =_{CR} t_{31}$).

In summary, if $t_1 =_C t_2$ holds, then $t_1 =_{\{CR,G\}} t_2$ are not present in the specification.

The same strategy can be used to generate also the $=_G$ kind of equations. Conceptually, this could be done with a semantic transformation equations. Conceptually, this could be done with a semantic transformation which replaces each free variable in all computed result with all its ground instances. In practice, we can use a completely dual approach, were we use a variable to represent all its possible ground instancies. The transformation which corresponds to this representation

- retains only the most general instancies of the original semantics (removing computed results which are instancies of others) and,
- replaces a set of computed results R with its common anti-instance r when appropriate. This happens when the set of all ground instancies of r is the same as that of the union of all ground instancies of all elements in R. This can be implemented by checking if we have a set with all the constructors of a given type (applied to free variables), then, we replace the set of constructors by a free variable and then we repeat the process until we reach a fix point.

In this way the semantics are transformed by removing further internal structure and again classes may collapse and new equations (w.r.t. $=_G$) are generated.

4.1 Effectivity and efficiency considerations

In a semantic-based approach, one of the main problems to be tackled is effectiveness. The semantics of a program is in general infinite and thus we use abstract interpretation [ ] in order to have a terminating method. More specifically, in this work we use a correct abstraction of the semantics of [,] over the *depth*(k) abstract domain. In the *depth*(k) abstraction, terms (occurring in the nodes of the semantic trees) are "cut" at depth k by replacing them with *cut variables*, distinct from program variables. Hence, for a given signature Σ, the universe of abstract semantic trees is finite (although it increases exponentially w.r.t. k). Therefore, the finite convergence of the computation of the abstract semantics is guaranteed.

The presence of cut variables in the nodes of the abstract semantics denotes that the (partial) computed result has been abstracted. However, if no cut variable occurs in a node, we know that it coincides with a node in the concrete semantics. Thanks to this structure, *depth*(k) semantics is technically an over approximation of the semantics, but simultaneously it can be very precise (concrete) when computed results show up without "cuts".

Therefore, equations coming from equivalence classes whose *depth*(k) semantics does not contain cut variables are *correct* equations, while for the others we do not know (yet). If we use a bigger k, the latter can definitively become valid or not. Thus, equations involving approximation are equations that *have not been falsified up to that point*, analogously to what happens in the testing-based approach. We call these equations *unfalsified* equations. When showing the specification, we mark the latter with a special equivalence symbol $=_C^\alpha$. Unfalsified equations are the only kind of equations that testing-based approaches can compute in general.

The main advantage of our proposal w.r.t. the testing-based approaches is the fact that we are able to distinguish when an equation *certainly* holds, and when it just *can* hold. Moreover, we can deal with non terminating programs.

Since the overall construction is (almost) independent of the actual structure of the abstract semantics, it would be possible in the future to use other abstract domains to reach a better trade-off between efficiency of the computation and accuracy of the specifications.

5. Case Studies

Let us start by discussing the results for a more elaborated example. The following Curry program implements a two-sided queue where it is possible to insert or delete elements on both left and right sides:

```
data Queue a = Q [a] [a]

new = Q [] []

inl x (Q xs ys) = Q (x:xs) ys
inr x (Q xs ys) = Q xs (x:ys)

outl (Q [] ys) = Q (tail (reverse ys)) []
outl (Q (_:xs) ys) = Q xs ys

outr (Q xs []) = Q [] (tail (reverse xs))
outr (Q xs (_:ys)) = Q xs ys

null (Q [] []) = True
null (Q (_:_) _) = False
null (Q [] (_:_)) = False

eqQ (Q xs ys) (Q xs' ys') =
  (xs++reverse ys) =:= (xs'++reverse ys')
```

The queue is implemented as two lists where the first list corresponds to the first part of the queue and the second list is the second part of the queue reversed. The `inl` function adds the new element to the head of the first list, whereas the `inr` function adds the new element to the head of the second list (the last element of the queue). The `outl` (`outr`) function drops one element from the left (right) list, unless the list is empty, in which case it reverses the other list and then swaps the two lists before removal. If we include all the functions in the API and by assuming $k \geq 3$ for the abstraction, an extract of the inferred specification for this program is the following one:

$$\texttt{null new} =_C \texttt{True} \quad (5.1)$$

$$\texttt{new} =_C \texttt{outl (inl x new)} =_C \texttt{outr (inr x new)} \quad (5.2)$$

$$\texttt{outl (inl x q)} =_C \texttt{outr (inr x q)} \quad (5.3)$$

$$\texttt{outr (inl x new)} =_C \texttt{outl (inr x new)} \quad (5.4)$$

$$\texttt{inr x (inl y q)} =_C \texttt{inl y (inr x q)} \quad (5.5)$$

$$\texttt{inl x (outl (inl y q))} =_G^\alpha \texttt{outr (inl x (inr y q))} \quad (5.6)$$

$$\texttt{outl (inl x (outl q))} =_G^\alpha \texttt{outl (outl (inl x q))} \quad (5.7)$$

$$\texttt{outr (outl (inl x q))} =_C \texttt{outl (inl x (outr q))} \quad (5.8)$$

$$\texttt{null (inl x new)} =_C \texttt{null (inr x new)} =_C \texttt{False} \quad (5.9)$$

$$\texttt{eqQ (inr x new) y} =_C \texttt{eqQ (inl x new) y} \quad (5.10)$$

We can see different kinds of equations in the specifications. The asymmetry in the definition of the queue makes that Equation (5.6) holds only for ground instances. Moreover, the semantics for terms in Equations (5.6) and (5.7) is abstracted (in fact, the semantics tree is infinite for these cases). Equations (5.2), (5.3) and (5.4) state that adding and removing one element produces always the same result independently from the side in which we add and remove it. Equations (5.5), (5.6), (5.7) and (5.8) show a sort of *restricted* commutativity between functions. Finally, Equation (5.10) shows that, w.r.t. the user defined predicate `eqQ`, that identifies queues which contain the same elements, `inr x new` is equivalent to `inl x new`, although the internal structure of the queue differs.

In Section 4, we have shown how we avoid much redundancy by using a single representative for each equivalence class. However, there is a situation in which equations may show some redundancy. The Queue example allows us to better illustrate this fact:

EXAMPLE 5.1

Assume we are computing the specification for the Queue example with relevant API $\Sigma^r = \{\texttt{inl, outl}\}$ following our method. The initial partition computes four equivalence classes: one for each of the two terms from the API and one for each of the two free variables `q` and `x` of type `Queue a` and `a`, respectively.

$$ec_{1.1} = \langle s_{1.1}, \texttt{inl x q}, \{\texttt{inl x q}\}\rangle$$
$$ec_{1.2} = \langle s_{1.2}, \texttt{outl q}, \{\texttt{outl q}\}\rangle$$
$$ec_{1.3} = \langle s_{1.3}, \texttt{q}, \{\texttt{q}\}\rangle$$
$$ec_{1.4} = \langle s_{1.4}, \texttt{x}, \{\texttt{x}\}\rangle$$

During the second iteration, the term `inl x (outl q)` is built as the instantiation of the representative of $ec_{1.1}$ with the representative of $ec_{1.2}$. This term adds a new equivalence class to the partition:

$$ec_{2.1} = \langle s_{2.1}, \texttt{inl x (outl q)}, \{\texttt{inl x (outl q)}\}\rangle$$

During the same iteration, also the term `outl (inl x q)` is built. For the sake of this discussion, we assume that it has the same semantics of `q`:

$$ec_{1.3} = \langle s_{1.3}, \texttt{q}, \{\texttt{q,outl (inl x q)}\}\rangle$$

This means that the equation `outl (inl x q)` $=_C$ `q` will be generated from $ec_{1.3}$. Then, in the third iteration, the term `outl (inl x (outl q))` is built as the instance of the representative of $ec_{1.2}$ with the representative of $ec_{2.1}$. The semantics of this new term coincides with that of `outl q`, thus $ec_{1.2}$ is updated:

$$ec_{1.2} = \langle s_{1.2}, \texttt{outl q}, \{\texttt{outl q,outl (inl x (outl q))}\}\rangle$$

As a consequence, the equation `outl (inl x (outl q))` $=_C$ `outl q` is generated. However, this equation is redundant because it is an instance of the equation already generated from $ec_{1.3}$, `outl (inl x q)` $=_C$ `q`. We recall that we have used the representatives for building the term, thus we cannot avoid this kind of redundancy with the strategy of just using the representatives.

Nevertheless, as we have already mentioned, these redundant equations are not common. The example above is not a real one since in our example the generated equation is `q` $=_G$ `outl (inl x q)`. Moreover, the eventual presence of these redundant equations does not propagate to other equations since, when these (greater) terms are introduced, they are not used for building other terms, but only the representative of the class.

It is worth noticing that the unfalsified equations for the Queue example (Equations (5.6) and (5.7) above), represent properties that actually hold for the program. However, it might occur that unfalsified equations correspond to *false* properties of the program, as the following example shows.

Consider the following program that computes the double of numbers in Peano notation:

```
data Nat = Z | S Nat

double, double' :: Nat -> Nat
double Z = Z
double (S x) = S (S (double x))

double' x = plus x x

plus :: Nat -> Nat -> Nat
plus Z y = y
plus (S x) y = S (plus x y)
```

Some of the inferred equations for the program are:

$$\texttt{double' (double' (double x))} =^{\alpha}_{CR}$$
$$=^{\alpha}_{CR} \texttt{double' (double (double' x))} \quad (5.11)$$
$$\texttt{double x} =^{\alpha}_{CR} \texttt{double' x} \quad (5.12)$$
$$\texttt{double' (double' x)} =^{\alpha}_{CR} \texttt{double' (double x)} =^{\alpha}_{CR}$$
$$=^{\alpha}_{CR} \texttt{double (double' x)} =^{\alpha}_{CR}$$
$$=^{\alpha}_{CR} \texttt{double (double x)} \quad (5.13)$$
$$\texttt{(S (double x))} =^{\alpha}_{CR} \texttt{double (S x)} \quad (5.14)$$
$$\texttt{plus (double x) y} =^{\alpha}_{CR} \texttt{plus (double' x) y} \quad (5.15)$$

We can observe that, in this case, all the equations are unfalsified due to the nature of the example. Moreover, all equations hold with the $=_{CR}$ relation. This is due to the asymmetry in the definition of the two versions of double: although the computed results of both versions are the same, there exist contexts in which the terms behave differently. This characteristic of the program is not easy to realize by just looking at the code, thus this is an example of the usefulness of having different notions of equivalence.

Finally, Equation (5.14) is an unfalsified equation that states a property which is false for the program. This is due to the approximation of the abstraction. It is worth noting that we would need to completely compute the (infinite) concrete semantics in order to discard the equation from the specification.

We do not remove unfalsified equations from the specifications since they have their own interest. Although it might be unfeasible to guarantee correctness of some equations (as in the example above), unfalsified equations may nevertheless show behaviors of the program which are actually correct. This is the only possible situation that arises in testing-based approaches, where all the equations must to be considered unfalsified since it is impossible to distinguish them from correct equations. In any case, we can try to prove correctness of these equations by using a complementary verification or validation technique.

5.1 AbsSpec: The prototype

We have implemented the basic functionality of this methodology in a prototype written in Haskell. The core of the AbsSpec 1.0 prototype[8] consists of about 800 lines of code implementing the tasks of generating and classifying terms. The inference core of AbsSpec 1.0 is generic w.r.t. the abstract domain, i.e., the operations implementing the abstract domain are passed to the generic inference process. Note that the AbsSpec 1.0 prototype invokes the semantics' prototype implementation, which consists of about 7500 additional lines of code. On top of the core part of the prototype, the interface module implements some functions that allow the user both to check if a specific set of equations hold, or to get the whole specification. It is worth noting that, although in this paper we consider as input Curry programs, the prototype also accepts programs written in (the first order fragment of) Haskell (which are automatically converted by orthogonalization into Curry equivalent programs).

Unfortunately, we do not know of sets of benchmarks in the literature to be used to evaluate the prototype. Hence, we wrote some examples as a proof of concept in order to get some impressions on the efficacy of our proposal. Since the prototype does not han-

[8] Available at `http://safe-tools.dsic.upv.es/absspec`.

dle built-in arithmetic operators yet, we tested it on both Curry and Haskell programs which do not involve arithmetics (mainly implementation of abstract data structures like queues, binary trees, arrays, heaps, *etc.*).

The experiments were conducted on an Intel Core2 Quad CPU Q9300(2.50GHz) with 6 Gigabytes of RAM. AbsSpec 1.0 was compiled with version 6.12.3 of the Glorious Glasgow Haskell Compilation System (GHC). Table 1 shows the execution times for the inference of each program example with some additional information. Column *Program* shows the name of the example program. The first three cases correspond to the examples shown in this paper. The fourth example is a more elaborated logic example where a data structure representing formulas is defined; column *Rules* shows the number of rules defining the program; column *API size* shows the number of operations included in the *relevant* API for the experiment. For the Booleans example, the experiment includes the operator for the logic implication defined explicitly (not in terms of the other boolean operators); column *Terms* shows the number of terms generated (thus, whose semantics is computed) during the inference process; columns $=_C$, and $=_{CR}$ show, respectively, the number of $=_C$, and $=_{CR}$ equivalence classes with more than one term that have been generated.[9]

Our preliminary experiments show that many interesting properties hold over the $depth(k)$ domain with low k values (we run the prototype with depth 7 by default). Also, many interesting properties show up with $max\_size = 3$. For example, we can see that for the Queue example, with $max\_size = 2$, only one equivalence class is defined whereas for $max\_size = 3$, 13 (sequences of) equations belong to the specification. We have used also $max\_size = 4$, but specifications tend to be less comprehensible for the user (64 equivalence classes for the same Queue example). Hence, increasing this value should be done only when bigger terms make sense, being at the same time very careful in choosing a sufficiently small API. The Double example illustrates the usefulness of the $=_{CR}$ equations: with $max\_size = 2$ we have already five of these equations.

The last example illustrates the fact that with a complex data structure, the high number of generated terms penalizes the inference process. Not that the increase of the number of generated terms depends, not only on the number of elements included in the relevant API (and on the number of arguments of the functions in the API), but also on the semantics of the program. Intuitively, if we have a program in which many terms share the same semantics, then fewer terms will be generated.

We also made some experiments on programs which use arithmetics by simulating the arithmetical operations using Peano's notation but, as one would expect, we got poor results.

A serious evaluation of the prototype should be done on a number of standard benchmarks (hopefully) not written by ourselves, and we hope to get several contributions in this sense by the international community.

6. Related Work

To the best of our knowledge, in the functional logic setting there are currently no proposals for specification synthesis. There is a testing tool, EasyCheck [ ], in which specifications are *used* as the input for the testing process. Given the properties, EasyCheck executes ground tests in order to check whether the property holds. This tool could be used as a companion tool of ours in order to check if the unfalsified $=_G$ equations can be actually falsified. However EasyCheck is not capable of checking the $=_C$ and $=_{CR}$ equations because it is based only on the execution of ground tests.

[9] The prototype does not compute the $=_G$ equations yet.

The mentioned tool QuickSpec [ ] computes an algebraic specification for Haskell programs by means of (almost black-box) testing. Like our approach, its inferred specifications are complete up to a certain depth of the analyzed terms because of its exhaustiveness. However, the equations in their specification are all unfalsified equations due to the use of testing for the equation generation. Instead, we follow a (glass-box) semantic-based approach that allows us to compute specifications as complete as those of QuickSpec, but with correctness guarantees on part of them (depending on the abstraction). We have not done an exhaustive comparison, but performance of QuickSpec is better than that of our prototype for similar programs. However, we have to recall that our purpose is more ambitious since, for the case of functional-logic languages, using just the ground equivalence is not enough: important behaviors regarding the loss of contextual closeness would not show up, as shown by the `double` example. Moreover, we can deal with non terminating programs.

Finally, a previous work ([ ]) identifies the additional difficulties for the inference of high level (property-based) specifications for the functional-logic paradigm.

7. Conclusions and Future Work

This paper presents a method to automatically infer high-level, property-oriented (algebraic) specifications in a functional logic setting. A specification represents relations that hold between operations (nested calls) in the program.

The method computes a concise specification of program properties from the source code of the program. We hope to have convinced the reader that we reached our main goal, that is to get a concise and clear specification that is useful for the programmer in order to detect possible errors, or to check that the program corresponds to the intended behavior.

The computed specification is particularly well suited for program understanding since it allows to discover non-evident behaviors, and also to be combined with testing. In the context of (formal) verification, the specification can be used to ease the verification tasks, for example by using the correct equations as annotations, or unfalsified equations as candidate axioms to be proven.

The approach relies on the computation of the semantics. Therefore, to achieve effectiveness and good performance results, we use a suitable abstract semantics instead of the concrete one. This means that we may not guarantee correctness of all the equations in the specification, but we can nevertheless infer correct equations thanks to a good compromise between correctness and efficiency.

We have developed a prototype that implements the basic functionality of the approach. We are working on the inclusion of all the functionality described in this paper.

As future work, we plan to add another notion of equivalence class $=_{Ueq}$. More specifically, when dealing with a user-defined data type, the user may have defined a specific notion of equivalence by means of an "equality" function. In this context, some interesting equations could show up. For instance, in the Queue example, the predicate `eqQ` identifies queues which contain the same elements and Equation (5.10) should be presented as **`inl x new`** $=_{Ueq}$ **`inr x new`**. These equivalence classes would depend on how the user defines the equality notion, thus we will surely need some assumptions (to ensure that indeed the user-defined function induces an equality relation) in order to get useful specifications.

Acknowledgments

M. A. Feliú and A. Villanueva have been partially supported by the EU (FEDER), the Spanish MICINN/MINECO under grant TIN2010-21062-C02-02, the Spanish MEC FPU grant AP2008-00608, and by the Generalitat Valenciana, ref. PROMETEO2011/052.

Program	Rules	API size	Term size	Terms	$=_C$ (# classes)	$=_{CR}$ (# classes)	Time
Booleans	9	5	2	121	65	1	0m0.130s
			3	2549	410	1	0m6.550s
			4	6399	1378	1	0m42.320s
Queue	11	6	2	34	1	0	0m0.080s
			3	132	12	1	0m0.180s
			4	473	56	8	0m0.580s
Double	5	3	2	25	0	5	0m0.110s
			3	676	55	157	0m19.860s
			4	2638	410	344	0m43.710s
BooleanDataStruct	8	4	2	42	0	0	3m53.980s
			3	1648	2	0	9m0.140s
			4	-	-	-	-

Table 1. Inference process of example programs

References

[1] E. Albert, M. Hanus, F. Huch, J. Oliver, and G. Vidal. Operational Semantics for Declarative Multi-Paradigm Languages. *Journal of Symbolic Computation*, 40(1):795–829, 2005.

[2] G. Ammons, R. Bodík, and J. R. Larus. Mining specifications. In *29th ACM SIGPLAN-SIGACT symposium on Principles of programming languages (POPL'02)*, pages 4–16, New York, NY, USA, 2002. Acm. ISBN 1-58113-450-9. doi: http://doi.acm.org/10.1145/503272.503275. URL `http://doi.acm.org/10.1145/503272.503275`.

[3] G. Bacci. *An Abstract Interpretation Framework for Semantics and Diagnosis of Lazy Functional-Logic Languages*. PhD thesis, Dipartimento di matematica e Informatica, Università di Udine, 2011.

[4] G. Bacci and M. Comini. A Compact Goal-Independent Bottom-Up Fixpoint Modeling of the Behaviour of First Order Curry. Technical Report DIMI-UD/06/2010/RR, Dipartimento di Matematica e Informatica, Università di Udine, 2010. URL `http://www.dimi.uniud.it/comini/Papers/`.

[5] G. Bacci and M. Comini. Abstract Diagnosis of First Order Functional Logic Programs. In M. Alpuente, editor, *Logic-based Program Synthesis and Transformation, 20th International Symposium*, volume 6564 of *Lecture Notes in Computer Science*, pages 215–233, Berlin, 2011. Springer-Verlag. ISBN 9783642205507. doi: 10.1007/978-3-642-20551-4_14.

[6] G. Bacci, M. Comini, M. A. Feliú, and A. Villanueva. The additional difficulties for the automatic synthesis of specifications posed by logic features in functional-logic languages. In *ICLP (Technical Communications)*, volume To appear of *LIPIcs*. Schloss Dagstuhl - Leibniz-Zentrum Fuer Informatik, 2012.

[7] J. Christiansen and S. Fischer. Easycheck – test data for free. In *Proceedings of the 9th International Symposium on Functional and Logic Programming (FLOPS'08)*, volume 4989 of *Lecture Notes in Computer Science*, pages 322–336. Springer, 2008.

[8] K. Claessen, N. Smallbone, and J. Hughes. QuickSpec: Guessing Formal Specifications using Testing. In *4th International Conference on Tests and Proofs (TAP 2010)*, volume 6143, pages 6–21, 2010. ISBN 978-3-642-13976-5.

[9] P. Cousot and R. Cousot. Abstract Interpretation: A Unified Lattice Model for Static Analysis of Programs by Construction or Approximation of Fixpoints. In *Proceedings of the 4th ACM SIGACT-SIGPLAN symposium on Principles of programming languages, Los Angeles, California, January 17–19*, pages 238–252, New York, NY, USA, 1977. ACM Press.

[10] P. Cousot and R. Cousot. Systematic Design of Program Analysis Frameworks. In *Proceedings of the 6th ACM SIGACT-SIGPLAN symposium on Principles of programming languages, San Antonio, Texas, January 29–31*, pages 269–282, New York, NY, USA, 1979. ACM Press.

[11] C. Ghezzi and A. Mocci. Behavior model based component search: an initial assessment. In *Proceedings of 2010 ICSE Workshop on Search-driven Development: Users, Infrastructure, Tools and Evaluation (SUITE'10)*, pages 9–12, New York, NY, USA, 2010. Acm. ISBN 978-1-60558-962-6.

[12] C. Ghezzi, A. Mocci, and M. Monga. Synthesizing intensional behavior models by graph transformation. In *31st International Conference on Software Engineering (ICSE'09)*, pages 430–440, 2009.

[13] M. Hanus. A unified computation model for functional and logic programming. In *24th ACM Symposium on Principles of Programming Languages (POPL 97)*, pages 80–93, 1997.

[14] M. Hanus. Curry: An integrated functional logic language (vers. 0.8.2), 2006. Available at URL: `http://www.informatik.uni-kiel.de/~curry`.

[15] J. Henkel, C. Reichenbach, and A. Diwan. Discovering documentation for java container classes. *IEEE Transactions on Software Engineering*, 33(8):526–542, 2007.

[16] A. A. Khwaja and J. E. Urban. A property based specification formalism classification. *The Journal of Systems and Software*, 83:2344–2362, 2010.

[17] I. Nunes, A. Lopes, and V. Vasconcelos. Bridging the Gap between Algebraic Specification and Object-Oriented Generic Programming. In S. Bensalem and D. Peled, editors, *9th International Workshop on Runtime Verification (RV 2009)*, volume 5779 of *Lecture Notes in Computer Science*, pages 115–131. Springer, 2009.

[18] S. Peyton Jones. *Haskell 98 Language and Libraries - The Revised Report*. Cambridge University Press, Cambridge, UK, 2003. ISBN 0521826144. Available at `http://www.haskell.org/definition/`.

[19] D. Rayside, A. Milicevic, K. Yessenov, G. Dennis, and D. Jackson. Agile specifications. In *Companion to the 24th Annual ACM SIGPLAN Conference on Object-Oriented Programming, Systems, Languages, and Applications (OOPSLA 2009)*, pages 999–1006. Acm, 2009.

[20] H. van Vliet. *Software Engineering–Principles and Practice*. John Wiley, 1993.

[21] J. M. Wing. A specifier's introduction to formal methods. *Computer*, 23(9):10–24, 1990.

[22] B. Yu, L. Kong, Y. Zhang, and H. Zhu. Testing Java Components based on Algebraic Specifications. In *First International Conference on Software Testing, Verification, and Validation (ICST 2008)*, pages 190–199. IEEE Computer Society, 2008.

Goal-Directed Execution of Answer Set Programs

Kyle Marple
University of Texas at Dallas
800 W. Campbell Road
Richardson, TX, USA
kbm072000@utdallas.edu

Ajay Bansal
Arizona State University
7231 E. Sonoran Arroyo Mall
Mesa, Arizona, USA
Ajay.Bansal@asu.edu

Richard Min
University of Texas at Dallas
800 W. Campbell Road
Richardson, TX, USA
min75243@hotmail.com

Gopal Gupta
University of Texas at Dallas
800 W. Campbell Road
Richardson, TX, USA
gupta@utdallas.edu

Abstract

Answer Set Programming (ASP) represents an elegant way of introducing non-monotonic reasoning into logic programming. ASP has gained popularity due to its applications to planning, default reasoning and other areas of AI. However, none of the approaches and current implementations for ASP are *goal-directed*. In this paper we present a technique based on *coinduction* that can be employed to design SLD resolution-style, goal-directed methods for executing answer set programs. We also discuss advantages and applications of such goal-directed execution of answer set programs, and report results from our implementation.

Categories and Subject Descriptors D.1.6 [*Programming Techniques*]: Logic Programming

General Terms Algorithms

Keywords Answer set programming, goal-directed execution, coinduction

1. Introduction

Answer Set Programming (ASP) is an elegant way of developing non-monotonic reasoning applications. ASP has gained wide acceptance, and considerable research has been done in developing the paradigm as well as its implementations and applications. ASP has been applied to important areas such as planning, scheduling, default reasoning, reasoning about actions [3], etc. Numerous implementations of ASP have been developed, ranging from *DLV* ([17]) and *smodels* [22] to SAT-based solvers such as *cmodels* [13] and the conflict-driven solver *clasp* [10]. However, these implementations compute the whole answer set: i.e., *they are not goal-directed* in the fashion of Prolog. Given an answer set program and a query goal `Q`, a goal-directed execution will systematically enumerate—via SLD style call expansions and backtracking—all answer sets that contain the propositions/predicates in `Q`. Other efforts have been made to realize goal-directed implementations (e.g., [5]), however, these approaches can handle only a limited class of programs and/or queries.

In this paper we describe a goal-directed execution method that works for any answer set program as well as for any query. The method relies on *coinductive logic programming* (co-LP) [14]. Co-LP can be regarded as providing an operational semantics, termed co-SLD resolution, for computing greatest fixed points (*gfp*) of logic programs. Co-SLD resolution systematically computes elements of the *gfp* of a program via backtracking [14, 27]. Additionally, calls are allowed to *coinductively succeed* if they unify with one of their ancestor calls [27]. To permit this, each call is stored in the *coinductive hypothesis set* (CHS) as the call is made. A more detailed introduction to co-LP and co-SLD resolution can be found in Appendix A.

A goal-directed method for executing answer set programs is analogous to top-down, SLD style resolution for Prolog, while current popular methods for ASP are analogous to bottom-up methods that have been used for evaluating Prolog (and Datalog) programs [25]. A goal-directed execution method for answering queries for an answer set program has several advantages. The main advantage is that it paves the way to lifting the restriction to finitely groundable programs, and allows realization of ASP with full first-order predicates [20].

In the rest of the paper we develop a goal-directed strategy for executing answer set programs, and prove that it is sound and complete with respect to the method of Gelfond and Lifschitz. We restrict ourselves to only propositional (grounded) answer set programs in this paper; work is in progress to extend our goal-directed method to predicate answer set programs [20, 21]. Note that the design of a top-down goal-directed execution strategy for answer set programs has been regarded as quite a challenging problem [3]. As pointed out in [6], the difficulty in designing a goal-directed method for ASP comes about due to the absence of a *relevance property* in *stable model semantics*, on which answer set programming is based [6, 23, 24]. We will introduce a modified relevance property that holds for our goal-directed method and guarantees that partial answer sets computed by our method can be extended to complete answer sets.

PPDP'12, September 19–21, 2012, Leuven, Belgium.

2. Answer Set Programming (ASP)

Answer Set Programming (ASP) [12] (A-Prolog [11] or AnsProlog [3]) is a declarative logic programming paradigm which encapsulates non-monotonic or common sense reasoning. The rules in an ASP program are of the form:

$$\texttt{p :- } q_1\texttt{, ..., } q_m\texttt{, not } r_1\texttt{, ..., not } r_n\texttt{.}$$

where $m \geq 0$ and $n \geq 0$. Each of p and q_i ($\forall i \leq m$) is a literal, each not r_j ($\forall j \leq n$) is a *naf-literal* (not is a logical connective called *negation as failure (naf)* or *default negation*). The semantics of an Answer Set program P is given via the Gelfond-Lifschitz method [3] in terms of the answer sets of the program ground(P), obtained by grounding the variables in the program P.

Gelfond-Lifschitz Transform (GLT) Given a grounded Answer Set program P and a candidate answer set A, a residual program R is obtained by applying the following transformation rules: for all literals $L \in A$,

1. Delete all rules in P which have not L in their body.
2. Delete all the remaining naf-literals (of the form not M) from the bodies of the remaining rules.

The least fixed-point (say, F) of the residual program R is next computed. If F = A, then A is a *stable model* or an *answer set* of P.

ASP can also have rules of the form:

$$\texttt{:- } q_1\texttt{, ..., } q_m\texttt{, not } r_1\texttt{, ..., not } r_n\texttt{.}$$
$$\texttt{p :- } q_1\texttt{, ..., } q_m\texttt{, not } r_1\texttt{, ..., not } r_n\texttt{, not p.}$$

These rules capture the non-monotonic aspect of Answer Set Programming. Consider an example rule:

```
p :- q, not p.
```

Following the Gelfond-Lifschitz method (GL method) outlined above, this rule restricts q (and p) to not be in the answer set (unless p happens to be in the answer set via other rules, in which case due to presence of not p this rule will be removed while generating the residual program). Note that even though an answer set program can have other rules to establish that q is in the answer set, adding the rule above forces q to not be in the answer set unless p succeeds through another rule, thus making ASP non-monotonic.

3. Goal-directed ASP Issues

Any normal logic program can also be viewed as an answer set program. However, ASP adds complexity to a normal logic program in two ways. In addition to the standard Prolog rules, it allows:

1. Cyclical rules which when used to expand a call to a subgoal G lead to a recursive call to G through an even (but non-zero) number of negations. For example, given the program P1 below:

   ```
   p :- not q.      ... Rule P1.a
   q :- not p.      ... Rule P1.b
   ```

   Ordinary logic programming execution for the query ?- p. (or ?- q.) will lead to non-termination. However, ASP will produce two answer sets: {p, not q} and {q, not p}[1]. Expanding the call p using Rule P1.a in the style of SLD resolution will lead to a recursive call to p that is in scope of two negations (p $\rightarrow$ not q $\rightarrow$ not not p). Such rules are termed *ordinary rules*. Rule P1.b is also an ordinary rule, since if used for expanding the call to q, it will lead to a recursive call to q through two negations. For simplicity of presentation, all non-cyclical rules will also be classified as ordinary rules.

2. Cyclical rules which when used to expand a call to subgoal G lead to a recursive call to G that is in the scope of an odd number of negations. Such recursive calls are known as *odd loops over negation* (OLONs). For example, given the program P2 below:

   ```
   p :- q, not p, r.   ... Rule P2.a
   ```

   a call to p using Rule P2.a will eventually lead to a call to not p. Under ordinary logic programming execution, this will lead to non-termination. Under ASP, however, the program consisting of Rule P2.a has {not p, not q, not r} as its answer set. For brevity, we refer to rules containing OLONs as *OLON rules*.

Note that a rule can be both an ordinary rule and an OLON rule, since given a subgoal G, its expansion can lead to a recursive call to G through both even and odd numbers of negations along different expansion paths. For example in program P3 below, Rule P3.a is both an ordinary rule and an OLON rule.

```
p :- q, not r.      ... Rule P3.a
r :- not p.         ... Rule P3.b
q :- t, not p.      ... Rule P3.c
```

Our top-down method requires that we properly identify and handle both ordinary and OLON rules. We will look at each type of rule in turn, followed by the steps taken to ensure that our method remains faithful to the GL method.

3.1 Ordinary Rules

Ordinary rules such as rules P1.a and P1.b in program P1 above exemplify the cyclical reasoning in ASP. The rules in the example force p and q to be mutually exclusive, i.e., either p is true or q is true, but not both. One can argue the reasoning presented in such rules is cyclical: If p is in the answer set, then q cannot be in the answer set, and if q is not in the answer set, then p must be in the answer set.

Given a goal, G, and an answer set program comprised of only ordinary rules, G can be executed in a top-down manner using coinduction, through the following steps:

- Record each call in the CHS. The recorded calls constitute the coinductive hypothesis set, which is the potential answer set.
- If at the time of the call, the call is already found in the CHS, it succeeds coinductively and finishes.
- If the current call is not in the CHS, then expand it in the style of ordinary SLD resolution (recording the call in the CHS prior to expansion).
- Simplify not not p to p, whenever possible, where p is a proposition occurring in the program.
- If success is achieved with no goals left to expand, then the coinductive hypothesis set contains the (partial) answer set.

The top-down resolution of query p with program P1 will proceed as follows.

:- p	CHS = {}
	(expand p by Rule P1.a)
:- not q	CHS = {p}
	(expand q by Rule P1.b)
:- not not p	CHS = {p, not q}
	(simplify not not p $\rightarrow$ p)
:- p	CHS = {p, not q}
	(coinductive success: p $\in$ CHS)
:- $\square$	success: answer set is {p, not q}

[1] Note that we will list all literals that are true in a given answer set. Conventionally, an answer set is specified by listing only the positive literals that are true; those not listed in the set are assumed to be false.

Note that the maintenance of the coinductive hypothesis set (CHS) is critical. If a call is encountered that is already in the CHS, it should not be expanded, it should simply (coinductively) succeed. Note that the query q will produce the other answer set {q, not p} in a symmetrical manner. Note also that the query not q will also produce the answer set {p, not q} as shown below. Thus, answers to negated queries can also be computed, *if we apply the coinductive hypothesis rule to negated goals also, i.e., a call to not p succeeds, if an ancestor call to not p is present*:

:- not q	CHS = {}
	(expand q by Rule P1.b)
:- not not p	CHS = {not q}
	(not not p $\rightarrow$ p)
:- p	CHS = {p, not q}
	(expand p by Rule P1.a)
:- not q	CHS = {p, not q}
	(coinductive success for not q)
:- $\square$	success: answer set is {p, not q}

3.2 OLON Rules

Our goal-directed procedure based on coinduction must also work with OLON rules. OLON rules are problematic because their influence on answer sets is indirect. Under ASP, rules of the form

```
p :- q1, q2, ..., qk, not p.
```

hold only for those (stable) models in which p succeeds through other rules in the program or at least one of the q_i's is false. Note that a headless rule of the form:

```
:- q1, q2, ..., qn.
```

is another manifestation of an OLON rule, as it is equivalent to the rule:

```
p :- q1, q2, ..., qn, not p.
```

where p is a literal that does not occur anywhere else in the program, in the sense that the stable models for the two rules are identical.

Without loss of generality, consider the simpler rule:

```
p :- q, not p.
```

For an interpretation to be a (stable) model for this rule, either p must succeed through other rules in the program or q must be false. Two interesting cases arise: (i). p is true through other rules in the program. (ii) q is true through other rules in the program.

For case (i), if p is true through other means in the program, then according to the Gelfond-Lifschitz method, it is in the answer set, and the OLON rule is taken out of consideration due to the occurrence of not p in its body. For case (ii), if q is true through other means and the rule is still in consideration due to p not being true through other rules in the program, then there are no answer sets, as q is both true and false. Thus, the answer set of the program P4 below is: {p, not q}.

```
p :- q, not p.      ... Rule P4.1
p.                  ... Rule P4.2
```

while there is no answer set for program P5 below:

```
p :- q, not p.      ... Rule P5.1
q.                  ... Rule P5.2
```

Given an OLON rule with p as its head and the query p, execution based on co-SLD resolution will fail, *if we require that the coinductive hypothesis set (CHS) remains consistent at all times.* That is, if we encounter the goal g (resp. not g) during execution and not g $\in$ CHS (resp. g $\in$ CHS), then the computation fails and backtracking ensues.

As another example, consider the program containing rule P4.1 (which has p in its head), but not rule P4.2, and the query :- p. When execution starts, p will be added to the CHS and then expanded by rule P4.1; if the call to q fails, then the goal p also fails. Alternatively, if q succeeds due to other rules in the program, then upon arriving at the call not p, failure will ensue, since not p is inconsistent with the current CHS (which equals {p, q} prior to the call not p).

Thus, OLON rules do not pose any problems in top-down execution based on coinduction, however, given an OLON rule with p as its head, if p can be inferred by other means (i.e., through ordinary rules) then the query p should succeed. Likewise, if q succeeds by other means and p does not, then we should report a failure (rather, report the absence of an answer set; note that given our conventions, CHS = {} denotes no answer set). We discuss how top-down execution of OLON rules is handled in Section 3.4.

3.3 Coinductive Success Under ASP

While our technique's use of co-SLD resolution has been outlined above, it requires some additional modification to be faithful to the Gelfond-Lifschitz method. Using normal coinductive success, our method will compute the *gfp* of the residual program after the GL transform, while the GL method computes the *lfp*. Consider Program P6 below:

```
p :- q.             ... Rule P6.1
q :- p.             ... Rule P6.2
```

Our method based on coinduction will succeed for queries :- p and :- q producing the answer set {p, q} while under the GL method, the answer set for this program is {not p, not q}. Our top-down method based on coinduction really computes the *gfp* of the original program. The GL method computes a fixed point of the original program (via the GL transformation and then computation of the *lfp* of the residual program) that is in between the *gfp* and the *lfp* of the original program. In the GL method, *direct cyclical reasoning is not allowed, however, cyclical reasoning that goes through at least one negated literal is allowed.* Thus, under the GL method, the answer set of program P6 does not contain a single positive literal, while there are two answer sets for the program P1 given earlier, each with exactly one positive literal, even though both programs P1 and P6 have only cyclical rules.

Our top-down method can be modified so that it produces answer sets consistent with the GL method: *a coinductive recursive call can succeed only if it is in the scope of at least one negation.* In other words, the path from a successful coinductive call to its ancestor call must include a call to not.

This restriction disallows inferring p from rules such as

```
p :- p.
```

With this operational restriction in place, the CHS will never contain a positive literal that is in the *gfp* of the residual program obtained after the GLT, but not in its *lfp*. To show this, let us assume that, for some ASP program, a call to p will always encounter at least one recursive call to p with no intervening negation. In such a case, p will never be part of any answer set:

- Under our goal-directed method, any call to p will fail when a recursive call is encountered with no intervening negation.
- Under the GL method, p will never be in the *lfp* of the residual. Even if a rule for p is present in the residual and all other dependencies are satisfied, the rule will still depend on the recursive call to p.

3.4 NMR Consistency Check

To summarize, the workings of our goal-directed strategy are as follows: given a goal G, perform co-SLD resolution while restricting coinductive success as outlined in Section 3.3. The CHS serves as the potential answer set. A successful answer will be computed only through ordinary rules, as all OLON rules will lead to failure due to the fact that `not h` will be encountered with proposition `h` present in the CHS while expanding with an OLON rule whose head is `h`. Once success is achieved, the answer set is the CHS. As discussed later, this answer set may be partial.

The answer set produced by the process above is only a potential answer set. Once a candidate answer set has been generated by co-SLD resolution as outlined above, the set has to be checked to see that it will not be rejected by an OLON rule. Suppose there are n OLON rules in the program of the form:

q_i :- B_i.

where $1 \leq i \leq n$ and each B_i is a conjunction of goals. Each B_i must contain a direct or indirect call to the respective q_i which is in the scope of odd number of negations in order for q_i :- B_i. to qualify as an OLON rule.

If a candidate answer set contains q_j ($1 \leq j \leq n$), then each OLON rule whose head matches q_j must be taken out of consideration (this is because B_j leads to not(q_j) which will be false for this candidate answer set). For all the other OLON rules whose head proposition q_k ($1 \leq j \leq n$) is not in the candidate answer set, their bodies must evaluate to false w.r.t. the candidate answer set, i.e., for each such rule, B_k must evaluate to false w.r.t. the candidate answer set.

The above restrictions can be restated as follows: a candidate answer set must satisfy the formula $q_i \vee$ not B_i ($1 \leq i \leq n$) for each OLON rule q_i :- B_i. ($1 \leq i \leq n$) in order to be reported as the final answer set. Thus, for each OLON rule, the check

chk_q_i :- q_i.
chk_q_i :- not B_i.

is constructed by our method. Furthermore, not B_i will be expanded to produce a chk_q_i clause for each literal in B_i. For example, if B_i represented the conjunction of literals `s, not r, t` in the above example, the check created would be:

chk_q_i :- q_i.
chk_q_i :- not s.
chk_q_i :- r.
chk_q_i :- not t.

A candidate answer set must satisfy each of these checks in order to be reported as a solution. This is enforced by rolling the checks into a single call, termed `nmr_chk`:

nmr_chk :- chk_q_1, chk_q_2, ...chk_q_n.

Now each query `Q` is transformed to `Q, nmr_chk.` before it is posed to our goal-directed system. One can think of `Q` as the generator of candidate answer sets and `nmr_chk` as the filter. If `nmr_chk` fails, then backtracking will take place and `Q` will produce another candidate answer set, and so on. Backtracking can also take place within `Q` itself when a call to `p` (resp. `not p`) is encountered and `not p` (resp. `p`) is present in the CHS. Note that the CHS must be a part of the execution state, and be restored upon backtracking.

4. Goal-directed Execution of Answer Set Programs

We next describe our general goal-directed procedure for computing answer sets.

4.1 Dual Rules

For simplicity, we add one more step to the process. Similarly to Alferes et al [1], for each rule in the program, we introduce its dual. That is, given a proposition H's definition (B_i's are conjunction of literals):

H :- B_1.
H :- B_2.
...
H :- B_n.

we add the dual rule

not H :- not B_1, not B_2, ..., not B_n.

If a proposition `q` appears in the body of a rule but not in any of the rule heads, then the fact

not q.

is added. Note that adding the dual rules is not necessary; it only makes the exposition of our goal-directed method easier to present and understand.

4.2 Goal-directed Method for Computing Answer Sets

Given a propositional query `:- Q` and a propositional answer set program `P`, the goal-directed procedure works as described below. Note that the execution state is a pair (G, S), where G is the current goal list, and S the current CHS.

1. Identify the set of ordinary rules and OLON rules in the program.
2. Assert a chk_q_i rule for every OLON rule with q_i as its head and build the `nmr_check` as described in Section 3.4.
3. For each ordinary rule and chk_q_i rule, construct its dual version.
4. Append the `nmr_check` to the query.
5. Set the initial execution state to: (:- G_1, ..., G_n, {}).
6. Non-deterministically reduce the execution state using the following rules:
   (a) *Call Expansion:*
   (:- G_1, .., G_i, .., G_n, S)
   $\rightarrow$ (:- G_1, .., B_1, .., B_m, .., G_n, S $\cup$ {G_i})
   where G_i matches the rule G_i :- B_1, ..., B_m. in P, G_i $\notin$ S and not $G_i \notin$ S.
   (b) *Coinductive Success:*
   (:- G_1, .., G_{i-1}, G_i, G_{i+1}, .., G_n, S)
   $\rightarrow$ (:- G_1, .., G_{i-1}, G_{i+1}, .., G_n, S)
   if $G_i \in$ S and either:
      i. G_i is not a recursive call or
      ii. G_i is a recursive call in the scope of a non-zero number of intervening negations.
   (c) *Inductive Success:*
   (:- G_1, .., G_{i-1}, G_i, G_{i+1}, .., G_n, S)
   $\rightarrow$ (:- G_1, .., G_{i-1}, G_{i+1}, .., G_n, S $\cup$ {G_i})
   if G_i matches a fact.
   (d) *Coinductive Failure:*
   (:- G_1, .., G_i, .., G_n, S) $\rightarrow$ (fail, S)
   if either:
      i. not $G_i \in$ S or
      ii. $G_i \in$ S and G_i is a recursive call without any intervening negations.
   (e) *Inductive Failure:*
   (:- G_1, .., G_i, .., G_n, S) $\rightarrow$ (fail, S)
   if G_i has no matching rule in P.
   (f) *Print Answer:*
   (:- `true`, S) $\rightarrow$ success: S is the answer set
   where ':- `true`' $\equiv$ empty goal list

Note that when all the goals in the query are exhausted, execution of `nmr_chk` begins. Upon failure, backtracking ensues, the state is restored and another rule tried. Note that negated calls are expanded using dual rules as in [1], so it is not necessary to check whether the number of intervening negations between a recursive call and its ancestor is even or odd. (See the call expansion rule above). A detailed example of goal-directed execution can be found in Appendix B. Next we discuss a few important issues:

Identifying OLON and Ordinary Rules Given a propositional answer set program P, OLON rules and ordinary rules can be identified by constructing and traversing the call graph. The complexity of this traversal is $O(|P| * n)$, where n is the number of propositional symbols occurring in the head of clauses in P and |P| is a measure of the program size. Note also that during the execution of a query Q, we need not make a distinction between ordinary and OLON rules; knowledge of OLON rules is needed only for creating the `nmr_chk`.

Partial Answer Set Our top-down procedure might not generate the entire answer set. It may generate only the part of the answer set that is needed to evaluate the query. Consider program P7:

```
p :- not q.
q :- not p.
r :- not s.
s :- not r.
```

Under goal-directed execution, the query `:- q.` for program P7 will produce only {`q, not p`} as the answer since the rules defining `r` and `s` are completely independent of rules for `p` and `q`. One could argue that this is an advantage of a goal-directed execution strategy rather than a disadvantage, as only the relevant part of the program will be explored. In contrast, if the query is `:- q, s`, then the right answer {`q, not p, s, not r`} will be produced by the goal-directed execution method. Thus, the part of the answer set that gets computed depends on the query. Correct maintenance of the CHS throughout the execution is important as it ensures that only consistent and correct answer sets are produced.

5. Soundness and Correctness of the Goal-directed Method

We will now show the correctness of our goal-directed execution method by showing it to be sound and complete with respect to the GL method. First, we will examine the modified relevance property which holds for our method.

5.1 Relevance

As we stated in the introduction, one of the primary problems with developing a goal-directed ASP implementation is the lack of a relevance property in stable model semantics. Dix introduces relevance by stating that, "given any semantics SEM and a program P, it is perfectly reasonable that the truth-value of a literal L, with respect to SEM(P), only depends on the subprogram formed from the relevant rules of P with respect to L" [6]. He formalizes this using the dependency-graph of P, first establishing that

- "$dependencies\_of(X) :=$ {A : X depends on A}, and
- rel_rul(P,X) is the set of relevant rules of P with respect to X, i.e. the set of rules that contain an $A \in dependencies\_of(X)$ in their heads" [6]

and noting that the dependencies and relevant rules of $\neg X$ are the same as those of X [6]. He then defines relevance as, for all literals L:

$$SEM(P)(L) = SEM(rel\_rul(P, L))(L) \quad (1)$$

The relevance property is desirable because it would ensure that a partial answer set computed using only relevant rules for each literal could be extended into a complete answer set. However, stable model semantics do not satisfy the definition as given. This is because OLON rules can alter the meaning of a program and the truth values of individual literals without occurring in the set of relevant rules [6, 23]. For instance, an irrelevant rule of the form `p :- not p.` when added to an answer set program P, where P has one or more stable models and `p` does not occur in P, results in a program that has no stable models.

Approaches such as [23] have addressed the lack of a relevance property by modifying stable model semantics to restore relevance. However, our implementation can be viewed as restoring relevance by expanding the definition of relevant rules to include all OLON rules in a program. Because the NMR check processes every OLON rule, it has the effect of making the truth value of every literal in a program dependent on such rules. That is,

$$\begin{aligned} nmr\_rel\_rul(P, L) &= rel\_rul(P, L) \cup O, \\ O &= \{ \text{ R: R is an OLON rule in P } \} \end{aligned} \quad (2)$$

Using nmr_rel_rul(P,L) in place of rel_rul(P,L), a modified version of equation 1 above holds for our semantics:

$$SEM(P)(L) = SEM(nmr\_rel\_rule(P, L))(L) \quad (3)$$

As a result, any partial model returned by our semantics is guaranteed to be a subset of one or more complete models.

5.2 Soundness

Theorem 1. *For the non-empty set X returned by successful top-down execution of some program P, the set of positive literals in X will be an answer set of R, the set of rules of P used during top-down execution.*

Proof. Let us assume that top-down execution of a program P has succeeded for some query Q consisting of a set of literals in P, returning a non-empty set of literals X. We can observe that $R \subseteq \bigcup_{L \in Q} nmr\_rel\_rul(P, L)$: for each positive literal in Q, one rule with the literal in its head will need to succeed, for each negative literal in Q all rules with the the positive form of the literal in their head will need to fail, and the resulting set must satisfy the NMR check. We will show that X is a valid answer set of R using the GL method. First, because X may contain negative literals and the residual program produced by the GL method is a positive one, let us remove any rules in R containing the positive version of such literals as a goal, and then remove the negated literals from X to obtain X'. Because our algorithm allows negative literals to succeed if and only if all rules for the positive form fail or no such rules exist, only rules which failed during execution will be removed by this step. Next, let us apply the GL transformation using X' as the candidate answer set to obtain the residual program R'. This will remove rules containing the negation of any literal in X' and remove any negated goals from the remaining rules.

We know that X' will be an answer set of R if and only if X' = LFP(R'). Now let us examine the properties of R'. As positive literals, we know that each literal in X' must occur as the head of a rule in R which succeeded during execution. Because such rules would have failed if the negation of any goal was present in the CHS, we know that such rules would not have been eliminated from the residual program by the GL transformation, and are thus still present in R' save for the removal of any negated goals. Because any rules containing the negation of a literal in X had to fail during execution, at least one goal in each of these rules must have failed, resulting in the negation of the goal being added to the CHS. Furthermore, because the NMR check applies the negation of each OLON rule, again the negation of some goal in each such rule must have been added to the CHS. Thus any rule which failed during execution and yet was included in R will have been removed from R'. Finally, because our algorithm allows coinductive success to occur only in the scope of at least one negation, the removal of negated goals from the residual program will ensure that R' contains no loops. Because the remaining rules in R' must have succeeded during execution, their goals must have been added to the CHS, and therefore those goals consisting of positive literals form X'. Thus R' is a positive program with no loops, and each literal in X' must appear as the head of some rule in R' which is either a fact or whose goals consist only of other elements in X'. Therefore the least fixed point of R' must be equal to X', and X' must be an answer set of R. □

Theorem 2. *Our top-down execution algorithm is sound with respect to the GL method. That is, for the non-empty set of literals X returned by successful execution of some program P, the set of positive literals in X is a subset of one or more answer sets of P.*

Proof. As shown above, the positive literals in the set returned by successful execution of P will be an answer set of $R \subseteq \bigcup_{L \in Q} nmr\_rel\_rul(P, L)$. Because R will always contain all OLON rules in P, no unused rules in P are capable of affecting the truth values of the literals in X. Thus the modified definition of relevance holds for all literals in X under our semantics and the partial answer set returned by our algorithm is guaranteed to be extensible to a complete one. Thus our algorithm for top-down execution is sound with respect to the GL method. □

5.3 Completeness

Theorem 3. *Our top-down execution algorithm is complete with respect to the GL method. That is, for a program P, any answer set valid under the GL method will succeed if used as a query for top-down execution. In addition, the set returned by successful execution will contain no additional positive literals.*

Proof. Let X be a valid answer set of P obtained via the GL method. Then there exists a resultant program P' obtained by removing those rules in P containing the negation of any literal in X and removing any additional negated literals from the goals of the remaining rules. Furthermore, because X is a valid answer set of P, X = LFP(P'). This tells us that for every literal $L \in X$ there is a rule in P' with L as its head, which is either a fact or whose goals consist only of other literals in X.

Let us assume that X is posed as a query for top-down execution of P. As we know that each $L \in X$ has a rule in P' with L as its head and whose positive goals are other literals in X, we know that such a rule also exists in P, with the possible addition of negated literals as goals. However, we know that these negated literals must succeed, that is, all rules with the positive form of such literals in their heads must fail, either by calling the negation of some literal in the answer set or by calling their heads recursively without an intervening negation. Were this not the case, these rules would remain in P', their heads would be included in LFP(P') and X would not be a valid answer set of P. Therefore, a combination of rules may be found such that each literal in X appears as the head of at least one rule which will succeed under top-down execution, and whose positive goals are all other literals in X. Furthermore, because each literal in the query must be satisfied and added to the CHS, and any rule with a goal whose negation is present in the CHS will fail, such a combination of rules will eventually be executed by our algorithm. Because such rules would also be present in P', we know that they cannot add additional positive literals to the CHS, as these would be part of LFP(P'), again rendering X invalid.

This leaves the NMR check, which ensures the set returned by our algorithm satisfies all OLON rules in P. However, we know this is the case, as the subset of positive literals in the CHS is equal to X. Because X is a valid answer set of P, there cannot be any rule in P which renders X invalid, and thus the NMR check must be satisfiable by a set of literals containing X. We also know that the NMR check will not add additional positive literals to the CHS, as any rules able to succeed would be present in P' and thus present in LFP(P').

Therefore any valid answer set X of a program P must succeed if posed as a query for top-down execution of P. Thus our top-down algorithm is complete with respect to the GL method. □

Table 1. N-Queens Problem; Times in Seconds

Problem	*Galliwasp*	*clasp*	*cmodels*	*smodels*
queens-12	0.033	0.019	0.055	0.112
queens-13	0.034	0.022	0.071	0.132
queens-14	0.076	0.029	0.098	0.362
queens-15	0.071	0.034	0.119	0.592
queens-16	0.293	0.043	0.138	1.356
queens-17	0.198	0.049	0.176	4.293
queens-18	1.239	0.059	0.224	8.653
queens-19	0.148	0.070	0.272	3.288
queens-20	6.744	0.084	0.316	47.782
queens-21	0.420	0.104	0.398	95.710
queens-22	69.224	0.112	0.472	N/A
queens-23	1.282	0.132	0.582	N/A
queens-24	19.916	0.152	0.602	N/A

Table 2. MxN-Pigeons Problem (No Solution for M>N)

Problem	*Galliwasp*	*clasp*	*cmodels*	*smodels*
pigeon-10x10	0.020	0.009	0.020	0.025
pigeon-20x20	0.050	0.048	0.163	0.517
pigeon-30x30	0.132	0.178	0.691	4.985
pigeon-8x7	0.123	0.072	0.089	0.535
pigeon-9x8	0.888	0.528	0.569	4.713
pigeon-10x9	8.339	4.590	2.417	46.208
pigeon-11x10	90.082	40.182	102.694	N/A

Table 3. MxN-Coloring problem (No Solution for M=3)

Problem	*Galliwasp*	*clasp*	*cmodels*	*smodels*
mapclr-4x20	0.018	0.006	0.011	0.013
mapclr-4x25	0.021	0.007	0.014	0.016
mapclr-4x29	0.023	0.008	0.016	0.018
mapclr-4x30	0.026	0.008	0.016	0.019
mapclr-3x20	0.022	0.005	0.009	0.008
mapclr-3x25	0.065	0.006	0.011	0.010
mapclr-3x29	0.394	0.006	0.012	0.011
mapclr-3x30	0.342	0.007	0.012	0.011

6. Performance Results

The goal-directed method described in this paper has been implemented in our system *Galliwasp*. In addition to the goal-directed method presented here, *Galliwasp* incorporates various other techniques to improve performance, including incremental enforcement of the NMR check [19]. Tables 1, 2 and 3 give performance results for some example programs. For the purpose of comparison, results for *clasp*, *cmodels* and *smodels* are also given.

The *Galliwasp* system consists of two programs, a compiler and an interpreter. The times given are for our interpreter using a compiled program and for the other solvers reading a program grounded by lparse. Neither compilation nor grounding times are factored into the results. A timeout of 600 seconds was enforced, with the instances which timed out listed as N/A in the tables.

As these results demonstrate, our goal-directed method is practical and can be efficiently implemented. While additional performance increases are possible, the *Galliwasp* interpreter is already significantly faster than *smodels* in almost every case and comparable to *clasp* and *cmodels* in most cases.

7. Discussion and Related Work

There are many advantages of top-down goal-directed execution of answer set programs, the main one being that it paves the way to answer set programming with predicates. The first step is to extend our method to *datalog answer set programs*, i.e., programs that allow only constants and variables as arguments in the predicates they contain [20].

Another advantage of goal-directed execution is that answer set programming can be made to work more naturally with other extensions that have been developed within logic programming, such as constraint programming, abduction, parallelism, probabilistic reasoning, etc. This leads to more sophisticated applications. Timed planning, i.e., planning in the presence of real-time constraints, is one such example [2].

With respect to related work, a top-down, goal-directed execution strategy for ASP has been the aim of many researchers in the past. Descriptions of some of these efforts can be found in [1, 4, 5, 8, 9, 15, 23, 24, 26]. The strategy presented in this paper is based on one presented by several of this paper's authors in previous work [14, 21]. However, the strategy presented in those works was limited to call-consistent or order-consistent programs. While the possibility of expansion to arbitrary ASP programs was mentioned, it was not expanded upon, and the proofs of soundness and completeness covered only the restricted cases [21].

A query-driven procedure for computing answer sets via an abductive proof procedure has been explored [7, 16]: a consistency check via integrity constraints is done before a negated literal is added to the answer set. However, "this procedure is not always sound with respect to the above abductive semantics of NAF" [16]. Alferes et al [1] have worked in a similar direction, though this is done in the context of abduction and again goal-directedness of ASP is not the main focus. Gebser and Schaub have developed a tableau based method which can be regarded as a step in this direction, however, the motivation for their work is completely different [9].

Bonatti, Pontelli and Tran [5] have proposed credulous resolution, an extension of earlier work of Bonatti [4], that extends SLD resolution for ASP. However, they place restrictions on the type of programs allowed and the type of queries allowed. Their method can be regarded as allowing coinductive success to be inferred only for negated goals. Thus, given query `:- p` and program P1, the execution will look as follows: `p` $\rightarrow$ `not q` $\rightarrow$ `not not p` $\rightarrow$ `not q` $\rightarrow$ `success`. Compared to our method, their method performs extra work. For example, if rule P1.1 is changed to `p :- big_goal, not q`, then `big_goal` will be executed twice. The main problem in their method is that since it does not take coinduction for positive goals into account, knowing when to succeed inductively and when to succeed coinductively is undecidable. For this reason, their method works correctly only for a limited class of answer set programs (for example, answers to negated queries such `?-not p` cannot be computed in a top-down manner). In contrast, our goal-directed method works correctly for all types of answer set programs and all types of queries.

Pereira's group has done significant work on defining semantics for normal logic programs and implementing them, including implementation in a top-down fashion [1, 23, 24]. However, their approach is to modify stable model semantics so that the property of relevance is restored [23]. For this modified semantics, goal-directed procedures have been designed [24]. In contrast, our goal is to stay faithful to stable model semantics and answer set programming.

8. Conclusions

The main contribution of our paper is to present a practical, top-down method for goal-directed execution of Answer Set programs along with proofs of soundness and completeness. Our method stays faithful to ASP, and works for arbitrary answer set programs as well as arbitrary queries. Other methods in the literature either change the semantics, or work for only restricted programs or queries. Our method achieves this by relying on the coinductive logic programming paradigm. Details of our method were presented, along with proofs of soundness and correctness, and some preliminary performance results. A goal-directed procedure has many advantages, the main one being that execution of answer set programs does not have to be restricted to only finitely groundable ones. Our work thus paves the way for developing execution procedures for ASP over predicates. A goal-directed strategy permits an easier integration with other extensions of logic programming, which in turn makes it possible to develop more interesting applications of ASP and non-monotonic reasoning. Our current work is focused on refining our implementation to improve efficiency and add support for features such as constraints and predicates.

9. Acknowledgments

Thanks to Michael Gelfond, Vladimir Lifschitz, Enrico Pontelli and Feliks Kluźniak for discussions and feedback.

References

[1] J. J. Alferes, L. M. Pereira, and T. Swift. Abduction in Well-Founded Semantics and Generalized Stable Models via Tabled Dual Programs. *Theory and Practice of Logic Programming*, 4:383–428, July 2004.

[2] A. Bansal. *Towards Next Generation Logic Programming Systems*. PhD thesis, University of Texas at Dallas, 2007.

[3] C. Baral. *Knowledge Representation, Reasoning and Declarative Problem Solving*. Cambridge University Press, 2003.

[4] P. A. Bonatti. Resolution for Skeptical Stable Model Semantics. *Journal of Automated Reasoning*, 27:391–421, November 2001.

[5] P. A. Bonatti, E. Pontelli, and T. C. Son. Credulous Resolution for Answer Set Programming. In *Proceedings of the 23rd national conference on Artificial Intelligence - Volume 1*, AAAI'08, pages 418–423. AAAI Press, 2008.

[6] J. Dix. A Classification Theory of Semantics of Normal Logic Programs: II. Weak Properties. *Fundamenta Informaticae*, 22:257–288, 1995.

[7] K. Eshghi and R. A. Kowalski. Abduction compared with negation by failure. In *ICLP*, pages 234–254, 1989.

[8] J. Fernández and J. Lobo. A Proof Procedure for Stable Theories. In *CS-TR-3034*, Computer Science Technical Report Series. University of Maryland, 1993.

[9] M. Gebser and T. Schaub. Tableau Calculi for Answer Set Programming. In *Proceedings of the 22nd international conference on Logic Programming*, ICLP'06, pages 11–25. Springer-Verlag, 2006.

[10] M. Gebser, B. Kaufmann, A. Neumann, and T. Schaub. Clasp: A Conflict-Driven Answer Set Solver. In *Proceedings of the 9th international conference on Logic Programming and Nonmonotonic Reasoning*, LPNMR'07, pages 260–265. Springer-Verlag, 2007.

[11] M. Gelfond. Representing Knowledge in A-Prolog. In *Computational Logic: Logic Programming and Beyond, Essays in Honour of Robert A. Kowalski, Part II*, pages 413–451. Springer-Verlag, 2002.

[12] M. Gelfond and V. Lifschitz. The Stable Model Semantics for Logic Programming. In *Proceedings of the Fifth international conference on Logic Programming*, pages 1070–1080. MIT Press, 1988.

[13] E. Giunchiglia, Y. Lierler, and M. Maratea. SAT-Based Answer Set Programming. In *Proceedings of the 19th national conference on Artifical Intelligence*, AAAI'04, pages 61–66. AAAI Press, 2004.

[14] G. Gupta, A. Bansal, R. Min, L. Simon, and A. Mallya. Coinductive Logic Programming and Its Applications. In *Proceedings of the 23rd international conference on Logic Programming*, ICLP'07, pages 27–44. Springer-Verlag, 2007.

[15] A. Kakas and F. Toni. Computing Argumentation in Logic Programming. *Journal of Logic and Computation*, 9(4):515–562, 1999.

[16] A. C. Kakas, R. A. Kowalski, and F. Toni. Abductive Logic Programming. *Journal of Logic and Computation*, 2(6):719–770, 1992.

[17] P. G. Leone, N. and W. Faber. DLV. `http://www.dbai.tuwien.ac.at/proj/dlv`.

[18] J. Lloyd. *Foundations of Logic Programming*. Symbolic Computation: Artificial Intelligence. Springer-Verlag, 1987.

[19] K. Marple and G. Gupta. Galliwasp: A Goal-Directed Answer Set Solver. Technical report, University of Texas at Dallas, 2012. `http://www.utdallas.edu/~kbm072000/galliwasp/publications/galliwasp.pdf`.

[20] R. Min. *Predicate Answer Set Programming with Coinduction*. PhD thesis, University of Texas at Dallas, 2010.

[21] R. Min, A. Bansal, and G. Gupta. Towards Predicate Answer Set Programming via Coinductive Logic Programming. In *AIAI*, pages 499–508. Springer, 2009.

[22] I. Niemelä and P. Simons. Smodels - An Implementation of the Stable Model and Well-Founded Semantics for Normal Logic Programs. In *Logic Programming And Nonmonotonic Reasoning*, volume 1265 of *Lecture Notes in Computer Science*, pages 420–429. Springer-Verlag, 1997.

[23] L. Pereira and A. Pinto. Revised Stable Models - A Semantics for Logic Programs. In *Progress in Artificial Intelligence*, volume 3808 of *Lecture Notes in Computer Science*, pages 29–42. Springer-Verlag, 2005.

[24] L. Pereira and A. Pinto. Layered Models Top-Down Querying of Normal Logic Programs. In *Practical Aspects of Declarative Languages*, volume 5418 of *Lecture Notes in Computer Science*, pages 254–268. Springer-Verlag, 2009.

[25] K. Sagonas, T. Swift, and D. Warren. XSB as an Efficient Deductive Database Engine. In *ACM SIGMOD Record*, volume 23, pages 442–453. ACM, 1994.

[26] Y. Shen, J. You, and L. Yuan. Enhancing Global SLS-Resolution with Loop Cutting and Tabling Mechanisms. *Theoretical Computer Science*, 328(3):271–287, 2004.

[27] L. Simon. *Extending Logic Programming with Coinduction*. PhD thesis, University of Texas at Dallas, 2006.

A. Co-SLD Resolution

As mentioned in the introduction, our goal-directed method relies on *coinductive logic programming* (co-LP) [14]. Co-SLD resolution, the operational semantics of coinduction, is briefly described below. The semantics is limited to *regular proofs*, i.e., those cases where the infinite behavior is obtained by infinite repetition of a finite number of finite behaviors.

Consider the logic programming definition of a stream (list) of numbers as in program R1 below:

```
stream([]).
stream([H|T]) :- number(H), stream(T).
```

Under SLD resolution, the query `?- stream(X)` will systematically produce all finite streams one by one starting from the `[]` stream. Suppose now we remove the base case and obtain the program R2:

```
stream([H|T]) :- number(H), stream(T).
```

In the program R2, the meaning of the query `?- stream(X)` is semantically null under standard logic programming. In the co-LP paradigm the declarative semantics of the predicate `stream/1` above is given in terms of *infinitary Herbrand (or co-Herbrand) universe, infinitary Herbrand (or co-Herbrand) base [18], and maximal models (computed using greatest fixed-points)* [27]. The operational semantics under coinduction is as follows [27]: a predicate call $p(\bar{t})$ succeeds if it unifies with one of its ancestor calls. Thus, every time a call is made, it has to be remembered. This set of ancestor calls constitutes the *coinductive hypothesis set* (CHS). Under co-LP, infinite *rational* answers can be computed, and infinite rational terms are allowed as arguments of predicates. Infinite terms are represented as solutions to unification equations and the occurs check is omitted during the unification process: for example, `X = [1 | X]` represents the binding of `X` to an infinite list of 1's. Thus, in co-SLD resolution, given a single clause

```
p([ 1 | X ]) :- p(X).
```

The query `?- p(A)` will succeed in two resolution steps with the answer `A = [1 | A]`, which is a finite representation of the infinite answer `A = [1, 1, 1, ....]`. Under coinductive interpretation of R2, the query `?- stream(X)` produces all infinite sized streams as answers, e.g., `X = [1 | X]`, `X = [1, 2 | X ]`, etc. Thus, the semantics of R2 is not null, but proofs may be of infinite length. If we take a coinductive interpretation of program R1, then we get all finite and infinite streams as answers to the query `?- stream(X)`.

B. Detailed Execution Example

We now present a larger, more complex example of execution using our goal-directed method. Consider program A1:

```
p :- not q.        ... Rule A1.1
q :- not r.        ... Rule A1.2
r :- not p.        ... Rule A1.3
q :- not p.        ... Rule A1.4
```

Rules A1.1, A1.2 and A1.3 are OLON rules, as calls to propositions `p`, `q`, and `r` in the heads of these rules lead to recursive calls to `p`, `q` and `r` respectively that are in the scope of odd numbers of negations. A1.1 is also an ordinary rule, since in conjunction with rule A1.4, a call to `p` resolved via rule A1.1 will lead to a call to `p` in rule A1.4 that is in the scope of an even number of negations. Thus, the `nmr_check` rule can be defined as:

```
nmr_check :- not chk_p, not chk_q, not chk_r.
chk_p :- not p, not q.
chk_q :- not q, not r.
chk_r :- not r, not p.
```

The duals of the above rules are as follows:

```
not p :- q.            ... Rule A1.6
not q :- r, p.         ... Rule A1.7
not r :- p.            ... Rule A1.8
not chk_p :- p; q....  Rule A1.9
not chk_q :- q; r....  Rule A1.10
not chk_r :- r; p....  Rule A1.11
```

Negated calls are resolved using these dual rules. Now the query `q` will be extended to `q, nmr_chk` and executed as follows:

```
:- q, nmr_chk.        CHS = {}; Rule A1.2
:- not r, nmr_chk     CHS = {q}; Rule A1.8
:- p, nmr_chk.        CHS = {q, not r}; Rule A1.1
:- not q, nmr_chk     CHS = {q, not r}
                      fail: backtrack to step 1
:- q, nmr_chk.        CHS = {}; Rule A1.4
:- not p, nmr_chk     CHS = {q, not p}; Rule A1.6
:- q, nmr_chk.        CHS = {q, not p}
                      coinductive success
:- nmr_chk.           CHS = {q, not p}
                      execution of q finished
:- not chk_p, not chk_q, not chk_r.
```

```
                     CHS = {q, not p}
                     nmr_chk rule
:- (p ; q), not chk_q, not chk_r.
                     CHS = {q, not p}
                     not p is in CHS
:- q, not chk_q, not chk_r.
                     CHS = {q, not p}
                     coinductive success for q
:- not chk_q, not chk_r.
                     CHS = {q, not p}; Rule A1.10
:- (q ; r), not chk_r.
                     CHS = {q, not p}
                     coinductive success for q
:- not chk_r.        CHS = {q, not p}; Rule A1.11

:- r ; p.            CHS = {q, not p, r}; Rule A1.3

:- not p ; p.        CHS = {q, not p, r}
                     coinductive success for not p
:- □.                success.
                     answer set is {q, not p, r}
```

Layered Fixed Point Logic

Piotr Filipiuk Flemming Nielson Hanne Riis Nielson
Technical University of Denmark
{pifi,nielson,riis}@imm.dtu.dk

Abstract

We present a logic for the specification of static analysis problems that goes beyond the logics traditionally used. Its most prominent feature is the direct support for both inductive computations of behaviors as well as co-inductive specifications of properties. Two main theoretical contributions are a Moore Family result and a parametrized worst case time complexity result. We show that the logic and the associated solver can be used for rapid prototyping of analyses and illustrate a wide variety of applications within Static Analysis, Constraint Satisfaction Problems and Model Checking. In all cases the complexity result specializes to the worst case time complexity of the classical methods.

Categories and Subject Descriptors F.3.1 [*Theory of Computation*]: LOGICS AND MEANINGS OF PROGRAMS—Specifying and Verifying and Reasoning about Programs; F.4.3 [*Theory of Computation*]: MATHEMATICAL LOGIC AND FORMAL LANGUAGES—Formal Languages; D.1.6 [*Software*]: PROGRAMMING TECHNIQUES—Logic Programming; D.2.4 [*Software*]: SOFTWARE ENGINEERING—Software/Program Verification

General Terms Theory, Verification

Keywords Static analysis, model checking, abstract interpretation

1. Introduction

As software systems become more complex, there is an increasing need for more powerful and sophisticated analyses to ensure system correctness. Unfortunately, developing new analysis specifications and implementations is often difficult and error-prone. In order to remedy that problem it should be possible to implement prototypes of analyses that are easy to analyse for complexity and correctness. Since analysis specifications are generally written in a declarative style, logic programming presents an attractive model for producing executable specifications of analyses. A logical framework for prototyping new analyses would allow to build an early implementation of analyses, test the concepts and learn from them. It would also allow for the rapid delivery of functioning analyses.

Static analysis [16, 28] is a successful approach to the validation of properties of programming languages. It can be seen as a two-phase process where we first transform the analysis problem into a set of constraints that, in the second phase, is solved to produce the analysis result of interest. The constraints may be expressed in a language tailored to the problem at hand, or they may be expressed in a general purpose constraint language such as Datalog [1, 6] or ALFP [29].

Model checking [2, 17] is an automatic technique for verifying hardware and more recently software systems. Specifications are expressed in modal logic, whereas the system is modeled as a transition system or a Kripke structure. Given a system description the model checking algorithm either proves that the system satisfies the property, or reports a counterexample that violates it.

Constraint Satisfaction Problems (CSPs) [25] are the subject of intense research in e.g. artificial intelligence and operations research. They consist of variables with constraints on them, and many real-world problems can be described as CSPs. A major challenge in constraint programming is to develop efficient generic approaches to solve instances of the CSP.

In this paper we present a framework that facilitates rapid prototyping of new analyses. The approach taken falls within the Abstract Interpretation [9, 10] framework, thus there always is a unique best solution to the analysis problem considered. The framework consists of the Layered Fixed Point Logic (LFP) and an associated solver. The most prominent feature of the LFP logic is the direct support for both inductive computations of behaviors as well as co-inductive specifications of properties. The solver is implemented in continuation passing style and uses symbolic representation of the state space by means of Binary Decision Diagrams (BDDs) [5]. The applicability of the framework is illustrated by presenting a variety of applications within Static Analysis, Constraint Satisfaction Problems and Model Checking. Due to the fact that problems from both static analysis and model checking can be succinctly expressed within one framework, we believe that this article enhances our understanding of the interplay between static analysis and model checking — to the extent that they can be seen as essentially equivalent to each other.

The LFP logic is similar to modal μ-calculus [17, 20], which is extensively used in various areas of computer science such as e.g computer-aided verification. Its defining feature is the addition of least and greatest fixpoint operators to modal logic; thus it achieves a great increase in expressive power, but at the same time an equally great increase in difficulty of understanding. The expressiveness of LFP logic is equivalent to the alternation free fragment of modal μ-calculus, however we find LFP more intuitive for prototyping new analyses.

The paper is organized as follows. In Section 2 we define the syntax and semantics of LFP. In Section 3 we establish a Moore Family result and estimate the worst case time complexity. Section 4 shows an application of LFP to Static Analysis. We continue in Section 5 with an application to the Constraint Satisfaction Problem. An application to Model Checking in presented in Section 6. Section 7 describes the solving algorithm developed for LFP. We review related work in Section 8 and conclude in Section 9.

PPDP'12, September 19–21, 2012, Leuven, Belgium.

2. Syntax and Semantics

In this section, we introduce Layered Fixed Point Logic (abbreviated LFP). The LFP formulae are made up of layers. Each layer can either be a *define* formula which corresponds to the inductive definition, or a *constrain* formula corresponding to the co-inductive specification. The following definition introduces the syntax of LFP.

DEFINITION 1. *Given a fixed countable set $\mathcal{X}$ of variables, a non-empty universe $\mathcal{U}$, a finite set of function symbols $\mathcal{F}$, and a finite alphabet $\mathcal{R}$ of predicate symbols, we define the set of LFP formulae, cls, together with clauses, cl, conditions, cond, constrains, con, definitions, def, and terms u by the grammar:*

$$
\begin{array}{lcl}
u & ::= & x \mid f(\vec{u}) \\
cond & ::= & R(\vec{x}) \mid \neg R(\vec{x}) \mid cond_1 \wedge cond_2 \mid cond_1 \vee cond_2 \\
 & \mid & \exists x : cond \mid \forall x : cond \mid true \mid false \\
def & ::= & cond \Rightarrow R(\vec{u}) \mid \forall x : def \mid def_1 \wedge def_2 \\
con & ::= & R(\vec{u}) \Rightarrow cond \mid \forall x : con \mid con_1 \wedge con_2 \\
cl_i & ::= & define(def) \mid constrain(con) \\
cls & ::= & cl_1, \ldots, cl_s
\end{array}
$$

Here $x \in \mathcal{X}$, $R \in \mathcal{R}$, $f \in \mathcal{F}$ and $1 \leq i \leq s$. We say that s is the order of the LFP formula $cl_1, \ldots, cl_s$.

We allow to write $R(\vec{u})$ for $true \Rightarrow R(\vec{u})$, $\neg R(\vec{u})$ for $R(\vec{u}) \Rightarrow false$ and we abbreviate zero-arity functions $f()$ as $f \in \mathcal{U}$. Occurrences of $R(\vec{x})$ and $\neg R(\vec{x})$ in conditions are called positive and negative queries, respectively. Occurrences of $R(\vec{u})$ on the right hand side of the implication in define formulas are called defined occurrences. Occurrences of $R(\vec{u})$ on the left hand side of the implication in constrain formulas are called constrained occurrences. Defined and constrained occurrences are jointly called assertions. In the following we refer to LFP relations interchangeably as relations or predicates.

In order to ensure desirable theoretical and pragmatic properties in the presence of negation, we impose a notion of *stratification* similar to the one in Datalog [1, 6]. Intuitively, stratification ensures that a negative query is not performed until the predicate has been fully asserted (defined or constrained). This is important for ensuring that once a condition evaluates to true it will continue to be true even after further assertions of predicates.

DEFINITION 2. *The formula $cl_1, \ldots, cl_s$ is stratified if for all $i = 1, \ldots, s$ the following properties hold:*

- *Relations asserted in cl_i must not be asserted in $cl_{i+1}, \ldots, cl_s$*
- *Relations occurring in positive queries in cl_i must not be asserted in $cl_{i+1}, \ldots, cl_s$*
- *Relations occurring in negative queries in cl_i must not be asserted in $cl_i, \ldots, cl_s$*

The function $rank : \mathcal{R} \to \{0, \ldots, s\}$ is then uniquely defined as

$$rank(R) = \max(\{0\} \cup \{i \mid R \text{ is asserted in } cl_i\})$$

Intuitively, the definition states that every relation can be asserted in at most one clause. The relations not asserted in any clause (relations that are given) have rank 0. Furthermore the definition ensures that a negative query is not performed until the predicate has been fully asserted. The following example illustrates the use of negation in the LFP formulae.

EXAMPLE 1. *Using the notion of stratification we can define equality eq and non-equality neq predicates as follows*

$$define(\forall x : true \Rightarrow eq(x,x)),$$
$$define(\forall x : \forall y : \neg eq(x,y) \Rightarrow neq(x,y))$$

According to Definition 2 the formula is stratified, since predicate eq is negatively used only in the layer above the one that defines it. More precisely, the predicate eq is fully defined before it is negatively queried in the clause asserting predicate neq.

Alternatively, we can use a greatest fixed point formulation (using constrain clause) to specify equality and non-equality predicates

$$constrain(\forall x : neq(x,x) \Rightarrow false),$$
$$constrain(\forall x : \forall y : \neg neq(x,y) \Rightarrow eq(x,y))$$

Again the formula is stratified, since predicate neq is negatively used only in the layer above the one that asserts it.

To specify the semantics of LFP we introduce the interpretations ρ, ζ and ς of predicate symbols, function symbols and variables, respectively. Formally we have

$$
\begin{array}{rl}
\rho : & \prod_k \mathcal{R}_{/k} \to \mathcal{P}(\mathcal{U}^k) \\
\zeta : & \prod_k \mathcal{F}_{/k} \to \mathcal{U}^k \to \mathcal{U} \\
\varsigma : & \mathcal{X} \to \mathcal{U}
\end{array}
$$

In the above $\mathcal{R}_{/k}$ stands for a set of predicate symbols of arity k, then $\mathcal{R}$ is a disjoint union of $\mathcal{R}_{/k}$, hence $\mathcal{R} = \biguplus_k \mathcal{R}_{/k}$. Similarity $\mathcal{F}_{/k}$ is a set of function symbols of arity k and $\mathcal{F} = \biguplus_k \mathcal{F}_{/k}$. The interpretation of variables is given by $[\![x]\!](\zeta, \varsigma) = \varsigma(x)$, where $\varsigma(x)$ is the element from $\mathcal{U}$ bound to $x \in \mathcal{X}$. Furthermore, the interpretation of function terms is defined as $[\![f(\vec{u})]\!](\zeta, \varsigma) = \zeta(f)([\![\vec{u}]\!](\zeta, \varsigma))$. It is generalized to sequences $\vec{u}$ of terms in a point-wise manner by taking $[\![a]\!](\zeta, \varsigma) = a$ for all $a \in \mathcal{U}$, and $[\![(u_1, \ldots, u_k)]\!](\zeta, \varsigma) = ([\![u_1]\!](\zeta, \varsigma), \ldots, [\![u_k]\!](\zeta, \varsigma))$.

The satisfaction relations for conditions *cond*, definitions *def* and constrains *con* are specified by:

$$(\rho, \varsigma) \models cond, \quad (\rho, \zeta, \varsigma) \models def \quad \text{and } (\rho, \zeta, \varsigma) \models con$$

The formal definition is given in Table 1; here $\varsigma[x \mapsto a]$ stands for the mapping that is as ς except that x is mapped to a.

3. Optimal Solutions

Moore Family First we establish a Moore family result for LFP, which guarantees that there always is a unique best solution for LFP formulae.

DEFINITION 3. *A Moore family is a subset Y of a complete lattice $L = (L, \sqsubseteq)$ that is closed under greatest lower bounds: $\forall Y' \subseteq Y : \bigsqcap Y' \in Y$.*

It follows that a Moore family always contains a least element, $\bigsqcap Y$, and a greatest element, $\bigsqcap \emptyset$, which equals the greatest element, $\top$, from L; in particular, a Moore family is never empty. The property is also called the model intersection property, since whenever we take a *meet* of a number of models we still get a model.

Let $\Delta = \{\rho \mid \rho : \prod_k \mathcal{R}_{/k} \to \mathcal{P}(\mathcal{U}^k)\}$ denote the set of interpretations ρ of predicate symbols in $\mathcal{R}$ over $\mathcal{U}$. We define a lexicographical ordering $\sqsubseteq$ defined by $\rho_1 \sqsubseteq \rho_2$ if and only if there is some $0 \leq j \leq s$, where s is the order of the formula (number of layers), such that the following properties hold:

(a) $\rho_1(R) = \rho_2(R)$ for all $R \in \mathcal{R}$ with $rank(R) < j$,

(b) $\rho_1(R) \subseteq \rho_2(R)$ for all $R \in \mathcal{R}$ with $rank(R) = j$ and either $j = 0$ or R is a *defined* relation,

(c) $\rho_1(R) \supseteq \rho_2(R)$ for all $R \in \mathcal{R}$ with $rank(R) = j$ and R is a *constrained* relation,

(d) either $j = s$ or $\rho_1(R) \neq \rho_2(R)$ for some relation $R \in \mathcal{R}$ with $rank(R) = j$.

Observe that relations that are not asserted are assumed to be *defined*. Moreover, due to the syntax of LFP for a given j, (b) and (c) cannot apply at the same time. In the case $s = 1$ the

(ρ,ς)	$\models$	$R(\vec{x})$	iff	$[\![\vec{x}]\!]([\,],\varsigma) \in \rho(R)$
(ρ,ς)	$\models$	$\neg R(\vec{x})$	iff	$[\![\vec{x}]\!]([\,],\varsigma) \notin \rho(R)$
(ρ,ς)	$\models$	$cond_1 \wedge cond_2$	iff	$(\rho,\varsigma) \models cond_1$ and $(\rho,\varsigma) \models cond_2$
(ρ,ς)	$\models$	$cond_1 \vee cond_2$	iff	$(\rho,\varsigma) \models cond_1$ or $(\rho,\varsigma) \models cond_2$
(ρ,ς)	$\models$	$\exists x : cond$	iff	$(\rho,\varsigma[x \mapsto a]) \models cond$ for some $a \in \mathcal{U}$
(ρ,ς)	$\models$	$\forall x : cond$	iff	$(\rho,\varsigma[x \mapsto a]) \models cond$ for all $a \in \mathcal{U}$
(ρ,ς)	$\models$	$true$	iff	true
(ρ,ς)	$\models$	$false$	iff	false
(ρ,ζ,ς)	$\models$	$R(\vec{u})$	iff	$[\![\vec{u}]\!](\zeta,\varsigma) \in \rho(R)$
(ρ,ζ,ς)	$\models$	$def_1 \wedge def_2$	iff	$(\rho,\zeta,\varsigma) \models def_1$ and $(\rho,\zeta,\varsigma) \models def_2$
(ρ,ζ,ς)	$\models$	$cond \Rightarrow R(\vec{u})$	iff	$(\rho,\zeta,\varsigma) \models R(\vec{u})$ whenever $(\rho,\varsigma) \models cond$
(ρ,ζ,ς)	$\models$	$\forall x : def$	iff	$(\rho,\zeta,\varsigma[x \mapsto a]) \models def$ for all $a \in \mathcal{U}$
(ρ,ζ,ς)	$\models$	$R(\vec{u})$	iff	$[\![\vec{u}]\!](\zeta,\varsigma) \in \rho(R)$
(ρ,ζ,ς)	$\models$	$con_1 \wedge con_2$	iff	$(\rho,\zeta,\varsigma) \models con_1$ and $(\rho,\zeta,\varsigma) \models con_2$
(ρ,ζ,ς)	$\models$	$R(\vec{u}) \Rightarrow cond$	iff	$(\rho,\varsigma) \models cond$ whenever $(\rho,\zeta,\varsigma) \models R(\vec{u})$
(ρ,ζ,ς)	$\models$	$\forall x : con$	iff	$(\rho,\zeta,\varsigma[x \mapsto a]) \models con$ for all $a \in \mathcal{U}$
(ρ,ζ,ς)	$\models$	$cl_1,\dots,cl_s$	iff	$(\rho,\zeta,\varsigma) \models cl_i$ for all $1 \le i \le s$

Table 1. Semantics of LFP.

ordering $\sqsubseteq$ coincides with the ordering $\subseteq$ for *defined* relations and with the ordering $\supseteq$ for the *constrained* relations. The use of the dual orderings for *defined* and *constrained* relations stems from the fact that we are interested in the smallest solution for the *defined* relations and the greatest solution for the *constrained* ones. Intuitively, the lexicographical ordering $\sqsubseteq$ orders the relations layer by layer starting with the layer 0. It is essentially analogous to the lexicographical ordering on strings, which is based on the alphabetical order of their characters.

LEMMA 1. *$\sqsubseteq$ defines a partial order.*

PROOF 1. *For proof refer to [14].*

LEMMA 2. *$(\Delta,\sqsubseteq)$ is a complete lattice with the greatest lower bound given by*

$$(\sqcap M)(R) = \begin{cases} \bigcap\{\rho(R) \mid \rho \in M_j\} & \text{if } rank(R) = j \text{ and either } j = 0 \text{ or } R \text{ is defined in } cl_j. \\ \bigcup\{\rho(R) \mid \rho \in M_j\} & \text{if } rank(R) = j \text{ and } R \text{ is constrained in } cl_j. \end{cases}$$

where

$$M_j = \{\rho \in M \mid \forall R' : rank(R') < j \Rightarrow (\sqcap M)(R') = \rho(R')\}$$

PROOF 2. *For proof refer to [14].*

Note that $\sqcap M$ is well defined by induction on j observing that $M_0 = M$ and $M_j \subseteq M_{j-1}$.

PROPOSITION 1. *Assume cls is a stratified LFP formula, ς_0 and ζ_0 are interpretations of the free variables and function symbols in cls, respectively. Furthermore, ρ_0 is an interpretation of all relations of rank 0. Then $\{\rho \mid (\rho,\zeta_0,\varsigma_0) \models cls \wedge \forall R : rank(R) = 0 \Rightarrow \rho(R) \supseteq \rho_0(R)\}$ is a Moore family.*

PROOF 3. *For proof refer to [14].*

The result ensures that the approach falls within the framework of Abstract Interpretation [9, 10]; hence we can be sure that there always is a single best solution for the analysis problem under consideration, namely the one defined in Proposition 1.

Complexity The least model for LFP formulae guaranteed by Proposition 1 can be computed efficiently as summarized in the following result.

PROPOSITION 2. *For a finite universe $\mathcal{U}$, the best solution ρ such that $\rho_0 \sqsubseteq \rho$ of a LFP formula $cl_1,\dots,cl_s$ (w.r.t. an interpretation of the constant symbols) can be computed in time*

$$O(|\rho_0| + \sum_{1 \le i \le s} |cl_i||\mathcal{U}|^{k_i})$$

where k_i is the maximal nesting depth of quantifiers in the cl_i and $|\rho_0|$ is the sum of cardinalities of predicates $\rho_0(R)$ of rank 0. We also assume unit time hash table operations (as in [26]).

PROOF 4. *For proof refer to [14].*

For *define* clauses a straightforward method that achieves the above complexity proceeds by instantiating all variables occurring in the input formula in all possible ways. The resulting formula has no free variables thus it can be solved by classical solvers for alternation-free Boolean equation systems [13] in linear time.

In case of *constrain* clauses we first dualize the problem by transforming the co-inductive specification into the inductive one. The transformation increases the size of the input formula by a constant factor. Thereafter, we proceed in the same way as for the define clauses.

In addition we need to take into account the number of known facts, which equals to the cardinality of all predicates of rank 0. As a result we get the complexity from Proposition 2.

4. Application to Data Flow Analysis

Datalog has already been used for program analysis in compilers [33, 35, 38]. In this section we present how the LFP logic can be used to specify analyses that are instances of Bit-Vector Frameworks, which are a special case of the Monotone Frameworks [18, 28].

A Monotone Framework consists of (a) a property space that usually is a complete lattice L satisfying the Ascending Chain Condition, and (b) transfer functions, i.e. monotone functions from L to L. The property space is used to represent the data flow information, whereas transfer functions capture the behavior of actions. In the Bit-Vector Framework, the property space is a power set of some finite set and all transfer functions are of the form $f_n(x) = (x \setminus kill_n) \cup gen_n$.

Throughout the section we assume that a program is represented as a control flow graph [19, 28], which is a directed graph with one entry node (having no incoming edges) and one exit node (having no outgoing edges), called extremal nodes. The remaining nodes represent statements and have transfer functions associated with them.

Backward may analyses Let us first consider backward may analyses expressed as an instance of the Monotone Frameworks. In the analyses, we require the least sets that solve the equations and we are able to detect properties satisfied by at least one path leading to the given node. The analyses use the reversed edges in the flow graph; hence the data flow information is propagated *against* the flow of the program starting at the exit node. The data flow equations are defined as follows

$$A(n) = \begin{cases} \iota & \text{if } n = n_{exit} \\ \bigcup\{f_n(A(n')) \mid (n,n') \in E\} & \text{otherwise} \end{cases}$$

where $A(n)$ represents data flow information at the entry to the node n, E is a set of edges in the control flow graph, and ι is the initial analysis information. The first case in the above equation, initializes the exit node with the initial analysis information, whereas the second one joins the data flow information from different paths (using the reversed flow). We use $\bigcup$ since we want be able detect properties satisfied by at least one path leading to the given node.

The LFP specification for backward may analyses consists of two conjuncts corresponding to two cases in the data flow equations. Since in case of may analyses we aim at computing the least solution, the specification is defined in terms of a *define* clause. The formula is obtained as

$$define \left(\begin{array}{c} \forall x : \iota(x) \Rightarrow A(n_{exit},x) \land \\ \bigwedge_{(s,t)\in E} \begin{array}{l} \forall x : (A(t,x) \land \neg kill_s(x)) \lor gen_s(x) \\ \qquad \Rightarrow A(s,x) \end{array} \end{array} \right)$$

The first conjunct initializes the exit node with initial analysis information, denoted by the predicate ι. The second one propagates data flow information agains the edges in the control flow graph, i.e. whenever we have an edge (s,t) in the control flow graph, we propagate data flow information from t to s, by applying the corresponding transfer function.

Notice that there is no explicit formula for joining analysis information from different paths, as it is the case in the data flow equations, but rather it is done implicitly. Suppose there are two distinct edges (s,p) and (s,q) in the flow graph, then we get

$$\forall x : \underbrace{(A(p,x) \land \neg kill_s(x)) \lor gen_s(x)}_{cond_p(x)} \Rightarrow A(s,x)$$
$$\forall x : \underbrace{(A(q,x) \land \neg kill_s(x)) \lor gen_s(x)}_{cond_q(x)} \Rightarrow A(s,x)$$

which is equivalent to

$$\forall x : cond_p(x) \lor cond_q(x) \Rightarrow A(s,x)$$

Forward must analyses Let us now consider the general pattern for defining forward must analyses. Here we require the largest sets that solve the equations and we are able to detect properties satisfied by all paths leading to a given node. The analyses propagate the data flow information along the edges of the flow graph starting at the entry node. The data flow equations are defined as follows

$$A(n) = \begin{cases} \iota & \text{if } n = n_{entry} \\ \bigcap\{f_n(A(n')) \mid (n',n) \in E\} & \text{otherwise} \end{cases}$$

where $A(n)$ represents analysis information at the exit from the node n. Since we require the greatest solution, the greatest lower bound $\bigcap$ is used to combine information from different paths.

The corresponding LFP specification is obtained as follows

$$constrain \left(\begin{array}{c} \forall x : A(n_{entry},x) \Rightarrow \iota(x) \land \\ \bigwedge_{(s,t)\in E} \begin{array}{l} \forall x : A(t,x) \Rightarrow \\ \qquad (A(s,x) \land \neg kill_t(x)) \lor gen_t(x) \end{array} \end{array} \right)$$

Since we aim at computing the greatest solution, the analysis is given by means of *constrain* clause. The first conjunct initializes the entry node with the initial analysis information, whereas the second one propagates the information along the edges in the control flow graph, i.e. whenever we have an edge (s,t) in the control flow graph, we propagate data flow information from s to t, by applying the corresponding transfer function.

The specifications of forward may and backward must analyses follow similar pattern. In case of forward may analyses the data flow information is propagated along the edges of the flow graph and since we aim at computing the least solution, the analyses are given by means of *define* clauses. Backward must analyses, on the other hand, use reversed edges in the flow graph and are specified using *constrain* clauses.

In order to compute the least solution of the data flow equations, one can use a general iterative algorithm for Monotone Frameworks. The worst case complexity of the algorithm is $O(|E|h)$, where $|E|$ is the number of edges in the control flow graph, and h is the height of the underlying lattice [28]. For Bit-Vector Frameworks the lattice is a powerset of a finite set U; hence h is $O(|U|)$. This gives the complexity $O(|E||U|)$.

According to Proposition 2 the worst case time complexity of the LFP specification is $O(|\rho_0| + \Sigma_{1\leq i\leq|E|}|U||cl_i|)$. Since the size of the clause cl_i is constant and the sum of cardinalities of predicates of rank 0 is $O(|N|)$, where N is the number of nodes in the control flow graph, we get $O(|N| + |E||U|)$. Provided that $|E| > |N|$ we achieve $O(|E||U|)$ i.e. the same worst case complexity as the standard iterative algorithm.

At this point it is worth mentioning that the Bit-Vector Frameworks can also be expressed using other logics such as Datalog or ALFP. Here we show an alternative specification by means of ALFP. The specification of forward may analyses could be given by

$$\forall x : \iota(x) \Rightarrow A(n_{entry},x) \land$$
$$\bigwedge_{(s,t)\in E} \forall x : (A(s,x) \land \neg kill_t(x)) \lor gen_t(x) \Rightarrow A(t,x)$$

Hence, it is exactly as the corresponding LFP specification except that there is no explicit *define* keyword. It is implicit, since in the case of ALFP we always compute the least solution. In the case of the backward must analyses the corresponding ALFP specification is more complicated since there is no direct support for the greatest fixpoints in the logic. To remedy that problem we need to dualize the specification, hence we give a specification that defines the complement of the relation of interest i.e. $A^{\complement}$. The idea is based on the following condition: $A^{\complement}(n,x)$ holds if and only if $\neg A(n,x)$ holds. The complement relation $A^{\complement}$ is defined as follows

$$\forall x : \neg\iota(x) \Rightarrow A^{\complement}(n_{exit},x) \land$$
$$\bigwedge_{(s,t)\in E} \forall x : (A^{\complement}(t,x) \lor kill_s(x)) \land \neg gen_s(x) \Rightarrow A^{\complement}(s,x)$$

Now we obtain the definition of the relation of interest by complementing the $A^{\complement}$ predicate for each node in the corresponding control flow graph as follows

$$\bigwedge_{n\in N} \forall x : \neg A^{\complement}(n,x) \Rightarrow A(n,x)$$

where N is a set of nodes in the control flow graph. Based on the ALFP specification, it is evident that the use of LFP has many benefits. Firstly, the LFP specifications are particularly intuitive and can easily be extracted from the classical data flow equations, which is a great convenience for the programmer writing the specification. In contrast, the ALFP formulations of must analyses require more complicated encodings. Secondly, due to direct support for the co-inductive specifications, in practice the analysis result can be computed more efficiently using LFP solver. This is because we do not need to compute the complement of the relation of interest first and then complement it, which in the case the relation $A^{\complement}$ is sparse can be very expensive.

It is common in the compiler optimization that various analyses are performed at the same time. Since LFP logic has direct support for both least fixed points and greatest fixed points, we can perform both may and must analyses at the same time by splitting the analyses into separate layers.

5. Application to Constraint Satisfaction

Arc consistency is a basic technique for solving Constraint Satisfaction Problems (CSP) and has various applications within e.g. Artificial Intelligence. Formally a CSP [25, 40] problem can be defined as follows.

DEFINITION 4. *A Constraint Satisfaction Problem* (N,D,C) *consists of a finite set of variables* $N = \{x_1,\ldots,x_n\}$*, a set of finite non-empty domains* $D = \{D_1,\ldots,D_n\}$*, where* x_i *ranges over* D_i*, and a set of constraints* $C \subseteq \{c_{ij} \mid i,j \in N\}$*, where each constraint* c_{ij} *is a binary relation between variables* x_i *and* x_j.

For simplicity we consider binary constraints only. Furthermore, we can represent a CSP problem as a directed graph in the following way.

DEFINITION 5. *A constraint graph of a CSP problem* (N,D,C) *is a directed graph* $G = (V,E)$ *where* $V = N$ *and* $E = \{(x_i,x_j) \mid c_{ij} \in C\}$.

Thus vertices of the graph correspond to the variables and an edge in the graph between nodes x_i and x_j corresponds to the constraint $c_{ij} \in C$.

The arc consistency problem is formally stated in the following definition.

DEFINITION 6. *Given a CSP* (N,D,C)*, an arc* (x_i,x_j) *of its constraint graph is arc consistent if and only if* $\forall x \in D_i$*, there exists* $y \in D_j$ *such that* $c_{ij}(x,y)$ *holds, as well as* $\forall y \in D_j$*, there exists* $x \in D_i$ *such that* $c_{ij}(x,y)$ *holds. A CSP* (N,D,C) *is arc consistent if and only if each arc in its constraint graph is arc consistent.*

The basic and widely used arc consistency algorithm is the AC-3 algorithm proposed in 1977 by Mackworth [25]. The complexity of the algorithm is $O(ed^3)$, where e is the number of constraints and d the size of the largest domain. The algorithm is used in many constraint solvers due to its simplicity and fairly good efficiency [36].

Now we show the LFP specification of the arc consistency problem. A domain of a variable x_i is represented as a unary relation D_i, and for each constraint $c_{ij} \in C$ we have a binary relation $C_{ij} \subseteq D_i \times D_j$. Then we obtain

$$constrain\left(\bigwedge_{c_{ij}\in C} \begin{array}{l} (\forall x : D_i(x) \Rightarrow \exists y : D_j(y) \wedge C_{ij}(x,y))\wedge \\ (\forall y : D_j(y) \Rightarrow \exists x : D_i(x) \wedge C_{ij}(x,y)) \end{array} \right)$$

which exactly captures the conditions from Definition 6.

According to the Proposition 2 the above specification gives rise to the worst case complexity $O(ed^2)$. The original AC-3 algorithm was optimized in [40] where it was shown that it achieves the worst case optimal time complexity of $O(ed^2)$. Hence LFP specification is as efficient as the improved version of the AC-3 algorithm.

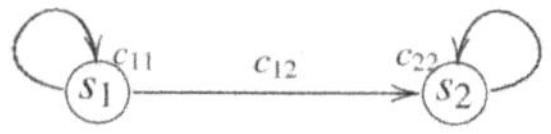

Figure 1. Arc consistency.

EXAMPLE 2. *As an example let us consider the following problem. Assume we have two processes* P_1 *and* P_2 *that need to be finished before 8 time units have elapsed. The process* P_1 *is required to run for 3 or 4 time units, the process* P_2 *is required to run for precisely 2 time units, and* P_2 *should start at the exact moment when* P_1 *finishes.*

The problem can be defined as an instance of CSP (N,D,C) *where* $N = \{s_1,s_2\}$ *denoting the starting times of the corresponding process. Since both processes need to be completed before 8 time units have elapsed we have* $D_1 = D_2 = \{0,\ldots,8\}$*. Moreover, we have the following constrains* $C = \{c_{12} = (3 \leq s_2 - s_1 \leq 4), c_{11} = (0 \leq s_1 \leq 4), c_{22} = (0 \leq s_2 \leq 6)\}$*. We can represent the above CSP problem as a constraint graph depicted in Figure 1. Furthermore it can be specified as the following LFP formulae*

$$define\left(\bigwedge_{0\leq x\leq 4} C_1(x) \wedge \bigwedge_{0\leq y\leq 6} C_2(y) \wedge \bigwedge_{3\leq z\leq 4} C_{12}(z) \right),$$
$$constrain\left(\begin{array}{l} (\forall x : D_1(x) \Rightarrow \exists y : D_2(y) \wedge C_{12}(y-x))\wedge \\ (\forall y : D_2(y) \Rightarrow \exists x : D_1(x) \wedge C_{12}(y-x)) \end{array} \right)$$

where we write $y-x$ *for a function* $f_{sub}(y,x)$.

6. Application to Model Checking

This section is concerned with the application of the LFP logic to the model checking problem [2]. In particular we show how LFP can be used to specify a prototype model checker for a special purpose modal logic of interest. Here we illustrate the approach on the familiar case of Computation Tree Logic (CTL) [8]. Throughout this section, we assume that the transition system is finite and has no terminal states.

CTL distinguishes between state formulae and path formulae. CTL state formulae over the set AP of atomic propositions are formed according to the following grammar

$$\Phi ::= true \mid a \mid \Phi_1 \wedge \Phi_2 \mid \neg\Phi \mid \mathbf{E}\varphi \mid \mathbf{A}\varphi$$

where $a \in AP$ and φ is a path formula. CTL path formulae are formed according to the following grammar

$$\varphi ::= \mathbf{X}\Phi \mid \Phi_1\mathbf{U}\Phi_2 \mid \mathbf{G}\Phi$$

where Φ, Φ_1 and Φ_2 are state formulae. The satisfaction relation $\models$ is defined for state formula by

$$\begin{array}{lll} s \models \mathbf{true} & \underline{\texttt{iff}} & true \\ s \models a & \underline{\texttt{iff}} & a \in L(s) \\ s \models \neg\Phi & \underline{\texttt{iff}} & \text{not } s \models \Phi \\ s \models \Phi_1 \wedge \Phi_2 & \underline{\texttt{iff}} & s \models \Phi_1 \text{ and } s \models \Phi_2 \\ s \models \mathbf{E}\varphi & \underline{\texttt{iff}} & \pi \models \varphi \text{ for some } \pi \in Paths(s) \\ s \models \mathbf{A}\varphi & \underline{\texttt{iff}} & \pi \models \varphi \text{ for all } \pi \in Paths(s) \end{array}$$

where $Paths(s)$ denote the set of maximal path fragments π starting in s. The satisfaction relation $\models$ for path formulae is defined by

$$\begin{array}{lll} \pi \models \mathbf{X}\Phi & \underline{\texttt{iff}} & \pi[1] \models \Phi \\ \pi \models \Phi_1\mathbf{U}\Phi_2 & \underline{\texttt{iff}} & \exists j \geq 0 : (\pi[j] \models \Phi_2 \wedge \\ & & \quad (\forall 0 \leq k < j : \pi[k] \models \Phi_1)) \\ \pi \models \mathbf{G}\Phi & \underline{\texttt{iff}} & \forall j \geq 0 : \pi[j] \models \Phi \end{array}$$

where for path $\pi = s_0 s_1 \ldots$ and an integer $i \geq 0$, $\pi[i]$ denotes the $(i+1)$th state of π, i.e. $\pi[i] = s_i$.

The CTL model checking amounts to a recursive computation of the set $Sat(\Phi)$ of all states satisfying Φ, which is sometimes referred to as *global* model checking. The algorithm boils down to a bottom-up traversal of the abstract syntax tree of the CTL formula Φ. The nodes of the abstract syntax tree correspond to the sub-formulae of Φ, and leaves are either a constant *true* or an atomic proposition $a \in AP$.

Now let us consider the LFP specification, where for each formula Φ we define a relation $Sat_\Phi \subseteq S$ characterizing states where Φ hold. The specification is defined in Table 2. The clause for *true* is straightforward and says that *true* holds in all states. The clause for an atomic proposition a expresses that a state satisfies a whenever it is in L_a, where we assume that we have a predicate $L_a \subseteq S$ for each $a \in AP$. The clause for $\Phi_1 \wedge \Phi_2$ captures that a state satisfies $\Phi_1 \wedge \Phi_2$ whenever it satisfies both Φ_1 and Φ_2. Similarly a state satisfies $\neg\Phi$ if it does not satisfy Φ. The formula for $\mathbf{EX}\Phi$ captures that a state s satisfies $\mathbf{EX}\Phi$, if there is a transition to state s' such that s' satisfies Φ. The formula for $\mathbf{AX}\Phi$ expresses that a state s satisfies $\mathbf{AX}\Phi$ if for all states s': either there is no transition from s to s', or otherwise s' satisfies Φ. The formula for $\mathbf{E}[\Phi_1\mathbf{U}\Phi_2]$ captures two possibilities. If a state satisfies Φ_2 then it also satisfies $\mathbf{E}[\Phi_1\mathbf{U}\Phi_2]$. Alternatively if the state s satisfies Φ_1 and there is a transition to a state satisfying $\mathbf{E}[\Phi_1\mathbf{U}\Phi_2]$ then s also satisfies $\mathbf{E}[\Phi_1\mathbf{U}\Phi_2]$. The formula $\mathbf{A}[\Phi_1\mathbf{U}\Phi_2]$ also captures two cases. If a state satisfies Φ_2 then it also satisfies $\mathbf{A}[\Phi_1\mathbf{U}\Phi_2]$. Alternatively state s satisfies $\mathbf{A}[\Phi_1\mathbf{U}\Phi_2]$ if it satisfies Φ_1 and for all states s' either there is no transition from s to s' or $\mathbf{A}[\Phi_1\mathbf{U}\Phi_2]$ is valid in s'. Let us now consider the formula for $\mathbf{EG}\Phi$. Since the set of states satisfying $\mathbf{EG}\Phi$ is defined as a largest set satisfying the semantics of $\mathbf{EG}\Phi$, the property is defined by means of constrain clause. The first conjunct expresses that whenever a state satisfies $\mathbf{EG}\Phi$ it also satisfies Φ. The second conjunct says that if a state satisfies $\mathbf{EG}\Phi$ then there exists a transition to a state s' such that s' satisfies $\mathbf{EG}\Phi$. Finally let us consider the formula for $\mathbf{AG}\Phi$, which is also defined in terms of constrain clause and distinguishes between two cases. In the first one whenever a state satisfies $\mathbf{AG}\Phi$, it also satisfies Φ. Alternatively, if a state s satisfies $\mathbf{AG}\Phi$ then for all states s': either there is no transition from s to s' or otherwise s' satisfies $\mathbf{AG}\Phi$.

The generation of clauses for Sat_Φ is performed in the postorder traversal over Φ; hence the clauses defining sub-formulas of Φ are defined in the lower layers. It is important to note that the specification in Table 2 is both correct and precise. It follows that an implementation of the given specification of CTL by means of the LFP solver constitutes a model checker for CTL.

We may estimate the worst case time complexity of model checking performed using LFP. Consider a CTL formula Φ of size $|\Phi|$; it is immediate that the LFP clause has size $O(|\Phi|)$, and the nesting depth is at most 2. According to Proposition 2 the worst case time complexity of the LFP specification is $O(|S| + |S|^2|\Phi|)$, where $|S|$ is the number of states in the transition system. Using a more refined reasoning than that of Proposition 2 we obtain $O(|S| + |T||\Phi|)$, where $|T|$ is the number of transitions in the transition system. It is due to the fact that the "double quantifications" over states in Table 2 really correspond to traversing all possible transitions rather than all pairs of states. Thus our LFP model checking algorithm has the same worst case complexity as classical model checking algorithms [2].

EXAMPLE 3. *As an example let us consider the Bakery mutual exclusion algorithm [22]. Although the algorithm is designed for an arbitrary number of processes, we consider the simpler setting with two processes. Let P_1 and P_2 be the two processes, and x_1 and x_2 be two shared variables both initialized to* 0. *We can represent the algorithm as an interleaving of two program graphs [2], which are directed graphs where actions label the edges rather than the nodes. The algorithm is as follows*

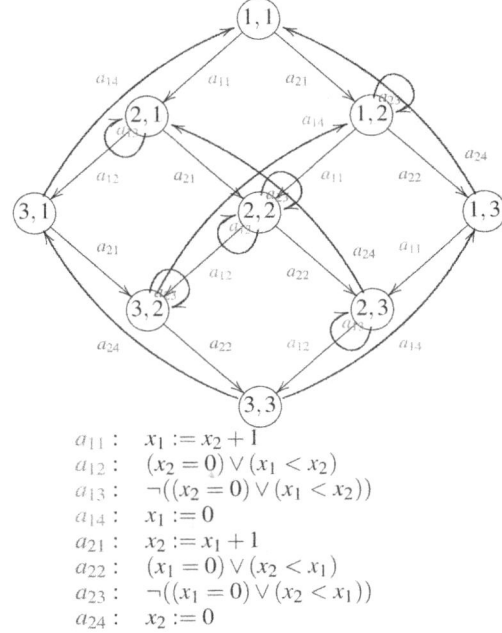

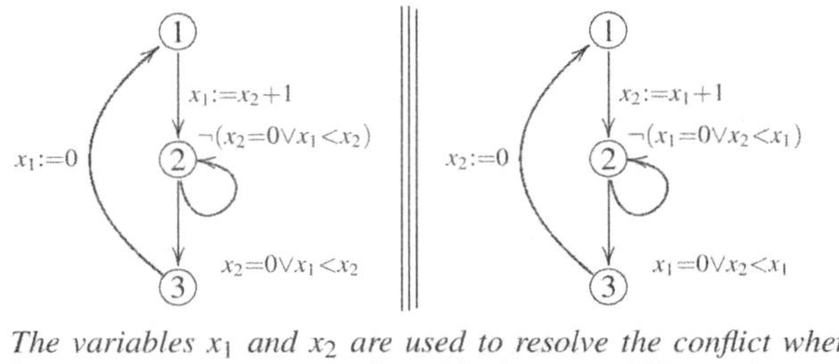

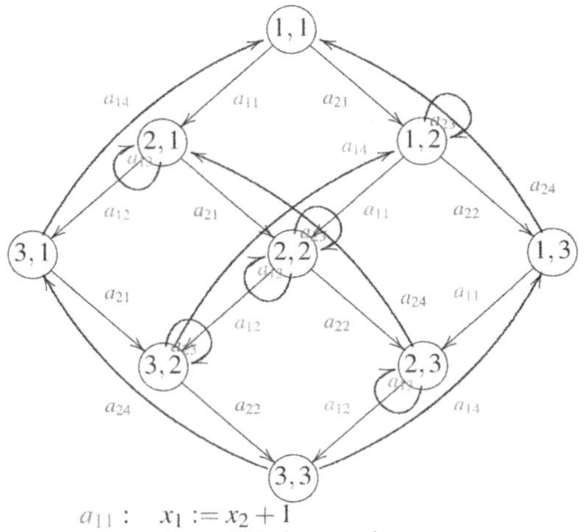

$a_{11}: \quad x_1 := x_2 + 1$
$a_{12}: \quad (x_2 = 0) \vee (x_1 < x_2)$
$a_{13}: \quad \neg((x_2 = 0) \vee (x_1 < x_2))$
$a_{14}: \quad x_1 := 0$
$a_{21}: \quad x_2 := x_1 + 1$
$a_{22}: \quad (x_1 = 0) \vee (x_2 < x_1)$
$a_{23}: \quad \neg((x_1 = 0) \vee (x_2 < x_1))$
$a_{24}: \quad x_2 := 0$

Figure 2. Interleaved program graph.

The variables x_1 and x_2 are used to resolve the conflict when both processes want to enter the critical section. When x_i is equal to zero, the process P_i is not in the critical section and does not attempt to enter it — the other one can safely proceed to the critical section. Otherwise, if both shared variables are non-zero, the process with smaller "ticket" (i.e. value of the corresponding variable) can enter the critical section. This reasoning is captured by the conditions of busy-waiting loops. When a process wants to enter the critical section, it simply takes the next "ticket" hence giving priority to the other process.

From the algorithm above, we can obtain a program graph corresponding to the interleaving of the two processes, which is depicted in Figure 2.

The CTL formulation of the mutual exclusion property is $AG\neg(crit_1 \wedge crit_2)$, which states that along all paths globally it is never the case that $crit_1$ and $crit_2$ hold at the same time.

As already mentioned, in order to specify the problem we proceed bottom up by specifying formulae for the sub problems. After a bit of simplification we obtain the following LFP clauses

$$define(\forall s : L_{crit_1}(s) \wedge L_{crit_2}(s) \Rightarrow Sat_{crit}(s)),$$
$$constrain\begin{pmatrix} (\forall s : Sat_{AG(\neg crit)}(s) \Rightarrow \neg Sat_{crit}(s)) \wedge \\ (\forall s : Sat_{AG(\neg crit)}(s) \Rightarrow \\ \quad (\forall s' : \neg T(s,s') \vee Sat_{AG(\neg crit)}(s'))) \end{pmatrix}$$

where relation L_{crit_1} (respectively L_{crit_1}) characterizes states in the interleaved program graph that correspond to process P_1 (respec-

$$define(\forall s : Sat_{true}(s))$$
$$define(\forall s : L_a(s) \Rightarrow Sat_a(s))$$
$$define(\forall s : Sat_{\Phi_1}(s) \wedge Sat_{\Phi_2}(s) \Rightarrow Sat_{\Phi_1 \wedge \Phi_2}(s))$$
$$define(\forall s : \neg Sat_{\Phi}(s) \Rightarrow Sat_{\neg\Phi}(s))$$

$$define(\forall s : (\exists s' : T(s,s') \wedge Sat_{\Phi}(s')) \Rightarrow Sat_{\mathbf{EX}\Phi}(s))$$

$$define(\forall s : (\forall s' : \neg T(s,s') \vee Sat_{\Phi}(s')) \Rightarrow Sat_{\mathbf{AX}\Phi}(s))$$

$$define\left(\begin{array}{l}(\forall s : Sat_{\Phi_2}(s) \Rightarrow Sat_{\mathbf{E}[\Phi_1 \mathbf{U} \Phi_2]}(s)) \wedge \\ (\forall s : Sat_{\Phi_1}(s) \wedge (\exists s' : T(s,s') \wedge Sat_{\mathbf{E}[\Phi_1 \mathbf{U} \Phi_2]}(s')) \Rightarrow Sat_{\mathbf{E}[\Phi_1 \mathbf{U} \Phi_2]}(s))\end{array}\right)$$

$$define\left(\begin{array}{l}(\forall s : Sat_{\Phi_2}(s) \Rightarrow Sat_{\mathbf{A}[\Phi_1 \mathbf{U} \Phi_2]}(s)) \wedge \\ (\forall s : Sat_{\Phi_1}(s) \wedge (\forall s' : \neg T(s,s') \vee Sat_{\mathbf{A}[\Phi_1 \mathbf{U} \Phi_2]}(s')) \Rightarrow Sat_{\mathbf{A}[\Phi_1 \mathbf{U} \Phi_2]}(s))\end{array}\right)$$

$$constrain\left(\begin{array}{l}(\forall s : Sat_{\mathbf{EG}\Phi}(s) \Rightarrow Sat_{\Phi}(s)) \wedge \\ (\forall s : Sat_{\mathbf{EG}\Phi}(s) \Rightarrow (\exists s' : T(s,s') \wedge Sat_{\mathbf{EG}\Phi}(s')))\end{array}\right)$$

$$constrain\left(\begin{array}{l}(\forall s : Sat_{\mathbf{AG}\Phi}(s) \Rightarrow Sat_{\Phi}(s)) \wedge \\ (\forall s : Sat_{\mathbf{AG}\Phi}(s) \Rightarrow (\forall s' : \neg T(s,s') \vee Sat_{\mathbf{AG}\Phi}(s')))\end{array}\right)$$

Table 2. LFP specification of satisfaction sets.

tively P_2) being in the critical section. Furthermore, the AG modality is defined by means of a constrain clause. The first conjunct expresses that whenever a state satisfies a mutual exclusion property $AG(\neg crit)$ it does not satisfy crit. The second one states that if a state satisfies a mutual exclusion property then all successors do as well, i.e. for an arbitrary state, it is either not a successor or else satisfies the mutual exclusion property.

7. The Algorithm

In this section we present a state-of-the-art solver for LFP, which is implemented in continuation passing style using Haskell. The solver computes the least model guaranteed by Proposition 1 and has a worst case time complexity as given by Proposition 2. In our experience, for many clauses it exhibits a running time substantially lower than the theoretical worst case time complexity. The algorithm is based on BDD representation of relations and it extends the BDD based algorithm for ALFP, presented in [15].

The algorithm operate with (intermediate) representations of the two interpretations ς and ρ of the semantics presented in Table 1; we call them `env` and `result`, respectively. In the algorithm `result` is an imperative data structure that is updated as we progress. The data structure `env` is supplied as a parameter to the functions of the algorithms. Both data structures are represented as reduced ordered binary decision diagrams (ROBDD's). Consequently the algorithm operates on entire relations, rather than on individual tuples. Furthermore, the cost of the BDD operations depends on the size of the BDD and not the number of tuples in the relation; hence dense relations can be computed efficiently as long as their encoded representations are compact.

Each BDD is defined over a finite sequence of distinct domain names. The main operations on BDD's, to be used in the following, are given by means of operations on the relations they represent. Given two relations with the same domain names, the operations *union*, $\cup$, and *non-equality testing*, $\neq$, are defined as a corresponding operations on the set of their tuples. The *projection* operation, π, selects the subset of domains from the relation and removes all other domains. The *select* operation, σ_b, selects all tuples from the relation for which the given condition b holds. The *complement* operation, $\complement$, on the relation R returns a new relation containing tuples that are not in R. Given two relations with pairwise disjoint domain names, the *product* operation, $\times$, is defined as a Cartesian product of their tuples. The operation $\forall_{d_i}$ is the universal quantification of variables in domain d_i. It removes tuples from the relation by universal quantification over domain d_i.

In order to keep track of the domain names of the BDD's the environments and predicates are annotated with subscript $[d_1, \cdots, d_k]$ denoting a list of pairwise disjoint domain names. In the case of environments $\texttt{env}_{[x_1,\cdots,x_n]}$ the domain names represent the variables currently in the scope.

Since ρ is not completely determined from the beginning it may happen that a query $R(v_1, \cdots, v_k)$ inside a condition *cond* fails to be satisfied at the given point in time, but may hold in the future when the interpretation of R is updated. If we are not careful we will then lose the consequences that the change of the interpretation of R will have on the contents of other predicates. This gives rise to introducing yet another global data structure `infl` that records computations that have to be resumed for the new tuples; these future computations will be called consumers. In the algorithm the `infl` data structure is implemented as a mapping from predicate names to functions (consumers) that are used to resume computations when the interpretation of the given predicate is updated. The `infl` data structure has two main operations REGISTER and RESUME for adding new consumers and invoking registered computations, respectively.

We have one function for each of the syntactic categories. The function SOLVE takes a clause sequence as input and calls the function EXECUTE on each of the individual clauses. It takes the form

$$\text{SOLVE}(cl_1, \cdots, cl_s) \quad = \quad \text{EXECUTE}(cl_1); \cdots; \text{EXECUTE}(cl_s);$$

The function does not make use of an explicit stack (or worklist) to keep track of clauses that need to be executed. Instead, the algorithm makes use of data structure `infl`, introduced above, to organize the computations.

The function EXECUTE takes a clause *cl* as a parameter and calls the appropriate function depending whether a given clause is a define or a constrain clause. The pseudo code is as follows

$$\begin{aligned}\text{EXECUTE}(\mathit{define}(cl)) &= \text{EXECUTE}_{\text{DEF}}(cl)[\,]\\ \text{EXECUTE}(\mathit{constrain}(cl)) &= \text{EXECUTE}_{\text{CON}}(cl)[\,]\end{aligned}$$

where we write [ ] for the empty environment reflecting that we have no free variables in the clause sequences.

The function $\text{EXECUTE}_{\text{DEF}}$ takes a define clause *def* as a parameter and a representation env of the interpretation of the variables. We have one case for each of the forms of *def*. Let us consider the case of the assertion first. The function is defined as follows

$$\begin{aligned}&\text{EXECUTE}_{\text{DEF}}\ R_{[d_1,\dots,d_k]}(v_1,\dots,v_k)\ \texttt{env}_{[x_1,\dots,x_n]} =\\ &\quad \textbf{for}\ i=1\ to\ k\ \textbf{do}\\ &\qquad \texttt{env}_{[x_1,\dots,x_n,d_1,\dots,d_i]}\\ &\qquad\qquad \leftarrow \sigma_{v_i=d_i}(\texttt{env}_{[x_1,\dots,x_n,d_1,\dots,d_{i-1}]}\times U_{[d_i]})\\ &\quad oldR_{[d_1,\dots,d_k]} \leftarrow \texttt{result}[R]\\ &\quad \texttt{result}[R] \leftarrow oldR_{[d_1,\dots,d_k]}\\ &\qquad\qquad \cup\pi_{[d_1,\dots,d_k]}(\texttt{env}_{[x_1,\dots,x_n,d_1,\dots,d_k]})\\ &\quad \textbf{if}\ oldR_{[d_1,\dots,d_k]} \neq \texttt{result}[R]\ \textbf{then}\\ &\qquad \texttt{infl}.\text{RESUME}\ R\end{aligned}$$

In the for loop the function incrementally builds a product of the current environment and a relation representing the universe, and simultaneously selects the tuples compatible with the arguments $(v_1,\cdots,v_k)$. Then, the resulting relation is projected to the domain names of R, and the content of R is updated with the newly derived tuples. Additionally, if the interpretation of predicate R has changed, we invoke the consumers registered for predicate R in the data structure `infl` by calling the RESUME function.

The case of conjunction is straightforward as we have to inspect both clauses in the same environment $\mathbf{env}_{[x_1,\dots,x_n]}$. The pseudo code is as follows

$$\begin{aligned}&\text{EXECUTE}_{\text{DEF}}(\mathit{def}_1\wedge\mathit{def}_2)\mathbf{env}_{[x_1,\dots,x_n]} =\\ &\quad \text{EXECUTE}_{\text{DEF}}(\mathit{def}_1)\mathbf{env}_{[x_1,\dots,x_n]}\\ &\quad \text{EXECUTE}_{\text{DEF}}(\mathit{def}_2)\mathbf{env}_{[x_1,\dots,x_n]}\end{aligned}$$

In the case of implication we make use of the function CHECK that in addition to the condition and the environment also takes the continuation $\text{EXECUTE}_{\text{DEF}}(\mathit{def})$ as an argument. The function is defined as

$$\begin{aligned}&\text{EXECUTE}_{\text{DEF}}(cond\Rightarrow R_{[d_1,\dots,d_k]}(v_1,\dots,v_k))\mathbf{env}_{[x_1,\dots,x_n]} =\\ &\quad \text{CHECK}(cond,\\ &\qquad\quad \text{EXECUTE}_{\text{DEF}}(R_{[d_1,\dots,d_k]}(v_1,\dots,v_k)))\mathbf{env}_{[x_1,\dots,x_n]}\end{aligned}$$

The case of universal quantification is of the following form

$$\begin{aligned}&\text{EXECUTE}_{\text{DEF}}(\forall x:\mathit{def})\ \texttt{env}_{[x_1,\dots,x_n]} =\\ &\quad \text{EXECUTE}_{\text{DEF}}\ \mathit{def}\ (\texttt{env}_{[x_1,\dots,x_n]}\times U_{[x]})\end{aligned}$$

The function simply extends the current environment with a domain for the quantified variable, and then executes the define clause *def*.

Now let us focus on the function $\text{EXECUTE}_{\text{CON}}$, which takes a constrain clause *con* and an environment ENV as parameters. The function is similar to the $\text{EXECUTE}_{\text{DEF}}$ function and we have one case for each of the forms of *con*. Let us first consider the case of the assertion, which is the most interesting. The function is defined as follows

$$\begin{aligned}&\text{EXECUTE}_{\text{CON}}\ R_{[d_1,\dots,d_k]}(v_1,\dots,v_k)\ \texttt{env}_{[x_1,\dots,x_n]} =\\ &\quad \texttt{env}'_{[x_1,\dots,x_n]} \leftarrow \complement\texttt{env}_{[x_1,\dots,x_n]}\\ &\quad \textbf{for}\ i=1\ to\ k\ \textbf{do}\\ &\qquad \texttt{env}'_{[x_1,\dots,x_n,d_1,\dots,d_i]}\\ &\qquad\qquad \leftarrow \sigma_{v_i=d_i}(\texttt{env}'_{[x_1,\dots,x_n,d_1,\dots,d_{i-1}]}\times U_{[d_i]})\\ &\quad oldR_{[d_1,\dots,d_k]} \leftarrow \texttt{result}[R]\\ &\quad \texttt{result}[R] \leftarrow oldR_{[d_1,\dots,d_k]}\\ &\qquad\qquad \cap\complement(\pi_{[d_1,\dots,d_k]}(\texttt{env}'_{[x_1,\dots,x_n,d_1,\dots,d_k]}))\\ &\quad \textbf{if}\ oldR_{[d_1,\dots,d_k]} \neq \texttt{result}[R]\ \textbf{then}\\ &\qquad \texttt{infl}.\text{RESUME}\ R\end{aligned}$$

The function begins with complementing the current environment and assigning the result to variable $\texttt{env}'_{[x_1,\dots,x_n]}$. In the for loop the function incrementally builds a product of the complemented environment and a relation representing the universe, and simultaneously selects the tuples compatible with the arguments $(v_1,\cdots,v_k)$. Since we aim at computing the greatest set of tuples for relation R, we assign the content of R with an intersection of the current interpretation of R and the complement of the relation denoted by $\texttt{env}'_{[x_1,\dots,x_n,d_1,\dots,d_i]}$ projected to the domain names of R. Additionally, if the interpretation of predicate R has changed, the invoke the consumers registered for predicate R in the data structure `infl` by calling the RESUME function.

The case of conjunction is straightforward as we again have to inspect both clauses in the same environment $\mathbf{env}_{[x_1,\dots,x_n]}$. The pseudo code is as follows

$$\begin{aligned}&\text{EXECUTE}_{\text{CON}}(con_1\wedge con_2)\mathbf{env}_{[x_1,\dots,x_n]} =\\ &\quad \text{EXECUTE}_{\text{CON}}(con_1)\mathbf{env}_{[x_1,\dots,x_n]}\\ &\quad \text{EXECUTE}_{\text{CON}}(con_2)\mathbf{env}_{[x_1,\dots,x_n]}\end{aligned}$$

In the case of implication we check the condition *cond* in the environment $\mathbf{env}_{[x_1,\dots,x_n]}$. As a continuation to the CHECK function we pass $\text{EXECUTE}_{\text{CON}}(R_{[d_1,\dots,d_k]}(v_1,\dots,v_k))$. The function is defined as

$$\begin{aligned}&\text{EXECUTE}_{\text{CON}}(R_{[d_1,\dots,d_k]}(v_1,\dots,v_k)\Rightarrow cond)\mathbf{env}_{[x_1,\dots,x_n]} =\\ &\quad \text{CHECK}(cond,\\ &\qquad\quad \text{EXECUTE}_{\text{CON}}(R_{[d_1,\dots,d_k]}(v_1,\dots,v_k)))\mathbf{env}_{[x_1,\dots,x_n]}\end{aligned}$$

The case of universal quantification is of the following form:

$$\begin{aligned}&\text{EXECUTE}_{\text{CON}}(\forall x:con)\ \texttt{env}_{[x_1,\dots,x_n]} =\\ &\quad \text{EXECUTE}_{\text{CON}}\ con\ (\texttt{env}_{[x_1,\dots,x_n]}\times U_{[x]})\end{aligned}$$

The function extends the current environment with a domain for the quantified variable, and then it executes the constrain clause *con*.

The function CHECK takes a condition, a continuation and an environment as parameters. We have one case for each of the forms of *cond*. Let us consider the case of positive query first. The pseudo code is as follows

$$\begin{aligned}&\text{CHECK}\ (R_{[d_1,\dots,d_k]}(v_1,\dots,v_k),next)\ \texttt{env}_{[x_1,\dots,x_n]} =\\ &\quad \texttt{infl}.\text{REGISTER}\ R\ \text{CONSUMER}\\ &\quad \texttt{env'}_{[x_1,\dots,x_n,d_1,\dots,d_k]} \leftarrow \texttt{env}_{[x_1,\dots,x_n]}\times\texttt{result}[R]\\ &\quad \textbf{for}\ i=1\ to\ k\ \textbf{do}\\ &\qquad \texttt{env'}_{[x_1,\dots,x_n,d_1,\dots,d_k]} \leftarrow \sigma_{v_i=d_i}(\texttt{env'}_{[x_1,\dots,x_n,d_1,\dots,d_k]})\\ &\quad \texttt{env'}_{[x_1,\dots,x_n]} \leftarrow \pi_{[x_1,\dots,x_n]}(\texttt{env'}_{[x_1,\dots,x_n,d_1,\dots,d_k]})\\ &\quad next\ \texttt{env'}_{[x_1,\dots,x_n]}\end{aligned}$$

First, the function registers a consumer for the relation R. Then, it creates an auxiliary relation, which is a product of the relations representing the current environment and the predicate R. The for loop selects tuples that are compatible with the arguments $(v_1,\cdots,v_k)$ producing a new relation that is then projected to the domain names of $\texttt{env}_{[x_1,\cdots,x_n]}$. The resulting relation is then applied to continuation *next*.

The case of negated query is similar, except that the predicate is complemented first. The algorithm for this case is of the following form:

$$\begin{aligned}&\text{CHECK}\ (\neg R_{[d_1,\dots,d_k]}(v_1,\dots,v_k),next)\ \texttt{env}_{[x_1,\dots,x_n]} =\\ &\quad \texttt{env'}_{[x_1,\dots,x_n,d_1,\dots,d_k]} \leftarrow \texttt{env}_{[x_1,\dots,x_n]}\times(\complement\ \texttt{result}[R])\\ &\quad \textbf{for}\ i=1\ to\ k\ \textbf{do}\\ &\qquad \texttt{env'}_{[x_1,\dots,x_n,d_1,\dots,d_k]} \leftarrow \sigma_{v_i=d_i}(\texttt{env'}_{[x_1,\dots,x_n,d_1,\dots,d_k]})\\ &\quad \texttt{env'}_{[x_1,\dots,x_n]} \leftarrow \pi_{[x_1,\dots,x_n]}(\texttt{env'}_{[x_1,\dots,x_n,d_1,\dots,d_k]})\\ &\quad next\ \texttt{env'}_{[x_1,\dots,x_n]}\end{aligned}$$

Notice that in the case of negative queries we do not register a consumer for the relation R. This is because the stratification condition introduced in Definition 2 ensures that the relation is fully evaluated before it is queried negatively. Thus, there is no need to register future computations since the interpretation of R will not change.

The CHECK function for disjunction of conditions is as follows:

$$\begin{aligned}&\text{CHECK}\ (cond_1 \vee cond_2, next)\ \text{env}_{[x_1,\dots,x_n]} = \\ &\quad \text{CHECK}\ (cond_1, \lambda\text{env}^1_{[x_1,\dots,x_n]}. \\ &\quad\quad \text{CHECK}\ (cond_2, \lambda\text{env}^2_{[x_1,\dots,x_n]}. \\ &\quad\quad\quad next\ (\text{env}^1_{[x_1,\dots,x_n]} \cup \text{env}^2_{[x_1,\dots,x_n]})) \\ &\quad\quad\quad\quad \text{env}_{[x_1,\dots,x_n]})\ \text{env}_{[x_1,\dots,x_n]}\end{aligned}$$

The function first checks both conditions $cond_1$ and $cond_2$ in the current environment $\text{env}_{[x_1,\cdots,x_n]}$. Then the continuation $next$ is evaluated in the union of $\text{env}^1_{[x_1,\cdots,x_n]}$ and $\text{env}^2_{[x_1,\cdots,x_n]}$, which were produced by calls to the function CHECK for conditions $cond_1$ and $cond_2$ respectively.

In the case of existential quantification in condition, the algorithm is as follows:

$$\begin{aligned}&\text{CHECK}\ ((\exists x : cond, next)\ \text{env}_{[x_1,\dots,x_n]} = \\ &\quad \text{CHECK}\ (cond, next \circ \pi_{[x_1,\dots,x_n]})\ (\text{env}_{[x_1,\dots,x_n]} \times U_{[x]})\end{aligned}$$

The function first extends the current environment with a domain for the quantified variable, in which the condition is checked. Furthermore, before calling the continuation $next$, the domain for the quantified variable is projected out.

The universal quantification is dealt in the following way:

$$\begin{aligned}&\text{CHECK}\ (\forall x : cond, next)\ \text{env}_{[x_1,\dots,x_n]} = \\ &\quad \text{CHECK}\ (cond, next \circ \forall_x)(\text{env}_{[x_1,\dots,x_n]} \times U_{[x]})\end{aligned}$$

The algorithm utilizes universal quantification of variables in a given domain, denoted by $\forall_x$, which is a standard BDD operation provided by the BDD package [24]. The operation removes tuples from the given relation by universal quantification over the given domain. In the above pseudo-code the CHECK function first extends the current environment with a quantified variable and then checks the condition in the extended environment. Thereafter it performs universal quantification on the returned environment and calls the continuation $next$.

8. Related Work

The use of logic for specifying analysis problems is far from being new. Dawson, Ramakrishnan, and Warren [11] showed how some program analyses can be cast in the form of evaluating minimal models of logic programs. Their results suggested that practical analysers can be built using general purpose logic programming systems. They also argued that logic programming is expressive enough to formulate many common analyses.

It was also demonstrated by Reps [34] that many data flow analyses may be formulated as graph reachability. Based on the correspondence between context-free languages and declarative programs that recognize them, his approach implies existence of declarative specifications of these analyses. This observation gives an opportunity for analysis tools to take advantage of techniques from deductive databases and logic programming.

There is also an immense amount of work on pointer analysis using logic programming; hence we restrict our discussion to a few representatives. Whaley et al. [21, 37, 39] developed an implementation of Datalog based on BDDs, called bddbddb. Thanks to the use of BDDs, they were able to exploit redundancy in the analysis relations in order to solve large problems efficiently.

PADDLE framework [23] is a highly flexible framework for context-sensitive analyses. It is also based on BDDs and represents the state of the art in context sensitive pointer analyses, in terms of both semantic completeness (language features support) and scalability.

Finally, DOOP [4] raised the bar for precise context sensitive analyses. It is a purely declarative points-to analysis framework and achieves remarkable performance due to a novel optimization methodology of Datalog programs. Unlike two previous frameworks, DOOP uses an explicit representation of relations and thus it enhances our understanding on how to implement efficient points-to analyses.

There is also interesting work on formalizing model checking using logic programming. Ramakrishna et al. [32] presented an implementation of a model checker called XMC using logic programming system XSB. In their system, a CCS-like language is used to describe the model of the system under consideration, whereas properties are expressed in the alternation free fragment of the modal μ-calculus. The results presented in [31] indicate that XMC, although implemented in a general purpose logic programming system, can compete with the state-of-the-art model checkers.

An alternative approach to model checking using logic programming is described by Charatonik and Podelski [7], where they demonstrated verification technique for infinite-state systems. Their approach uses set-based analysis to compute approximations of CTL formulae. Furthermore, Delzanno and Podelski [12] explored formulation of safety and liveness properties in terms of logic programs. Their approach uses constraint logic programming to encode both the transition system and the properties to be checked. Using their approach, they were able to verify well-known examples of infinite-state programs over integers.

Finally, the ALFP logic of Nielson et al. [29] is closely related to the LFP logic presented in this paper. ALFP has successfully been used as the constraint language for sophisticated analyses of many programming paradigms including imperative, functional, concurrent and mobile languages and more recently for model checking [3, 27]. However, in contrast to LFP logic introduced in this article, ALFP logic does not have direct support for greatest fixed point specifications. This leads to more complex formulations in the case of co-inductive specifications and run-time overhead during their evaluation.

9. Conclusions

In the paper we introduced the Layered Fixed Point Logic, which is a suitable formalism for specifying analysis problems. Its most prominent feature is the direct support for both inductive as well as co-inductive specifications of properties. The declarative style of the specifications makes them easy to analyse for complexity and correctness.

We established a Moore Family result that guarantees that there always is a best solution for the LFP formulae. More generally this ensures that the approach taken falls within the general Abstract Interpretation framework. Another theoretical contribution is the parametrized worst case time complexity result, which provide a simple characterization of the running time of the LFP programs.

We developed a state-of-the-art solving algorithm for LFP, which is a continuation passing style algorithm based on OBDD representations of relations. The solver achieves the best known theoretical complexity bounds, and for many clauses exhibit a running time substantially lower than the worst case time complexity.

We showed that the logic and the associated solver can be used for rapid prototyping of new analyses by presenting applications within Static Analysis, Constraint Satisfactions Problems and Model Checking. In all cases the complexity result specializes to the worst case time complexity of classical results.

As a future work we plan to implement a front-end to automatically extract analysis relations from program source code, and perform experiments on real-world programs in order to evaluate the performance of the LFP solver.

References

[1] K. R. Apt, H. A. Blair, and A. Walker. Towards a theory of declarative knowledge. In Foundations of Deductive Databases and Logic Programming., pages 89–148. Morgan Kaufmann, 1988. ISBN 0-934613-40-0.

[2] C. Baier and J.-P. Katoen. Principles of Model Checking (Representation and Mind Series). The MIT Press, 2008. ISBN 026202649X, 9780262026499.

[3] C. Bodei, M. Buchholtz, P. Degano, F. Nielson, and H. R. Nielson. Static validation of security protocols. Journal of Computer Security, 13(3):347–390, 2005.

[4] M. Bravenboer and Y. Smaragdakis. Strictly declarative specification of sophisticated points-to analyses. In S. Arora and G. T. Leavens, editors, OOPSLA, pages 243–262. ACM, 2009. ISBN 978-1-60558-766-0.

[5] R. E. Bryant. Symbolic boolean manipulation with ordered binary-decision diagrams. ACM Comput. Surv., 24(3):293–318, 1992.

[6] A. K. Chandra and D. Harel. Computable queries for relational data bases. J. Comput. Syst. Sci., 21(2):156–178, 1980.

[7] W. Charatonik and A. Podelski. Set-based analysis of reactive infinite-state systems. In B. Steffen, editor, TACAS, volume 1384 of Lecture Notes in Computer Science, pages 358–375. Springer, 1998. ISBN 3-540-64356-7.

[8] E. M. Clarke and E. A. Emerson. Design and synthesis of synchronization skeletons using branching-time temporal logic. In D. Kozen, editor, Logic of Programs, volume 131 of Lecture Notes in Computer Science, pages 52–71. Springer, 1981. ISBN 3-540-11212-X.

[9] P. Cousot and R. Cousot. Abstract interpretation: A unified lattice model for static analysis of programs by construction or approximation of fixpoints. In POPL, pages 238–252, 1977.

[10] P. Cousot and R. Cousot. Systematic design of program analysis frameworks. In POPL, pages 269–282, 1979.

[11] S. Dawson, C. R. Ramakrishnan, and D. S. Warren. Practical program analysis using general purpose logic programming systems - a case study. In C. N. Fischer, editor, PLDI, pages 117–126. ACM, 1996. ISBN 0-89791-795-2.

[12] G. Delzanno and A. Podelski. Model checking in clp. In R. Cleaveland, editor, TACAS, volume 1579 of Lecture Notes in Computer Science, pages 223–239. Springer, 1999. ISBN 3-540-65703-7.

[13] W. F. Dowling and J. H. Gallier. Linear-time algorithms for testing the satisfiability of propositional horn formulae. J. Log. Program., 1(3): 267–284, 1984.

[14] P. Filipiuk. Succinct Approach to Static Analysis and Model Checking. PhD thesis, Technical University of Denmark, 2012.

[15] P. Filipiuk, H. R. Nielson, and F. Nielson. Explicit versus symbolic algorithms for solving ALFP constraints. Electr. Notes Theor. Comput. Sci., 267(2):15–28, 2010.

[16] M. S. Hecht. Flow Analysis of Computer Programs. North Holland, 1977.

[17] E. M. C. (Jr.), O. Grumberg, and D. A. Peled. Model Checking. MIT Press, 1999.

[18] J. B. Kam and J. D. Ullman. Monotone data flow analysis frameworks. Acta Inf., 7:305–317, 1977.

[19] G. A. Kildall. A unified approach to global program optimization. In POPL, pages 194–206, 1973.

[20] D. Kozen. Results on the propositional mu-calculus. Theor. Comput. Sci., 27:333–354, 1983.

[21] M. S. Lam, J. Whaley, V. B. Livshits, M. C. Martin, D. Avots, M. Carbin, and C. Unkel. Context-sensitive program analysis as database queries. In C. Li, editor, PODS, pages 1–12. ACM, 2005. ISBN 1-59593-062-0.

[22] L. Lamport. A new solution of Dijkstra's concurrent programming problem. Commun. ACM, 17(8):453–455, 1974.

[23] O. Lhoták and L. J. Hendren. Evaluating the benefits of context-sensitive points-to analysis using a BDD-based implementation. ACM Trans. Softw. Eng. Methodol., 18(1), 2008.

[24] J. Lind-Nielsen. Buddy, a binary decision diagram package. URL `http://sourceforge.net/projects/buddy/`.

[25] A. K. Mackworth. Consistency in networks of relations. Artif. Intell., 8(1):99–118, 1977.

[26] D. A. McAllester. On the complexity analysis of static analyses. J. ACM, 49(4):512–537, 2002.

[27] F. Nielson and H. R. Nielson. Model checking *is* static analysis of modal logic. In C.-H. L. Ong, editor, FOSSACS, volume 6014 of Lecture Notes in Computer Science, pages 191–205. Springer, 2010. ISBN 978-3-642-12031-2.

[28] F. Nielson, H. R. Nielson, and C. Hankin. Principles of Program Analysis. Springer-Verlag New York, Inc., Secaucus, NJ, USA, 1999. ISBN 3540654100.

[29] F. Nielson, H. Seidl, and H. R. Nielson. A Succinct Solver for ALFP. Nord. J. Comput., 9(4):335–372, 2002.

[30] W. Pugh and C. Chambers, editors. Proceedings of the ACM SIGPLAN 2004 Conference on Programming Language Design and Implementation 2004, Washington, DC, USA, June 9-11, 2004, 2004. ACM. ISBN 1-58113-807-5.

[31] Y. S. Ramakrishna, C. R. Ramakrishnan, I. V. Ramakrishnan, S. A. Smolka, T. Swift, and D. S. Warren. Efficient model checking using tabled resolution. In O. Grumberg, editor, CAV, volume 1254 of Lecture Notes in Computer Science, pages 143–154. Springer, 1997. ISBN 3-540-63166-6.

[32] C. R. Ramakrishnan, I. V. Ramakrishnan, S. A. Smolka, Y. Dong, X. Du, A. Roychoudhury, and V. N. Venkatakrishnan. Xmc: A logic-programming-based verification toolset. In E. A. Emerson and A. P. Sistla, editors, CAV, volume 1855 of Lecture Notes in Computer Science, pages 576–580. Springer, 2000. ISBN 3-540-67770-4.

[33] T. W. Reps. Demand interprocedural program analysis using logic databases. In Workshop on Programming with Logic Databases (Book), ILPS, pages 163–196, 1993.

[34] T. W. Reps. Program analysis via graph reachability. Information & Software Technology, 40(11-12):701–726, 1998.

[35] J. D. Ullman. Bottom-Up Beats Top-Down for Datalog. In A. Silberschatz, editor, PODS, pages 140–149. ACM Press, 1989. ISBN 0-89791-308-6.

[36] R. J. Wallace. Why AC-3 is almost always better than AC4 for establishing arc consistency in csps. In IJCAI, pages 239–247, 1993.

[37] J. Whaley and M. S. Lam. Cloning-based context-sensitive pointer alias analysis using binary decision diagrams. In Pugh and Chambers [30], pages 131–144. ISBN 1-58113-807-5.

[38] J. Whaley and M. S. Lam. Cloning-based context-sensitive pointer alias analysis using binary decision diagrams. In Pugh and Chambers [30], pages 131–144. ISBN 1-58113-807-5.

[39] J. Whaley, D. Avots, M. Carbin, and M. S. Lam. Using Datalog with Binary Decision Diagrams for Program Analysis. In K. Yi, editor, APLAS, volume 3780 of Lecture Notes in Computer Science, pages 97–118. Springer, 2005. ISBN 3-540-29735-9.

[40] Y. Zhang and R. H. C. Yap. Making AC-3 an optimal algorithm. In B. Nebel, editor, IJCAI, pages 316–321. Morgan Kaufmann, 2001. ISBN 1-55860-777-3.

A Polynomial Time λ-calculus with Multithreading and Side Effects *

Antoine Madet

Univ Paris Diderot, Sorbonne Paris Cité
PPS, UMR 7126, CNRS, F-75205 Paris, France
madet@pps.univ-paris-diderot.fr

Abstract

The framework of *light logics* has been extensively studied to control the complexity of higher-order functional programs. We propose an extension of this framework to multithreaded programs with side effects, focusing on the case of polynomial time. After introducing a modal λ-calculus with parallel composition and *regions*, we prove that a realistic call-by-value evaluation strategy can be computed in polynomial time for a class of well-formed programs. The result relies on the simulation of call-by-value by a polynomial *shallow-first* strategy which preserves the evaluation order of side effects. Then, we provide a polynomial type system that guarantees that well-typed programs do not go wrong. Finally, we illustrate the expressivity of the type system by giving a programming example of concurrent iteration producing side effects over an inductive data structure.

Categories and Subject Descriptors D.3 [*Programming Languages*]: Formal Definitions and Theory; F.2 [*Analysis of Algorithms and Problem Complexity*]: General

Keywords λ-calculus, side effect, region, thread, resource analysis.

1. Introduction

Quantitative resource analysis of programs is a challenging task in computer science. Besides being essential for the development of safety-critical systems, it provides interesting viewpoints on the structure of programs.

The framework of *light logics* (see *e.g.* **LLL** [12], **ELL** [10], **SLL** [13]) which originates from Linear Logic [11], have been deeply studied to control the complexity of higher-order functional programs. In particular, polynomial time λ-calculi [5, 18] have been proposed as well as various type systems [8, 9] guaranteeing complexity bounds of functional programs. Recently, Amadio and the author proposed an extension of the framework to a higher-order functional language with multithreading and side effects [16], focusing on the case of elementary time (**ELL**).

In this paper, we consider a more reasonable complexity class: polynomial time. The functional core of the language is the *light* λ-calculus [18] that features the modalities *bang* (written '!') and *paragraph* (written '§') of **LLL**. The notion of *depth* (the number of nested modalities) which is standard in light logics is used to control the duplication of data during the execution of programs. The language is extended with side effects by means of read and write operations on *regions* which were introduced to represent areas of the store [15]. Threads can be put in parallel and interact through a shared state.

There appears to be no direct combinatorial argument to bound a call-by-value evaluation strategy by a polynomial. However, the *shallow-first* strategy (*i.e.* redexes are eliminated in a depth-increasing order) is known to be polynomial in the functional case [4, 12]. Using this result, Terui shows [18] that a class of *well-formed* light λ-terms strongly terminates in polynomial time (*i.e.* every reduction strategy is polynomial) by proving that any reduction sequence can be simulated by a *longer* one which is shallow-first. Following this method, our contribution is to show that a class of well-formed call-by-value programs with side effects and multithreading can be simulated in polynomial time by shallow-first reductions. The bound covers any scheduling policy and takes thread generation into account.

Reordering a reduction sequence into a shallow-first one is non-trivial: the evaluation order of side effects must be kept unchanged in order to preserve the semantics of the program. An additional difficulty is that reordering produces non call-by-value sequences but fails for an arbitrary larger relation (which may even require exponential time). We identify an intermediate *outer-bang* relation $\longrightarrow_{\mathsf{ob}}$ which can be simulated by shallow-first ordering and this allows us to simulate the call-by-value relation $\longrightarrow_{\mathsf{v}}$ which is contained in the outer-bang relation. We illustrate this development in Figure 1.

The paper is organized as follows. We start by presenting the language with multithreading and regions in Section 2 and define the largest reduction relation. Then, we introduce a *polynomial depth system* in Section 3 to control the depth of program occurrences. Well-formed programs in the depth system follow Terui's discipline [18] on the functional side and the *stratification of regions* by depth level that we introduced previously [16]. We prove in Section 4 that the class of outer-bang strategies (containing call-by-value) can be simulated by shallow-first reductions of exactly the same length. We review the proof of polynomial soundness of the shallow-first strategy in Section 5. We provide a *polynomial type system* in Section 6 which results from a simple decoration of the polynomial depth system with linear types. We derive the stan-

* Work partially supported by project ANR-08-BLANC-0211-01 "COMPLICE" and the Future and Emerging Technologies (FET) programme within the Seventh Framework Programme for Research of the European Commission, under FET-Open grant number: 243881 (project CerCo).

PPDP'12, September 19–21, 2012, Leuven, Belgium.

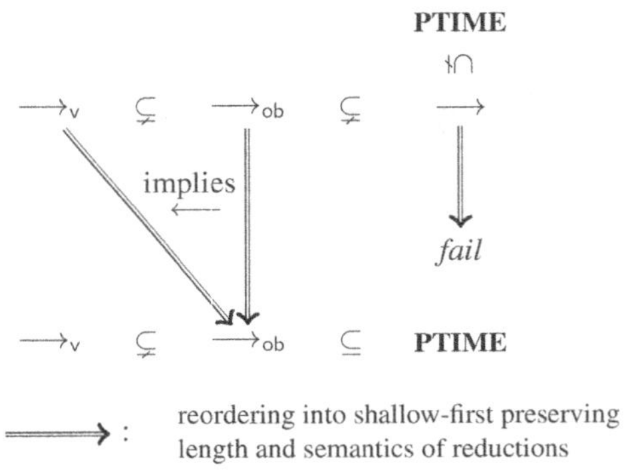

Figure 1. Simulation by shallow-first ordering

dard subject reduction proposition and progress proposition which states that well-types programs reduce to values. Finally, we illustrate the expressivity of the type system in Section 7 by showing that it is polynomially complete in the extensional sense and we give a programming example of a concurrent iteration producing side effects over an inductive data structure.

2. A modal λ-calculus with multithreading and regions

As mentioned previously, the functional core of the language is a modal λ-calculus with constructors and destructors for the modalities '!' and '§' that are used to control the duplication of data. The global store is partitioned into a finite number of regions where each region abstracts a set of memory locations. Following [1], side effects are produced by read and write operators on regions. A parallel operator allows to evaluate concurrently several terms which can communicate through regions. As we shall see in Section 7, this abstract non-deterministic language entails complexity bounds for languages with concrete memory locations representing *e.g.* references, channels or signals.

The syntax of the language is presented in Figure 2. We have

$$
\begin{array}{llll}
\text{-variables} & x, y, \ldots & & \\
\text{-regions} & r, r', \ldots & & \\
\text{-terms} & M & ::= & x \mid r \mid \star \mid \lambda x.M \mid MM \mid !M \mid \S M \\
 & & & \mathsf{let}\ !x = M \ \mathsf{in}\ M \mid \mathsf{let}\ \S x = M \ \mathsf{in}\ M \\
 & & & \mathsf{get}(r) \mid \mathsf{set}(r, M) \mid (M \parallel M) \\
\text{-stores} & S & ::= & r \Leftarrow M \mid (S \parallel S) \\
\text{-programs} & P & ::= & M \mid S \mid (P \parallel P)
\end{array}
$$

Figure 2. Syntax of the language

the usual set of variables $x, y, \ldots$ and a set of regions $r, r', \ldots$ The set of terms M contains variables, regions, the terminal value (unit) $\star$, λ-abstractions, applications, modal terms $!M$ and $\S M$ (resp. called !-terms and §-terms) and the associated let !-binders and let §-binders. We have an operator $\mathsf{get}(r)$ to read a region r, an operator $\mathsf{set}(r, M)$ to assign a term M to a region r and a parallel operator $(M \parallel N)$ to evaluate M and N in parallel. A store S is the composition of several assignments $r \Leftarrow M$ in parallel and a program P is the combination of several terms and stores in parallel. Note that stores are global, *i.e.* they always occur in empty contexts.

In the following we write $\dagger$ for $\dagger \in \{!, \S\}$ and we define $\dagger^0 M = M$ and $\dagger^{n+1} M = \dagger(\dagger^n M)$. Terms $\lambda x.M$ and let $\dagger x = N$ in M bind occurrences of x in M. The set of free variables of M is denoted by $\mathsf{FV}(M)$. The number of free occurrences of x in M is denoted by $\mathsf{FO}(x, M)$. The number of free occurrences in M is denoted by $\mathsf{FO}(M)$. $M[N/x]$ denotes the term M in which each free occurrence of x has been substituted by N.

Each program has an *abstract syntax tree* where variables, regions and unit constants are leaves, λ-abstractions and $\dagger$-terms have one child, and applications and let $\dagger$-binders have two children. An example is given in Figure 3. A path starting from the root to a

$$P = \mathsf{let}\ !x = \mathsf{get}(r) \ \mathsf{in}\ \mathsf{set}(r, (!x)(\S x)) \parallel r \Leftarrow !(\lambda x.x\star)$$

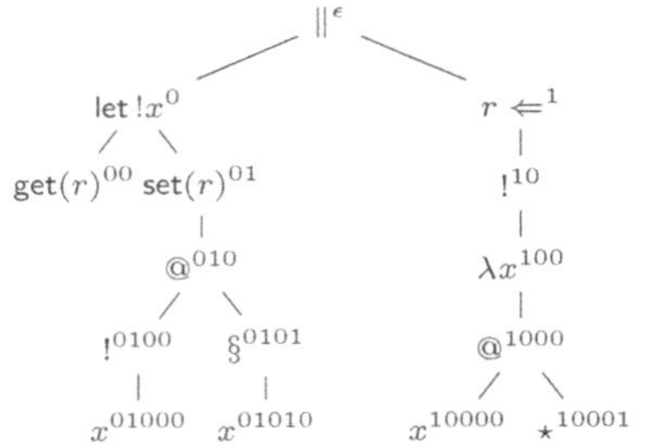

Figure 3. Syntax tree and addresses of P

node of the tree denotes an *occurrence* of the program whose address is a word $w \in \{0,1\}^*$ hereby denoted in exponent form. We write $w \sqsubseteq w'$ when w is a prefix of w'. We denote the number of occurrences in P by $|P|$.

The operational semantics of the language is given in Figure 4. In order to prove the later simulation result, the largest reduction relation $\longrightarrow$ (which shall contain call-by-value) is presented.

-structural rules-

$$
\begin{array}{rcl}
P \parallel P' & \equiv & P' \parallel P \\
(P \parallel P') \parallel P'' & \equiv & P \parallel (P' \parallel P'')
\end{array}
$$

-evaluation contexts-

$$
\begin{array}{lll}
E & ::= & [\cdot] \mid \lambda x.E \mid EM \mid ME \mid !E \mid \S E \\
 & & \mathsf{let}\ !x = E \ \mathsf{in}\ M \mid \mathsf{let}\ \S x = E \ \mathsf{in}\ M \\
 & & \mathsf{let}\ !x = M \ \mathsf{in}\ E \mid \mathsf{let}\ \S x = M \ \mathsf{in}\ E \\
 & & \mathsf{set}(r, E) \mid r \Leftarrow E \mid (E \parallel P) \mid (P \parallel E)
\end{array}
$$

-reduction rules-

$$
\begin{array}{lrcl}
(\beta) & E[(\lambda x.M)N] & \longrightarrow & E[M[N/x]] \\
(!) & E[\mathsf{let}\ !x = !N \ \mathsf{in}\ M] & \longrightarrow & E[M[N/x]] \\
(\S) & E[\mathsf{let}\ \S x = \S N \ \mathsf{in}\ M] & \longrightarrow & E[M[N/x]] \\
(\mathsf{get}) & E[\mathsf{get}(r)] \parallel r \Leftarrow M & \longrightarrow & E[M] \\
(\mathsf{set}) & E[\mathsf{set}(r, M)] & \longrightarrow & E[\star] \parallel r \Leftarrow M \text{-if } \mathsf{FV}(M) = \emptyset \\
(\mathsf{gc}) & E[\star \parallel M] & \longrightarrow & E[M]
\end{array}
$$

Figure 4. Operational semantics

Programs are considered up to a structural equivalence $\equiv$ which contains the equations for α-renaming, commutativity and associativity of parallel composition. Reduction rules apply modulo structural equivalence, in an evaluation context E which can be any program with exactly one occurrence of a special variable '$[\cdot]$', called the *hole*. We write $E[M]$ for $E[M/[\cdot]]$. Each rule is identified by its name. (β) is the usual β-reduction. $(\dagger)$ are rules for filtering modal terms. (get) is for *consuming* a term from a region. (set) is for *assigning* a closed term to a region. (gc) is for *erasing* a terminated thread.

First, note that the reduction rule (set) generates a *global* assignment, that is out of the evaluation context E. In turn, we require M

to be closed such that it does not contain variables bound in E. Second, several terms can be assigned to a single region. This cumulative semantics allows the simulation of several memory locations by a single region. In turn, reading a region consists in consuming *non-deterministically* one of the assigned terms.

The reduction is very 'liberal' with side effects. The contexts $(P \parallel E)$ and $(E \parallel P)$ embed any scheduling of threads. Moreover, contexts of the shape $r \Leftarrow E$ allow evaluation in the store as exemplified in the following possible reduction:

$$\begin{aligned}\mathsf{set}(r, \lambda x.\mathsf{get}(r)) \parallel r \Leftarrow M &\longrightarrow \star \parallel r \Leftarrow \lambda x.\mathsf{get}(r) \parallel r \Leftarrow M \\ &\longrightarrow \star \parallel r \Leftarrow \lambda x.M\end{aligned}$$

In the rules (β), $(\dagger)$, (gc), the *redex* denotes the term inside the context of the left hand-side and the *contractum* denotes the term inside the context of the right hand-side. In the rule (get), the redex is $\mathsf{get}(r)$ and the contractum is M. In the rule (set), the redex is $\mathsf{set}(r, M)$ and the contractum is M. Finally, $\longrightarrow^+$ denotes the transitive closure of $\longrightarrow$ and $\longrightarrow^*$ denotes the reflexive closure of $\longrightarrow^+$.

3. A polynomial depth system

In this section, we first review the principles of well-formed light λ-terms (Subsection 3.1) and then the stratification of regions by depth level (Subsection 3.2). Eventually we combine the two as a set of inference rules that characterizes a class of *well-formed* programs (Subsection 3.3).

3.1 On light λ-terms

First, we define the notion of depth.

Definition 1. *The* depth $d(w)$ *of an occurrence* w *in a program* P *is the number of* $\dagger$ *labels that the path leading to the end node crosses. The depth* $d(P)$ *of program* P *is the maximum depth of its occurrences.*

With reference to Figure 3, $d(01000) = d(01010) = d(100) = d(1000) = d(10000) = d(10001) = 1$, whereas other occurrences have depth 0. In particular, $d(0100) = d(0101) = d(10) = 0$; what matters in computing the depth of an occurrence is the number of $\dagger$'s that precede strictly the end node. Thus $d(P) = 1$. In the sequel, we say that a program *occurs* at depth i when it corresponds to an occurrence of depth i. For example, $\mathsf{get}(r)$ occur at depth 0 in P. We write $\xrightarrow{i}$ when the redex occurs at depth i; we write $|P|_i$ for the number of occurrences at depth i of P.

Then we can define *shallow-first* reductions.

Definition 2. *A* shallow-first reduction sequence $P_1 \xrightarrow{i_1} P_2 \xrightarrow{i_2} \dots \xrightarrow{i_n} P_n$ *is such that* $m < n$ *implies* $i_m \leq i_n$. *A* shallow-first strategy *is a strategy that produces shallow-first sequences.*

The polynomial soundness of shallow-first strategies relies on the following properties: when $P \xrightarrow{i}{}^* P'$,

$$d(P') \leq d(P) \quad (3.1)$$

$$|P'|_j \leq |P|_j \text{ for } j < i \quad (3.2)$$

$$|P'|_i < |P|_i \quad (3.3)$$

$$|P'| \leq |P|^2 \quad (3.4)$$

To see this in a simple way, assume P is a program such that $d(P) = 2$. By properties (3.1),(3.2),(3.3) we can eliminate all the redexes of P with the shallow-first sequence $P \xrightarrow{0}{}^* P' \xrightarrow{1}{}^* P'' \xrightarrow{2}{}^* P'''$. By property (3.4), $|P'''| \leq |P|^8$. By properties (3.3) the length l of the sequence is such that $l \leq |P| + |P'| + |P''| = p$. Since we can show that $p \leq |P|^8$ we conclude that the shallow-first evaluation of P can be computed in polynomial time.

The well-formedness criterions of light λ-terms are intended to ensure the above four properties. These criterions can be summarized as follows:

- λ-abstraction is affine: in $\lambda x.M$, x may occur at most once and at depth 0 in M.
- $\mathsf{let}\,!$-binders are for duplication: in $\mathsf{let}\ !x = M \ \mathsf{in}\ N$, x may occur arbitrarily many times and at depth 1 in N.
- $\mathsf{let}\,\S$-binders are affine: in $\mathsf{let}\ \S x = M \ \mathsf{in}\ N$, x may occur at most once and at depth 1 in N. The depth of x must be due to a $\S$ modality.
- a !-term may contain at most one occurrence of free variable, whereas a $\S$-term can contain many occurrences of free variables.

By the first three criterions, we observe the following. The depth of a term never increases (property (3.1)) since the reduction rules (β),(!) and $(\S)$ substitute a term for a variable occurring at the same depth. Reduction rules (β) and $(\S)$ are strictly size-decreasing since the corresponding binders are affine. A reduction (!) is strictly size-decreasing at the depth where the redex occurs but potentially size-increasing at deeper levels. Therefore properties (3.2) and (3.3) are also guaranteed. The fourth criterion is intended to ensure a quadratic size increase (property (3.4)). Indeed, take the term Z borrowed from [18] that respects the first three criterions but not the fourth:

$$\begin{gathered} Z = \lambda x.\mathsf{let}\ !x = x \ \mathsf{in}\ !(xx) \\ \underbrace{Z \dots (Z(Z}_{n \text{ times}}!y)) \longrightarrow^* !(\underbrace{yy\dots y}_{2^n \text{ times}}) \end{gathered} \quad (3.5)$$

It may trigger an exponential size explosion by repeated application of the duplicating rule (!). The following term

$$\begin{aligned} &Y = \lambda x.\mathsf{let}\ !x = x \ \mathsf{in}\ \S(xx) \\ &\underbrace{Y \dots (Y(Y}_{n \text{ times}}!y)) \\ &\longrightarrow^* \underbrace{Y \dots (Y(Y}_{n-2 \text{ times}}(\mathsf{let}\ !x = \S(yy) \ \mathsf{in}\ \S(xx)))) \not\rightarrow \end{aligned} \quad (3.6)$$

respects the four criterions but cannot be used to apply (!) exponentially.

3.2 On the stratification of regions by depth

In our previous work on elementary time [16], we analyzed the impact of side effects on the depth of occurrences and remarked that arbitrary reads and writes could increase the depth of programs. In the reduction sequence

$$\begin{aligned}(\lambda x.\mathsf{set}(r, x) \parallel \S\mathsf{get}(r))!M &\longrightarrow^* \S\mathsf{get}(r) \parallel r \Leftarrow !M \\ &\longrightarrow \S!M\end{aligned} \quad (3.7)$$

the occurrence M moves from depth 1 to depth 2 during the last reduction step, because the read occurs at depth 0 while the write occurs at depth 1.

Following this analysis, we introduced *region contexts* in order to constrain the depth at which side effects occur. A region context

$$R = r_1 : \delta_1, \dots, r_n : \delta_n$$

associates a natural number δ_i to each region r_i in a finite set of regions $\{r_1, \dots, r_n\}$ that we write $dom(R)$. We write $R(r_i)$ for δ_i. Then, the rules of the elementary depth system were designed in such a way that $\mathsf{get}(r_i)$ and $\mathsf{set}(r_i, M)$ may only occur at depth δ_i, thus rejecting (3.7).

Moreover, we remarked that since stores are global, that is they always occur at depth 0, assigning a term to a region breaks stratification whenever $\delta_i > 0$. Indeed, in the reduction

$$\S\mathsf{set}(r, M) \longrightarrow \S\star \parallel r \Leftarrow M \tag{3.8}$$

where $R(r)$ should be 1, the occurrence M moves from depth 1 to depth 0. Therefore, we revised the definition of depth as follows.

Definition 3. *Let P be a program and R a region context where $dom(R)$ contains all the regions of P. The* revised depth $d(w)$ *of an occurrence w of P is the number of $\dagger$ labels that the path leading to the end node crosses, plus $R(r)$ if the path crosses a store label $r \Leftarrow$. The revised depth $d(P)$ of a program P is the maximum revised depth of its occurrences.*

By considering this revised definition of depth, in (3.8) the occurrence M stays at depth 1. In Figure 3 we now get $d(01000) = d(01010) = 1$, $d(10) = R(r)$ and $d(100) = d(1000) = d(10000) = d(10001) = R(r) + 1$. Other occurrences have depth 0. From now on we shall say depth for the revised definition of depth.

3.3 Inference rules

Now we introduce the inference rules of the polynomial depth system. First, we define region contexts R and variable contexts Γ as follows:

$$\begin{array}{rcl} R & = & r_1 : \delta_1, \ldots, r_n : \delta_n \\ \Gamma & = & x_1 : u_1, \ldots, x_n : u_n \end{array}$$

Regions contexts are described in the previous subsection. A variable context associates each variable with a usage $u \in \{\lambda, \S, !\}$ which constrains the variable to be bound by a λ-abstraction, a let $\S$-binder or a let !-binder respectively. We write Γ_u if $dom(\Gamma)$ only contains variables with usage u. A depth judgement has the shape

$$R; \Gamma \vdash^{\delta} P$$

where δ is a natural number. It should entail the following:

- if $x : \lambda \in \Gamma$ then x occurs at depth δ in $\dagger^{\delta} P$,
- if $x : \dagger \in \Gamma$ then x occurs at depth $\delta + 1$ in $\dagger^{\delta} P$,
- if $r : \delta' \in R$ then $\mathsf{get}(r)$/$\mathsf{set}(r)$ occur at depth δ' in $\dagger^{\delta} P$.

The inference rules of the depth system are presented in Figure 5. We comment on the handling of usages. Variables are introduced with usage λ. The construction of !-terms updates the usage of variables to ! if they all previously had usage λ. The construction of $\S$-terms updates the usage of variables to $\S$ for one part and ! for the other part if they all previously had usage λ. In both constructions, contexts with other usages can be weakened. As a result, λ-abstractions bind variables occurring at depth 0, let !-binders bind variables occurring at depth 1 in !-terms or $\S$-terms, and let $\S$-binders bind variables occurring at depth 1 in $\S$-terms.

To control the duplication of data, the rules for binders have predicates which specify how many occurrences can be bound. λ-abstractions and let $\S$-binders are linear by predicate $\mathsf{FO}(x, M) = 1$ and let !-binders are at least linear by predicate $\mathsf{FO}(x, M) \geq 1$.

The depth δ of the judgement is decremented when constructing $\dagger$-terms. This allows to stratify regions by depth level by requiring that $\delta = R(r)$ in the rules for $\mathsf{get}(r)$ and $\mathsf{set}(r, M)$. A store assignment $r \Leftarrow M$ is global hence its judgement has depth 0 whereas the premise has depth $R(r)$ (this reflects the revised notion of depth).

Definition 4. *(Well-formedness) A program P is* well-formed *if a judgement $R; \Gamma \vdash^{\delta} P$ can be derived for some R, Γ and δ.*

$$\frac{x : \lambda \in \Gamma}{R; \Gamma \vdash^{\delta} x} \qquad \frac{}{R; \Gamma \vdash^{\delta} \star} \qquad \frac{}{R; \Gamma \vdash^{\delta} r}$$

$$\frac{\mathsf{FO}(x, M) = 1 \quad R; \Gamma, x : \lambda \vdash^{\delta} M}{R; \Gamma \vdash^{\delta} \lambda x.M} \qquad \frac{R; \Gamma \vdash^{\delta} M \quad R; \Gamma \vdash^{\delta} N}{R; \Gamma \vdash^{\delta} MN}$$

$$\frac{\mathsf{FO}(M) \leq 1 \quad R; \Gamma_{\lambda} \vdash^{\delta+1} M}{R; \Gamma_{!}, \Delta_{\S}, \Psi_{\lambda} \vdash^{\delta} !M} \qquad \frac{\mathsf{FO}(x, N) \geq 1 \quad R; \Gamma \vdash^{\delta} M \quad R; \Gamma, x : ! \vdash^{\delta} N}{R; \Gamma \vdash^{\delta} \mathsf{let}\ !x = M\ \mathsf{in}\ N}$$

$$\frac{R; \Gamma_{\lambda}, \Delta_{\lambda} \vdash^{\delta+1} M}{R; \Gamma_{!}, \Delta_{\S}, \Psi_{\lambda} \vdash^{\delta} \S M} \qquad \frac{\mathsf{FO}(x, N) = 1 \quad R; \Gamma \vdash^{\delta} M \quad R; \Gamma, x : \S \vdash^{\delta} N}{R; \Gamma \vdash^{\delta} \mathsf{let}\ \S x = M\ \mathsf{in}\ N}$$

$$\frac{r : \delta \in R}{R; \Gamma \vdash^{\delta} \mathsf{get}(r)} \qquad \frac{r : \delta \in R \quad R; \Gamma \vdash^{\delta} M}{R; \Gamma \vdash^{\delta} \mathsf{set}(r, M)}$$

$$\frac{r : \delta \in R \quad R; \Gamma \vdash^{\delta} M}{R; \Gamma \vdash^{0} r \Leftarrow M} \qquad \frac{i = 1, 2 \quad R; \Gamma \vdash^{\delta} P_i}{R; \Gamma \vdash^{\delta} (P_1 \parallel P_2)}$$

Figure 5. A polynomial depth system

Example 1. *The program P of Figure 3 is well-formed by composition of the two derivation trees of Figure 6. The program Z given in (3.5) is not well-formed.*

The depth system is strictly linear in the sense that it is not possible to bind 0 occurrences. We shall see in Section 4 that it allows for a major simplification of the proof of simulation. However, this impossibility to discard data is a notable restriction over light λ-terms. In a call-by-value setting, the sequential composition $M; N$ is usually encoded as the non well-formed term $(\lambda z.N)M$ where $z \notin \mathsf{FV}(N)$ is used to discard the terminal value of M. We show that side effects can be used to simulate the discarding of data even though the depth system is strictly linear. Assume that we dispose of a specific region gr collecting 'garbage' values at each depth level of a program. Then $M; N$ could be encoded as the well-formed program $(\lambda z.\mathsf{set}(gr, z) \parallel N)M$. Using a call-by-value semantics, we would observe the following reduction sequence

$$\begin{array}{l} M; N \longrightarrow^{*} V; N \longrightarrow \mathsf{set}(gr, V) \parallel N \longrightarrow \star \parallel N \parallel gr \Leftarrow V \\ \qquad \longrightarrow N \parallel gr \Leftarrow V \end{array}$$

where $\star$ has been erased by (gc) and V has been garbage collected into gr.

Finally we derive the following lemmas on the depth system in order to get the subject reduction proposition.

Lemma 1 (Weakening and Substitution)**.**

1. *If $R; \Gamma \vdash^{\delta} P$ then $R; \Gamma, \Gamma' \vdash^{\delta} P$.*
2. *If $R; \Gamma, x : \lambda \vdash^{\delta} M$ and $R; \Gamma \vdash^{\delta} N$ then $R; \Gamma \vdash^{\delta} M[N/x]$.*
3. *If $R; \Gamma, x : \S \vdash^{\delta} M$ and $R; \Gamma \vdash^{\delta} \S N$ then $R; \Gamma \vdash^{\delta} M[N/x]$.*
4. *If $R; \Gamma, x : ! \vdash^{\delta} M$ and $R; \Gamma \vdash^{\delta} !N$ then $R; \Gamma \vdash^{\delta} M[N/x]$.*

Proposition 1 (Subject reduction)**.** *If $R; \Gamma \vdash^{\delta} P$ and $P \longrightarrow P'$ then $R; \Gamma \vdash^{\delta} P'$ and $d(P) \geq d(P')$.*

$$\dfrac{\dfrac{\dfrac{}{r:0;-\vdash^0 r}}{r:0;-\vdash^0 \mathsf{get}(r)} \qquad \dfrac{\dfrac{}{r:0;x:!\vdash^0 r} \qquad \dfrac{\dfrac{\dfrac{}{r:0;x:\lambda\vdash^1 x}}{r:0;x:!\vdash^0 !x} \qquad \dfrac{\dfrac{}{r:0;x:\lambda\vdash^1 x}}{r:0;x:!\vdash^0 \S x}}{r:0;x:!\vdash^0 !x\S x}}{r:0;x:!\vdash^0 \mathsf{set}(r,!x\S x)}}{r:0;-\vdash^0 \mathsf{let}\ !x=\mathsf{get}(r)\ \mathsf{in}\ \mathsf{set}(r,!x\S x)} \qquad \dfrac{\dfrac{\dfrac{\dfrac{\dfrac{}{r:0;x:\lambda\vdash^1 x} \qquad \dfrac{}{r:0;x:\lambda\vdash^1 \star}}{r:0;x:\lambda\vdash^1 x\star}}{r:0;-\vdash^1 \lambda x.x\star}}{r:0;-\vdash^0 !(\lambda x.x\star)}}{r:0;-\vdash^0 r\Leftarrow !(\lambda x.x\star)}$$

Figure 6. Derivation trees

4. Simulation by shallow-first

In this section, we first explain why we need a class of *outer-bang* reduction strategies (Subsection 4.1). Then, we prove that shallow-first simulates any outer-bang strategy and that the result applies to call-by-value (Subsection 4.2).

4.1 Towards outer-bang strategies

Reordering a reduction sequence into a shallow-first one is an iterating process where each iteration consists in commuting two consecutive reduction steps which are applied in 'deep-first' order.

First, we show that this process requires a reduction which is strictly larger than an usual call-by-value relation. Informally, assume $\dagger V$ denotes a value. The following two reduction steps in call-by-value style

$$\mathsf{set}(r,\dagger M) \xrightarrow{1} \mathsf{set}(r,\dagger V) \xrightarrow{0} \star \parallel r \Leftarrow \dagger V$$

commute into the shallow-first sequence

$$\mathsf{set}(r,\dagger M) \xrightarrow{0} \star \parallel r \Leftarrow \dagger M \xrightarrow{1} \star \parallel r \Leftarrow \dagger V$$

which is obviously not call-by-value: first, we write a non-value $\dagger M$ to the store and second we reduce *in* the store! As another example, the following two reduction steps in call-by-value style

$$(\lambda x.\lambda y.xy)\dagger M \xrightarrow{1} (\lambda x.\lambda y.xy)\dagger V \xrightarrow{0} \lambda y.(\dagger V)y$$

commute into the shallow-first sequence

$$(\lambda x.\lambda y.xy)\dagger M \xrightarrow{0} \lambda y.(\dagger M)y \xrightarrow{i} \lambda y.(\dagger V)y$$

which is not call-by-value: we need to reduce inside a λ-abstraction and this is not compatible with the usual notion of value.

Second, we show that an arbitrary relation like $\longrightarrow$ is too large to be simulated by shallow-first sequences. For instance, consider the following reduction of a well-formed program:

$$\begin{array}{l} \mathsf{let}\ !x = !\mathsf{get}(r)\ \mathsf{in}\ \S(xx) \parallel r \Leftarrow M \\ \xrightarrow{1} \mathsf{let}\ !x = !M\ \mathsf{in}\ \S(xx) \\ \xrightarrow{0} \S(MM) \end{array} \tag{4.1}$$

This sequence is deep-first; it can be reordered into a shallow-first one as follows:

$$\begin{array}{l} \mathsf{let}\ !x = !\mathsf{get}(r)\ \mathsf{in}\ \S(xx) \parallel r \Leftarrow M \\ \xrightarrow{0} \S(\mathsf{get}(r)\mathsf{get}(r)) \parallel r \Leftarrow M \\ \xrightarrow{1} \S(M\mathsf{get}(r)) \not\rightarrow \end{array} \tag{4.2}$$

However, the sequence cannot be confluent with the previous one for we try to read the region two times by duplicating the redex $\mathsf{get}(r)$. It turns out that a non shallow-first strategy may require exponential time in the presence of side effects. Consider the well-formed λ-abstraction

$$F = \lambda x.\mathsf{let}\ \S x = x\ \mathsf{in}\ \S\mathsf{set}(r,x); !\mathsf{get}(r)$$

which transforms a $\S$-term into a !-term (think of the type $\S A \multimap !A$ that would be rejected in **LLL**). Then, building on program Z given in (3.5), take

$$Z' = \lambda x.\mathsf{let}\ !x = x\ \mathsf{in}\ F\S(xx)$$

We observe an exponential explosion of the size of the following well-formed program:

$$\begin{array}{l} \underbrace{Z'Z'\ldots Z'}_{n \text{ times}}!\star \\ \longrightarrow^* \underbrace{Z'Z'\ldots Z'}_{n-1 \text{ times}}(F\S(\star\star)) \\ \longrightarrow^* \underbrace{Z'Z'\ldots Z'}_{n-1 \text{ times}}(!(\star\star)) \parallel gr \Leftarrow \S\star \\ \longrightarrow^* !(\underbrace{\star\star\ldots\star}_{2^n \text{ times}}) \parallel \underbrace{gr \Leftarrow \S\star \parallel \ldots \parallel gr \Leftarrow \S\star}_{n \text{ times}} \end{array}$$

where gr is a region collecting the garbage produced by the sequential composition operator of F. This previous sequence is not shallow-first since the redexes $\mathsf{set}(r,M)$ and $\mathsf{get}(r)$ occurring at depth 1 are alternatively applied with other redexes occurring at depth 0. A shallow-first strategy would produce the reduction sequence

$$\underbrace{Z'Z'\ldots Z'}_{n \text{ times}}!\star \longrightarrow^* !(\star\star\underbrace{\mathsf{get}(r)\mathsf{get}(r)\ldots\mathsf{get}(r)}_{n-1 \text{ times}}) \parallel S$$

where S is the same garbage store as previously but we observe no size explosion.

Following these observations, our contribution is to identify an intermediate *outer-bang* reduction relation that can be simulated by shallow-first sequences. The keypoint is to prevent reductions inside !-terms like in sequence (4.1). For this, we define the *outer-bang* evaluation contexts F in Figure 7. They are not decomposable in a context of the shape $E[!E']$ and thus cannot be used to reduce in !-terms. In the sequel, $\longrightarrow_{\mathsf{ob}}$ denotes reduction modulo evaluation contexts F.

$$\begin{array}{lcl} F & ::= & [\cdot] \mid \lambda x.F \mid FM \mid MF \mid \S F \\ & & \mathsf{let}\ \dagger x = F\ \mathsf{in}\ M \mid \mathsf{let}\ \dagger x = M\ \mathsf{in}\ F \\ & & \mathsf{set}(r,F) \mid (F \parallel M) \mid (M \parallel F) \mid r \Leftarrow F \end{array}$$

Figure 7. Outer-bang evaluation contexts

4.2 Simulation of outer-bang strategies

After identifying a proper outer-bang relation $\longrightarrow_{\mathsf{ob}}$, the main difficulty is to preserve the evaluation order of side effects by shallow-first reordering. For example, the following two reduction steps do not commute:

$$\begin{array}{l} F_1[\mathsf{set}(r,Q)] \parallel F_2[\mathsf{get}(r)] \\ \xrightarrow{i} F_1[\star] \parallel F_2[\mathsf{get}(r)] \parallel r \Leftarrow Q \\ \xrightarrow{j} F_1[\star] \parallel F_2[Q] \end{array} \tag{4.3}$$

We claim that this is not an issue since the depth system enforces that side effects on a given region can only occur at fixed depth, hence that $i = j$. Therefore, we should never need to 'swap' a read with a write on the same region.

We can prove the following crucial lemma.

Lemma 2 (Swapping). *Let P be a well-formed program such that $P \xrightarrow{i}_{\mathsf{ob}} P_1 \xrightarrow{j}_{\mathsf{ob}} P_2$ and $i > j$. Then, there exists P' such that $P \xrightarrow{j}_{\mathsf{ob}} P' \xrightarrow{i}_{\mathsf{ob}} P_2$.*

Proof. We write M the contractum of the reduction $P \xrightarrow{i}_{\mathsf{ob}} P_1$ and N the redex of the reduction $P_1 \xrightarrow{j}_{\mathsf{ob}} P_2$. Assume they occur at addresses w_m and w_n in P_1. We distinguish three cases: (1) M and N are separated (neither $w_m \sqsubseteq w_n$ nor $w_m \sqsupseteq w_n$); (2) M contains N ($w_m \sqsubseteq w_n$); (3) N strictly contains M ($w_m \sqsupseteq w_n$ and $w_m \neq w_n$). For each of them we discuss a crucial subcase:

1. Assume M is the contractum of a (set) rule and that N is the redex of a (get) rule related to the same region. This case has been introduced in example (4.3) where M and N are separated by a parallel node. By well-formedness of P, the redexes $\mathsf{get}(r)$ and $\mathsf{set}(r, Q)$ must occur at the same depth, that is $i = j$, and we conclude that we do not need to swap the reductions.
2. If the contractum M contains the redex N, N may not exist yet in P which makes the swapping impossible. We remark that, for any well-formed program Q such that $Q \xrightarrow{d}_{\mathsf{ob}} Q'$, both the redex and the contractum occur at depth d. In particular, this is true when a contractum occurs in the store as follows:
$$Q = F[\mathsf{set}(r, T)] \xrightarrow{d}_{\mathsf{ob}} Q' = F[\star] \parallel r \Leftarrow T$$
By well-formedness of Q, there exists a region context R such that $R(r) = d$ and the redex $\mathsf{set}(r, T)$ occurs at depth d. By the revised definition of depth, the contractum T occurs at depth d in the store. As a result of this remark, M occurs at depth i and N occurs at depth j. Since $i > j$, it is clear that the contractum M cannot contain the redex N and this case is void.
3. Let N be the redex let $\S x = \S R$ in Q and let the contractum M appears in R as in the following reduction sequence
$$\begin{aligned} P &= F[\mathsf{let}\ \S x = \S R'\ \mathsf{in}\ Q] \\ &\xrightarrow{i}_{\mathsf{ob}} P_1 = F[\mathsf{let}\ \S x = \S R\ \mathsf{in}\ Q] \\ &\xrightarrow{j}_{\mathsf{ob}} P_2 = F[Q[R/x]] \end{aligned}$$
By well-formedness, x occurs exactly once in Q. This implies that applying first $P \xrightarrow{j} P'$ cannot discard the redex in R'. Hence, we can produce the following shallow-first sequence of the same length:
$$\begin{aligned} P = F[\mathsf{let}\ \S x = \S R'\ \mathsf{in}\ Q] &\xrightarrow{j}_{\mathsf{ob}} P' = F[Q[R'/x]] \\ &\xrightarrow{i}_{\mathsf{ob}} P_2 = F[Q[R/x]] \end{aligned}$$
Moreover, the reduction $P' \xrightarrow{i}_{\mathsf{ob}} P_2$ must be outer-bang for x cannot occur in a !-term in Q. □

There are two notable differences with Terui's swapping procedure. First, our procedure returns sequences of exactly the same length as the original ones while his may return longer sequences. The reason is that outer-bang contexts force redexes to be duplicated before being reduced, as in reduction (4.2), hence our swapping procedure cannot lengthen sequences more. The other difference is that his calculus is affine whereas ours is strictly linear. Therefore his procedure might shorten sequences by discarding redexes and this breaks the argument for *strong* polynomial termination. His solution is to introduce an auxiliary calculus with explicit discarding for which swapping lengthens sequences. This is at the price of introducing commutation rules which require quite a lot of extra work to obtain the simulation result. We conclude that strict linearity brings major proof simplifications while we have seen it does not cause a loss of expressivity if we use garbage collecting regions.

Using the swapping lemma, we show that any reduction sequence that uses outer-bang evaluation contexts can be simulated by a shallow-first sequence.

Proposition 2 (Simulation by shallow-first). *To any reduction sequence $P_1 \xrightarrow{*}_{\mathsf{ob}} P_n$ corresponds a shallow-first reduction sequence $P_1 \xrightarrow{*}_{\underline{\mathsf{ob}}} P_n$ of the same length.*

Proof. By simple application of the bubble sort algorithm: traverse the original sequence from P_1 to P_n, compare the depth of each consecutive reduction steps, swap them by Lemma 2 if they are in deep-first order. Repeat the traversal until no swap is needed. Note that we never need to swap two reduction steps of the same depth, which implies that we never need to reverse the order of dependent side effects. For example, in Figure 8, the sequence $P \xrightarrow{2}_{\mathsf{ob}} P' \xrightarrow{1}_{\mathsf{ob}} P'' \xrightarrow{0}_{\mathsf{ob}} P'''$ is reordered into $P \xrightarrow{0}_{\mathsf{ob}} C \xrightarrow{1}_{\mathsf{ob}} B \xrightarrow{2}_{\mathsf{ob}} P'''$ by 3 traversals. □

$$\begin{array}{ccccccc} P & \xrightarrow{2}_{\mathsf{ob}} & P' & \xrightarrow{1}_{\mathsf{ob}} & P'' & \xrightarrow{0}_{\mathsf{ob}} & P''' \\ P & \xrightarrow{1}_{\mathsf{ob}} & A & \xrightarrow{2}_{\mathsf{ob}} & P'' & \xrightarrow{0}_{\mathsf{ob}} & P''' \\ P & \xrightarrow{1}_{\mathsf{ob}} & A & \xrightarrow{0}_{\mathsf{ob}} & B & \xrightarrow{2}_{\mathsf{ob}} & P''' \\ P & \xrightarrow{0}_{\mathsf{ob}} & C & \xrightarrow{1}_{\mathsf{ob}} & B & \xrightarrow{2}_{\mathsf{ob}} & P''' \end{array}$$

Figure 8. Reordering of $P \xrightarrow{*}_{\mathsf{ob}} P'''$ in shallow-first

As an application, we show that the simulation result applies to a call-by-value operational semantics that we define in Figure 9. We

$$\begin{array}{llll} \text{-values} & V & ::= & x \mid \star \mid r \mid \lambda x.M \mid \dagger V \\ \text{-terms} & M & ::= & V \mid MM \mid \S M \mid \mathsf{let}\ \dagger x = M\ \mathsf{in}\ M \\ & & & \mathsf{get}(r) \mid \mathsf{set}(r, M) \mid (M \parallel M) \\ \text{-stores} & S & ::= & r \Leftarrow V \mid (S \parallel S) \\ \text{-programs} & P & ::= & M \mid S \mid (P \parallel P) \\ \text{-contexts} & F_{\mathsf{v}} & ::= & [\cdot] \mid F_{\mathsf{v}}M \mid VF_{\mathsf{v}} \mid \S F_{\mathsf{v}} \\ & & & \mathsf{let}\ \dagger x = F_{\mathsf{v}}\ \mathsf{in}\ M \mid \mathsf{set}(r, F_{\mathsf{v}}) \\ & & & (F_{\mathsf{v}} \parallel P) \mid (P \parallel F_{\mathsf{v}}) \end{array}$$

-reduction rules-

$$\begin{array}{lrcl} (\beta_{\mathsf{v}}) & F_{\mathsf{v}}[(\lambda x.M)V] & \longrightarrow_{\mathsf{v}} & F_{\mathsf{v}}[M[V/x]] \\ (!_{\mathsf{v}}) & F_{\mathsf{v}}[\mathsf{let}\ !x = !V\ \mathsf{in}\ M] & \longrightarrow_{\mathsf{v}} & F_{\mathsf{v}}[M[V/x]] \\ (\S_{\mathsf{v}}) & F_{\mathsf{v}}[\mathsf{let}\ \S x = \S V\ \mathsf{in}\ M] & \longrightarrow_{\mathsf{v}} & F_{\mathsf{v}}[M[V/x]] \\ (\mathsf{get}_{\mathsf{v}}) & F_{\mathsf{v}}[\mathsf{get}(r)] \parallel r \Leftarrow V & \longrightarrow_{\mathsf{v}} & F_{\mathsf{v}}[V] \\ (\mathsf{set}_{\mathsf{v}}) & F_{\mathsf{v}}[\mathsf{set}(r, V)] & \longrightarrow_{\mathsf{v}} & F_{\mathsf{v}}[\star] \parallel r \Leftarrow V \\ (\mathsf{gc}_{\mathsf{v}}) & F_{\mathsf{v}}[\star \parallel M] & \longrightarrow_{\mathsf{v}} & F_{\mathsf{v}}[M] \end{array}$$

Figure 9. CBV syntax and operational semantics

revisit the syntax of programs with a notion of value V that may be a variable, unit, a region, a λ-abstraction or a $\dagger$-value. Terms and programs are defined as previously (see Figure 2) except that $!M$ cannot be constructed unless M is a value. Store assignments are restricted to values. Evaluation contexts F_{v} are left-to-right call-by-value (obviously we do not evaluate in stores). The call-by-value reduction relation is denoted by $\longrightarrow_{\mathsf{v}}$ and is defined modulo F_{v} and $\equiv$.

From a programming viewpoint, we shall only duplicate values. This explains why we do not want to construct $!M$ if M is not a value.

Call-by-value contexts F_{v} are outer-bang contexts since F_{v} cannot be decomposed as $E[!E']$. This allows the relation $\longrightarrow_{\mathsf{ob}}$ to contain the relation $\longrightarrow_{\mathsf{v}}$. As a result, we obtain the following corollary.

Corollary 1 (Simulation of CBV). *To any reduction sequence $P_1 \longrightarrow_{\mathsf{v}}^{*} P_n$ corresponds a shallow-first reduction sequence $P_1 \longrightarrow_{\mathsf{ob}}^{*} P_n$ of the same length.*

Remark that we may obtain a non call-by-value sequence but that the semantics of the program is preserved (we compute P_n).

5. Polynomial soundness of shallow-first

In this section we prove that well-formed programs admit polynomial bounds with a shallow-first strategy. We stress that this subsection is similar to Terui's [18]; the main difficulty has been to design the polynomial depth system such that we could adopt a similar proof method.

As a first step, we define an *unfolding* transformation on programs.

Definition 5. *(Unfolding) The* unfolding *at depth i of a program P, written $\sharp^i(P)$, is defined as follows:*

$$\begin{array}{rcl} \sharp^i(x) &=& x \\ \sharp^i(r) &=& r \\ \sharp^i(\star) &=& \star \\ \sharp^i(\lambda x.M) &=& \lambda x.\sharp^i(M) \\ \sharp^i(MN) &=& \sharp^i(M)\sharp^i(N) \end{array}$$

$$\sharp^i(\dagger M) = \begin{cases} \dagger\sharp^{i-1}(M) & \text{if } i > 0 \\ \dagger M & \text{if } i = 0 \end{cases}$$

$$\sharp^i(\mathsf{let}\ \dagger x = M\ \mathsf{in}\ N) = \begin{cases} \text{if } i = 0, M = !M' \text{ and } \dagger = ! : \\ \mathsf{let}\ !x = \underbrace{MM\dots M}_{k \text{ times}}\ \mathsf{in}\ \sharp^0(N) \\ \text{where } k = \mathsf{FO}(x, \sharp^0(N)) \\ \\ \text{otherwise:} \\ \mathsf{let}\ \dagger x = \sharp^i(M)\ \mathsf{in}\ \sharp^i(N) \end{cases}$$

$$\begin{array}{rcl} \sharp^i(\mathsf{get}(r)) &=& \mathsf{get}(r) \\ \sharp^i(\mathsf{set}(r, M)) &=& \mathsf{set}(r, \sharp^i(M)) \\ \sharp^i(r \Leftarrow M) &=& r \Leftarrow \sharp^i(M) \\ \sharp^i(P_1 \parallel P_2) &=& \sharp^i(P_1) \parallel \sharp^i(P_2) \end{array}$$

This unfolding procedure is intended to duplicate statically the occurrences that will be duplicated by redexes occurring at depth i. For example, in the following reductions occurring at depth 0:

$$P = \mathsf{let}\ !x = !M\ \mathsf{in}\ (\mathsf{let}\ !y = !x\ \mathsf{in}\ \S(yy) \parallel \mathsf{let}\ !y = !x\ \mathsf{in}\ \S(yy))$$
$$\overset{0}{\longrightarrow}{}^{*}\ \S(MM) \parallel \S(MM)$$

the well-formed program P duplicates the occurrence M four times. We observe that the unfolding at depth 0 of P reflects this duplication:

$$\sharp^0(P) = \mathsf{let}\ !x = !M!M!M!M\ \mathsf{in}$$
$$(\mathsf{let}\ !y = !x!x\ \mathsf{in}\ \S(yy) \parallel \mathsf{let}\ !y = !x!x\ \mathsf{in}\ \S(yy))$$

Unfolded programs are not intended to be reduced. However, the size of an unfolded program can be used as a non increasing measure in the following way.

Lemma 3. *Let P be a well-formed program such that $P \overset{i}{\longrightarrow} P'$. Then $|\sharp^i(P')| \leq |\sharp^i(P)|$.*

Proof. First, we assume the occurrences labelled with '$\parallel$' and '$r \Leftarrow$' do not count in the size of a program and that '$\mathsf{set}(r)$' counts for two occurrences, such that the size strictly decreases by the rule (set). Then, it is clear that (!) is the only reduction rule that can make the size of a program increase, so let

$$P = F[\mathsf{let}\ !x = !N\ \mathsf{in}\ M] \overset{i}{\longrightarrow} P' = F[M[N/x]]$$

We have

$$\sharp^i(P) = F'[\mathsf{let}\ !x = \underbrace{!N!N\dots!N}_{n \text{ times}}\ \mathsf{in}\ \sharp^0(M)]$$
$$\sharp^i(P') = F'[\sharp^0(M[N/x])]$$

for some context F' and $n = \mathsf{FO}(x, \sharp^0(M))$. Therefore we are left to show

$$|\sharp^0(M[N/x])| \leq |\mathsf{let}\ !x = \underbrace{!N!N\dots!N}_{n \text{ times}}\ \mathsf{in}\ \sharp^0(M)|$$

which is clear since N must occur n times in $\sharp^0(M[N/x])$. □

We observe in the following lemma that the size of an unfolded program bounds quadratically the size of the original program.

Lemma 4. *If P is well-formed, then for any depth $i \leq d(P)$:*

1. $\mathsf{FO}(\sharp^i(P)) \leq |P|$,
2. $|\sharp^i(P)| \leq |P| \cdot (|P| - 1)$,

Proof. By induction on P and i. □

We can then bound the size of a program after reduction.

Lemma 5 (Squaring). *Let P be a well-formed program such that $P \overset{i}{\longrightarrow}{}^{*} P'$. Then:*

1. $|P'| \leq |P| \cdot (|P| - 1)$
2. *the length of the sequence is bounded by $|P|$*

Proof.

1. By Lemma 3 it is clear that $|\sharp^i(P')| \leq |\sharp^i(P)|$. Then by Lemma 4-2 we obtain $|\sharp^i(P')| \leq |P| \cdot (|P| - 1)$. Finally it is clear that $|P'| \leq |\sharp^i(P')|$ thus $|P'| \leq |P| \cdot (|P| - 1)$.
2. It suffices to remark $|P'|_i < |P|_i \leq |P|$. □

Finally we obtain the following theorem for a shallow-first strategy using any evaluation context.

Theorem 1 (Polynomial bounds). *Let P be a well-formed program such that $d(P) = d$ and $P \longrightarrow^{*} P'$ is shallow-first. Then:*

1. $|P'| \leq |P|^{2^d}$
2. *the length of the reduction sequence is bounded by $|P|^{2^d}$*

Proof. The reduction $P \longrightarrow^{*} P'$ can be decomposed as $P = P_0 \overset{0}{\longrightarrow}{}^{*} P_1 \overset{1}{\longrightarrow}{}^{*} \dots \overset{d-1}{\longrightarrow}{}^{*} P_d \overset{d}{\longrightarrow}{}^{*} P_{d+1} = P'$. To prove (1), we observe that by iterating Lemma 5-1 we obtain $|P_d| \leq |P_0|^{2^d}$. Moreover it is clear that $|P_{d+1}| \leq |P_d|$. Hence $|P'| \leq |P|^{2^d}$. To prove (2), we first prove by induction on d that $|P_0| + |P_1| + \dots + |P_d| \leq |P_0|^{2^d}$. By Lemma 5-2, it is clear that the length of the reduction $P \longrightarrow^* P'$ is bounded by $|P_0| + |P_1| + \ldots + |P_d|$, which is in turn bounded by $|P_0|^{2^d}$. □

It is worth noticing that the first bound takes the size of all the threads into account and that the second bound is valid for any thread interleaving.

Corollary 2 (Call-by-value is polynomial). *The call-by-value evaluation of a well-formed program P of size n and depth d can be computed in time $O(n^{2^d})$.*

Proof. Let $P \longrightarrow_{\mathsf{v}}^* P'$ be the call-by-value reduction sequence of the well-formed program P. By Corollary 1 we can reorder the sequence into a shallow-first sequence $P \longrightarrow_{\mathsf{ob}}^* P'$ of the same length. By Theorem 1 we know that its length is bounded by $|P|^{2^d}$ and that $|P'| \leq |P|^{2^d}$. □

6. A polynomial type system

The depth system entails termination in polynomial time but does *not* guarantee that programs 'do not go wrong'. In particular, the well-formed program in (3.6) get stuck on a non-value. In this section, we propose a solution to this problem by introducing a polynomial type system as a simple decoration of the polynomial depth system with linear types. Then, we derive a progress proposition which guarantees that well-typed programs cannot deadlock (except when trying to read an empty region).

We define the syntax of types and contexts in Figure 10. Types

-type variables	$t, t', \ldots$		
-types	α	$::=$	$\mathbf{B} \mid A$
-res. types	A	$::=$	$t \mid \mathbf{1} \mid A \multimap \alpha \mid \dagger A \mid \forall t.A \mid \mathsf{Reg}_r A$
-var. contexts	Γ	$::=$	$x_1 : (u_1, A_1), \ldots, x_n : (u_n, A_n)$
-reg. contexts	R	$::=$	$r_1 : (\delta_1, A_1), \ldots, r_n : (\delta_n, A_n)$

Figure 10. Syntax of types, effects and contexts

are denoted with $\alpha, \alpha', \ldots$. Note that we distinguish a special *behaviour* type $\mathbf{B}$ which is given to the entities of the language which are not supposed to return a result (such as a store or several terms in parallel) while types of entities that may return a result are denoted with A. Among the types A, we distinguish type variables $t, t', \ldots$, a terminal type $\mathbf{1}$, a linear functional type $A \multimap \alpha$, the type $!A$ of terms of type A that may be duplicated, the type $\S A$ of terms of type A that may have been duplicated, the type $\forall t.A$ of polymorphic terms and the type $\mathsf{Reg}_r A$ of regions r containing terms of type A. Hereby types may depend on regions.

In contexts, usages play the same role as in the depth system. Writing $x : (u, A)$ means that the variable x ranges on terms of type A and can be bound according to u. Writing $r : (\delta, A)$ means that the region r contain terms of type A and that $\mathsf{get}(r)$ and $\mathsf{set}(r, M)$ may only occur at depth δ. The typing system will additionally guarantee that whenever we use a type $\mathsf{Reg}_r A$ the region context contains a hypothesis $r : (\delta, A)$.

Because types depend on regions, we have to be careful in stating in Figure 11 when a region-context and a type are compatible ($R \downarrow \alpha$), when a region context is well-formed ($R \vdash$), when a type is well-formed in a region context ($R \vdash \alpha$) and when a context is well-formed in a region context ($R \vdash \Gamma$). A more informal way to express the condition is to say that a judgement $r_1 : (\delta_1, A_1), \ldots, r_n : (\delta_n, A_n) \vdash \alpha$ is well formed provided that: (1) all the region constants occurring in the types $A_1, \ldots, A_n, \alpha$ belong to the set $\{r_1, \ldots, r_n\}$, (2) all types of the shape $\mathsf{Reg}_{r_i} B$ with $i \in \{1, \ldots, n\}$ and occurring in the types $A_1, \ldots, A_n, \alpha$ are such that $B = A_i$.

$$\frac{}{R \downarrow t} \qquad \frac{}{R \downarrow \mathbf{1}} \qquad \frac{}{R \downarrow \mathbf{B}} \qquad \frac{R \downarrow A \quad R \downarrow \alpha}{R \downarrow (A \multimap \alpha)}$$

$$\frac{R \downarrow A}{R \downarrow \dagger A} \qquad \frac{r : (\delta, A) \in R}{R \downarrow \mathsf{Reg}_r A} \qquad \frac{R \downarrow A \quad t \notin R}{R \downarrow \forall t.A}$$

$$\frac{\forall r : (\delta, A) \in R \quad R \downarrow A}{R \vdash} \qquad \frac{R \vdash \quad R \downarrow \alpha}{R \vdash \alpha} \qquad \frac{\forall x : (\delta, A) \in \Gamma \quad R \vdash A}{R \vdash \Gamma}$$

Figure 11. Types and contexts

Example 2. *One may verify that the judgment $r : (\delta, \mathbf{1} \multimap \mathbf{1}) \vdash \mathsf{Reg}_r(\mathbf{1} \multimap \mathbf{1})$ can be derived while judgements $r : (\delta, \mathbf{1}) \vdash \mathsf{Reg}_r(\mathbf{1} \multimap \mathbf{1})$ and $r : (\delta, \mathsf{Reg}_r \mathbf{1}) \vdash \mathbf{1}$ cannot.*

We notice the following substitution property on types.

Proposition 3. *If $R \vdash \forall t.A$ and $R \vdash B$ then $R \vdash A[B/t]$.*

A typing judgement takes the form: $R; \Gamma \vdash^\delta P : \alpha$. It attributes a type α to the program P occurring at depth δ, according to region context R and variable context Γ. Figure 12 introduces the polynomial type system. We comment on some of the rules. A λ-abstraction may only take a term of result-type as argument, *i.e.* two threads in parallel are not considered an argument. The typing of $\dagger$-terms is limited to result-types for we may not duplicate several threads in parallel. There exists two rules for typing parallel programs. The one on the left indicates that a program P_2 in parallel with a store or a thread producing a terminal value should have the type of P_2 since we might be interested in its result (note that we omit the symmetric rule for the program $(P_2 \parallel P_1)$). The one on the right indicates that two programs in parallel cannot reduce to a single result.

Example 3. *The program of Figure 3 is well-typed according to the following derivable judgement:*

$$R; - \vdash^\delta \mathsf{let}\ !x = \mathsf{get}(r)\ \mathsf{in}\ \mathsf{set}(r, (!x)(\S x)) \parallel r \Leftarrow !(\lambda x.x\star) : \mathbf{1}$$

where $R = r : (\delta, \forall t.!((\mathbf{1} \multimap t) \multimap t))$. Whereas the program in (3.6) is not.

Remark 1. *We can easily see that a well-typed program is also well-formed.*

The polynomial type system enjoys the subject reduction property for the largest relation $\longrightarrow \supseteq \longrightarrow_{\mathsf{ob}} \supseteq \longrightarrow_{\mathsf{v}}$.

Lemma 6 (Substitution).

1. *If $R; \Gamma, x : (\lambda, A) \vdash^\delta M : B$ and $R; \Gamma \vdash^\delta N : A$ then $R; \Gamma \vdash^\delta M[N/x] : B$.*
2. *If $R; \Gamma, x : (\S, A) \vdash^\delta M : B$ and $R; \Gamma \vdash^\delta \S N : \S A$ then $R; \Gamma \vdash^\delta M[N/x] : B$.*
3. *If $R; \Gamma, x : (!, A) \vdash^\delta M : B$ and $R; \Gamma \vdash^\delta !N : !A$ then $R; \Gamma \vdash^\delta M[N/x] : B$.*

Proposition 4 (Subject Reduction). *If $R; \Gamma \vdash^\delta P : \alpha$ and $P \longrightarrow P'$ then $R; \Gamma \vdash^\delta P' : \alpha$.*

$$\frac{R \vdash \Gamma \quad x : (\lambda, A) \in \Gamma}{R; \Gamma \vdash^{\delta} x : A} \qquad \frac{R \vdash \Gamma}{R; \Gamma \vdash^{\delta} \star : \mathbf{1}} \qquad \frac{R \vdash \Gamma}{R; \Gamma \vdash^{\delta} r : \mathsf{Reg}_r A} \qquad \frac{\mathsf{FO}(x, M) = 1 \quad R; \Gamma, x : (\lambda, A) \vdash^{\delta} M : \alpha}{R : \Gamma \vdash^{\delta} \lambda x.M : A \multimap \alpha}$$

$$\frac{R; \Gamma \vdash^{\delta} M : A \multimap \alpha \quad R; \Gamma \vdash^{\delta} N : A}{R; \Gamma \vdash^{\delta} MN : \alpha} \qquad \frac{\mathsf{FO}(M) \leq 1 \quad R; \Gamma_{\lambda} \vdash^{\delta+1} M : A}{R; \Gamma_{!}, \Delta_{\S}, \Psi_{\lambda} \vdash^{\delta} !M : !A} \qquad \frac{R; \Gamma \vdash^{\delta} M : !A \quad \mathsf{FO}(x, N) \geq 1 \quad R; \Gamma, x : (!, A) \vdash^{\delta} N : \alpha}{R; \Gamma \vdash^{\delta} \mathsf{let}\ !x = M\ \mathsf{in}\ N : \alpha} \qquad \frac{R; \Gamma_{\lambda}, \Delta_{\lambda} \vdash^{\delta+1} M : A}{R; \Gamma_{\S}, \Delta_{!}, \Psi_{\lambda} \vdash^{\delta} \S M : \S A}$$

$$\frac{R; \Gamma \vdash^{\delta} M : \S A \quad \mathsf{FO}(x, N) = 1 \quad R; \Gamma, x : (\S, A) \vdash^{\delta} N : \alpha}{R; \Gamma \vdash^{\delta} \mathsf{let}\ \S x = M\ \mathsf{in}\ N : \alpha} \qquad \frac{t \notin (R; \Gamma) \quad R; \Gamma \vdash^{\delta} M : A}{R; \Gamma \vdash^{\delta} M : \forall t.A} \qquad \frac{R; \Gamma \vdash^{\delta} M : \forall t.A \quad R \vdash B}{R; \Gamma \vdash^{\delta} M : A[B/t]} \qquad \frac{R \vdash \Gamma \quad r : (\delta, A) \in R}{R; \Gamma \vdash^{\delta} \mathsf{get}(r) : A}$$

$$\frac{r : (\delta, A) \quad R; \Gamma \vdash^{\delta} M : A}{R; \Gamma \vdash^{\delta} \mathsf{set}(r, M) : \mathbf{1}} \qquad \frac{r : (\delta, A) \quad R; \Gamma \vdash^{\delta} M : A}{R; \Gamma \vdash^{0} r \Leftarrow M : \mathbf{B}} \qquad \frac{R; \Gamma \vdash^{\delta} P_1 : \mathbf{1} \text{ or } P_1 = S \quad R; \Gamma \vdash^{\delta} P_2 : \alpha}{R; \Gamma \vdash^{\delta} (P_1 \parallel P_2) : \alpha} \qquad \frac{R; \Gamma \vdash^{\delta} P_i : \alpha_i}{R; \Gamma \vdash^{\delta} (P_1 \parallel P_2) : \mathbf{B}}$$

Figure 12. A polynomial type system

Finally, we establish a progress proposition which shows that any well-typed call-by-value program (*i.e.* defined from Figure 9) reduces to several threads in parallel which are values or deadlocking reads.

Proposition 5 (Progress). *Suppose P is a closed typable call-by-value program which cannot reduce. Then P is structurally equivalent to a program*

$$M_1 \parallel \cdots \parallel M_m \parallel S_1 \parallel \cdots \parallel S_n \quad m, n \geq 0$$

where M_i is either a value or can only be decomposed as a term $F_{\mathsf{v}}[\mathsf{get}(r)]$ such that no value is associated with the region r in the stores $S_1, \ldots, S_n$.

7. Expressivity

We now illustrate the expressivity of the polynomial type system. First we show that our system is complete in the extensional sense: every polynomial time function can be represented (Subsection 7.1). Then we introduce a language with memory locations representing higher-order references for which the type system can be easily adapted (Subsection 7.2). Building on this language, we give an example of polynomial programming (Subsection 7.3).

As a first step, we define some Church-like encodings in Figure 13 where we abbreviate $\lambda x.\mathsf{let}\ \dagger x = x\ \mathsf{in}\ M$ by $\lambda^{\dagger} x.M$. We have natural numbers of type Nat, binary natural number of type BNat and lists of type $\mathsf{List}\ A$ that contain values of type A.

7.1 Polynomial completeness

The representation of polynomial functions relies on the representation of binary words. The precise notion of representation is spelled out in the following definitions.

Definition 6. *(Binary word representation) Let $- \vdash^{\delta} M : \S^{p}\mathsf{BNat}$ for some $\delta, p \in \mathbb{N}$. We say M* represents *$w \in \{0,1\}^*$, written $M \Vdash w$, if $M \longrightarrow^* \S^{p}\overline{w}$.*

Definition 7. *(Function representation) Let $- \vdash^{\delta} F : \mathsf{BNat} \multimap \S^{d}\mathsf{BNat}$ where $\delta, d \in \mathbb{N}$ and $f : \{0,1\}^* \to \{0,1\}^*$. We say F* represents *f, written $F \Vdash f$, if for any M and $w \in \{0,1\}^*$ such that $- \vdash^{\delta} M : \mathsf{BNat}$ and $M \Vdash w$, $FM \Vdash f(w)$.*

The following theorem is a restatement of Girard [12] and Asperti [4].

$$\begin{array}{rcl}
\mathsf{Nat} & = & \forall t.!(t \multimap t) \multimap \S(t \multimap t) \\
\overline{n} & : & \mathsf{Nat} \\
\overline{n} & = & \lambda^{!} f.\S(\lambda x.\underbrace{f(\ldots(fx))}_{n \text{ times}}) \\
 & & \\
\mathsf{add} & : & \mathsf{Nat} \multimap \mathsf{Nat} \multimap \mathsf{Nat} \\
\mathsf{add} & = & \lambda m.\lambda n.\lambda^{!} f.\mathsf{let}\ \S y = m!f\ \mathsf{in} \\
 & & \mathsf{let}\ \S z = n!f\ \mathsf{in}\ \S(\lambda x.y(zx)) \\
 & & \\
\mathsf{BNat} & = & \forall t.!(t \multimap t) \multimap !(t \multimap t) \multimap \S(t \multimap t) \\
\text{for } w = i_0 \ldots i_n \in \{0,1\}^* & & \\
\overline{w} & : & \mathsf{BNat} \\
\overline{w} & = & \lambda^{!} x_0.\lambda x_1^{!}.\S(\lambda z.x_{i_0}(\ldots(x_{i_n} z))) \\
 & & \\
\mathsf{List}\ A & = & \forall t.!(A \multimap t \multimap t) \multimap \S(t \multimap t) \\
[u_1, \ldots, u_n] & : & \mathsf{List}\ A \\
[u_1, \ldots, u_n] & = & \lambda f^{!}.\S(\lambda x.fu_1(fu_2 \ldots (fu_n x))) \\
 & & \\
\mathsf{list_it} & : & \forall u.\forall t.!(u \multimap t \multimap t) \multimap \mathsf{List}\ u \multimap \S t \multimap \S t \\
\mathsf{list_it} & = & \lambda f.\lambda l.\lambda^{\S} x.\mathsf{let}\ \S y = lf\ \mathsf{in}\ \S(yx)
\end{array}$$

Figure 13. Church encodings

Theorem 2 (Polynomial completeness).
Every function $f : \{0,1\}^* \to \{0,1\}^*$ which can be computed by a Turing machine in time bounded by a polynomial of degree d can be represented by a term of type $\mathsf{BNat} \multimap \S^{d}\mathsf{BNat}$.

7.2 A language with higher-order references

Next, we give an application of the language with abstract regions by presenting a connection with a language with dynamic memory locations representing higher-order references.

The differences with the region-based system are presented in Figure 14. We introduce terms of the form $\nu x.M$ to generate a fresh memory location x whose scope is M. Contexts are call-by-value and allow evaluation under ν binders. The structural rule (ν) is for scope extrusion. Region constants have been removed from the syntax of terms hence reduction rules (get_{ν}) and (set_{ν}) relate to memory locations. The operational semantics of references is adopted: when assigning a value to a memory location, the previous value is *overwritten*, and when reading a memory location, the

$$\begin{array}{rcl} M & ::= & \ldots \mid \nu x.M \\ F_\nu & ::= & F_{\mathsf{v}} \mid \nu x.F_\nu \end{array}$$

$$(\nu) \qquad F_\nu[\nu x.M] \equiv \nu x.F_\nu[M] \quad \text{if } x \notin \mathsf{FV}(F_\nu)$$

$$\begin{array}{llcl} (\mathsf{get}_\nu) & F_\nu[\mathsf{get}(x)] \parallel x \Leftarrow V & \longrightarrow_\nu & F_\nu[V] \parallel x \Leftarrow V \\ (\mathsf{set}_\nu) & F_\nu[\mathsf{set}(x,V)] \parallel x \Leftarrow V' & \longrightarrow_\nu & F_\nu[\star] \parallel x \Leftarrow V \end{array}$$

$$\frac{R;\Gamma, x : (u, \mathsf{Reg}_r !A) \vdash^\delta M : B}{R;\Gamma \vdash^\delta \nu x.M : B} \qquad \frac{R(r) = (\delta, !A) \quad R;\Gamma \vdash^\delta x : \mathsf{Reg}_r !A}{R;\Gamma \vdash^\delta \mathsf{get}(x) : !A}$$

$$\frac{R(r) = (\delta, !A) \quad R;\Gamma \vdash^\delta x : \mathsf{Reg}_r !A \quad R;\Gamma \vdash^\delta M : !A}{R;\Gamma \vdash^\delta \mathsf{set}(x, M) : \mathbf{1}} \qquad \frac{R(r) = (\delta, !A) \quad R;\Gamma \vdash^\delta x : \mathsf{Reg}_r !A \quad R;\Gamma \vdash^\delta V : !A}{R;\Gamma \vdash^0 x \Leftarrow V : \mathbf{B}}$$

Figure 14. A call-by-value system with references

value is *copied* from the store. We see in the typing rules that region constants still appear in region types and that a memory location must be a free variable that relates to an abstract region r by having the type $\mathsf{Reg}_r A$.

There is a simple translation from the language with memory locations to the language with regions. It consists in replacing the (free or bound) variables with a region type of the shape $\mathsf{Reg}_r A$ by the constant r. We then observe that read access and assignments to references are mapped to several reduction steps in the system with regions. It requires the following observation: in the typing rules, memory locations only relate to regions with duplicable content of type $!A$. This allows us to simulate the *copy from memory* mechanism of references by decomposing it into a *consume* and *duplicate* mechanism in the language with regions. More precisely: an occurrence of $\mathsf{get}(x)$ where x relates to region r is translated into

$$\mathsf{let}\ !y = \mathsf{get}(r)\ \mathsf{in}\ \mathsf{set}(r, !y) \parallel !y$$

such that

$$\begin{array}{l} F_{\mathsf{v}}[\mathsf{let}\ !y = \mathsf{get}(r)\ \mathsf{in}\ \mathsf{set}(r, !y) \parallel !y] \parallel r \Leftarrow !V \\ \longrightarrow_{\mathsf{v}}^{+} F[!V] \parallel r \Leftarrow !V \end{array}$$

simulates the reduction (get_ν). Also, it is easy to see that a reduction step (set_ν) can be simulated by exactly one reduction step ($\mathsf{set}_{\mathsf{v}}$). Since typing is preserved by translation, we conclude that any time complexity bound can be lifted to the language with references.

Note that this also works if we adopt the operational semantics of communication channels; in that case, memory locations can also relate to regions containing non-duplicable content since reading a channel means *consuming* the value.

7.3 Polynomial programming

Using higher-order references, we show that it is possible to program the iteration of operations producing a side effect on an inductive data structure, possibly in parallel.

Here is the function update taking as argument a memory location x related to region r and incrementing the numeral stored at that location:

$$\begin{array}{l} r : (3, !\mathsf{Nat}); - \vdash^2 \mathsf{update} : !\mathsf{Reg}_r !\mathsf{Nat} \multimap \S\mathbf{1} \multimap \S\mathbf{1} \\ \mathsf{update} = \lambda^! x.\lambda^\S z.\S(\mathsf{set}(x, \mathsf{let}\ !y = \mathsf{get}(x)\ \mathsf{in}\ !(\mathsf{add}\ \overline{2}\ y)) \parallel z) \end{array}$$

The second argument z is to be garbage collected. Then we define the program run that iterates the function update over a list $[!x, !y, !z]$ of 3 memory locations:

$$\begin{array}{l} r : (3, !\mathsf{Nat}) \vdash^1 \mathsf{run} : \S\S\mathbf{1} \\ \mathsf{run} = \mathsf{list\_it}\ !\mathsf{update}\ [!x, !y, !z]\ \S\S\star \end{array}$$

All addresses have type $!\mathsf{Reg}_r !\mathsf{Nat}$ and thus relate to the same region r. Finally, the program run in parallel with some store assignments reduces as expected:

$$\begin{array}{l} \mathsf{run} \parallel x \Leftarrow !\overline{m} \parallel y \Leftarrow !\overline{n} \parallel z \Leftarrow !\overline{p} \\ \longrightarrow_\nu^* \S\S\star \parallel x \Leftarrow !\overline{2+m} \parallel y \Leftarrow !\overline{2+n} \parallel z \Leftarrow !\overline{2+p} \end{array}$$

Note that due to the Church-style encoding of numbers and lists, we assume that the relation $\longrightarrow_\nu$ may reduce under binders when required.

Building on this example, suppose we want to write a program of three threads where each thread concurrently increments the numerals pointed by the memory locations of the list. Here is the function gen_threads taking a functional f and a value x as arguments and generating three threads where x is applied to f:

$$\begin{array}{l} r : (3, !\mathsf{Nat}) \vdash^0 \mathsf{gen\_threads} : \forall t.\forall t'.!(t \multimap t') \multimap !t \multimap \mathbf{B} \\ \mathsf{gen\_threads} = \lambda^! f.\lambda^! x.\S(fx) \parallel \S(fx) \parallel \S(fx) \end{array}$$

We define the functional F like run but parametric in the list:

$$\begin{array}{l} r : (3, !\mathsf{Nat}) \vdash^1 \mathsf{F} : \mathsf{List}\ !\mathsf{Reg}_r !\mathsf{Nat} \multimap \S\S\mathbf{1} \\ \mathsf{F} = \lambda l.\mathsf{list\_it}\ !\mathsf{update}\ l\ \S\S\star \end{array}$$

Finally the concurrent iteration is defined in run_threads:

$$\begin{array}{l} r : (3, !\mathsf{Nat}) \vdash^0 \mathsf{run\_threads} : \mathbf{B} \\ \mathsf{run\_threads} = \mathsf{gen\_threads}\ !\mathsf{F}\ ![!x, !y, !z] \end{array}$$

The program is well-typed for side effects occurring at depth 3 and it reduces as follows:

$$\begin{array}{l} \mathsf{run\_threads} \parallel x \Leftarrow !\overline{m} \parallel y \Leftarrow !\overline{n} \parallel z \Leftarrow !\overline{p} \\ \longrightarrow_\nu^* \S\S\S\star \parallel x \Leftarrow !\overline{6+m} \parallel y \Leftarrow !\overline{6+n} \parallel z \Leftarrow !\overline{6+p} \end{array}$$

Note that different thread interleavings are possible but in this particular case they are confluent.

8. Conclusion and Related work

We have proposed a type system for a higher-order functional language with multithreading and side effects that guarantees termination in polynomial time, covering any scheduling of threads and taking account of thread generation. To the best of our knowledge, there appears to be no other characterization of polynomial time in such a language. The polynomial soundness of the call-by-value strategy relies on the simulation of call-by-value by a shallow-first strategy which is proved to be polynomial. The proof is a significant adaptation of Terui's methodology [18]: it is greatly simplified by a strict linearity condition and based on a clever analysis of the evaluation order of side effects which is shown to be preserved.

Related work The framework of light logics has been previously applied to a higher-order π-calculus [14] and a functional language with pattern-matching and recursive definitions [6]. The notion of *stratified region*[1] has been proposed [1, 7] to ensure the termination of a higher-order multithreaded language with side effects . In the setting of *synchronous* computing, static analyses have been developed to bound resource consumption in a synchronous π-calculus [2] and a multithreaded first-order language [3]. Recently, the framework of *complexity information flow* have been applied to characterize polynomial multithreaded imperative programs [17].

[1] Here we speak of stratification by means of a type-and-effect discipline, this is not to be confused with the notion of stratification *by depth level* that is used in the present paper.

Acknowledgments The author wishes to thank Roberto Amadio for his precious help on the elaboration of this work and Patrick Baillot for his careful reading of the paper.

References

[1] R. M. Amadio. On stratified regions. In Z. Hu, editor, *APLAS*, volume 5904 of *Lecture Notes in Computer Science*, pages 210–225. Springer, 2009. ISBN 978-3-642-10671-2. 2, 8

[2] R. M. Amadio and F. Dabrowski. Feasible reactivity in a synchronous pi-calculus. In M. Leuschel and A. Podelski, editors, *PPDP*, pages 221–230. ACM, 2007. ISBN 978-1-59593-769-8. 8

[3] R. M. Amadio and S. Dal-Zilio. Resource control for synchronous cooperative threads. *Theoretical Computer Science*, 358(2-3):229–254, 2006. 8

[4] A. Asperti. Light affine logic. In *LICS*, pages 300–308. IEEE Computer Society, 1998. ISBN 0-8186-8506-9. 1, 7.1

[5] P. Baillot and V. Mogbil. Soft lambda-calculus: A language for polynomial time computation. In I. Walukiewicz, editor, *FoSSaCS*, volume 2987 of *Lecture Notes in Computer Science*, pages 27–41. Springer, 2004. ISBN 3-540-21298-1. 1

[6] P. Baillot, M. Gaboardi, and V. Mogbil. A polytime functional language from light linear logic. In A. D. Gordon, editor, *ESOP*, volume 6012 of *Lecture Notes in Computer Science*, pages 104–124. Springer, 2010. ISBN 978-3-642-11956-9. 8

[7] G. Boudol. Typing termination in a higher-order concurrent imperative language. *Information and Computation*, 208(6): 716–736, 2010. 8

[8] P. Coppola and S. Martini. Optimizing optimal reduction: A type inference algorithm for elementary affine logic. *ACM Transaction on Computational Logic*, 7:219–260, April 2006. ISSN 1529-3785. 1

[9] P. Coppola, U. Dal Lago, and S. Ronchi Della Rocca. Light logics and the call-by-value lambda calculus. *Logical Methods in Computer Science*, 4(4), 2008. 1

[10] V. Danos and J.-B. Joinet. Linear logic and elementary time. *Information and Computation*, 183(1):123 – 137, 2003. ISSN 0890-5401. 1

[11] J.-Y. Girard. Linear logic. *Theoretical Computer Science*, 50: 1–102, 1987. 1

[12] J.-Y. Girard. Light linear logic. *Information and Computation*, 143(2):175–204, 1998. 1, 7.1

[13] Y. Lafont. Soft linear logic and polynomial time. *Theoretical Computer Science*, 318(1-2):163–180, 2004. 1

[14] U. D. Lago, S. Martini, and D. Sangiorgi. Light logics and higher-order processes. In S. B. Fröschle and F. D. Valencia, editors, *EXPRESS*, volume 41 of *EPTCS*, pages 46–60, 2010. 8

[15] J. M. Lucassen and D. K. Gifford. Polymorphic effect systems. In J. Ferrante and P. Mager, editors, *POPL*, pages 47–57. ACM, 1988. ISBN 0-89791-252-7. 1

[16] A. Madet and R. M. Amadio. An elementary affine λ-calculus with multithreading and side effects. In C.-H. L. Ong, editor, *TLCA*, volume 6690 of *Lecture Notes in Computer Science*, pages 138–152. Springer, 2011. ISBN 978-3-642-21690-9. 1, 1, 3.2

[17] J.-Y. Marion and R. Péchoux. Complexity information flow in a multi-threaded imperative language. *CoRR*, abs/1203.6878, 2012. 8

[18] K. Terui. Light affine lambda calculus and polynomial time strong normalization. *Archive for Mathematical Logic*, 46(3-4):253–280, 2007. 1, 1, 3.1, 5, 8

Modeling Datalog Fact Assertion and Retraction in Linear Logic *

Edmund S. L. Lam
Carnegie Mellon University
sllam@qatar.cmu.edu

Iliano Cervesato
Carnegie Mellon University
iliano@cmu.edu

Abstract

Practical algorithms have been proposed to efficiently recompute the logical consequences of a Datalog program after a new fact has been asserted or retracted. This is essential in a dynamic setting where facts are frequently added and removed. Yet while assertion is logically well understood as incremental inference, the monotonic nature of first-order logic is ill-suited to model retraction. As such, the traditional logical interpretation of Datalog offers at most an abstract specification of Datalog systems, but has tenuous relations to the algorithms that perform efficient assertions and retractions in practical implementations. This paper proposes a logical interpretation of Datalog based on linear logic. It not only captures the meaning of Datalog updates, but also provides an operational model that underlies the dynamic changes of the set of inferable facts, all within the confines of logic. We prove the correctness of this interpretation with respect to its traditional counterpart.

Categories and Subject Descriptors F.3.2 [*Theory of Computation*]: Logics and Meanings of Programs—Semantics of Programming Languages

General Terms Languages, Performance, Theory

Keywords Datalog, Assertion, Retraction, Linear Logic

1. Introduction

Datalog, a logic programming language defined in the early 1980s, was originally used to describe and implement deductive databases [8]. Given a set $\mathcal{B}$ that represents the data in the database, a Datalog program $\mathcal{P}$ specified recursive views that a user can query over $\mathcal{B}$. Logically, $\mathcal{B}$ is a set of ground atomic formulas (facts) and $\mathcal{P}$ a set of implicational formulas of a restricted form (Horn clauses). The semantics of such a Datalog system, as well as some actual implementations [4], was given by the set of the atomic logical consequences of $\mathcal{P}$ with respect to $\mathcal{B}$, in symbols $\{p(\vec{t}) \mid \mathcal{P}, \mathcal{B} \vdash p(\vec{t})\}$ — a beautifully pure use of logic.

In the last ten years, Datalog has had a resurgence in a variety of domains other than databases: to provide user authentication [13], to implement network protocols [10, 14], to program cyber-physical systems [1] and to support deductive spreadsheets [5], just to cite a few. In these applications, the contents of the fact base $\mathcal{B}$ is highly dynamic, at least compared to the relatively static databases of the 1980s. This requires efficient algorithms to assert new facts and to retract stale facts. While such algorithms have been proposed [1, 7, 11, 14, 16], the connection with logic has lagged behind, especially for retraction. Indeed, although it is easy to give a logical specification of assertion and retraction, as done in Figure 1, a direct implementation of these specifications is horribly inefficient as it involves recomputing logical consequences from scratch after each assertion or retraction.

$$\begin{array}{llcl} \textbf{Assertion:} & \mathcal{P}(\mathcal{B}) & \overset{+a}{\Longrightarrow}_{\mathcal{P}} & \mathcal{P}(\mathcal{B}, a) \\ \textbf{Retraction:} & \mathcal{P}(\mathcal{B}, a) & \overset{-a}{\Longrightarrow}_{\mathcal{P}} & \mathcal{P}(\mathcal{B}) \end{array}$$

where $\mathcal{P}(\mathcal{B}) = \{p(\vec{t}) \mid \mathcal{P}, \mathcal{B} \vdash p(\vec{t})\}$.

Figure 1. Logical Specification of Datalog Updates

In this paper, we propose a logical interpretation of Datalog that supports updates internally. Like with the traditional reading, the semantics of a Datalog system $(\mathcal{P}, B)$ will be the set $\{p(\vec{t}) \mid \mathcal{P}, B \vdash p(\vec{t})\}$ of its logical consequences (plus some bookkeeping information). However, the assertion or retraction of a fact a will trigger a small number of logical inferences to determine the new set of logical consequences rather than performing a full recalculation. In this way, the proposed encoding not only constitutes a logical specification of the static and dynamic aspects of a Datalog system, but it can also be viewed as an efficient algorithm to compute updates. Because retraction results in the removal of inferred facts, we base our encoding on a fragment of first-order linear logic rather than on the traditional predicate calculus.

The main contributions of this paper are therefore 1) the definition of an encoding of Datalog which models the assertion and retraction of facts within logic, and 2) a proof of its correctness with respect to the traditional interpretation.

The rest of this paper is organized as follows: Section 2 reviews Datalog and linear logic. Section 3 illustrates our approach with an example. Section 4 introduces an initial linear logic interpretation of Datalog that focuses just on assertion. Section 5 extends it to capture retraction as well. We discuss related work in Section 6, while Section 7 outlines directions of future work.

2. Preliminaries

This section provides a brief review of Datalog and linear logic. We first recall some common mathematical notions that we will use throughout this paper.

* Funded by the Qatar National Research Fund as project NPRP 09-667-1-100 (Effective Programming for Large Distributed Ensembles)

PPDP'12, September 19–21, 2012, Leuven, Belgium.

Terms:	t	$::=$	$x \mid c$
Facts:	a, b, h	$::=$	$p(\vec{t})$
Clause:	D	$::=$	$r : \forall \vec{x}.\ B \supset h$
Clause bodies:	B	$::=$	$b \wedge B \mid b$
Programs:	$\mathcal{P}$	$::=$	$D,\ \mathcal{P} \mid \cdot$
Fact bases:	$\mathcal{B}$	$::=$	$p(\vec{c}),\ \mathcal{B} \mid \cdot$

Figure 2. Syntax of Datalog

2.1 Notations

In this paper, we will refer to both sets and multisets. We write $\wr a_1, ..., a_n \int$ for a multiset with elements $a_1, ..., a_n$ (possibly repeated) and $S \uplus S'$ for the multiset union of S and S'. We use $\emptyset$ to denote both the empty set and the empty multiset. Given a multiset S, we write $set(S)$ for the set of the elements of S (without duplicates). We write $\bar{a}$ for a generic set or multiset, disambiguating as needed. Sequences will be written as $(a_1, ..., a_n)$ or $\vec{a}$, with ϵ for the empty sequence and S, S' for the concatenation of two sequences S and S'. A substitution $[t_1/x_1, .., t_n/x_n]$, denoted θ, is a mapping of variables x_i to terms t_i. Given a collection S (set, multiset or sequence) of formulas and $\theta = [t_1/x_1, ..., t_n/x_n]$, we denote with $\theta(S)$ the simultaneous substitution of all free occurrences of x_i in S with t_i. We denote the set of free variables in S as $FV(S)$.

2.2 Datalog

Datalog is a declarative rule-based language, founded on traditional first-order logic. Its syntax is given in Figure 2. A *Datalog system* consists of a fact base, $\mathcal{B}$, and a program, $\mathcal{P}$. A *fact base* is a set of ground atomic formulas, called *facts*, of the form $p(\vec{c})$, where p is a predicate of fixed arity and $\vec{c}$ is a sequence of constants drawn from a fixed and finite signature Σ. A *Datalog program* is a set of *clauses* of the form $r : \forall \vec{x}.\ b_1 \wedge \ldots \wedge b_n \supset h$ where h and b_i are atomic formulas possibly mentioning variables among $\vec{x}$, and r is a unique label acting as the rule's name. We call h the *head* of r and $b_1 \wedge \ldots \wedge b_n$ its *body*. In this paper, we consider Datalog in its "purest" form: Datalog clauses are a restricted form of Horn clauses: the body cannot be empty, the arguments of each predicate must be either constants or variables (function symbols are disallowed), and each variable in h must appear in the antecedent $b_1 \wedge \ldots \wedge b_n$ (variables are *range-restricted*). We do not consider negated literals. Furthermore, to keep the presentation simple, we shall assume that no two body atoms have common instances.

Datalog classifies predicates p into *base predicates*, whose values are supplied by the user and can appear only in the body of a clause, and *inferred predicates* corresponding to views computed by the system. Clearly, all heads have inferred predicates. We classify the facts built from these predicates into *base facts* and *inferred facts*, respectively. The set of all facts that can be built from the signature Σ and the predicates mentioned in a program $\mathcal{P}$ is traditionally called the *Herbrand base* of $\mathcal{P}$. We denote it $herbrand(\mathcal{P})$. Furthermore, we write $herbrand_B(\mathcal{P})$ and $herbrand_I(\mathcal{P})$ for the portions of $herbrand(\mathcal{P})$ that contain base and inferred facts, respectively. The common assumption that both Σ and $\mathcal{P}$ are finite ensures that these sets are finite as well.

The semantics of a Datalog system $(\mathcal{P}, \mathcal{B})$ is defined as the set of all atomic logical consequences of $\mathcal{P}$ and $\mathcal{B}$, formally $\{p(\vec{t}) \mid \mathcal{P}, \mathcal{B} \vdash p(\vec{t})\}$. This set, the *inferential closure* of $\mathcal{P}$ and $\mathcal{B}$, consists of both base and inferred facts. We will denote it as $\mathcal{P}(\mathcal{B})$, thereby emphasizing that a fixed program $\mathcal{P}$ can be viewed as a function that maps a fact base $\mathcal{B}$ to the set of its logical consequences. This is particularly convenient given that this paper focuses on the effect of dynamic updates to the fact base of a Datalog system.

Given a fact base $\mathcal{B}$, the *assertion* of a fact a yields the updated fact base $\mathcal{B}' = \mathcal{B} \cup \{a\}$ (which we abbreviate "$\mathcal{B}, a$"). Similarly, the *retraction* of a from $\mathcal{B}$ produces $\mathcal{B}' = \mathcal{B} \setminus \{a\}$. For convenience, we will assume that $a \notin \mathcal{B}$ in the first case and $a \in \mathcal{B}$ in the second. The effect of either type of update is to change the set $\mathcal{P}(\mathcal{B})$ to $\mathcal{P}(\mathcal{B}')$. We denote this as $\mathcal{P}(\mathcal{B}) \overset{\alpha}{\Longrightarrow}_{\mathcal{P}} \mathcal{P}(\mathcal{B}')$ where the *action* α is $+a$ in the case of assertion and $-a$ for retraction. The logical meaning of both forms of update is summarized in Figure 1. Although it is possible to compute $\mathcal{P}(\mathcal{B}')$ from scratch on the basis of $\mathcal{P}$ and $\mathcal{B}'$, it is generally much more efficient to do so starting from $\mathcal{P}(\mathcal{B})$. Although a number of algorithms have been proposed to do exactly this [1, 7, 11, 14, 16], they lack a logical justification, especially in the case of retraction. This paper provides such a justification.

2.3 Linear Logic: LV^{obs} and LV^{obs-}

Linear logic [9] is a substructural refinement of traditional logic. In traditional logic, assumptions grow monotonically during proof search. By restricting the use of the structural rules of contraction and weakening, linear logic enables the context to grow and shrink as inference rules are applied. This permits interpreting formulas as *resources* that are produced and consumed during the process of constructing a derivation. The result is a rich logic that is well-suited for modeling concurrent and dynamic systems [6].

In linear logic, the usage pattern of a formula is made explicit by replacing the connectives of traditional logic with a new set of operators. For instance, multiplicative conjunction or tensor ($A \otimes B$) denotes the simultaneous occurrence of A and B, and additive conjunction ($A \& B$) denotes the exclusive occurrence of either A or B. Hence $\otimes$ and $\&$ models two understandings of "conjunction" on resources. Traditional logic implication $A \supset B$ is replaced by $A \multimap B$ which preserves the idea of deducing B from A, but differs in that A is consumed upon the application of $A \multimap B$. An atom $p(\vec{t})$ is defined as in Figure 2. The fragment of linear logic used in this paper is shown in the top part of Figure 3. With the exception of the $\multimap_a$ operator (discussed below), it is a subset of the linear logic system, known as LV^{obs} [6], that has been used to faithfully encode concurrent languages and rewriting systems.

We use the judgment $\Gamma; \Delta \longrightarrow C$ to express that the linear logic formula C is derivable from the *unrestricted context* Γ (a set of formulas that can be used as often as needed) and the *linear context* Δ (a multiset of formulas that must be used exactly once) [6, 18]. The proof system defining this judgment is given in the bottom part of Figure 3. Rules (obs), $(\multimap_L)$ and $(\multimap_L^-)$ make use of the *tensorial closure* $\bigotimes \Delta$ of a context Δ, defined as follows:

$$\begin{array}{lcl} \bigotimes(.) & = & 1 \\ \bigotimes(A, \Delta) & = & A \otimes (\bigotimes \Delta) \end{array}$$

The language used in this paper, LV^{obs-}, adds one construct to LV^{obs} (highlighted in Figure 3): *guarded implication*, written $A \multimap_a B$, where A and B are any formulas and a is an atomic formula. Its left rule $(\multimap_L^-)$ differs from that of regular implication in that it is applicable only when the linear context *does not* contain the atomic formula a; moreover, once applied, a is inserted into the context alongside the consequent B. It can be thought of as an implication with *negation-as-absence* on an atomic formula a (i.e., $\neg a \otimes A \multimap B \otimes a$).

A formula of the form $A \multimap B \otimes A$ is called *reassertive* in that applying it consumes A from the linear context Δ but immediately restores it there. If $A \multimap B \otimes A$ is in the unrestricted context Γ, it can then be applied again and again, producing arbitrarily many copies of B. By contrast, the *guarded reassertive formula* $A \multimap_a B \otimes A$ can be used at most once and produce a single B, even if it is unrestricted. Indeed, it is enabled only if $a \notin \Delta$ but its application adds a to Δ thereby preventing additional uses.

$$
\begin{array}{rrcl}
\textit{Atomic formulas:} & a, b & ::= & p(\vec{t}) \\
\textit{Formulas:} & A, B, C & ::= & a \mid 1 \mid A \otimes B \mid A \& B \mid A \multimap B \mid \forall x.A \mid \boxed{A \multimap_a B} \\
\textit{Unrestricted contexts:} & \Gamma & ::= & . \mid \Gamma, A \\
\textit{Linear contexts:} & \Delta & ::= & . \mid \Delta, A
\end{array}
$$

$$
\frac{}{\Gamma; \Delta \longrightarrow \bigotimes \Delta}(obs) \qquad \frac{\Gamma, A; \Delta, A \longrightarrow C}{\Gamma, A; \Delta \longrightarrow C}(clone) \qquad \frac{\Gamma; \Delta \longrightarrow C}{\Gamma; \Delta, 1 \longrightarrow C}(1_L)
$$

$$
\frac{\Gamma; \Delta, A_1, A_2 \longrightarrow C}{\Gamma; \Delta, A_1 \otimes A_2 \longrightarrow C}(\otimes_L) \qquad \frac{\Gamma; \Delta, A_i \longrightarrow C}{\Gamma; \Delta, A_1 \& A_2 \longrightarrow C}(\&_{L_i}) \qquad \frac{t \in \Sigma \quad \Gamma; \Delta, [t/x]A \longrightarrow C}{\Gamma; \Delta, \forall x.A \longrightarrow C}(\forall_L)
$$

$$
\frac{\Gamma; \Delta, B \longrightarrow C}{\Gamma; \Delta, \Delta', (\bigotimes \Delta') \multimap B \longrightarrow C}(\multimap_L) \qquad \boxed{\frac{a \notin \Delta \quad \Gamma; \Delta, B, a \longrightarrow C}{\Gamma; \Delta, \Delta', (\bigotimes \Delta') \multimap_a B \longrightarrow C}(\multimap_L^-)}
$$

Figure 3. LV^{obs} and LV^{obs-} Intuitionistic Linear Logic

$$
\mathcal{P} = \begin{cases} r_1 : \forall x, y.\ E(x, y) \supset P(x, y) \\ r_2 : \forall x, y, z.\ E(x, y) \wedge P(y, z) \supset P(x, z) \end{cases}
$$

Linear Logic Interpretation (Simplified):

$$
[\![\mathcal{P}]\!]' = \begin{cases}
\forall x, y.\ E(x, y) & \\
\quad \multimap \quad P(x, y) \otimes E(x, y) \otimes & \\
\qquad \boxed{(\tilde{E}(x, y) \multimap \tilde{P}(x, y) \otimes \tilde{E}(x, y))} & -\mathcal{I}_1 \\
\forall x, y, z.\ E(x, y) \otimes P(y, z) & \\
\quad \multimap \quad P(x, z) \otimes E(x, y) \otimes P(y, z) \otimes & \\
\qquad \boxed{(\tilde{E}(x, y) \multimap \tilde{P}(x, z) \otimes \tilde{E}(x, y))} \ \& & -\mathcal{I}_2 \\
\qquad \boxed{(\tilde{P}(y, z) \multimap \tilde{P}(x, z) \otimes \tilde{P}(y, z))} &
\end{cases}
$$

$$
\mathcal{A}_{\mathcal{P}} = \begin{cases} \forall x, y.\ E(x, y) \otimes \tilde{E}(x, y) \multimap 1 & -\mathcal{A}_1 \\ \forall x, y.\ P(x, y) \otimes \tilde{P}(x, y) \multimap 1 & -\mathcal{A}_2 \end{cases}
$$

Figure 4. Example of Linear Logic Interpretation

Therefore, a can act both as a guard and a witness of the application of this rule. We will make abundant use of guarded reassertive formulas and choose the witness a in such a way that distinct instances can be used at most once in a derivation.

Given unrestricted context Γ and linear context Δ, the pair (Γ, Δ) is *quiescent*, denoted $Quiescent(\Gamma, \Delta)$, if, whenever $\Gamma; \Delta \longrightarrow \bigotimes \Delta'$ is derivable, it must be the case that $\Delta = \Delta'$. In the sequel, we will be encoding Datalog clauses as guarded reassertive implications in Γ and facts as atomic formulas in Δ. Because the rules in Figure 3 operate exclusively on the left-hand side of a sequent, the inferential closure of a fact base will be obtained when these contexts reach quiescence. The primary purpose of guarded implications is indeed to allow us to reach quiescence. This is crucial to our results in Section 4.

3. Example

Consider the Datalog program $\mathcal{P}$ shown in Figure 4, together with a simplified version $[\![\mathcal{P}]\!]'$ of its linear logic interpretation. This program computes the paths in a graph: the base predicate $E(x, y)$ means that there is an edge between nodes x and y, while the inferred predicate $P(x, y)$ indicates that there is a path between them. Each Datalog clause is represented by an unrestricted linear implication called an *inference rule* ($\mathcal{I}_1$ and $\mathcal{I}_2$). Intuitively, Datalog facts are not quite *linear* in that they should not be consumed when applied to inference rules, yet we do not want to model them as *unrestricted* formulas in Γ because they are subject to retraction. Hence we model Datalog facts as *linear* atomic formulas in Δ which can be consumed, and Datalog clauses as reassertive implications. In Figure 4, we model the retraction of a fact $E(x, y)$ by defining an equal and opposite fact $\tilde{E}(x, y)$ that will consume a copy of the atomic formula $E(x, y)$[1]. Each inference rule, modeling the inference of the head, embeds one or more scoped linear implications called a *retraction rule* (highlighted in boxes), that deals with the retraction of this same fact.

Embedded retraction rules prepare for the retraction of the head of the corresponding clause in the event of the retraction of one of its body elements. For instance, the retraction rule in $\mathcal{I}_1$ states that if $E(x, y)$ is retracted — represented by $\tilde{E}(x, y)$, we shall retract $P(x, y)$ — represented by $\tilde{P}(x, y)$. Similarly, inference rule $\mathcal{I}_2$ contains two embedded retraction rules, each preparing for the retraction of its consequent $\tilde{P}(x, z)$ in the event of the retraction of either of its antecedents ($\tilde{E}(x, y)$ or $\tilde{P}(y, z)$, respectively). These two retraction rules are connected by the $\&$ operator, thereby strictly enforcing the exclusive use of either of the rules and hence ensuring that we introduce at most a single $\tilde{P}(x, z)$ in the event of the retraction of either of $P(x, z)$'s antecedents. Retraction rules enter a derivation as *linear* formulas, which means that they disappear the moment they are used. The retraction of some base fact $E(a, b)$ will trigger a cascade of applications of retraction rules, effectively retracting all paths $P(c, d)$ that are causally dependent on $E(a, b)$. Notice that retraction rules are reassertive (their antecedents appear as in their consequent). This is because a single retraction atom $\tilde{E}(x, y)$ might be responsible for producing more than one retraction atoms (e.g. $\tilde{E}(1, 2)$ might need to produce $\tilde{P}(1, 2)$ and $\tilde{P}(1, 3)$) hence the actual consumption of a retraction atom $\tilde{E}(x, y)$ cannot be the responsibility of a retraction rule, but is pushed to an *absorption rule* (e.g., $\mathcal{A}_1$ and $\mathcal{A}_2$), which models the annihilation of equal and opposite atoms.

The interpretation $[\![\mathcal{P}]\!]'$ illustrated in Figure 4 is a simplified form of our approach. Indeed, some additional bookkeeping information needs to be included to guarantee quiescence and correctness. Sections 4 and 5 will describe refinements that will provide such guarantees.

[1] $\tilde{E}$ and $\tilde{P}$ are ordinary predicates. The notation is meant to indicate that they are related to E and P, respectively.

$$
\begin{array}{rlcl}
\text{Fact} & \lceil p(\vec{t})\rceil & = & p(\vec{t}) \\
\text{Program} & \left\{ \begin{array}{l} \lceil D\,,\,\mathcal{P}\rceil \\ \lceil\cdot\rceil \end{array}\right. & \begin{array}{c} = \\ = \end{array} & \begin{array}{l} \lceil D\rceil, \lceil\mathcal{P}\rceil \\ . \end{array} \\
\text{Conjunction} & \lceil b\wedge B\rceil & = & \lceil b\rceil \otimes \lceil B\rceil \\
\text{Clause} & \left\{ \begin{array}{l} \lceil r : \forall\vec{x}.\ B\supset h\rceil \quad = \\ \qquad \forall\vec{x}.\ \lceil B\rceil \multimap_{r^\sharp(\vec{x})} \lceil h\rceil \otimes \lceil B\rceil \end{array}\right. & & \\
\text{Fact base} & \left\{ \begin{array}{l} \lceil \mathcal{B}, a\rceil \\ \lceil\emptyset\rceil \end{array}\right. & \begin{array}{c} = \\ = \end{array} & \begin{array}{l} \lceil\mathcal{B}\rceil, \lceil a\rceil \\ . \end{array}
\end{array}
$$

Figure 5. llD^{Assert} Interpretation of Datalog

4. Modeling Datalog Assertion

In this section, we define a linear logic interpretation of Datalog program which focuses only on assertions. We call this interpretation llD^{Assert}. It maps a Datalog assertions inference $\mathcal{P}(\mathcal{B}) \stackrel{+a}{\Longrightarrow}_{\mathcal{P}} \mathcal{P}(\mathcal{B}, a)$ to a derivation of an LV^{obs-} sequent $\Gamma; \Delta \longrightarrow \bigotimes\Delta'$ where Γ encodes $\mathcal{P}$, Δ encodes $\mathcal{P}(\mathcal{B})$ together with a, and Δ' encodes $\mathcal{P}(\mathcal{B}, a)$.

4.1 Inference Rules and Interpretation

We model a Datalog clause as a guarded implication in the unrestricted context and a Datalog fact as a linear atomic formula. Given a Datalog clause $r : \forall\vec{x}.\ b_1 \wedge ... \wedge b_n \supset h$, we interpret it as a linear logic implication $\forall\vec{x}.\ b_1 \otimes ... \otimes b_n \multimap_{r^\sharp(\vec{x})} h \otimes b_1 \otimes ... \otimes b_n$ which we call an *inference rule* (denoted by $\mathcal{I}$). The witness $r^\sharp(\vec{x})$ serves the purpose of reaching quiescence — it is discussed in detail below. While inference rules are unrestricted formulas that can be applied as many times as needed (more precisely, as many times as the $(\multimap_L^-)$ rule permits), Datalog facts are linear atomic formulas. The responsibility of modeling their non-linearity is achieved by making inference rule reassertive. This choice is taken in anticipation to extending our logic interpretation with retraction in Section 5.

Figure 5 formalizes the encoding function $\lceil - \rceil$ which takes a Datalog program $\mathcal{P}$ and returns the corresponding linear logic interpretation $\lceil\mathcal{P}\rceil$. Datalog facts are mapped to atomic formulas, and multisets of facts are mapped to linear contexts of atomic formulas. A Datalog clause is mapped to a guarded reassertive implication.

Inference rules are guarded by an *atomic formula witness* $r^\sharp(\vec{x})$ where r is the unique name of the clause and $\vec{x}$ are all the variables of the clause. Note that $r^\sharp$ is not a Datalog predicate but an artifact of the encoding. In particular $r^\sharp(\vec{c}) \notin herbrand(\mathcal{P})$ for any $\vec{c}$. We write $\Delta^\sharp$ for a context fragment consisting only of rule witnesses. An llD^{Assert} state is a multiset of facts and witnesses. Specifically, given a Datalog program $\mathcal{P}$, a multiset of facts $F \subseteq herbrand(\mathcal{P})$ and a multiset of rule witnesses $\Delta^\sharp$, an llD^{Assert} *state* is defined as the set of linear formula $\lceil F\rceil, \Delta^\sharp$. Moreover, given base facts $\mathcal{B} \subseteq herbrand_{\mathcal{B}}(\mathcal{P})$, the state $\lceil F\rceil, \Delta^\sharp$ is *reachable* from $\mathcal{B}$ if $\lceil\mathcal{P}\rceil; \lceil\mathcal{B}\rceil \longrightarrow \bigotimes\lceil F\rceil \otimes \bigotimes\Delta^\sharp$ is derivable. Note that $\lceil\mathcal{B}\rceil$ is always reachable from $\mathcal{B}$ — it is called an *initial state*.

To model the application of a Datalog clause D, we consider the sequence of linear logic derivation steps that corresponds to the cloning and instantiation of inference rule $\lceil D\rceil$, followed by the actual application of the inference rule instance and assembly of the tensor closure of consequents into atomic formulas. Figure 6 factors out the mapping of this sequence of linear logic derivation steps into a *macro rule* $(\mathcal{I}_L)$. Lemma 1 in Section 4.3 entails

$$
\begin{array}{lrcl}
\text{Let} & \lceil\mathcal{P}\rceil & \equiv & \Gamma, \mathcal{I} \\
 & \mathcal{I} & \equiv & \forall\vec{x}.\ \bigotimes\Delta \multimap_{r^\sharp(\vec{x})} h \otimes \bigotimes\Delta
\end{array}
$$

$$
\frac{r^\sharp(\vec{t}) \notin \Delta' \quad \lceil\mathcal{P}\rceil; [\vec{t}/\vec{x}]h, [\vec{t}/\vec{x}]\Delta, r^\sharp(\vec{t}), \Delta' \longrightarrow C}{\lceil\mathcal{P}\rceil; [\vec{t}/\vec{x}]\Delta, \Delta' \longrightarrow C} \; (\mathcal{I}_L)
$$

which decomposes into:

$$
\dfrac{\dfrac{\dfrac{r^\sharp(\vec{t}) \notin \Delta' \quad \dfrac{\lceil\mathcal{P}\rceil; [\vec{t}/\vec{x}]h, [\vec{t}/\vec{x}]\Delta, r^\sharp(\vec{t}), \Delta' \longrightarrow C}{\lceil\mathcal{P}\rceil; [\vec{t}/\vec{x}](h \otimes \bigotimes\Delta), r^\sharp(\vec{t}), \Delta' \longrightarrow C}\,(\otimes_L)^*}{\lceil\mathcal{P}\rceil; [\vec{t}/\vec{x}]\mathcal{I}, [\vec{t}/\vec{x}]\Delta, \Delta' \longrightarrow C}\,(\multimap_L^-)}{\lceil\mathcal{P}\rceil; \mathcal{I}, [\vec{t}/\vec{x}]\Delta, \Delta' \longrightarrow C}\,(\forall_L)^*}{\lceil\mathcal{P}\rceil; [\vec{t}/\vec{x}]\Delta, \Delta' \longrightarrow C}\,(\text{clone})
$$

Figure 6. llD^{Assert} Inference Macro Rule

that any derivation on LV^{obs-} states has an equivalent derivation comprised of only $(\mathcal{I}_L)$ and (obs) derivation steps.

We informally define a transition $\Delta \stackrel{+a}{\Longrightarrow}{}^{LL}_{\lceil\mathcal{P}\rceil} \Delta'$ that maps a state Δ to another state Δ' such that Δ' has reached quiescence and $\mathcal{P}; \Delta, a \longrightarrow \bigotimes\Delta'$. We will extend it to retraction in Section 5 and formally define it in Section 5.3.

4.2 Quiescence and Complete Inference

Figure 7 illustrates an example LV^{obs-} derivation based on the llD^{Assert} interpretation of our example in Figure 4. It features two successive assertion steps from an empty state. For clarity, we highlight (using boxes) the formula fragments that are acted upon in each derivation step. The first derivation represents the assertion of $E(1,2)$ from the empty state, during which the inference rule instance $\mathcal{I}_1^{(1,2)}$ is applied and we produce the state Δ. Note that without the guards $I_1^\sharp(x,y)$ and $I_2^\sharp(x,y,z)$, the inference rules would allow the derivation of goal formulas with arbitrarily many copies of the head of the clauses that have been applied. Instead, from $E(1,2)$ we can only derive a single instance of $P(1,2)$ because an application of $\mathcal{I}_1^{(x,y)}$ introduces the atomic formula $I_1^\sharp(1,2)$ which, by rule $(\multimap_L^-)$, prevents further application of $\mathcal{I}_1^{(x,y)}$. In fact, derivations such as this will always reach quiescence. The second derivation represents the assertion of $E(2,3)$ from the state Δ obtained in the previous derivation. Here, we reach quiescence with Δ' after applying inference rule instances $\mathcal{I}_1^{(2,3)}$ and $\mathcal{I}_2^{(1,2,3)}$.

Given a Datalog program $\mathcal{P}$, a state Δ reachable from fact base $\mathcal{B}$ and some new fact a, to derive the inferential closure of $(\mathcal{B}, a)$, we construct the derivation of $\lceil\mathcal{P}\rceil; \Delta, a \longrightarrow \bigotimes\Delta'$ such that Δ' is quiescent with respect to $\lceil\mathcal{P}\rceil$.

4.3 Correctness

In this section, we argue for the soundness and completeness of the llD^{Assert} linear logic interpretation of Datalog program. Detailed proofs can be found in [12].

As mentioned earlier, for LV^{obs-} sequents of the form we are interested in, we can always find a normalized LV^{obs-} derivation that consist just of $(\mathcal{I}_L)$ and (obs) rules. This simplifies the proof of the correctness of our interpretation.

LEMMA 1 (Normalized Derivations). *Given a Datalog program $\mathcal{P}$ and states $\lceil F_1\rceil, \Delta_1^\sharp$ and $\lceil F_2\rceil, \Delta_2^\sharp$, a sequent $\lceil\mathcal{P}\rceil; \lceil F_1\rceil, \Delta_1^\sharp \longrightarrow \bigotimes\lceil F_2\rceil \otimes \bigotimes\Delta_2^\sharp$ has a derivation consisting of only applications of $(\mathcal{I}_L)$ and (obs) derivation steps.*

$$\mathcal{P} \quad = \quad I_1 : \forall x,y.\, E(x,y) \supset P(x,y) \quad , \quad I_2 : \forall x,y,z.\, E(x,y) \wedge P(y,z) \supset P(x,z)$$

$$\begin{array}{lcl} \lceil\mathcal{P}\rceil & = & \forall x,y.\,\mathcal{I}_1^{(x,y)}, \forall x,y,z.\,\mathcal{I}_2^{(x,y,z)} \\ \mathcal{I}_1^{(x,y)} & = & E(x,y) \multimap_{I_1^\sharp(x,y)} P(x,y) \otimes E(x,y) \\ \mathcal{I}_2^{(x,y,z)} & = & E(x,y) \otimes P(y,z) \multimap_{I_2^\sharp(x,y,z)} P(x,z) \otimes E(x,y) \otimes P(y,z) \end{array}$$

Assertion of $E(1,2)$: $\emptyset \xrightarrow{+E(1,2)}{}^{LL}_{\lceil\mathcal{P}\rceil} \Delta$ **where** $\Delta = \lbag P(1,2), E(1,2), I_1^\sharp(1,2) \rbag$

$$\mathcal{I}_1^{(1,2)}\ \dfrac{\dfrac{}{\lceil\mathcal{P}\rceil; P(1,2), E(1,2), I_1^\sharp(1,2) \longrightarrow \bigotimes\Delta}\ (obs)}{\lceil\mathcal{P}\rceil; E(1,2) \longrightarrow \bigotimes\Delta}\ (\mathcal{I}_L)$$

Assertion of $E(2,3)$: $\Delta \xrightarrow{+E(2,3)}{}^{LL}_{\lceil\mathcal{P}\rceil} \Delta'$ **where** $\Delta' = \lbag P(1,2), P(2,3), P(1,3), E(1,2), E(2,3), I_1^\sharp(1,2), I_1^\sharp(2,3), I_2^\sharp(1,2,3) \rbag$

$$\mathcal{I}_1^{(2,3)}\ \dfrac{\mathcal{I}_2^{(1,2,3)}\ \dfrac{\dfrac{}{\lceil\mathcal{P}\rceil; P(1,2), P(2,3), P(1,3), E(1,2), E(2,3), I_1^\sharp(1,2), I_1^\sharp(2,3), I_2^\sharp(1,2,3) \longrightarrow \bigotimes\Delta'}\ (obs)}{\lceil\mathcal{P}\rceil; P(1,2), P(2,3), E(1,2), E(2,3), I_1^\sharp(1,2), I_1^\sharp(2,3) \longrightarrow \bigotimes\Delta'}\ (\mathcal{I}_L)}{\lceil\mathcal{P}\rceil; P(1,2), E(1,2), E(2,3), I_1^\sharp(1,2) \longrightarrow \bigotimes\Delta'}\ (\mathcal{I}_L)$$

Figure 7. LV^{obs-} derivations of an example llD^{Assert} interpretation

$$\mathcal{P} \quad = \quad I : \forall x.\, A(x) \wedge B(x) \supset D(x)$$

$$\begin{array}{lcl} \lceil\mathcal{P}\rceil' & = & \forall x.\,\mathcal{I}_1^{(x)} \\ \mathcal{I}_1^{(x)} & = & A(x) \otimes B(x) \multimap_{I^\sharp(x)} D(x) \otimes A(x) \otimes B(x) \otimes \mathcal{R}_1^{(x)} \\ \mathcal{R}_1^{(x)} & = & (\tilde{A}(x) \otimes I^\sharp(x) \multimap \tilde{D}(x) \otimes \tilde{A}(x)) \& \\ & & (\tilde{B}(x) \otimes I^\sharp(x) \multimap \tilde{D}(x) \otimes \tilde{B}(x)) \end{array} \qquad \begin{array}{lcl} \mathcal{A}_\mathcal{P} & = & \forall x.\,\mathcal{A}_A^{(x)}, \forall x.\,\mathcal{A}_B^{(x)}, \forall x.\,\mathcal{A}_D^{(x)} \\ \mathcal{A}_A^{(x)} & = & A(x) \otimes \tilde{A}(x) \multimap 1 \\ \mathcal{A}_B^{(x)} & = & B(x) \otimes \tilde{B}(x) \multimap 1 \\ \mathcal{A}_D^{(x)} & = & D(x) \otimes \tilde{D}(x) \multimap 1 \end{array}$$

Assertion of $B(5)$

$\lbag A(5) \rbag \xrightarrow{+B(5)}{}^{LL}_{\lceil\mathcal{P}\rceil} \Delta'$ where $\Delta' = \lbag A(5), B(5), D(5), \mathcal{R}_1^{(5)}, I^\sharp(5) \rbag$

$$\mathcal{I}_1^{(5)}\ \dfrac{\dfrac{}{\lceil\mathcal{P}\rceil', \mathcal{A}_\mathcal{P}; A(5), B(5), D(5), \mathcal{R}_1^{(5)}, I^\sharp(5) \longrightarrow \bigotimes\Delta'}\ (obs)}{\lceil\mathcal{P}\rceil', \mathcal{A}_\mathcal{P}; A(5), B(5) \longrightarrow \bigotimes\Delta'}$$

Retraction of $A(5)$

$\Delta' \xrightarrow{-A(5)}{}^{LL}_{\lceil\mathcal{P}\rceil} \Delta''$ where $\Delta'' = \lbag B(5) \rbag$

$$\mathcal{R}_1^{(5)}\ \dfrac{\mathcal{A}_D^{(5)}\ \dfrac{\mathcal{A}_A^{(5)}\ \dfrac{\dfrac{}{\lceil\mathcal{P}\rceil', \mathcal{A}_\mathcal{P}; B(5) \longrightarrow \bigotimes\Delta''}\ (obs)}{\lceil\mathcal{P}\rceil', \mathcal{A}_\mathcal{P}; A(5), B(5), \tilde{A}(5) \longrightarrow \bigotimes\Delta''}}{\lceil\mathcal{P}\rceil', \mathcal{A}_\mathcal{P}; A(5), B(5), D(5), \tilde{A}(5), \tilde{D}(5) \longrightarrow \bigotimes\Delta''}}{\lceil\mathcal{P}\rceil', \mathcal{A}_\mathcal{P}; A(5), B(5), D(5), \mathcal{R}_1^{(5)}, I^\sharp(5), \tilde{A}(5) \longrightarrow \bigotimes\Delta''}$$

Figure 8. An Example of llD^{Full-} Interpretation with Assertion/Retraction Derivations

Lemma 2 states the redundancy of having multiple copies of facts, with respect to Datalog inference. Essentially a consequence of the invertibility of the left contraction rule, this lemma allows us to safely go back and forth between the multisets of facts of LV^{obs-} and the sets of facts in traditional logic, in our soundness proof (Theorem 3). In the reverse direction of the proof, it allows us to focus on traditional logic proofs that are sufficiently *saturated*, meaning that multiple applications of the same instance of Horn clauses do not provide more information. This is crucial for our completeness proof (Theorem 4), given that in the llD^{Assert} interpretation of Datalog clauses, inference rules are guarded implications that will reach quiescence, preventing multiple applications of same implication rule instances.

LEMMA 2 (Redundancy). *Given a Datalog program $\mathcal{P}$, states $\Delta_1 \equiv \lceil F_1 \rceil, \Delta_1^\sharp$ and $\Delta_2 \equiv \lceil F_2 \rceil, \Delta_2^\sharp$ and some fact $b \in herbrand(\mathcal{P})$, we have the following:*

1. $\mathcal{P}, b, b, F_1 \vdash \bigwedge F_2$ *if and only if* $\mathcal{P}, b, F_1 \vdash \bigwedge F_2$
2. $\lceil\mathcal{P}\rceil; \lceil b \rceil, \lceil b \rceil, \Delta_1 \longrightarrow \lceil b \rceil \otimes \bigotimes \Delta_2$ *if and only if* $\lceil\mathcal{P}\rceil; \lceil b \rceil, \Delta_1 \longrightarrow \bigotimes \Delta_2$

Given a Datalog program and a multiset of facts, every valid LV^{obs-} derivation built from the llD^{Assert} interpretation has a corresponding valid traditional logic derivation. Therefore, our linear logic interpretation is sound with respect to the traditional semantics of Datalog.

THEOREM 3 (Soundness). *Given a Datalog program $\mathcal{P}$, fact base $\mathcal{B}$ and reachable llD^{Assert} state $\lceil F \rceil, \Delta^\sharp$, if $\lceil \mathcal{P} \rceil; \lceil \mathcal{B} \rceil \longrightarrow \bigotimes \lceil F \rceil \otimes \bigotimes \Delta^\sharp$, then $\mathcal{P}, \mathcal{B} \vdash \bigwedge F$.*

Proof: Given Lemma 1, we can safely focus on normalized derivations. Then this proof proceeds by structural induction on normalized LV^{obs-} derivations: for any $(\mathcal{I}_L)$ derivation step we can find a corresponding sequence of traditional logic derivation steps that mimics application of Horn clauses, while (*obs*) derivation steps corresponds to a combination of weakening and identity rules in traditional logic sequent calculus. □

Given a Datalog program and a set of facts, every valid traditional logic derivation built from the traditional Horn clause interpretation of Datalog, has a corresponding LV^{obs-} derivation built from its llD^{Assert} interpretation. Our interpretation is therefore also complete.

THEOREM 4 (Completeness). *Given a Datalog program $\mathcal{P}$, fact base $\mathcal{B}$ and $F \subseteq herbrand(\mathcal{P})$, if $\mathcal{P}, \mathcal{B} \vdash \bigwedge F$, then there is $\Delta^\sharp$ such that $\lceil \mathcal{P} \rceil; \lceil \mathcal{B} \rceil \longrightarrow \bigotimes \lceil F \rceil \otimes \bigotimes \Delta^\sharp$.*

Proof: With permutability properties of traditional logic derivation steps [15], we safely focus on normalized derivations, which comprise of a sequence of derivations modeling applications of Horn clauses, while weakening rules and identity rules are permuted upwards. The proof proceeds by structural induction on normalized traditional logic derivations. Thanks to Lemma 2, derivation steps which corresponds to application of Horn clauses can always be mapped to $(\mathcal{I}_L)$ macro rules. The combination of weakening and identity rules are mapped to the (*obs*) rule. □

From Theorems 4 and 3, we have that, given a fact base $\mathcal{B}$, we can always derive a state $\lceil F \rceil, \lceil \Delta^\sharp \rceil$ such that the set interpretation of $\lceil F \rceil$ (denoted $set(F)$) is equal to $\mathcal{P}(\mathcal{B})$ and this state is quiescent. Furthermore, there can only be one such quiescent state.

THEOREM 5 (Correctness). *Let $\mathcal{P}$ be a Datalog program and $\mathcal{B}$ a collection of base facts.*

1. *There are $\lceil F \rceil$ and $\Delta^\sharp$ such that $\lceil \mathcal{P} \rceil; \lceil \mathcal{B} \rceil \longrightarrow \bigotimes \lceil F \rceil \otimes \bigotimes \Delta^\sharp$ and $Quiescent(\lceil \mathcal{P} \rceil, (\lceil F \rceil, \Delta^\sharp))$ and $set(F) = \mathcal{P}(\mathcal{B})$.*
2. *For any state Δ, if $\lceil \mathcal{P} \rceil; \lceil \mathcal{B} \rceil \longrightarrow \bigotimes \lceil \Delta \rceil$ and $Quiescent(\lceil \mathcal{P} \rceil, \Delta)$, then there is $\Delta^\sharp$ such that $\Delta = \lceil F \rceil, \Delta^\sharp$ and $set(F) = \mathcal{P}(\mathcal{B})$.*

Proof: (1) From Theorem 4, we can conclude that since $\mathcal{P}, \mathcal{B} \vdash \bigwedge \mathcal{P}(\mathcal{B})$, then we have $\lceil \mathcal{P} \rceil; \lceil \mathcal{B} \rceil \longrightarrow \bigotimes \lceil F \rceil \otimes \bigotimes \Delta^\sharp$ for some $\Delta^\sharp$ and $set(F) = \mathcal{P}(\mathcal{B})$. Furthermore we must have $Quiescent(\lceil \mathcal{P} \rceil, (\lceil F \rceil, \Delta^\sharp))$ since all inference rules must have applied to reach quiescence, and $\mathcal{P}(\mathcal{B})$ contains the inferential closure of $\mathcal{B}$.

(2) By contradiction, suppose that $Quiescent(\lceil \mathcal{P} \rceil, \Delta)$ and $set(F)$ contains some fact b not in $\mathcal{P}(\mathcal{B})$. Yet by Theorem 3, we have $\mathcal{P}, \mathcal{B} \vdash \bigwedge F$ with F containing facts that are not in $\mathcal{P}(\mathcal{B})$ hence contradicting that $\mathcal{P}(\mathcal{B})$ is the inferential closure of $\mathcal{B}$. □

These results are incremental steps towards achieving the main goal of this paper, which is to formalize an interpretation of both assertion and retraction in Datalog, done in Section 5.

5. Modeling Datalog Retraction

In this section, we extend our linear logic interpretation of Datalog assertion to also account for the retraction of facts. We first illustrate our technique in Section 5.1 by informally introducing a simplified version called llD^{Full-}. Unfortunately, this simplified version admits LV^{obs-} sequent derivations that correspond to incomplete retraction of facts, meaning that when such a derivation reaches quiescence there is no guarantee that the state we obtain corresponds to a valid Datalog object. In Section, 5.2, we modify it into the llD^{Full} interpretation that provides guarantees of completeness when quiescence is achieved. Then in Section 5.3, we formally define the llD^{Full} interpretation that incorporates this modification and correctly models Datalog assertion and retraction.

5.1 Retraction and Absorption Rules

We model the removal of facts by means of *anti-predicates*. An anti-predicate $\tilde{p}$ is an ordinary predicate that is meant to be *equal and opposite* to p. While p applied to terms $\vec{t}$ forms a *fact*, $\tilde{p}$ applied to terms form a *retraction fact*. For instance, recalling the reachability example from Figure 4, the predicates E and P will have equal and opposite anti-predicates $\tilde{E}$ and $\tilde{P}$ respectively. The intent is that an atom $\tilde{p}(\vec{t})$ will ultimately absorb its equal and opposite atom $p(\vec{t})$. To model this property, we define *absorption rules* of the form $\forall \vec{x}.\ p(\vec{x}) \otimes \tilde{p}(\vec{x}) \multimap 1$. We illustrate this by means of an example, displayed in Figure 8, which shows a Datalog program $\mathcal{P}$ and its llD^{Full-} interpretation. We have three absorption rules $\mathcal{A}_{\_}^{(x)}$, one for each predicate of this Datalog program. Also demonstrated here, we enrich the linear logic interpretation of Datalog programs with *retraction rules*: Each Datalog clause $r : \forall \vec{x}.\ p_1(\vec{t_1}) \wedge \ldots \wedge p_n(\vec{t_n}) \supset p_h(\vec{t_h})$ is modeled by an inference rule that contains an additional consequent, the additive conjunction of n retraction rules, each of which is uniquely associated with one of the antecedents $p_i(\vec{t_i})$. For instance, inference rule $\mathcal{I}_1^{(x)}$ has an embedded retraction rule $\mathcal{R}_1^{(x)}$ in its consequent and $\mathcal{R}_1^{(x)}$ contains two linear implications, joined by the & operator. Each of these linear implications produces a retraction of $D(x)$ (i.e. $\tilde{D}(x)$) in the event that we have a retraction of $B(x)$ or $C(x)$ respectively.

In the llD^{Full-} interpretation of Datalog programs, we can always find a valid LV^{obs-} derivation that represents each assertion or retraction of facts. Figure 8 illustrates two such derivations, starting from a state containing just the fact $A(5)$, the first derivation shows a derivation in the llD^{Full-} interpretation of this program, that models the assertion of a new fact $B(5)$. As such, we consider the derivation starting from the initial state, consisting of $A(5)$ and the newly asserted fact $B(5)$. We highlight (using boxes) the active fragments of the sequent which contributes to the application of the derivation step. Notice that when the inference rule instance $\mathcal{I}_1^{(5)}$ applies, we have not only the inferred fact $D(5)$, but we have the retraction rule instance $\mathcal{R}_1^{(5)}$ as well. This retraction rule is bookkeeping information that will facilitate the retraction of $D(5)$, in the event that either $A(5)$ or $B(5)$ is retracted. To illustrate this, the second derivation of this figure models the retraction of fact $A(5)$. We consider the state Δ' (obtained in the previous derivation) with the retraction atom $\tilde{A}(5)$ inserted. $\tilde{A}(5)$ and $I^\sharp(5)$ triggers the first additive conjunction component $\tilde{A}(5) \otimes I^\sharp(5) \multimap \tilde{D}(5) \otimes \tilde{A}(5)$ of the retraction rule instance $\mathcal{R}_1^{(5)}$ and produces $\tilde{D}(5)$ while retaining $\tilde{A}(5)$. The purpose of retaining $\tilde{A}(5)$ is that in the general case, $\tilde{A}(5)$ might be necessary for triggering the retraction of other atoms, yet we consume $I^\sharp(5)$ to allow future applications of inference rule instance $I^\sharp(5)$ should $A(5)$ be re-asserted by future updates. Joining the linear implications of retraction rule $\mathcal{R}_2^{(x)}$ with the & operator allows the creation of exactly *one* $\tilde{D}(5)$ atom from the retraction of $B(5)$ or $C(5)$. Hence we will not be left with a "dangling" copy of $\tilde{D}(5)$ should $C(5)$ be retracted as well (since $\mathcal{R}_1^{(5)}$ has completely been consumed by $\tilde{B}(5)$). We finally complete the derivation by applying the absorption of $D(5)$ and $A(5)$ by $\tilde{D}(5)$ and $\tilde{A}(5)$, via absorption rules $\mathcal{A}_D^{(5)}$ and $\mathcal{A}_A^{(5)}$ respectively.

$$
\begin{array}{rcl}
\mathcal{P} & = & I : \forall x.\, A(x) \wedge B(x) \supset D(x) \\
\mathcal{I}_1^{(x)} & = & A(x) \otimes B(x) \multimap_{I^\sharp(x)} D(x) \otimes A(x) \otimes B(x) \otimes \mathcal{R}_1^{(x)} \otimes \\
 & & \boxed{A^\sharp(x) \otimes B^\sharp(x)} \\
\mathcal{R}_1^{(x)} & = & (\tilde{A}(x) \otimes \boxed{A^\sharp(x) \otimes B^\sharp(x)} \multimap \tilde{D}(x) \otimes \tilde{A}(x))\ \& \\
 & & (\tilde{B}(x) \otimes \boxed{A^\sharp(x) \otimes B^\sharp(x)} \multimap \tilde{D}(x) \otimes \tilde{B}(x))
\end{array}
\qquad
\begin{array}{rcl}
\llbracket \mathcal{P} \rrbracket & = & \forall x.\, \mathcal{I}_1^{(x)} \\
\mathcal{A}_{\mathcal{P}} & = & \forall x.\, \mathcal{A}_A^{(x)}, \forall x.\, \mathcal{A}_B^{(x)}, \forall x.\, \mathcal{A}_D^{(x)} \\
\mathcal{A}_A^{(x)} & = & A(x) \otimes \tilde{A}(x) \boxed{\multimap_{A^\sharp(x)}} \boxed{(A^\sharp(x) \multimap 1)} \\
\mathcal{A}_B^{(x)} & = & B(x) \otimes \tilde{B}(x) \boxed{\multimap_{B^\sharp(x)}} \boxed{(B^\sharp(x) \multimap 1)} \\
\mathcal{A}_D^{(x)} & = & D(x) \otimes \tilde{D}(x) \boxed{\multimap_{D^\sharp(x)}} \boxed{(D^\sharp(x) \multimap 1)}
\end{array}
$$

Assertion of $B(5)$**:** $\lfloor A(5) \rfloor \overset{+B(5)}{\Longrightarrow}{}^{LL}_{\llbracket \mathcal{P} \rrbracket} \Delta'$ **where** $\Delta' = \lfloor A(5), B(5), D(5), \mathcal{R}_1^{(5)}, I^\sharp(5), A^\sharp(5), B^\sharp(5) \rfloor$

$$
\cfrac{\cfrac{}{\llbracket \mathcal{P} \rrbracket, \mathcal{A}_{\mathcal{P}};\ \boxed{A(5), B(5), D(5), \mathcal{R}_1^{(5)}, I^\sharp(5), A^\sharp(5), B^\sharp(5)} \longrightarrow \boxed{\bigotimes \Delta'}}\ (obs)}{\boxed{\llbracket \mathcal{P} \rrbracket}, \mathcal{A}_{\mathcal{P}};\ \boxed{A(5), B(5)} \longrightarrow \bigotimes \Delta'}\ \mathcal{I}_1^{(5)}
$$

Retraction of $A(5)$**:** $\Delta' \overset{-A(5)}{\Longrightarrow}{}^{LL}_{\llbracket \mathcal{P} \rrbracket} \Delta''$ **where** $\Delta'' = \lfloor B(5) \rfloor$

$$
\cfrac{\cfrac{\cfrac{\cfrac{}{\llbracket \mathcal{P} \rrbracket, \mathcal{A}_{\mathcal{P}};\ \boxed{B(5)} \longrightarrow \boxed{\bigotimes \Delta''}}\ (obs)}{\llbracket \mathcal{P} \rrbracket, \boxed{\mathcal{A}_{\mathcal{P}}};\ \boxed{A(5)}, B(5), \boxed{\tilde{A}(5)} \longrightarrow \bigotimes \Delta''}\ \mathcal{A}_A^{(5)}}{\llbracket \mathcal{P} \rrbracket, \boxed{\mathcal{A}_{\mathcal{P}}};\ A(5), B(5), \boxed{D(5)}, \tilde{A}(5), \boxed{\tilde{D}(5)} \longrightarrow \bigotimes \Delta''}\ \mathcal{A}_D^{(5)}}{\llbracket \mathcal{P} \rrbracket, \mathcal{A}_{\mathcal{P}};\ A(5), B(5), D(5), \boxed{\mathcal{R}_1^{(5)}, I^\sharp(5), \tilde{A}(5), A^\sharp(5), B^\sharp(5)} \longrightarrow \bigotimes \Delta''}\ \mathcal{R}_1^{(5)}
$$

Figure 9. An Example of llD^{Full} Interpretation

$$
\begin{array}{lrcl}
\text{Fact} & \llbracket p(\vec{t}) \rrbracket & = & p(\vec{t}) \\
\text{Program} & \llbracket D, \mathcal{P} \rrbracket & = & \llbracket D \rrbracket, \llbracket \mathcal{P} \rrbracket \\
 & \llbracket . \rrbracket & = & . \\
\text{Conjunction} & \llbracket b \wedge B \rrbracket & = & \llbracket b \rrbracket \otimes \llbracket B \rrbracket \\
\text{Clause} & \multicolumn{3}{l}{\llbracket r : \forall \vec{x}.\, B \supset h \rrbracket =} \\
 & \multicolumn{3}{l}{\quad \forall \vec{x}.\, \llbracket B \rrbracket \multimap_{r^\sharp(\vec{x})} \llbracket h \rrbracket \otimes \llbracket B \rrbracket \otimes \llbracket B^\sharp \rrbracket \otimes} \\
 & \multicolumn{3}{r}{Ret(B, B, r^\sharp(\vec{x}), h)} \\
\text{Fact base} & \llbracket \mathcal{B}, a \rrbracket & = & \llbracket \mathcal{B} \rrbracket, \llbracket a \rrbracket \\
 & \llbracket \emptyset \rrbracket & = & .
\end{array}
$$

where

$$
\begin{array}{l}
Ret(b \wedge B', B, r^\sharp(\vec{x}), h) = \\
\quad (\llbracket \tilde{b} \rrbracket \otimes r^\sharp(\vec{x}) \otimes \llbracket B^\sharp \rrbracket \multimap \llbracket \tilde{h} \rrbracket \otimes \llbracket \tilde{b} \rrbracket)\ \&\ Ret(B', B, r^\sharp(\vec{x}), h) \\
Ret(b, B, r^\sharp(\vec{x}), h) = \\
\quad (\llbracket \tilde{b} \rrbracket \otimes r^\sharp(\vec{x}) \otimes \llbracket B^\sharp \rrbracket \multimap \llbracket \tilde{h} \rrbracket \otimes \llbracket \tilde{b} \rrbracket)
\end{array}
$$

Figure 10. llD^{Full} Interpretation of Datalog

Note that Δ and Δ' are *quiescent* with respect to the llD^{Full-} interpretation of the Datalog program.

5.2 Quiescence and Complete Retraction

In this section we address a shortcoming of the llD^{Full-} interpretation: we cannot guarantee that reachable states derived by valid LV^{obs-} derivations model complete retraction of Datalog facts when they reach quiescence.

Refer to Figure 8 again. In the second derivation, which corresponds to the retraction of $A(5)$ starting from state $\Delta', \tilde{A}(5)$, rather than applying retraction rule $\mathcal{R}_1^{(5)}$, we could have instead immediately applied the absorption rule instance $\mathcal{A}_1^{(5)}$, yielding a state of quiescence and bypassing the retraction of $D(5)$. This state, however, would be an incorrect representation of the effect of retracting $A(5)$, hence such derivations should somehow be disallowed. In general, any pair of equal and opposite atoms $p(\vec{t})$ and $\tilde{p}(\vec{t})$ should be applied to (and consumed by) their corresponding absorption rule only when all retraction rules that can be applied to $p(\vec{t})$ have been applied. In other words, we must ***inhibit*** the application of absorption rules until all such retraction rules have been applied. To do so, we use the same technique with which we achieved quiescence in the presence of reassertive inference rules: guarded linear implications. Specifically we require that for each inference rule that is applied, for each antecedent $p(\vec{t})$ of this inference rule we produce a witness atom $p^\sharp(\vec{t})$; retraction rules additionally consume these witnesses $p^\sharp(\vec{t})$. We define absorption rules as guarded implications $p(\vec{x}) \otimes \tilde{p}(\vec{x}) \multimap_{p^\sharp(\vec{x})} (p^\sharp(\vec{x}) \multimap 1)$. The witnesses inhibit absorption rules until they are finally removed by retraction rules. Notice that an absorption rule produces a peculiar consequent $p^\sharp(\vec{x}) \multimap 1$. The purpose for this is to consume the atom $p^\sharp(\vec{x})$ produced as a consequent of applying the $(\multimap_L^-)$ rule.

Figure 9 illustrates this idea on our last example. The boxes highlight the components added on top of the llD^{Full-} interpretation example of Figure 8. We call it the llD^{Full} interpretation, implemented by the function $\llbracket - \rrbracket$, defined in Section 5.3. Specifically inference rule $\mathcal{I}_1^{(x)}$ has two additional consequents $A^\sharp(x)$ and $B^\sharp(x)$, which are witness atoms for antecedents $A(x)$ and $B(x)$ respectively. Absorption rules are now guarded linear implications with witness atoms as inhibitors. For instance, $\mathcal{A}_A^{(x)}$ can only apply if there are no witnesses $A^\sharp(x)$ in the context. Finally, on top of consuming inference witness $I^\sharp(x)$ and producing retraction atom

$$\text{Let}\quad \llbracket\mathcal{P}\rrbracket \equiv \Gamma, \mathcal{I}$$
$$\mathcal{I} \equiv \forall\vec{x}.\ \bigotimes\Delta \multimap_{r^\sharp(\vec{x})} h \otimes \bigotimes\Delta \otimes \mathcal{R}_r \otimes \bigotimes\Delta^\sharp$$

$$\frac{r^\sharp(\vec{t}) \notin \Delta' \qquad \llbracket\mathcal{P}\rrbracket, \mathcal{A}_\mathcal{P}; [\vec{t}/\vec{x}](h, \Delta, \mathcal{R}_r, \Delta^\sharp), r^\sharp(\vec{t}), \Delta' \longrightarrow C}{\llbracket\mathcal{P}\rrbracket, \mathcal{A}_\mathcal{P}; [\vec{t}/\vec{x}]\Delta, \Delta' \longrightarrow C}\ (\mathcal{I}_L)$$

which decomposes into:

$$\dfrac{\dfrac{r^\sharp(\vec{t}) \notin \Delta' \qquad \dfrac{\llbracket\mathcal{P}\rrbracket, \mathcal{A}_\mathcal{P}; [\vec{t}/\vec{x}](h, \Delta, \mathcal{R}_r), r^\sharp(\vec{t}), [\vec{t}/\vec{x}]\Delta^\sharp, \Delta' \longrightarrow C}{\llbracket\mathcal{P}\rrbracket, \mathcal{A}_\mathcal{P}; [\vec{t}/\vec{x}](h \otimes \bigotimes\Delta \otimes \mathcal{R}_r \otimes \bigotimes\Delta^\sharp), r^\sharp(\vec{t}), \Delta' \longrightarrow C}\ (\otimes_L)^*}{\dfrac{\llbracket\mathcal{P}\rrbracket, \mathcal{A}_\mathcal{P}; [\vec{t}/\vec{x}]\mathcal{I}, [\vec{t}/\vec{x}]\Delta, \Delta' \longrightarrow C}{\dfrac{\llbracket\mathcal{P}\rrbracket, \mathcal{A}_\mathcal{P}; \mathcal{I}, [\vec{t}/\vec{x}]\Delta, \Delta' \longrightarrow C}{\llbracket\mathcal{P}\rrbracket, \mathcal{A}_\mathcal{P}; [\vec{t}/\vec{x}]\Delta, \Delta' \longrightarrow C}\ (\text{clone})}\ (\forall_L)^*}\ (\multimap_L^-)$$

Figure 11. llD^{Full} Inference Macro Rule

$\tilde{D}(x)$, the retraction rules in $\mathcal{R}_1^{(x)}$ have the additional responsibility of consuming witness atoms $A^\sharp(x)$ and $B^\sharp(x)$.

Figure 9 shows derivations for the llD^{Full} interpretation of our last example (Figure 8). The first derivation corresponds to the assertion of $B(5)$ starting from a state containing a single $A(5)$ and is similar to that in Figure 8 except we additionally infer witness atoms $A^\sharp(5)$ and $B^\sharp(5)$. The next derivation illustrates the subsequent retraction of $A(5)$. Now absorption rule $\mathcal{A}_A^{(5)}$ cannot be applied to $\tilde{A}(5)$ and $A(5)$ as there is a witness atom $A^\sharp(5)$ inhibiting $\mathcal{A}_A^{(5)}$. The only possible way forward is the application of retraction rule $\mathcal{R}_1^{(5)}$, which on top of producing retraction atom $\tilde{D(5)}$ and consuming inference witness $I^\sharp(5)$, consumes witness atoms $A^\sharp(5)$ and $B^\sharp(5)$, thereby unlocking the applicability of $\mathcal{A}_A^{(5)}$.

5.3 The llD^{Full} Interpretation

We now formalize the llD^{Full} interpretation of Datalog programs. For each atom representing a fact $p(\vec{t})$, we define its equal and opposite retraction atom $\tilde{p}(\vec{t})$. We will extend this notation to collections of atoms, hence for a multiset of atoms Δ, we denote a multiset of all equal and opposite retraction atoms of Δ by $\tilde{\Delta}$. Beside the rule witnesses $r^\sharp(\vec{x})$ of Section 4.1, for each atom $p(\vec{x})$ we have another type of witnesses, the *fact witness* $p^\sharp(\vec{x})$. While a rule witness $r^\sharp(\vec{t})$ witnesses the application of an inference rule instance of r, a fact $p^\sharp(\vec{t})$ witnesses a use of $p(\vec{t})$ to infer some other fact. Given a Datalog program $\mathcal{P}$, for each predicate p of some arity n, we define the set of all absorption rules $\mathcal{A}_\mathcal{P}$ as follows:

$$\mathcal{A}_\mathcal{P} = \wr \forall\vec{x}.p(\vec{x}) \otimes \tilde{p}(\vec{x}) \multimap_{p^\sharp(\vec{x})} (p^\sharp(\vec{x}) \multimap 1) \mid p \text{ in } \mathcal{P} \wr$$

Figure 10 formalizes the llD^{Full} interpretation of Datalog programs as the function $\llbracket - \rrbracket$. The main difference between this function and the function $\lceil - \rceil$ of llD^{Full-} is that Datalog clauses are inference rules that include two additional types of consequents. Specifically, a retraction rule which is an additive conjunction of linear implications defined by the function Ret and a tensor closure of inference fact witnesses derived from the antecedents of the inference rule. Altogether, given a Datalog clause $r : \forall\vec{x}.\ B \supset h$, its corresponding inference rule in llD^{Full} interpretation infers three types of bookkeeping information, namely, the retraction rule $\mathcal{R}_r$, the rule witness $r^\sharp(\vec{x})$ and fact witnesses $B^\sharp$.

$$\frac{a \notin \Delta \quad \llbracket\mathcal{P}\rrbracket, \mathcal{A}_\mathcal{P}; \Delta, a \longrightarrow \bigotimes\Delta' \quad Quiescent((\llbracket\mathcal{P}\rrbracket, \mathcal{A}_\mathcal{P}), \Delta')}{\Delta \overset{+a}{\Longrightarrow}{}^{LL}_{\llbracket\mathcal{P}\rrbracket} \Delta'}\ (Infer)$$

$$\frac{a \in \Delta \quad \llbracket\mathcal{P}\rrbracket, \mathcal{A}_\mathcal{P}; \Delta, \tilde{a} \longrightarrow \bigotimes\Delta' \quad Quiescent((\llbracket\mathcal{P}\rrbracket, \mathcal{A}_\mathcal{P}), \Delta')}{\Delta \overset{-a}{\Longrightarrow}{}^{LL}_{\llbracket\mathcal{P}\rrbracket} \Delta'}\ (Retract)$$

Figure 12. Assertion and Retraction, in llD^{Full}

Given Datalog program $\mathcal{P}$, multiset of facts $F \subseteq herbrand(\mathcal{P})$, multiset of retraction rules $\Delta^\mathcal{R}$ and multiset of witness atoms $\Delta^\sharp$, a llD^{Full} state of this Datalog program is an LV^{obs-} linear context $\llbracket F\rrbracket, \Delta^\mathcal{R}, \Delta^\sharp$. Given base facts $\mathcal{B} \subseteq herbrand_\mathcal{B}(\mathcal{P})$, the state $\lceil F\rceil, \Delta^\mathcal{R}, \Delta^\sharp$ is *reachable* from $\mathcal{B}$ if $\llbracket\mathcal{P}\rrbracket; \lceil\mathcal{B}\rceil \longrightarrow \bigotimes\llbracket F\rrbracket \otimes \bigotimes\Delta^\mathcal{R} \otimes \bigotimes\Delta^\sharp$ is derivable. Note that $\llbracket\mathcal{B}\rrbracket$ is always reachable from $\mathcal{B}$ — it is again called an *initial state*.

Similarly to Figure 6, Figure 11 defines the inference macro derivation rule for the llD^{Full} interpretation.

Figure 13 introduces the retraction macro step, which models the retraction of some fact h. As defined in Figure 10 by the function Ret, a retraction rule $\mathcal{R}_r$ is an additive conjunction of linear implications of the form $\tilde{a}_i \otimes r(\vec{t}) \otimes \bigotimes\Delta^\sharp \multimap \tilde{a}_i \otimes \tilde{h}$, which are reassertive (antecedent $\tilde{a}_i$ appears as consequent) and the only component that varies among the linear implications is the antecedent $\tilde{a}_i$. As such, retraction rule $\mathcal{R}_r$ can be viewed as a formula that reacts to any $\tilde{a}_i$ which is an antecedent of one of its linear implications and, when applied, consumes rule witness $r(\vec{t})$ and fact witnesses $\Delta^\sharp$, and produces $\tilde{h}$.

Figure 14 defines the last of the three macro derivation steps of the llD^{Full} interpretation. It models the absorption of an atom $p(\vec{t})$ and the equal and opposite $\tilde{p}(\vec{t})$, but only in the absence of any witness $p^\sharp(\vec{t})$.

Figure 12 illustrates the top-level formulation of the main goal of this paper, defining $\Longrightarrow^{LL}_{\llbracket\mathcal{P}\rrbracket}$, our linear logic specification of Datalog assertion and retraction in terms of LV^{obs-} derivations. In contrast to the logical specification $\Longrightarrow_\mathcal{P}$ in Figure 1 which defines assertion and retraction based on inferential closures of base facts, $\Longrightarrow^{LL}_{\llbracket\mathcal{P}\rrbracket}$ is defined as follows: the assertion of a new base fact a to a state Δ maps to the derivation with fact a inserted into the original state, while the retraction an existing base fact a from state Δ maps to a derivation with $\tilde{a}$ inserted. In both cases, we consider only resulting states which are quiescent. Theorem 12 in Section 5.5 states the correspondence of the llD^{Full} interpretation that formally prove the correctness this logical specification.

5.4 Cycles and Re-assertion

In this section, we analyze two aspects of the llD^{Full} interpretation. Specifically, we discuss *cycles* in Datalog inference and the need for *re-assertion* when doing retraction.

Quiescence in Cycles: One important issue to consider for the llD^{Full} interpretation, is whether quiescence can be achieved for Datalog programs with cycles. Figure 15 shows one such example modified from the graph example of Figure 7, along with its linear logic interpretation (we omit the absorption rules for brevity). This example attempts to generate reflexive paths $P(x, y)$ from base facts $E(x, y)$ that represent edges. Figure 15 also illustrates an LV^{obs-} derivation which represents the assertion of $E(4, 5)$ which in fact, achieves quiescence: We infer the facts $P(4, 5)$ and $P(5, 4)$ through inference rule instances $\mathcal{I}_1^{(4,5)}$ and $\mathcal{I}_2^{(4,5)}$, as well

$$\mathcal{P} \;=\; I_1 : \forall x, y.\ E(x,y) \supset P(x,y) \quad , \quad I_2 : \forall x, y.\ P(x,y) \supset P(y,x)$$

$$\begin{array}{lcl} \llbracket \mathcal{P} \rrbracket & = & \forall x, y.\ \mathcal{I}_1^{(x,y)},\ \forall x, y.\ \mathcal{I}_2^{(x,y)} \\ \mathcal{I}_1^{(x,y)} & = & E(x,y) \multimap_{I_1^\sharp(x,y)} P(x,y) \otimes E(x,y) \otimes E^\sharp(x,y) \otimes \mathcal{R}_1^{(x,y)} \\ \mathcal{R}_1^{(x,y)} & = & \tilde{E}(x,y) \otimes I_1^\sharp(x,y) \otimes E^\sharp(x,y) \multimap \tilde{P}(x,y) \otimes \tilde{E}(x,y) \\ \mathcal{I}_2^{(x,y)} & = & P(x,y) \multimap_{I_2^\sharp(x,y)} P(y,x) \otimes P(x,y) \otimes P^\sharp(x,y) \otimes \mathcal{R}_2^{(x,y)} \\ \mathcal{R}_2^{(x,y)} & = & \tilde{P}(x,y) \otimes I_2^\sharp(x,y) \otimes P^\sharp(x,y) \multimap \tilde{P}(y,x) \otimes \tilde{P}(x,y) \end{array}$$

Assertion of $E(4,5)$: $\emptyset \xrightarrow{+E(4,5)}_{\mathcal{P}} \Delta$ **where** $\Delta = \wr P(4,5), P(5,4), P(4,5), E(4,5), I_1^\sharp(4,5), I_2^\sharp(4,5), I_2^\sharp(5,4), ..\int$

$$\dfrac{\dfrac{\dfrac{\dfrac{}{\llbracket \mathcal{P} \rrbracket, \mathcal{A}_\mathcal{P};\ P(4,5), P(5,4), P(4,5), E(4,5), I_1^\sharp(4,5), I_2^\sharp(4,5), I_2^\sharp(5,4), .. \longrightarrow \bigotimes \Delta}\ (obs)}{\llbracket \mathcal{P} \rrbracket, \mathcal{A}_\mathcal{P};\ P(5,4), P(4,5), E(4,5), I_1^\sharp(4,5), I_2^\sharp(4,5), .. \longrightarrow \bigotimes \Delta}\ \mathcal{I}_2^{(5,4)}\ (\mathcal{I}_L)}{\llbracket \mathcal{P} \rrbracket, \mathcal{A}_\mathcal{P};\ P(4,5), E(4,5), I_1^\sharp(4,5), .. \longrightarrow \bigotimes \Delta}\ \mathcal{I}_2^{(4,5)}\ (\mathcal{I}_L)}{\llbracket \mathcal{P} \rrbracket, \mathcal{A}_\mathcal{P};\ E(4,5) \longrightarrow \bigotimes \Delta}\ \mathcal{I}_1^{(4,5)}\ (\mathcal{I}_L)$$

Figure 15. Example of Quiescence in the Presence of Cycles

Let $\mathcal{R}_i \equiv \tilde{a}_i \otimes r(\vec{t}) \otimes \bigotimes \Delta^\sharp \multimap \tilde{a}_i \otimes \tilde{h}$

$$\dfrac{\llbracket \mathcal{P} \rrbracket, \mathcal{A}_\mathcal{P}; \tilde{a}_k, \tilde{h}, \Delta \longrightarrow C}{\llbracket \mathcal{P} \rrbracket, \mathcal{A}_\mathcal{P}; \tilde{a}_k, \&_{i=1}^n \mathcal{R}_i, r(\vec{t}), \Delta^\sharp, \Delta \longrightarrow C}\ (\mathcal{R}_L)$$

for some $k \geq 1$ and $k \leq n$, which decomposes into:

$$\dfrac{\dfrac{\dfrac{\llbracket \mathcal{P} \rrbracket, \mathcal{A}_\mathcal{P}; \tilde{a}_k, \tilde{h}, \Delta \longrightarrow C}{\llbracket \mathcal{P} \rrbracket, \mathcal{A}_\mathcal{P}; \tilde{a}_k \otimes \tilde{h}, \Delta \longrightarrow C}\ (\otimes_L)}{\llbracket \mathcal{P} \rrbracket, \mathcal{A}_\mathcal{P}; \tilde{a}_k, \mathcal{R}_k, r(\vec{t}), \Delta^\sharp, \Delta \longrightarrow C}\ (\multimap_L)}{\llbracket \mathcal{P} \rrbracket, \mathcal{A}_\mathcal{P}; \tilde{a}_k, \&_{i=1}^n \mathcal{R}_i, r(\vec{t}), \Delta^\sharp, \Delta \longrightarrow C}\ (\&_L)^*$$

Figure 13. llD^{Full} Retraction Macro Rule

Let $\forall \vec{x}.\ p(\vec{x}) \otimes \tilde{p}(\vec{x}) \multimap_{p^\sharp(\vec{x})} (p^\sharp(\vec{x}) \multimap 1) \in \mathcal{A}_\mathcal{P}$

$$\dfrac{p^\sharp(\vec{t}) \notin \Delta \quad \llbracket \mathcal{P} \rrbracket, \mathcal{A}_\mathcal{P}; \Delta \longrightarrow C}{\llbracket \mathcal{P} \rrbracket, \mathcal{A}_\mathcal{P}; p(\vec{t}), \tilde{p}(\vec{t}), \Delta \longrightarrow C}\ (\mathcal{A}_L)$$

which decomposes into:

$$\dfrac{\dfrac{\dfrac{p^\sharp(\vec{t}) \notin \Delta \quad \dfrac{\dfrac{\llbracket \mathcal{P} \rrbracket, \mathcal{A}_\mathcal{P}; \Delta \longrightarrow C}{\llbracket \mathcal{P} \rrbracket, \mathcal{A}_\mathcal{P}; 1, \Delta \longrightarrow C}\ (1_L)}{\llbracket \mathcal{P} \rrbracket, \mathcal{A}_\mathcal{P}; (p^\sharp(\vec{t}) \multimap 1), p^\sharp(\vec{t}), \Delta \longrightarrow C}\ (\multimap_L)}{\llbracket \mathcal{P} \rrbracket, \mathcal{A}_\mathcal{P};\ (p(\vec{t}) \otimes \tilde{p}(\vec{t}) \multimap_{p^\sharp(\vec{t})} (p^\sharp(\vec{t}) \multimap 1)), p(\vec{t}), \tilde{p}(\vec{t}), \Delta \longrightarrow C}\ (\multimap_L^-)}{\llbracket \mathcal{P} \rrbracket, \mathcal{A}_\mathcal{P}; \mathcal{A}_p, p(\vec{t}), \tilde{p}(\vec{t}), \Delta \longrightarrow C}\ (\forall_L)^*}{\llbracket \mathcal{P} \rrbracket, \mathcal{A}_\mathcal{P}; p(\vec{t}), \tilde{p}(\vec{t}), \Delta \longrightarrow C}\ (clone)$$

Figure 14. llD^{Full} Absorption Macro Rule

as an additional copy of $P(4,5)$ through $\mathcal{I}_2^{(5,4)}$, before we reach quiescence. We omit fact witnesses and retraction rules as they are inessential in this discussion. In general, as long as Datalog clauses are well-formed and the set Σ of all possible constants is finite, the llD^{Full} interpretation of Datalog programs will reach quiescence under LV^{obs-} derivations. This is because the possible combinations of rule instances are finite, and since for each rule instance we can apply it at most once in a derivation, all LV^{obs-} derivations of well-formed Datalog programs reach quiescence.

Re-assertion during Retraction: In some cases, re-assertion of facts occurs during retraction while working towards quiescence. Figure 16 illustrates a Datalog program which exhibits such a behavior. From either base facts $A(x)$ or $B(x)$, we can infer $C(x)$. We consider an initial state Δ where $A(2)$ and $B(2)$ has been asserted. Hence, inference rule instances $\mathcal{I}_1^{(2)}$, $\mathcal{I}_2^{(2)}$ and $\mathcal{I}_3^{(2)}$ has been applied before reaching quiescence at state Δ. Note that while we have two copies of $C(2)$ (from $\mathcal{I}_1^{(2)}$ and $\mathcal{I}_2^{(2)}$), we only have one copy of $D(2)$, since rule instance $\mathcal{I}_3^{(2)}$ is only permitted to be applied once. Next we consider the situation when $A(2)$ is retracted, triggering the application of retraction rules $\mathcal{R}_1^{(2)}$ and $\mathcal{R}_3^{(2)}$ which ultimately absorbs $A(2)$, $C(2)$ and $D(2)$. This leads us to a seemingly inconsistent state, where $B(2)$ and $C(2)$ exists, yet $D(2)$ has been completely retracted as part of the retraction closure of $A(2)$. However, quiescence is only achieved when inference rule instance $\mathcal{I}_3^{(2)}$ is re-applied, re-asserting another copy of $D(2)$. While re-assertion guarantees the re-completion of assertion closures of the llD^{Full} interpretation, it arguably adds overheads. One of our future objectives is to refine the llD^{Full} interpretation to overcome the need for re-assertion during retraction.

5.5 Correctness

In this section, we highlight the proofs of correspondence of the llD^{Full} linear logic interpretation of Datalog program. Details of the proofs can be found in the full version of this paper [12].

For any LV^{obs-} sequents constructed from the llD^{Full} interpretations of Datalog assertion, we can always find a normalized LV^{obs-} derivation that consists only of $(\mathcal{I}_L)$ and (obs) derivation rules. Similarly, for sequents from llD^{Full} interpretations of Datalog retraction, we can find normalized derivations that consist strictly only of $(\mathcal{I}_L)$, $(\mathcal{R}_L)$, $(\mathcal{A}_L)$ and (obs) derivation rules. This will simplify the proof of the correctness of our interpretation.

$$\begin{array}{lcl} \mathcal{P} & = & I_1 : \forall x.\, A(x) \supset C(x) \quad I_2 : \forall x.\, B(x) \supset C(x) \quad I_3 : \forall x.\, C(x) \supset D(x) \\ \llbracket \mathcal{P} \rrbracket & = & \forall x.\, \mathcal{I}_1^{(x)},\ \forall x.\, \mathcal{I}_2^{(x)},\ \forall x.\, \mathcal{I}_3^{(x)} \end{array}$$

$$\begin{array}{lcl lcl} \mathcal{I}_1^{(x)} & = & A(x) \multimap_{I_1^\sharp(x)} C(x) \otimes A(x) \otimes A^\sharp(x) \otimes \mathcal{R}_1^{(x)} & \mathcal{R}_1^{(x)} & = & \tilde{A}(x) \otimes I_1^\sharp(x) \otimes A^\sharp(x) \multimap \tilde{C}(x) \otimes \tilde{A}(x) \\ \mathcal{I}_2^{(x)} & = & B(x) \multimap_{I_2^\sharp(x)} C(x) \otimes B(x) \otimes B^\sharp(x) \otimes \mathcal{R}_2^{(x)} & \mathcal{R}_2^{(x)} & = & \tilde{B}(x) \otimes I_2^\sharp(x) \otimes B^\sharp(x) \multimap \tilde{C}(x) \otimes \tilde{B}(x) \\ \mathcal{I}_3^{(x)} & = & C(x) \multimap_{I_3^\sharp(x)} D(x) \otimes C(x) \otimes C^\sharp(x) \otimes \mathcal{R}_3^{(x)} & \mathcal{R}_3^{(x)} & = & \tilde{C}(x) \otimes I_3^\sharp(x) \otimes C^\sharp(x) \multimap \tilde{D}(x) \otimes \tilde{C}(x) \end{array}$$

Retraction of $A(2)$: $\Delta \xRightarrow{-A(2)}{}^{LL}_{\llbracket \mathcal{P} \rrbracket} \Delta'$ **where** $\Delta' = \lbag D(2), B(2), C(2), I_3^\sharp(2), I_2^\sharp(2), C^\sharp(2), B^\sharp(2), \mathcal{R}_3^{(2)}, \mathcal{R}_2^{(2)} \rbag$

$$\llbracket \mathcal{P} \rrbracket, \mathcal{A}_\mathcal{P};\ D(2), B(2), C(2), I_3^\sharp(2), I_2^\sharp(2), C^\sharp(2), B^\sharp(2), \mathcal{R}_3^{(2)}, \mathcal{R}_2^{(2)} \longrightarrow \bigotimes \Delta'$$

$$\mathcal{I}_3^{(2)} \quad (\mathcal{I}_L)$$

$$\llbracket \mathcal{P} \rrbracket, \mathcal{A}_\mathcal{P}; B(2), C(2), I_2^\sharp(2), B^\sharp(2), \mathcal{R}_2^{(2)} \longrightarrow \bigotimes \Delta'$$

$$\mathcal{A}_C^{(2)} \quad (\mathcal{A}_L)$$

$$\llbracket \mathcal{P} \rrbracket, \mathcal{A}_\mathcal{P}; \tilde{C}(2), B(2), C(2), C(2), I_2^\sharp(2), B^\sharp(2), \mathcal{R}_2^{(2)} \longrightarrow \bigotimes \Delta'$$

$$\mathcal{A}_D^{(2)} \quad (\mathcal{A}_L)$$

$$\llbracket \mathcal{P} \rrbracket, \mathcal{A}_\mathcal{P}; \tilde{D}(2), \tilde{C}(2), B(2), C(2), C(2), D(2), I_2^\sharp(2), B^\sharp(2), \mathcal{R}_2^{(2)} \longrightarrow \bigotimes \Delta'$$

$$\mathcal{R}_3^{(2)} \quad (\mathcal{R}_L)$$

$$\llbracket \mathcal{P} \rrbracket, \mathcal{A}_\mathcal{P}; \tilde{C}(2), B(2), C(2), C(2), D(2), I_2^\sharp(2), I_3^\sharp(2), B^\sharp(2), C^\sharp(2), \mathcal{R}_2^{(2)}, \mathcal{R}_3^{(2)} \longrightarrow \bigotimes \Delta'$$

$$\mathcal{A}_A^{(2)} \quad (\mathcal{A}_L)$$

$$\llbracket \mathcal{P} \rrbracket, \mathcal{A}_\mathcal{P}; \tilde{C}(2), \tilde{A}(2), A(2), B(2), C(2), C(2), D(2), I_2^\sharp(2), I_3^\sharp(2), B^\sharp(2), C^\sharp(2), \mathcal{R}_2^{(2)}, \mathcal{R}_3^{(2)} \longrightarrow \bigotimes \Delta'$$

$$\mathcal{R}_1^{(2)} \quad (\mathcal{R}_L)$$

$$\llbracket \mathcal{P} \rrbracket, \mathcal{A}_\mathcal{P}; \begin{array}{l} \tilde{A}(2), A(2), B(2), C(2), C(2), D(2), I_1^\sharp(2), I_2^\sharp(2), I_3^\sharp(2), \\ A^\sharp(2), B^\sharp(2), C^\sharp(2), \mathcal{R}_1^{(2)}, \mathcal{R}_2^{(2)}, \mathcal{R}_3^{(2)} \end{array} \longrightarrow \bigotimes \Delta'$$

Figure 16. Example of re-assertion during retraction

LEMMA 6 (Normalized Derivations). *Given Datalog program $\mathcal{P}$, llD^{Full} states $\llbracket F_1 \rrbracket, \Delta_1^\mathcal{R}, \Delta_1^\sharp$ and $\llbracket F_2 \rrbracket, \Delta_2^\mathcal{R}, \Delta_2^\sharp$, a LV^{obs-} derivation $\llbracket \mathcal{P} \rrbracket, \mathcal{A}_\mathcal{P}; \llbracket F_1 \rrbracket, \Delta_1^\mathcal{R}, \Delta_1^\sharp \longrightarrow \bigotimes \llbracket F_1 \rrbracket \otimes \bigotimes \Delta_2^\mathcal{R} \otimes \bigotimes \Delta_2^\sharp$ has a proof consisting of only applications of $(\mathcal{I}_L)$, $(\mathcal{R}_L)$, $(\mathcal{A}_L)$ and (obs) derivation rules.*

For every llD^{Full} derivation that models the assertion of facts (excluding retraction), we have a corresponding llD^{Assert} derivation and vice versa. Both directions depend on the fact that witness facts and retraction rules have no effects on the assertion of new facts.

LEMMA 7 (Soundness and Completeness of Assertion). *Given a Datalog Program $\mathcal{P}$, for any fact base $\mathcal{B}$, multiset of facts $F \subseteq herbrand(\mathcal{P})$, multiset of rule witnesses $\Delta_R^\sharp$, multiset of fact witnesses $\Delta_F^\sharp$ and multiset of retraction rules $\Delta^\mathcal{R}$,*

$$\begin{array}{l} \llbracket \mathcal{P} \rrbracket, \mathcal{A}_\mathcal{P}; \llbracket \mathcal{B} \rrbracket \longrightarrow \bigotimes \llbracket F \rrbracket \otimes \bigotimes \Delta^\mathcal{R} \otimes \bigotimes \Delta_R^\sharp \otimes \bigotimes \Delta_F^\sharp \\ \textit{if and only if} \quad \lceil \mathcal{P} \rceil; \lceil \mathcal{B} \rceil \longrightarrow \bigotimes \lceil F \rceil \otimes \bigotimes \Delta_R^\sharp \end{array}$$

Similarly to Theorem 5, for any fact base $\mathcal{B}$, we can derive a quiescent state which is an inferential closure of $\mathcal{B}$. Further more this there can only be one such quiescent state.

THEOREM 8 (Correctness of Assertion). *Let $\mathcal{P}$ be a Datalog program and $\mathcal{B}$ a collection of base facts,*

1. *There is $\llbracket F \rrbracket, \Delta^\mathcal{R}, \Delta^\sharp$ such that $\llbracket \mathcal{P} \rrbracket, \mathcal{A}_\mathcal{P}; \llbracket \mathcal{B} \rrbracket \longrightarrow \bigotimes \llbracket F \rrbracket \otimes \bigotimes \Delta^\mathcal{R} \otimes \bigotimes \Delta^\sharp$ and $Quiescent((\llbracket \mathcal{P} \rrbracket, \mathcal{A}_\mathcal{P}), (\llbracket F \rrbracket, \Delta^\mathcal{R}, \Delta^\sharp))$ and $set(F) = \mathcal{P}(\mathcal{B})$.*
2. *For any state Δ, if we have $\llbracket \mathcal{P} \rrbracket; \llbracket \mathcal{B} \rrbracket \longrightarrow \bigotimes \llbracket \Delta \rrbracket$ and $Quiescent((\llbracket \mathcal{P} \rrbracket, \mathcal{A}_\mathcal{P}), \Delta)$, then there is $\Delta^\mathcal{R}, \Delta^\sharp$ such that $\Delta = \lceil F \rceil, \Delta^\mathcal{R}, \Delta^\sharp$ and $set(F) = \mathcal{P}(\mathcal{B})$.*

Proof: This follows from Lemma 7, which states the correspondence between llD^{Full} and llD^{Assert} assertions. As such, since Theorem 5 holds, then we must have Theorem 8 as well. □

While $(\mathcal{I}_L)$ macro derivation rules in llD^{Full} corresponds to llD^{Assert}, applications of the $(\mathcal{I}_L)$ macro rules in llD^{Full} that models assertion of facts provides certain properties that facilitates the retraction of facts. Lemma 9 states these properties of assertion. Similarly, retraction rules and absorption rules are defined in a manner which provides some important properties that help to guarantee the correctness of retraction. Lemma 10 formally asserts these properties.

LEMMA 9 (Properties of Assertion). *Given a Datalog Program $\mathcal{P}$, for any llD^{Full} state $\Delta, \Delta^\mathcal{R}, \Delta^\sharp$, and for some Δ', if $\llbracket \mathcal{P} \rrbracket, \mathcal{A}_\mathcal{P}; \Delta, \Delta^\mathcal{R}, \Delta^\sharp \longrightarrow \bigotimes \Delta'$ and $Quiescent((\llbracket \mathcal{P} \rrbracket, \mathcal{A}_\mathcal{P}), \Delta')$ we have the following properties:*

1. *For each $a \in \Delta'$ such that $a \in herbrand_I(\mathcal{P})$ (i.e. a is inferred), there must exist some retraction rule $\&_{i=1}^n(\tilde{a}_i \otimes r(\vec{t}) \otimes \bigotimes B^\sharp \multimap \tilde{a}_i \otimes \tilde{h}) \in \Delta'$ such that $a = h$.*
2. *For each retraction rule $\&_{i=1}^n(\tilde{a}_i \otimes r(\vec{t}) \otimes \bigotimes B^\sharp \multimap \tilde{a}_i \otimes \tilde{h}) \in \Delta'$, we must have for each $\tilde{a}_i$ such that equal and opposite $a_i \in \Delta'$.*
3. *For each retraction rule $\mathcal{R} = \&_{i=1}^n(\tilde{a}_i \otimes r(\vec{t}) \otimes \bigotimes B^\sharp \multimap \tilde{a}_i \otimes \tilde{h})$, $\mathcal{R} \in \Delta'$ if and only if $B^\sharp \in \Delta'$ and $r(\vec{t}) \in \Delta'$ as well.*
4. *Always exists some Δ' such that $Quiescent((\mathcal{P}, \mathcal{A}_\mathcal{P}), \Delta')$.*

Proof: The proof of these properties rely entirely on the definition of inference rules in $\llbracket \mathcal{P} \rrbracket$ (Figure 11). Recall that they are of the form: $\forall \vec{x}.\ \bigotimes B \multimap_{r(\vec{x})} h \otimes \bigotimes B \otimes \bigotimes B^\sharp \otimes \mathcal{R}$ such that

$\mathcal{R} = \&_{i=1}^{n}(\tilde{a}_i \otimes r(\vec{x}) \otimes \bigotimes B^\sharp \multimap \tilde{a}_i \otimes \tilde{h})$. Details of the proof for each property follow.

1. For any fact $a \in \Delta'$, if a is not a base fact then it must be the product of an application of an inference rule instance from $\llbracket \mathcal{P} \rrbracket$. As such, by the definition of inference rule, for every $h = a$ fact inferred, we have a corresponding retraction rule $\mathcal{R} = \&_{i=1}^{n}(\tilde{a}_i \otimes r(\vec{x}) \otimes \bigotimes B^\sharp \multimap \tilde{a}_i \otimes \tilde{a})$ as a by-product. Hence we have property (1).
2. Since, by definition, retraction rules are only introduced by inference rules, each inference rule $\forall \vec{x}.\ \bigotimes B \multimap_{r(\vec{x})} h \otimes \bigotimes B \otimes \bigotimes B^\sharp \otimes \mathcal{R}$ introduces retraction rule $\mathcal{R}$ such that each $\tilde{a}_i$ that appears in each implication of the retraction rule is the equal and opposite of a unique atom in B. Hence we have property (2).
3. Similarly, since retraction rules are only introduced by inference rules, by the definition of inference rule, each retraction rule $\mathcal{R} = \&_{i=1}^{n}(\tilde{a}_i \otimes r(\vec{x}) \otimes \bigotimes B^\sharp \multimap \tilde{a}_i \otimes \tilde{h})$ is introduced explicitly with $B^\sharp$ as accompanying consequents, while the formulation of $(\multimap_L^-)$ rule dictates the introduction of inhibiting atom $r(\vec{t})$. Hence we have property (3).
4. We argue that all inference rules are guarded implication rules inhibited by a unique rule instance $r(\vec{t})$. Since all well-formed Datalog program we consider have finite number of clauses and finite constants, there are a finite number of rule instances $r(\vec{t})$. As such, we can apply a finite number of $(\mathcal{I}_L)$ macro derivation steps and hence all derivations modeling assertion will reach quiescence.

This concludes the proof of this lemma. □

LEMMA 10 (Properties of Retraction). *Given a Datalog program $\mathcal{P}$, for any llD^{Full} state that represent an intermediate state of retraction $\Delta, \Delta^{\mathcal{R}}, \Delta^\sharp$ such that $\Delta = \llbracket F \rrbracket, \llbracket a \rrbracket, \llbracket F' \rrbracket, \llbracket \tilde{F'} \rrbracket, \llbracket \tilde{a} \rrbracket$ and $F, F' \subseteq herbrand(\mathcal{P})$ and $a \in herbrand(\mathcal{P})$, and for some Δ', if we have the sequent $\llbracket \mathcal{P} \rrbracket, \mathcal{A}_{\mathcal{P}}; \Delta, \Delta^{\mathcal{R}}, \Delta^\sharp \longrightarrow \bigotimes \Delta'$, we have the following properties:*

1. *For each retraction rule $\mathcal{R} = \&_{i=1}^{n}(\tilde{a}_i \otimes r(\vec{t}) \otimes \bigotimes B^\sharp \multimap \tilde{a}_i \otimes \tilde{h})$, $\mathcal{R} \in \Delta'$ if and only if $B^\sharp \in \Delta'$ and $r(\vec{t}) \in \Delta'$.*
2. *If $\tilde{a} \notin \Delta'$, then there does not exist any retraction rule $\&_{i=1}^{n}(\tilde{a}_i \otimes r(\vec{t}) \otimes \bigotimes B^\sharp \multimap \tilde{a}_i \otimes \tilde{h}) \in \Delta'$, such that $\tilde{a} = \tilde{a}_i$ for some $i \geq 1$ and $i \leq n$.*
3. *There exists some Δ' such that $Quiescent((\mathcal{P}, \mathcal{A}_{\mathcal{P}}), \Delta')$.*
4. *If $Quiescent((\llbracket \mathcal{P} \rrbracket, \mathcal{A}_{\mathcal{P}}), \Delta')$, then there not exists any $\tilde{b} \in \Delta'$.*

Proof: The proofs of these properties rely on guarantees provided by assertions (Lemma 9) and the definition of retraction rules and absorption rules (Figure 13 and 14 respectively). Details of the proof for each property follow.

1. Since all retraction rules are only introduced by inference rules and $\Delta, \Delta^{\mathcal{R}}, \Delta^\sharp$ is a reachable state, property 3 of Lemma 9 guarantees that initially, each retraction rule in $\&_{i=1}^{n}(\tilde{a}_i \otimes r(\vec{t}) \otimes \bigotimes B^\sharp \multimap \tilde{a}_i \otimes \tilde{h}) \in \Delta^{\mathcal{R}}$ has a complete set of witnesses in $\Delta^\sharp$ (i.e. $r(\vec{t}), B^\sharp \subseteq \Delta^\sharp$). During retraction, each application of a retraction $\mathcal{R}$ consumes the retraction rule itself as well as the exact set of witnesses $B^\sharp$ and $r(\vec{t})$ (and nothing more) which was introduced together with $\mathcal{R}$ in the same inference rule instance. Hence, the property that any remaining retraction rule has its full set of witnesses in the context is preserved throughout intermediate retraction states.
2. If $\tilde{a} \notin \Delta'$, absorption rule $a \otimes \tilde{a} \multimap_{a^\sharp} (a^\sharp \multimap 1)$ must have been applied, since it is the only way to consume an $\tilde{a}$. In order for the absorption rule to apply, the context must not have had any occurrence of $a^\sharp$, and the only way to have achieved this is that all retraction rules $\&_{i=1}^{n}(\tilde{a}_i \otimes r(\vec{t}) \otimes \bigotimes B^\sharp \multimap \tilde{a}_i \otimes \tilde{h})$ such that $\tilde{a} = \tilde{a}_i$ for some $i \geq 1$ and $i \leq n$ and $a^\sharp \in B^\sharp$ were applied to consume all instance of $a^\sharp$, hence allowing the absorption rule to be applied.
3. We argue that retraction rules are linear, hence there always exist a derivation which involves an exhaustive and finite application of the retraction macro steps $(\mathcal{R}_L)$. Since we can apply a finite number of $(\mathcal{R}_L)$ rules, we can generate a finite numbers of retraction atoms $\tilde{a}$. As such, we can apply a finite number of absorption $(\mathcal{A}_L)$ macro derivation steps as well. Yet in retraction, we may need to reassert facts via $(\mathcal{I}_L)$. By property (4) of Lemma 9 we can conclude that there are also finite a number of reassertion steps. Hence we can always reach quiescence.
4. From 1, we argue that all retraction rules at any intermediate reachable states always have their accompanying witnesses $B^\sharp$ and $r(\vec{t})$. As such we can exhaustively apply retraction rules to remove all witnesses inhibiting absorption rules from being applicable, after which all $\tilde{b} \in \Delta$ will be consumed. Hence if Δ' is quiescent, we must have removed all retraction atom $\tilde{b}$.

This concludes the proof of this lemma. □

Inserting a set of retraction atoms $\tilde{\mathcal{B}}$ in a llD^{Full} state $\llbracket F \rrbracket, \llbracket \mathcal{B} \rrbracket, \Delta^{\mathcal{R}}, \Delta^\sharp$ will ultimately result in the derivation of the state Δ_1 which excludes $\llbracket \mathcal{B} \rrbracket$. Recall that we disallow the insertion of a retraction atom $\tilde{b}$ if b does not exist in the state.

THEOREM 11 (Correctness of Retraction). *Given a Datalog Program $\mathcal{P}$ and a base fact $b \in herbrand_B(\mathcal{P})$ and llD^{Full} states Δ_1,*

1. *Exists some state $\llbracket F \rrbracket, \Delta^{\mathcal{R}}, \Delta^\sharp$, and Δ_1, Δ_2, such that*

$$\begin{array}{l} \llbracket \mathcal{P} \rrbracket, \mathcal{A}_{\mathcal{P}}; \llbracket F \rrbracket, \llbracket b \rrbracket, \Delta^{\mathcal{R}}, \Delta^\sharp \longrightarrow \bigotimes \Delta_1 \otimes \bigotimes \Delta_2 \text{ and} \\ Quiescent((\llbracket \mathcal{P} \rrbracket, \mathcal{A}_{\mathcal{P}}), (\Delta_1, \Delta_2)) \text{ and} \\ \llbracket \mathcal{P} \rrbracket, \mathcal{A}_{\mathcal{P}}; \llbracket F \rrbracket, \Delta^{\mathcal{R}}, \Delta^\sharp \longrightarrow \bigotimes \Delta_1 \text{ and} \\ Quiescent((\llbracket \mathcal{P} \rrbracket, \mathcal{A}_{\mathcal{P}}), \Delta_1) \text{ and} \\ \llbracket \mathcal{P} \rrbracket, \mathcal{A}_{\mathcal{P}}; \llbracket F \rrbracket, \llbracket b \rrbracket, \Delta^{\mathcal{R}}, \Delta^\sharp, \llbracket \tilde{b} \rrbracket \longrightarrow \bigotimes \Delta_1 \end{array}$$

2. *For all states $\llbracket F \rrbracket, \Delta^{\mathcal{R}}, \Delta^\sharp$, there exists some Δ_1, Δ_2, such that*

$$\begin{array}{ll} \textit{if} & \llbracket \mathcal{P} \rrbracket, \mathcal{A}_{\mathcal{P}}; \llbracket F \rrbracket, \llbracket b \rrbracket, \Delta^{\mathcal{R}}, \Delta^\sharp, \llbracket \tilde{b} \rrbracket \longrightarrow \bigotimes \Delta_1 \\ & \text{and } Quiescent((\llbracket \mathcal{P} \rrbracket, \mathcal{A}_{\mathcal{P}}), \Delta_1) \\ \textit{then} & \llbracket \mathcal{P} \rrbracket, \mathcal{A}_{\mathcal{P}}; \llbracket F \rrbracket, \llbracket b \rrbracket, \Delta^{\mathcal{R}}, \Delta^\sharp \longrightarrow \bigotimes \Delta_1 \otimes \bigotimes \Delta_2 \\ & \text{and } Quiescent((\llbracket \mathcal{P} \rrbracket, \mathcal{A}_{\mathcal{P}}), (\Delta_1, \Delta_2)) \\ & \text{and } \llbracket \mathcal{P} \rrbracket, \mathcal{A}_{\mathcal{P}}; \llbracket F \rrbracket, \Delta^{\mathcal{R}}, \Delta^\sharp \longrightarrow \bigotimes \Delta_1 \end{array}$$

Proof: First, by relying on property 4 of Lemma 9, we can conclude that there exists an assertion state Δ_1, Δ_2 such that $Quiescent((\llbracket \mathcal{P} \rrbracket, \mathcal{A}_{\mathcal{P}}), (\Delta_1, \Delta_2))$ and by property 3 of Lemma 10 we can conclude that there exists a retraction state Δ_1 such that $Quiescent((\llbracket \mathcal{P} \rrbracket, \mathcal{A}_{\mathcal{P}}), \Delta_1)$. We now need to show that there exist such quiescent assertion and retraction states where $\llbracket \mathcal{P} \rrbracket, \mathcal{A}_{\mathcal{P}}; \llbracket F \rrbracket, \llbracket b \rrbracket, \Delta^{\mathcal{R}}, \Delta^\sharp, \llbracket \tilde{b} \rrbracket \longrightarrow \bigotimes \Delta_1$. We assume that $\llbracket \mathcal{P} \rrbracket, \mathcal{A}_{\mathcal{P}}; \llbracket F \rrbracket, \llbracket b \rrbracket, \Delta^{\mathcal{R}}, \Delta^\sharp, \llbracket \tilde{b} \rrbracket \longrightarrow \bigotimes \Delta_3$ for some Δ_3, then proceed to show that if $\Delta_1 = \Delta_3$, our assumption still holds. Property 4 of Lemma 10 states that quiescent retraction states have no retraction atoms, hence we know for sure Δ_3 contains no retraction atoms. By property 2 of Lemma 10, since $\tilde{b} \notin \Delta_3$, we can safely assert that no retraction rule $\mathcal{R} = \&_{i=1}^{n}(\tilde{a}_i \otimes r(\vec{t}) \otimes \bigotimes B^\sharp \multimap \tilde{a}_i \otimes \tilde{h}) \in \Delta^{\mathcal{R}}$ such that $\tilde{a}_i = \tilde{b}$ for some i is in Δ_3 as well. With all such retraction rule removed, property 1 of Lemma 10 further states that corresponding witnesses of these retraction rules are not present in Δ_3 either. Finally, we know that to remove all retraction atoms $\tilde{a}$ from the context, Δ_3 was the result of several $(\mathcal{A}_L)$ macro derivation steps that removed b and its consequent facts. Hence, we can conclude that Δ_3 can be intermediately obtained by removing b and all its consequents (facts, retraction rules and witnesses) from $\llbracket F \rrbracket, \Delta^{\mathcal{R}}, \Delta^{\sharp}$, yielding some Δ_4 which contains no retraction atoms. From Δ_4 we can apply $(\mathcal{I}_L)$ macro steps to reassert facts common to b's consequents and by Theorem 5 we can guarantee that we can find a unique quiescent state Δ_3 since this quiescent state must be unique, hence $\Delta_1 = \Delta_3$. □

Corollary 12 formally asserts the bridge between our llD^{Full} interpretation of Datalog in linear logic LV^{obs-} and the traditional interpretation (Figure 1 and 12). It is directly derived from Theorems 8 and 11.

COROLLARY 12 (Correctness). *Given a Datalog Program $\mathcal{P}$, for reachable states $\Delta_1, \Delta_1^{\mathcal{R}}, \Delta_1^{\sharp}$ and $\Delta_2, \Delta_2^{\mathcal{R}}, \Delta_2^{\sharp}$ such that $\Delta_1 = \llbracket \mathcal{P}(\mathcal{B}_1) \rrbracket$ and $\Delta_2 = \llbracket \mathcal{P}(\mathcal{B}_2) \rrbracket$, then we have the following:*

$$(\Delta_1, \Delta_1^{\mathcal{R}}, \Delta_1^{\sharp}) \overset{\alpha}{\Longrightarrow}{}^{LL}_{\llbracket \mathcal{P} \rrbracket} (\Delta_2, \Delta_2^{\mathcal{R}}, \Delta_2^{\sharp}) \text{ iff } \mathcal{P}(\mathcal{B}_1) \overset{\alpha}{\Longrightarrow}_{\mathcal{P}} \mathcal{P}(\mathcal{B}_2)$$

6. Related Work

Early work on Datalog focused on efficient support for querying the logical consequences of a static fact base [4] although some of it also supported assertions. Examples include the semi-naive strategy [2], QSQ [19], and magic sets [3]. Recently, there has been a trend in the parallel and distributed programming research community to develop high-level declarative programming languages which are based on (or inspired by) Datalog. For instance, NetLog [10] and Network Datalog (*NDLog*) [14] target the development of networking protocols, Meld [1] for programming of large ensembles of embedded robotic devices, and the system in [13] enables distributed user authentication. To varying extents, all of these works credit the declarative nature of Datalog as a main motivation, mitigating the notorious complexities of parallel and distributed programming. These new application areas are characterized by frequent assertions *and* retractions. For example, the Nexcel language of [5] uses a dialect of Datalog to compute derived data in a spreadsheet as the user types.

These works contributed efficient algorithms and implementations to efficiently compute inferential closures incrementally as facts are dynamically added or removed [1, 7, 11, 14, 16]. However we are unaware of any work that bridges these algorithms back to formal logic. As such, our efforts here complement these developments.

7. Conclusions and Future Work

In this paper, we have given a logical interpretation of Datalog in linear logic, which captures assertion and retraction of facts within the confines of logic. It directly maps assertion and retraction steps to derivations in linear logic, thereby functioning not only as an abstract specification, but as an operational blueprint for practical implementations of Datalog systems. Indeed, we prove the llD^{Full} interpretation corresponds with the traditional logic interpretation of Datalog programs.

In the future, we plan to implement a Datalog system based on llD^{Full} and exploiting ideas in [6]. We believe that this can be a foundationally strong approach for deriving expressive and powerful concurrent logic programming languages to be applied to highly parallel systems such as Claytronics [1]. We also wish to further investigate re-assertion during retraction, briefly discussed in Section 5.4. Specifically, we are interested in exploring the possibility of deriving a linear logic interpretation of Datalog programs that removes the need for re-assertion during fact retraction, thereby providing a more streamlined and efficient operational semantics for practical implementation. We intend to explore the use of other variants of linear logic, in the attempt to streamline our interpretation of Datalog. (E.g. representing Datalog facts as consumable subexponentials [17] and using polarized presentations of linear logic).

References

[1] M. P. Ashley-Rollman, P. Lee, S. C. Goldstein, P. Pillai, and J. D. Campbell. A language for large ensembles of independently executing nodes. In *Proc. of ICLP'09*, volume 5649/2009, pages 265–280. Springer-Verlag, 2009.

[2] I. Balbin and K. Ramamohanarao. A generalization of the differential approach to recursive query evaluation. *J. Log. Program.*, 4(3):259–262, 1987.

[3] F. Bancilhon, D. Maier, Y. Sagiv, and J. D. Ullman. Magic sets and other strange ways to implement logic programs (extended abstract). In *Proc. of PODS'86*, pages 1–15. ACM, 1986.

[4] S. Ceri, G. Gottlob, and L. Tanca. What you always wanted to know about datalog (and never dared to ask). *IEEE Trans. on Knowl. and Data Eng.*, 1(1):146–166, March 1989.

[5] I. Cervesato. NEXCEL, a Deductive Spreadsheet. *The Knowledge Engineering Review*, 22:221–236, 2007.

[6] I. Cervesato and A. Scedrov. Relating state-based and process-based concurrency through linear logic. *Inf. Comput.*, 207(10):1044–1077, 2009.

[7] F. Cruz, M. P. Ashley-Rollman, S. C. Goldstein, Ricardo Rocha, and F. Pfenning. Bottom-up logic programming for multicores. In Vítor Santos Costa, editor, *Proc. of DAMP 2012 - Short Papers*. ACM Digital Library, January 2012.

[8] H. Gallaire, J. Minker, and J. M. Nicolas. Logic and databases: A deductive approach. *ACM Comput. Surv.*, 16(2):153–185, June 1984.

[9] J. Y. Girard. Linear logic. *Theor. Comput. Sci.*, 50:1–102, 1987.

[10] S. Grumbach and F. Wang. Netlog, a rule-based language for distributed programming. In *Proc. of PADL'10*, volume 5937/2010, pages 88–103. Springer-Verlag, 2010.

[11] A. Gupta, I. S. Mumick, and V. S. Subrahmanian. Maintaining views incrementally. In *Proc. of SIGMOD'93*, pages 157–166. ACM, 1993.

[12] E. S. L. Lam and I. Cervesato. Modeling datalog assertion and retraction in linear logic (full-version). Technical Report CMU-CS-QTR-113/CMU-CS-12-126, Carnegie Mellon University, Jun 2012.

[13] Ninghui Li and John C. Mitchell. Datalog with constraints: A foundation for trust-management languages. In *Proc. of PADL'03*, volume 2562/2003, pages 58–73. Springer-Verlag, 2003.

[14] B. T. Loo, T. Condie, M. Garofalakis, D. E. Gay, J. M. Hellerstein, P. Maniatis, R. Ramakrishnan, T. Roscoe, and I. Stoica. Declarative networking: language, execution and optimization. In *Proc. of SIGMOD '06*, pages 97–108. ACM, 2006.

[15] D. Miller, G. Nadathur, F. Pfenning, and A. Scedrov. Uniform proofs as a foundation for logic programming. *Proc. of APAL'91*, 51:125–157, 1991.

[16] V. Nigam, L. Jia, B. T. Loo, and A. Scedrov. Maintaining distributed logic programs incrementally. In *Proc. of PPDP'11*, pages 125–136. ACM, 2011.

[17] V. Nigam and D. Miller. Algorithmic specifications in linear logic with subexponentials. In *Proc. of PPDP'09*, pages 129–140. ACM, 2009.

[18] F. Pfenning. Structural cut elimination. In *Proc. of LICS'95*, pages 156–166. IEEE Press, 1995.

[19] L. Vieille. Recursive axioms in deductive databases: The query/subquery approach. In *Expert Database Conf.*, pages 253–267. Benjamin Cummings, 1986.

Regular Expression Sub-Matching using Partial Derivatives

Martin Sulzmann
Hochschule Karlsruhe - Technik und Wirtschaft
martin.sulzmann@gmail.com

Kenny Zhuo Ming Lu
Nanyang Polytechnic
luzhuomi@gmail.com

Abstract

Regular expression sub-matching is the problem of finding for each sub-part of a regular expression a matching sub-string. Prior work applies Thompson and Glushkov NFA methods for the construction of the matching automata. We propose the novel use of derivatives and partial derivatives for regular expression sub-matching. Our benchmarking results show that the run-time performance is promising and that our approach can be applied in practice.

Categories and Subject Descriptors F.1.1 [**Computation by Abstract Devices**]: Models of Computation—Automata; F.4.3 [**Mathematical Logic and Formal Languages**]: Formal Languages—Operations on languages

General Terms Algorithms, Languages, Performance

Keywords Regular expression, Automata, Matching

1. Introduction

Regular expression matching is the problem of checking if a word matches a regular expression. For example, consider the word $ABAAC$ comprising of letters A, B and C and the regular expression $(A+AB)(BAA+A)(AC+C)$. Symbol $+$ denotes the choice operator. Concatenation is implicit. It is straightforward to see that $ABAAC$ matches the regular expression.

Specifically, we are interested in sub-matchings where for each sub-part of a regular expression we seek for a matching sub-word. To refer to sub-parts we are interested in, we annotate our regular expression with distinct variables:

$$(x_1 : (A+AB))(x_2 : (BAA+A))(x_3 : (AC+C))$$

These variables will be bound to the sub-matchings. For example, the first two letters AB of the input word $ABAAC$ will be bound to x_1, the third letter A to x_2 and the remainder AC to x_3.

Many of the real-world implementations of regular expression (sub)matching are very slow for even simple matching problems. For example, consider the pattern $A?^n A^n$ and the input string A^n where A^n stands for repeating the letter A n-times. As reported in [5], Perl shows some exponential behavior for this example because of its back-tracking matching algorithm. However, the running time of the matching algorithm can be linear in the size of the input string if proper automata-based methods are applied.

The works in [5, 12] advocate the use of Thompson NFAs [24]. The NFA non-deterministically searches for possible matchings without having to back-track. Thus, a linear running time can be guaranteed. There are several other NFA constructions which can serve as a basis to build the matching automata. For example, the work in [7] relies on Glushkov NFAs for finding (sub)matchings.

In this work, we propose the novel use of Brzozowski's regular expression derivatives [3] and Antimirov's partial derivative NFAs [2] for sub-matching which in our view leads to a particular elegant formalization of regular expression sub-matching. We obtain the proof of correctness of regular expression sub-matching by construction. The further advantage of partial derivatives is that on the average the partial derivative NFA is smaller than the Glushkov NFA. There are no ϵ-transitions compared to Thompson NFAs. We can thus build a highly efficient implementation in Haskell which is the fastest among all Haskell implementations of regular expression sub-matching we are aware of. Our implementation incorporates many of the extensions found in real world regular expressions and we are competitive compared to state-of-the art C-based implementations such as RE2 and PCRE.

In summary, we make the following contributions:

- We give a rigorous treatment of regular expression sub-matching (Section 3).
- We extend Brzozowski's regular expression derivatives [3] and Antimirov's partial derivative [2] to obtain algorithms which implement POSIX and greedy left-most matching (Sections 4 and 5).
- We give a comparison among Thompson, Glushkov and partial derivatives NFA approaches (Section 5.4).
- We show that our approach can support the many extensions typically found in real world regular expressions (Section 6).
- We have built an optimized implementation of regular expression sub-matching with partial derivatives and provide empirical evidence that our implementation yields competitive performance results (Section 7).

All our implementations, including reference implementations of greedy left-most matching using Thompson and Glushkov NFAs, are available via

`http://hackage.haskell.org/package/regex-pderiv`

Related work is discussed in Section 8. Section 9 concludes.

2. The Key Ideas

We motivate the key ideas of our regular expression sub-matching approach via some examples. Our starting point are Brzozowski's derivatives [3] which have recently been rediscovered for matching a word against a regular expression [16].

A word w matches a regular expression r if w is an element of the language described by r, written $w \in L(r)$. This problem can be elegantly solved via derivatives as follows. The idea is that

$$lw \in L(r) \text{ iff } w \in L(r\backslash l)$$

where $r\backslash l$ is the derivative of r with respect to l. In language terms, $L(r\backslash l) = \{w \mid lw \in L(r)\}$. Constructively, we obtain $r\backslash l$

PPDP'12, September 19–21, 2012, Leuven, Belgium.

from r by taking away the letter l while traversing the structure of r. We will shortly see examples explaining the workings of the derivative operator $(\cdot\backslash\cdot)$. To check that word $l_1...l_n$ matches regular expression r, we simply build $r\backslash l_1\backslash...\backslash l_n$ and test if this regular expression accepts the empty string.

Our idea is to transfer derivatives to the pattern sub-matching problem. Patterns p are regular expressions annotated with pattern variables as shown in the introduction. Variable environments Γ hold the bindings of these pattern variables. The derivative operation in this setting is as follows:

$$lw \vdash p \leadsto \Gamma \text{ iff } w \vdash p\backslash l \leadsto \Gamma$$

Word lw matches the pattern p and yields environment Γ iff w matches the pattern derivative of p with respect to l. The construction of pattern derivatives $p\backslash l$ is similar to regular expressions. The crucial difference is that we also take care of sub-matchings.

As an example we consider pattern $(x : A + y : AB + z : B)^*$ and the to be matched input AB. To be clear, the pattern's meaning is $((x : A) + (y : AB) + (z : B))^*$ but we generally avoid parentheses around pattern variable bindings. Next, we show the individual derivative steps where notation $p_1 \xrightarrow{l} p_2$ denotes that p_2 is the derivative of p_1 with respect to l. For the first step, we also show the intermediate steps indicated by subscript notation. We write $p_1 \xrightarrow{l}_i p_2$ to denote the ith intermediate step.

$$\begin{array}{ll} & (x : A + y : AB + z : B)^* \\ \xrightarrow{\epsilon}_1 & (x : A + y : AB + z : B)(x : A + y : AB + z : B)^* \\ \xrightarrow{\epsilon}_2 & (x_1 : A + y_1 : AB + z_1 : B)(x : A + y : AB + z : B)^* \end{array}$$

$$\begin{array}{ll} A \xrightarrow{A} \epsilon & x_1 : A \xrightarrow{A} x_1|A : \epsilon \\ AB \xrightarrow{A} B & y_1 : AB \xrightarrow{A} y_1|A : B \\ B \xrightarrow{A} \phi & z_1 : B \xrightarrow{A} z_1|A : \phi \end{array}$$

$$\begin{array}{ll} \xrightarrow{A}_3 & (x_1|A : \epsilon + y_1|A : B + z_1|A : \phi) \\ & (x : A + y : AB + z : B)^* \end{array}$$

For space reasons, we put the concatenated expressions $(x_1|A : \epsilon + y_1|A : B + z_1|A : \phi)$ and $(x : A + y : AB + z : B)^*$ below each other.

The purpose of the intermediate steps are: (1) We unfold the Kleene star, (2) generate for clarity fresh variables for each iteration and (3) we apply the derivative operation to each subcomponent. The sub-matchings are stored within in the sub-pattern. This saves us from keeping track of an additional variable environment which describes the current match. For example, $z_1|A : \phi$ denotes that z_1 is so far bound to A and ϕ (the empty regular expression) is the residue of the derivative operation.

We continue with step $\xrightarrow{B}$ starting with

$$\underbrace{(x_1|A : \epsilon + y_1|A : B + z_1|A : \phi)}_{p_1}\underbrace{(x : A + y : AB + z : B)^*}_{p_2}$$

In case of concatenated expressions p_1p_2 the derivative operation is applied to the leading expression p_1. Hence, we find

$$\begin{array}{ll} & (x_1|A : \epsilon + y_1|A : B + z_1|A : \phi) \\ & (x : A + y : AB + z : B)^* \\ \xrightarrow{B} & (x_1|AB : \phi + y_1|AB : \epsilon + z_1|AB : \phi) \\ & (x : A + y : AB + z : B)^* \end{array} \qquad (1)$$

For our example, the leading expression p_1 matches the empty word and therefore the derivative operation is also applicable to p_2. The individual steps are similar to the steps above, unrolling Kleene star etc. In p_1, we must replace sub-parts which match the empty word by ϵ, otherwise, ϕ. This is to ensure that any matches involving letter take place 'behind' p_1.

$$\begin{array}{ll} & (x_1|A : \epsilon + y_1|A : B + z_1|A : \phi) \\ & (x : A + y : AB + z : B)^* \\ \xrightarrow{B} & (x_1|A : \epsilon + y_1|A : B + z_1|A : \phi) \\ & (x_2|B : \phi + y_2|B : \phi + z_2|B : \epsilon) \\ & (x : A + y : AB + z : B)^* \end{array} \qquad (2)$$

Both cases (1) and (2) are combined via choice.

$$\begin{array}{ll} & (x_1|A : \epsilon + y_1|A : B + z_1|A : \phi) \\ & (x : A + y : AB + z : B)^* \\ \xrightarrow{B} & \left(\begin{array}{l} (x_1|AB : \phi + y_1|AB : \epsilon + z_1|AB : \phi) \\ (x : A + y : AB + z : B)^* \end{array} \right) \\ & + \\ & \left(\begin{array}{l} (x_1|A : \epsilon + y_1|A : B + z_1|A : \phi) \\ (x_2|B : \phi + y_2|B : \phi + z_2|B : \epsilon) \\ (x : A + y : AB + z : B)^* \end{array} \right) \end{array}$$

We simplify the final pattern by removing parts which are connected to ϕ. The thus simplified pattern is

$$\begin{array}{c} (y_1|AB : \epsilon)(x : A + y : AB + z : B)^* \\ + \\ (x_1|A : \epsilon + y_1|A : B)(z_2|B : \epsilon)(x : A + y : AB + z : B)^* \end{array}$$

We can directly read out the sub-matchings and collect them in some variable environments. Of course, we only consider sub-matchings whose residue matches the empty word which applies here to all cases. Hence, the first match is $\Gamma_1 = \{y_1 : AB\}$ and the second match is $\Gamma_2 = \{x_1 : A, z_2 : B\}$.

To guarantee that there is a unique, unambiguous match, we impose a specific matching policy such as POSIX or greedy left-most as found in Perl. In the above example, the first match is the POSIX match whereas the second match is the greedy left-most match.

As we will see, the first match reported by our derivative matching algorithm is always the POSIX match. Obtaining the greedy left-most match via the derivative matching algorithm is non-trivial because the derivative operation maintains the structure of the pattern whereas the greedy left-most match policy effectively ignores the structure.

To obtain the greedy left-most match, we make use of Antimirov's partial derivatives [2]. Partial derivatives are related to derivatives like non-deterministic automata (NFAs) are related to deterministic automata (DFAs). Derivatives represent the states of a deterministic automata whereas partial derivatives represent the states of a non-deterministic automata. The partial derivative operation $\cdot\backslash_p\cdot$ yields a set of regular expressions partial derivatives. The connection to the derivative operation $\cdot\backslash\cdot$ in terms of languages is as follows:

$$L(r\backslash l) \quad = \quad L(r_1 + ... + r_n)$$

where $r\backslash_p l = \{r_1, ..., r_n\}$

One of Antimirov's important results is that the set of partial derivatives of a regular expression and its descendants is finite. For our running example $(x : A + y : AB + z : B)^*$ we obtain the partial derivatives

$$\begin{array}{lcl} p_1 & = & (x : A + y : AB + z : B)^* \\ p_2 & = & (y : B, (x : A + y : AB + z : B)^*) \end{array}$$

For example,

$$\begin{array}{ll} p_1\backslash_p A = \{ & (x : \epsilon)(x : A + y : AB + z : B)^*, \\ & (y : B)(x : A + y : AB + z : B)^*\} \end{array}$$

That is, choice '+' is broken up into a set. We can further simplify $(x : \epsilon)(x : A+y : AB+z : B)^*$ to p_1. Hence, after simplifications $p_1\backslash_p A = \{p_1, (y : B)p_1\}$.

Partial derivatives p_1 and p_2 are states of an NFA where p_1 is the starting as well as final state. The NFA transitions are given in

$$
\begin{array}{lll}
\text{(T1)} & p_1 \xrightarrow{x \mapsto A} & p_1 \\
\text{(T2)} & p_1 \xrightarrow{y \mapsto A} & p_2 \\
\text{(T3)} & p_1 \xrightarrow{z \mapsto B} & p_1 \\
\text{(T4)} & p_2 \xrightarrow{y \mapsto B} & p_1
\end{array}
$$

Figure 1. Transitions for $(x : A + y : AB + z : B)^*$

Figure 1. Each transition carries a specific match. Matches associated to transitions are incremental. For example, in case of (T3) the current input B will be added to the current match binding of z. The above represents a non-deterministic, finite match automata in style of Laurikari's NFAs with tagged transitions [12].

Via the partial derivative NFA match automata it is straightforward to compute the greedy left-most match. We follow NFA states, i.e. apply transitions, from left to right in the order as computed by the pattern partial derivative function $\cdot\backslash_p\cdot$. Each resulting state is associated with an environment. We label each environment with the corresponding state. The initial state has the empty environment $\{\}^{p_1}$. In each transition step, the match function is applied to the environment yielding an updated environment.

For input AB, we find the following derivation steps

$$
\begin{array}{lll}
 & \{p_1\} & \{\}^{p_1} \\
\xrightarrow{A} & \{p_1, p_2\} & \{x : A\}^{p_1} \ \{y : A\}^{p_2} \\
\xrightarrow{B} & \{p_1, p_1'\} & \{x : A, z : B\}^{p_1} \\
 & & \{y : AB\}^{p_1'} \\
\longrightarrow & & \text{keep left-most match} \\
 & \{p_1\} & \{x : A, z : B\}^{p_1}
\end{array}
$$

In the second derivation step, we could reach p_1 from p_1 and p_2 but we only keep the first p_1 resulting from transition (T1) due to the left-to-right traversal order. The second p_1' is discarded. State p_1 is final. Hence, we obtain the greedy left-most match $\{x : A, z : B\}$.

To summarize, the derivative operation maintains the pattern structure whereas the partial derivative operation ignores the pattern structure by for example breaking apart choice. This becomes clear when consider derivative and partial derivative of p_1 w.r.t. A:

$$p_1 \backslash_p A \quad = \{p_1, (y : B)p_1\}$$

$$p_1 \backslash A \quad = (x|A : \epsilon + y|A : B)p_1$$

Under a greedy matching policy, we try to maximize the left-most match. As can be seen from our example, matching via derivatives still respects the original pattern structure and therefore we obtain the POSIX match. Partial derivatives break apart the original pattern structure. Therefore, we obtain the greedy left-most match as found in Perl.

Next, we formalize this idea.

3. Regular Expression Pattern Sub-Matching

Figure 2 defines the syntax of words, regular expressions, patterns and environments. Σ refers to a finite set of alphabet symbols A, B, etc. To avoid confusion with the EBNF symbol "|", we write "+" to denote the regular expression choice operator. The pattern language consists of variables, pair, choice and star patterns. The treatment of extensions such as character classes, back-references is postponed until the later Section 6. Environments are ordered multi-sets, i.e. lists. We write $\uplus$ to denote multi-set union, i.e. list concatenation. The reason for using multi-sets rather than sets is that we record multiple bindings for a variable x. See the upcoming match rule for Kleene star patterns. The reason for using an ordered multi-set is that we will compare the matchings in the order they appear, e.g. from left-to-right.

Words:

$$
\begin{array}{rcll}
w & ::= & \epsilon & \text{Empty word} \\
 & | & l \in \Sigma & \text{Letters} \\
 & | & lw & \text{Concatenation}
\end{array}
$$

Regular expressions:

$$
\begin{array}{rcll}
r & ::= & r + r & \text{Choice} \\
 & | & (r, r) & \text{Concatenation} \\
 & | & r^* & \text{Kleene star} \\
 & | & \epsilon & \text{Empty word} \\
 & | & \phi & \text{Empty language} \\
 & | & l \in \Sigma & \text{Letters}
\end{array}
$$

Patterns:

$$
\begin{array}{rcll}
p & ::= & (x : r) & \text{Variables Base} \\
 & | & (x : p) & \text{Variables Group} \\
 & | & (p, p) & \text{Pairs} \\
 & | & (p + p) & \text{Choice} \\
 & | & p^* & \text{Kleene Star}
\end{array}
$$

Environments:

$$
\begin{array}{rcll}
\Gamma & ::= & \{x : w\} & \text{Variable binding} \\
 & | & \Gamma \uplus \Gamma & \text{Ordered multi-set of variable bindings}
\end{array}
$$

Language:

$$
\begin{array}{lcl}
L(r_1 + r_2) & = & L(r_1) \cup L(r_2) \\
L(r_1, r_2) & = & \{w_1 w_2 \mid w_1 \in L(r_1), w_2 \in L(r_2)\} \\
L(r^*) & = & \{\epsilon\} \cup \{w_1 ... w_n | i \in \{1, .., n\} \ w_i \in L(r)\} \\
L(\epsilon) & = & \{\epsilon\} \\
L(\phi) & = & \{\} \\
L(l) & = & \{l\}
\end{array}
$$

Figure 2. Regular Expressions Syntax and Language

Concatenation among regular expressions and patterns is often left implicit. That is, we may write the shorter form $r_1 r_2$ instead of (r_1, r_2). To omit parentheses we assume that $+$ has a lower precedence than concatenation. Hence, $A + AB$ is a short-hand for $A + (A, B)$ and $x : A + y : AB$ is a short-hand for $(x : A) + (y : AB)$.

Figure 3 defines regular expression matching in terms of $w \vdash p \rightsquigarrow \Gamma$ where word w and pattern p are input arguments and matching environment Γ is the output argument, mapping variables to matched sub-parts of the word. The matching relation as defined is indeterministic, i.e. ambiguous, for the following reasons.

In case of choice, we can arbitrarily match a word either against the left or right pattern. See rules (ChoiceL) and (ChoiceR). Indeterminism also arises in case of (Pair) and (Star) where the input word w can be broken up arbitrarily. Next, we consider some examples to discuss these points in more detail.

For pattern $(xyz : (x : A + y : AB + z : B)^*)$ and input ABA the following matchings are possible:

- $\{xyz : ABA, x : A, z : B, x : A\}$.

  In the first iteration, we match A (bound by x), then B (bound by z), and then again A (bound by x). For each iteration step we record a binding and therefore treat bindings as lists. We write the bindings in the order as they appear in the pattern, starting with the left-most binding.

- $\{xyz : ABA, y : AB, x : A\}$.

  We first match AB (bound by y) and in the final last iteration then A (bound by x).

$$\text{(VarBase)} \quad \frac{w \in L(r)}{w \vdash x : r \rightsquigarrow \{x : w\}}$$

$$\text{(VarGroup)} \quad \frac{w \vdash p \rightsquigarrow \Gamma}{w \vdash x : p \rightsquigarrow \{x : w\} \uplus \Gamma}$$

$$\text{(Pair)} \quad \frac{\begin{array}{c} w = w_1 w_2 \\ w_1 \vdash p_1 \rightsquigarrow \Gamma_1 \\ w_2 \vdash p_2 \rightsquigarrow \Gamma_2 \end{array}}{w \vdash (p_1, p_2) \rightsquigarrow \Gamma_1 \uplus \Gamma_2}$$

$$\text{(ChoiceL)} \quad \frac{w \vdash p_1 \rightsquigarrow \Gamma_1}{w \vdash p_1 + p_2 \rightsquigarrow \Gamma_1}$$

$$\text{(ChoiceR)} \quad \frac{w \vdash p_2 \rightsquigarrow \Gamma_2}{w \vdash p_1 + p_2 \rightsquigarrow \Gamma_2}$$

$$\text{(Star)} \quad \frac{\begin{array}{c} w = w_1 ... w_n \\ w_i \vdash p \rightsquigarrow \Gamma_i \quad \text{for } i = 1..n \end{array}}{w \vdash p^* \rightsquigarrow \Gamma_1 \uplus ... \uplus \Gamma_n}$$

Figure 3. Pattern matching relation: $w \vdash p \rightsquigarrow \Gamma$

For pattern $(xyz : (xy : (x : A + AB, y : BAA + A), z : AC + C))$ and input $ABAAC$ we find the following matchings:

- $\{xyz : ABAAC, xy : ABAA, x : A, y : BAA, z : C\}$.
- $\{xyz : ABAAC, xy : ABA, x : AB, y : A, z : AC\}$.

Next, we formalize greedy left-most matching (like in Perl) followed by POSIX matching to obtain a deterministic matching relation.

3.1 Greedy Left-Most Matching

The greedy left-most matching strategy is implemented by Perl and by the PCRE library. We present here a formalization of greedy left-most matching in terms of our notation of patterns and regular expressions.

We start off by establishing some basic definitions. The first definition establishes an ordering relation $\geq$ among structured words w_1 and w_2 which are represented as tuples. For example, we wish that $ABB \geq (AB, B)$ but $AB \not\geq (AB, B)$. That is, the ordering relation $\geq$ favors the longest (matching) word, starting from left to right.

DEFINITION 1 (Ordering among Word Tuples). *Let $|w|$ denote the length, i.e. number of symbols, of word w. Then, we inductively define the (partial) ordering among tuples $(w_1, ..., w_n)$ of words as follows:*

- $w_1 \geq w_2$ *iff* $|w_1| \geq |w_2|$
- $(w_1, ..., w_n) \geq (w'_1, ..., w'_m)$ *iff*
  1. $|w_1| > |w'_1|$, *or*
  2. $|w_1| = |w'_1| \wedge n > 1 \wedge m > 1 \wedge$ $(w_2, ..., w_n) \geq (w'_2, ..., w'_m))$

The ordering relation $\geq$ will only be applied on tuples $(w_1, ..., w_n)$ and $(w'_1, ..., w'_m)$ where flattening the tuples will either result in the same sequence of letters or one is a prefix of the other.

The next definition extends the ordering relation among structured words to an ordering among environments. We will write $(x_{i_j} : w_{i_j}) \in \Gamma_i$ to refer to each binding in $\Gamma_i = \{x_{i_1} : w_{i_1}, ..., x_{i_n} : x_{i_n}\}$.

DEFINITION 2 (Ordering among Environments). *Let $(x_{i_j} : w_{i_j}) \in \Gamma_i$ for $i \in \{1, ..., n\}$ and $(x'_{i_j} : w'_{i_j}) \in \Gamma'_i$ for $i \in \{1, ..., m\}$. The sequence of variables in $\Gamma'_1 \uplus ... \uplus \Gamma'_m$ is a prefix of the sequence of variables in $\Gamma_1 \uplus ... \uplus \Gamma_n$. Recall that bindings are ordered multi-sets. Then, $(\Gamma_1, ..., \Gamma_n) \geq (\Gamma'_1, ..., \Gamma'_m)$ iff $(w_{1_1}, ..., w_{n_{l_n}}) \geq (w'_{1_1}, ..., w'_{m_{l_m}})$.*

Environments are ordered multi-sets (lists) as well. Hence, the order of w_{i_j} and w'_{i_j} is fixed by the order of their corresponding environment variables x_{i_j}.

For comparison, we may only consider selected environment variables. We write $\Gamma_{|V}$ to restrict the environment to those variables mentioned in V. That is, $\Gamma_{|V} = \{x : w | x : w \in \Gamma \quad x \in V\}$. We write $(\Gamma_1, ..., \Gamma_n)_{|V}$ as a short-hand notation for $(\Gamma_{1_{|V}}, ..., \Gamma_{n_{|V}})$.

For all pattern variables we record the match in some environment. We compute those variables via function fv. See the upcoming definition. To decide which environment is the greedy left-most match, we only consider variables of base patterns $x : r$. We compute these variables via function $baseFv$.

DEFINITION 3 (Free Pattern Variables). *The set of free pattern variables is defined as follows:*

$$\begin{array}{lcl} fv(x : r) & = & \{x\} \\ fv(x : p) & = & \{x\} \cup fv(p) \\ fv(p_1, p_2) & = & fv(p_1) \cup fv(p_2) \\ fv(p^*) & = & fv(p) \\ fv(p_1 + p_2) & = & fv(p_1) \cup fv(p_2) \end{array}$$

The set of free variables belonging to base patterns $x : r$ is defined as follows:

$$\begin{array}{lcl} baseFv(x : r) & = & \{x\} \\ baseFv(x : p) & = & baseFv(p) \\ baseFv(p_1, p_2) & = & baseFv(p_1) \cup baseFv(p_2) \\ baseFv(p^*) & = & baseFv(p) \\ baseFv(p_1 + p_2) & = & baseFv(p_1) \cup baseFv(p_2) \end{array}$$

We have everything at hand to formalize greedy left-most matching in Figure 4. Judgment $\cdot \vdash_{lm} \cdot \rightsquigarrow \cdot$ performs the matching for all intermediate nodes. The rules strictly favor the left-most match as shown by rules (LM-ChoiceL) and (LM-ChoiceR). In case of (LM-ChoiceR), we append the empty binding Γ_1 ahead of the right match Γ_2. This guarantees that we cover all pattern variables even if they only contribute the empty binding and all bindings reflect the order of the variables in the pattern. This is the basis for the greedy left-most comparison in rules (LM-Star) and (LM).

In case of the Kleene star, we greedily follow the left-most matching policy. See rule (LM-Star). Recall that the bindings in Γ are ordered in the left-to-right matching order.

The top judgment $\cdot \vdash_{lm_{top}} \cdot \rightsquigarrow \cdot$ and rule (LM) finally select the greedy left-most match. For selection, we must only consider the base bindings resulting from sub-patterns $x : r$ because of the depth-first left-to-right nature of greedy left-most matching.

For example, $\{xyz : ABAAC, xy : ABA, x : AB, y : A, z : AC\}$ is the greedy left-most match for pattern $(xyz : (xy : (x : A + AB, y : BAA + A), z : AC + C))$ and input $ABAAC$.

A subtle point is that this is not strictly enough to ensure that we compute the 'Perl-style' greedy left-most match. The reason is that we do not require to fully annotate a pattern with variables.

For example, consider pattern $(x : (A + AB), y : (B + \epsilon))$ and input AB where we find that

$$AB \vdash_{lm_{top}} (x : (A + AB), y : (B + \epsilon)) \rightsquigarrow \{x : AB, y : \epsilon\}$$

This match arises because we do not look further inside the base pattern $x : (A + AB)$. However, this is not quite the Perl-style match which is $\{x : A, y : B\}$.

$$\boxed{w \vdash_{lm} p \rightsquigarrow \Gamma}$$

(LM-VarBase) $$\frac{w \in L(r)}{w \vdash_{lm} x : r \rightsquigarrow \{x : w\}}$$

(LM-VarGroup) $$\frac{w \vdash_{lm} p \rightsquigarrow \Gamma}{w \vdash_{lm} x : p \rightsquigarrow \{x : w\} \uplus \Gamma}$$

(LM-Pair) $$\frac{\begin{array}{c} w = w_1 w_2 \\ w_1 \vdash_{lm} p_1 \rightsquigarrow \Gamma_1 \\ w_2 \vdash_{lm} p_2 \rightsquigarrow \Gamma_2 \end{array}}{w \vdash_{lm} (p_1, p_2) \rightsquigarrow \Gamma_1 \uplus \Gamma_2}$$

(LM-ChoiceL) $$\frac{\begin{array}{c} w \vdash_{lm} p_1 \rightsquigarrow \Gamma_1 \\ fv(p_2) = \{x_1, .., x_n\} \\ \Gamma_2 = \{x_1 : \epsilon, ..., x_n : \epsilon\} \end{array}}{w \vdash_{lm} p_1 + p_2 \rightsquigarrow \Gamma_1 \uplus \Gamma_2}$$

(LM-ChoiceR) $$\frac{\begin{array}{c} \text{there is no } \Gamma_1 \text{ s.t. } w \vdash_{lm} p_1 \rightsquigarrow \Gamma_1 \\ w \vdash_{lm} p_2 \rightsquigarrow \Gamma_2 \\ fv(p_1) = \{x_1, .., x_n\} \\ \Gamma'_1 = \{x_1 : \epsilon, ..., x_n : \epsilon\} \end{array}}{w \vdash_{lm} p_1 + p_2 \rightsquigarrow \Gamma'_1 \uplus \Gamma_2}$$

(LM-Star) $$\frac{\begin{array}{c} w = w_1 ... w_n \\ w_i \vdash_{lm} p \rightsquigarrow \Gamma_i \quad \text{for } i = 1..n \\ \text{for all } (w'_1, \Gamma'_1), ..., (w'_m, \Gamma'_m) \text{ such that} \\ \bullet w_1 ... w_n = w'_1 ... w'_m, \text{ and} \\ \bullet w'_i \vdash p \rightsquigarrow \Gamma'_i \text{ for } i = 1, ..., m \\ \text{we have that} \\ (\Gamma_1, ..., \Gamma_n)_{|baseFv(p)} \geq (\Gamma'_1, ..., \Gamma'_m)_{|baseFv(p)} \end{array}}{w \vdash_{lm} p^* \rightsquigarrow \Gamma_1 \uplus ... \uplus \Gamma_n}$$

(LM) $$\frac{\begin{array}{c} w \vdash_{lm} p \rightsquigarrow \Gamma \\ \text{for all } \Gamma' \text{ such that } w \vdash_{lm} p \rightsquigarrow \Gamma' \\ \text{we have that } \Gamma_{|baseFv(p)} \geq \Gamma'_{|baseFv(p)} \end{array}}{w \vdash_{lm_{top}} p \rightsquigarrow \Gamma}$$

Figure 4. Greedy Left-Most Matching

To obtain the Perl-style match, we must simply fully annotate the pattern with variables:

$$(x : (x_1 : A + x_2 : AB), y : (y_1 : B + y_2 : \epsilon))$$

By fully annotating the pattern we guarantee that the input letter A is matched against the left-most occurrence of A in $A + AB$. Thus, we obtain the desired match $\{x : A, x_1 : A, y : B, y_1 : B\}$.

We conclude this section by stating some elementary properties and also consider a few further examples.

PROPOSITION 3.1 (Greedy Left-Most Completeness). *Let w be a word, p be a pattern and Γ be a binding such that $w \vdash p \rightsquigarrow \Gamma$. Then, $w \vdash_{lm_{top}} p \rightsquigarrow \Gamma'$ for some Γ' such that $\Gamma(x) = \Gamma'(x)$ for all $x \in dom(\Gamma)$.*

PROPOSITION 3.2 (Greedy Left-Most Determinism). *Let w be a word, p be a pattern and Γ_1, Γ_2 be two bindings such that $w \vdash_{lm_{top}} p \rightsquigarrow \Gamma_1$ and $w \vdash_{lm_{top}} p \rightsquigarrow \Gamma_2$. Then, $\Gamma_1 = \Gamma_2$.*

PROPOSITION 3.3 (Greedy Left-Most Correctness). *Let w be a word, p be a pattern and Γ be a binding such that $w \vdash_{lm_{top}} p \rightsquigarrow \Gamma$. Then, $w \vdash p \rightsquigarrow \Gamma'$ for some Γ' such that $\Gamma(x) = \Gamma'(x)$ for all $x \in dom(\Gamma')$.*

$$\boxed{w \vdash_{POSIX} p \rightsquigarrow \Gamma}$$

(POSIX-VarBase) $$\frac{w \in L(r)}{w \vdash_{POSIX} x : r \rightsquigarrow \{x : w\}}$$

(POSIX-VarGroup) $$\frac{w \vdash_{POSIX} p \rightsquigarrow \Gamma}{w \vdash_{POSIX} x : p \rightsquigarrow \{x : w\} \uplus \Gamma}$$

(POSIX-ChoiceL) $$\frac{w \vdash_{POSIX} p_1 \rightsquigarrow \Gamma}{w \vdash_{POSIX} p_1 + p_2 \rightsquigarrow \Gamma}$$

(POSIX-ChoiceR) $$\frac{\begin{array}{c} \text{there is no } \Gamma_1 \text{ s.t. } w \vdash_{POSIX} p_1 \rightsquigarrow \Gamma_1 \\ w \vdash_{POSIX} p_2 \rightsquigarrow \Gamma \end{array}}{w \vdash_{POSIX} p_1 + p_2 \rightsquigarrow \Gamma}$$

(POSIX-Pair) $$\frac{\begin{array}{c} w = w_1 w_2 \\ w_1 \vdash_{POSIX} p_1 \rightsquigarrow \Gamma_1 \\ w_2 \vdash_{POSIX} p_2 \rightsquigarrow \Gamma_2 \\ w_1, w_2 \text{ is the maximal word match} \end{array}}{w \vdash_{POSIX} (p_1, p_2) \rightsquigarrow \Gamma_1 \uplus \Gamma_2}$$

(POSIX-Star) $$\frac{\begin{array}{c} w = w_1 ... w_n \\ w_i \vdash_{POSIX} p \rightsquigarrow \Gamma_i \quad \text{for } i = 1..n \\ w_1,...,w_n \text{ is the maximal word match} \end{array}}{w \vdash_{POSIX} p^* \rightsquigarrow \Gamma_1 \uplus \ ... \uplus \ \Gamma_n}$$

Figure 5. POSIX Matching

Because we also record empty bindings resulting from choice patterns, see rules (LM-ChoiceL) and (LM-ChoiceR), the greedy left-most binding Γ represents a superset of the binding Γ' computed via Figure 3. Therefore, we compare Γ and Γ' with respect to the variable bindings in Γ'. For convenience, we treat bindings like functions and write $dom(\Gamma')$ to denote the function domain of Γ'. The co-domain is the power set over the language of words because of repeated bindings in case of the pattern star iteration. For instance, for $\Gamma'' = \{x : A, x : B\}$ we have that $\Gamma''(x) = \{A, B\}$.

It is easy to see that the greedy left-most match is stable under associativity of concatenation. Consider rule (LM-Pair) rule and the case $((p_1, p_2), p_3)$ versus $(p_1, (p_2, p_3))$. We have that $\uplus$ is associative and therefore for each case we obtain the same binding.

PROPOSITION 3.4 (Greedy Left-Most Associative Stability). *Let w be a word, p_1, p_2, p_3 be patterns and Γ and Γ' be bindings such that $w \vdash_{lm_{top}} ((p_1, p_2), p_3) \rightsquigarrow \Gamma$ and $w \vdash_{lm_{top}} (p_1, (p_2, p_3)) \rightsquigarrow \Gamma'$. Then, we have that $\Gamma = \Gamma'$.*

3.2 POSIX Matching

POSIX matching favors the longest word match $w_1,...,w_n$ relative to some pattern structure $p_1,...,p_n$ where each sub-word w_i matches sub-pattern p_i. We say that $w_1,...,w_n$ is the maximal (longest) word match if for any other matching sequence $w'_1,...,w'_n$ we have that $w'_1,...,w'_n$ is smaller than $w_1,...,w_n$ w.r.t. to the ordering relation $\geq$ among word tuples. The precise definition follows.

DEFINITION 4 (Maximal Word Match). *We say that $w_1,...,w_n$ is the maximal (word) match w.r.t. patterns $p_1,...,p_n$ and environment $\Gamma_1,...,\Gamma_n$ iff*

1. $w_i \vdash p_i \rightsquigarrow \Gamma_i$ for $i = 1, ..., n$, and

$$
\begin{array}{lcl}
\phi\backslash l & = & \phi \\
\epsilon\backslash l & = & \phi \\
l_1\backslash l_2 & = & \left\{ \begin{array}{ll} \epsilon & \text{if } l_1 == l_2 \\ \phi & \text{otherwise} \end{array} \right. \\
(r_1 + r_2)\backslash l & = & r_1\backslash l + r_2\backslash l \\
(r_1, r_2)\backslash l & = & \left\{ \begin{array}{ll} (r_1\backslash l, r_2) + r_2\backslash l & \text{if } \epsilon \in L(r_1) \\ (r_1\backslash l, r_2) & \text{otherwise} \end{array} \right. \\
r^*\backslash l & = & (r\backslash l, r^*)
\end{array}
$$

Figure 6. Regular Expression Derivatives

2. *for all* $(w'_1, \Gamma'_1), ..., (w'_m, \Gamma'_m)$ *such that*
   - $w_1...w_n = w'_1...w'_m$, *and*
   - $w'_i \vdash p_i \rightsquigarrow \Gamma'_i$ *for* $i = 1, ..., m$

   we have that $(w_1, ..., w_n) \geq (w'_1, ..., w'_m)$.

PROPOSITION 3.5 (Maximal Word Match Existence and Uniqueness). *The maximal word match exists and is unique because the ordering relation among word matches and environment matches is well-founded.*

POSIX Matching favors the left-most match which respects the pattern structure. Figure 5 formalizes this requirement. The maximal word match condition in rule (POSIX-Pair) ensures that the first pattern p_1 is matched by the longest sub-part of w. Similarly, rule (POSIX-Star) demands that in each iteration we match the longest sub-word. For each iteration we record the binding and therefore use multi-sets, i.e. lists.

We state some elementary properties about POSIX matching. The first property states that if there is a match there is also a POSIX match

PROPOSITION 3.6 (POSIX Completeness). *Let* w *be a word,* p *be a pattern and* Γ *a binding such that* $w \vdash p \rightsquigarrow \Gamma$. *Then, there exists* Γ' *such that* $w \vdash_{POSIX} p \rightsquigarrow \Gamma'$

Determinism of POSIX matching follows from the fact that the maximal match is unique and we favor the left-match in case of choice patterns.

PROPOSITION 3.7 (POSIX Determinism). *Let* w *be a word,* p *be a pattern and* Γ_1 *and* Γ_2 *be two bindings such that* $w \vdash_{POSIX} p \rightsquigarrow \Gamma_1$ *and* $w \vdash_{POSIX} p \rightsquigarrow \Gamma_2$. *Then,* $\Gamma_1 = \Gamma_2$.

A straightforward induction shows that every POSIX match is still a valid match w.r.t the earlier indeterministic matching relation in Figure 3.

PROPOSITION 3.8 (POSIX Correctness). *Let* w *be a word,* p *be a pattern and* Γ *a binding such that* $w \vdash_{POSIX} p \rightsquigarrow \Gamma$. *Then,* $w \vdash p \rightsquigarrow \Gamma$

Unlike greedy left-most, POSIX matching is not stable under associativity of concatenation. For example, $\{x : A, y : BAA, z : C\}$ is the POSIX match for pattern $((x : A + AB, y : BAA + A), z : AC{+}C)$ and input $ABAAC$. For pattern $(x : A{+}AB, (y : BAA + A, z : AC + C))$, we find the different POSIX match $\{x : AB, y : A, z : AC\}$.

4. Derivatives for Sub-Matching

We formalize the derivatives matching algorithm motivated in Section 2. Figure 6 summarizes all cases for building regular expression derivatives. For example, $l\backslash l = \epsilon$ and $(r_1 + r_2)\backslash\, l = r_1\backslash l{+}r_2\backslash l$. The pair case checks if the first component r_1 is empty or not. If empty, the letter l can be taken away from either r_1 or r_2. If non-empty, we take away l from r_1. In case of the Kleene star, we unfold r^* to (r, r^*) and take away the leading l from r.

$$
\begin{array}{lcll}
p & ::= & (x|w : r) & \text{Base variable with match } w \\
 & | & (x|w : p) & \text{Group variable with match } w \\
 & | & (p, p) & \text{Pairs} \\
 & | & (p + p) & \text{Choice} \\
 & | & p^* & \text{Kleene Star}
\end{array}
$$

Pattern derivative of letter: $\cdot\backslash\cdot :: p \to l \to p$

$$
\begin{array}{lcl}
(x|w : r)\backslash l & = & (x|w{+}{+}\,[l] : r\backslash l) \\
(x|w : p)\backslash l & = & (x|w{+}{+}\,[l] : p\backslash l) \\
(p_1 + p_2)\backslash l & = & p_1\backslash l + p_2\backslash l \\
(p_1, p_2)\backslash l & = & \left\{ \begin{array}{ll} (p_1\backslash l, p_2) + ({p_1}_\epsilon, p_2\backslash l) & \text{if } \epsilon \in L(p_1\downarrow) \\ (p_1\backslash l, p_2) & \text{otherwise} \end{array} \right. \\
p^*\backslash l & = & (p\backslash l, p^*)
\end{array}
$$

Pattern derivative of word: $\cdot\backslash\cdot :: p \to w \to p$

$$
\begin{array}{lcl}
p\backslash\epsilon & = & p \\
p\backslash lw & = & (p\backslash l)\backslash w
\end{array}
$$

Empty pattern of shape p: $\cdot_\epsilon :: p \to p$

$$
\begin{array}{lcl}
(x|w : r)_\epsilon & = & \left\{ \begin{array}{ll} (x|w : \epsilon) & \text{if } \epsilon \in L(r) \\ (x|w : \phi) & \text{otherwise} \end{array} \right. \\
(x|w : p)_\epsilon & = & (x|w : p_\epsilon) \\
p_1 + {p_2}_\epsilon & = & {p_1}_\epsilon + {p_2}_\epsilon \\
(p_1, p_2)_\epsilon & = & ({p_1}_\epsilon, {p_2}_\epsilon) \\
{p^*}_\epsilon & = & (p_\epsilon)^*
\end{array}
$$

Extract regular expression from p: $\cdot\downarrow :: p \to r$

$$
\begin{array}{lcl}
(x|w : r)\downarrow & = & r \\
(x|w : p)\downarrow & = & p\downarrow \\
p_1 + p_2\downarrow & = & p_1\downarrow + p_2\downarrow \\
(p_1, p_2)\downarrow & = & (p_1\downarrow, p_2\downarrow) \\
p^*\downarrow & = & (p\downarrow)^*
\end{array}
$$

Figure 7. Pattern Derivatives

$env(\cdot) :: p \to \{\Gamma\}$

$$
\begin{array}{lcl}
env((x|w : r)) & = & \left\{ \begin{array}{ll} \{\{(x, w)\}\} & \text{if } \epsilon \in L(r) \\ \{\} & \text{otherwise} \end{array} \right. \\
env((x|w : p)) & = & \{\{(x, w)\} \uplus es | es \in env(p)\} \\
env((p_1, p_2)) & = & \{e_1 \uplus e_2 | e_1 \in env(p_1), e_2 \in env(p_2)\} \\
env((p_1 + p_2)) & = & env(p_1) \uplus env(p_2) \\
env(p^*) & = & env(p)
\end{array}
$$

$match(\cdot, \cdot) :: p \to w \to \{\Gamma\}$

$$
match(p, w) \quad = \quad env(p\backslash w)
$$

Figure 8. Derivative Matching

Figure 7 formalizes the construction of pattern derivatives $p\backslash l$. In case of a pattern variable, we build the derivative of the regular expression (base variable) or inner pattern (group variable). The match is recorded in the pattern itself by appending l to the already matched word w. The pattern syntax in case of variables is therefore slightly extended. The cases for choice and star are similar to the regular expression case. The pattern match for star records the binding for each iteration.

The pair case differs compared to the regular expression case. The $\cdot\downarrow$ helper function extracts the regular expression to test if the first pattern p_1 is empty. If empty, all further matchings will only consider p_2. However, we can't simply drop p_1 because we record the variable binding in the pattern itself. Instead, we make the pattern empty such that the resulting pattern can't match any further input. See helper function $\cdot_\epsilon$.

Pattern equality: $\cdot = \cdot :: p \to p \to Bool$

$$
\begin{array}{lll}
(x|_- : r_1) = (x|_- : r_1) & \text{iff} & L(r_1) = L(r_2) \\
(x|_- : p_1) = (x|_- : p_2) & \text{iff} & p_1 = p_2 \\
(p_1, p_2) = (p_3, p_4) & \text{iff} & p_1 = p_3 \wedge p_2 = p_4 \\
p_1 + p_2 = p_3 + p_4 & \text{iff} & p_1 = p_3 \wedge p_2 = p_4 \\
p_1{}^* = p_2{}^* & \text{iff} & p_1 = p_2
\end{array}
$$

Simplifications:

$$
\begin{array}{lllll}
(S1) & p_1 + p_2 & \longrightarrow & p_2 & \text{where } L(p_1 \downarrow) = \emptyset \\
(S2) & p_1 + p_2 & \longrightarrow & p_1 & \text{where } L(p_2 \downarrow) = \emptyset \\
(S3) & p_1 + p_2 & \longrightarrow & p_1 & \text{where } p_1 = p_2
\end{array}
$$

Figure 9. Pattern Simplifications

Figure 8 puts the pieces together. The pattern derivative function $\cdot\backslash\cdot$ builds the derivative of pattern p w.r.t the input word w. Function $env(\cdot)$ computes the list of all bindings of the resulting pattern (we treat multi-sets like lists). We assume that initially the matched words in patterns are empty (ϵ).

Soundness and completeness of matching with derivatives follow immediately.

PROPOSITION 4.1 (Pattern Derivative Soundness). *Let w be a word, p be a pattern and Γ a binding such that $w \vdash p \rightsquigarrow \Gamma$. Then, $\Gamma \in env(p\backslash w)$.*

PROPOSITION 4.2 (Pattern Derivative Completeness). *Let w be a word and p be a pattern. For all $\Gamma \in env(p\backslash w)$ we have that $w \vdash p \rightsquigarrow \Gamma$.*

As motivated earlier, the first match obtained via the derivative matcher must also be the POSIX match. This is the case because derivatives don't break apart the pattern structure. Via derivatives we greedily match the left-most parts of the pattern. Hence, this must be the POSIX match.

PROPOSITION 4.3 (Pattern Derivative POSIX Match). *Let w be a word, p be a pattern and Γ be an environment such that Γ is the first environment in $env(p\backslash w)$. Then, Γ is the POSIX match.*

A well-known problem with the derivative approach is that derivatives may grow exponentially. For example, consider the following example where we again use the earlier notation $\cdot \xrightarrow{l} \cdot$ to denote the derivative step.

$$
\begin{array}{ll}
 & (x|\epsilon : A^*, y|\epsilon : A^*) \\
\xrightarrow{A} & (x|A : A^*, y|\epsilon : A^*) + (x|\epsilon : A^*, y|A : A^*) \\
\xrightarrow{A} & ((x|AA : A^*, y|\epsilon : A^*) + (x|A : A^*, y|A : A^*))+ \\
 & ((x|A : A^*, y|A : A^*) + (x|\epsilon : A^*, y|AA : A^*)) \\
\xrightarrow{A} & \ldots
\end{array}
$$

This exponential blow-up is not surprising given that via the derivative approach, we can compute all possible matchings. Given that our main interest is in the (first) POSIX match, we can apply some simplifications which have been identified in [20] in the context of testing regular language membership.

If we ignore the accumulated matchings, we can see that the underlying regular expressions of each pattern in

$$
\begin{array}{l}
((x|AA : A^*, y|\epsilon : A^*) + (x|A : A^*, y|A : A^*))+ \\
((x|A : A^*, y|A : A^*) + (x|\epsilon : A^*, y|AA : A^*))
\end{array}
$$

are identical and equivalent to (A^*, A^*). Hence, it suffices to keep only the left-most pattern which is

$$(x|AA : A^*, y|\epsilon : A^*)$$

$\cdot\backslash_p\cdot :: r \to l \to \{r\}$

$$
\begin{array}{lll}
\phi\backslash_p l & = & \{\} \\
\epsilon\backslash_p l & = & \{\} \\
l_1\backslash_p l_2 & = & \begin{cases} \{\epsilon\} & \text{if } l_1 == l_2 \\ \{\} & \text{otherwise} \end{cases} \\
(r_1 + r_2)\backslash_p l & = & r_1\backslash_p l \cup r_2\backslash_p l \\
(r_1, r_2)\backslash_p l & = & \begin{cases} \{(r, r_2) | r \in r_1\backslash_p l\} \cup r_2\backslash_p l & \text{if } \epsilon \in L(r_1) \\ \{(r, r_2) | r \in r_1\backslash_p l\} & \text{otherwise} \end{cases} \\
r^*\backslash_p l & = & \{(r', r^*) \mid r' \in r\backslash_p l\}
\end{array}
$$

Figure 10. Regular Expression Partial Derivatives

Figure 9 formalizes the simplifications for the pattern case. (S1) and (S2) remove failed matches. (S3) favors the left-most match. These simplifications should be applied after each derivative step. For our running example, we obtain then the following derivation.

$$
\begin{array}{ll}
 & (x|\epsilon : A^*, y|\epsilon : A^*) \\
\xrightarrow{A} & (x|A : A^*, y|\epsilon : A^*) \\
\xrightarrow{A} & (x|AA : A^*, y|\epsilon : A^*) \\
\xrightarrow{A} & \ldots
\end{array}
$$

Thus, we achieve a reasonable performance. However, in our experience the partial derivative matching approach appears to be superior in terms of performance. In general, it is more effective to build a (partial derivative) automata whose size is per construction at most linear in the size of the regular expression pattern, instead of constructing a potentially exponentially large (derivative) automata which needs to be simplified. Hence, we will take a closer look at the partial derivative approach next.

5. Partial Derivatives for Sub-Matching

Our goal is to construct a NFA match automata as outlined in Section 2. The states of the NFA are pattern partial derivatives.

5.1 Pattern Partial Derivatives

First, we repeat the definition of regular expression partial derivatives in Figure 10. Operator $\cdot\backslash_p\cdot$ computes partial derivatives and is similar to the derivative $\cdot\backslash\cdot$ operator. The crucial difference is that we now put sub-results into a set instead of combining them via the choice operator $+$.

For expression A^* we find

$$A^*\backslash_p A = \{(\epsilon, A^*)\} =_{simplification} \{A^*\}$$

For brevity, we omit some obvious simplifications, e.g. $(\epsilon, A^*) \longrightarrow A^*$, to reduce the number of partial derivatives. We can restate the following result already reported in [2].

PROPOSITION 5.1 (Antimirov). *For a finite alphabet Σ and regular expression r, the set of partial derivatives of r and its descendants is finite. The size of the set is linear in the size of the regular expression.*

The construction of pattern partial derivatives follows closely the construction of regular expression partial derivatives. Instead of recording the pattern match in the pattern itself as in the derivative case, we associate a pattern matching function f to each partial derivative. Figure 11 contains the details.

In case of $x : r$, we compute the partial derivatives r' of the base regular expression r. The resulting set consists of elements $(x : r', x \mapsto l)$ where $x \mapsto l$ records that letter l is consumed by some pattern variable x. In case of a variable group pattern, we compose the matchings f of the partial derivatives of the underlying pattern p with the outer group match $x \mapsto l$.

$\cdot\backslash_p\cdot :: p \to l \to \{(p, x \to l)\}$

$$
\begin{array}{lcl}
(x:r)\backslash_p l & = & \{(x:r', x \mapsto l) \mid r' \in r\backslash_p l\} \\
(x:p)\backslash_p l & = & \{(p', (x \mapsto l) \circ f) \mid (p', f) \in p\backslash_p l\} \\
(p_1 + p_2)\backslash_p l & = & p_1\backslash_p l \cup p_2\backslash l \\
(p_1, p_2)\backslash_p l & = & \left\{ \begin{array}{ll} \{((p', p_2), f) \mid (p', f) \in p_1\backslash_p l\} \cup p_2\backslash_p l & \text{if } \epsilon \in L(p_1 \downarrow) \\ \{(q, p_2) \mid q \in p_1\backslash_p l\} & \text{otherwise} \end{array} \right. \\
p^*\backslash_p l & = & \{((p', p^*), f \circ iterate_{fv(p)}) \mid (p', f) \in p\backslash_p l\}
\end{array}
$$

Figure 11. Pattern Partial Derivatives with Matching Function

The cases for choice and concatenation are straightforward. In case of the Kleene star, the purpose of $iterate_{fv(p)}$ is to keep track of the number of iterations in case of a star pattern. Thus, we can customize the matcher to keep all matchings concerning $fv(p)$ or only keep the last match (which is the typical case). For example, consider pattern $(x : AB + C)^*$. and input $ABCAB$. If $iterate_{fv(p)}$ is customized to keep the last match, then we obtain $\{x : AB\}$. If $iterate_{fv(p)}$ accumulates the individual matchings then the result will be $\{x : AB, x : C, x : AB\}$.

DEFINITION 5 (Star Pattern All Matchings). *We follow the* star pattern all matchings *policy if* $iterate_{fv(p)}$ *accumulates all matchings of each the individual iteration step.*

DEFINITION 6 (Star Pattern Last Match). *We follow the* star pattern last match *policy if* $iterate_{fv(p)}$ *removes the bindings for all variables in* $fv(p)$ *besides the last, i.e. current, match.*

Antimirov's result straightforwardly transfers to the regular expression pattern setting.

PROPOSITION 5.2 (Finiteness of Pattern Partial Derivatives). *For a finite alphabet* $\Sigma = \{l_1, ..., l_n\}$ *and pattern* p*, the set* P *of pattern partial derivatives of* p *and its descendants computed via* $\cdot\backslash_p\cdot$ *is finite. The set* P *can be described as the least fix point of the following equation*

$$\mathcal{P}(p) = \{q \mid (q, f) \in p\backslash_p l_1...l_n\} \cup \{q' \mid q \in \mathcal{P}(p), q' \in q\backslash_p l_1...l_n\}$$

where $q\backslash_p l_1...l_n = q\backslash_p l_1 \cup ... \cup q\backslash_p l_n$*. The size of the set* $\mathcal{P}(p)$ *is linear in the size of the pattern.*

We consider construction of partial derivatives for our earlier example $(x : A + y : AB + z : B)^*$. We start with $p_1 = (x : A + y : AB + z : B)^*$. Next,

$$
\begin{array}{rcl}
p_1\backslash_p A & = & \{((x:\epsilon)p_1, x \mapsto A), ((y:B)p_1, y \mapsto A)\} \\
& & \text{simplification} \\
& = & \{(p_1, x \mapsto A), (\underbrace{(y:B)p_1}_{p_2}, y \mapsto A)\}
\end{array}
$$

Like in the regular expression case, we apply some simplifications. The remaining calculations are as follows.

$$
\begin{array}{rcl}
p_1\backslash_p B & = & \{((z:\epsilon)p_1, z \mapsto B)\} \\
& & \text{simplification} \\
& = & \{(p_1, z \mapsto B)\} \\
p_2\backslash_p A & = & \{\} \\
p_2\backslash_p B & = & \{((y:\epsilon)p_1, y \mapsto B)\} \\
& & \text{simplification} \\
& = & \{(p_1, y \mapsto B)\}
\end{array}
$$

We have reached a fix point.

5.2 NFA Match Automata

The above result allows us to build a non-deterministic, finite match automata in style of Laurikari's NFAs with tagged transitions [12].

DEFINITION 7 (NFA Match Automata). *We define the NFA match automata for pattern* p *as follows. Pattern* p *is the initial state. The set of final states equals*

$$\{q \mid q \in \mathcal{P}(p), \epsilon \in L(q \downarrow)\}$$

That is, a pattern is final if its underlying regular expression contains the empty word.

The NFA transitions result from the pattern partial derivative operation as follows. For each $(p', f) \in (p\backslash_p l)$*, we introduce a transition*

$$p \xrightarrow{(l,f)} p'$$

We use a Mealy automata where the letter l *is the triggering condition and the match function* f *is the output function applied to the match environment.*

For our running example $(x : A + y : AB + z : B)^*$, the NFAs transitions are shown in Figure 1.

5.3 Greedy Left-Most Matching Algorithm

DEFINITION 8 (Greedy Left-Most Matching Algorithm). *The greedy left-most matching algorithm for pattern* p *and input word* w *is defined as the left-to-right traversal of the NFA match automata resulting from* p *for input word* w*. Sink states of transitions are kept in the order as they appear in the set of partial derivatives. Duplicate states are removed, only the left-most state is kept.*

Precisely, transitions operate on configurations

$$\{p_1, ..., p_n\} \ \Gamma_1^{p_1}...\Gamma_n^{p_n}$$

For transitions

$$
\begin{array}{c}
p \xrightarrow{(l,f_1)} p'_1 \\
... \\
p \xrightarrow{(l,f_m)} p'_m
\end{array}
$$

where $\{(p'_1, f_1), ..., (p'_m, f_m)\} = p\backslash_p l$ *and configuration*

$$\{p_1, ..., p, ..., p_n\} \ \Gamma_1^{p_1}...\Gamma^{p}...\Gamma_n^{p_n}$$

we obtain the (intermediate) derivation step

$$
\begin{array}{ll}
& \{p_1, ..., p, ..., p_n\} \ \Gamma_1^{p_1}...\Gamma^{p}...\Gamma_n^{p_n} \\
\xrightarrow{l} & \{p_1, ..., p'_1, ..., p'_m, ..., p_n\} \ \Gamma_1^{p_1}...f_1(\Gamma)^{p'_1}...f_m(\Gamma)^{p'_m}...\Gamma_n^{p_n}
\end{array}
$$

Of course, we need to reduce the remaining p_i*'s w.r.t. letter* l *to obtain a complete derivation step.*

In a configuration, the resulting set of states is simplified by removing duplicate states where we keep the left-most state. That is, $P_1 \cup \{p\} \cup P_2 \cup \{p\} \cup P_3$ *is simplified to* $P_1 \cup \{p\} \cup P_2 \cup P_3$ *until there are no duplicates.*

We elaborate on a few aspects of the algorithm.

To guarantee the greedy left-most matching order, it is important that transitions are executed as in the (left-to-right) order of partial derivatives $\{(p'_1, f_1), ..., (p'_m, f_m)\}$ as computed by $p\backslash_p l$.

Our algorithm does not require to fully annotate the pattern. The reason is that the construction of pattern partial derivatives strictly breaks apart the pattern structure. Consider the base case $(x : r)$ from Figure 11

$$(x:r)\backslash_p l = \{(x:r', x \mapsto l) \mid r' \in r\backslash_p l\}$$

For $p = (x : (A + AB), y : (B + \epsilon))$, we obtain (after simplification)

$$p\backslash_p A = \{(y:(B+\epsilon), x \mapsto A), ((x:B)(y:(B+\epsilon)), y \mapsto B)\}$$

This guarantees that we compute the greedy left-most match $\{x : A, y : B\}$ for input AB.

The set of NFA states is a constant, bound by the size of p. Hence, the running time of the algorithm is linear in the size of the input. In summary, we can state the following results. By construction, the algorithm follows the greedy left-to-right matching policy.

PROPOSITION 5.3 (Greedy Algorithm Correctness and Complexity). *The greedy left-most matching algorithm implements the greedy left-most matching policy and it's running time is linear in the size of the input. The space required to store the final and all intermediate match environments is a constant, bound by the size of the pattern.*

5.4 NFA Comparison

In Figure 12 we show the size of the resulting match automata for Thompson, Glushkov and partial derivative NFAs. Our focus is on the specific automata construction method without any post-simplification step. As can be seen, the partial derivative NFA is 'smaller' compared to the other NFAs. This is confirmed through [1], [2] and [21]. Thompson NFAs often have the largest sets of states and transitions due to the ϵ transitions. According to [21], for large alphabet sets, partial derivative NFAs are about half the sizes of Glushkov NFAs in terms of states and transitions.

In the last example, we use Σ to denote the union of all ASCII characters. In this particular case, the Glushkov NFA construction scales the worst. This is due to the fact that each character creates a state in the NFA [15]. Due to the Kleene star, there are at least 256*256 transitions. The Thompson NFA does not scale well in terms of states, either. Our implementation de-sugars $(A+B+C)$ to $(A+(B+C))$ and therefore more states will be generated. Of course, the size of the Thompson NFA could be significantly reduced if we avoid this de-sugaring step.

We have built reference implementations of greedy left-most matching for all three NFA approaches. Basic measurements show that the matcher based on partial derivatives is generally much faster. These are 'non-optimized' reference implementations. Hence, the result is not necessarily conclusive but is an indication that matching with partial derivatives is promising. We provide conclusive evidence in the later Section 7.

6. Extensions for Real world Applications

So far, we have presented the core of a system to support regular expression pattern matching. Regular expression patterns used in the real world applications require some extensions. For instance, patterns with sub-match binding is expressed implicitly in the regular expression pattern via groups, and the concatenation requires no constructor. In the following section, we use `p` (in text mode) to denote a pattern in the real world application syntax, and p (in math mode) to denote a pattern in our internal syntax defined earlier. The syntax of `p` will be explained by examples in the following paragraphs

6.1 Group Matching

In many mainstream languages that support regular expression pattern matchings, such as Perl, python, awk and sed, programmers are allowed to use "group operator", $(\cdot)$ to mark a sub-pattern from the input pattern, and the sub strings matched by the sub pattern can be retrieved by making reference to integer index of the group. For instance, `(a*)(b*)` is equivalent to pattern $(x : a^*, y : b^*)$ in our notation. Sending the input "aab" to `(a*)(b*)`. yields $["aa", "b"]$, where the first element in the list refers to the binding of the first group `(a*)` and the second element refers to the binding of the second group `(b*)`. Group matching is supported in our implementation by translating the groups into patterns with pattern variables.

6.2 Character Classes

Character class is another extension we consider. For instance, `[0-9]` denotes a single numeric character. `[A-Za-z]` denotes one alphabet character. We translate these two types of character classes into regular expressions via the choice operation $+$. There are some other type of character classes that require more work to support. Character classes can be negated. `[^0-9]` denotes any non-numeric character. Another related extension that is available in real world application is the dot symbol `.`, which can be used to represent any character. There are two different approaches to support the dot symbol and negative character classes. One approach is to translate the dot symbol into a union of all ASCII characters and to translate negative character classes to unions of all ASCII characters excluding those characters mentioned in the negated character classes. The other approach is to introduce these two notations `.` and $\texttt{[\^{}}l_1...l_n\texttt{]}$ to our internal regular expression pattern language, such that

$$.\backslash_p l = \{\epsilon\}$$

$$\texttt{[\^{}}l_1...l_n\texttt{]}\backslash_p l = \begin{cases} \{\epsilon\} & \text{if } l \in \{l_1, ..., l_n\} \\ \{\} & \text{otherwise} \end{cases}$$

In our implementation, we adopt the latter because the resulting regular expressions are smaller in size hence it is more efficient.

6.3 Non-Greedy Match

The symbol `?` in the pattern `(a*?)(a*)` indicates that the first sub pattern `a*` is matched non-greedily, i.e. it matches with the shortest possible prefix, as long as the suffix can be consumed by the sub pattern that follows.

Non-greedy matching can be neatly handled in our implementation. To obtain a non-greedy match for a pair pattern (p_1, p_2) where p_1 is not greedy, we simply reorder the two partial derivatives coming from $(p_1, p_2)\backslash_p l$. We extend the pair pattern case of $\cdot\backslash_p\cdot$ in Figure 11 as follows,

$$(p_1, p_2)\backslash_p l = \begin{cases} p_2\backslash_p l \ \cup & \\ \{((p', p_2), f) | (p', f) \in p_1\backslash_p l\} & \text{if } \epsilon \in L(p_1 \downarrow) \\ & \wedge \neg greedy(p_1) \\ \{((p', p_2), f) | (p', f) \in p_1\backslash_p l\} & \\ \cup\ p_2\backslash_p l & \text{if } \epsilon \in L(p_1 \downarrow) \\ & \wedge greedy(p_1) \\ \{(y, p_2) | y \in p_1\backslash_p l\} & \text{otherwise} \end{cases}$$

Extending our pattern language with the greediness symbol is straight-forward and the definition of $greedy(\cdot) :: p \rightarrow bool$ is omitted for brevity.

6.4 Anchored and Unanchored Match

Given a pattern `p`, `^p$` denotes an anchored regular expression pattern. The match is successful only if the input string is fully matched by `p`. A pattern which is not starting with `^` and not ending with `$` is considered unanchored. An unanchored pattern can match with any sub-string of the given input, under some matching policy. Our implementation clearly supports anchored matches. To support unanchored match, we could rewrite the unanchored pattern `p` into an equivalent anchored form, `^.*?p.*$`, and proceed with anchored match.

6.5 Repetition Pattern

Repetition patterns can be viewed as the syntactic sugar of sequence patterns with Kleene star. `p{m}` repeats the pattern `p` for `m` times; `p{n,m}` repeats the pattern `p` for at least `n` times and at maximum `m` times. It is obvious that the repetition pattern can be "compiled" away using the composition of sequence and Kleene star operators.

Other extensions such as unicode encoding and back references are not considered in this work.

7. Experimental Results

We measure the performance of our regular expression sub-matching approach based on partial derivatives. We have built an optimized implementation of greedy left-to-right matching. Our

Pattern	Thompson NFA		Glushkov NFA		Partial Derivative NFA	
	# states	# transitions	# states	# transitions	# states	# transitions
$(x : A + AB, (y : BAA + A, z : AC + C))$	23	24	11	14	8	11
$(x : A^*, y : A^*)$	6	7	3	5	3	5
$(x : (A + B)^*, y : (A, (A + \epsilon), B))$	14	16	6	12	5	9
$(x : \Sigma^*)$	768	1023	257	65792	2	512

Figure 12. NFA Match Automata Comparison

implementation is entirely written in Haskell and we employ several (fairly standard) optimizations such as hashing of states etc.

The benchmarkings were conducted on a Mac OSX 10.6.8 with 2.4GHz Core 2 Duo and 8GB RAM. The benchmark programs were compiled using GHC 7.0.4. We divide the benchmarkings into two groups. In the first group, we compare our implementation with other native Haskell implementation. In the second group, we challenge the C implementations.

The complete set of the benchmark results can be located via

`http://code.google.com/p/xhaskell-library/`

in which the broader scope of comparison is considered.

7.1 Contenders and Benchmark Examples

The contenders are:

- PD-GLR our greedy left-to-right matching implementation.
- Weighted [7], the native Haskell implementation of regular expression matching. Weighted's sub matching is fairly limited because it only supports one variable pattern, i.e. `_ :: .* ( x :: r ) _ :: .*`. Nevertheless, we included Weighted in the comparison. [1] The implementation is accessible via the Haskell package Text.Regex.Weighted;
- TDFA, the native Haskell implementation of [11]. It is accessible via the library Text.Regex.TDFA [19].
- RE2, the google library re2;
- PCRE, the pcre library, accessible via the Haskell wrapper Text.Regex.PCRE [17];
- PCREL, the light-weight wrapper to the pcre library, accessible via Text.Regex.PCRE.Light [18]

The benchmark sets consist of examples adopted from [6], and some others being extracted from the real world applications that we encountered. For the up-coming performance measurements, we select the following representative examples:

1. A simple pattern which involves no choice, in which our implementation does not take any advantage;
2. A contrived pattern which builds up a lot of choices, in which our algorithm out-performs PCRE's and is on par with RE2's;
3. Two real world application examples in which we assess the practicality of our implementation.

7.2 Competing with Native Haskell Implementations

In Figure 13, Figure 14 and Figure 15, we compare the run-time performance of PD-GLR, TDFA and Weighted. As a convention in all figures, the x-axis measures the size of the input; the y-axis measures the time taken to complete the match, measured in seconds.

Figure 13 shows the results of matching the pattern `^.*$` against some randomly generated text. PD-GLR's performance is on par

[1] Other implementations, e.g. Text.Regex.Parsec, Text.Regex.DFA and Text.Regex.TRE couldn't be compiled at the time when this paper was written. Text.RegexPR didn't scale at all for any of our examples. Therefore, we exclude these packages from our benchmark comparison.

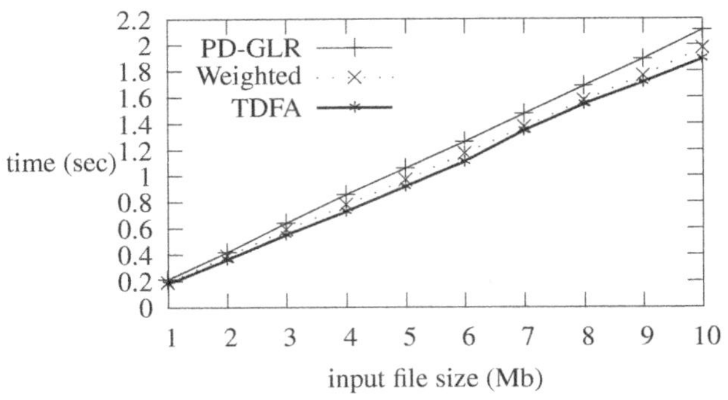

Figure 13. Native Haskell benchmark `^.*$`

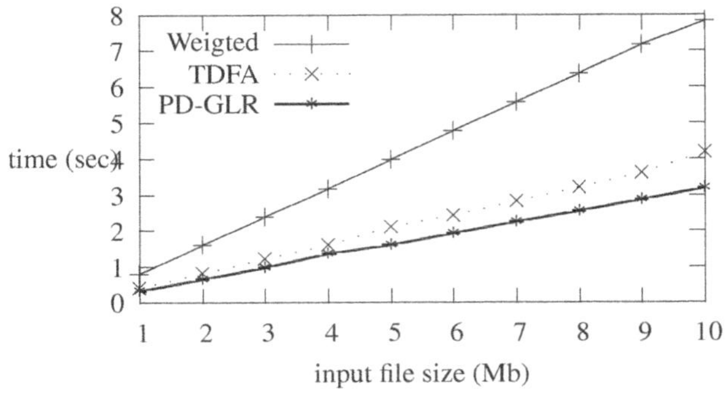

Figure 14. Native Haskell benchmark `^.*foo=([0-9]+).*bar=([0-9]+).*$`

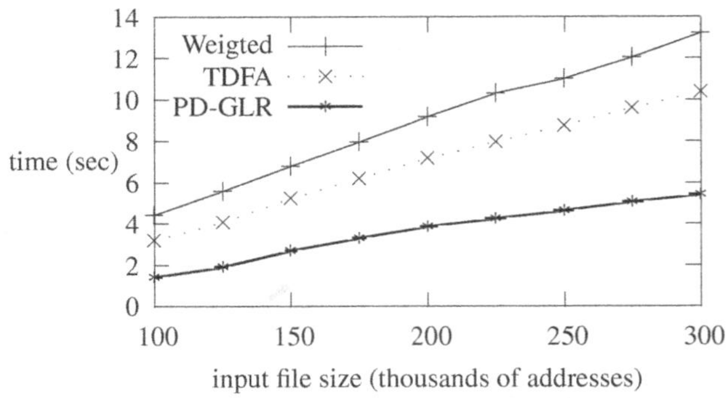

Figure 15. Native Haskell benchmark `^(.*) ([A-Za-z]{2}) ([0-9]{5})(-[0-9]{4})?$`

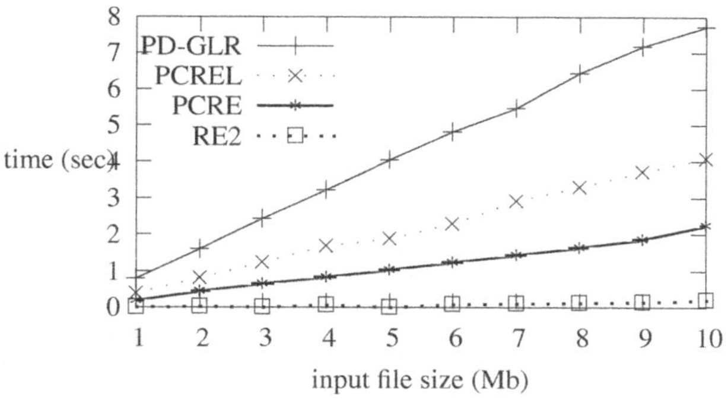

Figure 16. C benchmark `(.*)$`

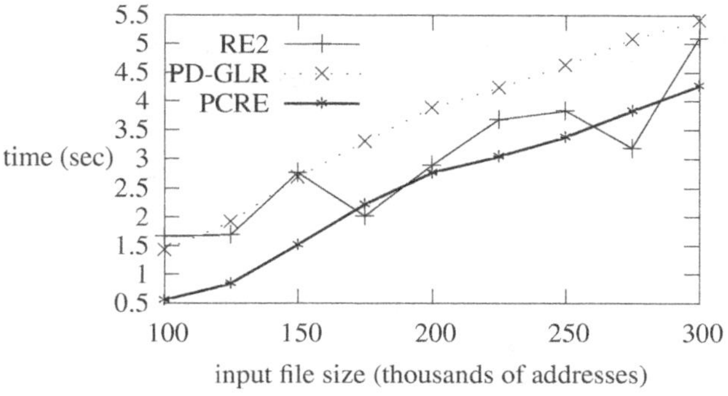

Figure 17. C benchmark `^(.*) ([A-Za-z]{2}) ([0-9]{5})(-[0-9]{4})?$`

with others because the pattern is simple.[2] In Figure 14 and Figure 15, we use two examples extracted from some real world applications. The pattern in Figure 14,

```
^.*foo=([0-9]+).*bar=([0-9]+).*$
```

extracts the values of some HTTP URL Get parameters, `foo` and `bar`, from the random input strings. For example, the string "http://www.mysite.com/?foo=123&bar=567" matches with the above pattern.

The pattern in Figure 15

```
^(.*) ([A-Za-z]{2}) ([0-9]{5})(-[0-9]{4})?$
```

extracts the US addresses from the input. For instance, the address "Mountain View, CA 90410" matches with the pattern. Note that the x-axis in Figure 15 measures the number of addresses in the input. The charts show that in case of complex patterns, PD-GLR out-performs Weighted thanks to the smaller automata. PD-GLR performs marginally better than TDFA in these examples.

7.3 Competing with C Implementation and Wrappers

In this section, we challenge ourselves by benchmarking against some implementation directly using C or wrapping around the C PCRE library.

In Figure 16, we use a wild card pattern `(.*)$` to match with some randomly generated text. PD-GLR's performance is slightly worse than PCRE and PCREL. RE2 is taking the lead by a factor

[2] Weighted does not support the anchor extension. In the actual benchmark code, we mimic it by using the `fullMatch` function. Further more, Weighted does not support group matching via (), which is automatically ignored by the regular expression compiler.

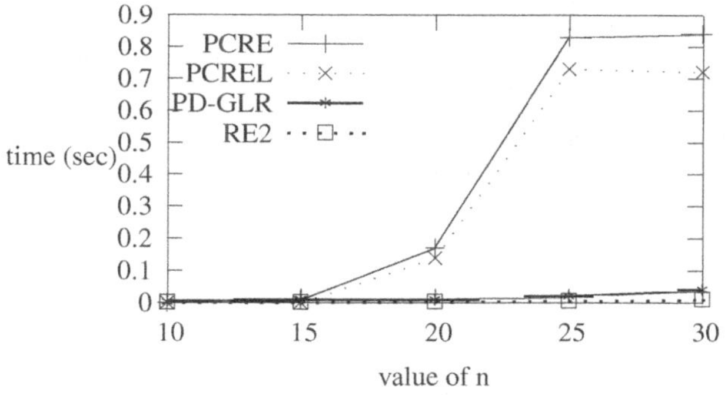

Figure 18. C benchmark `^(a?){n}(a){n}$`

of ten. Profiling PD-GLR for this example shows that most time is spent in de-composing the input ByteString [4], which is of course less efficient than the C counterparts which have direct access to the character array.

In Figure 17, we re-apply the example from Figure 15 to PCRE and RE2. It shows that PD-GLR and RE2 perform slightly worse than PCRE. The difference is about 1 second, due to the ByteString decomposition. Note that the run-time statistics of PCREL is omitted in Figure 17. In this particular example, PCREL performs the worst. The difference is by hundreds of seconds compared to others.

In the last example in Figure 18, we match a string with `n` "a"s against the pattern `^(a?){n}(a){n}$`. The x-axis measures the value of input `n`. For instance, let `n` is 2, we match "aa" with `^(a?){2}(a){2}$`. The sub-pattern `(a?){2}` will *not* match anything. PCRE does not scale well because of back-tracking. When the input `n` reaches 30, the program exits with a segmentation fault. PCREL shares the same behavior as PCRE since they share the same C backend library. The non-backtracking algorithms PD-GLR and RE2 show the similar performance. What is omitted in Figure 18 is that, when `n > 30`, PD-GLR is performing non-linearly. Profiling reveals that the overhead is arising from the compilation phase. We plan to address this issue in the future work.

7.4 Performance Measurement Summary

Our measurements show that ours is the fastest native Haskell implementation of regular expression sub-matching. Compared to state-of-the art C-based implementations RE2 and PCRE, our implementation has a fairly competitive performance.

8. Related Work and Discussion

Our use of derivatives and partial derivatives for regular expression matching is inspired by our own prior work [14, 22] where we derive up-cast and down-cast coercions out of a proof system describing regular expression containment based on partial derivatives. The goal of this line of work is to integrate a XDuce-style language [9] into a variant of Haskell [23]. The focus of the present work is on regular expression sub-matching and some specific matching policies such as greedy and POSIX.

Regular expression derivatives have recently attracted again some attention. The work in [16] employs derivatives for scanning, i.e. matching a word against a regular expression. To the best of our knowledge, we are the first to transfer the concept of derivatives and partial derivatives to the regular expression sub-matching setting.

Prior work relies on mostly Thompson NFAs [24] for the construction of the matching automata. For example, Frisch and Cardelli [8] introduce a greedy matching algorithm. They first run the input from right-to-left to prune the search space. A similar approach is pursued in some earlier work by Kearns [10].

Laurikari [12, 13] devises a POSIX matching automata and introduces the idea of tagged transitions. A tag effectively corresponds to our incremental matching functions which are computed as part of partial derivative operation $\cdot\backslash_p\cdot$.

Kuklewicz has implemented Laurikari style tagged NFAs in Haskell. He [11] discusses various optimizations techniques to bound the space for matching histories which are necessary in case of (forward) left-to-right POSIX matching.

Cox [6] reports on a high-performance implementation of regular expression matching and also gives a comprehensive account of the history of regular expression match implementations. We refer to [6] and the references therein for further details. He introduces the idea of right-to-left scanning of the input for POSIX matching.

As said, all prior work on efficient regular expression matching relies mostly on Thompson NFAs or variants of it. Partial derivatives are a form of NFA with no ϵ-transitions. For a pattern of size n, the partial derivative NFA has $O(n)$ states and $O(n^2)$ transitions. Thompson NFAs have $O(n)$ states as well but $O(n)$ transitions because of ϵ-transitions.

The work in [8] considers ϵ-transitions as problematic for the construction of the matching automata. Laurikari [12, 13] therefore first removes ϵ-transitions whereas Cox [6] builds the ϵ-closure. Cox algorithm has a better theoretical complexity in the range of $O(n * m)$ where m is the input language. In each of the m steps, we must consider $O(n)$ transitions. With partial derivatives we cannot do better than $O(n^2 * m)$ because there are $O(n^2)$ transitions to consider. However, as shown in [2] the number of partial derivatives states is often smaller than the number of states obtained via other NFA constructions. Our performance comparisons indicate that partial derivatives are competitive.

Fischer, Huch and Wilke [7] discuss a rewriting-based approach to support regular expressions based on Glushkov NFAs. They build the matching automata incrementally during the actual matching whereas we build a classic matching automata based on partial derivative NFAs. There exists a close connection between Glushkov and partial derivative NFAs, e.g. see [1]. However, as our benchmark results show it appears that matching via partial derivative NFAs is superior. As mentioned earlier, the Fischer et. al. approach is fairly limited when it comes to sub-matching. Three matching policies are discussed (leftmost, leftlong and longest). Longest seems closest to POSIX and greedy left-most but not formal investigations on this topic are conducted in [7].

9. Conclusion

Our work shows that regular expression sub-matching can be elegant using derivatives and partial derivatives. The Haskell implementation of our partial derivative matching algorithm is the fastest among all native in Haskell implementations we are aware of. Our performance results show that we are competitive compared to state-of-the-art C-based implementations such as PCRE and RE2. Our extensive set of benchmarks show that our approach yields competitive performance results.

Acknowledgments

We thank Christopher Kuklewicz for useful discussions about his TDFA system, Christian Urban for his comments and Russ Cox for pointing us to some related work. We are grateful to some ICFP'10, ICFP'11 and PPDP'12 reviewers for their helpful comments on previous versions of this paper.

References

[1] C. Allauzen and M. Mohri. A unified construction of the Glushkov, follow, and Antimirov automata. In *Proc. of MFCS'06*, volume 4162 of *LNCS*, pages 110–121. Springer, 2006.

[2] V. M. Antimirov. Partial derivatives of regular expressions and finite automaton constructions. *Theoretical Computer Science*, 155(2):291–319, 1996.

[3] J. A. Brzozowski. Derivatives of regular expressions. *J. ACM*, 11(4):481–494, 1964.

[4] bytestring: Fast, packed, strict and lazy byte arrays with a list interface. `http://www.cse.unsw.edu.au/~dons/fps.html`.

[5] R. Cox. Regular expression matching can be simple and fast (but is slow in java, perl, php, python, ruby, ...), 2007. `http://swtch.com/~rsc/regexp/regexp1.html`.

[6] R. Cox. Regular expression matching in the wild, 2010. `http://swtch.com/~rsc/regexp/regexp3.html`.

[7] S. Fischer, F. Huch, and T. Wilke. A play on regular expressions: functional pearl. In *Proc. of ICFP'10*, pages 357–368. ACM Press, 2010.

[8] A. Frisch and L. Cardelli. Greedy regular expression matching. In *Proc. of ICALP'04*, pages 618– 629. Spinger-Verlag, 2004.

[9] H. Hosoya and B. C. Pierce. Regular expression pattern matching for XML. In *Proc. of POPL '01*, pages 67–80. ACM Press, 2001.

[10] S. M. Kearns. Extending regular expressions with context operators and parse extraction. *Software - Practice and Experience*, 21(8):787–804, 1991.

[11] C. Kuklewicz. Forward regular expression matching with bounded space, 2007. `http://haskell.org/haskellwiki/RegexpDesign`.

[12] V. Laurikari. NFAs with tagged transitions, their conversion to deterministic automata and application to regular expressions. In *SPIRE*, pages 181–187, 2000.

[13] V. Laurikari. Efficient submatch addressing for regular expressions, 2001. Master thesis.

[14] K. Z. M. Lu and M. Sulzmann. An implementation of subtyping among regular expression types. In *Proc. of APLAS'04*, volume 3302 of *LNCS*, pages 57–73. Springer-Verlag, 2004.

[15] G. Navarro and M. Raffinot. Compact dfa representation for fast regular expression search. In *Proc. of Algorithm Engineering'01*, volume 2141 of *LNCS*, pages 1–12. Springer, 2001.

[16] S. Owens, J. Reppy, and A. Turon. Regular-expression derivatives reexamined. *Journal of Functional Programming*, 19(2):173–190, 2009.

[17] regex-pcre: The pcre backend to accompany regex-base. `http://hackage.haskell.org/package/regex-pcre`.

[18] pcre-light: A small, efficient and portable regex library for perl 5 compatible regular expressions. `http://hackage.haskell.org/package/pcre-light`.

[19] regex-tdfa: A new all haskell tagged dfa regex engine, inspired by libtre. `http://hackage.haskell.org/package/regex-tdfa`.

[20] G. Rosu and M. Viswanathan. Testing extended regular language membership incrementally by rewriting. In *Proc. of RTA'03*, volume 2706 of *LNCS*, pages 499–514. Springer, 2003.

[21] Nelma Moreira Sabine Broda, Antonio Machiavelo and Rogerio Reis. Study of the average size of glushkov and partial derivative automata, Octorber 2011.

[22] M. Sulzmann and K. Z. M. Lu. A type-safe embedding of XDuce into ML. In *Proc. of ACM SIGPLAN Workshop on ML*, Electronic Notes in Computer Science, pages 229–253, 2005.

[23] M. Sulzmann and K. Z. M. Lu. Xhaskell - adding regular expression types to haskell. In *Proc. of IFL'07*, volume 5083 of *LNCS*, pages 75–92. Springer-Verlag, 2007.

[24] K. Thompson. Programming techniques: Regular expression search algorithm. *Commun. ACM*, 11(6):419–422, 1968.

Functional Semantics of Parsing Actions, and Left Recursion Elimination as Continuation Passing

Hayo Thielecke
University of Birmingham, UK
H.Thielecke@cs.bham.ac.uk

Abstract

Parsers, whether constructed by hand or automatically via a parser generator tool, typically need to compute some useful semantic information in addition to the purely syntactic analysis of their input. Semantic actions may be added to parsing code by hand, or the parser generator may have its own syntax for annotating grammar rules with semantic actions. In this paper, we take a functional programming view of such actions. We use concepts from the semantics of mostly functional programming languages and adapt them to give meaning to the actions of the parser. Specifically, the semantics is inspired by the categorical semantics of lambda calculi and the use of premonoidal categories for the semantics of effects in programming languages. This framework is then applied to our leading example, the transformation of grammars to eliminate left recursion. The syntactic transformation of left-recursion elimination leads to a corresponding semantic transformation of the actions for the grammar. We prove the semantic transformation correct and relate it to continuation passing style, a widely studied transformation in lambda calculi and functional programming.

Categories and Subject Descriptors D.3.1 [*Programming Languages*]: Formal Definitions and Theory—Semantics

General Terms Theory

Keywords Continuations; functional programming; lambda calculus; parsing; semantics; types; verification

1. Introduction

When writing interpreters or denotational semantics of programming languages, one aims to define the meaning of an expression in a clean, compositional style. As usually understood in computer science, the principle of compositionality states that the meaning of an expression arises as the meaning of its constituent parts.

For example, in a compositional semantics for arithmetic expressions, the semantic definitions may even appear trivial and no more than a font change:

$$[\![E_1\texttt{-}E_2]\!] = [\![E_1]\!] - [\![E_2]\!]$$

Of course, the simplicity of such rules is due to the fact that the semantic operations (in this case subtraction $-$) and the syntax (in this case `-`) that they interpret are chosen to be as similar as possible. A more formal statement of this idea is initial algebra semantics [8]. The constructors for the syntax trees form the initial algebra, so that any choice of corresponding semantic operations induces a unique algebra homomorphism. Intuitively, the initial algebra property means that we take our syntax tree for a given expression, replace syntactic operation (say, `-`) everywhere by their semantic counterpart (subtraction in this case), and then collapse the resulting tree by evaluating it to an integer.

The simple picture of semantics as tree node replacement followed by evaluation assumes that parsing has been taken care of, in a reasonable separation of concerns. If, however, parsing is taken into account, the situation becomes more complicated. We would still hope any semantics to be as compositional as possible (sometimes called "syntax-directed" in compiling [1]), but now the grammar must be suitable for the parsing technology at hand. Many of the grammars widely used in semantics are not, including the example above, assuming a grammar rule $E :- E\texttt{-}E$, or the usual grammar for lambda calculus with the rule for application as juxtaposition, $M :- M\,M$. Both these rules exhibit left recursion (and also result in an ambiguous grammar). There are standard techniques for transforming grammars to make them more amenable to parsing. If we take compositionality seriously, the sematics should also change to reflect the new grammar; moreover the transformation should be correct relative to the old grammar and its compositional semantics. The old grammar, while unsuitable for parsing, may give a more direct meaning to the syntactic constructs where the intended meaning may be more evident than for the transformed grammar and its semantics.

Our running example of left recursion elimination and its semantics will be a simple expression grammar. We first discuss it informally, in the hope that it already provides some intuition of continuations arising in parsing.

Example 1.1 Consider the following grammar rules, where the rule (2) has an immediate left-recursion for E:

$$E \;:-\; \texttt{1} \tag{1}$$

$$E \;:-\; E - E \tag{2}$$

Eliminating left recursion from this grammar involves the introduction of a new grammar symbol E' (together with some rules for it), and replacing (1) with a new grammar rule that uses the new symbol in the rightmost position:

$$E \;:-\; \texttt{1}\,E' \tag{3}$$

The semantics of E' needs an argument for receiving the value of its left context. For example in (3), the value 1 needs to be passed to the semantic action for E'. Now compare the original (1) to the transformed (3). The original rule is in direct style, in the sense that 1 is returned as the value of the occurrence of E. By contrast, the

PPDP'12, September 19–21, 2012, Leuven, Belgium.

transformed rule (3) is in continuation passing style, in that 1 is not *returned* here; rather, it is passed to its continuation, given by E'.

As research communities, parsing and semantics can be quite separated, with (to put it crudely) the former using formal language theory and the latter lambda calculi. The contribution of the present paper is in bridging the gap between parsing a language and its semantics. To do so, we use formal tools that were originally developed on the semantic side. One such semantic tool is category theory. Due to its abstract nature, it can capture both syntax and semantics.

One of these formal tools will be premonoidal categories [22], which were originally developed as an alternative to Moggi's monads as notions of computation [17] for the semantics of functional languages with effects (such as ML). Much as monads in category theory are related to monads in Haskell, premonoidal categories have a functional programming analogue, Hughes's arrows [10, 20].

The idea of the "tensor" $\otimes$ in premonoidal categories is easy to grasp from a functional programming point of view. Suppose we have a function $f : X_1 \to X_2$. Then we can still run the same function while carrying along an additional value of type Y. That gives us two new functions, by multiplying f with Y from the left or right, as it were:

$$\begin{array}{rcl} f \otimes Y & = & \lambda(x : X_1, y : Y).(f(x), y)) \\ & : & (X_1 \otimes Y) \longrightarrow (X_2 \otimes Y) \end{array}$$

$$\begin{array}{rcl} Y \otimes f & = & \lambda(y : Y, x : X_1).(y, f(x)) \\ & : & (Y \otimes X_1) \longrightarrow (Y \otimes X_2) \end{array}$$

(For the notational conventions we will use regarding letters, arrows, etc, see Figure 1.) While category theory can be used to structure functional programs and to reason about their meaning algebraically, categories are not restricted to morphisms being functions. Syntactic structures, such as strings, sequences, paths, traces, etc, can also be used to construct categories. For our purposes here, it will be useful to define a $\otimes$ that simply concatenates strings:

$$w \otimes \beta \stackrel{\text{def}}{=} w\,\beta$$

This operation will be used to characterise leftmost derivations. Suppose we have a grammar rule $A :- \alpha$. By multiplying it with some string w not containing any non-terminals on the left, and a string β (possibly containing non-terminals), we get a leftmost derivation step:

$$(w\,A\,\beta) \longrightarrow (w\,\alpha\,\beta)$$

Leftmost and rightmost derivations characterise the two main classes of parser generators, LL and LR [1]. The former include for example ANTLR [19], while the latter include LALR(1) parsers generators such as yacc.

Usually it is more convenient to calculate with lambda terms rather than translate them into their categorical semantics in a Cartesian closed category. For our purposes here, however, diagram chases are convenient and perspicuous. Since the meaning of a string to be parsed is generated compositionally from its derivation, we can take the derivation, translate it into the corresponding semantic diagram, and chase morphisms to reason about semantic equality.

Background and prerequisites

This paper assumes only basic familiarity with grammars and parsing, at the level of an undergraduate compiling course. To the extent that it is needed, some category theory will be presented as a form of simply-typed functional programming. Familiarity with the semantics of lambda calculus in a Cartesian closed category will be useful (as covered in programming language semantics texts, e.g. by Gunter [9]). The category theory used in this paper is elementary and closely related to functional programming. Readers who prefer type theory can safely view it as a form of type system that emphasizes sequential composition and lends itself to proof by diagram chase.

A, B, C, E, L	:	nonterminal symbols of a grammar
a, b	:	terminal symbols of a grammar
f, g, k	:	functions, variables of function type
x, y, z, p	:	variables
X, Y, X_1	:	types, objects in a category
$X \otimes Y$	:	product type, premonoidal functor
(x, y)	:	pair of type $X \otimes Y$
$()$	:	empty tuple of type **Unit**
$\alpha, \beta, \gamma, \delta, \varphi, \psi$	:	strings of terminal or nonterminals
ε	:	empty string
λ	:	lambda-abstraction; not used for strings
v, w, w_1, w_2	:	Strings of terminal symbols
$\alpha\,\beta$	:	concatenation of strings α and β
$A :- \alpha$	:	grammar rule for replacing A by α
$f : X \to Y$	:	f is a morphism from X to Y
$\alpha \to_{\mathcal{G}} \beta$	:	derivation of string β from α (a special case of a morphism)
$\rightsquigarrow$	:	abstract machine transition step
$\langle w, \sigma, k \rangle$	:	abstract machine configuration
$f \cdot g$	:	composition of morphisms in diagrammatic order: first$f$, then g
$[\,]$	:	empty list or path
$[\![\alpha]\!]$	:	semantics of a string α as a type or set
$[\![d]\!]$	:	semantics of a derivation d as a function

Figure 1. Notational conventions

Outline of the paper

Section 2 describes parser generators in terms of simple abstract machines. Section 3 casts the notion of leftmost derivation (fundamental for LL parsers) into a mathematical form adapted from premonoidal categories. The semantics of derivations is then defined compositionally from their associated parsing actions in Section 4. With the framework in place, Section 5 then uses it on the leading example: the elimination of left recursion induces a semantic transformation. We prove the correctness of the semantic transformation (Section 6) and reconstruct it as a form of continuation passing in Section 7. Section 8 concludes with a discussion of related work and directions for further research.

2. Parser generators

We recall some definitions, as can be found in any compiling text. A grammar is of the form

$$\mathcal{G} = (\mathbf{T}_{\mathcal{G}}, \mathbf{N}_{\mathcal{G}}, \mathbf{S}_{\mathcal{G}}, :-)$$

where $\mathbf{T}_{\mathcal{G}}$ is a finite set of terminal symbols, $\mathbf{N}_{\mathcal{G}}$ is a finite set of non-terminal symbols, $\mathbf{S}_{\mathcal{G}}$ is the start symbol, and $:-$ is a finite binary relation between non–terminal symbols and strings of symbols.

LL parsers attempt to construct a leftmost derivation of the string they are parsing [1]. If we leave open the question of *how* the parser decides on its next move, we can formulate LL parsers as a (remarkably simple) abstract machine, albeit a non-deterministic one. Given a grammar, an LL parser is an abstract machine of the following form. Configurations are pairs $\langle w, \sigma \rangle$. Here w is the remaining input string, consisting of terminal symbols, and σ is the parsing stack, consisting of a sequence of grammar symbols (each of which can be terminal or non-terminal). We write the top of the parsing stack on the left. The parser has two kind of transitions: matching and predicting. In a matching transition, an input symbol a is removed both from the stack and the input. In a predicting transition, a non-terminal A at the top of the parsing stack is popped off and replaced by the right-hand-side of a grammar rule $A :\!- \alpha$ for it.

$$\begin{array}{rcl} \langle a\,w, a\,\sigma \rangle & \leadsto & \langle w, \sigma \rangle \\ \langle w, A\,\sigma \rangle & \leadsto & \langle w, \alpha\,\sigma \rangle \\ & & \text{if there is a rule } A :\!- \alpha \end{array}$$

The initial configuration consists of the initial input w and the parsing stack holding start symbol S of the grammar, that is $\langle w, S \rangle$. The accepting configuration has both an empty input and an empty parsing stack $\langle \varepsilon, \varepsilon \rangle$. As defined here, the machine is highly non-deterministic, since for a given A at the top of the parsing stack there may be many different rules $A \to \alpha_1, \ldots, A \to \alpha_n$ with different right-hand sides. Given bad choices, the machine may get stuck in a state of the form $\langle a\,w, b\,\sigma \rangle$ for some $a \neq b$.

In parser construction, the problem is how to make the above non-deterministic machine deterministic. For LL parsers, the choice between rules is made using lookahead, leading to parser classes such as LL(1) or LL(k), using 1 or some larger numbers of symbols in the input w. In particular, some modern parser generator such as ANTLR [19] use large lookaheads where required.

Here we are not concerned with the parser construction; on the contrary, we assume that there is a parser generator that successfully generates a parser for the grammar at hand. In other words, the above abstract machine is *assumed* to be deterministic, for example by looking at the first k symbols of the input.

The problem that this paper aims to address is how to bridge the gap between the parsing abstract machine and the semantics of the language that is being parsed. We extend the parsing abstract machine with a third component that iteratively computes meaning during the parsing. The extended machine makes a transition

$$\langle w, A\,\sigma, k_1 \rangle \quad \leadsto \quad \langle w, \alpha\,\sigma, k_2 \rangle$$

whenever the parsing machine decides to make a prediction transition using a rule $A \to \alpha$. (In ANTLR, semantic information can also be used to guide the choice of predictive transition, in addition to lookahead. We do not model this feature.) Each such rule has an associated semantic action $[\![A :\!- \alpha]\!]$ that tells us how to compute the new semantic component k_2 from the preceding one k_1. As usual in programming language theory, the semantic actions will be idealised using λ-calculus. The semantic actions should arise in a compositional way from the syntactic transitions of the parser constructing a leftmost derivation. Ideally, the connection between syntax and semantics should be maintained even if the grammar needs to be transformed. Grammars may have to be rewritten to make them suitable for parsing. Specifically, left recursion is a problem for parsers relying on lookahead [1]. There is a standard grammar transformation, left recursion elimination, that removes the problem for many useful grammars (such as expressions in arithmetic). It is easy enough to understand if we are only interested in the language as a set of strings; but if we take a more fine-grained view of derivations and their semantic actions, the semantic transformation corresponding to the grammar refactoring is quite subtle. It involves introducing explicit dependence on context, which we show to be a form of a widely studied semantic transformation, continuation-passing style (CPS) [21, 28, 29].

3. From grammars to L-categories

For each grammar, we define a category with some structure that will be useful for defining the semantic actions.

Definition 3.1 (L-category of a grammar) Given a grammar $\mathcal{G}$, we define a directed graph $\mathbf{Graph}(\mathcal{G})$ as follows:

- The nodes of $\mathbf{Graph}(\mathcal{G})$ are strings of grammar symbols α.
- Whenever there is a grammar rule $A :\!- \alpha$, a terminal string w and a string β, $\mathbf{Graph}(\mathcal{G})$ has an edge from $w\,A\,\beta$ to $w\,\alpha\,\beta$.

The L-category for $\mathcal{G}$ is defined as the path category [16] for the graph $\mathbf{Graph}(\mathcal{G})$. Morphisms in the L-category are called leftmost derivations.

We write morphisms in the L-category as lists of pairs of the form $(w\,A\,\beta, w\,\alpha\,\beta)$. Composition of morphisms is by list concatenation. The identity morphism $\mathrm{id}_\alpha : \alpha \longrightarrow \alpha$ is given by the empty list. Each morphism in a category has a unique domain and codomain. As they are not evident in case of the empty list, we need to tag each morphism with its domain and codomain. However, as long as they are evident from the context, we omit these additional tags and represent morphisms as lists.

The reason for defining leftmost derivations via L-categories rather than in the style found in most compiler construction texts [1] is that they allow us to introduce some extra structure.

For each string of grammar symbols α of $\mathcal{G}$, the L-category has an endofunctor, written as $- \otimes \alpha$. That is to say, for each leftmost derivation $d : \beta \to \gamma$, there is a leftmost derivation

$$(d \otimes \alpha) : (\beta \otimes \alpha) \to (\gamma \otimes \alpha)$$

On objects, $- \otimes \alpha$ is string concatenation, that is,

$$\beta \otimes \alpha \stackrel{\text{def}}{=} \beta\,\alpha$$

On morphisms, $\otimes\alpha$ extends each step in the derivation with α. Writing list :: for list cons, as in ML, we define:

$$\begin{array}{rcl} [\,] \otimes \alpha & \stackrel{\text{def}}{=} & [\,] \\ ((w\,A\,\gamma, w\,\delta\,\beta)::p) \otimes \alpha & \stackrel{\text{def}}{=} & ((w\,A\,\gamma\,\alpha, w\,\delta\,\beta\,\alpha)::(p \otimes \alpha) \end{array}$$

Notice that we do not generally define a functor $\alpha \otimes -$ that works symmetrically. If α contains non-terminal symbols, then adding it *on the left* of a leftmost derivation does not produce a leftmost derivation. However, for string w consisting entirely of terminal symbols, the leftmost character of a derivation is preserved if we add such a string everywhere on the left. Hence we define an endofunctor $w \otimes -$ for each terminal string w. For a leftmost derivation $d : \beta \to \gamma$, we have

$$(w \otimes d) : (w\,\beta) \to (w\,\gamma)$$

defined by

$$\begin{array}{rcl} w \otimes [\,] & \stackrel{\text{def}}{=} & [\,] \\ w \otimes ((w_2\,A\,\gamma, w_2\,\delta\,\beta)::p) & \stackrel{\text{def}}{=} & ((w\,w_2\,A\,\gamma\,\alpha, w\,w_2\,\delta\,\beta\,\alpha) \\ & & ::(w \otimes p) \end{array}$$

$$\frac{A :- \alpha}{[(A,\alpha)] : A \to \alpha}$$

$$\frac{}{[\,] : \alpha \to \alpha} \qquad \frac{d_1 : \alpha \to \beta \qquad d_2 : \beta \to \gamma}{d_1 \cdot d_2 : \alpha \to \gamma}$$

$$\frac{d : \alpha \to \beta}{w \otimes d : w\,\alpha \to w\,\beta} \qquad \frac{d : \beta \to \gamma}{d \otimes \alpha : \beta\,\alpha \to \gamma\,\alpha}$$

Figure 2. Type system for leftmost derivations

$$X_1 \xrightarrow{\quad f \quad} X_2$$

$$
\begin{array}{ccc}
Y_1 & X_1 \otimes Y_1 \xrightarrow{\quad f \otimes Y_1 \quad} X_2 \otimes Y_1 \\
\downarrow g & \big\downarrow X_1 \otimes g \qquad\qquad \big\downarrow X_2 \otimes g \\
Y_2 & X_1 \otimes Y_2 \xrightarrow{\quad f \otimes Y_2 \quad} X_2 \otimes Y_2
\end{array}
$$

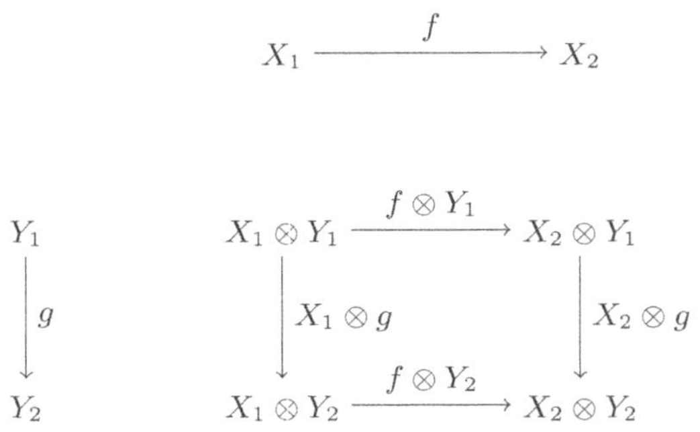

Figure 3. A morphism f is called *central* if the square commutes for all g

The definition of L-category is inspired of Power and Robinson's premonoidal categories [22, 23] and by Lambek's syntactic calculus [13]. In particular, the idea of a functor $- \otimes \alpha$ for each object comes from premonoidal categories, whereas the distinction between left and right functors is reminiscent of the non-commutative contexts in Lambek's calculus.

It is worth noting that L-categories have a very substructural flavour, as it were. We do not even assume a symmetry isomorphism

$$\alpha \otimes \beta \cong \beta \otimes \alpha$$

In premonoidal categories, which are intended for modelling programming languages with effects, a symmetry is a natural ingredient, as it models swapping two values. In an L-category for an arbitrary grammar, there is no reason to expect a leftmost derivation leading from $\alpha\,\beta$ to $\beta\,\alpha$.

Readers who prefer types to categories may refer to Figure 2, presenting the L-category construction as types for derivations. The first rule lifts grammar rules to derivations. The next two rules construct paths, and the final two rules introduce the two tensors. As the leftmost derivations are lists, we can always break a morphism down into its derivation steps. Each such step gives us a grammar rule $A :- f$ together with the left context w and the right context γ in which it was applied. We will use this decomposition for giving semantics to morphisms in L-categories.

4. Semantic actions

A grammar only defines a language, in the sense of a set of strings. It does not say what those strings mean. To give meaning to the strings in the language, we need to associate a semantic action to each grammar rule, so that the meaning of a string can be constructed by parsing the string.

The language in which the semantic actions are written is a simply-typed lambda calculus with finite products. We will use this lambda calculus as a semantic meta-language, without committing to any particular model. For simply-typed lambda calculus, the set-theoretic semantics is so straightforward that we think of any semantic action

$$[\![d]\!] : [\![\beta]\!] \to [\![\alpha]\!]$$

term as just a function between sets $[\![\beta]\!]$ and $[\![\alpha]\!]$.

However, it is not necessary that the lambda calculus is pure. It could be a call-by-value lambda calculus with side effects, such as state. Such a lambda calculus could be interpreted using the Kleisli category of a monad [17] or a Freyd category [24]. The details of categorical semantics are beyond the scope of this paper, but there is one aspect that is immediately relevant here: the notion of *central* morphisms [22]. A morphism f is called central if for all g, the two ways of composing f and g given in Figure 3 are the same. Programs with effects are usually not central. For example, suppose f writes to some shared variable and g reads from it: then the order of f or g coming first is observable, and the square does not commute. When lambda abstractions are interpreted in a Freyd category via the adjunction

$$\frac{f : (X \otimes Y) \to Z}{\lambda f : X \to (Y \to Z)}$$

then the λf is always central. This reflects the situation in call-by-value or computational lambda calculi, where a lambda abstraction $\lambda x . M$ is always a value [17, 21].

For each non-terminal symbol A, we assume a type $[\![A]\!]$ for the semantic values of strings derived from that symbol.

Definition 4.1 (Semantic action for a grammar) Given a grammar $\mathcal{G}$, a semantic action $[\![-]\!]$ consists of

- For each non-terminal symbols A of $\mathcal{G}$, a type $[\![A]\!]$. For a terminal symbol a, its semantic type is the unit type containing only the empty tuple:

$$[\![a]\!] \stackrel{\text{def}}{=} \mathbf{Unit} = \{\,(\,)\,\}$$

The types are extended to strings of symbols $X_1 \ldots X_n$ by taking the product of the types of the X_j:

$$[\![X_1 \ldots X_n]\!] \stackrel{\text{def}}{=} [\![X_1]\!] \otimes \cdots \otimes [\![X_n]\!]$$

- For each grammar rule $A :- \alpha$, there is a function (going in the opposite direction) of type

$$[\![A :- \alpha]\!] : [\![\alpha]\!] \longrightarrow [\![A]\!]$$

Definition 4.2 (Semantic action of a derivation) Let $\mathcal{G}$ be a grammar with a semantic action $[\![-]\!]$. For each derivation $d : \alpha \to_{\mathcal{G}} \beta$, we define the semantic action of d as as morphism $[\![d]\!] : [\![\beta]\!] \longrightarrow [\![\alpha]\!]$ as follows:

- If d is the empty derivation of a string α from itself, $d = [\![[\,]]\!] : \alpha \to_{\mathcal{G}} \alpha$, then its semantic action is the identity function on the semantic of the string α:

$$[\![d]\!] \stackrel{\text{def}}{=} \mathsf{id}_{[\![\alpha]\!]}$$

- If d is not empty, we decompose it into its first derivation step using some rule $A :- \alpha$ and the remaining derivation d_1:

$$d = ((w\,A\,\beta, w\,\alpha\,\beta) :: d_1$$

Then $[\![d]\!]$ is defined as follows:

$$[\![d]\!] \stackrel{\text{def}}{=} [\![d_1]\!] \cdot (([\![w]\!]) \otimes [\![A :- \alpha]\!] \otimes [\![\beta]\!])$$

Note that Definition 4.2 is just the evident inductive extension of a semantic action from rules to all derivations. We could even have omitted the induction and just appealed to the initial property of the

$$\langle w, S, \lambda x.x\rangle \xrightarrow{\leadsto^*} \langle w_1, A\,\sigma_1, k_1\rangle \xrightarrow{\leadsto} \langle w_1, \alpha\,\sigma_1, ([\![A :\!-\ \alpha]\!] \otimes [\![\sigma_1]\!])\cdot k_1\rangle \xrightarrow{\leadsto^*} \langle \varepsilon, \varepsilon, k_2\rangle$$

$$S \xrightarrow{\quad d_1 \quad} v_1\,A\,\sigma \xrightarrow{\quad v_1 \otimes (A :\!-\ \alpha) \otimes \sigma_1 \quad} v_1\,\alpha\,\sigma_1$$

$$[\![S]\!] \xleftarrow{\quad [\![d_1]\!] = k_1 \quad} [\![A]\!] \otimes [\![\sigma_1]\!] \xleftarrow{\quad [\![A :\!-\ \alpha]\!] \otimes [\![\sigma_1]\!] \quad} [\![\alpha]\!] \otimes [\![\sigma_1]\!]$$

Figure 4. WSK machine move for a grammar rule $A :\!-\ \alpha$ with syntactic and semantic invariants

path category [16]. Also note that a derivation is already identified by the sequence of grammar rules $a :\!-\ \alpha$ that it uses. The reason for explicitly including the left context w and the right context β in Defintion 3.1 is that it makes it easier to define the action of a derivation in Definition 4.2. The values of types $[\![w]\!]$ and $[\![\beta]\!]$ are simply carried along when we define the meaning of a grammar rule application in this context:

$$[\![(w\,A\,\beta, w\,\alpha\,\beta)]\!] : ([\![w]\!] \otimes [\![\alpha]\!] \otimes [\![\beta]\!]) \longrightarrow ([\![w]\!] \otimes [\![A]\!] \otimes [\![\beta]\!])$$

Since the semantics of terminal symbols is the unit type, $[\![a]\!] \stackrel{\text{def}}{=}$ **Unit**, it follows that $[\![w]\!] \cong$ **Unit**, so that $[\![w]\!] \otimes -$ contributes little to a semantics action.

The benefit of having defined a semantic action $[\![d]\!]$ for each derivation d is this: we can now return to the abstract machines from Section 2 and extend them with a semantic component that computes the effect of all the parsing moves.

Like the SECD [14] and CEK [7] machines, the WSK machine is named for its components: a remaining input word w, a stack s, and a semantic continuation k. The latter is a continuation in the sense that it represents a function to the final answer, as the K in the CEK machine.

Definition 4.3 (WSK machine) Given a grammar $\mathcal{G}$ with a semantic action $[\![-]\!]$, the parsing machine with semantic actions is defined as follows:

- The machine has configurations of the form
$$\langle w, \sigma, k\rangle$$
Here w is the remaining input (a string of terminals), σ is the parsing stack (a string of grammar symbols), and k is a function.
- The initial configuration of the machine for a given input w is
$$\langle w, S, \lambda x.x\rangle$$
The initial parsing stack consists only of the start symbol S of $\mathcal{G}$, and the initial semantic action is the identity $\lambda x.x$.
- An accepting configuration of the machine is of the form
$$\langle \varepsilon, \varepsilon, k\rangle$$
with an empty input and parsing stack.
- The transitions of the machine are predicting and matching moves:
$$\begin{array}{rcl} \langle w, A\,\sigma, k\rangle & \leadsto & \langle w, \alpha\,\sigma, ([\![A :\!-\ \alpha]\!] \otimes [\![\sigma]\!])\cdot k\rangle \\ \langle a\,w, a\,\sigma, k\rangle & \leadsto & \langle w, \sigma, \mathbf{unitleft}\cdot k\rangle \end{array}$$
Here **unitleft** is the left identity for the unit type:
$$\mathbf{unitleft} : (\mathbf{Unit} \otimes [\![\sigma]\!]) \longrightarrow [\![\sigma]\!]$$
As a term, $\mathbf{unitleft} = (\lambda(\,(), x).x)$.

Theorem 4.4 (WSK machine correctness) For each input string w, if the WSK machine accepts the input with final configuration $\langle \varepsilon, \varepsilon, k\rangle$, then it has constructed a leftmost derivation $d : S \to w$ and the final answer $k = [\![d]\!]$.

Proof We prove an invariant that holds for each configuration reachable from the initial configuration. The syntactic invariant is as follows: for each reachable configuration $\langle w_1, \sigma_1, k_1\rangle$, there is a leftmost derivation

$$d_1 : S \to_{\mathcal{G}} v_1\,\sigma_1$$

where v_1 represents the input that the machine has already consumed, so that $w = v_1\,w_1$. Moreover $k = [\![d_1]\!]$. The proof is by induction on the length of d_1. The most interesting inductive step is a predict move, as depicted in Figure 4. Note that when the machine terminates with a configuration of the form

$$\langle \varepsilon, \varepsilon, k\rangle$$

by Lemma 4.4, the type of the final action is k : **Unit** $= [\![\varepsilon]\!] \to [\![S]\!]$. Hence we have an element of the semantic type $[\![S]\!]$ of the start symbols as the final answer computed by the parser using the actions given by $[\![-]\!]$ for the grammar.

As discussed in Section 2, we assume that the parser generator turns the non-deterministic WSK machine for a given grammar and its action into a deterministic parser. For example, ANTLR guides the predict moves by computing appropriate lookaheads, and it implements the parsing rules as Java methods, so that both the parsing stack σ and the semantic k are managed by the call stack of the programming language. The same holds if a recursive descent parser is written by hand.

Example 4.5 Consider the following grammar $\mathcal{G}$:

$$\begin{array}{rcl} A & :\!- & B\,\alpha \\ A & :\!- & B\,\beta \end{array}$$

Because both rules for A start with the same B, this grammar has a FIRST/FIRST conflict, causing problems for LL parsers relying on lookahead [1]. A simple solution is to refactor the grammar using a fresh non-terminal C. The resulting grammar $\mathcal{F}$ has these rules:

$$\begin{array}{rcl} A & :\!- & B\,C \\ C & :\!- & \alpha \\ C & :\!- & \beta \end{array}$$

But what about the semantic actions? The new symbol C depends on some left context given by B, so we add an argument to pass in the corresponding semantic information:

$$[\![C]\!] \stackrel{\text{def}}{=} [\![B]\!] \to [\![A]\!]$$

For all other symbols X, we let $[\![X]\!] = [\![X]\!]$, and we write simply $[\![X]\!]$ for both. Let

$$\begin{array}{rcl} f & \stackrel{\text{def}}{=} & [\![A :\!-\ B\,\alpha]\!] : ([\![B]\!] \otimes [\![\alpha]\!]) \to [\![A]\!] \\ g & \stackrel{\text{def}}{=} & [\![A :\!-\ B\,\beta]\!] : ([\![B]\!] \otimes [\![\beta]\!]) \to [\![A]\!] \end{array}$$

Original rules for L:

$$\begin{array}{lll} L & :- & \psi_1 \\ & \vdots & \\ L & :- & \psi_m \\ L & :- & L\,\varphi_1 \\ & \vdots & \\ L & :- & L\,\varphi_n \end{array}$$

Transformed rules:

$$\begin{array}{lll} L & :- & \psi_1\,L' \\ & \vdots & \\ L & :- & \psi_m\,L' \\ L' & :- & \varphi_1\,L' \\ & \vdots & \\ L' & :- & \varphi_n\,L' \\ L' & :- & \varepsilon \end{array}$$

Figure 5. Transformation of grammar rules

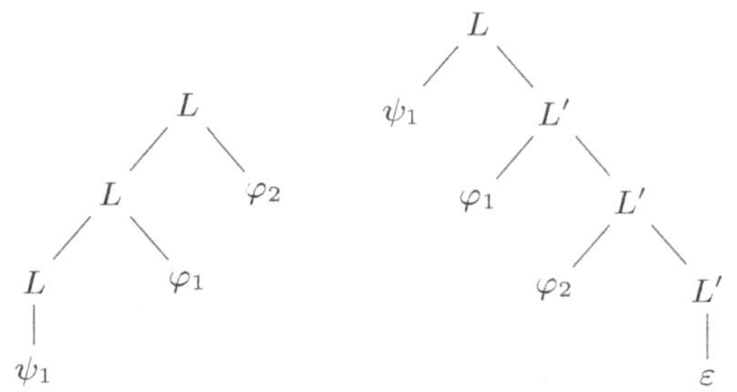

Figure 6. Parse trees for $L \to_{\mathcal{G}} \psi_1\,\varphi_1\,\varphi_2$ and $L \to_{\mathcal{F}} \psi_1\,\varphi_1\,\varphi_2$ in the original and transformed grammar

We define the semantic actions $[\![-]\!]$ in the new grammar $\mathcal{F}$ as follows:

$$\begin{array}{rcl} [\![C :- \alpha]\!] & \stackrel{\text{def}}{=} & \lambda x.\lambda y.f(y,x) \\ & : & [\![\alpha]\!] \to ([\![B]\!] \to [\![A]\!]) \\ \\ [\![C :- \beta]\!] & \stackrel{\text{def}}{=} & \lambda x.\lambda y.g(y,x) \\ & : & [\![\beta]\!] \to ([\![B]\!] \to [\![A]\!]) \\ \\ [\![A :- B\,C]\!] & \stackrel{\text{def}}{=} & \lambda x.\lambda f.f(x) \\ & : & ([\![B]\!] \otimes \underbrace{([\![B]\!] \to [\![A]\!])}_{[\![C]\!]}) \to [\![A]\!] \end{array}$$

To prove correctness of this transformation, we need to consider all leftmost derivations

$$\begin{array}{lll} d_1 & : & A \to_{\mathcal{G}} w \\ d_2 & : & A \to_{\mathcal{F}} w \end{array}$$

and show that $[\![d_1]\!] = [\![d_2]\!]$.

5. Left recursion elimination

We recall the standard definition of (immediate) left-recursion elimination as presented in compiling texts [1]. Left recursion could also occur indirectly via other symbols, but that indirection can be eliminated.

Definition 5.1 (Left recursion) Given a grammar $\mathcal{G}$ and a non-terminal symbols L of $\mathcal{G}$, a non-terminal L is called *immediately left-recursive* if there is a rule of the form $L :- L\,\varphi_i$ for some string φ_i.

Left-recursion elimination for L in $\mathcal{G}$ produces a new grammar $\mathcal{F}$. Let the left-recursive rules for L in $\mathcal{G}$ be

$$L :- L\,\varphi_i$$

and let the remaining rules for L in $\mathcal{G}$ be

$$L :- \psi_j$$

Then $\mathcal{F}$ is constructed by adding a new non-terminal symbol L' and replacing the rules for L as given in Figure 5.

Note that since L' is chosen to be distinct from all other grammar symbols, it is at the right of the new rules and does not occur in φ_i or ψ_j, whereas L may occur anywhere in L or ψ_j, except in the left-most position of ψ_j.

The resulting grammar $\mathcal{F}$ generates the same language as the original grammar $\mathcal{G}$. The usual proof sketch for this fact points out that the rules for L' resemble the translation of Kleene star to grammars, in that L' can either terminate with the ε-rule, or go around the loop once more to generate another φ_i. One can then picture L as follows:

$$L \quad :- \quad \overbrace{(\psi_1 \mid \ldots \mid \psi_m)\,\underbrace{(\varphi_1 \mid \ldots \mid \varphi_n)^*}_{L'}}^{L}$$

This simple intuition for left-recursion elimination works for the language generated by the grammars, as the language is a set of strings, with no further structure. If we take a more intensional or fine-grained view of derivations or parse trees, the effect of the transformation is less easy to grasp. As shown in Figure 6, parse trees are rotated. If we compute the meaning of a string by way of a tree walk, as in compositional semantics, the semantics is transformed globally.

Example 5.2 The standard example of left-recursion elimination found in many compiling texts consists of expressions in arithmetic with various binary operators for addition, multiplication, subtraction, etc. For simplicity, we take the subset given by a single binary operator `-` and a single constant `1`. This gives us one grammar rule with, and one without, left recursion. Let the grammar $\mathcal{G}$ be given by the following rules:

$$\begin{array}{lll} E & :- & \mathtt{1} \\ E & :- & E - E \end{array}$$

In the notation of the left-recursion elimination construction, we have the following case:

$$L = E \qquad \psi_j = \mathtt{1} \qquad \varphi_i = \mathtt{-}\,E$$

Consequently, the construction adds a fresh non-terminal symbol E', and the rules of the transformed grammar $\mathcal{F}$ are as follows:

$$\begin{array}{lll} E & :- & \mathtt{1}\,E' \\ E' & :- & \mathtt{-}\,E\,E' \\ E' & :- & \varepsilon \end{array}$$

When a parser generator parses a string, it does not just construct a derivation. It also performs semantic actions associated with each grammar rule. For the simple expression grammar, it is clear what these actions should be. For a rule

$$E :- E\ \mathtt{-}\ E$$

each of the occurrences of E on the right-hand side returns an integer, and the whole subtree (corresponding to the occurrence of E on the left-hand side of the rule) should return the difference of these two numbers.

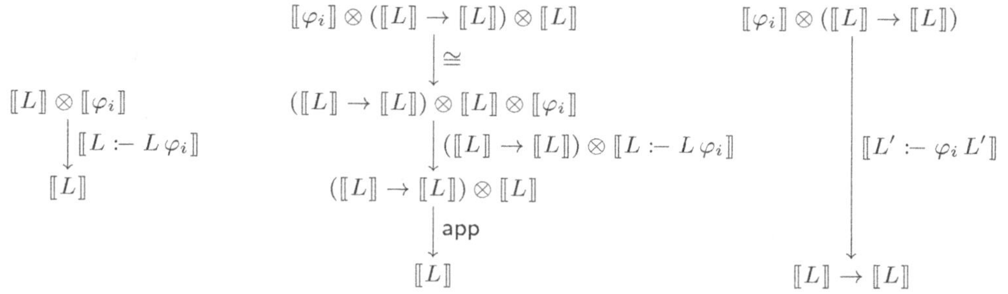

Figure 7. From $[\![L :- L\,\varphi_i]\!]$ to $[\![L' :- \varphi_i\,L']\!]$

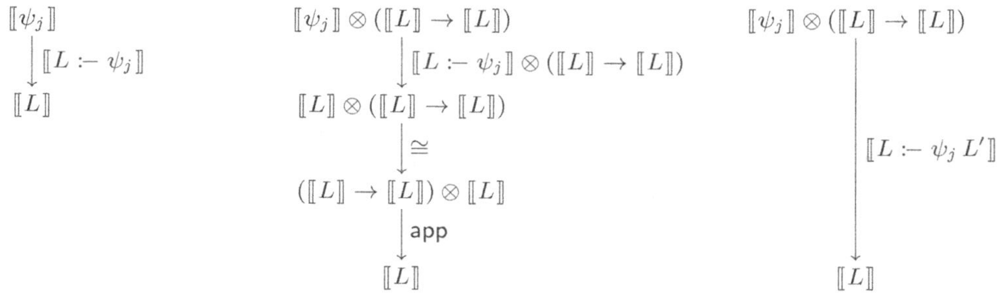

Figure 8. From $[\![L :- \psi_j]\!]$ to $[\![L :- \psi_j\,L']\!]$

Definition 5.3 (Transformation of semantic actions) Let $\mathcal{G}$ be a grammar with a semantic action $[\![-]\!]$. We assume that $\mathcal{G}$ contains left recursion for a non-teminal L. Let $\mathcal{F}$ be the grammar that is constructed from $\mathcal{G}$ by the left-recursion elimination transformation as in Definition 5.1. We define a semantic action $[\![-]\!]$ for $\mathcal{F}$ that matches how grammar rules are transformed in Figure 5.

- For the new non-terminal L', we define its semantic type as

$$[\![L']\!] \stackrel{\text{def}}{=} [\![L]\!] \longrightarrow [\![L]\!]$$

- For a left-recursive grammar rule rule $L :- L\,\varphi_i$ in $\mathcal{G}$, let its action be

$$f \stackrel{\text{def}}{=} [\![L :- L\,\varphi_i]\!] : ([\![L]\!] \otimes [\![\varphi_i]\!]) \longrightarrow [\![L]\!]$$

As shown in Figure 7, we first construct a morphism (in the middle) column

$$([\![\varphi_i]\!] \otimes ([\![L]\!] \to [\![L]\!]) \otimes [\![L]\!]) \to [\![L]\!]$$

Lambda abstraction of $[\![L]\!]$ gives us

$$\begin{array}{ll} & [\![L' :- \varphi_i\,L']\!] \\ : & ([\![\varphi_i]\!] \otimes ([\![L]\!] \to [\![L]\!])) \to ([\![L]\!] \to [\![L]\!]) \end{array}$$

Equivalently, using lambda calculus syntax, we write

$$[\![L' :- \varphi_i\,L']\!] \stackrel{\text{def}}{=} \lambda(p,k).\lambda x.k(f(x,p))$$

Here the types are:

$$p : [\![\varphi_i]\!] \qquad k : [\![L]\!] \longrightarrow [\![L]\!] \qquad x : [\![L]\!]$$

- For a rule $L :- \psi_j$ in $\mathcal{G}$ that is not left-recursive, let its action be

$$g \stackrel{\text{def}}{=} [\![L :- \psi_j]\!] : [\![\psi_j]\!] \to [\![L]\!]$$

As shown in Figure 8, we add a parameter of type $[\![L]\!] \to [\![L]\!]$ and apply it to the result of g, which gives us a morphism

$$\begin{array}{ll} & [\![L :- \psi_j\,L']\!] \\ : & ([\![\psi_j]\!] \otimes ([\![L]\!] \to [\![L]\!])) \to [\![L]\!] \end{array}$$

Writing the same with lambda terms, we have:

$$[\![L :- \psi_j\,L']\!] \stackrel{\text{def}}{=} \lambda(p,k).k(g(p))$$

- For the additional ε-rule for L', we take the isomorphism

$$\textbf{unitleft} : (\textbf{Unit} \otimes [\![L]\!]) \to L$$

and lambda-abstract, to give

$$\begin{array}{ll} & [\![L' :- \varepsilon]\!] \\ : & [\![\varepsilon]\!] \to ([\![L]\!] \to [\![L]\!]) \end{array}$$

Written as a lambda term, $[\![L' :- \varepsilon]\!] \stackrel{\text{def}}{=} (\lambda\,().(\lambda x.x))$.

- For all other non-terminals and grammar rules, the action of $\mathcal{F}$ is defined to be equal to that of $\mathcal{G}$.

Example 5.4 We continue Example 5.2 by extending it with semantic actions: we have $[\![E]\!] = \mathbb{N}$ and the semantic functions as follows:

$$\begin{array}{rcl} [\![E :- \mathtt{1}]\!] & \stackrel{\text{def}}{=} & \lambda(()).1 \\ [\![E :- E - E]\!] & \stackrel{\text{def}}{=} & \lambda(x,(),y).x - y \end{array}$$

Left-recursion elimination introduces a fresh non-terminal E'. Its semantic type is:

$$[\![E']\!] \stackrel{\text{def}}{=} \mathbb{N} \longrightarrow \mathbb{N}$$

The semantic actions for the transformed grammar rules can be written as lambda-terms as follows:

$$[\![E :- \mathbf{1}\ E']\!] \stackrel{\text{def}}{=} \lambda((), k).k(1)$$
$$: (\mathbf{Unit} \otimes (\mathbb{N} \to \mathbb{N})) \to \mathbb{N}$$

$$[\![E' :- \mathbf{-}\ E\ E']\!] \stackrel{\text{def}}{=} \lambda((), x, k).\lambda y.k(y - x)$$
$$: (\mathbf{Unit} \otimes \mathbb{N} \otimes (\mathbb{N} \to \mathbb{N})) \to (\mathbb{N} \to \mathbb{N})$$

$$[\![E' :- \varepsilon]\!] \stackrel{\text{def}}{=} \lambda().\lambda x.x$$
$$: \mathbf{Unit} \to (\mathbb{N} \to \mathbb{N})$$

6. Correctness of the transformation

We first note that the transformed grammar simulates derivations of the original grammar. The simulation is then extended from syntax to semantics. The proof relies on the fact that the semantics $[\![-]\!]$ preserves the relevant structure, so that a diagram of derivations gives rise to a diagram of their semantics actions. Correctness amounts to showing that the resulting semantic diagram commutes.

Lemma 6.1 Let d be a derivation $d : \alpha \to_{\mathcal{F}} w$ where L' does not occur in α. Then one of the following holds:

- No rules for L or L' are used in d.
- The derivation d contains a derivation of a terminal string from L. Moreover, this sub-derivation is of the form $L \to_{\mathcal{F}} w\, L'$ followed by $L' :- \varepsilon$.

Consider a leftmost derivation where the next step is a rule for L:

$$w\, L\, \gamma \to_{\mathcal{F}} w\, \psi_j\, L'\, \gamma$$

The only way we can reach a string not containing L' from $w\, \psi_j\, L'\, \gamma$ is via the rule $L' :- \varepsilon$. In a leftmost derivation, all non-terminals to the left of the occurrence of L' must first have been eliminated by way of a derivation $d : \psi_j \to_{\mathcal{F}} w_2$. This gives us a derivation

$$w\, L\, \gamma \to_{\mathcal{F}} w\, \psi_j\, L'\, \gamma \to_{\mathcal{F}} w\, w_2\, L'\, \gamma \to_{\mathcal{F}} w\, w_2\, \gamma$$

Lemma 6.2 Derivations in $\mathcal{F}$ can be simulated by those in $\mathcal{G}$ while the semantics is preserved, in the following sense.

1. For each derivation $d : \alpha \to_{\mathcal{F}} w$ where L' does not occur in α, there is a derivation $d^{\triangle} : \alpha \to_{\mathcal{G}} w$ such that $[\![d^{\triangle}]\!] = [\![d]\!]$.
2. For each derivation $d : L \to_{\mathcal{F}} w\, L'$ there is a derivation $d^{\triangle} : L \to_{\mathcal{G}} w$ such that for all $k : [\![L]\!] \longrightarrow [\![L]\!]$, the following diagram commutes:

$$
\begin{array}{ccc}
[\![L]\!] & \xleftarrow{\quad [\![d]\!] \quad} & [\![w]\!] \otimes ([\![L]\!] \to [\![L]\!]) \\
{\scriptstyle k} \Big\uparrow & & \Big\uparrow {\scriptstyle [\![w]\!] \otimes \lambda k} \\
[\![L]\!] \otimes [\![\alpha]\!] & \xleftarrow{\ [\![d^{\triangle}]\!] \otimes [\![\alpha]\!]\ } & [\![w]\!] \otimes [\![\alpha]\!]
\end{array}
$$

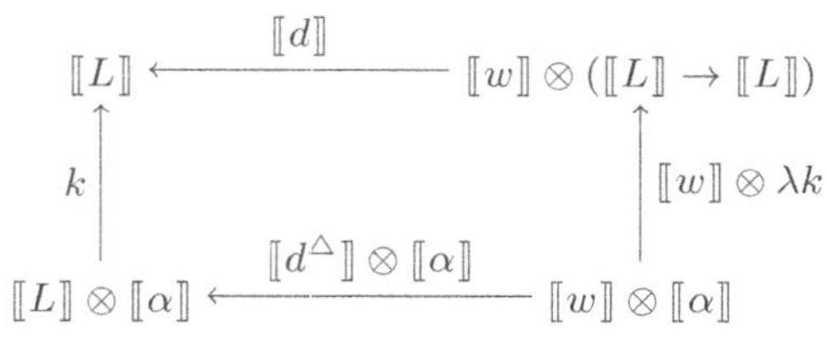

Proof We prove both statements of the lemma by simultaneous induction on the length of the derivation. Details are omitted, except for the three most difficult inductive steps, using rules involving L'.

1. Assume we have a derivation $d_1 : L \to_{\mathcal{F}} w\, L'$, and we extend it to a derivation d by using the rule $L' :- \varepsilon$. By the induction hypothesis, we have a derivation $d_1^{\triangle}$ making the square above commute for all k. In particular, it commutes for k being the

isomorphism $[\![L]\!] \otimes \mathbf{Unit} \cong [\![L]\!]$. Hence the following diagram commutes by the definition of $[\![L' :- \varepsilon]\!]$ in Definition 5.3:

$$
\begin{array}{ccc}
[\![L]\!] & \xleftarrow{\quad [\![d_1]\!] \quad} & [\![w]\!] \otimes ([\![L]\!] \to [\![L]\!]) \\
{\scriptstyle \cong} \Big\uparrow & & \Big\uparrow {\scriptstyle [\![w]\!] \otimes [\![L' :- \varepsilon]\!]} \\
[\![L]\!] \otimes [\![\varepsilon]\!] & \xleftarrow{\ [\![d_1^{\triangle}]\!] \otimes [\![\varepsilon]\!]\ } & [\![w]\!] \otimes [\![\varepsilon]\!]
\end{array}
$$

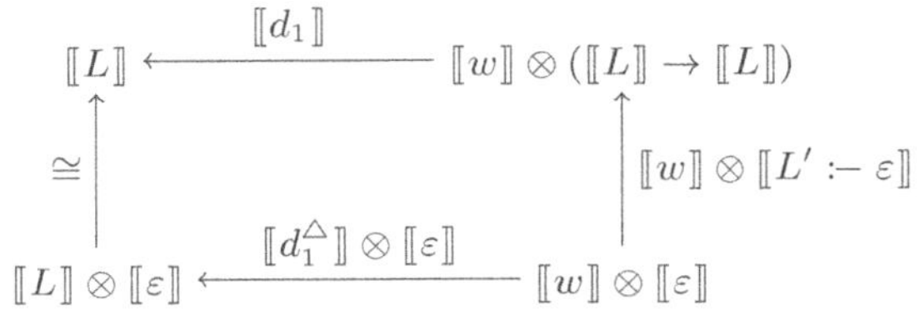

We define $d^{\triangle} \stackrel{\text{def}}{=} d_1^{\triangle}$. From the diagram, we have $[\![d^{\triangle}]\!] = [\![d]\!]$, as required.

2. Consider a derivation of the form $d : L \to_{\mathcal{F}} w\, L'$. The first step of all such derivations must be $L :- \psi_j\, L'$. This must be followed by a derivation $d_1 : \psi_j \to_{\mathcal{F}} w$ for some word w. We apply the induction hypothesis to d_1, which gives us derivation $d_1^{\triangle}$ with the same semantics, $[\![d_1^{\triangle}]\!] = [\![d_1]\!]$. Figure 9 gives the property we need to prove for d. The right rectangle commutes because $[\![d^{\triangle}]\!] = [\![d]\!]$. The left rectangle commutes due to the construction of $L :- \psi_j\, L'$ in Figure 8).

3. Now suppose we have a derivation $d_1 : L \to w_1\, L'$, and the next derivation step uses the rule $L' :- \varphi_i\, L'$. In a leftmost derivation, we must now take φ_i to some terminal string w_2 via a derivation d_2. We apply the induction hypothesis to the derivations d_1, giving $d_1^{\triangle}$ and to d_2, giving $d_2^{\triangle}$. Overall we have the following derivations:

$$
\begin{array}{ccccc}
L & \xrightarrow{\quad d_1 \quad} & w_1\, L' & & \\
\Big\downarrow & & \Big\downarrow {\scriptstyle w_1 \otimes (L' :- \varphi_i\, L')} & & \\
{\scriptstyle L :- L\, \varphi_i} & & w_1\, \varphi_i\, L' & \xrightarrow{\ w_1 \otimes d_2 \otimes L'\ } & w_1\, w_2\, L' \\
\Big\downarrow & & & & \\
L\, \varphi_i & \xrightarrow{\ d_1^{\triangle} \otimes \varphi_i\ } & w_1\, \varphi_i & \xrightarrow{\ w_1 \otimes d_2^{\triangle}\ } & w_1\, w_2
\end{array}
$$

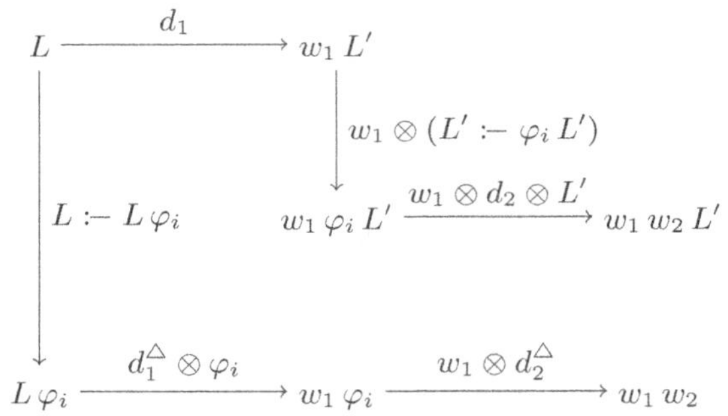

The property we need to prove is given in Figure 10. The right rectangle commutes because $[\![d_2^{\triangle}]\!] = [\![d_2]\!]$. The left rectangle commutes because $[\![L' :- \varphi_i\, L']\!]$ is central and due to its definition (see Figure 7).

Given Lemma 6.2, we have the desired result for complete derivations, which correspond to accepting computations of the WSK machine.

Theorem 6.3 Derivations $S \to_{\mathcal{F}} w$ in $\mathcal{F}$ (after left-recursion elimination) can be simulated by those in the original grammar $\mathcal{G}$ such that the semantics is preserved.

The converse of Theorem 6.3 does not hold. There could be derivations in the original grammar that do not correspond to any after transformation. This is due to the fact that the transformation can reduce the ambiguity of the grammar. For example, the grammar in Example 5.2 can parse $\mathbf{1} - \mathbf{1} - \mathbf{1}$ in two different ways, giving two different parse trees, or equivalently, two different left-most derivations. But removing the ambiguity is beneficial [1]; af-

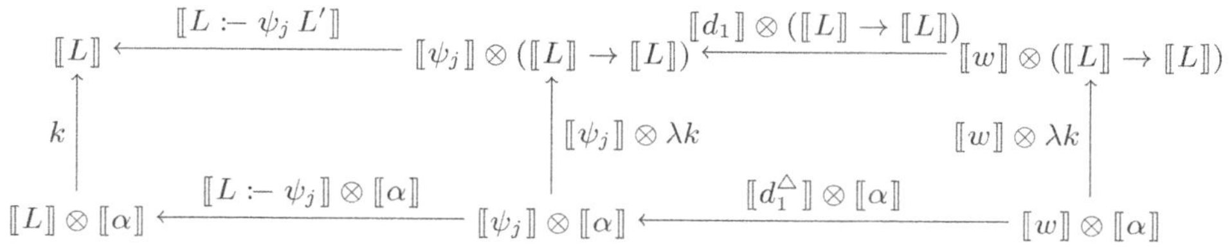

Figure 9. Simulation for a $L :- \psi_j L'$ step

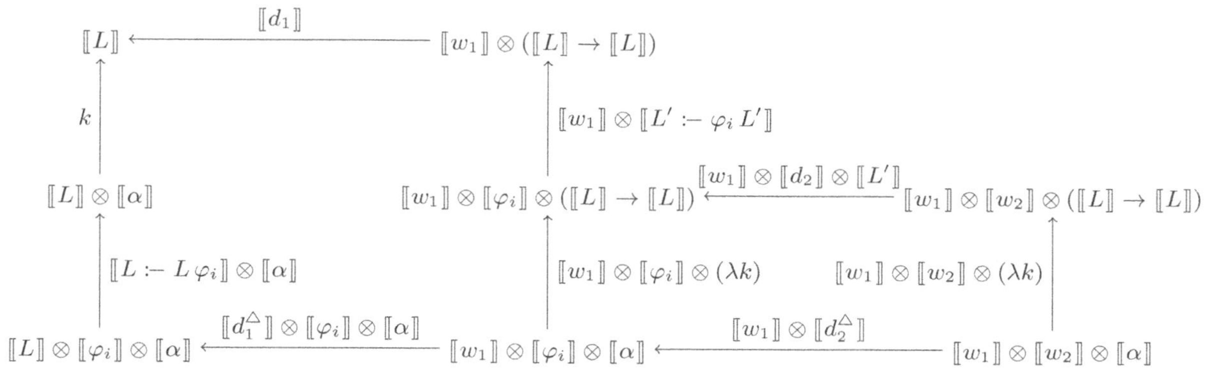

Figure 10. Simulation for a derivation d_1 followed by a $L' :- \varphi_i\, L'$ step

ter all, we would not want a compiler to choose randomly how to evaluate expressions.

7. Relation to continuation passing style

If one thinks of continuations in terms of control operators such as `call/cc` in Scheme, it may be surprising to find them in left-recursion elimination. In this section, some parallels to continuations, as expressed via transformations on lambda calculi, are drawn.

Consider Example 5.4 again, and compare it to a CPS transform for the semantics of the original grammar. An expression M is transformed into $\overline{M}$ as follows:

$$\begin{aligned} \overline{1} &= \lambda k.k\,1 \\ \overline{M_1 - M_2} &= \lambda k.\overline{M_1}\,(\lambda x.\overline{M_2}(\lambda y.k(x-y))) \end{aligned}$$

For each transformed M, its type is

$$\overline{M} : (\mathbb{N} \to \mathbb{N}) \to \mathbb{N}$$

To evaluate a term in CPS to a number, we supply the identity as the top-level continuation $\overline{M}\,(\lambda x.x)$.

Reading Example 5.4 in continuation terms, note that the semantics of the fresh non-terminal E' is that of continuations for $[\![E]\!] = \mathbb{N}$:

$$[\![E']\!] \quad = \quad \mathbb{N} \longrightarrow \mathbb{N}$$

Up to some uncurrying and reordering of parameters, the above CPS transform gives us essentially the semantic actions for the transformed grammar:

$$\begin{aligned} [\![E :- \texttt{1}\ E']\!] &= \lambda((),k).k(1) \\ [\![E' :- \texttt{-}\ E\ E']\!] &= \lambda((),x,k).\lambda y.k(y-x) \\ [\![E' :- \varepsilon]\!] &= \lambda().\lambda x.x \end{aligned}$$

For the last rule, we know that the ε-rule is applied at the end of a sub-derivation when we are done with expanding the E' and switch back to the original grammar by deleting E'. At this point in the derivation, the continuation-passing style ends, which is a form of control delimiter. A variety of such control delimiters, with subtle differences, have been defined and investigated, for instance by Danvy and Filinksi [6] and Felleisen et. al. [27]. A common feature is that the identity $\lambda x.x$ is supplied when expressions in continuation-passing style are interfaced with those in direct style.

More generally, we revisit the rotation of parse trees from Figure 6 in terms of semantic actions in Figure 11. Here the actions of the original rules for L are assumed to be g_1, f_1, and f_2. To compensate for the rotation, the transformed semantic actions take a parameter k that works as a continuation. Corresponding to the syntactic rotation of the parse tree, on the semantic actions we have the "inside-out" composition typical of continuation passing. In the first tree, f_2 is added to the top of the tree, in direct style. In the second tree, it is added near the bottom, in the continuation. Since the remainder of the tree will apply its continuation k in tail position, the two ways of adding f_2 are equivalent. The continuations move semantic actions around the tree, but they are not used for control effects like copying or discarding the current continuation: they are *linearly used* [5].

The equations that we need to prove correctness of the semantic transform lend themselves to answer type polymorphism [31]. Recall the transformation of semantic actions from Definition 5.3. For an action in the original grammar,

$$f = [\![L :- L\,\varphi_i]\!]$$

the transformed grammar has the action

$$[\![L' :- \varphi_i\, L']\!] = \lambda(p,k).\lambda x.k(f(x,p))$$

So far, we have typed this term with $k : [\![L]\!] \longrightarrow [\![L]\!]$. But the answer type of the continuation need not be $[\![L]\!]$. It could be a type

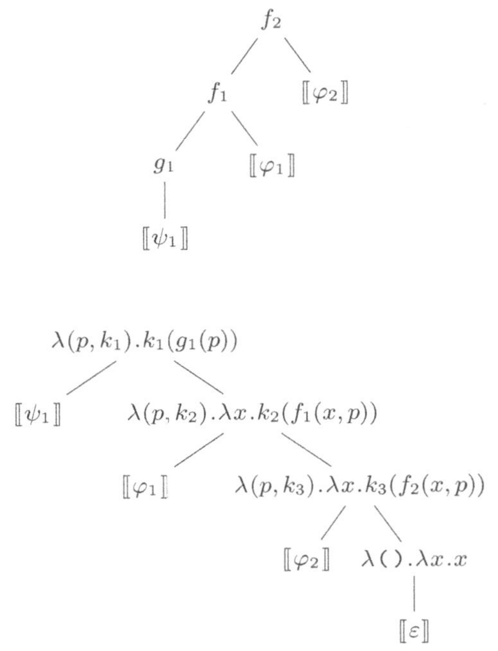

Figure 11. Semantic actions for original and transformed parse trees for $\psi_1\ \varphi_1\ \varphi_2$

variable χ. We give the term the following polymorphic type that is parametric in the answer type χ:

$$\lambda(p,k).\lambda x.k(f(x,p)) : \forall\chi.([\![\varphi_i]\!] \otimes ([\![L]\!] \to \chi)) \to \chi$$

Just from the type, we can infer that the action satisfies certain equations by using parametricity reasoning in the style that Wadler calls "Theorems for free" [32]. Developing answer type parametricity for the transformation is beyond the scope of the present paper, but it could give an alternative proof technique to the diagram chases in Figures 9 and 10. In continuation terms, the commuting diagrams in the simulation of transformed derivations can be explained as the relation between a direct-style program and its continuation passing equivalent. Supplying a continuation k as a value (via the λk on the right) to the continuation passing program is the same as post-composing k to the program in direct style (via the k on the left of the diagram).

8. Conclusions

The immediate motivation for this paper was the desire to relate the syntactic transformation of left-recursion elimination to the well-understood semantic transformation of continuation passing. The intuitive idea of left-recursion elimination (as well as other grammar transformations) is to introduce a fresh non-terminal L' that represents *part* of some rule for L. The intuitive idea of continuations is that they represent the meaning of the rest of the computation [29]. To bridge the gap between syntax and semantics, it helps to have a framework that presents them in analogous terms.

The diagram chases emphasise what properties of the language for semantic actions are needed. It need not be a pure lambda calculus, but can also be a call-by-value lambda calculus with effects. Parsing actions often refer to a symbol table, which represents a global mutable state.

8.1 Related work

The fact that the semantics of the language needs to be adapted when left recursion is eliminated appears to be part of compiling folklore. For instance, Aho et. al. [1] discuss L-attribute grammars, and Appel [2] gives an example of a hand-written LL(1) parser in Java where the parsing methods have been adapted by taking additional arguments.

Lohmann, Riedewald and Stoy [15] show how to transform semantic rules during left recursion elimination. They use the traditional compiler construction framework of Attribute Grammars [12], so that their semantics of grammar rules consists of equations between attributes. Some of their observations about moving such attribute rules across the transformed trees are closely related to the present paper (particularly Figure 11). In this paper, however, we use structures from the semantics of programming languages, such as categorical semantics, premonoidal categories and continuations, so that the results are quite different to theirs. Roughly speaking, inherited attributes push information down the parse tree towards the leaves, whereas synthesised attributes push information up towards the roots [1]. In the framework of L-categories, the semantics of a node $[\![A\ :-\ \alpha]\!]$ takes a value of type $[\![\alpha]\!]$ and returns value $[\![A]\!]$, thereby pushing information towards the root. If $[\![A]\!]$ is itself a function type, its parameter pushes information down the parse tree. ANTLR as well as some other modern parser generators are not based on attribute grammars, but on grammar rules having arguments and return values, which is closer to the approach of the present paper of modelling semantic actions as functions. Attribute grammars have been related to functional parsing actions [18].

Functional programming for parser construction is a well established stream of research, going back at least to the 1960s. However, here the idea is not to construct a parser. Instead, the parser should ideally be constructed automatically. We are only concerned about *that* the grammar can be parsed, rather than *how*, so that research on constructing parsers in Haskell [11] is only distantly related to the aims of this paper. In the context of parsing combinators in Haskell [30], Swierstra and coauthors have defined typed transformations of semantic actions [3], including left-recursion elimination and related transformations. The categorical framework defined in the present paper may be applicable to proving the correctness of their constructions involving more general grammar transformations in addition to left recursion elimination. Unlike parsing combinators in Haskell, the semantics of parsing actions presented here is geared towards call-by-value languages with effects (not all morphisms are required to be central, permitting the actions to have computational effects such as updating state). Such call-by-value parsing actions are arguably closer to tools such as ANTLR. On the other hand, since arrows [10, 20] have been related to Freyd-categories, they may provide a link to parsing in Haskell.

The idea to seek analogues of continuation passing in syntax was inspired by continuations in natural language (see Barker's survey [4]) and Lambek's pioneering syntactic calculus [13], where left and right $\otimes$ are not symmetric. In addition to the left/right distinction, Lambek's calculus is also linear. Since the new grammar symbol L' introduced by left recursion elimination occurs only in a right-linear position, it is another instance of linearly used continuations [5].

8.2 Directions for further research

The use of lambda calculus for the semantic actions is not always realistic, even though lambda calculus is commonly used as a tractable idealisation of programming languages. While there are parser generator tools for functional languages, other widely used tools support Java or C, and one may wish to use C for efficiency. There are two ways the actions could be refined to be closer to such parser generator tools. The first possibility is to use a variant of lambda calculus, either a syntactic restriction or perhaps a substructural type system. The other possibility is to represent lambda terms in a way that is suitable for a language lacking first-class functions. This would essentially be a form of defunctionalization [26] and explicitly representing closures as data structures. For example, instead of a lambda term $\lambda y.x - y$, we would need to build a data structure recording both the current value of x and the fact that some future value y will need to be subtracted from it. Modern tools support Java as the language in which semantic actions are written, so that function closures could be simulated by way of objects.

The category theory used in this paper was kept deliberately naive on a "need-to-know" basis, so to speak. It should be possible to give a more axiomatic definition of L-category along the same lines as premonoidal category [22], and the semantic action $[\![-]\!]$ as a contravariant functor to a Freyd category [24] preserving the functor $\otimes$. Likewise, coherence isomorphisms have been glossed over in the present paper and could be addressed more formally. For syntax, the operation $\otimes$ is strictly associative, but its semantic counterpart is only associative up to isomorphism. Coherence as developed for premonoidal categories could be adapted to the latter situation.

References

[1] A. V. Aho, R. Sethi, and J. D. Ullman. *Compilers - Principles, Techniques and Tools*. Addison Wesley, 1985.

[2] A. W. Appel and J. Palsberg. *Modern Compiler Implementation in Java*. Cambridge University Press, 1997.

[3] A. Baars, S. Doaitse Swierstra, and M. Viera. Typed transformations of typed grammars: The left corner transform. *Electron. Notes Theor. Comput. Sci.*, 253:51–64, September 2010. ISSN 1571-0661. doi: http://dx.doi.org/10.1016/j.entcs.2010.08.031. URL `http://dx.doi.org/10.1016/j.entcs.2010.08.031`.

[4] C. Barker. Continuations in natural language. In *Proceedings of the Fourth ACM SIGPLAN Continuations Workshop (CW'04)*. University of Birmingham Computer Science technical report CSR-04-1, 2004.

[5] J. Berdine, P. W. O'Hearn, U. Reddy, and H. Thielecke. Linear continuation passing. *Higher-order and Symbolic Computation*, 15 (2/3):181–208, 2002.

[6] O. Danvy and A. Filinski. Representing control, a study of the CPS transformation. *Mathematical Structures in Computer Science*, 2(4): 361–391, Dec. 1992.

[7] M. Felleisen and D. P. Friedman. Control operators, the SECD-machine, and the λ-calculus. In M. Wirsing, editor, *Formal Description of Programming Concepts*, pages 193–217. North-Holland, 1986.

[8] J. A. Goguen, J. W. Thatcher, E. G. Wagner, and J. B. Wright. Initial algebra semantics and continuous algebras. *Journal of the ACM*, 24 (1):68–95, 1977.

[9] C. A. Gunther. *Semantics of Programming Languages*. MIT Press, 1992.

[10] J. Hughes. Generalising monads to arrows. *Science of Computer. Programming*, 37(1-3):67–111, 2000.

[11] G. Hutton and E. Meijer. Monadic parsing in Haskell. *Journal of Functional Programming*, 8(4):437–444, 1998.

[12] D. E. Knuth. Semantics of context-free languages. *Mathematical Systems Theory*, 2(2):127–145, 1968.

[13] J. Lambek. The mathematics of sentence structure. *American Mathematical Monthly*, 65(3):154–170, 1958.

[14] P. J. Landin. The mechanical evaluation of expressions. *The Computer Journal*, 6(4):308–320, Jan. 1964.

[15] W. Lohmann, G. Riedewald, and M. Stoy. Semantics-preserving migration of semantic rules during left recursion removal in attribute grammars. *Electronic Notes in Theoretical Compututer Science*, 110: 133–148, 2004.

[16] S. Mac Lane. *Categories for the Working Mathematician*. Springer Verlag, 1971.

[17] E. Moggi. Computational lambda calculus and monads. In *Proceedings, Fourth Annual Symposium on Logic in Computer Science (LICS)*, pages 14–23, 1989. ISBN 0-8186-1954-6.

[18] K. B. Oege de Moor and S. D. Swierstra. First class attribute grammars. *Informatica: An International Journal of Computing and Informatics*, 24(2):329–341, June 2000. ISSN ISSN 0350-5596. Special Issue: Attribute grammars and their Applications.

[19] T. Parr and K. Fisher. LL(*): the foundation of the ANTLR parser generator. In *PLDI*. ACM, 2011. ISBN 978-1-4503-0663-8.

[20] R. Paterson. A new notation for arrows. In *ICFP*. ACM, 2001. ISBN 1-58113-415-0.

[21] G. D. Plotkin. Call-by-name, call-by-value, and the λ-calculus. *Theoretical Computer Science*, 1(2):125–159, 1975.

[22] J. Power and E. Robinson. Premonoidal categories and notions of computation. *Mathematical Structures in Computer Science*, 7(5): 453–468, 1997.

[23] J. Power and H. Thielecke. Environments, continuation semantics and indexed categories. In M. Abadi and T. Ito, editors, *Proceedings TACS'97*, number 1281 in LNCS, pages 391–414. Springer Verlag, 1997.

[24] J. Power and H. Thielecke. Closed Freyd- and kappa-categories. In J. Wiedermann, P. van Emde Boas, and M. Nielsen, editors, *Proceedings 26th International Colloquium on Automata, Languages and Programming (ICALP)*, number 1644 in LNCS, pages 625–634. Springer Verlag, 1999.

[25] J. C. Reynolds. Definitional interpreters for higher-order programming languages. In *Proceedings of the 25th ACM National Conference*, pages 717–740. ACM, Aug. 1972.

[26] J. C. Reynolds. Definitional interpreters for higher-order programming languages. *Higher-Order and Symbolic Computation*, 11(4):363–397, 1998. Reprint of a conference paper [25].

[27] D. Sitaram and M. Felleisen. Control delilmiters and their hierarchies. *Lisp and Symbolic Computation*, 3(1):67–99, 1990.

[28] G. Steele. Rabbit: A compiler for Scheme. Technical Report AI TR 474, Artificial Intelligence Laboratory, Massachusetts Institute of Technology, May 1978.

[29] C. Strachey and C. P. Wadsworth. Continuations: A mathematical semantics for handling full jumps. Technical Monograph PRG-11, Oxford University Computing Laboratory, Jan. 1974.

[30] S. D. Swierstra. Combinator parsers: a short tutorial. In A. Bove, L. Barbosa, A. Pardo, , and J. Sousa Pinto, editors, *Language Engineering and Rigorous Software Development*, volume 5520 of *LNCS*, pages 252–300. Spinger, 2009.

[31] H. Thielecke. From control effects to typed continuation passing. In *Principles of Programming Languages (POPL'03)*, pages 139–149. ACM, 2003.

[32] P. Wadler. Theorems for free! In *Proceedings of the 4th International Conference on Functional Programming and Computer Architecture (FPCA'89), London, 11–13 September 1989*, pages 347–359. ACM Press, New York, 1989.

Tor

Extensible Search with Hookable Disjunction

Tom Schrijvers
Ghent University
tom.schrijvers@ugent.be

Markus Triska
Vienna University of Technology
triska@dbai.tuwien.ac.at

Bart Demoen
KU Leuven
bart.demoen@cs.kuleuven.be

Abstract

Horn Clause Programs have a natural depth-first procedural semantics. However, for many programs this procedural semantics is ineffective. In order to compute useful solutions, one needs the ability to modify the search method that explores the alternative execution branches.

Tor, a well-defined hook into Prolog disjunction, provides this ability. It is light-weight thanks to its library approach and efficient because it is based on program transformation. Tor is general enough to mimic search-modifying predicates like ECLiPSe's `search/6`. Moreover, Tor supports modular composition of search methods and other hooks. Our library is already provided and used as an add-on to SWI-Prolog.

Categories and Subject Descriptors F.3.3 [*Logics and Meanings of Programs*]: Studies of Program Constructs

General Terms Languages

Keywords Prolog, disjunction, search, modularity

1. Introduction

Kowalski's well-known adage [9] crisply captures the essence of programming in the equation:

ALGORITHM = LOGIC + CONTROL

In Prolog, the LOGIC part is captured in the programmer-supplied rules or clauses that have a first-order logic interpretation. The CONTROL component is supplied by the Prolog engine and essentially consists of *search*. In order to answer queries, a Prolog engine performs a backward-chaining depth-first tree search.

Prolog's default search strategy is in practice inadequate to effectively scour large search spaces. As a consequence, the programmer often has to complement Prolog's CONTROL with additional hints or heuristics in the form of extra code. This is particularly prevalent in the context of Constraint Logic Programming where it is common practice for the programmer to complement a constraint model with a search specification.

Unfortunately, it is not all that easy to cleanly separate LOGIC and CONTROL when implementing search heuristics in Prolog. When one discovers that Prolog's CONTROL is ineffective, it is often impossible to orthogonally add one's own CONTROL without touching the existing LOGIC. The problem is that syntactically logic and control in Prolog are generally tightly coupled, and adding a different control means cross-cutting existing code.

In this paper we present a novel approach to adding, in an orthogonal manner, CONTROL. Our solution features the following properties:

- It is a light-weight library-based approach that is easily portable to different Prolog systems: it is currently an SWI-Prolog library [22]
- Our approach has all the benefits of modularity: search methods can be composed and the library of these heuristics is (user-)extensible.
- Its overhead is minimal, as we demonstrate on benchmarks: this is achieved through `term_expansion/2`, a feature present in most Prolog systems.

With Tor, we capture all common search methods in CLP(FD) libraries such as ECLiPSe's `search/6` [13]. This approach is indeed particularly suitable for Constraint Logic Programming, but also useful for general Prolog programs with a large search space.

2. Problem Statement

We illustrate the heart of the matter on a simple labeling predicate `label/1` written against SWI-Prolog's `clpfd` library [18] (see Fig. 1, left). `label/1` defines a search tree where the branches are created by the disjunction.[1]

Suppose that for a certain call `label([`X_1`,...,`X_n`])` the search tree is too large to fully explore. In order to get some useful answers, we may decide to leave certain parts of the tree unexplored, conceptually pruning the tree. One particular way in which we can do this is by reaping the low-hanging solutions only, and pruning the subtrees that are below a certain depth. Hence, we impose a *depth bound* on Prolog's depth first search. This is achieved by modifying the `label/1` code to that of `label/2` (Fig. 1, right) where the second parameter is the depth bound.

Imposing a depth bound may or may not be a successful approach to getting useful answers. If it turns out to be unsuccessful, we can try other pruning strategies like imposing a node bound or a discrepancy bound. Each of these requires rewriting the `label/1` predicate to incorporate a different pruning technique. In general, we follow an explorative process whereby we write and evaluate several different variants of the labeling code until we find an effective pruning strategy.

[1] `fd_inf/2` returns the smallest value in a variable's finite domain.

PPDP'12, September 19–21, 2012, Leuven, Belgium.

```
label([]).
label([Var|Vars]) :-
  ( var(Var) ->
      fd_inf(Var,Value),
      ( Var #= Value,
        label(Vars)
      ;
        Var #\= Value,
        label([Var|Vars])
      )
  ;
      label(Vars)
  ).
```

```
label([] ,_ ).
label([Var|Vars] ,D ) :-
  ( var(Var) ->
      D > 0,
      ND is D - 1,
      fd_inf(Var,Value),
      ( Var #= Value,
        label(Vars ,ND )
      ;
        Var #\= Value,
        label([Var|Vars] ,ND )
      )
  ;
      label(Vars ,D )
  ).
```

Figure 1. Labeling predicate: plain (left) and with depth bound (right).

2.1 Problems with this Approach

The problems with the above approach should be apparent:

- The approach follows the well-known copy-paste-modify anti-pattern. Variants of the labeling code are copied all over the place, potentially propagating bugs and rendering maintenance into a nightmare. Working code is modified.
- The same heuristic is implemented over and over in different settings (different applications, different labeling predicates, different Prolog systems, ...). This process is error-prone, wastes precious programmer time and is bound to yield non-optimal code quality.
- The effort and expertise required to combine working labeling code with various search heuristics is non-trivial. This means that fewer combinations are explored by programmers under time pressure or unfamiliar with particular heuristics. The end result is that suboptimal solutions are obtained.
- As soon as the labeling code spans several different predicates or multiple invocations of the same predicate, the complexity of adding search heuristics increases drastically.

2.2 Current Solutions

Most of the current solutions are specific to CLP, but we are aware of one general Prolog approach.

CLP Solutions In the context of CLP **ECLiPSe** [13] copes with this problem by providing a number of search methods in the `search/6` predicate. This predicate lets the user control through its various arguments the selection method, the choice method and the search method: the former two decide on which variable is used during labeling, and which value it is assigned first. They do not concern us here. The search method controls how the search tree is explored, e.g., depth-bounded, node-bounded or limited discrepancy search. Apart from individual search methods, only a fixed number of compositions is supported, such as changing strategy when a depth bound is reached. In this setting users can extend the set of supported heuristics and combinations by reprogramming parts of the `search/6` predicate.

We see the same approach in other Prolog systems' CLP(FD) libraries, albeit to a more limited extent. **SICStus** Prolog [2] allows imposing discrepancy and time limits, and **B-Prolog** [23] provides only a time limit. **GNU Prolog** [3] and **Ciao**'s new `clpfd` library provide no limits on top of depth-first search.

All CLP(FD) libraries do provide one extra search method: optimization with respect to an objective value. Optimization is typically implemented as either branch-and-bound or by restarting the whole search with a new bound whenever a solution is found.

Typically these approaches only support adding search heuristics to a simple goal made up of a labeling predicate defined in the corresponding CLP library. This means that complex goals made up of a conjunction of labeling calls or custom labeling predicates are not supported.

Prolog Solution We are aware of one other approach to modify Prolog's own search method: the breadth-first and iterative deepening program transformations in Ciao [6]. These modify annotated predicates in place and are not compositional.

All in all the available library support that Prolog systems provide is very limited indeed. As soon as users face a constraint problem that requires a non-trivial search method, they are forced to write all their search code from scratch, and it can be very daunting to combine different search methods.

2.3 Our Solution

We propose to solve the above modularity problem concerning search methods by decoupling the code that defines the *search tree* (e.g., `labeling/1`) from the code that defines the *search method* (e.g., `depth_bound/2` and `lds/1`[2]). We emphasize that solver-specific heuristics for defining the search tree (e.g., variable and value selection strategies for CLP(FD)) are not in the scope of Tor. Tor's search methods specify how a search tree is visited, e.g., what parts are pruned.

Tor combines the search tree and search method specifications by means of the `search/1` predicate. For instance, we express three different scenarios as:

```
?- search(label([X1,...,Xn])).
?- search(depth_bound(10,label([X1,...,Xn]))).
?- search(lds(label([X1,...,Xn]))).
```

This approach does not suffer from the many disadvantages of the copy-paste-modify approach discussed above. In particular, the code for `label/1` is not touched, and the code for `depth_bound/2`

[2] `lds` stands for `limited-discrepancy search`

and `lds/1` is provided in a library or supplied by the user. Existing search tree descriptions and search methods are easily and independently reused and maintained, with all the benefits of increased productivity and code quality.

Moreover, our approach is truly compositional. With the same three components we can express an additional search heuristic that combines a depth bound with lds:

```
?- search(depth_bound(10,lds(label([X1,...,Xn])))).
```

At the same time, it is not limited to a single invocation of `label/1`. For instance, we can apply a search heuristic to a conjunction of labelings.

```
?- search(depth_bound(10,lds((label([X1,...,Xn])
                              ,label([Y1,...,Ym]))))).
```

Only small syntactic changes are necessary to use our highly modular library based approach: Instead of using Prolog's disjunction `(;)/2`, the search tree description must use our library's disjunction predicate `tor/2`.

In the next section we reveal the technical details of our solution.

3. Basic Solution

Many variants of Prolog's default search method are most easily expressed as an action to be taken at the moment the alternative branches are entered, and possibly modifying the branches themselves.

Basically, we achieve this in a general way by providing a hook into disjunction as follows:

- programmers load our `library(tor)` and use the Tor-disjunction at appropriate places in their code, i.e., instead of `(;)/2` they use `tor/2`
- the library contains a definition of the Tor-disjunction – this definition can be partially evaluated away in many cases
- the library provides a means to specify what action needs to be taken in entering one of the tor-disjunctive branches: the definition of the Tor-disjunction uses these actions
- the system provides a set of useful and common actions; the user can implement additional actions himself, without the need to modify the library; neither does the user need to know to which program this new action will be applied

We illustrate the basics of Tor on the labeling example with depth bound.

```
tor_label([]).
tor_label([Var|Vars]) :-
  ( var(Var) ->
      fd_inf(Var,Value),
      (    Var #= Value,
           tor_label(Vars)
       tor
           Var #\= Value,
           tor_label([Var|Vars])
      )
  ;
      tor_label(Vars)
  ).
```

Instead of the regular Prolog disjunction we use Tor's `tor/2` disjunction for non-determinism. This predicate is defined as:

```
G1 tor G2 :-
  ( b_getval(left,Left),
    call(Left,G1)   % conceptually: Left(G1)
  ;
    b_getval(right,Right),
    call(Right,G2)  % conceptually: Right(G2)
  ).
```

This definition provides two hooks into the disjunction by means of global variables `left` and `right`.[3] In these hooks the programmer installs *handlers* for the left and right branches to control the search. These handlers are *higher-order* predicates that take a goal and execute it in a (possibly) modified manner.

We obtain standard Prolog disjunction, if we use `call/1` as handler.

```
?- findall(X, ( X in 1..10
              , b_setval(left,call)
              , b_setval(right,call)
              , label([X])
              ), Values).
Values = [1,2,3,4,5,6,7,8,9,10].
```

Things get more interesting when we use a different handler. For instance, the following handler limits the depth:

```
dbs_handler(Branch) :-
   b_getval(depth_limit,Depth),
   NewDepth is Depth - 1,
   NewDepth > 0,
   b_setval(depth_limit,NewDepth),
   call(Branch).
```

In addition to calling the `Branch` goal, this handler also maintains a depth limit in the global variable `depth_limit`. When this limit reaches zero, the handler *replaces* the branch goal by failure. In other words, the handler prunes the search tree below the depth limit.

We use this depth-bounded search handler as follows:

```
?- findall(X, ( X in 1..10
              , b_setval(depth_limit, 4)
              , b_setval(left,  dbs_handler)
              , b_setval(right, dbs_handler)
              , label([X])
              ), Values).
Values = [1,2,3,4].
```

The above way to specify and invoke handlers is clearly too clumsy. The next sections remedy this by introducing much more convenient infrastructure.

4. Advanced Infrastructure

The basic approach we have presented in the previous section is rather primitive to use directly. In this section, we provide a layer of additional infrastructure that makes using Tor a much more pleasant and high-level experience.

4.1 Implicit Disjunctions

The `tor/1` declaration implicitly adds Tor-disjunctions between the clauses of a predicate. For instance, the Tor variant of `member/2` can be written conventionally as:

```
:- tor tor_member/2.
tor_member(X,[X|_]).
tor_member(X,[_|Xs]) :- tor_member(X,Xs).
```

[3] Note that `b_getval/2` and `b_putval/2` are SWI-Prolog builtins for reading and writing global mutable variables, whose names are atoms. Their non-backtrackable counterparts are `nb_getval/2` and `nb_putval/2`.

instead of

```
tor_member(X,[Y|Ys]) :-
  (
      X = Y
  tor
      tor_member(X,Ys)
  ).
```

4.2 Default Handler

The convenient predicate `search/1` sets up the default handler for both hooks: `call/1`.

```
search(Goal) :-
  b_setval(left,call),
  b_setval(right,call),
  call(Goal).
```

With this default handler, `tor/2` corresponds simply to plain disjunction `(;)/2`.[4] For instance, with `search/1` we recover the behavior of `label/1` of Fig. 1 from the Tor-variant.

`search(tor_label(Vars))` $\equiv$ `label(Vars)`

4.3 Custom Handlers

In order to facilitate installing new handlers, we provide two convenient predicates.

Firstly, `tor_handlers/3` composes the currently installed handlers with the ones provided. Then it runs the provided goal and finally, it resets the installed handlers.

```
tor_handlers(Goal,Left,Right) :-
  b_getval(left,LeftHandler),
  b_getval(right,RightHandler),
  b_setval(left,compose(LeftHandler,Left)),
  b_setval(right,compose(RightHandler,Right)),
    call(Goal),
  b_setval(left,LeftHandler),
  b_setval(right,RightHandler).

compose(G1,G2,Goal) :- call(G1,call(G2,Goal)).
  % conceptually: G1(G2(Goal))
```

Section 5.8 shows that this approach enables composing different search methods.

Secondly, in many cases, the handler only needs to precede the actual branch goal by its own goal, much like *before-advice* in Aspect Oriented Programming [8]. For that purpose we introduce the `tor_before_handlers/3` predicate.

```
tor_before_handlers(Goal,Left,Right) :-
  tor_handlers(Goal,before(Left),before(Right)).

before(G1,G2) :- G1, G2.
```

Note that `before/2` is an alias for Prolog conjunction `(,)/2` which is convenient to use in partially applied form.

We illustrate the use of `tor_before_handlers/3` on the query example we've seen earlier:

```
?- findall(X, ( X in 1..10
              , b_setval(depth_limit, 4)
              , tor_before_handlers(label([X])
                                   ,dbs_handler
                                   ,dbs_handler)
              ), Values).
   Values = [1,2,3,4].
```

where `dbs_handler/0` now is no longer responsible for calling the branch goal:

```
dbs_handler :-
   b_getval(depth_limit,Depth),
   NewDepth is Depth - 1,
   NewDepth > 0,
   b_setval(depth_limit,NewDepth).
```

We will see examples of `tor_handlers/3` in Section 5.

4.4 Reference Cells

Usually a handler maintains some *stateful information*. For instance, the depth bounded handler maintains the current depth in the search tree. Generally, it is considered good style to declaratively thread such state through predicate calls by means of input and/or output arguments. This is the case in the `label/2` predicate, where the second argument captures the current depth.

However, Tor decouples the handler code from the labeling code. This means there is no explicit static control flow from one invocation of the handler to the next. Hence, there is no way in which state arguments can be threaded explicitly. In order to overcome this problem, we turn to a non-declarative solution: the use of mutable variables. These mutable variables provide an implicit channel of communication between successive invocations of a handler.

While mutable variables are notoriously error-prone and detrimental to the overall declarative nature of a Prolog program, Tor aims to contain the danger to a reasonable level. In particular, users of off-the-shelf handlers should not be exposed directly or indirectly to the fact that mutable variables are used internally. Only handler implementors, i.e., advanced users of the Tor library, should deal with them.

Moreover, Tor provides handler implementors with *reference cells* for mutable variables. These prevent implementors from shooting themselves in the foot in the most obvious ways and handler instances from interfering in unexpected ways. To illustrate the problem, consider again the naive use of the mutable global variable `depth_limit`. This global variable is problematic for two important reasons:

- We cannot ensure that no other part of the program, e.g., a different handler, uses the same name for other purposes.
- We cannot use two instances of the same variable simultaneously, e.g., to impose one depth bound on the overall search tree and another one on the top part of the tree.

In both cases, the issue is one of interference. While we can consider the first case as somewhat unlucky, the latter clearly limits usability.

In order to avoid the interference problem we advocate the use of reference cells, implemented by means of mutable terms, as proposed by Aggoun and Beldiceanu [1]. Our implementation for creating, reading and writing such variables is as follows:

```
new_bvar(InitialValue,Var) :-
  var(Var),
  Var = bvar(InitialValue).

b_put(Var,Value) :-
  Var = bvar(_),
  setarg(1,Var,Value).

b_get(bvar(Value),Value).
```

[4] Apart from the scope of any cuts in the alternative branches

The depth-bounded search method now becomes:

```
dbs(Depth,Goal) :-
  new_bvar(Depth,Var),
  tor_before_handlers(Goal,dbs_handler(Var)
                         ,dbs_handler(Var)).

dbs_handler(Var) :-
  b_get(Var,N),
  N > 0,
  N1 is N - 1,
  b_put(Var,N1).
```

Note that `dbs_handler/1` now takes the mutable variable as a parameter. We make use of a *wrapper* predicate `dbs/2` to create the mutable variable and install the handlers. Now our query example becomes very compact indeed:

```
?- findall(X, ( X in 1..10
              , dbs(4,label([X]))
              ), Values).
Values = [1,2,3,4].
```

Because some handler information has to persist across backtracking, we also provide a non-backtrackable variant of reference cells.

```
new_nbvar(InitialValue,Var) :-
  var(Var),
  Var = nbvar(InitialValue).

nb_put(Var,Value) :-
  Var = nbvar(_),
  nb_setarg(1,Var,Value).

nb_get(nbvar(Value),Value).
```

We will see examples of their use in the next section.

5. Handler Library

With the Tor infrastructure, it is easy to write various search methods in a modular way. While the user can write custom ones himself, Tor already provides a substantial library of handlers. We cover several of them here.

5.1 Depth Bounded Search

We have already developed a depth-bounded search handler in the previous section. Here we only remind the reader that it recovers the behavior of `label/2` of Fig. 1 as follows:

```
search(dbs(Depth,tor_label(Vars)))
              ≡
       label(Vars,Depth)
```

5.2 Discrepancy-Bounded Search

The discrepancy-bounded search heuristic is a small variant of depth-bounded search: the bound is only updated in right branches.

```
dibs(Discrepancies,Goal) :-
  (dib,Var),
  new_bvar(Discrepancies,Var),
  tor_before_handlers(Goal,true,dbs_handler(Var)).
```

5.3 Iterative Deepening

Iterative deepening emulates breadth-first search by means of increasing depth-bounds. The implementation below makes use of two variables: `DVar` to keep track of the current depth, and `PVar` to record whether the depth limit has been enforced in the current iteration. The handler `id_handler/2` checks and updates these variables in every node of the search tree. The driver `id_loop/2` initiates each iteration and, if pruning occurred, starts the next one.

```
id(Goal) :-
  new_bvar(0,DVar),
  new_nbvar(not_pruned,PVar),
  id_loop(Goal,DVar,0,PVar).

id_loop(Goal,DVar,Depth,PVar) :-
  b_put(DVar,Depth),
  nb_put(PVar,not_pruned),
  Handler = id_handler(DVar,PVar),
  ( tor_before_handlers(Goal,Handler,Handler)
  ;
    nb_get(PVar,Value),
    Value == pruned,
    NDepth is Depth + 1,
    id_loop(Goal,DVar,NDepth,PVar)
  ).

id_handler(DVar,PVar) :-
  b_get(DVar,N),
  ( N > 0 ->
      N1 is N - 1,
      b_put(DVar,N1)
  ;
      nb_put(PVar,pruned),
      false
  ).
```

5.4 Limited Discrepancy Search and Factored Iteration

The traditional limited discrepancy search [5] is a minor variant of iterative deepening. It applies the depth-bound only in right branches. Put differently, limited discrepancy search is to discrepancy-bounded search what iterative deepening is to depth-bounded search.

With some abstraction, we can factor out the common iteration part of iterative deepening and limited discrepancy search:

```
iterate(PGoal) :-
  with_pruned(
    iterate_loop(0,PGoal)).

iterate_loop(N,PGoal) :-
  (
    call(PGoal,N)
  ;
    is_pruned,
    reset_pruned,
    M is N + 1,
    iterate_loop(M,PGoal)
  ).
```

This iteration pattern runs a goal `PGoal` that is parameterized in a natural number `N`. The goal uses this number as a bound and applies pruning when the bound is exceeded. The iteration repeatedly restarts the goal with successive values for `N` until the goal completes without pruning.

With this iteration pattern we can express iterative deepening and limited discrepancy search as follows:

```
id(Goal)  :- iterate(flip(dbs,Goal)).
lds(Goal) :- iterate(flip(dibs,Goal)).

flip(Goal,Y,X) :- call(Goal,X,Y).
```

There is only one complicating factor: we need to communicate the pruning from the handler to the iteration. Despite the negative aspects of global variables, we opt for them due to their minimally intrusive nature.

```
prune :-
  set_pruned(true),
  fail.

reset_pruned :-
  set_pruned(false).

is_pruned :-
  get_pruned(true).

get_pruned(Flag) :-
  nb_getval(pruned,Flag).

set_pruned(Flag) :-
  nb_setval(pruned,Flag).

with_pruned(Goal) :-
  get_pruned(OldFlag),
  ( reset_pruned,
    call(Goal)
  ;
    set_pruned(OldFlag),
    fail
  ).

pruned_union(true,_,true).
pruned_union(false,true,true).
pruned_union(false,false,false).
```

With the imperative ugliness hidden in the above definitions, `prune` elegantly replaces `fail` in the handler code:

```
dbs_handler(Var) :-
  b_get(Var,N),
  ( N > 0 ->
      N1 is N - 1,
      b_put(Var,N1)
  ;
      prune
  ).
```

5.5 Branch-and-Bound Optimization

This well-known optimization approach posts constraints in the intermediate nodes of the search tree to find increasingly better solutions. Our implementation uses Tor to access those intermediate nodes and generate increasingly larger values of the `Objective` variable. It uses two variables, `BestVar` and `CurrentVar`. The former keeps track of the overall best solution so far, while the latter is the solution that the current node tries to improve upon.

Both the overall and current best solution are initialized to a value smaller than the infimum of the objective variable's domain. Whenever a solution is found, the overall best solution is updated. Whenever we backtrack into a Tor choicepoint, the handler synchronizes the current best solution with the overall best solution. If the current best solution was out of sync, the handler also imposes a new lower bound on the objective variable. Note that `inf` denotes negative infinity.

```
bab(Objective,Goal) :-
  fd_inf(Objective,Inf),
  Best is Inf - 1,
  new_nbvar(Best,BestVar),
  new_bvar(Best,CurrentVar),
  Handler = bab_handler(Objective,BestVar,CurrentVar),
  tor_before_handlers(Goal,Handler,Handler),
  nb_put(BestVar,Objective).

bab_handler(Objective,BestVar,CurrentVar) :-
  nb_get(BestVar,Best),
  b_get(CurrentVar,Current),
  ( Best \= inf , (Current == inf ; Best > Current ) ->
      Objective #> Best,
      b_put(CurrentVar,Best)
  ;
      true
  ).
```

5.6 Search Tree Observation

Tor does not only allow us to manipulate the traversal of the search tree in various search heuristics. It also enables us to observe the search tree in different ways in order to gain insight in the search process for (performance) debugging purposes.

Statistics Similar to SWI-Prolog's `profile/1`, `time/1` and `statistics/0` predicates, we can provide different components that monitor various metrics of the search tree and provide us with a convenient summary.

```
?- length(Xs,4), Xs ins 1..4,
   search(statistics((tor_label(Xs),writeln(Xs)))),
   false.
...
[4,4,4,4]
% Number of solutions: ....... 256
% Number of nodes: ........... 510
% Number of failures: .......... 0
```

The code for `statistics/1` is in the Tor library.

To support users who want to check whether they have successfully replaced all regular disjunctions with Tor, we also provide a tool that uses SWI-Prolog's choice point inspection primitives (like `prolog_current_choice/1`) to verify this.

Visualisation In addition to summarized data of the search tree, we can also visualize the actual search tree itself. For that purpose, we provide a predicate that emits a textual representation, a log, of the search tree:

```
log(Goal) :-
  tor_handlers(Goal,log_handler(left)
                   ,log_handler(right)),
  writeln(solution).

log_handler(Side,Goal) :-
  ( writeln(Side),  call(Goal)
  ;
    writeln(false), false).
```

A complimentary tool that turns this log into a PDF image is also available from our public code repository.

Fig. 2 shows the complete search tree for labeling 3 variables with domains of size 3 that are not involved in any constraints. The symbol $\top$ denotes that a solution is found at this node.

Fig. 3 shows two search trees for the 8-queens puzzle: The left one was created with depth limit (search strategy `dbs`) 4, and the right one with depth limit 7, where we stopped the search after finding the first solution. The symbol $\bot$ denotes pruning due to constraint propagation, and ! denotes a node that is not explored because the depth limit is exceeded at this level of the search tree.

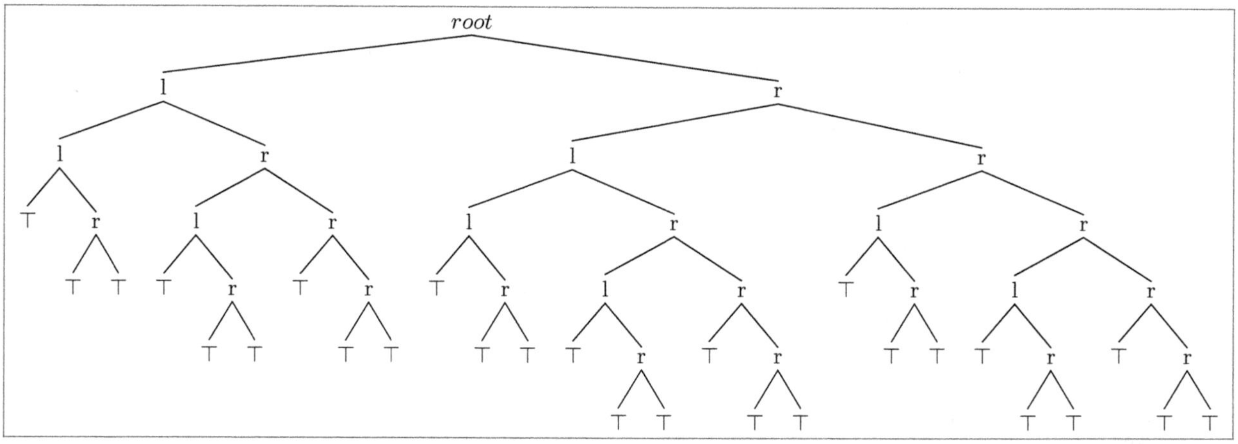

Figure 2. Search tree of `Xs = [_,_,_], Xs ins 1..3, search(log(tor_label(Xs)))`

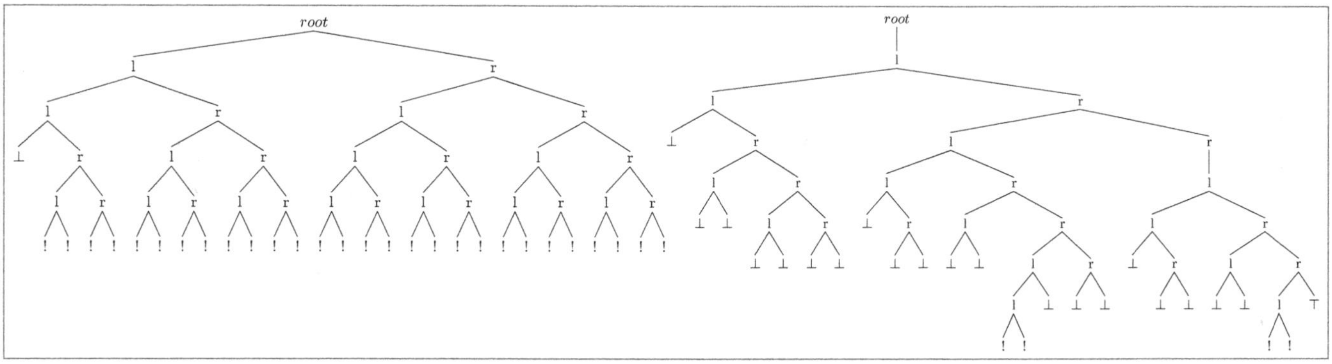

Figure 3. Search trees of 8-queens with depth bound 4 and 7

5.7 More and Higher-Order Handlers

We have implemented many other orthogonal search methods with tor, including all those offered by ECLiPSe's `search/6` predicate. In particular, several *higher-order search methods* are provided; these are search methods that are parametrized by other search methods.

An example of that is the following `dbs/3` variant on depth-bounded search. When it reaches the depth bound, it does not prune the remaining subtree, but activates the search method `Method`. A typical example is to limit the discrepancy once we reach a certain level in the search tree. This is achieved with `dbs(Level,lds(Discrepancies),Goal)`.

```
dbs(Level, Method, Goal) :-
  new_bvar(yes(Level),Var),
  tor_handlers(Goal,dbs_handler(Var,Method)
                   ,dbs_handler(Var,Method)).

dbs_handler(Var,Method,Goal) :-
  b_get(Var,MDepth),
  dbs_handler_(MDepth,Var,Method,Goal).

dbs_handler_(yes(Depth),Var,Method,Goal) :-
  ( Depth > 1 ->
      NDepth is Depth - 1,
      b_put(Var,yes(NDepth)),
      call(Goal)
  ;
      b_put(Var,no),
      call(Method,Goal)
  ).
dbs_handler_(no,_,_,Goal) :-
      call(Goal).
```

We recover the original first-order search method `dbs/2` with `dbs(Level,prune,Goal)` where:

```
prune(Goal) :- prune.
```

In ECLiPSe, only a fixed number of parameters can be supplied to these higher-order search methods, and `search/6` explicitly caters for each separate combination in its implementation. Not so with Tor. There is no restriction on the possible combinations; the higher-order search methods are truly parametric.

See our online code supplement for more handlers: `http://users.ugent.be/~tschrijv/tor`.

5.8 Composing Handlers

The beauty of Tor is that handlers can be composed. Below, we illustrate three kinds of composition.

Firstly, several handlers can be active at the same Tor-disjunction. For instance, we can perform branch-and-bound optimization with a depth-bound as follows:

```
?- ...,
   search(bab(Objective
             ,dbs(DepthLimit,tor_label(Vars)))).
```

Secondly, different handlers can be used for different parts of the search space. For instance, we can label the Xs and Ys variables each with their own depth limit:

```
?- ...,
   search((dbs(XsLimit,tor_label(Xs))
          ,dbs(YsLimit,tor_label(Ys)))).
```

Note that the global variables necessary for the two depth bounds exist simultaneously, but, because we use different ones, they do not interfere.

Finally, one handler can relinquish control to another one. For instance, inspired by ECLiPSe's `search/6` predicate, we provide a variant `dbs/3` of depth-bounded search that does not fail when the bound is reached, but switches to another strategy. While ECLiPSe only offers two alternatives for the other strategy, Tor allows any handler. For instance, once the depth-limit is reached, we visit only a fixed number of nodes with:

```
?- ...,
   search(dbs(DepthLimit
             ,nbs(NodeLimit,tor_label(Vars)))).
```

6. Plain Prolog Example

While the application of Tor to CLP problems is obvious, we wish to emphasize that Tor is not limited to CLP.

For that reason we illustrate the use of Tor on the well-known problem of the wolf, the goat and the cabbage. The following code, adapted from Sterling and Shapiro [16], implements this decision problem in plain Prolog (without constraints). Naive depth-first execution of this code loops infinitely.

```
wgc :-
  initial_state(State),
  wgc(State).

wgc(State) :-
  final_state(State), !.
wgc(State) :-
  move(State,Move),
  update(State,Move,State1),
  legal(State1),
  wgc(State1).

initial_state(wgc(left, [wolf, goat, cabbage], [])).

final_state(wgc(right, [], [wolf, goat, cabbage])).

move(wgc(Bank, Left, Right),Move) :-
  ( Bank == left,
    tor_member(Move, Left)
  tor
    Bank == right,
    tor_member(Move, Right )
  tor
    Move = alone
  ).

:- tor tor_member/2.
tor_member(X,[X|_]).
tor_member(X,[_|Xs]) :- tor_member(X,Xs).

update(wgc(B,L,R), Cargo, wgc(B1, L1, R1)) :-
  update_boat(B, B1),
  update_banks(Cargo, B, L, R, L1, R1).

update_boat(left, right).
update_boat(right, left).

update_banks(alone, _B, L, R, L, R) :- !.
update_banks(Cargo, left, L, R, L1, R1) :- !,
  select(Cargo, L, L1),
  insert(Cargo, R, R1).
update_banks(Cargo, right, L, R, L1, R1) :-
  select(Cargo, R, R1),
  insert(Cargo, L, L1).

insert(X,[Y|Ys], [X,Y|Ys]) :-
  precedes(X,Y), !.
insert(X, [Y|Ys], [Y|Zs]) :-
  precedes(Y,X), !,
  insert(X,Ys,Zs).
insert(X, [], [X]).

precedes(wolf, _X).
precedes(_X, cabbage).

legal(wgc(left, _L, R)) :- \+ illegal(R).
legal(wgc(right, L, _R)) :- \+ illegal(L).

illegal(Bank) :- memberchk(wolf, Bank),
                 memberchk(goat, Bank).
illegal(Bank) :- memberchk(goat, Bank),
                 memberchk(cabbage, Bank).
```

The nondeterministic enumeration in this code is situated in the `move/2` and `tor_member/2` predicates. In order to use Tor, we have replaced ordinary Prolog disjunction with `tor/2`.

To avoid the non-termination, we can apply a depth-bound and discover in finite time that the problem has a solution.

```
?- search(dbs(17,wgc)).
true.
```

7. Evaluation

To study Tor's overhead, we have performed a number of benchmarks on a MacBook Pro with a 2.4 GHz CPU and 4 GB RAM. We compare two Prolog systems with different performance characteristics. On the one hand we consider SWI-Prolog 5.11.7 in Mac OS X 10.6.7, a feature-rich, but relatively slow Prolog system with a CLP(FD) solver written in Prolog. On the other hand, we consider B-Prolog 7.5#3, one of the fastest Prolog systems with a highly optimized CLP(FD) implementation.

7.1 Pure Search

Figure 4 considers the extreme situation where the search is pure enumeration of *unconstrained* constraint variables: `length(N,Vars)`, `Vars ins 1..D`. Hence, no constraint propagators are activated due to choices. Values are simply enumerated.

The first column denotes the problem size, expressed in the number of variables N and their domain size D. The other three pairs of columns denote different implementations of labeling: 1) `label/1` as listed in this paper, 2) `label/1` from SWI-Prolog's `clpfd` library and the corresponding `labeling/1` provided by B-Prolog, and 3) `search/6` ported from ECLiPSe to SWI-Prolog and B-Prolog with minimal changes. For each of these, we show the absolute runtime of the standard/manual version (man) and the relative runtime of the Tor version (tor).

In both SWI-Prolog and B-Prolog the impact of Tor is pretty consistent across the problem sizes, but depends on the labeling implementation. In SWI-Prolog, the overhead is most prominent (140-180 %) in our barebones `label/1`, while it is less so (50-60 %) in `clpfd`'s `label/1`. The latter delegates to `labeling/2`, which in-

	our label/1		clpfd's label/1 B-Prolog's labeling/1		search/6	
	man	Tor	man	Tor	man	Tor
SWI-Prolog						
N=6,D= 8	1.80 s	240 %	2.08 s	151 %	2.55 s	132 %
N=6,D= 9	3.63 s	249 %	4.20 s	153 %	5.09 s	135 %
N=6,D=10	6.82 s	269 %	7.87 s	155 %	9.53 s	137 %
N=7,D= 8	14.44 s	244 %	16.63 s	153 %	20.40 s	134 %
N=7,D= 9	32.80 s	269 %	37.80 s	155 %	46.04 s	136 %
N=7,D=10	68.27 s	278 %	78.63 s	157 %	94.30 s	139 %
B-Prolog						
N=6,D= 8	0.49 s	156 %	0.09 s	276 %	0.12 s	223 %
N=6,D= 9	0.99 s	157 %	0.18 s	283 %	0.23 s	221 %
N=6,D=10	1.87 s	160 %	0.32 s	291 %	0.44 s	219 %
N=7,D= 8	4.56 s	144 %	0.71 s	306 %	0.94 s	220 %
N=7,D= 9	8.90 s	163 %	1.59 s	301 %	2.06 s	225 %
N=7,D=10	18.64 s	163 %	3.25 s	332 %	4.37 s	220 %

Figure 4. Labeling benchmarks without propagation

volves more generic option processing. Finally, in search/6 Tor compensates its overhead further (to 30-40 %) by not collecting search statistics when these are not demanded. In the original version, these statistics are collected regardless of demand.

In B-Prolog, the performance characteristics of the labeling predicates are markedly different. Firstly, the cost of the inequality (#\=)/2 in our label/1 is relatively high, which keeps the overhead of Tor low (60%). In contrast, the two other labeling predicates rely on B-Prolog's domain_inst_next/3 for enumeration, which compiles down to a single machine instruction. As a result the overhead of Tor is much higher, more so in the tight labeling/1 (170%-230%) than the more bloated search/6 (120%).

In summary, in these propagation-free benchmarks, the overhead of Tor goes up to about a factor three for tight labeling loops, but is lower for option-rich labeling predicates. Moreover, Tor is better behaved in SWI-Prolog than in B-Prolog. All in all, we find that this is a very reasonable price to pay for the extra flexibility that Tor provides. Still, invoking Tor's specializer (see the next section) is warranted to get rid of all overhead.

7.2 Search vs. Propagation

While the overhead of Tor is bounded in the previous benchmarks, the performance-wary user may not be willing to accept the overhead. However,the previous benchmarks are not representative of realistic CLP problems, that spend a lot of time on constraint propagation in every node of the search tree. All this extra work easily dwarfs the overhead of Tor. Figure 5 illustrates this observation on a number of typical CLP benchmarks.

For added realism, the benchmarks use the first-fail variable selection strategy, with hand-written labeling code ff_label/1, the two library predicates labeling/2 (SWI-Prolog) and labeling_ff/1 (B-Prolog), and the ported search/6. Because B-Prolog's CLP(FD) solver is orders of magnitude faster than SWI-Prolog's, it makes little sense to use exactly the same benchmarks for the two platforms. Instead, we resorted to different problem sizes or different benchmarks altogether.

	plain	lds	dibs-1	dibs-2	credit/bbs
N= 95	2.11 s	0.66 s	0.45 s	**0.28 s**	0.33 s
N= 96	**0.65 s**	4.98 s	4.89 s	1.13 s	1,04 s
N= 97	T/O	3.68 s	**3.56 s**	22.66 s	4,08 s
N= 98	T/O	15.67 s	† 5.71 s	10.16 s	**2.50 s**
N= 99	T/O	2.42 s	**2.22 s**	9.85 s	2.57 s

† no solution

Figure 6. N-Queens benchmarks with various search methods

In the case of SWI-Prolog, we see that Tor introduces no (significant) overhead; its runtime is marginal compared to that of constraint propagation. In the case of B-Prolog, the overhead of Tor is more noticeable, in the order of 10% for most benchmarks. Only in the case of the knapsack problem does it go up to 75% for the tightest labeling loop.

In summary, we see little reason not to use Tor for most CLP problems. Especially in SWI-Prolog there is no runtime price to pay. In the setting of B-Prolog, an extra 10% runtime is a cheap price for the extra flexibility that Tor provides. Moreover, in the next section we will see how we can eliminate Tor's overhead to the extent that we don't pay for it if we don't use its extra flexibility.

7.3 Search Methods

Finally, Figure 6 illustrates again why we want to use different search methods: they can have a significant impact on runtime. The figure shows the runtime of the **n_queens** benchmark in SWI-Prolog for 5 different problem sizes and 5 different search methods: (plain) plain depth-first search, (lds) limited discrepancy search, (dibs-1/-2) discrepancy bounds of 1 and 2, and (credit/bbs) credit-based search with 10,000 credits that switches to a bounded backtracking (1 backtrack) search when the credits are exhausted.

	our `ff_label/1`		`labeling/2`		`search/6`	
	man	Tor	man	Tor	man	Tor
SWI-Prolog						
`allinterval`	4.03 s	101 %	4.02 s	101 %	4.01 s	101 %
`golf`	3.93 s	99 %	3.92 s	100 %	3.96 s	99 %
`mhex`	18.59 s	102 %	18.61 s	101 %	18.46 s	101 %
`n_queens`	2.03 s	103 %	2.05 s	102 %	2.09 s	102 %
`sudoku`	2.14 s	101 %	2.15 s	101 %	3.40 s	100 %
B-Prolog						
`allinterval`	1.14 s	100 %	0.81 s	112 %	0.89 s	109 %
`knapsack`	3.94 s	125 %	2.11 s	175 %	2.17 s	172 %
`knight`	0.67 s	101 %	0.71 s	100 %	0.91 s	100 %
`mhex`	0.23 s	106 %	0.19 s	107 %	0.23 s	104 %
`n_queens`	1.01 s	107 %	0.89 s	107 %	1.03 s	106 %

Figure 5. Labeling benchmarks with propagation

8. Automatic Specialization

Tor encourages writing fairly abstract and generic code. This style clearly incurs some overhead (notably due to meta-calling) compared to specialized search code. Fortunately, in the case of CLP applications, this overhead is very modest compared to the bottleneck of constraint propagation. However, in the case of applications without constraint propagation, we do observe an overhead that is not insignificant. In order to mitigate that overhead, we exploit Prolog's homoiconic nature to provide a simple but effective automatic specializer.

Even though there is a large body of work on automatic program specialization for Prolog, notably involving partial evaluation, we decided to write our own program specializer. Its main tasks are 1) to perform *constant propagation* on the global variables `left` and `right`, 2) to replace instantiated meta-calls by direct calls and 3) to inline the handler code into the main search loop. For control we follow a light-weight approach based on declarations of what predicates to inline and specialize.

Example 1 Our specializer yields `label/1` for the generic composition `search(tor_label(Vars))`. Similarly, we recover SWI-Prolog's `labeling/2` by specializing its Tor variant. Hence, we do not pay if we do not use search methods.

Example 2 The specialized form of the goal `search(dbs(N, tor_label(Vars)))` is `new_bvar(N,DVar), label21(Vars, DVar)`, with:

```
label21([], _).
label21([Var|Vars], DVar) :-
  ( var(Var) ->
      fd_inf(Var, Val),
      ( b_get(DVar, Depth),
        Depth>0,
        NDepth is Depth+ -1,
        b_put(DVar, NDepth),
        Var#=Val,
        label21(Vars, DVar)
      ;
        b_get(DVar, G),
        G>0,
        NDepth is G+ -1,
        b_put(DVar, NDepth),
        Var#\=Val,
        label21([Var|Vars], DVar)
      )
  ;
      label21(Vars, DVar)
  ).
```

This code is slightly less efficient than that of `label/2`. Firstly, the overhead of mutable variables is not entirely eliminated here, as `DVar` is still present. Secondly, the two branches have some code in common that could be shared. However, there are no more meta-calls and all code is inlined in the recursive loop of `label21/2`.

In future work, we intend to get rid of the remaining inefficiencies by implementing additional transformations, including Peter Schachte's approach [12] for eliminating mutable variables adapted to our setting.

9. Related Work

We have already covered the most closely related work, existing approaches to search heuristics in Prolog, in Section 2.2. Here we cover other important related topics.

Earlier Work Tor is related to earlier work on *Monadic Constraint Programming* (MCP) [14] in the context of Haskell, and *Search Combinators* [15] in the context of C++ and the Gecode library[5]. In contrast to those works, Tor is tailored towards Prolog's built-in depth-first search and, as a consequence, consists of a much simpler and more elegant design.

Comet The imperative Comet language [19] features fully programmable search by means of *search controllers* [20]. There are too main differences between Tor and Comet's search controllers. Firstly, search controllers exchange simplicity for flexibility, providing more hooks and first-class continuations to manipulate the search. Secondly, search controllers are not intended to be used together, in contrast to Tor's handlers that are explicitly designed to be composed.

Aspect-Oriented Programming The Tor approach is closely related to Aspect-Oriented Programming (AOP) [8, 10]. AOP provides a generic approach for modularly *crosscutting* existing code

[5] `http://www.gecode.org`

with new code, so-called *advice*. This advice is injected in arbitrary *join points* (i.e., program points) based on a *pointcut* predicate.

Obviously Tor is more limited in scope, as only `tor/2` disjunctions are crosscut and only at the positions of the two hooks. However, we believe that these "limitations" are actually Tor's strength: its simplicity makes it easy to express all common search methods and its discipline favors compositionality.

10. Design Discussion

In this section we briefly discuss a number of design decisions of Tor as well as possible future extensions.

Increased Expressivity Simplicity has been a guiding principles in the design of Tor. In order to minimize the threshold for users, we keep the effort and complexity of defining and using search methods low. We pay for this simplicity with somewhat restricted expressivity. An example of a search method that cannot be expressed with Tor is swapping the order of branches in a disjunction. In order to overcome this limitation we would have to add extra complexity to the `tor/2` built-in in the form of an additional hook. Nevertheless, Tor is remarkably expressive as it is, covering all of the commonly found search methods in CLP(FD) libraries.

Multiway Disjunctions Tor currently only supports binary disjunctions; multiway disjunctions have to be decomposed into binary ones. For some applications, this decomposition can be somewhat unnatural. For instance, when enumerating all the values `V` of a constraint variable `X`, one might expect that all alternative assignments `X #= V` sit at the same level in the search tree. This is of course generally not the case in a binary decomposition. For that reason we are considering backward compatible ways to generalize the handler approach.

Declarative State Management We have already mitigated the dangers of mutable variables with reference cells. Nevertheless handler programming requires a rather imperative programming style. We are considering more declarative interfaces, inspired by definite clause grammars and the state monad [21], that better screen the handler programmer from the mutation side effect. The idea is to add behind the scenes an impure wrapper around pure handler code. There are two complicating factors in the matter: Tor's higher-order programming style and non-backtrackable state. The higher-order style complicates the boundaries of the handler code and thus increases the complexity of a pure interface to it. Non-backtrackable state updates are often followed immediately by failure. There is no idiomatic declarative alternative for this technique. However, we can turn to pure deterministic encodings of failure with non-backtrackable state, like Haskell's `ListT (State s)` monad [7] and use Filinski's reification/reflection technique [4] to translate to and from Prolog's native effects.

11. Conclusion

We have presented Tor, a light-weight library-based approach for modifying Prolog's depth-first search with reusable and compositional search methods.

On a more drastic account, we will investigate ways to replace the underlying depth-first queuing strategy. The stack freezing functionality of tabling systems like XSB [17] and YAP [11] provides interesting perspectives for this purpose.

Acknowledgements We are grateful to Rémy Haemmerlé and Jose Morales Caballero for our discussions on Tor, and to Neng-Fa Zhou for revealing B-Prolog's `labeling/1` code to us.

References

[1] Abderrahmane Aggoun and Nicolas Beldiceanu. Time stamps techniques for the trailed data in constraint logic programming systems. In Serge Bourgault and Mehmet Dincbas, editors, *SPLT'90, 8ème Séminaire Programmation en Logique, 16-18 mai 1990, Trégastel, France*, pages 487–510, 1990.

[2] Mats Carlsson and Per Mildner. SICStus Prolog - The first 25 years. *Theory and Practice of Logic Programming*, 12(1-2):35–66, 2012.

[3] Daniel Diaz, Salvador Abreu, and Philippe Codognet. On the implementation of GNU-Prolog. *Theory and Practice of Logic Programming*, 12(1-2):253–282, 2012.

[4] Andrzej Filinski. Monads in action. In Manuel V. Hermenegildo and Jens Palsberg, editors, *Proceedings of the 37th ACM SIGPLAN-SIGACT Symposium on Principles of Programming Languages (POPL 2010)*, pages 483–494. ACM, 2010.

[5] William D. Harvey and Matthew L. Ginsberg. Limited discrepancy search. In *Proceedings of the 15th International Joint Conferences on Artificial Intelligence (IJCAI 1995)*, pages 607–613, 1995.

[6] Manuel V. Hermenegildo, Francisco Bueno, Manuel Carro, Pedro López-García, Edison Mera, José F. Morales, and German Puebla. An overview of Ciao and its design philosophy. *Theory and Practice of Logic Programming*, 12(1-2):219–252, 2012.

[7] Mark P. Jones and Luc Duponcheel. Composing monads. Research Report YALEU/DCS/RR-1004, Yale University, Department of Computer Science, New Haven, Connecticut, December 1993.

[8] Gregor Kiczales, John Lamping, Anurag Menhdhekar, Chris Maeda, Christina V. Lopes, Jean-Marc Loingtier, and John Irwin. Aspect-oriented programming. In *Proceedings of the 11th European Conference on Object-Oriented Programming (ECOOP 1997)*, pages 220–242, 1997.

[9] Robert Kowalski. *Logic for Problem Solving*. North-Holland, 1979.

[10] Wolfgang Lohmann, Günter Riedewald, and Guido Wachsmuth. Aspect-Orientation in Prolog. In *Proceedings of the 16th International Symposium on Logic-based Program Synthesis and Transformation*, 2006.

[11] Vitor Santos Costa, Ricardo Rocha, and Luis Damas. The YAP Prolog system. *Theory and Practice of Logic Programming*, 12(1-2):5–34, 2012.

[12] Peter Schachte. Global variables in logic programming. In *Proceedings of the International Conference on Logic Programming (ICLP 1997)*, pages 3–17, 1997.

[13] Joachim Schimpf and Kish Shen. ECLiPSe From LP to CLP. *Theory and Practice of Logic Programming*, 12(1-2):127–156, 2012.

[14] Tom Schrijvers, Peter J. Stuckey, and Philip Wadler. Monadic constraint programming. *Journal of Functional Programming*, 19(6):663–697, 2009.

[15] Tom Schrijvers, Guido Tack, Pieter Wuille, Horst Samulowitz, and Peter Stuckey. Search Combinators. In *Proceedings of the 17th International Conference on Principles and Practice of Constraint Programming (CP 2011)*, volume 6876 of *Lecture Notes in Computer Science*, pages 774–788. Springer, 2011.

[16] Leon Sterling and Ehud Shapiro. *The Art of Prolog: Advanced Programming Techniques*. MIT Press, Cambridge, MA, 2. edition, 1994.

[17] Terrance Swift and David S. Warren. XSB: Extending Prolog with Tabled Logic Programming. *Theory and Practice of Logic Programming*, 12(1-2):157–187, 2012.

[18] Markus Triska. The finite domain constraint solver of SWI-Prolog. In *Proceedings of the 11th International Symposium on Functional and Logic Programming (FLOPS 2012)*, pages 307–316, 2012.

[19] Pascal Van Hentenryck and Laurent Michel. *Constraint-Based Local Search*. MIT Press, 2005.

[20] Pascal Van Hentenryck and Laurent Michel. Nondeterministic control for hybrid search. *Constraints*, 11(4):353–373, 2006.

[21] Philip Wadler. The essence of functional programming. In Ravi Sethi, editor, *Conference Record of the Nineteenth Annual ACM SIGPLAN-SIGACT Symposium on Principles of Programming Languages (POPL 1992)*, pages 1–14. ACM Press, 1992.

[22] Jan Wielemaker, Tom Schrijvers, Markus Triska, and Torbjörn Lager. SWI-Prolog. *Theory and Practice of Logic Programming*, 12(1-2):67–96, 2012.

[23] Neng-Fa Zhou. The language features and architecture of B-Prolog. *Theory and Practice of Logic Programming*, 12(1-2):189–218, 2012.

Linear Dependent Types in a Call-by-Value Scenario *

Ugo Dal Lago Barbara Petit
Università di Bologna & INRIA
{dallago,petit}@cs.unibo.it

Abstract

Linear dependent types [11] allow to precisely capture both the extensional behavior and the time complexity of λ-terms, when the latter are evaluated by Krivine's abstract machine. In this work, we show that the same paradigm can be applied to call-by-value computation. A system of linear dependent types for Plotkin's PCF is introduced, called $\mathsf{d}\ell\mathsf{PCF}_\mathsf{V}$, whose types reflect the complexity of evaluating terms in the so-called CEK machine. $\mathsf{d}\ell\mathsf{PCF}_\mathsf{V}$ is proved to be sound, but also relatively complete: every true statement about the extensional and intentional behavior of terms can be derived, provided all true index term inequalities can be used as assumptions.

Categories and Subject Descriptors F.3.2 [*Logics and Meaning of Programs*]: Semantics of Programming Languages—program analysis, operational semantics

Keywords Functional Programming, Linear Logic, Dependent Types, Implicit Computational Complexity

1. Introduction

A variety of methodologies for formally verifying properties of programs have been introduced in the last fifty years. Among them, *type systems* have certain peculiarities. On the one hand, the way type systems are defined makes the task of proving a given program to have a type reasonably simple and modular: a type derivation for a compound program usually consists of some type derivations for the components, appropriately glued together in a syntax-directed way (*i.e.*, attributing a type to a program can usually be done *compositionally*). On the other, the specifications that can be expressed through types have traditionally been weak, although stronger properties have recently become of interest, such as security [25, 26], termination [6], monadic temporal properties [20] or resource bounds [9, 19]. But contrarily to what happens with other formal methods (*e.g.* model checking or program logics), giving a type to a program t is a *sound* but *incomplete* way to prove t to satisfy a specification: there are correct programs which cannot be proved such by way of typing.

* This work is partially supported by the INRIA ARC Project "ETERNAL"

PPDP'12, September 19–21, 2012, Leuven, Belgium.

In other words, the tension between expressiveness and tractability is particularly evident in the field of type systems, where certain good properties the majority of type systems enjoy (*e.g.* syntax-directedness) are usually considered desirable (if not necessary), but also have their drawbacks: some specifications are intrinsically hard to verify locally and compositionally. One specific research field in which the just-described scenario manifests itself is complexity analysis, in which specifications are concrete or asymptotic bounds on the complexity of the underlying program. Many type systems have been introduced capturing, for instance, the class of polynomial time computable functions [4, 5, 18]. All of them, under mild assumptions, can be employed as tools to certify programs as asymptotically time efficient. However, a tiny slice of the polytime *programs* are generally typable, since the underlying complexity class **FP** is only characterized in a purely extensional sense — for every function in **FP** there is *at least one* typable program computing it.

Gaboardi and the first author have recently introduced [11] a type system for Plotkin's PCF, called $\mathsf{d}\ell\mathsf{PCF}_\mathsf{N}$, in which linearity and a restricted form of dependency in the spirit of Xi's DML [27] are present:

- **Linearity** makes it possible to finely control the number of times subterms are copied during the evaluation of a term t, itself a parameter which accurately reflects the time complexity of t [10].
- **Dependency** allows to type distinct (virtual) copies of a term with distinct types. This gives the type system an extra flexibility similar to that of intersection types [8, 14].

When mixed together, these two ingredients allow to precisely capture the extensional behavior of λ-terms *and* the time complexity of their evaluation by Krivine's abstract machine. Both soundness and relative completeness hold for $\mathsf{d}\ell\mathsf{PCF}_\mathsf{N}$.

One may argue, however, that the practical relevance of these results is quite limited, given that call-by-name evaluation and KAM are very inefficient: why would one be interested in verifying the complexity of evaluating concrete programs in such a setting?

In this work, we show that linear dependent types can also be applied to the analysis of call-by-value evaluation of functional programs. This is done by introducing another system of linear dependent types for Plotkin's PCF. The system, called $\mathsf{d}\ell\mathsf{PCF}_\mathsf{V}$, captures the complexity of evaluating terms by Felleisen and Friedman's CEK machine [15], a simple abstract machine for call-by-value evaluation. $\mathsf{d}\ell\mathsf{PCF}_\mathsf{V}$ is proved to have the same good properties enjoyed by its sibling $\mathsf{d}\ell\mathsf{PCF}_\mathsf{N}$, namely soundness and relative completeness: every true statement about the extensional behavior of terms can be derived, provided all true index term inequalities can be used as assumptions.

Actually, $\mathsf{d}\ell\mathsf{PCF}_\mathsf{V}$ is not merely a variation on $\mathsf{d}\ell\mathsf{PCF}_\mathsf{N}$: not only typing rules are different, but also the language of types itself must be modified. Roughly, $\mathsf{d}\ell\mathsf{PCF}_\mathsf{V}$ and $\mathsf{d}\ell\mathsf{PCF}_\mathsf{N}$ can be thought as being induced by translations of intuitionistic logic into linear logic: the latter corresponds to Girard's translation $A \Rightarrow B \equiv\ !A \multimap B$, while the former corresponds to $A \Rightarrow B \equiv !(A \multimap B)$. The strong link between translations of IL into ILL and notions of reduction for the λ-calculus is well-known (see *e.g.* [22]) and has been a guide in the design of $\mathsf{d}\ell\mathsf{PCF_V}$ (this is explained in Section. 2.2).

An extended version with more details and proofs is available [12].

2. Linear Dependent Types, Intuitively

Consider the following program:

$$\mathsf{dbl} = \mathtt{fix}\, f.\lambda x.\ \mathtt{ifz}\, x\, \mathtt{then}\, x\, \mathtt{else}\, \mathtt{s}(\mathtt{s}(f(\mathtt{p}(x)))).$$

In a type system like PCF [24], the term dbl receives type $\mathsf{Nat} \Rightarrow \mathsf{Nat}$. As a consequence, dbl computes a function on natural numbers without "going wrong": it takes in input a natural number, and (possibly) produces in output another natural number. The type $\mathsf{Nat} \Rightarrow \mathsf{Nat}$, however, does not give any information about *which* specific function on the natural numbers dbl computes.

Properties of programs which are completely ignored by ordinary type systems are termination and its most natural refinement, namely termination *in bounded time.* Typing a term t with $\mathsf{Nat} \Rightarrow \mathsf{Nat}$ does not guarantee that t, when applied to a natural number, terminates. Consider, as another example, a slight modification of dbl, namely

$$\mathsf{div} = \mathtt{fix}\, f.\lambda x.\ \mathtt{ifz}\, x\, \mathtt{then}\, x\, \mathtt{else}\, \mathtt{s}(\mathtt{s}(f(x))).$$

It behaves as dbl when fed with 0, but it diverges when it receives a positive natural number as argument. But look: div is not so different from dbl. Indeed, the latter can be obtained from the former by feeding not x but $\mathtt{p}(x)$ to f. And any type system in which dbl and div are somehow recognized as being fundamentally different must be able to detect the presence of p in dbl and deduce termination from it. Indeed, sized types [6] and dependent types [27] are able to do so. Going further, we could ask the type system to be able not only to guarantee termination, but also to somehow evaluate the time or space consumption of programs. For example, we could be interested in knowing that dbl takes a polynomial number of steps to be evaluated on any natural number, and actually some type systems able to control the complexity of higher-order programs exist. Good examples are type systems for amortized analysis [17, 19] or those using ideas from linear logic [4, 5]: in all of them, linearity plays a key role.

$\mathsf{d}\ell\mathsf{PCF_N}$ [11] combines some of the ideas presented above with the principles of bounded linear logic (BLL [16]): the cost of evaluating a term is measured by counting how many times function arguments need to be copied during evaluation, and different copies can be given distinct, although uniform, types. Making this information explicit in types permits to compute the cost step by step during the type derivation process. Roughly, typing judgments in $\mathsf{d}\ell\mathsf{PCF_N}$ are statements like

$$\vdash_{\mathrm{J}} t\ :\ !_{\mathrm{n}}\, \mathsf{Nat}[a] \multimap \mathsf{Nat}[\mathrm{I}],$$

where I and J depend on a and n is a natural number capturing the number of times t uses its argument. But this is not sufficient: analogously to what happens in BLL, $\mathsf{d}\ell\mathsf{PCF_N}$ makes types more parametric. A type like $!_{\mathrm{n}}\, \sigma \multimap \tau$ is replaced by the more parametric type $!_{a<\mathrm{n}}\sigma \multimap \tau$, which tells us that the argument will be used n times, and each instance has type σ *where, however* the variable a is substituted by a value less than n. This allows to type each copy of the argument differently but uniformly, since all instances of σ have the same PCF skeleton. This form of *uniform linear dependence* is actually crucial in obtaining the result which makes $\mathsf{d}\ell\mathsf{PCF_N}$ different from similar type systems, namely completeness. As an example, dbl can be typed as follows in $\mathsf{d}\ell\mathsf{PCF_N}$:

$$\vdash^{\mathcal{E}}_{a} \mathsf{dbl}\ :!_{b<a+1}\mathsf{Nat}[a] \multimap \mathsf{Nat}[2\times a].$$

This tells us that the argument will be used a times by dbl, namely a number of times equal to its value. And that the cost of evaluation will be itself proportional to a.

2.1 Why Another Type System?

The theory of λ-calculus is full of interesting results, one of them being the so-called Church-Rsser property: both β and $\beta\eta$ reduction are confluent, *i.e.*, if you fire two distinct redexes in a λ-term, you can always "close the diagram" by performing one *or more* rewriting steps. This, however, is not a *local* confluence result, and as such does *not* imply that all reduction strategies are computationally equivalent. Indeed, some of them are normalizing (like normal-order evaluation) while some others are not (like innermost reduction). But how about efficiency?

On the one hand, it is well known that optimal reduction *is* indeed possible [21], even if it gives rise to high overheads [2]. On the other, call-by-name can be highly inefficient. Consider, as an example, the composition of dbl with itself:

$$\mathsf{dbl2} = \lambda x.\mathsf{dbl}(\mathsf{dbl}\ x).$$

This takes quadratic time to be evaluated by the KAM: the evaluation of ($\mathsf{dbl}\ \underline{\mathrm{n}}$) is repeated a linear number of times, whenever it reaches the head position. This actually *can* be seen from within $\mathsf{d}\ell\mathsf{PCF_N}$, since

$$\vdash^{\mathcal{E}}_{\mathrm{J}} \mathsf{dbl2}\ :!_{b<\mathrm{I}}\mathsf{Nat}[a] \multimap \mathsf{Nat}[4\times a],$$

where both I and J are quadratic in a. Call-by-value solves this problem, at the price of not being normalizing. Indeed, eager evaluation of dbl2 when fed with a natural number n takes linear time in n. The relative efficiency of call-by-value evaluation, compared to call-by-name, is not a novelty: many modern functional programming languages (like OCaml and Scheme) are based on it, while very few of them evaluate terms in call-by-name order. A nice discussion about the relative efficiency of call-by-value and call-by-name evaluation can be found in [1].

For the reasons above, we strongly believe that designing a type system in the style of $\mathsf{d}\ell\mathsf{PCF_N}$, but able to deal with eager evaluation, is a step forward applying linear dependent types to actual programming languages.

2.2 Call-by-Value, Call-by-Name and Linear Logic

Various notions of evaluation for the λ-calculus can be seen as translations of intuitionistic logic (or of simply-typed λ-calculi) into Girard's linear logic. This correspondence has been investigated in the specific cases of call-by-name (CBN) and call-by-value (CBV) reduction (*e.g.* see the work of Maraist et al. [22]). In this section, we briefly introduce the main ideas behind the correspondence, explaining why linear logic has guided the design of $\mathsf{d}\ell\mathsf{PCF_V}$.

The general principle in such translations, is to guarantee that whenever a term *can* possibly be duplicated, it must be mapped to a box in the underlying linear logic proof. In the CBN translation (also called Girard's translation), *any* argument to functions can possibly be substituted for a variable and copied, so arguments are banged during the translation:

$$(A \Rightarrow B)^* \;=\; (!A^*) \multimap B^*$$

Adding the quantitative bound on banged types (as explained in the previous section) gives rise to the type $(!_{a<\mathrm{I}}\sigma) \multimap \tau$ for functions (written $[a < \mathrm{I}]\cdot\sigma \multimap \tau$ in [11]). In the same way, *contexts* are banged in the CBN translation: a typing judgment in $\mathsf{d}\ell\mathsf{PCF_N}$ have the following form:

$$x_1 : !_{a_1<\mathrm{I}_1}\sigma_1, \ldots, x_n : !_{a_n<\mathrm{I}_n}\sigma_n \ \vdash_{\mathrm{J}}\ t : \tau.$$

In the CBV translation, β-reduction should be performed only if the argument is a value. Thus, arguments are not automatically banged during the translation but values are, so that β-reduction remains blocked until the argument reduces to a value. In the λ-calculus values are functions, hence the translation of the intuitionistic arrow becomes

$$(A \Rightarrow B)^\circ \ = \ !(A^\circ \multimap B^\circ).$$

Function types in $\mathsf{d}\ell\mathsf{PCF_V}$ then become $!_{a<\mathrm{I}}(\sigma \multimap \tau)$, and a judgment has the form $x_1 : \sigma_1, \ldots, x_n : \sigma_n \ \vdash_{\mathrm{J}}\ t : \tau$. The syntax of types varies fairly much between $\mathsf{d}\ell\mathsf{PCF_N}$ and $\mathsf{d}\ell\mathsf{PCF_V}$, and consequently the two type systems are different, although both of them are greatly inspired by linear logic.

In both cases, however, the "target" of the translation is not the whole of ILL, but rather a restricted version of it, namely BLL, in which the complexity of normalization is kept under control by shifting from unbounded, infinitary, exponentials to finitary ones. For example, the BLL *contraction* rule allows to merge the first I copies of A, and the following J ones into the first I + J copies of A:

$$\frac{\Gamma, !_{a<\mathrm{I}}A, !_{a<\mathrm{J}}A\{\mathrm{I}+a/a\} \vdash B}{\Gamma, !_{a<\mathrm{I}+\mathrm{J}}A \vdash B}$$

We write $\sigma \uplus \tau = !_{a<\mathrm{I}+\mathrm{J}}A$ if $\sigma = !_{a<\mathrm{I}}A$ and $\tau = !_{a<\mathrm{J}}A\{\mathrm{I}+a/a\}$. Any time a contraction rule is involved in the CBV translation of a type derivation, a sum $\uplus$ appears at the same place in the corresponding $\mathsf{d}\ell\mathsf{PCF_V}$ derivation. Similarly, the *dereliction* rule allows to see any banged type as the first copy of itself:

$$\frac{\Gamma, A\{0/a\} \vdash B}{\Gamma, !_{a<1}A \vdash B}$$

hence any dereliction rule appearing in the translation of a typing judgment tells us that the corresponding type is copied once. Both contraction and dereliction appear while typing an application in $\mathsf{d}\ell\mathsf{PCF_V}$: the PCF typing rule

$$\frac{\Gamma \vdash t : AB \quad \Gamma \vdash u : A}{\Gamma \vdash tu : B}$$

corresponds to the ILL proof

$$\dfrac{\dfrac{\dfrac{\dfrac{z: A^\circ \multimap B^\circ \vdash z: A^\circ \multimap B^\circ}{!z: !(A^\circ \multimap B^\circ) \vdash z: A^\circ \multimap B^\circ} \quad \Gamma^\circ \vdash t^\circ : !(A^\circ \multimap B^\circ)}{\Gamma^\circ \vdash t^\circ : A^\circ \multimap B^\circ} \quad \Gamma^\circ \vdash u^\circ : A^\circ}{\Gamma^\circ, \Gamma^\circ \vdash t^\circ u^\circ : B^\circ}}{\Gamma^\circ \vdash t^\circ u^\circ : B^\circ}$$

which becomes the following, when appropriately decorated according to the principles of BLL (writing A_0 and B_0 for $A\{0/a\}$ and $B\{0/a\}$)

$$\dfrac{\dfrac{\dfrac{\dfrac{z: A_0^\circ \multimap B_0^\circ \vdash z: A_0^\circ \multimap B_0^\circ}{!z: !_{a<1}(A^\circ \multimap B^\circ) \vdash z: A_0^\circ \multimap B_0^\circ} \quad \Gamma^\circ \vdash t^\circ : !_{a<1}(A^\circ \multimap B^\circ)}{\Gamma^\circ \vdash t^\circ : A_0^\circ \multimap B_0^\circ} \quad \Gamma^\circ \vdash u^\circ : A_0^\circ}{\Gamma^\circ, \Gamma^\circ \vdash t^\circ u^\circ : B_0^\circ}}{\Gamma^\circ \uplus \Gamma^\circ \vdash t^\circ u^\circ : B_0^\circ}$$

The CBV translation of the application rule hence leads to the typing rule for applications in $\mathsf{d}\ell\mathsf{PCF_V}$:

$$\frac{\Gamma \vdash_{\mathrm{K}} t : !_{a<1}(\sigma \multimap \tau) \quad \Delta \vdash_{\mathrm{H}} u : \sigma\{0/a\}}{\Gamma \uplus \Delta \vdash_{\mathrm{K}+\mathrm{H}} tu : \tau\{0/a\}}$$

The same kind of analysis allows to derive the typing rule for abstractions (whose call-by-value translation requires the use of a promotion rule) in $\mathsf{d}\ell\mathsf{PCF_V}$:

$$\frac{\Gamma, x : \sigma \vdash_{\mathrm{K}} t : \tau}{\sum_{a<\mathrm{I}} \Gamma \vdash_{\mathrm{I}+\sum_{a<\mathrm{I}}\mathrm{K}} \lambda x.t : !_{a<\mathrm{I}}(\sigma \multimap \tau)}$$

One may wonder what I represents in this typing rule, and more generally in a judgment such as

$$\Gamma \vdash_{\mathrm{K}} t : \ !_{a<\mathrm{I}}A.$$

This is actually the main new idea of $\mathsf{d}\ell\mathsf{PCF_V}$: such a judgment intuitively means that the value to which t reduces will be used I times by the environment. If t is applied to an argument u, then t must reduce to an abstraction $\lambda x.s$, that is used by the argument without being duplicated. In that case, $\mathrm{I} = 1$, as indicated by the application typing rule. On the opposite, if t is applied to a function $\lambda x.u$, then the type of this function must be of the form (up to a substitution of b) $!_{b<1}((!_{a<\mathrm{I}}A) \multimap \tau)$. This means that $\lambda x.u$ uses I times its arguments, or, that x can appear at most I times in the reducts of u.

This suggests that the type derivation of a term is not unique in general: whether a term t has type $!_{a<\mathrm{I}}A$ or $!_{a<\mathrm{J}}A$ depends on the use we want to make of t. This intuition will direct us in establishing the typing rules for the other PCF constructs (namely conditional branching and fixpoints).

3. $\mathsf{d}\ell\mathsf{PCF_V}$, Formally

In this section, the language of programs and a type system $\mathsf{d}\ell\mathsf{PCF_V}$ for it will be introduced formally. While terms are just those of a fairly standard λ-calculus (which is very similar to Plotkin's PCF), types may include so-called *index terms*, which are first-order terms denoting natural numbers by which one can express properties about the extensional and intentional behavior of programs.

3.1 Index Terms and Equational Programs

Syntactically, index terms are built either from function symbols from a given untyped signature Θ or by applying any of two special term constructs:

$$\mathrm{I}, \mathrm{J}, \mathrm{K} \quad ::= \quad a \mid \mathrm{f}(\mathrm{I}_1, \ldots, \mathrm{I}_n) \mid \sum_{a<\mathrm{I}} \mathrm{J} \mid \mathop{\textcircled{\scriptsize$\triangle$}}_{a}^{\mathrm{I},\mathrm{J}} \mathrm{K}.$$

Here, f is a symbol of arity n from Θ and a is a variable drawn from a set $\mathcal{V}$ of *index variables*. We assume the symbols 0, 1 (with arity 0) and $+$, $-$ (with arity 2) are always part of Θ. An index term in the form $\sum_{a<\mathrm{I}} \mathrm{J}$ is a *bounded sum*, while one in the form $\textcircled{\scriptsize$\triangle$}_a^{\mathrm{I},\mathrm{J}}\,\mathrm{K}$ is a *forest cardinality*. For every natural number n, the index term n is just $\underbrace{1+1+\ldots+1}_{n \text{ times}}$.

Index terms are meant to denote natural numbers, possibly depending on the (unknown) values of variables. Variables can be instantiated with other index terms, *e.g.* $\mathrm{I}\{\mathrm{J}/a\}$. So, index terms can also act as first order functions. What is the meaning of the function symbols from the signature Θ? It is the one induced by an equational program $\mathcal{E}$. Formally, an *equational program* $\mathcal{E}$ over a signature Θ is a set of equations in the form $\mathrm{I} = \mathrm{J}$ where both I and J are index terms. We are interested in equational programs guaranteeing that, whenever symbols in Θ are interpreted as partial functions over $\mathbb{N}$ and 0, 1, $+$ and $-$ are interpreted in the usual way, the semantics of any function symbol f can be uniquely determined from $\mathcal{E}$. This can be guaranteed by, for example, taking $\mathcal{E}$ as an Herbrand-Gödel scheme [23] or as an orthogonal constructor term rewriting system [3]. The definition of index terms is parametric on Θ and $\mathcal{E}$: this way one can tune our type system from a highly undecidable but truly powerful machinery down to a tractable but less expressive formal system.

What about the meaning of bounded sums and forest cardinalities? The first is very intuitive: the value of $\sum_{a<\mathrm{I}} \mathrm{J}$ is simply the sum of all possible values of J with a taking the values from 0 up to I, excluded. Forest cardinalities, on the other hand, require some effort to be described. Informally, $\text{\textcircled{$\triangle$}}_a^{I,J}\,K$ is an index term denoting the number of nodes in a forest composed of J trees described using K. All the nodes in the forest are (uniquely) identified by natural numbers. These are obtained by consecutively visiting each tree in pre-order, starting from I. The term K has the role of describing the number of children of each forest node, *e.g.* , the number of children of the node 0 is $K\{0/a\}$. More formally, the meaning of a forest cardinality is defined by the following two equations:

$$\underset{a}{\overset{I,0}{\text{\textcircled{$\triangle$}}}} K = 0;$$

$$\underset{a}{\overset{I,J+1}{\text{\textcircled{$\triangle$}}}} K = \left(\underset{a}{\overset{I,J}{\text{\textcircled{$\triangle$}}}} K\right) + 1 + \left(\underset{a}{\overset{I+1+\text{\textcircled{$\triangle$}}_a^{I,J} K,\, K\{I+\text{\textcircled{$\triangle$}}_a^{I,J} K/a\}}{\text{\textcircled{$\triangle$}}}} K\right).$$

The first equation says that a forest of 0 trees contains no nodes. The second one tells us that a forest of J + 1 trees contains:

- The nodes in the first J trees;
- plus the nodes in the last tree, which are just one plus the nodes in the immediate subtrees of the root, considered themselves as a forest.

To better understand forest cardinalities, consider the following forest comprising two trees:

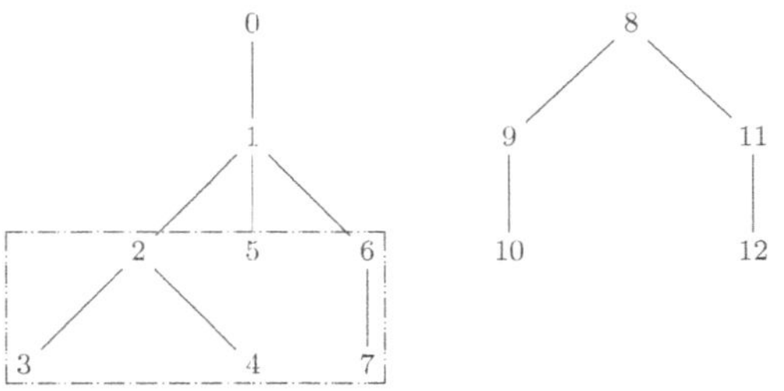

It is well described by an index term K with a free index variable a such that $K\{1/a\} = 3$; $K\{n/a\} = 2$ for $n \in \{2, 8\}$; $K\{n/a\} = 1$ when $n \in \{0, 6, 9, 11\}$; and $K\{n/a\} = 0$ when $n \in \{3, 4, 5, 7, 10, 12\}$. That is, K describes the number of children of each node. Then $\text{\textcircled{$\triangle$}}_a^{0,2}\,K = 13$ since it takes into account the entire forest; $\text{\textcircled{$\triangle$}}_a^{0,1}\,K = 8$ since it takes into account only the leftmost tree; $\text{\textcircled{$\triangle$}}_a^{8,1}\,K = 5$ since it takes into account only the second tree of the forest; finally, $\text{\textcircled{$\triangle$}}_a^{2,3}\,K = 6$ since it takes into account only the three trees (as a forest) within the dashed rectangle.

One may wonder what is the role of forest cardinalities in the type system. Actually, they play a crucial role in the treatment of recursion, where the unfolding of recursion produces a tree-like structure whose size is just the number of times the (recursively defined) function will be used *globally*. Note that the value of a forest cardinality could also be undefined. For instance, this happens when infinite trees, corresponding to diverging recursive computations, are considered.

The expression $[\![I]\!]_\rho^{\mathcal{E}}$ denotes the meaning of I, defined by induction along the lines of the previous discussion, where $\rho : \mathcal{V} \to \mathbb{N}$ is an assignment and $\mathcal{E}$ is an equational program giving meaning to the function symbols in I. Since $\mathcal{E}$ does not necessarily interpret such symbols as *total* functions, and moreover, the value of a forest cardinality can be undefined, $[\![I]\!]_\rho^{\mathcal{E}}$ can be undefined itself. A *constraint* is an inequality in the form $I \leqslant J$. Such a constraint is *true* in an assignment ρ if $[\![I]\!]_\rho^{\mathcal{E}}$ and $[\![J]\!]_\rho^{\mathcal{E}}$ are *both* defined and the first is smaller or equal to the latter. Now, for a subset ϕ of $\mathcal{V}$, and for a set Φ of constraints involving variables in ϕ, the expression

$$\phi; \Phi \models_{\mathcal{E}} I \leqslant J$$

denotes the fact that the truth of $I \leqslant J$ *semantically* follows from the truth of the constraints in Φ. To denote that I is well defined for $\mathcal{E}$ and any valuation ρ satisfying Φ, we may write $\phi; \Phi \models_{\mathcal{E}} I \Downarrow$ instead of $\phi; \Phi \models_{\mathcal{E}} I \leqslant I$.

$$\begin{aligned}
(\lambda x.t)\; v &\;_v\; t[x := v] \\
\mathtt{s}(\underline{n}) &\;_v\; \underline{n+1} \\
\mathtt{p}(\underline{n+1}) &\;_v\; \underline{n} \\
\mathtt{p}(\underline{0}) &\;_v\; \underline{0} \\
\mathtt{ifz}\; \underline{0}\; \mathtt{then}\; t\; \mathtt{else}\; u &\;_v\; t \\
\mathtt{ifz}\; \underline{n+1}\; \mathtt{then}\; t\; \mathtt{else}\; u &\;_v\; u \\
(\,\mathtt{fix}\, x.t)\; v &\;_v\; (t[x := \mathtt{fix}\, x.t])\; v
\end{aligned}$$

Figure 1. Call-by-value reduction of PCF terms.

3.2 Programs

Values and *terms* are generated by the following grammar:

$$\begin{aligned}
\text{Values:}\quad v, w &::= \underline{n} \mid \lambda x.t \mid \mathtt{fix}\, x.t \\
\text{Terms:}\quad s, t, u &::= x \mid v \mid tu \mid \mathtt{s}(t) \mid \mathtt{p}(t) \\
&\quad\;\; \mid \mathtt{ifz}\; t\; \mathtt{then}\; u\; \mathtt{else}\; s
\end{aligned}$$

Terms can be typed with a well-known type system called PCF: types are those generated by the basic type Nat and the binary type constructor $\Rightarrow$. Typing rules are standard (see [12]). A notion of (weak) call-by-value reduction $_v$ can be easily defined: take the rewriting rules in Figure 1 and close them under all applicative contexts. A term t is said to be a *program* if it can be given the PCF type Nat in the empty context. The *size* $|t|$ of a term t is defined as follows:

$$\begin{aligned}
|\underline{n}| = |x| &= 2; \\
|\lambda x.t| = |\,\mathtt{fix}\, x.t| &= |t| + 2; \\
|tu| &= |t| + |u| + 2; \\
|\mathtt{s}(t)| = |\mathtt{p}(t)| &= |t| + 2; \\
|\,\mathtt{ifz}\; t\; \mathtt{then}\; u\; \mathtt{else}\; s| &= |t| + |u| + |s| + 2.
\end{aligned}$$

In other words, every symbol counts for 2. The *multiplicative size* $\|t\|$ of a term t is defined as its size $|t|$ except on values, which have null multiplicative size (see Figure 9 for a formal definition). The reason why values are not taken into account by the multiplicative size, is that evaluation by the CEK abstract machine (see Section 3.4) proceeds by first *scanning* terms until a value is reached, and the cost of these initial steps is taken into account by the multiplicative size. This value is either erased (*e.g.* when a lambda abstraction is given an argument), or duplicated (*e.g.* when it is itself the argument to a lambda abstraction). The cost of this second phase is measured by the type system dℓPCF$_V$.

3.3 The Type System

The Language of Types. The type system dℓPCF$_V$ can be seen as a refinement of PCF obtained by a linear decoration of its type derivations. *Linear* and *modal types* are defined as follows:

$$\begin{aligned}
A, B &::= \sigma \multimap \tau && \text{linear types} \\
\sigma, \tau &::= [a < I] \cdot A \mid \mathtt{Nat}[I, J] && \text{modal types}
\end{aligned}$$

where I, J range over index terms and a ranges over index variables. Modal types need some comments. Natural numbers are freely duplicable, so Nat[I, J] is modal by definition. As a first approximation, $[a < I] \cdot A$ can be thought of as a universal quantification of A, and so a is bound in the linear type A. Moreover, the condition $a < I$ says that σ consists of all the instances of the linear type A where the variable a is successively instantiated with the values from 0 to I − 1, *i.e.*, $A\{0/a\}, \ldots, A\{I-1/a\}$. For those readers who are familiar with linear logic, and in particular with BLL, the modal type $[a < I] \cdot A$ is a generalization of the BLL

$$\frac{\phi;\Phi \models_{\mathcal{E}} \mathrm{K} \leqslant \mathrm{I} \qquad \phi;\Phi \models_{\mathcal{E}} \mathrm{J} \leqslant \mathrm{H}}{\phi;\Phi \vdash_{\mathcal{E}} \mathtt{Nat}[\mathrm{I},\mathrm{J}] \sqsubseteq \mathtt{Nat}[\mathrm{K},\mathrm{H}]} \qquad \frac{\phi;\Phi \vdash_{\mathcal{E}} \sigma' \sqsubseteq \sigma \qquad \phi;\Phi \vdash_{\mathcal{E}} \tau \sqsubseteq \tau'}{\phi;\Phi \vdash_{\mathcal{E}} \sigma \multimap \tau \sqsubseteq \sigma' \multimap \tau'} \qquad \frac{(a,\phi);(a<\mathrm{J},\Phi) \vdash_{\mathcal{E}} A \sqsubseteq B \qquad \phi;\Phi \models_{\mathcal{E}} \mathrm{J} \leqslant \mathrm{I}}{\phi;\Phi \vdash_{\mathcal{E}} [a<\mathrm{I}]\cdot A \sqsubseteq [a<\mathrm{J}]\cdot B}$$

Figure 2. Subtyping derivation rules of dℓPCF$_{\mathsf{V}}$.

$$\frac{}{\phi;\Phi;\Gamma,x:\sigma \vdash^{\mathcal{E}}_{0} x:\sigma}(Ax) \qquad \frac{\phi;\Phi;\Gamma \vdash^{\mathcal{E}}_{\mathrm{I}} t:\sigma \qquad \phi;\Phi \vdash_{\mathcal{E}} \Delta \sqsubseteq \Gamma \qquad \phi;\Phi \vdash_{\mathcal{E}} \sigma \sqsubseteq \tau \qquad \phi;\Phi \models_{\mathcal{E}} \mathrm{I} \leqslant \mathrm{J}}{\phi;\Phi;\Delta \vdash^{\mathcal{E}}_{\mathrm{J}} t:\tau}(Subs)$$

$$\frac{(a,\phi);(a<\mathrm{I},\Phi);\Gamma,x:\sigma \vdash^{\mathcal{E}}_{\mathrm{K}} t:\tau}{\phi;\Phi;\sum_{a<\mathrm{I}}\Gamma \vdash^{\mathcal{E}}_{\mathrm{I}+\sum_{a<\mathrm{I}}\mathrm{K}} \lambda x.t:[a<\mathrm{I}]\cdot\sigma \multimap \tau}(\multimap) \qquad \frac{\phi;\Phi;\Gamma \vdash^{\mathcal{E}}_{\mathrm{K}} t:[a<1]\cdot\sigma \multimap \tau \qquad \phi;\Phi;\Delta \vdash^{\mathcal{E}}_{\mathrm{H}} u:\sigma\{0/a\}}{\phi;\Phi;\Gamma \uplus \Delta \vdash^{\mathcal{E}}_{\mathrm{K}+\mathrm{H}} tu:\tau\{0/a\}}(App)$$

$$\frac{\phi;\Phi;\Gamma \vdash^{\mathcal{E}}_{\mathrm{M}} t:\mathtt{Nat}[\mathrm{J},\mathrm{K}] \qquad \phi;(\mathrm{J}\leqslant 0,\Phi);\Delta \vdash^{\mathcal{E}}_{\mathrm{N}} u:\tau \qquad \phi;(\mathrm{K}\geqslant 1,\Phi);\Delta \vdash^{\mathcal{E}}_{\mathrm{N}} s:\tau}{\phi;\Phi;\Gamma \uplus \Delta \vdash^{\mathcal{E}}_{\mathrm{M}+\mathrm{N}} \mathtt{ifz}\ t\ \mathtt{then}\ u\ \mathtt{else}\ s:\tau}(If)$$

$$\frac{}{\phi;\Phi;\Gamma \vdash^{\mathcal{E}}_{0} \underline{\mathrm{n}}:\mathtt{Nat}[\mathrm{n},\mathrm{n}]}(n) \qquad \frac{\phi;\Phi;\Gamma \vdash^{\mathcal{E}}_{\mathrm{M}} t:\mathtt{Nat}[\mathrm{I},\mathrm{J}]}{\phi;\Phi;\Gamma \vdash^{\mathcal{E}}_{\mathrm{M}} \mathtt{s}(t):\mathtt{Nat}[\mathrm{I}+1,\mathrm{J}+1]}(s) \qquad \frac{\phi;\Phi;\Gamma \vdash^{\mathcal{E}}_{\mathrm{M}} t:\mathtt{Nat}[\mathrm{I},\mathrm{J}]}{\phi;\Phi;\Gamma \vdash^{\mathcal{E}}_{\mathrm{M}} \mathtt{p}(t):\mathtt{Nat}[\mathrm{I}-1,\mathrm{J}-1]}(p)$$

$$\frac{(b,\phi);(b<\mathrm{H},\Phi);\Gamma,x:[a<\mathrm{I}]\cdot A \vdash^{\mathcal{E}}_{\mathrm{J}} t:[a<1]\cdot B \qquad (a,b,\phi);(a<\mathrm{I},b<\mathrm{H},\Phi) \vdash_{\mathcal{E}} B\{0/a\}\{\bigcirc\kern-0.78em\triangle_b^{b+1,a}\,\mathrm{I}+b+1/b\} \sqsubseteq A}{\phi;\Phi;\sum_{b<\mathrm{H}}\Gamma \vdash^{\mathcal{E}}_{\mathrm{H}+\sum_{b<\mathrm{H}}\mathrm{J}} \mathtt{fix}\ x.t:[a<\mathrm{K}]\cdot B\{0/a\}\{\bigcirc\kern-0.78em\triangle_b^{0,a}\,\mathrm{I}/b\}}(Fix)$$

(where $\mathrm{H} = \bigcirc\kern-0.78em\triangle_b^{0,\mathrm{K}}\,\mathrm{I}$)

Figure 3. Typing rules of dℓPCF$_{\mathsf{V}}$.

formula $!_{a<p}A$ to arbitrary index terms. As such it can be thought of as representing the type $A\{0/a\} \otimes \cdots \otimes A\{\mathrm{I}-1/a\}$. $\mathtt{Nat}[\mathrm{I}]$ is syntactic sugar for $\mathtt{Nat}[\mathrm{I},\mathrm{I}]$. In the typing rules we are going to define, modal types need to be manipulated in an algebraic way. For this reason, two operations on modal types need to be introduced. The first one is a binary operation $\uplus$ on modal types. Suppose that $\sigma = [a<\mathrm{I}]\cdot A\{a/c\}$ and that $\tau = [b<\mathrm{J}]\cdot A\{\mathrm{I}+b/c\}$. Their *sum* $\sigma \uplus \tau$ is naturally defined as a modal type consisting of the first $\mathrm{I}+\mathrm{J}$ instances of A, *i.e.* $[c<\mathrm{I}+\mathrm{J}]\cdot A$. Furthermore, $\mathtt{Nat}[\mathrm{I},\mathrm{J}] \uplus \mathtt{Nat}[\mathrm{I},\mathrm{J}]$ is just $\mathtt{Nat}[\mathrm{I},\mathrm{J}]$. An operation of bounded sum on modal types can be defined by generalizing the idea above: suppose that

$$\sigma = [b<\mathrm{J}]\cdot A\{b+\sum_{d<a}\mathrm{J}\{d/a\}/c\}.$$

Then its *bounded sum* $\sum_{a<\mathrm{I}}\sigma$ is just $[c<\sum_{a<\mathrm{I}}\mathrm{J}]\cdot A$. Finally, $\sum_{a<\mathrm{I}}\mathtt{Nat}[\mathrm{J},\mathrm{K}] = \mathtt{Nat}[\mathrm{J},\mathrm{K}]$, provided a is not free in J nor in K.

Subtyping. Central to dℓPCF$_{\mathsf{V}}$ is the notion of subtyping. An inequality relation $\sqsubseteq$ between (linear or modal) types can be defined using the formal system in Figure 2. This relation corresponds to lifting index inequalities at the type level. Please observe that $\sqsubseteq$ is a pre-order, *i.e.*, a reflexive and transitive relation.

Typing. A typing judgment is of the form

$$\phi;\Phi;\Gamma \vdash^{\mathcal{E}}_{\mathrm{K}} t:\tau,$$

where K is the *weight* of t, that is (informally) the maximal number of substitutions involved in the CBV evaluation of t. Φ is a set of constraints (*cf.* Section 3.1) that we call the *index context*, and Γ is a context assigning a modal type to (at least) each free variable of t. Both sums and bounded sums are naturally extended from modal types to contexts (with, for instance, $\{x:\sigma;y:\tau\} \uplus \{x:\zeta,z:\eta\} = \{x:\sigma\uplus\zeta;y:\tau;z:\eta\}$). There might be free index variables in Φ,Γ,τ and K, all of them from ϕ. Typing judgments can be derived from the rules of Figure 3. We are implicitly assuming that all index terms appearing in (derivable) typing judgments are defined in the appropriate index contexts.

Derivation rules for abstractions and applications have been informally presented in Section 2.2. The other ones are then intuitive, except the derivation rule for typing $\mathtt{fix}\ x.t$, that is worth an explanation: to simplify, assume we want to type only one copy of its type (that is, $\mathrm{K}=1$). To compute the weight of $\mathtt{fix}\ x.t$, we need to know the number of times t will be copied during the evaluation, that is the number of nodes in the tree of its recursive calls. This tree is described by I (as explained in Section 3.1), since each occurrence of x in t stands for a recursive call. It has, say, $\mathrm{H} = \bigcirc\kern-0.78em\triangle_b^{0,1}\,\mathrm{I}$ nodes. At each node b of this tree, the ath occurrence of x will be replaced by the ath son of b, *i.e.* by $b+1+\bigcirc\kern-0.78em\triangle_b^{b+1,a}\,\mathrm{I}$. The types have to match, and that is what the second premise expresses. Finally, the type of $\mathtt{fix}\ x.t$ is the type of the "main" copy of t, at the root of the tree (*i.e.*, at $b=0$). The weight counts all the recursive calls (*i.e.*, H) plus the weight of each copy of t (*i.e.*, the weight of t for each $b<\mathrm{H}$).

Last, the subsumption rule (*Subs*) allows to relax the precision standard of a typing judgment. One can also restrict the inequalities on indexes to equalities in this rule, and thereby construct only *precise* typing judgments. Observe that the set of all rules but this one is syntax directed. Moreover, the subsumption rule preserves the PCF skeleton of the types, and so the type system is itself syntax directed *up to* index inequalities.

3.4 An Abstract Machine for PCF

The call-by-value evaluation of PCF terms can be faithfully captured by an abstract machine in the style of CEK [15], which will be introduced in this section.

The internal state of the CEK$_{\mathsf{PCF}}$ machine consists of a closure and a stack, interacting following a set of rules. Formally, a *value closure* is a pair $\mathsf{v} = \langle v;\xi\rangle$ where v is a value and ξ is an *environment*, itself a list of assignments of value closures to variables:

$$\xi ::= \ \mid (x \mapsto \mathsf{v})\cdot\xi.$$

$$
\begin{array}{ccccccc}
\mathsf{v} & \star & \mathsf{arg}(\mathsf{c}\,,\,\pi) & \succ & \mathsf{c} & \star & \mathsf{fun}(\mathsf{v}\,,\,\pi) \\
\mathsf{v} & \star & \mathsf{fun}(\langle\, \lambda x.t\,;\,\xi\,\rangle\,,\,\pi) & \succ & \langle\, t\,;\,(x\mapsto \mathsf{v})\cdot\xi\,\rangle & \star & \pi \\
\mathsf{v} & \star & \mathsf{fun}(\langle\, \mathtt{fix}\, x.t\,;\,\xi\,\rangle\,,\,\pi) & \succ & \langle\, t\,;\,(x\mapsto\langle\, \mathtt{fix}\, x.t\,;\,\xi\,\rangle)\cdot\xi\,\rangle & \star & \mathsf{arg}(\mathsf{v}\,,\,\pi) \\
\langle\, \underline{0}\,;\,\xi'\,\rangle & \star & \mathsf{fork}(t\,,\,u\,,\,\xi\,,\,\pi) & \succ & \langle\, t\,;\,\xi\,\rangle & \star & \pi \\
\langle\, \underline{\mathrm{n}+1}\,;\,\xi'\,\rangle & \star & \mathsf{fork}(t\,,\,u\,,\,\xi\,,\,\pi) & \succ & \langle\, u\,;\,\xi\,\rangle & \star & \pi \\
\langle\, \underline{\mathrm{n}}\,;\,\xi\,\rangle & \star & \mathsf{s}(\pi) & \succ & \langle\, \underline{\mathrm{n}+1}\,;\,\varnothing\,\rangle & \star & \pi \\
\langle\, \underline{\mathrm{n}}\,;\,\xi\,\rangle & \star & \mathsf{p}(\pi) & \succ & \langle\, \underline{\mathrm{n}-1}\,;\,\varnothing\,\rangle & \star & \pi
\end{array}
$$

Figure 4. $\mathsf{CEK}_{\mathsf{PCF}}$ evaluation rules for value closures.

$$
\begin{array}{ccccccc}
\langle\, x\,;\,\xi\,\rangle & \star & \pi & \succ & \xi(x) & \star & \pi \\
\langle\, tu\,;\,\xi\,\rangle & \star & \pi & \succ & \langle\, t\,;\,\xi\,\rangle & \star & \mathsf{arg}(\langle\, u\,;\,\xi\,\rangle\,,\,\pi) \\
\langle\, \mathtt{s}(t)\,;\,\xi\,\rangle & \star & \pi & \succ & \langle\, t\,;\,\xi\,\rangle & \star & \mathsf{s}(\pi) \\
\langle\, \mathtt{p}(t)\,;\,\xi\,\rangle & \star & \pi & \succ & \langle\, t\,;\,\xi\,\rangle & \star & \mathsf{p}(\pi) \\
\langle\, \mathtt{ifz}\, t\, \mathtt{then}\, u\, \mathtt{else}\, s\,;\,\xi\,\rangle & \star & \pi & \succ & \langle\, t\,;\,\xi\,\rangle & \star & \mathsf{fork}(u\,,\,s\,,\,\xi\,,\,\pi)
\end{array}
$$

Figure 5. $\mathsf{CEK}_{\mathsf{PCF}}$ contextual evaluation rules.

A *closure* is a pair $\mathsf{c} = \langle\, t\,;\,\xi\,\rangle$ where t is a term (and not necessarily a value). *Stacks* are terms from the following grammar:

$$
\begin{aligned}
\pi ::= {} & \diamond \mid \mathsf{fun}(\mathsf{v}\,,\,\pi) \mid \mathsf{arg}(\mathsf{c}\,,\,\pi) \\
& \mid \mathsf{fork}(t\,,\,u\,,\,\xi\,,\,\pi) \mid \mathsf{s}(\pi) \mid \mathsf{p}(\pi).
\end{aligned}
$$

A *process* P is a pair $\mathsf{c} \star \pi$ of a closure and a stack.

Processes evolve according to a number of rules. Some of them (see Figure 4) describe how the $\mathsf{CEK}_{\mathsf{PCF}}$ machine evolves when the first component of the process is a value closure. Other rules (see Figure 5) prescribe the evolution of $\mathsf{CEK}_{\mathsf{PCF}}$ in all the other cases.

The following tells us that $\mathsf{CEK}_{\mathsf{PCF}}$ is an adequate methodology to evaluate PCF terms:

PROPOSITION 3.1 (Adequacy). *If t is a* PCF *term of type* Nat, *then* $t \Downarrow_v^* \underline{\mathrm{n}}$ *iff* $(\langle\, t\,;\,\varnothing\,\rangle \star \diamond) \succ^* (\langle\, \underline{\mathrm{n}}\,;\,\varnothing\,\rangle \star \diamond)$.

Weights and the $\mathsf{CEK}_{\mathsf{PCF}}$ ***Machine.*** As it will be formalized in Section 5.3, an upper bound for the evaluation of a given term in the $\mathsf{CEK}_{\mathsf{PCF}}$ machine can be obtained by multiplying its weight and its size. This result can be explained as follows: we have seen (in Section 3.3) that its weight represents the maximal number of substitutions in its CBV evaluation, and thereby the maximal number of steps of the form

$$
\begin{aligned}
& \mathsf{v} \star \mathsf{fun}(\langle\, \lambda x.t\,;\,\xi\,\rangle\,,\,\pi) \succ \langle\, t\,;\,(x\mapsto \mathsf{v})\cdot\xi\,\rangle \star \pi; \\
& \mathsf{v} \star \mathsf{fun}(\langle\, \mathtt{fix}\, x.t\,;\,\xi\,\rangle\,,\,\pi) \succ \\
& \qquad \langle\, t\,;\,(x\mapsto\langle\, \mathtt{fix}\, x.t\,;\,\xi\,\rangle)\cdot\xi\,\rangle \star \mathsf{arg}(\mathsf{v}\,,\,\pi);
\end{aligned}
$$

in its evaluation with the $\mathsf{CEK}_{\mathsf{PCF}}$. Between two such steps, the use of the other rules is not taken into account by the weight; however the other rules make the *size* of the process to decrease.

4. Examples

In this section we will see how to type some "real life" functions in $\mathsf{d}\ell\mathsf{PCF}_\mathsf{V}$, and what is the cost associated to them.

Addition. In PCF, addition can be computed as follows:

$$\mathsf{add} = \mathtt{fix}\, x.\lambda yz.\, \mathtt{ifz}\, y\, \mathtt{then}\, z\, \mathtt{else}\, \mathtt{s}(x\, \mathtt{p}(y)\, z),$$

and has type NatNatNat. A brief analysis of its evaluation, if we apply it to two values v and w in Nat, indicates that a correct annotation for this type in $\mathsf{d}\ell\mathsf{PCF}_\mathsf{V}$ would be

$$[a < 1]\cdot(\mathtt{Nat}[d] \multimap [c < 1]\cdot(\mathtt{Nat}[e] \multimap \mathtt{Nat}[d+e]))$$

where d and e are variable symbols representing the values of v and w respectively. Since we directly apply add, without copying this function, the index variables a and c are bounded by 1. This type is indeed derivable for add in $\mathsf{d}\ell\mathsf{PCF}_\mathsf{V}$, assuming that the equational program $\mathcal{E}$ is powerful enough to express the following index terms (they all depend on the index variables b and d):

$$
\begin{aligned}
\mathrm{I} &= \text{if } b < d \text{ then } 1 \text{ else } 0; \\
\mathrm{J} &= d - b - 1; \\
\mathrm{H} &= d - b; \\
\mathrm{K} &= d - b + 1.
\end{aligned}
$$

The derivation is given in Figure 6. We omit all the subsumption steps, but the index equalities they use are easy to check given that the number of nodes in the tree of recursive calls is $\triangle_b^{0,1}\,\mathrm{I} = d+1$. The final weight is equal to $3 \times (d+1)$.

Multiplication. Multiplication can be easily defined using addition:

$$\mathsf{mult} = \mathtt{fix}\, x.\lambda yz.\, \mathtt{ifz}\, y\, \mathtt{then}\, \underline{0}\, \mathtt{else}\, \mathsf{add}\, z\, (x\, \mathtt{p}(y)\, z).$$

Taking the indexes I,J,H and K defined as in the previous paragraph, and using the typing judgement for add with d replaced by e and e replaced by $\mathrm{J} \times e$, we can assign to mult the type

$$[a < 1]\cdot\mathtt{Nat}[d] \multimap [c < 1]\cdot(\mathtt{Nat}[e] \multimap \mathtt{Nat}[d \times e])$$

(see Figure 7). The weight of mult is equal to $3 \times (d+1) + \sum_{b<d+1} \mathrm{M}$, where the meaning of M is "if $b = d$ then 0 else $3e+1$". Thus the cost of the application of mult to two integers $\underline{\mathrm{n}}$ and $\underline{\mathrm{m}}$ in the $\mathsf{CEK}_{\mathsf{PCF}}$ machine is proportional to $n \times m$.

5. The Metatheory of $\mathsf{d}\ell\mathsf{PCF}_\mathsf{V}$

In this section, some metatheoretical results about $\mathsf{d}\ell\mathsf{PCF}_\mathsf{V}$ will be presented. More specifically, type derivations are shown to be modifiable in many different ways, all of them leaving the underlying term unaltered. These manipulations, described in Section 5.1, form a basic toolkit which is essential to achieve the main results of this paper, namely intentional soundness and completeness (which are presented in Section 5.3 and Section 5.4). Types are preserved by call-by-value reduction, as proved in Section 5.2.

5.1 Manipulating Type Derivations

First of all, the constraints Φ in index, subtyping and typing judgments can be made stronger without altering the rest:

LEMMA 5.1 (Strengthening). *If* $\phi; \Psi \models_{\mathcal{E}} \Phi$, *then the following implications hold:*

1. *If* $\phi; \Phi \models_{\mathcal{E}} \mathrm{I} \leqslant \mathrm{J}$, *then* $\phi; \Psi \models_{\mathcal{E}} \mathrm{I} \leqslant \mathrm{J}$;
2. *If* $\phi; \Phi \vdash_{\mathcal{E}} \sigma \sqsubseteq \tau$, *then* $\phi; \Psi \vdash_{\mathcal{E}} \sigma \sqsubseteq \tau$;

$$
\begin{aligned}
A &= \mathtt{Nat}[\mathrm{J}] \multimap [c < 1] \cdot (\mathtt{Nat}[e] \multimap \mathtt{Nat}[\mathrm{J} + e]) \\
C &= \mathtt{Nat}[\mathrm{H}] \multimap [c < 1] \cdot (\mathtt{Nat}[e] \multimap \mathtt{Nat}[\mathrm{H} + e]) \\
\Gamma &= \{x : [a < \mathrm{I}] \cdot A,\ y : \mathtt{Nat}[\mathrm{H}],\ z : \mathtt{Nat}[e]\} \\
\phi &= \{a, b, c, d, e\} \\
\Phi &= \{b < d + 1, a < 1, c < 1\}
\end{aligned}
$$

$$
\dfrac{\phi; (\mathrm{H} \geqslant 1, \Phi); x : [a < \mathrm{I}] \cdot A \vdash^{\mathcal{E}}_{0} x : [a < \mathrm{I}] \cdot A \qquad \dfrac{\phi; (\mathrm{H} \geqslant 1, \Phi); y : \mathtt{Nat}[\mathrm{H}] \vdash^{\mathcal{E}}_{0} y : \mathtt{Nat}[\mathrm{H}]}{\phi; (\mathrm{H} \geqslant 1, \Phi); y : \mathtt{Nat}[\mathrm{H}] \vdash^{\mathcal{E}}_{0} \mathtt{p}(y) : \mathtt{Nat}[\mathrm{J}]}\,(p)}{\phi; (\mathrm{H} \geqslant 1, \Phi); x : [a < \mathrm{I}] \cdot A, y : \mathtt{Nat}[\mathrm{H}] \vdash^{\mathcal{E}}_{0} x\,\mathtt{p}(y) : [c < 1] \cdot (\mathtt{Nat}[e] \multimap \mathtt{Nat}[\mathrm{J} + e])}\,(App)
$$

$$
(s)\,\dfrac{(App)\,\dfrac{\vdots \qquad \phi; (\mathrm{H} \geqslant 1, \Phi); z : \mathtt{Nat}[e] \vdash^{\mathcal{E}}_{0} z : \mathtt{Nat}[e]}{\phi; (\mathrm{H} \geqslant 1, \Phi); \Gamma \vdash^{\mathcal{E}}_{0} x\,\mathtt{p}(y)\,z : \mathtt{Nat}[\mathrm{J} + e]}}{\phi; (\mathrm{H} \geqslant 1, \Phi); \Gamma \vdash^{\mathcal{E}}_{0} \mathtt{s}(x\,\mathtt{p}(y)\,z) : \mathtt{Nat}[\mathrm{H} + e]}
$$

$$
(Fix)\,\dfrac{\dfrac{\dfrac{\dfrac{\phi; \Phi; y : \mathtt{Nat}[\mathrm{H}] \vdash^{\mathcal{E}}_{0} y : \mathtt{Nat}[\mathrm{H}] \qquad \phi; (\mathrm{H} \leqslant 0, \Phi); \Gamma \vdash^{\mathcal{E}}_{0} z : \mathtt{Nat}[\mathrm{H} + e] \qquad \vdots}{\phi; \Phi; \Gamma \vdash^{\mathcal{E}}_{0} \mathtt{ifz}\ y\ \mathtt{then}\ z\ \mathtt{else}\ \mathtt{s}(x\,\mathtt{p}(y)\,z) : \mathtt{Nat}[\mathrm{H} + e]}\,(If)}{(b, a); (b < d + 1, a < 1); (x : [a < \mathrm{I}] \cdot A; y : \mathtt{Nat}[\mathrm{H}]) \vdash^{\mathcal{E}}_{1} \lambda z.\ \mathtt{ifz}\ y\ \mathtt{then}\ z\ \mathtt{else}\ \mathtt{s}(x\,\mathtt{p}(y)\,z) : [c < 1] \cdot (\mathtt{Nat}[e] \multimap \mathtt{Nat}[\mathrm{H} + e])}\,(\multimap)}{b; b < d + 1; x : [a < \mathrm{I}] \cdot A \vdash^{\mathcal{E}}_{1+1} \lambda yz.\ \mathtt{ifz}\ y\ \mathtt{then}\ z\ \mathtt{else}\ \mathtt{s}(x\,\mathtt{p}(y)\,z) : [a < 1] \cdot C}\,(\multimap) \qquad b; b < d + 1 \vDash_{\mathcal{E}} C\{b + 1/b\} \equiv A}{\vdash^{\mathcal{E}}_{d+1+\sum_{b<d+1}(1+1)} \mathtt{add} : [a < 1] \cdot \mathtt{Nat}[d] \multimap [c < 1] \cdot (\mathtt{Nat}[e] \multimap \mathtt{Nat}[d + e])}
$$

Figure 6. A type derivation for add.

$$
\begin{aligned}
(\bigstar) &: \phi; (\mathrm{H} \geqslant 1, \Phi); \varnothing \vdash^{\mathcal{E}}_{3\times(e+1)} \mathtt{add} : [a < 1] \cdot \mathtt{Nat}[e] \multimap [c < 1] \cdot (\mathtt{Nat}[\mathrm{J} \times e] \multimap \mathtt{Nat}[e + \mathrm{J} \times e]) \\
A &= \mathtt{Nat}[\mathrm{J}] \multimap [c < 1] \cdot (\mathtt{Nat}[e] \multimap \mathtt{Nat}[\mathrm{J} \times e]) \\
C &= \mathtt{Nat}[\mathrm{H}] \multimap [c < 1] \cdot (\mathtt{Nat}[e] \multimap \mathtt{Nat}[\mathrm{H} \times e]) \\
\Gamma &= \{x : [a < \mathrm{I}] \cdot A,\ y : \mathtt{Nat}[\mathrm{H}],\ z : \mathtt{Nat}[e]\} \\
\phi &= \{a, b, c, d, e\} \\
\Phi &= \{b < d + 1, a < 1, c < 1\}
\end{aligned}
$$

$$
\dfrac{\phi; (\mathrm{H} \geqslant 1, \Phi); x : [a < \mathrm{I}] \cdot A \vdash^{\mathcal{E}}_{0} x : [a < \mathrm{I}] \cdot A \qquad \dfrac{\phi; (\mathrm{H} \geqslant 1, \Phi); y : \mathtt{Nat}[\mathrm{H}] \vdash^{\mathcal{E}}_{0} y : \mathtt{Nat}[\mathrm{H}]}{\phi; (\mathrm{H} \geqslant 1, \Phi); y : \mathtt{Nat}[\mathrm{H}] \vdash^{\mathcal{E}}_{0} \mathtt{p}(y) : \mathtt{Nat}[\mathrm{J}]}\,(p)}{\phi; (\mathrm{H} \geqslant 1, \Phi); x : [a < \mathrm{I}] \cdot A, y : \mathtt{Nat}[\mathrm{H}] \vdash^{\mathcal{E}}_{0} x\,\mathtt{p}(y) : [c < 1] \cdot (\mathtt{Nat}[e] \multimap \mathtt{Nat}[\mathrm{J} \times e])}\,(App)
$$

$$
\dfrac{\dfrac{(\bigstar) \qquad \phi; (\mathrm{H} \geqslant 1, \Phi); z : \mathtt{Nat}[e] \vdash^{\mathcal{E}}_{0} z : \mathtt{Nat}[e]}{\phi; (\mathrm{H} \geqslant 1, \Phi); \Gamma \vdash^{\mathcal{E}}_{3\times(e+1)} \mathtt{add}\ z : [c < 1] \cdot (\mathtt{Nat}[\mathrm{J} \times e] \multimap \mathtt{Nat}[e + \mathrm{J} \times e])} \qquad \dfrac{\vdots \qquad \phi; (\mathrm{H} \geqslant 1, \Phi); z : \mathtt{Nat}[e] \vdash^{\mathcal{E}}_{0} z : \mathtt{Nat}[e]}{\phi; (\mathrm{H} \geqslant 1, \Phi); \Gamma \vdash^{\mathcal{E}}_{0} x\,\mathtt{p}(y)\,z : \mathtt{Nat}[\mathrm{J} \times e]}\,(App)}{\phi; (\mathrm{H} \geqslant 1, \Phi); \Gamma \vdash^{\mathcal{E}}_{3\times(e+1)} \mathtt{add}\ z\ (x\,\mathtt{p}(y)\,z) : \mathtt{Nat}[\mathrm{H} \times e]}\,(App)
$$

$$
\dfrac{\dfrac{\dfrac{\dfrac{\phi; \Phi; y : \mathtt{Nat}[\mathrm{H}] \vdash^{\mathcal{E}}_{0} y : \mathtt{Nat}[\mathrm{H}] \qquad \phi; (\mathrm{H} \leqslant 0, \Phi); \Gamma \vdash^{\mathcal{E}}_{0} \underline{0} : \mathtt{Nat}[\mathrm{H} \times e] \qquad \vdots}{\phi; \Phi; \Gamma \vdash^{\mathcal{E}}_{\mathrm{M}} \mathtt{ifz}\ y\ \mathtt{then}\ \underline{0}\ \mathtt{else}\ \mathtt{add}\ (x\,\mathtt{p}(y)\,z)\ z : \mathtt{Nat}[\mathrm{H} \times e]}\,(If)}{(b, a); (b < d + 1, a < 1); (x : [a < \mathrm{I}] \cdot A; y : \mathtt{Nat}[\mathrm{H}]) \vdash^{\mathcal{E}}_{1+\mathrm{M}} \lambda z.\ \mathtt{ifz}\ y\ \mathtt{then}\ \underline{0}\ \mathtt{else}\ \mathtt{add}\ (x\,\mathtt{p}(y)\,z)\ z : [c < 1] \cdot (\mathtt{Nat}[g] \multimap \mathtt{Nat}[\mathrm{H} \times g])}\,(\multimap)}{b; b < d + 1; x : [a < \mathrm{I}] \cdot A \vdash^{\mathcal{E}}_{1+1+\mathrm{M}} \lambda yz.\ \mathtt{ifz}\ y\ \mathtt{then}\ \underline{0}\ \mathtt{else}\ \mathtt{add}\ (x\,\mathtt{p}(y)\,z)\ z : [a < 1] \cdot C}\,(\multimap)}{\vdash^{\mathcal{E}}_{d+1+\sum_{b<d+1}(1+1+\mathrm{M})} \mathtt{mult} : [a < 1] \cdot \mathtt{Nat}[d] \multimap [c < 1] \cdot (\mathtt{Nat}[e] \multimap \mathtt{Nat}[d \times e])}\,(Fix)
$$

Figure 7. A type derivation for mult.

$$\frac{}{\phi;\Phi \vdash_0^{\mathcal{E}} \diamond : (\tau,\tau)} \qquad \frac{\phi;\Phi \vdash_{\mathrm{I}}^{\mathcal{E}} \pi : (\sigma,\tau) \quad \phi;\Phi \vdash_{\mathcal{E}} \sigma' \sqsubseteq \sigma \quad \phi;\Phi \vdash_{\mathcal{E}} \tau \sqsubseteq \tau' \quad \phi;\Phi \models_{\mathcal{E}} \mathrm{I} \leqslant \mathrm{J}}{\phi;\Phi \vdash_{\mathrm{J}}^{\mathcal{E}} \pi : (\sigma',\tau')}$$

$$\frac{\phi;\Phi \vdash_{\mathrm{J}}^{\mathcal{E}} \mathsf{c} : \sigma\{0/a\} \qquad \phi;\Phi \vdash_{\mathrm{K}}^{\mathcal{E}} \pi' : (\tau\{0/a\},\tau')}{\phi;\Phi \vdash_{\mathrm{J+K}}^{\mathcal{E}} \mathsf{arg}(\mathsf{c}\,,\,\pi') : ([a<1]\cdot(\sigma \multimap \tau),\tau')} \qquad \frac{\phi;\Phi \vdash_{\mathrm{J}}^{\mathcal{E}} \mathsf{v} : [a<1]\cdot(\sigma \multimap \tau) \qquad \phi;\Phi \vdash_{\mathrm{K}}^{\mathcal{E}} \pi' : (\tau\{0/a\},\tau')}{\phi;\Phi \vdash_{\mathrm{J+K}}^{\mathcal{E}} \mathsf{fun}(\mathsf{v}\,,\,\pi') : (\sigma\{0/a\},\tau')}$$

$$\frac{\phi;\mathrm{N}=0,\Phi \vdash_{\mathrm{J}}^{\mathcal{E}} \langle t;\xi\rangle : \sigma \quad \phi;\mathrm{M}\geqslant 1,\Phi \vdash_{\mathrm{J}}^{\mathcal{E}} \langle u;\xi\rangle : \sigma \quad \phi;\Phi \vdash_{\mathrm{K}}^{\mathcal{E}} \pi' : (\sigma,\tau)}{\phi;\Phi \vdash_{\mathrm{J+K}}^{\mathcal{E}} \mathsf{fork}(t\,,\,u\,,\,\xi\,,\,\pi') : (\mathtt{Nat}[\mathrm{M},\mathrm{N}],\tau)}$$

$$\frac{\phi;\Phi \vdash_{\mathrm{I}}^{\mathcal{E}} \pi : (\mathtt{Nat}[\mathrm{M}+1,\mathrm{N}+1],\tau)}{\phi;\Phi \vdash_{\mathrm{I}}^{\mathcal{E}} \mathsf{s}(\pi) : (\mathtt{Nat}[\mathrm{M},\mathrm{N}],\tau)} \qquad \frac{\phi;\Phi \vdash_{\mathrm{I}}^{\mathcal{E}} \pi : (\mathtt{Nat}[\mathrm{M}-1,\mathrm{N}-1],\tau)}{\phi;\Phi \vdash_{\mathrm{I}}^{\mathcal{E}} \mathsf{p}(\pi) : (\mathtt{Nat}[\mathrm{M},\mathrm{N}],\tau)}$$

Figure 8. dℓPCF$_{\mathrm{V}}$: Lifting Typing to Stacks

3. *If* $\phi;\Phi;\Gamma \vdash_{\mathrm{I}}^{\mathcal{E}} t:\sigma$, *then* $\phi;\Psi;\Gamma \vdash_{\mathrm{I}}^{\mathcal{E}} t:\sigma$.

Proof. Point 1. is a trivial consequence of transitivity of implication in logic. Point 2. can be proved by induction on the structure of the proof of $\phi;\Phi \vdash_{\mathcal{E}} \sigma \sqsubseteq \tau$, using point 1. Point 3. can be proved by induction on a proof of $\phi;\Phi;\Gamma \vdash_{\mathrm{I}}^{\mathcal{E}} t:\sigma$, using points 1 and 3. □

Strengthening is quite intuitive: whatever appears on the right of $\vdash_{\mathcal{E}}$ should hold for all values of the variables in ϕ satisfying Φ, so strengthening corresponds to making the judgment weaker.

Fresh term variables can be added to the context Γ, leaving the rest of the judgment unchanged:

LEMMA 5.2 (Context Weakening). $\phi;\Phi;\Gamma \vdash_{\mathrm{I}}^{\mathcal{E}} t:\tau$ *implies* $\phi;\Phi;\Gamma,\Delta \vdash_{\mathrm{I}}^{\mathcal{E}} t:\tau$.

Proof. Again, this is an induction on the structure of a derivation for $\phi;\Phi;\Gamma \vdash_{\mathrm{I}}^{\mathcal{E}} t:\tau$. □

Please note that Δ is completely arbitrary. Another useful transformation on type derivations consists in substituting index variables for (defined) index terms.

LEMMA 5.3 (Index Substitution). *If* $\phi;\Phi \models_{\mathcal{E}} \mathrm{I} \Downarrow$, *then the following implications hold:*

1. *If* $(a,\phi);\Phi,\Psi \models_{\mathcal{E}} \mathrm{J} \leqslant \mathrm{K}$, *then* $\phi;\Phi,\Psi\{\mathrm{I}/a\} \models_{\mathcal{E}} \mathrm{J}\{\mathrm{I}/a\} \leqslant \mathrm{K}\{\mathrm{I}/a\}$ *;*
2. *If* $(a,\phi);\Phi,\Psi \vdash_{\mathcal{E}} \sigma \sqsubseteq \tau$, *then* $\phi;\Phi,\Psi\{\mathrm{I}/a\} \vdash_{\mathcal{E}} \sigma\{\mathrm{I}/a\} \sqsubseteq \tau\{\mathrm{I}/a\}$ *;*
3. *If* $(a,\phi);\Phi,\Psi;\Gamma \vdash_{\mathrm{J}}^{\mathcal{E}} t:\sigma$, *then* $\phi;\Phi,\Psi\{\mathrm{I}/a\};\Gamma\{\mathrm{I}/a\} \vdash_{\mathrm{J}\{\mathrm{I}/a\}}^{\mathcal{E}} t:\sigma\{\mathrm{I}/a\}$.

Observe that the only hypothesis is that $\phi;\Phi \models_{\mathcal{E}} \mathrm{I} \Downarrow$ (see Section 3.1 for a definition): we do not require I to be a value of a that satisfies Ψ. If it does not the constraints in $\Phi,\Psi\{\mathrm{I}/a\}$ become inconsistent, and the obtained judgments are vacuous.

5.2 Subject Reduction

What we want to prove in this subsection is the following result:

PROPOSITION 5.4 (Subject Reduction). *If* $t_{v}u$ *and* $\phi;\Phi;\varnothing \vdash_{\mathrm{M}}^{\mathcal{E}} t:\tau$, *then* $\phi;\Phi;\varnothing \vdash_{\mathrm{M}}^{\mathcal{E}} u:\tau$.

Subject Reduction can be proved in a standard way, by going through a Substitution Lemma, which only needs to be proved when the term being substituted is a *value*. Preliminary to the Substitution Lemma are two auxiliary results stating that derivations giving types to values can, if certain conditions hold, be split into two, or put in parametric form:

LEMMA 5.5 (Splitting). *If* $\phi;\Phi;\Gamma \vdash_{\mathrm{M}}^{\mathcal{E}} v:\tau_1 \uplus \tau_2$, *then there exist two indexes* $\mathrm{N}_1,\mathrm{N}_2$, *and two contexts* Γ_1,Γ_2, *such that* $\phi;\Phi;\Gamma_i \vdash_{\mathrm{N}_i}^{\mathcal{E}} v:\tau_i$, *and* $\phi;\Phi \models_{\mathcal{E}} \mathrm{N}_1+\mathrm{N}_2 \leqslant \mathrm{M}$ *and* $\phi;\Phi \vdash_{\mathcal{E}} \Gamma \sqsubseteq \Gamma_1 \uplus \Gamma_2$.

Proof. If v is a primitive integer $\underline{\mathtt{n}}$, the result is trivial as the only possible decomposition of a type for integers is $\mathtt{Nat}[\mathrm{I},\mathrm{J}] = \mathtt{Nat}[\mathrm{I},\mathrm{J}] \uplus \mathtt{Nat}[\mathrm{I},\mathrm{J}]$. If v is either an abstraction or a fixpoint, then its type derivation can be manipulated by way of strengthening and substitution until it reaches the desired form. □

LEMMA 5.6 (Parametric Splitting). *If* $\phi;\Phi;\Gamma \vdash_{\mathrm{M}}^{\mathcal{E}} v:\sum_{c<\mathrm{J}}\sigma$ *is derivable, then there exist an index* N *and a context* Δ *such that one can derive* $c,\phi;c<\mathrm{J},\Phi;\Delta \vdash_{\mathrm{N}}^{\mathcal{E}} v:\sigma$, *and* $\phi;\Phi \models_{\mathcal{E}} \sum_{c<\mathrm{J}}\mathrm{N} \leqslant \mathrm{M}$ *and* $\phi;\Phi \vdash_{\mathcal{E}} \Gamma \sqsubseteq \sum_{c<\mathrm{J}}\Delta$.

Proof. The proof uses the same technique as for Lemma 5.5. □

One can easily realize *why* these results are crucial for subject reduction: whenever the substituted value flows through a type derivation, there are various places where its type changes, namely when it reaches instances of the typing rules (*App*), ($\multimap$), (*If*) and (*Rec*): in all these cases the type derivation for the value must be modified, and the splitting lemmas certify that this is possible. We can this way reach the key intermediate result:

LEMMA 5.7 (Substitution). *If* $\phi;\Phi;\Gamma,x:\sigma \vdash_{\mathrm{M}}^{\mathcal{E}} t:\tau$ *and* $\phi;\Phi;\varnothing \vdash_{\mathrm{N}}^{\mathcal{E}} v:\sigma$ *are both derivable, then there is an index* K *such that* $\phi;\Phi;\Gamma \vdash_{\mathrm{K}}^{\mathcal{E}} t[x:=v]:\tau$ *and* $\phi;\Phi \models_{\mathcal{E}} \mathrm{K} \leqslant \mathrm{M}+\mathrm{N}$.

Proof. The proof goes by induction on the derivation of the judgment $\phi;\Phi;\Gamma,x:\sigma \vdash_{\mathrm{M}}^{\mathcal{E}} t:\tau$, making intense use of Lemma 5.5 and Lemma 5.6. □

Given Lemma 5.7, proving Proposition 5.4 is routine: the only two nontrivial cases are those where the fired redex is a β-redex or the unfolding of a recursively-defined function, and both consist in a substitution.

Observe how Subject Reduction already embeds a form of *extensional* soundness for dℓPCF$_{\mathrm{V}}$, since types are preserved by reduction. As an example, if one builds a type derivation for $\vdash_{\mathrm{I}}^{\mathcal{E}} t:\mathtt{Nat}[2,7]$, then the normal form of t (if it exists) is guaranteed to be a constant between 2 and 7. Observe, on the other hand, than nothing is known about the *complexity* of the underlying computational process yet, since the weight I does not necessarily decrease along reduction, although it cannot increase. This is the topic of the following section.

5.3 Intentional Soundness

In this section, we prove the following result:

Terms

$$\|\underline{\mathtt{n}}\| = \|\lambda x.t\| = \|\,\mathtt{fix}\,x.t\| = 0;$$
$$\|x\| = 2;$$
$$\|tu\| = \|t\| + \|u\| + 2;$$
$$\|\mathtt{s}(t)\| = \|\mathtt{p}(t)\| = \|t\| + 2;$$
$$\|\,\mathtt{ifz}\,t\,\mathtt{then}\,u\,\mathtt{else}\,s\| = \|t\| + \|u\| + \|s\| + 2;$$

Closures

$$|\langle t\,;\,\xi\rangle| = \|t\|;$$

Stacks

$$|\diamond| = 0;$$
$$|\mathsf{fun}(\mathsf{v}\,,\,\pi)| = |\mathsf{v}| + |\pi|;$$
$$|\mathsf{arg}(\mathsf{c}\,,\,\pi)| = |\mathsf{c}| + |\pi| + 1;$$
$$|\mathsf{fork}(t\,,\,u\,,\,\xi\,,\,\pi)| = \|t\| + \|u\| + |\pi| + 1;$$
$$|\mathsf{s}(\pi)| = |\pi| + 1;$$
$$|\mathsf{p}(\pi)| = |\pi| + 1;$$

Processes

$$|\mathsf{c} \star \pi| = |\mathsf{c}| + |\pi|.$$

Figure 9. Size of processes.

THEOREM 5.8 (Intensional soundness). *For any term t, if*

$$\vdash^{\mathcal{E}}_{\mathrm{H}} t : \mathtt{Nat}[\mathrm{I}, \mathrm{J}]$$

then $t \Downarrow^n \underline{\mathtt{m}}$ where $n \leqslant |t| \cdot (\llbracket \mathrm{H}\rrbracket^{\mathcal{E}} + 1)$ and $\llbracket \mathrm{I}\rrbracket^{\mathcal{E}} \leqslant m \leqslant \llbracket \mathrm{J}\rrbracket^{\mathcal{E}}$.

Roughly speaking, this means that dℓPCF$_\mathsf{V}$ also gives us some sensible information about the time complexity of evaluating typable PCF programs. The path towards Theorem 5.8 is not too short: it is necessary to lift dℓPCF$_\mathsf{V}$ to a type system for closures, environments and processes, as defined in Section 3.4. Actually, the type system can be easily generalized to closures by the rule below:

$$\frac{\phi; \Phi; x_1 : \sigma_1, \ldots, x_n : \sigma_n \vdash^{\mathcal{E}}_{\mathrm{K}} t : \tau \qquad \phi; \Phi \vdash^{\mathcal{E}}_{\mathrm{J}_i} \mathsf{v}_i : \sigma_i}{\phi; \Phi \vdash^{\mathcal{E}}_{\mathrm{K}+\sum_{1\leqslant i \leqslant n} \mathrm{J}_i} \langle t\,;\,\{x_1 \mapsto \mathsf{v}_1; \cdots; x_n \mapsto \mathsf{v}_n\}\rangle : \tau}$$

Lifting everything to stacks, on the other hand, requires more work, see Figure 8. We say that a stack π is *$(\phi; \Phi)$-acceptable* for σ with type τ and cost I (notation: $\phi; \Phi \vdash^{\mathcal{E}}_{\mathrm{I}} \pi : (\sigma, \tau)$) when it interacts well with closures of type σ to product a process of type τ. Indeed, a *process* can be typed as follows:

$$\frac{\phi; \Phi \vdash^{\mathcal{E}}_{\mathrm{J}} \pi : (\sigma, \tau) \qquad \phi; \Phi \vdash^{\mathcal{E}}_{\mathrm{K}} \mathsf{c} : \sigma}{\phi; \Phi \vdash^{\mathcal{E}}_{\mathrm{J}+\mathrm{K}} \mathsf{c} \star \pi : \tau}$$

This way, also the notion of weight has been lifted to processes, with the hope of being able to show that it strictly decreases at every evaluation step. Apparently, this cannot be achieved in full: sometimes the weight of a process does not change, but in that case another parameter is guaranteed to decrease, namely the process *size*. The size $|\mathsf{c} \star \pi|$ of $\mathsf{c} \star \pi$, is defined as $|\mathsf{c}| + |\pi|$, where:

- The size $|\mathsf{c}|$ of a closure $\langle t\,;\,\xi\rangle$ is the *multiplicative* size of t (see Section 3.2).
- The size of $|\pi|$ is the sum of the sizes of all closures appearing in π plus the number of occurrences of symbols (different from $\diamond$ and fun) in π.

The formal definition of $|\mathsf{c} \star \pi|$ is in Figure 9.

PROPOSITION 5.9 (Weighted Subject Reduction). *Assume $\mathrm{P} > \mathrm{R}$ and $\phi; \Phi \vdash^{\mathcal{E}}_{\mathrm{I}} \mathrm{P} : \tau$. Then $\phi; \Phi \vdash^{\mathcal{E}}_{\mathrm{J}} \mathrm{R} : \tau$ and:*

- *either $\phi; \Phi \models_{\mathcal{E}} \mathrm{I} = \mathrm{J}$ and $|\mathrm{P}| > |\mathrm{R}|$,*
- *or $\phi; \Phi \models_{\mathcal{E}} \mathrm{I} > \mathrm{J}$ and $|\mathrm{P}| + |s| > |\mathrm{R}|$, where s is a term appearing in P.*

Actually, Proposition 5.9 can be proved by carefully analyzing the various cases as for how P evolves to R, *i.e.*, the rules from Figure 4 and Figure 5. Only in two of them the weight decreases, namely the ones in which P is in the form $\mathsf{v} \star \mathsf{fun}(\mathsf{w}\,,\,\pi)$. By the way, these are the cases in which a box is opened up in the underlying linear logic proof. Splitting and parametric splitting play a crucial role here, once appropriately generalized to value closures.

Given Proposition 5.9, Theorem 5.8 is within reach: the natural number $|s|$ in Proposition 5.9 cannot be greater than the size of the term t we start from, since the only "new" terms created along reduction are constants in the form $\underline{\mathtt{n}}$ (which have null size).

5.4 (Relative) Completeness

In this section, we will prove some results about the expressive power of dℓPCF$_\mathsf{V}$, seen as a tool to prove intentional (but also extensional) properties of PCF terms. Actually, dℓPCF$_\mathsf{V}$ is extremely powerful: every first-order PCF program computing the function $f : \mathbb{N} \to \mathbb{N}$ in a number of steps bounded by $g : \mathbb{N} \to \mathbb{N}$ can be proved to enjoy these properties by way of dℓPCF$_\mathsf{V}$, provided two conditions are satisfied:

- On the one hand, the equational program $\mathcal{E}$ needs to be *universal*, meaning that every partial recursive function is expressible by some index terms. This can be guaranteed, as an example, by the presence of a universal program in $\mathcal{E}$.
- On the other hand, all *true* statements in the form $\phi; \Phi \models_{\mathcal{E}} \mathrm{I} \leqslant \mathrm{J}$ must be "available" in the type system for completeness to hold. In other words, one cannot assume that those judgments are derived in a given (recursively enumerable) formal system, because this would violate Gödel's Incompleteness Theorem. In fact, ours are completeness theorems *relative* to an oracle for the truth of those assumptions, which is precisely what happens in similar results for Floyd-Hoare logics [7].

PCF ***Typing.*** The first step towards completeness is quite easy: propositional type systems in the style of PCF for terms, closures, stacks and processes need to be introduced. All of them can be easily obtained by erasing the index information from dℓPCF$_\mathsf{V}$. As an example, the typing rule for the application looks like

$$\frac{\Gamma \vdash_{\mathsf{PCF}} t : \alpha \Rightarrow \beta \qquad \Gamma \vdash_{\mathsf{PCF}} u : \alpha}{\Gamma \vdash_{\mathsf{PCF}} tu : \beta}$$

while processes can be typed by the following rule

$$\frac{\vdash_{\mathsf{PCF}} \pi : (\alpha, \beta) \qquad \vdash_{\mathsf{PCF}} \mathsf{c} : \alpha}{\vdash_{\mathsf{PCF}} \mathsf{c} \star \pi : \beta}$$

Given any type σ (respectively, any type derivation δ) of dℓPCF$_\mathsf{V}$, the PCF type (respectively, the PCF type derivation) obtained by erasing all the index information will be denoted by $(\!|\sigma|\!)$ (respectively, by $(\!|\delta|\!)$). Of course both terms and processes enjoy subject reduction theorems with respect to PCF typing, and their proofs are much simpler than those for dℓPCF$_\mathsf{V}$. As an example, given a type derivation δ for $\vdash_{\mathsf{PCF}} \mathrm{P} : \mathtt{Nat}$ (we might write $\delta \rhd \vdash_{\mathsf{PCF}} \mathrm{P} : \mathtt{Nat}$)

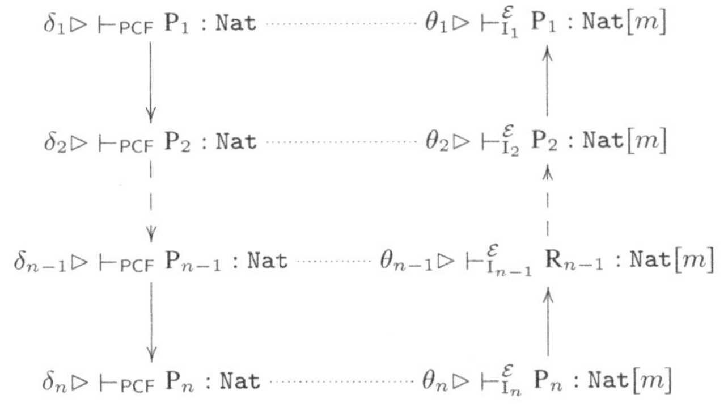

Figure 10. Completeness for programs, sketch of the Proof.

and $\mathrm{P} > \mathrm{R}$, a type derivation δ' for $\vdash_{\mathsf{PCF}} \mathrm{R} : \mathtt{Nat}$ can be easily built by manipulating in a standard way δ; we write $\delta > \delta'$.

Weighted Subject Expansion. The key ingredient for completeness is a dualisation of Weighted Subject Reduction:

PROPOSITION 5.10 (Weighted Subject Expansion). *Suppose that* $\delta \rhd \vdash_{\mathsf{PCF}} \mathrm{P} : \alpha$, *that* $\delta > \delta'$, *and that* $\theta' \rhd \phi; \Phi \vdash^{\mathcal{E}}_{\mathrm{I}} \mathrm{R} : \tau$ *where* $(\!|\theta'|\!) = \delta'$. *Then there is* $\theta \rhd \phi; \Phi \vdash^{\mathcal{E}}_{\mathrm{J}} \mathrm{P} : \tau$ *with* $(\!|\theta|\!) = \delta$ *and* $\phi; \Phi \models_{\mathcal{E}} \mathrm{J} \leqslant \mathrm{I} + 1$. *Moreover,* θ *can be effectively computed from* δ, θ' *and* δ'.

Proving Proposition 5.10 requires a careful analysis of the evolution of the $\mathsf{CEK_{PCF}}$ machine, similarly to what happened for Weighted Subject *Reduction*. But while in the latter it is crucial to be able to (parametrically) *split* type derivations for terms (and thus closures), here we need to be able to *join* them:

LEMMA 5.11 (Joining). *Suppose* $\mathcal{E}$ *is universal. If* $\delta_i \rhd \phi; \Phi; \Gamma_i \vdash^{\mathcal{E}}_{\mathrm{N}_i} v : \tau_i$, $(\!|\delta_1|\!) = (\!|\delta_2|\!)$, $\phi; \Phi \vdash_{\mathcal{E}} \Gamma \sqsubseteq \Gamma_1 \uplus \Gamma_2$, $\phi; \Phi \vdash_{\mathcal{E}} \tau_1 \uplus \tau_2 \sqsubseteq \tau$ *and* $\phi; \Phi \models_{\mathcal{E}} \mathrm{N}_1 + \mathrm{N}_2 \leqslant \mathrm{M}$, *then* $\phi; \Phi; \Gamma \vdash^{\mathcal{E}}_{\mathrm{M}} v : \tau$.

LEMMA 5.12 (Parametric Joining). *Suppose that* $\mathcal{E}$ *is universal. If* $a, \phi; a < \mathrm{I}, \Phi; \Delta \vdash^{\mathcal{E}}_{\mathrm{N}} v : \sigma$, $\phi; \Phi \vdash_{\mathcal{E}} \Gamma \sqsubseteq \sum_{a<\mathrm{I}} \Delta$, $\phi; \Phi \vdash_{\mathcal{E}} \sum_{a<\mathrm{I}} \sigma \sqsubseteq \tau$ *and* $\phi; \Phi \models_{\mathcal{E}} \sum_{a<\mathrm{I}} \mathrm{N} \leqslant \mathrm{M}$, *then* $\phi; \Phi; \Gamma \vdash^{\mathcal{E}}_{\mathrm{M}} v : \tau$.

Observe that the Joining Lemma requires the two type derivations to be joined to have the same PCF "skeleton". This is essential, because otherwise it would not be possible to unify them into one single type derivation.

Completeness for Programs. We now have all the necessary ingredients to obtain a first completeness result, namely one about programs (which are terms of type $\mathtt{Nat}$). Suppose that t is a PCF program and that $t^*_v m$, where m is a natural number. By Proposition 3.1, there is a sequence of processes

$$\mathrm{P}_1 > \mathrm{P}_2 > \ldots > \mathrm{P}_n,$$

where $\mathrm{P}_1 = (\langle t\,;\,\varnothing\rangle \star \diamond)$ and $\mathrm{P}_n = (\langle m\,;\,\varnothing\rangle \star \diamond)$. Of course, $\vdash \mathrm{P}_i : \mathtt{Nat}$ for every i. For obvious reasons, $\vdash^{\mathcal{E}}_{0} \mathrm{P}_n : \mathtt{Nat}[m]$. Moreover, by Weighted Subject Expansion, we can derive each of $\vdash^{\mathcal{E}}_{\mathrm{I}_i} \mathrm{P}_i : \mathtt{Nat}[m]$, until we reach $\vdash^{\mathcal{E}}_{\mathrm{I}_1} \mathrm{P}_1 : \mathtt{Nat}[m]$, where $\mathrm{I}_1 \leqslant n$. See Figure 10 for a graphical representation of the above argument. It should be now clear that one can reach the following:

THEOREM 5.13 (Completeness for Programs). *Suppose that* $\vdash_{\mathsf{PCF}} t : \mathtt{Nat}$, *that* $t \Downarrow^n \underline{\mathrm{m}}$ *and that* $\mathcal{E}$ *is universal. Then,* $\vdash^{\mathcal{E}}_{k} t : \mathtt{Nat}[\mathrm{m}]$, *where* $k \leqslant n$.

Uniformisation and Completeness for Functions. Completeness for programs, however, is not satisfactory: the fact (normalizing) PCF terms of type $\mathtt{Nat}$ can all be analyzed by $\mathsf{d\ell PCF_V}$ is not so surprising, and other type systems (like non-idempotent intersection types [14]) have comparable expressive power. Suppose we want to generalize relative completeness to first-order functions: we would like to prove that every term t having a PCF type $\mathtt{Nat} \Rightarrow \mathtt{Nat}$ (which terminates when fed with any natural number) can be typed in $\mathsf{d\ell PCF_V}$. How could we proceed? First of all, observe that the argument in Figure 10 could be applied to all *instances* of t, namely to all terms in $\{t\ \underline{\mathrm{n}} \mid n \in \mathbb{N}\}$. This way one can obtain, for every $n \in \mathbb{N}$, a type derivation δ_n for

$$\vdash^{\mathcal{E}}_{\mathrm{I}_n} t : [a < \mathrm{J}_n] \cdot \mathtt{Nat}[\mathrm{K}_n] \multimap \mathtt{Nat}[\mathrm{H}_n],$$

where J_n can be assumed to be 1, while K_n can be assumed to be n. Moreover, the problem of obtaining δ_n from n is recursive, *i.e.*, can be solved by an algorithm. Surprisingly, the infinitely many type derivations in $\{\delta_n \mid n \in \mathbb{N}\}$ can be turned into one:

PROPOSITION 5.14 (Uniformisation of type derivations). *Suppose that* $\mathcal{E}$ *is universal and that* $\{\delta_n\}_{n\in\mathbb{N}}$ *is a recursively enumerable collection of type derivations satisfying the following constraints:*

1. *For every* $n \in \mathbb{N}$, $\delta_n \rhd \vdash^{\mathcal{E}}_{\mathrm{I}_n} t : \sigma_n$;
2. *all derivations in* $\{\delta_n\}_{n\in\mathbb{N}}$ *have the same skeleton, i.e., for every* $n, m \in \mathbb{N}$, $(\!|\delta_n|\!) = (\!|\delta_m|\!)$.

Then there is a type derivation $\theta \rhd a; \varnothing; \varnothing \vdash^{\mathcal{E}}_{\mathrm{I}} t : \sigma$ *such that* $\models_{\mathcal{E}} \mathrm{I}\{\mathrm{n}/a\} = \mathrm{I}_n$ *and* $\models_{\mathcal{E}} \sigma\{\mathrm{n}/a\} \equiv \sigma_n$ *for all* n.

Uniformisation of type derivations should be seen as an extreme form of joining: not only a finite number of type derivations for the same term can be unified into one, but any recursively enumerable class of them can. Again, the universality of $\mathcal{E}$ is crucial here. We are now ready to give the following:

THEOREM 5.15 (Completeness for functions). *Suppose that* $\vdash_{\mathsf{PCF}} t : \mathtt{Nat} \Rightarrow \mathtt{Nat}$, *that* $t\,\underline{\mathrm{n}} \Downarrow^{k_n} \underline{\mathrm{m}_n}$ *for all* $n \in \mathbb{N}$ *and that* $\mathcal{E}$ *is universal. Then, there are index terms* I *and* H *such that* $a; \varnothing; \varnothing \vdash^{\mathcal{E}}_{\mathrm{I}} t : [b < 1] \cdot \mathtt{Nat}[a] \multimap \mathtt{Nat}[\mathrm{H}]$, *where* $\models_{\mathcal{E}} \mathrm{I}\{\mathrm{n}/a\} \leqslant \mathrm{k}_n$ *and* $\models_{\mathcal{E}} \mathrm{H}\{\mathrm{n}/a\} = \mathrm{m}_n$.

6. Further Developments

Relative completeness of $\mathsf{d\ell PCF_V}$, especially in its stronger form (Theorem 5.15) can be read as follows. Suppose that a sound, finitary formal C system deriving judgements in the form $\phi; \Phi \vdash_{\mathcal{E}} \mathrm{I} \leqslant \mathrm{J}$ is fixed and "plugged" into $\mathsf{d\ell PCF_V}$. What you obtain is a sound, but necessarily incomplete formal system, due to Gödel's incompleteness. However, this incompleteness is *only* due to C and not to the rules of $\mathsf{d\ell PCF_V}$, which are designed so as to reduce the problem of proving properties of programs to checking inequalities over $\mathcal{E}$ *without any loss of information.*

In this scenario, it is of paramount importance to devise techniques to *automatically* reduce the problem of checking whether a program satisfies a given intentional or extensional specification to the problem of checking whether a given set of inequalities over an equational program $\mathcal{E}$ hold. Indeed, many techniques and concrete tools are available for the latter problem (take, as an example, the immense literature on SMT solving), while the same cannot be said about the former problem. The situation, in a sense, is similar to the one in the realm of program logics for imperative programs, where logics are indeed very powerful [7], and great effort have been directed to devise efficient algorithms generating weakest preconditions [13].

Actually, at the time of writing, the authors are actively involved in the development of *relative type inference* algorithms for both $\mathsf{d\ell PCF_N}$ and $\mathsf{d\ell PCF_V}$, which can be seen as having the same role as algorithms computing weakest preconditions. This is however out of the scope of this paper.

7. $\mathsf{d}\ell\mathsf{PCF}_\mathsf{V}$ and Implicit Complexity

There is a price to pay for the kind of relative completeness $\mathsf{d}\ell\mathsf{PCF}_\mathsf{V}$ (and $\mathsf{d}\ell\mathsf{PCF}_\mathsf{N}$) enjoys: checking a type derivation for correctness is undecidable in general, simply because it relies on semantic assumptions in the form of inequalities between index terms, or on subtyping judgments, which themselves rely on the properties of the underlying equational program $\mathcal{E}$. Indeed, $\mathsf{d}\ell\mathsf{PCF}_\mathsf{V}$ should *not* be thought of as a type system, but rather as a framework in which various distinct type systems can be defined. Concrete type systems can be crafted by either concretely instantiating $\mathcal{E}$, or by choosing specific and sound formal systems for the verification of semantic assumptions. By the way, the just described problem is not peculiar to $\mathsf{d}\ell\mathsf{PCF}_\mathsf{V}$: Floyd-Hoare program logics are themselves undecidable.

The main motivation behind the introduction of linear dependent types comes from implicit computational complexity. Traditionally, what prevents (most) ICC techniques to find concrete applications along this line is their poor expressive power: the class of programs which can be recognized as being efficient by (tools derived from) ICC systems is often very small and does not include programs corresponding to natural, well-known algorithms. In this respect, $\mathsf{d}\ell\mathsf{PCF}_\mathsf{N}$ and $\mathsf{d}\ell\mathsf{PCF}_\mathsf{V}$ are completely different: *all* PCF programs with a certain complexity can be proved to be so by deriving a typing judgment for them.

8. Conclusions

Linear dependent types are shown to be applicable to the analysis of intentional and extensional properties of functional programs when the latter are call-by-value evaluated. More specifically, soundness and relative completeness results are proved for both programs a and functions. This generalizes previous work by Gaboardi and the first author [11], who proved similar results in the call-by-name setting. This shows that linear dependency not only provides an expressive formalism, but is also robust enough to be adaptable to calculi whose notions of reduction are significantly different (and more efficient) than normal order evaluation.

Topics for future work include some further analysis about the applicability of linear dependent types to languages with more features, including some form of inductive data types, or ground type references.

References

[1] A. Asperti and S. Guerrini. *The Optimal Implementation of Functional Programming Languages*. Cambridge University Press, 1998.

[2] A. Asperti and H. G. Mairson. Parallel beta reduction is not elementary recursive. *Inf. Comput.*, 170(1):49–80, 2001.

[3] F. Baader and T. Nipkow. *Term Rewriting and All That*. Cambridge University Press, 1998.

[4] P. Baillot and K. Terui. Light types for polynomial time computation in lambda calculus. *Inf. Comput.*, 207(1):41–62, 2009.

[5] P. Baillot, M. Gaboardi, and V. Mogbil. A polytime functional language from light linear logic. In *ESOP*, volume 6012 of *LNCS*, pages 104–124. Springer, 2010.

[6] G. Barthe, B. Grégoire, and C. Riba. Type-based termination with sized products. In *CSL*, volume 5213 of *LNCS*, pages 493–507. Springer, 2008.

[7] S. A. Cook. Soundness and completeness of an axiom system for program verification. *SIAM J. on Computing*, 7:70–90, 1978.

[8] M. Coppo and M. Dezani-Ciancaglini. An extension of the basic functionality theory for the λ-calculus. *Notre Dame J. Formal Logic*, 21(4):685–693, 1980.

[9] K. Crary and S. Weirich. Resource bound certification. In *POPL*, pages 184–198. ACM Press, 2000.

[10] U. Dal Lago. Context semantics, linear logic, and computational complexity. *ACM Trans. Comput. Log.*, 10(4), 2009.

[11] U. Dal Lago and M. Gaboardi. Linear dependent types and relative completeness. In *LICS*, pages 133–142. IEEE Comp. Soc., 2011.

[12] U. Dal Lago and B. Petit. Linear dependent types in a call-by-value scenario (long version). Available at `http://arxiv.org/abs/1207.5592`, 2012.

[13] J. W. de Bakker, A. de Bruin, and J. Zucker. *Mathematical theory of program correctness*. Prentice-Hall international series in computer science. Prentice Hall, 1980.

[14] D. de Carvalho. Execution time of lambda-terms via denotational semantics and intersection types. Available at `http://arxiv.org/abs/0905.4251`, 2009.

[15] M. Felleisen and D. P. Friedman. Control operators, the SECD-machine and the λ-calculus. Technical Report 197, Computer Science Department, Indiana University, 1986.

[16] J.-Y. Girard, A. Scedrov, and P. J. Scott. Bounded linear logic: A modular approach to polynomial-time computability. *Theor. Comput. Sci.*, 97(1):1–66, 1992.

[17] J. Hoffmann, K. Aehlig, and M. Hofmann. Multivariate Amortized Resource Analysis. In *POPL*, pages 357–370. ACM Press, 2011.

[18] M. Hofmann. Linear types and non-size-increasing polynomial time computation. In *LICS*, pages 464–473. IEEE Comp. Soc., 1999.

[19] S. Jost, K. Hammond, H.-W. Loid, and M. Hofmann. Static Determination of Quantitative Resource Usage for Higher-Order Programs. In *POPL*, pages 223–236. ACM Press, 2010.

[20] N. Kobayashi and C.-H. L. Ong. A type system equivalent to the modal mu-calculus model checking of higher-order recursion schemes. In *LICS*, pages 179–188. IEEE Comp. Soc., 2009.

[21] J. Lamping. An algorithm for optimal lambda calculus reduction. In *POPL*, pages 16–30. ACM Press, 1990.

[22] J. Maraist, M. Odersky, D. N. Turner, and P. Wadler. Call-by-name, call-by-value, call-by-need and the linear lambda calculus. *Electr. Notes Theor. Comput. Sci.*, 1:370–392, 1995.

[23] P. Odifreddi. *Classical Recursion Theory: the Theory of Functions and Sets of Natural Numbers*. Number 125 in Studies in Logic and the Foundations of Mathematics. North-Holland, 1989.

[24] G. D. Plotkin. LCF considerd as a programming language. *Theor. Comput. Sci.*, 5:225–255, 1977.

[25] A. Sabelfeld and A. C. Myers. Language-based information-flow security. *IEEE JSAC*, 21(1):5–19, 2003.

[26] D. M. Volpano, C. E. Irvine, and G. Smith. A sound type system for secure flow analysis. *JCS*, 4(2/3):167–188, 1996.

[27] H. Xi. Dependent types for program termination verification. In *LICS*, pages 231–246. IEEE Comp. Soc., 2001.

Transparent Function Types: Clearing up Opacity

Enrique Martin-Martin
Dpto. de Sistemas Informáticos y Computación
Universidad Complutense de Madrid
emartinm@fdi.ucm.es

Juan Rodríguez-Hortalá
Dpto. de Sistemas Informáticos y Computación
Universidad Complutense de Madrid
juan.rodriguez.hortala@gmail.com

Abstract

Functional logic programming (FLP) is a paradigm that comes from the integration of lazy functional programming and logic programming. Although most FLP systems use static typing by means of a direct adaptation of Damas-Milner type system, it is well-known that some FLP features like higher-order patterns or the equality operator lead to so-called opacity situations that are not properly handled by Damas-Milner type system, thus leading to the loss of type preservation. Previous works have addressed this problem either directly forbidding those HO patterns that are opaque or restricting its use. In this paper we propose a new approach that is based on eliminating the unintended opacity created by HO patterns and the equality operator by extending the expressiveness of the type language with decorations in the arrows of the functional types. We study diverse possibilities, which differ in the amount of information included in the decorations. The obtained type systems have different properties and expressiveness, but each of them recovers type preservation from simple extensions of Damas-Milner.

Categories and Subject Descriptors F.3.3 [*Logics and meanings of programs*]: Studies of Program Constructs—Type Structure; D.3.2 [*Programming Languages*]: Language Classifications—Multiparadigm languages; D.3.1 [*Programming Languages*]: Formal Definitions and Theory

General Terms Theory, Languages, Design

Keywords Functional-logic programming, type systems, higher-order patterns, opacity

1. Introduction

Functional logic programming (FLP) [2, 15, 29] is a paradigm that comes from the integration of the main features of lazy functional programming and logic programming. Hence, modern FLP languages like Toy [8, 23] or Curry [14] can be roughly described as a variant of Haskell 2010 [17] with some modifications and extensions at the semantic level. First of all, overlapping rules are not handled in a first fit approach like in Haskell, but they are tried in order using a backtracking mechanism in the line of Prolog. This leads to the definition of so-called *non-deterministic functions*, which may return more than one result for the same input. This combination of non-determinism and lazy evaluation gives rise to several semantic options, among which *call-time choice* semantics [12] is the option adopted by most modern FLP implementations. Call-time choice corresponds to *call-by-need* parameter passing [4] in the sense that different occurrences of the same variable in the body of a program rule *share* the same value. To illustrate this point let us consider the FLP program $\{coin \rightarrow z, coin \rightarrow s\ z, pair\ X \rightarrow (X, X)\}$ where z and s stand for the data constructors for Peano numbers[1]. Under a call-time choice semantics the values (z, z) and $(s\ z, s\ z)$ are correct for the expression $pair\ coin$, but the values $(z, s\ z)$ and $(s\ z, z)$ are incorrect because the occurrences of X in (X, X) must share the same value.

As a consequence of non-determinism, the notion of equality is also revised in FLP languages. Given two expressions e_1 and e_2 several interpretations for their equality are possible. For example we could ask for both expressions to have the same set of values, which is not very practical in a lazy language, as those sets can easily be infinite. The criterion adopted in modern FLP languages corresponds to the notion of joinability [12], so two expressions e_1 and e_2 are joinable, written $e_1 \bowtie e_2$, iff they can be reduced to the same value.

There are different approaches to functional-logic programming, but in this work we will use the same approach as Toy, which is based on the HO-CRWL[2] logic [12]. In FLP, due to the combination of higher order features, call-time choice and non-determinism, expressions that are *extensionally* equal—i.e., that have the same behavior when applied to the same arguments—can produce different values when placed in the same context [22]. The HO-CRWL logic follows an *intensional* approach that semantically distinguishes function symbols for extensionally equivalent functions whenever they are syntactically different. This intensionality leads to another important feature of the functional-logic language Toy, namely *higher-order patterns*. These patterns are composed by partial applications of function or constructor symbols to other patterns, thus generalizing the notion of patterns that can appear in left-hand sides of rules in Haskell. By using HO patterns, functions are not treated as black boxes [3] anymore but can be distinguished by matching. For example, programmers can define different sorting functions for lists, e.g. *quicksort* and *permutsort*. They correspond to the same extensional sorting function, however, *quicksort* and *permutsort* are two different intensional descriptions that can be distinguished in the left-hand side of a rule: $\{tractable\ quicksort \rightarrow true, tractable\ permutsort \rightarrow false\}$. Thanks to this ability to view functional expressions as data that can appear in left-hand sides of rules, HO patterns have been proved to be a useful and expressive feature [1, 5–7, 13, 16]. With the aim of providing standard tools for reasoning in FLP—like type-based rea-

PPDP'12, September 19–21, 2012, Leuven, Belgium.

[1] We will use an applicative syntax similar to Haskell syntax but employing uppercase for variables and lowercase for constructor and function symbols.

[2] HO-CRWL stands for *Higher-Order Constructor Based Rewriting Logic*, the higher order extension of CRWL [11].

soning via free theorems [30]—a new denotational semantics has been recently proposed [9]. This semantics, which does not consider HO patterns because it is proposed for the Curry language, is more "abstract" than HO-CRWL, considering as semantically equal functional expressions that are different in HO-CRWL like *id* and *map id*. However, in this work we have considered the HO-CRWL approach because it a well-established semantics for FLP [15] and it is at the core of the language Toy.

Regarding types, most FLP systems like Toy or the implementations of Curry use static typing by means of a direct adaptation of Damas-Milner type system [10], where the equality operator is added as a primitive of the language with type $(\bowtie) : \forall\alpha.\alpha \rightarrow \alpha \rightarrow bool$. The reason for that is twofold. First of all, overloading support by means of type classes is still in an experimental phase [24, 25]. But, more importantly, $\bowtie$ cannot be defined as an ordinary function because it has to compare expressions with variables, which contrary to Haskell and other functional languages, are valid run-time expressions. Therefore, no program rule can express that $X \bowtie X$ should be reduced to $true$ as establishes the notion of joinability of HO-CRWL semantics [12]—e.g. the rule $V \bowtie V \rightarrow true$ is not valid as it is not left-linear, a usual requirement in lazy functional languages.

Nevertheless, it is well-known [13] that some FLP features like the equality operator or the use of HO patterns lead to so-called opacity situations that are not properly handled by Damas-Milner typing, thus leading to the loss of type preservation. The following examples, which borrow some ideas from [13, 20], illustrate these problems.

Example 1. *Consider a function snd defined by the rule*

$$snd\ X\ Y \rightarrow Y$$

for which the classical Damas-Milner algorithm infers the type $snd : \forall\alpha,\beta.\alpha \rightarrow \beta \rightarrow \beta$. *The point is that in any partial application of* snd*, the type of its argument is not reflected in the type of the whole expression: for example* $snd\ z$ *has type* $\beta \rightarrow \beta$*, in which we cannot find the type* nat *that corresponds to* z.

This situation can be described using the terminology "opacity" [13], so a symbol is called opaque if the type of each of its arguments is not determined by the type of the application of the symbol to those arguments. This way the type of expressions placed in an opaque context is unknown. Opaque symbols are dangerous when using classical Damas-Milner typing because that type system is not prepared to manage opacity safely, which can be perversely exploited to define some "polymorphic casting" function that can be used to break type safety. This can be done by using the unpack function defined by the rule $unpack\ (snd\ X) \rightarrow X$*, for which a direct adaptation of Damas-Milner typing gives the type* $unpack : \forall\alpha,\beta.(\beta \rightarrow \beta) \rightarrow \alpha$*. Note the use of the HO pattern* $snd\ X$ *in the definition of* $unpack$*. The exploit is already performed by* $unpack$ *and it is reflected in its type: the type* α *for the returning value* X *does not appear in the type* $\beta \rightarrow \beta$ *for the pattern* $snd\ X$*, while at the value level the returning value* X *is just the same* X *that was wrapped by* snd *at the input. We can use this desynchronization between types and values to define the polymorphic casting function* cast *by the rule* $cast\ X \rightarrow unpack\ (snd\ X)$*: at the value level* cast *behaves like the identity function, as it just wraps and unwraps its input value with an application of* snd*, but at the type level it has the Damas-Milner type* $cast : \forall\alpha,\beta.\alpha \rightarrow \beta$*, because of the loss of information caused by opacity. With* cast *at hand type preservation is broken easily. For example with the usual definition for the boolean operator* not*, we have that* $not\ (cast\ z)$ *is well-typed because* $cast\ z$ *can be given the type* bool*, but after evaluating the call to* $cast\ z$ *we get the expression* $not\ z$*, which is ill-typed.*

Opacity is avoided in classical Damas-Milner typing by requiring constructor symbols to be transparent, i.e., not to be opaque, and in practical languages like Haskell 2010 or ML this is a consequence of the format of data type declarations. If we restrict ourselves to first order patterns this "transparency hypothesis" over constructors is enough to ensure the absence of opacity, but when HO patterns are used then opacity situations may occur, as no transparency constraint is imposed over function symbols. Another sample of the type problems generated by HO patterns can be seen in their combination with the equality operator as defined in Toy or in some Curry implementations (like PAKCS 1.10.0[3] or MCC 0.9.11[4]):[5]

Example 2. *Using the program from Example 1, the equality* $snd\ z \bowtie snd\ true$ *is well-typed by Damas-Milner typing because both sides admit the type* $\beta \rightarrow \beta$*. But to resolve that equality a decomposition step is performed, leading to the expression* $z \bowtie true$ *that is obviously ill-typed as it implies comparing expressions of different types. This situation was described in [13] as the problem of* opaque decomposition*, i.e., a decomposition step during the resolution of an equality in which some expressions are extracted from an opaque context. This problem is specially harmful, as the eventual occurrence of opaque decomposition is undecidable [13]. Hence, the equality operator can be used to break type preservation without the need of HO patterns in left-hand sides of rules or opaque assumptions for constructor symbols. The intuition behind this is that as the equality operator is also defined for the comparison of expressions with functional type, the definition for this primitive implicitly uses HO patterns.*

The problem in these examples is that the type system is not prepared to deal with opacity, so a solution could be extending the type system with a proper support for opacity. One option could be adapting to the FLP context the existential types extension of Damas-Milner typing [18, 27], where the transparency hypothesis is explicitly broken in data type declarations, so in this case opacity is intended in contrast with the examples above. This type system is able to handle opacity safely and it enables the creation of *abstract data types* whose implementations are first-class citizens, i.e., they can be passed as function parameters or returned by functions. Although existential types maybe could be adapted to safely handle the opacity caused by HO patterns in program rules, it is not clear how they could be adapted to avoid opaque decomposition, as the equality operator is not defined by a set of program rules that can be accepted or rejected separately by the type system. Therefore, the dangerous expression $snd\ z \bowtie snd\ true$ would still be a valid expression using an adaptation of existential types.

In the context of FLP, the seminal work [13] already identified those unintended opacity situations, so opaque patterns are forbidden and type preservation is only granted for computations with no opaque decomposition steps, which is undecidable. Some other works have been developed recently to allow safe uses of opaque HO patterns [19, 20]. They restrict the use of variables whose type has been hidden by opacity, employing techniques different from those used in existential types, obtaining type systems with diverse properties and possibilities for generic programming techniques. However, the use of the equality operator and the subsequent problem of opaque decomposition is not treated.

To the best of our knowledge there is no proposal for solving the problem of opaque decomposition. In this paper we propose a new

[3] `http://www.informatik.uni-kiel.de/~pakcs/`

[4] `http://danae.uni-muenster.de/~lux/curry/`

[5] Admittedly, equality between higher-order expressions is not specified in the Curry Report [14], however, it is supported in the mentioned implementations.

approach to overcome these problems that is based on *eliminating the unintended opacity* created by HO patterns and the equality operator, by proposing several different extensions of the type language. The resulting type systems are simple extensions of Damas-Milner typing that recover type preservation. The idea is, starting from the transparency hypothesis, to ensure transparency of patterns as an invariant during type inference of programs. The unexpected opacity might only appear in HO patterns, as it cannot be caused by partial applications of constructor symbols, because if a symbol is transparent then all its partial applications are transparent too. The problem lies in the partial applications of function symbols that appear in HO patterns: for each function of arity n there are $n-1$ possible partial applications that conceptually correspond to $n-1$ constructor symbols whose opacity does not obey the transparency hypothesis. How do we fix this? We take inspiration from what we would do in Haskell 2010[6] for the declaration `data t B = sndc A B`, that is rejected because the variable `A` does not appear as an argument of the type constructor `t`, which implies the opaque assumption $sndc : \forall \alpha, \beta.\alpha \rightarrow \beta \rightarrow t\ \beta$—which is very similar to the type for *snd* in Example 1. We can easily fix this by adding `A` as an additional argument for `t`, getting the transparent assumption $sndc : \forall \alpha, \beta.\alpha \rightarrow \beta \rightarrow t\ \alpha\ \beta$. As the type constructor for functions is the arrow $\rightarrow$, we can reproduce this solution for partial applications of functions by adding a new argument to $\rightarrow$, in particular one carrying the types of the arguments already applied to the function. As we will see in this paper $\forall \alpha, \beta.\alpha \rightarrow_{()} \beta \rightarrow_{(\alpha)} \beta$ is a valid type for the function *snd* in Example 1 according to our type systems, thus clearing up the opacity of *snd*. As a consequence, the function *cast* takes the type $cast : \forall \alpha.\alpha \rightarrow_{()} \alpha$, which corresponds to its actual behaviour, and the equality $snd\ z \bowtie snd\ true$ is rejected as $\beta \rightarrow_{(nat)} \beta$ is different to $\beta \rightarrow_{(bool)} \beta$. In fact the problem of opaque decomposition is avoided because there is no opacity at all—as they say, *"dead dogs don't bite"*.

The rest of the paper is organized as follows. Section 2 contains some technical preliminaries and notions about expressions, types and the operational semantics used in this paper. In Section 3, we present a type system using an approach that decorates arrows with complete types. We also show how it eliminates opacity from programs if we assume the transparency hypothesis, and provide a complete type inference procedure for expressions. We also prove its soundness w.r.t. the semantics. On the negative side, it considers ill-typed some safe programs using HO patterns. To overcome this limitation, in Section 4 we present a modification of the previous type system that reduces the amount of information included in arrow decorations. The resulting type system still preserves types, however it lacks closure under type substitutions, which is an important property since it is used intensively in the inference algorithm for expressions. Mixing the ideas of the two previous type systems, in Section 5 we present a type systems that preserves types and is also closed under type substitutions, so type inference for expressions is possible. In Section 6 we compare the presented type systems with previous proposals for FLP. Finally, Section 7 summarizes some conclusions and future work. The complete proofs of the results—as well as complementary material about type inference for programs—can be found in the extended version of this paper [26].

Symbol	$s ::=$	$X \mid c \mid f$
Pattern	$t ::=$	$X \mid c\ \overline{t_n}\ \ (n \leq ar(c))$
	$\mid$	$f\ \overline{t_n}\ \ (n < ar(f))$
Expression	$e ::=$	$X \mid c \mid f \mid e_1\ e_2$
	$\mid$	$let\ X = e_1\ in\ e_2$
Simple type	$\tau ::=$	$\alpha \mid C\ \overline{\tau_n}\ (ar(C) = n)$
		$\mid \tau_1 \rightarrow_\rho \tau_2$
Type decoration	$\rho ::=$	$\alpha \mid (\tau_1, \ldots, \tau_n)\ \ (n \geq 0)$
Type-scheme	$\sigma ::=$	$\forall \overline{\alpha_n}.\tau\ \ (n \geq 0)$

Figure 1. Syntax of expressions and types

2. Preliminaries

2.1 Expressions and Programs

We assume a signature $\Sigma = CS \cup FS$, where CS and FS are two disjoint sets of *data constructors* c and *function* symbols f respectively. Each symbol $h \in \Sigma$ has an associated arity $ar(h)$. We also assume a denumerable set $\mathcal{DV}$ of *data variables* X. Figure 1 shows the syntax of *patterns* $\in Pat$—our notion of *value*—and *expressions* $\in Expr$. We use the notation $\overline{o_n}$ for a sequence of n syntactic objects $o_1 \ldots o_n$, where o_i refers to the ith element of the sequence. If the number of elements is not relevant, we write simply $\overline{o}$. We split the set of patterns into two: *first-order patterns* $FOPat \ni fot ::= X \mid c\ \overline{fot_n}$, where $ar(c) = n$, and *higher-order patterns* $HOPat = Pat \setminus FOPat$. We also distinguish different classes of expressions: $X\ \overline{e_n}\ (n > 0)$ is a *variable application*, $c\ \overline{e_n}$ is a *junk expression* when $n > ar(c)$ and $f\ \overline{e_n}$ is an *active expression* when $n > ar(f)$. The set of *variables*—$var(e)$—and *free variables*—$fv(e)$—are defined in the usual way. Note that our let-expressions are not recursive, so $fv(let\ X = e_1\ in\ e_2) = fv(e_1) \cup (fv(e_2) \setminus \{X\})$.

A *program rule* R is defined as $f\ \overline{t_n} \rightarrow e$ where $ar(f) = n$ and $\overline{t_n}$ is linear, i.e., every variable occurs only once in all the patterns. Program rules also verify that $fv(e) \subseteq \bigcup_{i=1}^{n} fv(t_i)$, so *extra variables* are not considered in this work. *Programs* $\mathcal{P}$ are sets of rules $\{R_1, \ldots, R_n\}$. A *one-hole context* is defined as $\mathcal{C} ::= [\,] \mid \mathcal{C}\ e \mid e\ \mathcal{C} \mid let\ X = \mathcal{C}\ in\ e \mid let\ X = e\ in\ \mathcal{C}$, and its application to an expression—$\mathcal{C}[e]$—is defined in the usual way. The set of *bound variables of a context*—$bv(\mathcal{C})$—contains those variables bound by a let-expression in the context, and it is defined as $bv([\,]) = \emptyset$, $bv(\mathcal{C}\ e) = bv(\mathcal{C})$, $bv(e\ \mathcal{C}) = bv(\mathcal{C})$, $bv(let\ X = \mathcal{C}\ in\ e) = bv(\mathcal{C})$, $bv(let\ X = e\ in\ \mathcal{C}) = \{X\} \cup bv(\mathcal{C})$. A *data substitution* $\theta \in \mathcal{PS}ubst$ is a finite mapping from data variables to patterns $[\overline{X \mapsto t}]$. The *domain* and *variable range* of a data substitution are defined as $dom(\theta) = \{X \in \mathcal{DV} \mid X\theta \neq X\}$ and $vran(\theta) = \bigcup_{X \in dom(\theta)} fv(X\theta)$, respectively. Application of data substitutions is defined in the natural way.

2.2 Types

We assume a denumerable set $\mathcal{TV}$ of *type variables* α and a countable alphabet $\mathcal{TC}$ of *type constructors* C. Each type constructor C has an associated arity $ar(C)$. The syntax of *simple types* τ and *type-schemes* σ appears in Figure 1. The main novelty regarding the usual syntax of simple types is that arrows in functional types must be decorated with a type variable or a tuple—possibly empty—of types. For instance, $bool \rightarrow bool$ and $int \rightarrow_{int} [bool]$ are syntactically invalid types, while $bool \rightarrow_{()} bool$ and $int \rightarrow_{(int)} [bool]$ are correct ones. These *type decorations* ρ in the arrows are a crucial ingredient for removing opacity from higher-order patterns as

[6] For the sake of notation homogeneity we employ here a modification of Haskell's syntax that uses uppercase for variables and lowercase for constructors.

they are used to store the types of the arguments already applied in partial applications of functions, as we will see in Sections 3–5. The set of *free type variables* (ftv) of a simple type τ is defined in the usual way except for functional types, where it is defined as: $ftv(\tau_1 \rightarrow_\rho \tau_2) = ftv(\tau_1) \cup ftv(\tau_2) \cup ftv(\rho)$. For type-schemes, $ftv(\forall\overline{\alpha}.\tau) = ftv(\tau) \smallsetminus \{\overline{\alpha}\}$. A type-scheme $\sigma \equiv \forall\overline{\alpha}.\tau_1 \rightarrow_{\rho_1} \ldots \tau_k \rightarrow_{\rho_k} \tau'$ is called *k-transparent* if $ftv(\tau_1 \rightarrow_{\rho_1} \ldots \tau_k) \subseteq ftv(\tau')$, and *closed* if $ftv(\sigma) = \emptyset$. Notice that k-transparency implies j-transparency for any $j < k$, and every type-scheme is trivially 0-transparent.

A *set of assumptions* $\mathcal{A}$ is a set $\{\overline{s : \sigma}\}$ relating type-schemes to symbols. If $(s : \sigma) \in \mathcal{A}$ we write $\mathcal{A}(s) = \sigma$. Data constructors and function symbols appearing in $\mathcal{A}$ must be *transparent*, i.e., $\mathcal{A}(c)$ must be k_c-transparent if $k_c = ar(c)$, and $\mathcal{A}(f)$ must be k_f-transparent if $k_f = ar(f) - 1$. For function symbols we do not require transparency for their total application because function symbols can only appear partially applied in patterns. This transparency hypothesis is essential to guarantee type preservation with equality, as we will see in Section 3. The transparency requirement is common over data constructors, and forbids the use of *existential types* [18, 27], but it might seem too tight for functions, at first sight. Nevertheless, as we will see in Sections 3 and 5, when transparent assumptions are used our type systems only infer transparent types for functions. As in practice type inference for programs starts from a transparent set of assumptions for constructors—obtained from data type declarations—and infers the types for the functions in an order according to the dependencies in the call-graph, we may conclude that thanks to the "transparency invariant" that requirement is not limiting and always holds in practice. The set of free type variables of a set of assumptions is defined as $ftv(\{\overline{s_n : \sigma_n}\}) = \bigcup_{i=1}^{n} ftv(\sigma_i)$. The union of sets of assumptions is denoted by $\mathcal{A} \oplus \mathcal{A}'$ with the usual meaning: it contains the assumptions in $\mathcal{A}'$ as well as those in $\mathcal{A}$ for the symbols not appearing in $\mathcal{A}'$.

A *type substitution* π is a finite mapping from type variables to simple types $[\overline{\alpha \mapsto \tau}]$, whose application is defined in the usual way. The domain $dom(\pi)$ and variable range $vran(\pi)$ are defined as for data substitutions. We use ϵ to denote the identity substitution. A simple type τ' is a *generic instance* of $\sigma \equiv \forall\overline{\alpha}.\tau$ if $\tau' = \tau[\overline{\alpha \mapsto \tau''}]$ for some $\overline{\tau''}$, and we write $\sigma \succ \tau'$. Finally, we say τ' is a *variant* of $\sigma \equiv \forall\overline{\alpha}.\tau$ (written $\sigma \succ_{var} \tau'$) if $\tau' = \tau[\overline{\alpha \mapsto \beta}]$, where $\overline{\beta}$ are fresh type variables.

2.3 Operational Semantics

The operational semantics used in this work is based on let-rewriting [22]. This semantics, which is is sound and complete w.r.t. HO-CRWL, is a notion of reduction step that expresses call-time choice by means of sharing subexpressions using let-bindings. In Figure 2 we have extended the original let-rewriting relation with two rules to cope with an equality operator ($\bowtie$) that corresponds to the notion of joinability [12]. This equality behaves like the strict equality operator of Curry, so two expressions are equal when they can be reduced to the same value. However, notice that this operational semantics supports equality between functional expressions—its rules handle equality between HO patterns—in contrast with the specification of Curry [14], that only allows equalities for first-order expressions[7].

We assume that *true* and *false* are 0-arity constructor symbols, and $\wedge$ is a binary function symbol defined with the rule $true \wedge Y \rightarrow Y$. Regarding types, we assume that every set of assumptions contains: $\{true : bool,\ false : bool,\ (\wedge) : bool \rightarrow_{()} bool \rightarrow_{(bool)} bool,\ (\bowtie) : \forall\alpha.\alpha \rightarrow_{()} \alpha \rightarrow_{(\alpha)} bool\}$. The first five rules (LetIn)–(LetAp) do not use the program and just change the textual representation of the term graph implied by the let-bindings in order to enable the application of program rules or the equality operator, but keeping the implied term graph untouched. The (Fapp) rule performs function application. The rule (JoinS) reduces the equality of one-symbol patterns to *true*. It is important to force them to be patterns, otherwise the rule could be incorrectly applied to the equality of 0-arity function symbols—$coin \bowtie coin$—without evaluating them. On the other hand, the rule (JoinP) reduces the equality of compound patterns by decomposition. This step is the cause of the *opaque decomposition* problem mentioned in Section 1. Note that the rules (JoinS) and (JoinP) represent the same behavior as joinability. Therefore an equality involving two patterns $t_1 \bowtie t_2$ will be evaluated to $true$ iff both patterns are *syntactically* the same—including HO patterns. In addition to the new rules, (Contx) is modified to avoid the application of (JoinS) to bound variables, as bound variables do not correspond to totally defined values but to expressions whose evaluation is pending [22], and by definition joinability only holds for totally defined values [12]. Finally, we also assume that programs do not contain any rule for $\bowtie$, so (Fapp) cannot be used to evaluate an equality.

(LetIn) $e_1\ e_2 \rightarrow^l let\ X = e_2\ in\ e_1\ X$, if e_2 is junk, active, variable application or a let-expression; for X fresh.

(Bind) $let\ X = t\ in\ e \rightarrow^l e[X/t]$

(Elim) $let\ X = e_1\ in\ e_2 \rightarrow^l e_2$, if $X \notin fv(e_2)$

(Flat) $let\ X = (let\ Y = e_1\ in\ e_2)\ in\ e_3 \rightarrow^l let\ Y = e_1\ in\ (let\ X = e_2\ in\ e_3)$, if $Y \notin fv(e_3)$

(LetAp) $(let\ X = e_1\ in\ e_2)\ e_3 \rightarrow^l let\ X = e_1\ in\ e_2\ e_3$ if $X \notin fv(e_3)$

(Fapp) $f\ t_1\theta \ldots t_n\theta \rightarrow^l r\theta$, if $(f\ t_1 \ldots t_n \rightarrow r) \in \mathcal{P}$

(JoinS) $s \bowtie s \rightarrow^l true$, if $s \in Pat$

(JoinP) $(h\ \overline{t_n}) \bowtie (h\ \overline{t'_n}) \rightarrow^l (t_1 \bowtie t'_1) \wedge \ldots \wedge (t_n \bowtie t'_n)$ if $(h\ \overline{t_n}), (h\ \overline{t'_n}) \in Pat$ and $n > 0$

(Contx) $\mathcal{C}[e] \rightarrow^l \mathcal{C}[e']$, if $\mathcal{C} \neq [\ ]$, $e \rightarrow^l e'$ using any of the previous rules, and if the step is $X \bowtie X \rightarrow^l true$ using (JoinS) then $X \notin bv(\mathcal{C})$

Figure 2. Higher order let-rewriting relation with equality $\rightarrow^l$

3. Fully decorated type system

In this section we present a type system that decorates the arrows of functional types with the complete information about the types of the previous arguments. Although this simple approach leads to a type system that recovers type preservation and has a sound a complete type inference, we will show that it is not expressive enough and rejects some well-known programs using HO patterns. Sections 4 and 5 contain two different approaches trying to overcome this limitation.

We consider the type derivation relation $\vdash$ in Figure 3, where $\mathcal{A} \vdash e : \tau$ means that the expression e has type τ under the assumptions $\mathcal{A}$. Notice that, although they do not appear in the syntax presented in Figure 1 and they cannot appear in programs, Figure 3 includes a rule for λ-abstractions[8] (expressions with the shape

[7] However, some of the most important Curry implementations like PAKCS or MCC currently support equality between functional expressions, following the same joinability approach.

[8] λ-abstractions have been excluded because there is no consensus about the semantic and operational meaning of λ-abstractions, and they are supported neither in the original let-rewriting [22] nor its underlying HO-CRWL semantics [12].

$$\text{(ID)}\frac{}{\mathcal{A} \vdash s : \tau} \text{ if } \mathcal{A}(s) \succ \tau$$

$$\text{(APP)}\frac{\mathcal{A} \vdash e_1 : \tau_1 \rightarrow_\rho \tau \quad \mathcal{A} \vdash e_2 : \tau_1}{\mathcal{A} \vdash e_1\ e_2 : \tau}$$

$$(\Lambda)\frac{\mathcal{A} \oplus \{\overline{X_n : \tau_n}\} \vdash t : \tau_t \quad \mathcal{A} \oplus \{\overline{X_n : \tau_n}\} \vdash e : \tau}{\mathcal{A} \vdash \lambda t.e : \tau_t \rightarrow_{()} anArgs(k, \tau_t, \tau)}$$

where $\{\overline{X_n}\} = var(t)$ and $\lambda depth(e) = k$

$$\text{(LET)}\frac{\mathcal{A} \vdash e_1 : \tau_x \quad \mathcal{A} \oplus \{X : \tau_x\} \vdash e_2 : \tau}{\mathcal{A} \vdash let\ X = e_1\ in\ e_2 : \tau}$$

Figure 3. Type derivation rules

$$\text{(iID)}\frac{}{\mathcal{A} \Vdash s : \tau|\epsilon} \text{ if } \mathcal{A}(s) \succ_{var} \tau$$

$$\text{(iAPP)}\frac{\mathcal{A} \Vdash e_1 : \tau_1|\pi_1 \quad \mathcal{A}\pi_1 \Vdash e_2 : \tau_2|\pi_2}{\mathcal{A} \Vdash e_1\ e_2 : \alpha\pi|\pi_1\pi_2\pi}$$

where α, β fresh and $\pi = mgu(\tau_1\pi_2, \tau_2 \rightarrow_\beta \alpha)$

$$(\text{i}\Lambda)\frac{\mathcal{A} \oplus \{\overline{X_n : \alpha_n}\} \Vdash t : \tau_t|\pi_t \quad (\mathcal{A} \oplus \{\overline{X_n : \alpha_n}\})\pi_t \Vdash e : \tau|\pi}{\mathcal{A} \Vdash \lambda t.e : \tau_t\pi \rightarrow_{()} anArgs(k, \tau_t\pi, \tau)|\pi_t\pi}$$

where $\{\overline{X_n}\} = var(t)$, $\overline{\alpha_n}$ fresh and $\lambda depth(e) = k$

$$\text{(iLET)}\frac{\mathcal{A} \Vdash e_1 : \tau_x|\pi_x \quad \mathcal{A}\pi_x \oplus \{X : \tau_x\} \Vdash e_2 : \tau|\pi}{\mathcal{A} \Vdash let\ X = e_1\ in\ e_2 : \tau|\pi_x\pi}$$

Figure 4. Type inference rules

$\lambda t.e$). This kind of expressions have been included only for typing purposes, as they simplify the definition of *well-typed program rule*: a rule $f\ \overline{p_n} \rightarrow e$ is well-typed whenever its associated λ-abstraction $\lambda\overline{p_n}.e$ matches the type for f (see Definition 2). The type derivation relation in Figure 3 is based in our previous type system for FLP [20], so it is similar to Damas-Milner [10] modified to be syntax-directed. The main novelty lies in the treatment of λ-abstractions, as the rule (Λ) now decorates each of the arrows in the type obtained for a chain of λ-abstractions, with the complete types of its previous arguments. For that, (Λ) uses the $\lambda depth$ and $anArgs$ meta operators:

Definition 1 (λ-depth and type decoration).

$\lambda depth(s) = 0 \qquad \lambda depth(let\ X = e_1\ in\ e_2) = 0$
$\lambda depth(e_1\ e_2) = 0 \quad \lambda depth(\lambda t.e) = 1 + \lambda depth(e)$

$anArgs(0, \tau, \tau') = \tau'$
$anArgs(n, \tau, \tau_1 \rightarrow_{(\overline{\tau'})} \tau_2) = \tau_1 \rightarrow_{(\tau,\overline{\tau'})} anArgs(n-1, \tau, \tau_2)$
where $n > 0$

The $\lambda depth(e)$ operator simply counts the number of consecutive λ-abstractions occurring from the top of an expression e, and $anArgs(n, \tau, \tau')$ adds the type τ to all the decorations of the functional type τ', up to some depth n. The use of $\lambda depth$ in combination with $anArgs$ is important because we only want to decorate as many arrows as arguments the complete λ-abstraction has—corresponding to the number of arguments of the associated program rule. This avoids the incorrect decoration of arrows in the type of the right-hand side if it has a functional type, for example deriving $bool \rightarrow_{()} (\alpha \rightarrow_{(bool)} \beta \rightarrow_{(bool,\alpha)} \beta)$ for $\lambda true.snd$ instead of the expected type $bool \rightarrow_{()} (\alpha \rightarrow_{()} \beta \rightarrow_{(\alpha)} \beta)$. Notice that $anArgs$ is undefined for non-functional types when n is greater than 0. However this is not a problem because in type derivations $anArgs$ is always applied to functional types with enough arrows (see Lemma 4 in the Appendix B of the extended version of the paper [26] for a formal statement).

In essence, the rule (Λ) derives the usual Damas-Milner type but decorating the arrows with the types of the previous arguments. For example, the expression $\lambda X.\lambda Y.Y$—corresponding to the *snd* function of Example 1—have the standard Damas-Milner type $\alpha \rightarrow \beta \rightarrow \beta$, while (Λ) derives $\alpha \rightarrow_{()} \beta \rightarrow_{(\alpha)} \beta$. By keeping the types of the arguments safely stored in the decorations, we ensure that these are always available, even for partial applications. This, together with the notion of well-typed program that we will see in the next subsection, assures that every function symbol has a transparent type.

We say that an expression e has type τ w.r.t. $\mathcal{A}$ when $\mathcal{A} \vdash e : \tau$, and is *well-typed* w.r.t. $\mathcal{A}$—written $wt_{\mathcal{A}}(e)$—if $\mathcal{A} \vdash e : \tau$ for some type τ. Intuitively, if an expression has type $\tau_1 \rightarrow_{(\overline{\tau'_m})} \tau_2$ then it corresponds to a partial application of a symbol to m expressions of types $\overline{\tau'_m}$. On the other hand, types as $\tau_1 \rightarrow_\alpha \tau_2$ are used to allow HO parameters in functions without fixing the number of expressions (and the type) they are applied to. This situation is shown in the *map* function with type

$$\forall\alpha, \beta, \gamma.(\alpha \rightarrow_\gamma \beta) \rightarrow_{()} [\alpha] \rightarrow_{(\alpha \rightarrow_\gamma \beta)} [\beta]$$

The type $\alpha \rightarrow_\gamma \beta$ of the first argument allows passing partial applications of any arity. For example, expressions as $map\ not\ [true]$ and $map\ (and\ true)\ [false]$ are well-typed, although their first argument has types $bool \rightarrow_{()} bool$ and $bool \rightarrow_{(bool)} bool$ respectively.

Regarding type inference, Figure 4 shows the rules of $\Vdash$. We express $\Vdash$ with a relational style to show the close similarity to the type derivation $\vdash$. However $\mathcal{A} \Vdash e : \tau|\pi$ represents an algorithm—following the ideas of algorithm $\mathcal{W}$ [10]—which returns a simple type τ and a type substitution π from an expression e and assumptions $\mathcal{A}$, failing if any of the rules cannot be applied. Intuitively, τ is the most general type for e and π is the minimum substitution that $\mathcal{A}$ needs to be able to derive a type for e. The rules of $\Vdash$ are similar to those of $\vdash$ but inserting fresh type variables in the places where type derivation guesses types, variables that can be unified during inference. Notice that, similarly to $\vdash$, the application of $anArgs$ in the rule $(\text{i}\Lambda)$ is always defined—see Lemma 5 in the Appendix B of the extended version of the paper [26]. The most important properties of type inference are its soundness and completeness w.r.t. type derivation:

Theorem 1 (Soundness of $\Vdash$). *If* $\mathcal{A} \Vdash e : \tau|\pi$ *then* $\mathcal{A}\pi \vdash e : \tau$.

Theorem 2 (Completeness of $\Vdash$). *If* $\mathcal{A}\pi' \vdash e : \tau'$ *then* $\mathcal{A} \Vdash e : \tau|\pi$ *and there is some* π'' *verifying* $\mathcal{A}\pi\pi'' = \mathcal{A}\pi'$ *and* $\tau\pi'' = \tau'$.

A trivial consequence of Theorems 1 and 2 is that when $\mathcal{A}$ is closed—$ftv(\mathcal{A}) = \emptyset$—and $\mathcal{A} \vdash e : \tau'$ then $\mathcal{A} \Vdash e : \tau|\pi$ succeeds and τ is a *principal type* of e.

3.1 Well-typed programs

We have presented type derivation for expressions, however this notion cannot be directly extended to programs as in functional programming, because in our FLP setting let-expressions only performs pattern matching and λ-abstractions are not supported by the semantics. Therefore we need an explicit notion of *well-typed program*:

Definition 2 (Well-typed program). *A program rule $f\ \overline{t_n} \to e$ is well-typed w.r.t. $\mathcal{A}$ if $\mathcal{A} \vdash \lambda\overline{t_n}.e : \tau$ and τ is a variant of $\mathcal{A}(f)$. A program $\mathcal{P}$ is well-typed w.r.t. $\mathcal{A}$—written $wt_{\mathcal{A}}(\mathcal{P})$—if all its rules are well-typed w.r.t. $\mathcal{A}$.*

The previous definition is the same as the one in [20], but using the type derivation $\vdash$ presented in this paper. Program well-typedness proceeds rule by rule, independently of the order. Notice that forcing the derived types for the associated λ-abstraction to be a variant of the type of the function is essential to guarantee type preservation, as showed in [20].

Let us see how the proposed type system solves the opacity problems showed in Section 1. First, consider the rule for *snd* in Example 1. The most general type for its associated λ-abstraction $\lambda X.\lambda Y.Y$ is $\alpha \to_{()} \beta \to_{(\alpha)} \beta$—which is 1-transparent—so the most general type that makes the rule well-typed is $\forall\alpha,\beta.\alpha \to_{()} \beta \to_{(\alpha)} \beta$. This type is essentially the same as the usual type $\forall\alpha,\beta.\alpha \to \beta \to \beta$ for *snd*, but with the opacity removed owing to the decorations in the arrows. Therefore, the type of its application will always reveal the type of its argument: $snd\ true$ can have type $\beta \to_{(bool)} \beta$, $[bool] \to_{(bool)} [bool]$... but always containing a decoration in the arrow to reveal that it is applied to a boolean. Using this type $\forall\alpha,\beta.\alpha \to_{()} \beta \to_{(\alpha)} \beta$ for *snd*, the problems with $unpack\ (snd\ X) \to X$ are now solved. Any valid type for *unpack*, e.g. $\forall\alpha,\beta.(\beta \to_{(\alpha)} \beta) \to_{()} \alpha$, will show a connection between the type of the element contained in the pattern—which appears in the decoration of the arrow—and the result of the function. As a consequence of this connection, the *cast* function gets the same type as the identity function, i.e., $\forall\alpha.\alpha \to_{()} \alpha$, thus recovering the synchronization between types and the behavior at the value level. This can be easily checked by looking at its associated λ-abstraction $\lambda X.unpack\ (snd\ X)$ as, due to the types of *snd* and *unpack*, the type of the right-hand side must be the same as the type of the input variable X. Regarding Example 2, opaque decomposition is avoided because now there is no opacity anymore. As now snd takes the transparent type $\forall\alpha,\beta.\alpha \to_{()} \beta \to_{(\alpha)} \beta$, then the expression $(snd\ true) \bowtie (snd\ z)$ is ill-typed because $snd\ true$ has type $\beta \to_{(bool)} \beta$, which is different to the type $\beta \to_{(nat)} \beta$ for $snd\ z$. Hence we will never will be forced to compare expressions with different types like $true$ and z.

Using the default set of assumptions at the beginning of Section 2.3, the rule for $\wedge$ is well-typed in every set of assumptions, since $\mathcal{A} \vdash \lambda true.\lambda Y.Y : bool \to_{()} bool \to_{(bool)} bool$, which is exactly the type assumed for $\wedge$. Similarly, the rules for *map*—$map\ F\ [\,] \to [\,]$ and $map\ F\ (X : Xs) \to (F\ X) : (map\ F\ Xs)$—are well-typed w.r.t. set of assumptions containing $map : \forall\alpha,\beta,\gamma.(\alpha \to_{\gamma} \beta) \to [\alpha] \to [\beta]$, the type for *map* presented before.

A fundamental remark about Definition 2 is that, if a program is well typed w.r.t. $\mathcal{A}$, then all its function symbols are transparent w.r.t. $\mathcal{A}$. This fact is based in the following result about the types of λ-abstractions (notice that 0-ary function symbols are trivially transparent):

Lemma 1. *If $\mathcal{A} \vdash \lambda\overline{t_{n+1}}.e : \tau$ then τ is n-transparent. Similarly, if $\mathcal{A} \Vdash \lambda\overline{t_{n+1}}.e : \tau'|\pi'$ then τ' is n-transparent.*

An important result of the proposed type system regarding soundness w.r.t. the semantics is *type preservation*, stating that evaluation using well-typed programs preserves types:

Theorem 3 (Type Preservation). *If $wt_{\mathcal{A}}(\mathcal{P})$, $\mathcal{A} \vdash e : \tau$ and $e \to^{l} e'$ then $\mathcal{A} \vdash e' : \tau$.*

Notice that the constraint of transparent set of assumptions (which is a consequence of program well-typedness) is essential to guarantee type preservation, since it forces the type of every subpattern to be fixed by the type of the whole pattern. Otherwise, the steps (JoinP) or (Fapp) could easily produce ill-typed expressions, as we have seen in Examples 1 and 2.

The notion of well-typed program is based on type derivation, so it does not provide any operational mechanism to check program well-typedness or infer the types of its functions. However, we can use a type inference procedure for programs $\mathcal{B}$ similar to the one presented in [20]: it takes a set of assumptions $\mathcal{A}$ and a program $\mathcal{P}$ and returns a type substitution π. The set $\mathcal{A}$ must contain assumptions for all the symbols in the program, even for the functions defined in $\mathcal{P}$. For some of the functions—those for which we want to infer types—the assumption will be simply a fresh type variable to be instantiated by the inference process. For the rest, the assumption will be a closed type-scheme provided by the programmer to be checked by the procedure.

Definition 3 (Type Inference of a Program).
Given a program $\{R_1, \ldots, R_m\}$, the procedure $\mathcal{B}$ for type inference of is defined as:

$$\mathcal{B}(\mathcal{A}, \{R_1, \ldots, R_m\}) = \pi, \text{if}$$

1. *$\mathcal{A} \Vdash (\varphi(R_1), \ldots, \varphi(R_m)) : (\tau_1, \ldots, \tau_m)|\pi$.*
2. *Let $f^1 \ldots f^k$ be the function symbols of the rules R_i in $\mathcal{P}$ such that $\mathcal{A}(f^i)$ is a closed type-scheme, and τ^i the type obtained for R_i in step 1. Then τ^i must be a variant of $\mathcal{A}(f^i)$.*

φ is a transformation from rules to expressions defined as:

$$\varphi(f\ t_1 \ldots t_n \to e) = pair\ (\lambda t_1 \ldots \lambda t_n.e)\ f$$

using the special constructor pair *for "tuples" of two elements of the same type, with type $\forall\alpha.\alpha \to \alpha \to \alpha$.*

The following results show that $\mathcal{B}$ is sound and complete w.r.t. the notion of well-typed program:

Theorem 4 (Soundness of $\mathcal{B}$). *If $\mathcal{B}(\mathcal{A}, \mathcal{P}) = \pi$ then $wt_{\mathcal{A}\pi}(\mathcal{P})$.*

Theorem 5 (Completeness of $\mathcal{B}$). *If $wt_{\mathcal{A}\pi'}(\mathcal{P})$ then $\mathcal{B}(\mathcal{A}, \mathcal{P}) = \pi$ and $\mathcal{A}\pi' = \mathcal{A}\pi\pi''$ for some π''.*

Another important property of $\mathcal{B}$ is that, starting from transparent assumptions for constructor symbols—as it is usual for Haskell-like `data` declarations—the types inferred for the function symbols in the program will also be transparent, as the following transparency invariant states. This result follows easily from Theorem 4, as the substitution π found by $\mathcal{B}$ verifies $wt_{\mathcal{A}\pi}(\mathcal{P})$ and every function symbol in a well-typed program w.r.t. $\mathcal{A}\pi$ is transparent w.r.t. $\mathcal{A}\pi$.

Theorem 6 (Transparency invariant). *Consider a program $\mathcal{P}$ and a set of assumptions $\mathcal{A}$ satisfying the requirements of $\mathcal{B}$. If $\mathcal{B}(\mathcal{A}, \mathcal{P}) = \pi$ then $\mathcal{A}\pi(f)$ is transparent for every $f \in \mathcal{P}$.*

3.2 Limitations of the type system

Although the proposed type system solves the opacity problems generated by HO patterns, as Examples 1 and 2 show, there are situations where it rejects programs that do not generate any type problems. A sample of this situation is the classical program of boolean circuits from [13], that exploits the use of HO-patterns:

Example 3 (Boolean circuits). *Consider the program*

$$x1\ X\ Y \to X$$
$$x2\ X\ Y \to Y$$
$$notGate\ C\ X\ Y \to not\ (C\ X\ Y)$$

Functions $x1$ and $x2$ are basic circuits that copy one of their inputs to the output, while notGate *takes a circuit as parameter and builds a circuit corresponding to the logical* not *gate. Using these functions to build HO patterns, it is possible to write a function that computes the size of a circuit:*

$$\begin{array}{l} size\ x1 \rightarrow z \\ size\ x2 \rightarrow z \\ size\ (notGate\ C) \rightarrow s\ (size\ C) \end{array}$$

Using the type alias $circuit \equiv bool \rightarrow bool \rightarrow bool$, the functions $x1$ and $x2$ have type $circuit$ in standard Damas-Milner type systems for FLP, while $notGate$ has type $circuit \rightarrow circuit$. It is clear that there is no opacity problem here, as all the types are ground. Considering these types, $size$ would have type $circuit \rightarrow nat$ in standard Damas-Milner. However this function is not valid in our type system since the type decorations in the types of $x1/x2$ and $notGate\ C$ are different. A valid type for both $x1$ and $x2$ would be

$$circuit' \equiv bool \rightarrow_{()} bool \rightarrow_{(bool)} bool$$

Nevertheless, the type of $notGate$ cannot be $circuit' \rightarrow circuit'$ but a more complex type due to the decorations in the arrows:

$$\forall\alpha,\beta.\tau \rightarrow_{()} bool \rightarrow_{(\tau)} bool \rightarrow_{(\tau,bool)} bool$$

where $\tau \equiv bool \rightarrow_\alpha bool \rightarrow_\beta bool$. With these types it is clear that $x1/x2$ and $notGate\ C$ cannot have the same type, as they will differ in the type decorations:

$$\begin{array}{ll} x1/x2 :: & bool \rightarrow_{()} bool \rightarrow_{(bool)} bool \\ notGate\ C :: & bool \rightarrow_{(\tau')} bool \rightarrow_{(\tau',bool)} bool \end{array}$$

for some instance τ' of τ. Therefore, the function size *is ill-typed because there is not any type-scheme for* size*—$\mathcal{A}(size) = \sigma$— such that $\mathcal{A} \vdash \lambda x1.z : \tau_1$, $\mathcal{A} \vdash \lambda(notGate\ C).s\ (size\ C) : \tau_2$ and both τ_1, τ_2 are variants of σ.*

This example makes clear that if decorations in arrows reflect the arity then functions like *size*, whose arguments are HO patterns constructed with function symbols of different arity, will be ill-typed because their arguments will have different types. It also shows that type decorations are not always needed to remove opacity. Since some kind of type decorations are mandatory to remove opacity in some cases, it seems a good option to lighten type decorations, avoiding the use of the complete types of the previous arguments and reflecting the arity, while guaranteeing transparency in λ-abstractions. We develop this approach in the next section.

4. Decorations with variables

As we have seen in the previous section, if arrow decorations are a sequence of the types of previous arguments, then some functions involving HO patterns will be rejected. On the other hand, arrow decorations are essential because they provide transparency to functions, which guarantees type preservation when using the rules of evaluation (Fapp) or (JoinP). However, the transparency requirement for a function f demands that $\mathcal{A}(f)$ must be k-transparent if $k = ar(f) - 1$, i.e., $ftv(\tau_1 \rightarrow_{\rho_1} \ldots \tau_k) \subseteq ftv(\tau_{k+1} \rightarrow_{\rho_{k+1}} \tau')$ where $\mathcal{A}(f) = \forall\overline{\alpha}.\tau_1 \rightarrow_{\rho_1} \ldots \tau_k \rightarrow_{\rho_k} \tau_{k+1} \rightarrow_{\rho_{k+1}} \tau'$. In other words, transparency only affects free type variables, so concrete types included in type decorations do not play any role. Therefore to avoid the undesired rejection of programs as in Example 3 and preserve types during evaluation we need to modify arrow decorations in the types of functions: instead of sequences of types we have to use sequences of type variables. These sequences of type variables must only contain the type variables occurring in the type of the previous arguments similarly as we did in the Section 3 with the whole types of the arguments. The decoration ρ_{k+1} would

$$(\Lambda^v)\ \frac{\begin{array}{c}\mathcal{A} \oplus \{\overline{X_n : \tau_n}\} \vdash^v t : \tau_t \\ \mathcal{A} \oplus \{\overline{X_n : \tau_n}\} \vdash^v e : \tau\end{array}}{\mathcal{A} \vdash^v \lambda t.e : \tau_t \rightarrow_{()} anArgs^v(k, \tau_t, \tau)}$$

$$\text{where } \{\overline{X_n}\} = var(t) \text{ and } \lambda depth(e) = k$$

Figure 5. Type derivation rule for λ-abstractions

then contain the free type variables in $\tau_1 \ldots \tau_k$, so clearly the type $\forall\overline{\alpha}.\tau_1 \rightarrow_{\rho_1} \ldots \tau_k \rightarrow_{\rho_k} \tau_{k+1} \rightarrow_{\rho_{k+1}} \tau'$ would still be transparent.

To formalize the presented intuition we only need to modify how we derive types for λ-abstractions, forcing their arrow decorations to be sequences of type variables instead of types, as the notion of well-typed program relies on λ-abstractions to check the types of functions. Notice that this change does not modify the syntax of arrow decorations: they are still (possibly empty) sequences of simple types. We are only forcing that arrow decorations in the types of λ-abstractions—and therefore of any valid function—were sequences of type variables, but sequences of simple types can still arise as arrow decorations. For example, the expression *snd true* must have type $\tau \rightarrow_{(bool)} \tau$ (for some τ). Otherwise, it would not be possible to know from its type that it has been applied to a boolean, so an expression as $snd\ true \bowtie snd\ z$ would be incorrectly considered as well-typed. In the sequel we will use the metavariable χ to denote sequences of type variables, i.e., $\chi ::= (\overline{\alpha_n})$ where $n \geq 0$.

Regarding the type system, we provide a new type derivation relation $\vdash^v$ whose rules for symbols, applications and let-expressions are the same as the ones for $\vdash$ in Figure 3. For λ-abstractions, the typing rule appears in Figure 5. The (Λ^v) rule is very similar to the original rule (Λ), with the difference that it uses $anArgs^v$ instead of $anArgs$.

Definition 4 (Type decoration with variables)**.**

$anArgs^v(0, \tau, \tau') = \tau'$
$anArgs^v(n, \tau, \tau_1 \rightarrow_{(\chi)} \tau_2) = \tau_1 \rightarrow_{(\chi' \diamond \chi)} anArgs^v(n-1, \tau, \tau_2)$
where χ' is the sequence of free type variables in τ

The meta operator $anArgs^v(n, \tau, \tau')$ adds the type variables in τ to all the decorations of the functional type τ' up to some depth n. The sequence χ' contains the variables occurring in τ without repetitions and in the order in which they appear from left to right. To concatenate sequences of type variables we use the operator $\chi' \diamond \chi$, which generates a sequence without repetitions consisting of the sequence χ' followed by the sequence χ where all the variables that also appear in χ' have been removed.

In essence, the (Λ^v) rule derives the usual Damas-Milner type but decorating the arrows with the type variables of the previous arguments. In some cases the type derived for a λ-abstraction using $\vdash^v$ is the same as the one derived using $\vdash$. For example, $\mathcal{A} \vdash^v \lambda X.\lambda Y.Y : \alpha \rightarrow_{()} \beta \rightarrow_{(\alpha)} \beta$—corresponding to the *snd* function in Example 1. In this case the types coincide because the sequence of type variables in α is the same as the whole type α. However, if the types of the arguments are not type variables then the derived types will be different. Considering the rule for $(\wedge)$—the boolean conjunction used in the rewriting rule (JoinP) in Figure 2—we have that $\mathcal{A} \vdash^v \lambda true.\lambda Y.Y : bool \rightarrow_{()} bool \rightarrow_{()} bool$, whereas $\mathcal{A} \vdash \lambda true.\lambda Y.Y : bool \rightarrow_{()} bool \rightarrow_{(bool)} bool$. Notice that $\vdash^v$ does not add any decoration in the second arrow, as *bool* does not contain any type variable.

Based on this new type derivation relation, we provide a definition of *well-typed programs* that is the same as the one in Definition 2 but using $\vdash^v$ instead of $\vdash$.

Definition 5 (Well-typed program using $\vdash^v$).
A program rule $f\ \overline{t_n} \to e$ is well-typed w.r.t. $\mathcal{A}$ if $\mathcal{A} \vdash^v \lambda\overline{t_n}.e : \tau$ and τ is a variant of $\mathcal{A}(f)$. A program $\mathcal{P}$ is well-typed w.r.t. $\mathcal{A}$—written $wt^v_{\mathcal{A}}(\mathcal{P})$—if all its rules are well-typed w.r.t. $\mathcal{A}$.

As in the well-typed notion in the previous section, Definition 5 also assures that if $wt^v_{\mathcal{A}}(\mathcal{P})$ then every function in $\mathcal{P}$ is transparent w.r.t. $\mathcal{A}$. This fact is based in the following result about the types of λ-abstractions:

Lemma 2. *If $\mathcal{A} \vdash^v \lambda\overline{t_{n+1}}.e : \tau$ then τ is n-transparent.*

The most important property about the type system in this section is that it preserves types when evaluating expressions using well-typed programs:

Theorem 7 (Type Preservation). *If $wt^v_{\mathcal{A}}(\mathcal{P})$, $\mathcal{A} \vdash^v e : \tau$ and $e \to^l e'$ then $\mathcal{A} \vdash^v e' : \tau$.*

Notice that expressions to evaluate and programs cannot contain λ-abstractions. As the typing rules for these expressions are the same in $\vdash$ and $\vdash^v$, $\mathcal{A} \vdash e : \tau$ is equivalent to $\mathcal{A} \vdash^v e : \tau$. Therefore the only difference between the previous theorem and Theorem 3 is the notion of well-typed program. However, this new notion of well-typed program is more expressive than the one in the previous section, considering as well-typed the program of boolean circuits—Example 3—as well as all the motivating programs in Section 1.

Regarding boolean circuits, consider the set of assumptions $\mathcal{A} \equiv \{x1, x2 : circuit, notGate : circuit \to_{()} circuit\}$ where $circuit \equiv bool \to_{()} bool \to_{()} bool$. With these assumptions the rules for $x1/x2$ and *notGate* are well-typed, as $\mathcal{A} \vdash^v \lambda X.\lambda Y.X : circuit$, $\mathcal{A} \vdash^v \lambda X.\lambda Y.X : circuit$ and $\mathcal{A} \vdash^v \lambda C.\lambda X.\lambda Y.not\ (C\ X\ Y) : circuit \to_{()} circuit$. More important, these assumptions remove any information about the arity of the symbols, so the function *size* is now well-typed with the assumption $\{size : circuit \to_{()} nat\}$. The reason is that now the HO patterns $x1/x2$ and $notGate\ C$ have exactly the same type *circuit*, so all the rules for *size* have type $circuit \to_{()} nat$: $\mathcal{A} \vdash^v \lambda x1.z : circuit \to_{()} nat$, $\mathcal{A} \vdash^v \lambda x2.z : circuit \to_{()} nat$ and $\mathcal{A} \vdash^v \lambda(notGate\ C).s\ (size\ C) : circuit \to_{()} nat$.

Apart from boolean circuits, the type system in this section also solves the opacity problems presented in Section 1. Regarding the *snd* function in Example 1, it is still well-typed with the assumption $\{snd : \forall\alpha,\beta.\alpha \to_{()} \beta \to_{(\alpha)} \beta\}$ as $\mathcal{A} \vdash^v \lambda X.\lambda Y.Y : \alpha \to_{()} \beta \to_{(\alpha)} \beta$. This type is transparent, solving the problem of polymorphic casting using the *unpack* function as mentioned in the previous section. Regarding the loss of type preservation using the (JoinP) and HO patterns in Example 2, the type of *snd* also solves the problem because of its transparency. The expression $snd\ true \bowtie snd\ z$ is still ill-typed, avoiding the problematic step $snd\ true \bowtie snd\ z \to^l true \bowtie z$ that breaks type preservation. On the other hand, the rule for the $(\wedge)$ function used by the let-rewriting relation (Section 2.3) is well-typed with the assumption $\{(\wedge) : bool \to_{()} bool \to_{()} bool\}$, as $\mathcal{A} \vdash^v \lambda true.\lambda Y.Y : bool \to_{()} bool \to_{(bool)} bool$[9].

The type system based on $\vdash^v$ provides transparency to function symbols, solving the opacity situations that break type preservation, and it also overcomes the limitations of $\vdash$ when dealing with functions containing HO patterns as *size*. However it lacks an important property: closure under type substitutions.

Example 4. *Consider a set of assumptions $\mathcal{A}$ containing an assumption $\{f : \alpha \to_{()} \alpha\}$ for the function symbol f of arity 1, and the expression $e \equiv \lambda f.\lambda true.true$. We can build the type derivation*

$$\mathcal{A} \vdash^v e : (\alpha \to_{()} \alpha) \to_{()} bool \to_{(\alpha)} bool \equiv \tau$$

However, using the type substitution $\pi \equiv [\alpha \mapsto nat]$ we cannot build the type derivation $\mathcal{A}\pi \vdash^v e : \tau\pi$. The reason is that $\tau\pi \equiv (nat \to_{()} nat) \to_{()} bool \to_{(nat)} bool$ is an invalid type for a λ-abstraction using $\vdash^v$, as it decorates the final arrow with the type constructor nat instead of a sequence of type variables. Using the set of assumptions $\mathcal{A}\pi$, the only possible type for e is $(nat \to_{()} nat) \to_{()} bool \to_{()} bool$.

Closure under type substitutions is an essential property of the type system because it plays an important role in the soundness of the type inference. If this property does not hold, a type inference algorithm for expressions based on unification similar to $\Vdash$ (thus following the same ideas as algorithm $\mathcal{W}$ [10]) would be unsound. As type inference for programs is based on type inference for expressions, this means that following an approach similar to $\mathcal{B}$ in Definition 3 would also lead to unsoundness.

Example 4 shows that the typing relation $\vdash^v$ is not closed under type substitutions because the substitution can replace type variables in arrow decorations by types different from variables. If these variables appear in arrow decorations generated for λ-abstractions, the invariant that these decorations must be sequences of type variables is broken, and the type derivation $\mathcal{A}\pi \vdash^v e : \tau\pi$ is not possible. However, since the typing rules for symbols, applications and let-expression are the same in $\vdash$ and $\vdash^v$, it is important to note that $\vdash^v$ is closed under type substitutions for expressions no containing λ-abstractions.

It may seem from Example 4 that we only need to perform a "flattening" process that replaces arrow decorations by a sequence of its type variables after applying the type substitution to recover a result of closure: *if $\mathcal{A} \vdash^v e : \tau$ then $\mathcal{A}\pi \vdash^v e : flat(\tau\pi)$*. It would work in the previous example, since $flat(\tau\pi) = (nat \to_{()} nat) \to_{()} bool \to_{()} bool$, which is a valid type for e under $\mathcal{A}\pi$. However, not all arrow decorations should be flattened. As an example, consider a set of assumptions $\mathcal{A}'$ containing $\{snd :: \forall\alpha,\beta.\alpha \to_{()} \beta \to_{(\alpha)} \beta\}$. A valid type derivation is $\mathcal{A}' \vdash^v snd\ true : bool \to_{(bool)} bool$, whose type shows that it has been applied to a boolean. According to the tentative closure result proposed, the type derivation $\mathcal{A}'\pi \vdash^v snd\ true : bool \to_{()} bool$ should be correct for any π, as $flat((bool \to_{(bool)} bool)\pi) = bool \to_{()} bool$. However, this type derivation is incorrect: the only valid type for $snd\ true$ under $\mathcal{A}'\pi$ is $bool \to_{(bool)} bool$. Therefore, the flattening process cannot take only a type to flatten but also extra information about what arrows need to be flattened, which are exactly those generated in the type of a λ-abstraction.

5. Marked decorations

To solve the lack of closure under type substitutions shown in Example 4 and being able to define a type inference algorithm both for expressions and programs, in this section we propose a new type derivation relation $\vdash^m$. This relation is like $\vdash$ but marking with $\bullet$ those arrow decorations generated in the types of λ-abstractions. A later flattening process can then flatten marked decorations (which will be sequences of types as in $\vdash$), obtaining the same type as $\vdash^v$. The benefit of this separation of tasks is that, thanks to the closure under type substitutions of $\vdash^m$, we can develop a sound and complete marking type inference algorithm $\Vdash^m$ similar to $\Vdash$. This algorithm $\Vdash^m$ could then be used in a process $\mathcal{B}^\bullet$ for inferring types of programs.

In order to handle marked arrow decorations, we consider the following new syntactic categories:

$$\begin{array}{rcl} \tau^\bullet & ::= & \alpha \mid C\,\overline{\tau^\bullet_n}\ \text{ if } ar(C) = n \mid \tau^\bullet_1 \to_{\rho^\bullet} \tau^\bullet_2 \\ \rho^\bullet & ::= & \alpha \mid (\overline{\tau^\bullet_n})\ \text{ if } n \geq 0 \mid {}^\bullet(\overline{\tau^\bullet_n})\ \text{ if } n \geq 0 \end{array}$$

[9] As $(\wedge)$ is a predefined function used in let-rewriting rules, in this section we assume that every set of assumptions $\mathcal{A}$ contains $\{(\wedge) : bool \to_{()} bool \to_{()} bool\}$.

$$(\text{ID}^\bullet)\frac{}{\mathcal{A} \vdash^m s : \tau^\bullet} \text{ if } \mathcal{A}(s) \succ \tau^\bullet$$

$$(\text{APP}^\bullet)\frac{\mathcal{A} \vdash^m e_1 : \tau_1^\bullet \rightarrow_{\rho^\bullet} \tau^\bullet \quad \mathcal{A} \vdash^m e_2 : \tau_1^\bullet}{\mathcal{A} \vdash^m e_1\, e_2 : \tau^\bullet}$$

$$(\Lambda^\bullet)\frac{\mathcal{A} \oplus \{\overline{X_n : \tau_n^\bullet}\} \vdash^m t : \tau_t^\bullet \quad \mathcal{A} \oplus \{\overline{X_n : \tau_n^\bullet}\} \vdash^m e : \tau^\bullet}{\mathcal{A} \vdash^m \lambda t.e : \tau_t^\bullet \rightarrow_{\bullet()} anArgs^\bullet(k, \tau_t^\bullet, \tau^\bullet)}$$

where $\{\overline{X_n}\} = var(t)$ and $\lambda depth(e) = k$

$$(\text{LET}^\bullet)\frac{\mathcal{A} \vdash^m e_1 : \tau_x^\bullet \quad \mathcal{A} \oplus \{X : \tau_x^\bullet\} \vdash^m e_2 : \tau^\bullet}{\mathcal{A} \vdash^m let\ X = e_1\ in\ e_2 : \tau^\bullet}$$

Figure 6. Marked type derivation

We use $\rho^\bullet$ (*marked decorations*) for possibly marked arrow decorations, whereas ρ will still denote unmarked arrow decorations as in the previous sections. Similarly, we use $\tau^\bullet$ (*marked simple types*) to denote simple types with possibly marked arrow decorations and τ for simple types with unmarked arrow decorations. *Marked type substitutions* $\pi^\bullet$ are finite mappings from type variables to marked simple types: $\pi^\bullet ::= [\overline{\alpha_n \mapsto \tau_n^\bullet}]$. As types with marked arrow decorations have only been included to separate type derivation and flattening and they have not any particular meaning, in type derivations we consider that sets of assumptions contain type-schemes as defined in Figure 1, i.e., without marked arrow decorations.

Figure 6 contains the rules of the typing relation $\mathcal{A} \vdash^m e : \tau^\bullet$, which is very similar to the rules for $\vdash$ in Figure 3. Notice that in (ID$^\bullet$) we obtain a marked simple type $\tau^\bullet$ although set of assumptions contain unmarked type-schemes. The reason is that now we consider that generic instances are generated using marked type substitutions, i.e., $\sigma \succ \tau^\bullet$ iff $\sigma \equiv \forall \alpha_n.\tau'$ and $\tau'[\overline{\alpha_n \mapsto \tau_n^\bullet}]$. The rest of rules are very similar to those in Figure 3. The main difference is $(\Lambda^\bullet)$. This rule marks the empty decoration $^\bullet()$ included in the arrow, as it is a decoration generated for a λ-abstraction. If the expression belongs to a bigger λ-abstraction this decoration will be populated with a sequence of types by the function $anArgs^\bullet$, but as the whole decoration is marked with $^\bullet$ it will be flattened. The other difference is the use of the aforementioned $anArgs^\bullet$. This function is defined as $anArgs$ in Definition 1 but considering only marked decorations:

Definition 6 (Marked type decoration).

$$anArgs^\bullet(0, \tau^\bullet, \tau_2^\bullet) = \tau_2^\bullet$$
$$anArgs^\bullet(n, \tau^\bullet, \tau_1^\bullet \rightarrow_{\bullet(\overline{\tau_m^\bullet})} \tau_2^\bullet) =$$
$$\tau_1^\bullet \rightarrow_{\bullet(\tau^\bullet, \overline{\tau_m^\bullet})} anArgs^\bullet(n-1, \tau^\bullet, \tau_2^\bullet) \quad \textit{where } n > 0$$

Notice that $anArgs^\bullet$ includes simple types in arrow decorations up to some depth n, but these arrow decorations are always marked—they have been generated by the rule $(\Lambda^\bullet)$. As with $anArgs$, if $anArgs^\bullet(n, \tau^\bullet, \tau_2^\bullet)$ is used in $(\Lambda^\bullet)$ with $n > 0$ then $\tau_2^\bullet$ is guaranteed to be a functional type with enough marked arrow decorations.

Considering the *snd* function, using $\vdash^m$ we can build the following type derivation for its associated λ-abstraction: $\lambda X.\lambda Y.Y : \alpha \rightarrow_{\bullet()} \beta \rightarrow_{\bullet(\alpha)} \beta$. It is the same type derived using $\vdash$ but with marked arrow decorations. However a flattening process produces $\alpha \rightarrow_{()} \beta \rightarrow_{(\alpha)} \beta$, exactly the same type derived using $\vdash$ and $\vdash^v$. Regarding the operator $(\wedge)$—Section 2.3—we have the type derivation $\lambda true.\lambda Y.Y : bool \rightarrow_{\bullet()} bool \rightarrow_{\bullet(bool)} bool$. It is the same type derived using $\vdash$ but with marked arrow decorations, and it becomes the type derived using $\vdash^v$ after flattening $(bool \rightarrow_{()} bool \rightarrow_{()} bool)$. Considering a more complex example as function *notGate* in Example 3, a type derivation for its associated λ-abstraction is $\mathcal{A} \vdash^m \lambda C.\lambda X.\lambda Y.not\ C\ X\ Y : circuit \rightarrow_{\bullet()} bool \rightarrow_{\bullet(circuit)} bool \rightarrow_{\bullet(circuit,bool)} bool$, where $circuit \equiv bool \rightarrow_{()} bool \rightarrow_{()} bool$—notice that *circuit* is the guessed type for C in the λ-abstraction, so it is possible to use this unmarked simple type. However, if we flatten this type we obtain the same type derived using $\vdash^v$: $circuit \rightarrow_{()} circuit$.

As showed in the previous examples, flattening a valid type obtained for e using $\vdash^m$ results in a valid type for e using $\vdash^v$. This result is clear, as $\vdash^v$ flattens decorations when using $anArgs^v$ in the (Λ^v) rule, whereas $\vdash^m$ marks the decorations in the rule $(\Lambda^\bullet)$ and the final flattening stage obtains the same flattened arrow decorations. The following theorem formalizes this result, which uses the flattening function *flat*.

Definition 7 (Flattening).

$$flat(\alpha) = \alpha$$
$$flat(C\,\overline{\tau_n^\bullet}) = C\,\overline{flat(\tau_n^\bullet)}$$
$$flat(\tau_1^\bullet \rightarrow_\rho \tau_2^\bullet) = flat(\tau_1^\bullet) \rightarrow_\rho flat(\tau_2^\bullet)$$
$$flat(\tau_1^\bullet \rightarrow_{\bullet(\overline{\tau_m^\bullet})} \tau_2^\bullet) = flat(\tau_1^\bullet) \rightarrow_\chi flat(\tau_2^\bullet)$$

where χ is the sequence of type variables in $(\overline{\tau_m^\bullet})$ as they appear from left to right and without repetitions.

Theorem 8. *$\mathcal{A} \vdash^m e : \tau^\bullet$ and $\tau = flat(\tau^\bullet)$ iff $\mathcal{A} \vdash^v e : \tau$.*

As $\vdash^m$ behaves similar to $\vdash$ but marking arrow decorations that will be flattened afterward, it recovers closure under marked type substitutions:

Lemma 3 (Closure of $\vdash^m$). *If $\mathcal{A} \vdash^m e : \tau^\bullet$ then $\mathcal{A}\pi^\bullet \vdash^m e : \tau^\bullet\pi^\bullet$*

Using the type relation $\vdash^m$ we provide a definition of well-typed programs that assures type preservation. This definition is very similar to the previous one (Definitions 2 and 5) but it needs to flatten the obtained types for λ-abstractions associated to rules:

Definition 8 (Well-typed program using $\vdash^m$).
A program rule $f\ \overline{t_n} \rightarrow e$ is well-typed w.r.t. $\mathcal{A}$ if $\mathcal{A} \vdash^m \lambda\overline{t_n}.e : \tau^\bullet$, $flat(\tau^\bullet) = \tau$ and τ is a variant of $\mathcal{A}(f)$. A program $\mathcal{P}$ is well-typed w.r.t. $\mathcal{A}$—written $wt^m_{\mathcal{A}}(\mathcal{P})$—if all its rules are well-typed w.r.t. $\mathcal{A}$.

Theorem 9 (Type Preservation). *If $wt^m_{\mathcal{A}}(\mathcal{P})$, $\mathcal{A} \vdash^m e : \tau$ and $e \rightarrow^l e'$ then $\mathcal{A} \vdash^m e' : \tau$.*

It is important to note that the new definition of well-typed program using $\vdash^m$ and flattening is equivalent to the previous one using only $\vdash^v$ (Definition 5). It follows as a simple corollary from Theorem 8. Note also that in Theorem 9 we consider only unmarked simple types for the expression e to evaluate. As expressions to evaluate cannot contain λ-abstractions, it is easy to see that valid unmarked types for these expressions using $\vdash^m$ are the same as valid types using $\vdash^v$, i.e., $\mathcal{A} \vdash^m e : \tau$ iff $\mathcal{A} \vdash^v e : \tau$.[10] Finally, it is important to note that $wt^m_{\mathcal{A}}(\mathcal{P})$ assures that every function in $\mathcal{P}$ is transparent w.r.t. $\mathcal{A}$, as $wt^m_{\mathcal{A}}(\mathcal{P})$ and $wt^v_{\mathcal{A}}(\mathcal{P})$ are equivalent.

5.1 Marked type inference

Up to this point, the type relation $\vdash^m$ does not provide any clear advantage over $\vdash^v$ but closure under type substitutions. However,

[10] As showed in Section 4, the same equivalence holds for $\vdash$ and $\vdash^v$.

$$\text{(iID}^\bullet\text{)}\ \frac{}{\mathcal{A}^\bullet \Vdash^m s : \tau^\bullet | \epsilon}\ \text{if } \mathcal{A}^\bullet(s) \succ_{var} \tau^\bullet$$

$$\text{(iAPP}^\bullet\text{)}\ \frac{\mathcal{A}^\bullet \Vdash^m e_1 : \tau_1^\bullet | \pi_1^\bullet \qquad \mathcal{A}^\bullet \pi_1^\bullet \Vdash^m e_2 : \tau_2^\bullet | \pi_2^\bullet}{\mathcal{A}^\bullet \Vdash^m e_1\, e_2 : \alpha\pi^\bullet | \pi_1^\bullet \pi_2^\bullet \pi^\bullet}$$

where α, β fresh and $\pi^\bullet = mgu(\tau_1^\bullet \pi_2^\bullet, \tau_2^\bullet \to_\beta \alpha)$

$$\text{(i}\Lambda^\bullet\text{)}\ \frac{\mathcal{A}^\bullet \oplus \{\overline{X_n : \alpha_n}\} \Vdash^m t : \tau_t^\bullet | \pi_t^\bullet \qquad (\mathcal{A}^\bullet \oplus \{\overline{X_n : \alpha_n}\})\pi_t^\bullet \Vdash^m e : \tau^\bullet | \pi^\bullet}{\mathcal{A}^\bullet \Vdash^m \lambda t.e : \tau_t^\bullet \pi^\bullet \to_{()} anArgs^\bullet(k, \tau_t^\bullet \pi^\bullet, \tau^\bullet) | \pi_t^\bullet \pi^\bullet}$$

where $\{\overline{X_n}\} = var(t)$, $\overline{\alpha_n}$ fresh and $\lambda depth(e) = k$

$$\text{(iLET}^\bullet\text{)}\ \frac{\mathcal{A}^\bullet \Vdash^m e_1 : \tau_x^\bullet | \pi_x^\bullet \qquad \mathcal{A}^\bullet \pi_x^\bullet \oplus \{X : \tau_x^\bullet\} \Vdash^m e_2 : \tau^\bullet | \pi^\bullet}{\mathcal{A}^\bullet \Vdash^m let\ X = e_1\ in\ e_2 : \tau^\bullet | \pi_x^\bullet \pi^\bullet}$$

Figure 7. Marked type inference rules

we can develop a sound and complete marked type inference for expressions to be used in a type inference algorithm for programs.

Figure 7 shows the rules of the marked type inference for expressions $\mathcal{A}^\bullet \Vdash^m e : \tau^\bullet | \pi^\bullet$. It considers marked sets of assumptions $\mathcal{A}^\bullet$—i.e., set of assumptions that can contain marked simple types $\tau^\bullet$—marked simple types and marked type substitutions. Like $\Vdash$, marked type inference $\Vdash^m$ has a relational style to express the similarities with $\vdash^m$ although it is an algorithm: given a marked set of assumptions $\mathcal{A}^\bullet$ and expression e returns a marked simple type $\tau^\bullet$ and a marked type substitution $\pi^\bullet$, or it fails if no rule can be applied. The rules of $\Vdash^m$ are very similar to the rules of $\Vdash$ in Figure 4, with the exception of rule (i$\Lambda^\bullet$). This rule follows the same ideas as the typing rule ($\Lambda^\bullet$) in Figure 6, marking generated arrow decorations with $\bullet$ and using $anArgs^\bullet$ instead of $anArgs$ when including types in the arrows decorations.

Intuitively, $\Vdash^m$ returns a marked simple type $\tau^\bullet$ that is the most general type for e and a marked type substitution $\pi^\bullet$ that is the minimum substitution that $\mathcal{A}^\bullet$ needs to be able to derive a type for e w.r.t. $\vdash^m$. This intuition is stated in the next result:

Theorem 10 (Properties of $\Vdash^m$ w.r.t. $\vdash^m$).
• (Soundness) *If* $\mathcal{A}^\bullet \Vdash^m e : \tau^\bullet | \pi^\bullet$ *then* $\mathcal{A}^\bullet \pi^\bullet \vdash^m e : \tau^\bullet$.
• (Completeness) *If* $\mathcal{A}\pi_1^\bullet \vdash^m e : \tau_1^\bullet$ *then* $\mathcal{A}^\bullet \Vdash^m e : \tau^\bullet | \pi^\bullet$ *and there is some* $\pi_2^\bullet$ *verifying* $\mathcal{A}^\bullet \pi^\bullet \pi_2^\bullet = \mathcal{A}_1^\bullet$ *and* $\tau^\bullet \pi_2^\bullet = \tau_1^\bullet$.

These results follow easily from soundness and completeness of $\Vdash$ (Theorem 1 and 2), as the only difference between $\vdash$/$\vdash^m$ and $\Vdash$/$\Vdash^m$ are the marks in arrow decorations. Notice that, although not included in the presentation of marked type derivation $\vdash^m$, to be able to relate type inference and derivation we need to consider marked set of assumptions for type derivations. This is not a problem, as $\vdash^m$ supports marked set of assumptions directly (note that the only rule that uses assumptions is (ID$^\bullet$), which creates generic instances from assumptions using marked type substitutions).

Based on the type inference for expressions $\Vdash^m$, we can develop a sound—and conjectured complete—type inference algorithm for programs $\mathcal{B}^\bullet$ similar to $\mathcal{B}$ in Section 3. As the inference algorithm $\mathcal{B}^\bullet$ is sound the program is well-typed w.r.t. the resulting assumptions, so the transparency invariant holds also for $\mathcal{B}^\bullet$: the types inferred for the function symbols in the program will be transparent. The definition of $\mathcal{B}^\bullet$ and its properties can be found in Appendix A of the extended version of the paper [26].

6. Related type systems

Here we will discuss the permissiveness of our type systems compared to previous proposals of type systems for FLP, i.e., we will compare the different systems w.r.t. inclusion of the sets of well-typed programs in each typing. Regarding [13], that can be considered a canonical adaptation to FLP of Damas-Milner typing, and $\vdash$ from Section 3, none of these systems is more permissive than the other. It is shown by Example 1 (where *unpack* is rejected by [13], as it uses an opaque pattern) and the program using boolean circuits in Example 3 (accepted by [13] but not by $\vdash$). However the type system $\vdash^v$ from Section 4—which is equivalent to the type system in Section 5 regarding well-typed programs—is more permissive than the type system in [13], as it considers as well-typed the mentioned programs.

The systems from [20] and [19] also start from Damas-Milner typing and extend the system to safely support opacity. In [20] *parametricity* [28] can be broken in opaque program patterns, so a function f defined by the rules $f\ (snd\ z) \to true$ and $f\ (snd\ true) \to false\}$ is well typed with $f : \forall\alpha.(\alpha \to \alpha) \to bool$. That program is rejected by all the type systems presented in this paper because, according to the type of *snd* ($\forall\alpha,\beta.\alpha \to_{()} \beta \to_{(\alpha)} \beta$), the types of the rules for f are not a variant of the assumption for f, a condition needed to ensure parametricity. However, the type system in [20] rejects the polymorphic cast function in Example 1—accepted by all the type systems in this paper—because the rule for *unpack* has a *critical variable*. The same rules for f are accepted by [19], where parametricity can be broken freely in any pattern. However, the type system in [19] also rejects the polymorphic cast function from Example 1 because it is not type safe in absence of type decorations.

Finally, we consider that a comparison with existential types would be artificial, as our system uses HO patterns and tries to avoid opacity completely, while existential types embraces it, and usually employs first order patterns only. However it is important to remark that an approach similar to existential types [18, 27] could solve problems as the polymorphic cast function in Example 1 (it would reject the *unpack* function as the type systems in [19, 20]) however it cannot solve the problem of opaque decomposition (see Example 2) since the function ($\bowtie$) is not defined by rules.

7. Conclusions and Future Work

In this paper we extend Damas-Milner typing to eliminate the unintended opacity caused by HO patterns by enhancing the expressiveness of the type language. This is different from the approach followed by previous proposals as [13], where opaque patterns are forbidden from rules, or [19, 20], that try to deal with opacity safely. Starting from a set of transparent assumptions for constructor symbols—as it is usual in Damas-Milner typing—the type systems presented in this paper guarantee a transparency invariant that ensures that the type derived for subsequent functions will always be transparent. As a consequence, opacity disappears from programs and type preservation is recovered, since it was destroyed just by an improper handling of opacity. Besides, by recovering transparency the problem of opaque decomposition in equalities is avoided. This is an important aspect of the paper, since (to the best of our knowledge) there is no proposal for solving the opaque decomposition problem that appear in FLP computations in the presence of HO patterns.

To eliminate the unintended opacity caused by HO patterns we enhance the expressiveness of the type language by decorating the functional type constructors ($\to$). Using these decorations we can store type information about the previous arguments of the functions so that their types are transparent. We have explored two alternatives, which differ in the amount of information stored in arrows. In Section 3 we consider that arrows contains the types of all the previous arguments of the functions, i.e., they are $\forall\overline{\alpha_m}.\tau_1 \rightarrow_{()} \tau_2 \rightarrow_{(\tau_1)} \cdots \rightarrow_{(\overline{\tau_{n-2}})} \tau_n \rightarrow_{(\overline{\tau_{n-1}})} \tau$. Intuitively, an expression of type $\tau_1 \rightarrow_{(\overline{\tau'_m})} \tau_2$ corresponds to a partial application of a symbol to m expressions of types $\overline{\tau'_m}$. Although the obtained type system preserves types and enjoys a sound a complete type inference algorithm for expressions, it has the drawback that it rejects some safe programs using HO pattens as Example 3. To overcome this limitation, in Section 4 we reduce the amount of type information included in arrow decorations of the types of functions to the type variables of the previous arguments. We obtain a type system that also enjoys type preservation, however it lacks an important property: closure under type substitutions. As this property is essential for developing a type inference algorithm based on unification, in Section 5 we present a type system that unites the ideas behind the two previous ones. By separating the process of deriving a marked type from the process of flattening arrow decorations we obtain a type system that enjoys type preservation, is closed under type substitution—so type inference using unification as in algorithm $\mathcal{W}$ [10] is possible—and accepts the programs using HO patterns that were rejected in the first approach. All the presented type systems give a proper type to functions like the polymorphic casting function, which behaves like the identity and could only be rejected by previous proposals.

An important feature of modern FLP languages, not treated in the present work, is the support for logical variables, which are free variables that get bound during the computation by means of some narrowing mechanism [2]. The interactions between types and narrowing in FLP has not received much attention, with remarkable exceptions [3, 13]. In fact the combination of logical variables and equality constraints ($==$)—which replaces the equality operator ($\bowtie$) when dealing with logical variables—allows us to reproduce all the typing problems caused by opacity of HO patterns, even in languages without them like Curry (e.g. in PAKCS 1.10.0 and MCC 0.9.11), as any program rule $f\ \overline{p} \rightarrow e$ with HO patterns can be emulated by a strict version[11] $f\ \overline{X} \rightarrow cond\ (\overline{X} == \overline{p})\ e$. In [13] it was already detected that parametricity—there the more restrictive property of type generality is considered instead—is needed to ensure type safety with narrowing. We are convinced that our type system enjoys parametricity which, combined with the transparency warranties it provides, makes it a very promising candidate to provide a better type system for FLP with narrowing, when combined with our recent work in that subject [21]. That could improve previous proposals like [13], with tighter transparency requirements, and [3], restricted to monomorphic functions and program rules without extra variables—in contrast to [21]. We consider the approaches from [19, 20] less promising for this task because of their lack of parametricity, although they could be an interesting extension when confined to some parts of the program. Another possibility could be adapting existential types to FLP, but again it is not clear how might they cope with opaque decomposition.

As another line of future work we plan to integrate the type system of Section 5 into the FLP system Toy [23]. Using this system we could test the behavior of the type system with a broader set of programs. Arrow decorations are a novelty in the type language, so we wonder if they will fit easily in programmer intuition about types. Tests with the system will determine whether arrow decorations can be left as part of the types or it is better to hide them to programmers and use their information only in error messages.

[11] Similarly to $\bowtie$, equality constraints between functional expressions are not specified in the Curry report [14] but they are supported by the mentioned Curry implementations.

8. Acknowledgments

This work has been partially supported by the Spanish projects MICINN TIN2008-06622-C03-01/TIN, CM S2009/TIC-1465 and UCM-BSCH-GR35/10-A-910502. We would also want to thank Francisco J. López-Fraguas for his help and advice with some parts of this paper, and for the interesting discussions about some topics of FLP.

References

[1] J. M. Almendros-Jiménez, R. Caballero, Y. García-Ruiz, and F. Sáenz-Pérez. XQuery in the functional-logic language Toy. In *Proceedings of the 20th International Workshop on Functional and Constraint Logic Programming (WFLP '11)*, volume 6816 of *Lecture Notes in Computer Science*, pages 35–51. Springer, 2011.

[2] S. Antoy and M. Hanus. Functional logic programming. *Communications of the ACM*, 53(4):74–85, 2010.

[3] S. Antoy and A. Tolmach. Typed higher-order narrowing without higher-order strategies. In *Proceedings of the 4th International Symposium on Functional and Logic Programming (FLOPS '99)*, volume 1722 of *Lecture Notes in Computer Science*, pages 335–352. Springer, 1999.

[4] Z. Ariola, M. Felleisen, J. Maraist, M. Odersky, and P. Wadler. A call-by-need lambda calculus. In *Proceedings of the 22nd Annual ACM SIGACT-SIGPLAN Symposium on Principles of Programming Languages (POPL '95)*, pages 233–246. ACM, 1995.

[5] R. Caballero, Y. García-Ruiz, and F. Sáenz-Pérez. Integrating XPath with the functional-logic language toy. In *Proceedings of the 13th International Symposium on Practical Aspects of Declarative Languages (PADL '11)*, volume 6539 of *Lecture Notes in Computer Science*, pages 145–159. Springer, 2011.

[6] R. Caballero and F. López-Fraguas. A functional-logic perspective on parsing. In *Proceedings of the 4th International Symposium on Functional and Logic Programming (FLOPS '99)*, pages 85–99. Springer, 1999.

[7] R. Caballero and F. J. López-Fraguas. Functional logic parsers in Toy. Technical Report SIP-7498, Universidad Complutense de Madrid, April 1998. Available at `http://gpd.sip.ucm.es/fraguas/papers/TR-SIP-74-98-Toy-parsers.pdf`.

[8] R. Caballero, J. Sánchez, P. A. Sánchez, A. J. F. Leiva, A. G. Luezas, F. L. Fraguas, M. R. Artalejo, and F. S. Pérez. Toy, a multiparadigm declarative language. version 2.3.2, October 2011. Available at `http://toy.sourceforge.net`.

[9] J. Christiansen, D. Seidel, and J. Voigtländer. An adequate, denotational, functional-style semantics for typed FlatCurry. In *Proceedings of the 19th International Workshop on Functional and (Constraint) Logic Programming (WFLP '10), Revised Selected Papers*, volume 6559 of *Lecture Notes in Computer Science*, pages 119–136. Springer, 2011.

[10] L. Damas and R. Milner. Principal type-schemes for functional programs. In *Proceedings of the 9th ACM SIGPLAN-SIGACT Symposium on Principles of Programming Languages (POPL '82)*, pages 207–212. ACM, 1982.

[11] J. González-Moreno, T. Hortalá-González, F. López-Fraguas, and M. Rodríguez-Artalejo. An approach to declarative programming based on a rewriting logic. *Journal of Logic Programming*, 40(1):47–87, 1999.

[12] J. González-Moreno, T. Hortalá-González, and M. Rodríguez-Artalejo. A higher order rewriting logic for functional logic programming. In *Proceedings of the 14th International Conference on Logic Programming (ICLP '97)*, pages 153–167. MIT Press, 1997.

[13] J. González-Moreno, T. Hortalá-González, and M. Rodríguez-Artalejo. Polymorphic types in functional logic programming. *Journal of Functional and Logic Programming*, 2001(1), July 2001.

[14] M. Hanus. Curry: An integrated functional logic language (version 0.8.2). Available at `http://www.informatik.uni-kiel.de/~curry/report.html`, March 2006.

[15] M. Hanus. Multi-paradigm declarative languages. In *Proceedings of the 23rd International Conference on Logic Programming (ICLP '07)*, volume 4670 of *Lecture Notes in Computer Science*, pages 45–75. Springer, 2007.

[16] T. Hortalá-González, F. J. López-Fraguas, J. Sánchez-Hernández, and E. Ullán-Hernández. Declarative programming with real constraints. Technical Report SIP-5997, Universidad Complutense de Madrid, April 1997. Available at `http://gpd.sip.ucm.es/fraguas/papers/TR-DIA-5997-CFLPR.pdf`.

[17] P. Hudak, J. Hughes, S. Peyton Jones, and P. Wadler. A history of Haskell: Being lazy with class. In *Proceedings of the 3rd ACM SIGPLAN Conference on History of Programming Languages (HOPL III)*, pages 12–1–12–55. ACM, 2007.

[18] K. Läufer and M. Odersky. Polymorphic type inference and abstract data types. *ACM Transactions on Programming Languages and Systems*, 16:1411–1430, 1994.

[19] F. López-Fraguas, E. Martin-Martin, and J. Rodríguez-Hortalá. Liberal typing for functional logic programs. In *Proceedings of the 8th Asian Symposium on Programming Languages and Systems (APLAS '10)*, volume 6461 of *Lecture Notes in Computer Science*, pages 80–96. Springer, 2010.

[20] F. López-Fraguas, E. Martin-Martin, and J. Rodríguez-Hortalá. New results on type systems for functional logic programming. In *Proceedings of the 18th International Workshop on Functional and (Constraint) Logic Programming (WFLP '09), Revised Selected Papers*, volume 5979 of *Lecture Notes in Computer Science*, pages 128–144. Springer, 2010.

[21] F. López-Fraguas, E. Martin-Martin, and J. Rodríguez-Hortalá. Well-typed narrowing with extra variables in functional-logic programming. In *Proceedings of the 2012 ACM SIGPLAN Workshop on Partial Evaluation and Program Manipulation (PEPM '12)*, pages 83–92. ACM, 2012.

[22] F. López-Fraguas, J. Rodríguez-Hortalá, and J. Sánchez-Hernández. Rewriting and call-time choice: the HO case. In *Proceedings of the 9th International Symposium on Functional and Logic Programming (FLOPS '08)*, volume 4989 of *Lecture Notes in Computer Science*, pages 147–162. Springer, 2008.

[23] F. López-Fraguas and J. Sánchez-Hernández. Toy: A multiparadigm declarative system. In *Proceedings of the 10th International Conference on Rewriting Techniques and Applications (RTA '99)*, volume 1631 of *Lecture Notes in Computer Science*, pages 244–247. Springer, 1999.

[24] W. Lux. Adding Haskell-style overloading to Curry. In *Workshop of Working Group 2.1.4 of the German Computing Science Association GI*, pages 67–76, 2008.

[25] E. Martin-Martin. Type classes in functional logic programming. In *Proceedings of the 2011 ACM SIGPLAN Workshop on Partial Evaluation and Program Manipulation (PEPM '11)*, pages 121–130. ACM, 2011.

[26] E. Martin-Martin and J. Rodríguez-Hortalá. Transparent function types: Clearing up opacity (extended version). Technical Report SIC-11-12, Universidad Complutense de Madrid, July 2012. Available at `http://gpd.sip.ucm.es/enrique/publications/ppdp12/SIC-11-12.pdf`.

[27] J. C. Mitchell and G. D. Plotkin. Abstract types have existential type. *ACM Transactions on Programming Languages and Systems*, 10(3):470–502, 1988.

[28] J. C. Reynolds. Types, abstraction and parametric polymorphism. *Information Processing*, (83):513–523, 1983.

[29] M. Rodríguez-Artalejo. Functional and constraint logic programming. In *Constraints in Computational Logics: Theory and Applications. International Summer School (CCL99)*, volume 2002 of *Lecture Notes in Computer Science*, pages 202–270. Springer, 2001.

[30] P. Wadler. Theorems for free! In *Proceedings of the 4th International Conference on Functional Programming Languages and Computer Architecture (FPCA '89)*, pages 347–359. ACM, 1989.

Session Types Revisited

Ornela Dardha Elena Giachino Davide Sangiorgi
INRIA Focus Team / University of Bologna
{dardha, giachino, sangio}@cs.unibo.it

Abstract

Session types are a formalism to model structured communication-based programming. A session type describes communication by specifying the type and direction of data exchanged between two parties. When session types and session primitives are added to the syntax of standard π-calculus types and terms, they give rise to additional separate syntactic categories. As a consequence, when new type features are added, there is duplication of efforts in the theory: the proofs of properties must be checked both on ordinary types and on session types. We show that session types are encodable in ordinary π types, relying on linear and variant types. Besides being an expressivity result, the encoding (i) removes the above redundancies in the syntax, and (ii) the properties of session types are derived as straightforward corollaries, exploiting the corresponding properties of ordinary π types. The robustness of the encoding is tested on a few extensions of session types, including subtyping, polymorphism and higher-order communications.

Categories and Subject Descriptors D.3.1 [*Programming languages*]: Formal Definitions and Theory; F.1.2 [*Computation by abstract devices*]: Modes of Computation—Parallelism and concurrency; F.3.2 [*Logics and meanings of programs*]: Semantics of Programming Languages—Process models; F.3.3 [*Logics and meanings of programs*]: Studies of Program Constructs—Type structure

General Terms Languages, Theory

Keywords session types, linear types, π-calculus, encoding

1. Introduction

In complex distributed systems, participants willing to communicate should previously agree on a protocol to follow. The specified protocol describes the types of messages that are exchanged as well as their direction. In this context *session types* [3, 21] came into play: they describe a protocol as a type abstraction. Session types were originally designed for process calculi [7, 19, 22]. They have been studied also for other paradigms like multithreaded functional languages, object-oriented languages, Web Services and Contracts, WC3-CDL a language for choreography etc [3].

Session types are a formalism proposed as a theoretical foundation to describe and model structured communication-based programming, guaranteeing privacy as well as communication safety. They are an 'ad hoc' means to describe a *session*, namely a logical unit of data that are exchanged between two or more interacting participants.

Session types are defined as a sequence of input and output operations, explicitly indicating the types of messages being transmitted. This structured *sequentiality* of operations is what makes session types suitable to model protocols and distributed scenarios.

However, they offer more flexibility than just performing inputs and outputs: they permit choice, internal and external one. Branch and select are typical type (and term) constructs in the theory of session types, the former being the offering of a set of alternatives and the latter being the selection of one of the possible options on hand.

As mentioned above, session types guarantee privacy and communication safety. Privacy is guaranteed since session channels are known only to the agents involved in the communication. Such communication proceeds without any mismatch of direction and of message type. In order to achieve communication safety, a session channel is split by giving rise to two opposite endpoints, each of which is owned by one of the agents. These endpoints have dual behavior and thus have dual types. So, *duality* is a fundamental concept in the theory of session types as it is the ingredient that guarantees communication safety.

To better understand session types and the notion of duality, let us consider a simple example: a client and a server communicating over a session channel. The endpoints x and y of the channel are owned by the client and the server exclusively and should have dual types. To guarantee duality of types, static checks are performed by the type system. If the type of x is $?Int.?Int.!Bool.end$ — meaning that the process listening on channel x receives an integer value followed by another integer value and then sends back a boolean value — then the type of y should be $!Int.!Int.?Bool.end$ — meaning that the process listening on channel y sends an integer value followed by another integer value and then waits to receive back a boolean value — which is exactly the dual type.

There is a precise moment at which a session, between two agents, is established. It is the *connection*, when a fresh (private) session channel is created and its endpoints are bound to each communicating process. The connection is also the moment when the duality, hence compliance of two session types, is verified. In order to perform a connection, primitives for session channel creation, like `accept/request` or (νxy), are added to the syntax of terms [7, 19, 21].

Session types and session primitives are supposed to be added to the syntax of standard π-calculus types and terms, respectively. In doing so, sessions give rise to additional separate syntactic categories. Hence, the syntax of types need to be split into separate syntactic categories, one for session types and the other for standard π-calculus types [5, 7, 19, 22] (this often introduces a duplication of type environments, as well). Common typing features, such as products, records, subtyping, polymorphism, have then to be added to both syntactic categories. Also the syntax of processes will con-

PPDP'12, September 19–21, 2012, Leuven, Belgium.

tain both standard process constructs and session primitives (for example, the constructs mentioned above to create session channels). This redundancy in the syntax brings in redundancy also in the theory, and can make the proofs of properties of the language heavy. For instance, if a new type construct is added, the corresponding properties must be checked both on ordinary types and on session types.

In this paper we try to understand at which extent this redundancy is necessary, in the light of the following similarities between session constructs and standard π-calculus constructs. Consider $?Int.?Int.!Bool.end$. This type is assigned to a session channel (actually, as we said above, to one of its endpoints) and describes a structured sequence of inputs and outputs by specifying the type of messages that it can transmit. This way of proceeding reminds us of the *linearized* channels [14], which are channels used multiple times for communication but only in a sequential manner. Linearized types can be encoded, as shown in [14], into linear types—*i.e.*, channel types used *exactly once*.

The considerations above deal with input and output operations and the sequentiality of session types. Let us consider branch and select. These constructs give more flexibility by offering and selecting a range of possibilities. This brings in mind an already existing type construct in the π- calculus, namely the *variant* type [18].

Other analogies between session types and π types concern connection and duality. Connection can be seen as the *restriction* construct, since both are used to create and bind a new private session channel to the communication parties. As mentioned above, duality is checked when connection takes place. Duality describes the split of behavior of session channel endpoints. This reminds us of the split of *capabilities*: once a new channel is created by the ν construct, it can be used by two communicating processes owning the opposite capability each.

In this paper, by following Kobayashi [13], we define an interpretation of session types into π types and by exploiting this encoding, session types and all their theory are shown to be derivable from the theory of π-calculus. For instance, basic properties such as Subject Reduction and Type Safety become straightforward corollaries.

Intuitively, a session channel is interpreted as a linear channel transmitting a pair consisting of the original message and a new linear channel which is going to be used for the continuation of the communication.

Furthermore, we present an optimization of linear channels enabling the reuse of the same channel, instead of a new one, for the continuation of the communication.

As stated above, the encoding we adopt follows Kobayashi [13] and the constructs we use are not new (linear types and variants are well-known concepts in type theory and they are also well integrated in the π-calculus). Indeed the technical contribution of the paper may be considered minor (the main technical novelty being the optimization in linear channel usage mentioned above). Rather than technical, the contribution of the paper is meant to be foundational: we show that Kobayashi's encoding

(i) does permit to derive the session types and their basic properties; and

(ii) is a robust encoding.

As evidence for (ii), in the paper we examine, besides plain session types, a few extensions of them, adding subtyping, polymorphism and higher-order features. These are non-trivial extensions, which have been studied in dedicated session types papers [4, 5, 15]. In each case we show that we can derive the main results of the papers via the encoding, as straightforward corollaries.

While Kobayashi's encoding was generally known, its strength, robustness, and practical impact were not. This is witnessed by the plethora of papers on session types over the last 10-15 years, in which session types are always taken as primitives — we are not aware of a single work that explains the results on session types via an encoding of them into ordinary types. In our opinion, the reasons why Kobayashi's encoding had not caught attention are:

(a) Kobayashi did not prove any properties of the encoding and did not investigate its robustness;

(b) as certain key features of session types do not clearly show up in the encoding, the faithfulness of the encoding was unclear.

A good example for (b) is duality. In session types duality plays a central role: a session is identified by two channel end-points, and these have dual types. In the ordinary π-calculus, in contrast, there is no notion of duality on types. Indeed, in the encoding, dual session types (e.g., the branch type and the select type) are mapped onto the same type (e.g., the variant type). In general, dual session types will be mapped onto linear types that are identical except for the outermost I/O tag — duality on session types boils down to the duality between input and output capability of channels.

The results in the paper are not however meant to say that session types are useless, as they are very useful from a programming perspective. The work just tells us that, at least for the binary sessions and properties examined in the paper, session types and session primitives may be taken as macros.

The rest of the paper is structured as follows: Section 2 gives an overview of session types and π-calculus types as well as language terms, typing rules and operational semantics. Section 3 presents the encoding of both session types and session processes. Sections 4, 5 and 6 consider extensions to session types: subtyping, polymorphism and higher-order, respectively and analyze the encoding w.r.t. these extensions. Section 7 presents an optimization of linear channels usage. Section 8 examines the related work and concludes the paper.

2. Background

In this section we give an overview of the main technical concepts of the two theories we will be dealing with in the next sections: sessions and π-calculus.

2.1 Session Types

Type Syntax Generally, the syntax of types is given by two separate syntactic categories: one for session types and the other for standard π types, including session types, as well. Types are presented in Figure 1.

We use S to range over session types and T to range over basic types. Session types are: *end*, the type of a terminated session; $?T.S$ and $!T.S$ indicating respectively session channel types used to *receive* and *send* a value of type T and then proceed according to type S. *Branch* and *select* are sets of labelled session types, where the order of components does not matter and labels are all distinct. They indicate external and internal choice, respectively, i.e., what is offered and what is chosen. $\&\{l_1 : S_1, \ldots, l_n : S_n\}$ indicates the external choice, what is offered. Dually, select type $\oplus\{l_1 : S_1, \ldots, l_n : S_n\}$ indicates the internal choice, only one of the labels will be chosen. Types T include session types, standard channel types and other standard π type constructs. They may also include other basic types meant to be the types of exchanged messages, such as ground types, classes, etc. In [21] the syntax of types is given by a unique syntactic category. In order to distinguish between session types and standard ones, [21] uses *qualifiers* `lin`-linear and `un`-unrestricted. Linear types correspond to session types whereas unrestricted types correspond to the standard π types. We have decided to adopt the syntax above, inspired by [5] as it

Types $T ::=$			Session Types $S ::=$	end	termination
	S	session type		$?T.S$	input
	$\sharp T$	channel type		$!T.S$	output
	$\cdots$	other constructs		$\&\{l_1 : S_1, \ldots, l_n : S_n\}$	branch
				$\oplus\{l_1 : S_1, \ldots, l_n : S_n\}$	select

Processes $P ::=$	$x!\langle v\rangle.P$	output	$(\nu xy)P$	session restriction
	$x?(y).P$	input	$x \triangleleft l.P$	selection
	$P \mid Q$	composition	$x \triangleright \{l_1 : P_1, \ldots, l_n : P_n\}$	branching
	$\mathbf{0}$	inaction		
Values $v ::=$	x	variable	$true \mid false$	boolean values

Transitions	$(\nu xy)(x!\langle v\rangle.P \mid y?(z).Q) \longrightarrow (\nu xy)(P \mid Q\{v/z\})$	[*R-Com*]
	$(\nu xy)(x \triangleleft l_j.P \mid x \triangleright \{l_1 : P_1, \ldots, l_n : P_n\}) \longrightarrow (\nu xy)(P \mid P_j) \quad j \in 1 \ldots n$	[*R-Case*]

Figure 1. Syntax and Semantics for Sessions

$$\frac{}{\varnothing = \varnothing \circ \varnothing} \qquad \frac{\Gamma = \Gamma_1 \circ \Gamma_2}{\Gamma, x : S = (\Gamma_1, x : S) \circ \Gamma_2} \qquad \frac{\Gamma = \Gamma_1 \circ \Gamma_2}{\Gamma, x : S = \Gamma_1 \circ (\Gamma_2, x : S)}$$

$$\frac{}{\Gamma = \Gamma + \varnothing} \qquad \frac{\Gamma = \Gamma_1 + \Gamma_2}{\Gamma, x : S = (\Gamma_1, x : S) + \Gamma_2} \qquad \frac{\Gamma = \Gamma_1 \circ \Gamma_2}{\Gamma, x : S = \Gamma_1 + (\Gamma_2, x : S)}$$

Figure 2. Context split and Context update

underlines the separation of session types from standard channel types.

Language Syntax The syntax of terms presented in Figure 1 is inspired by Vasconcelos [21]. There are different ways of presenting session channel initiation and end-points, like `accept/request` [7], polarized channels [5] or by means of co-variables [21]. Standard communication (not involving sessions) is based on standard π channels [5, 7], whether in [21] it is based on co-variables, as well. In our work we have adopted the use of co-variables. Some comments on the syntax follow: We use P and Q to range over processes and v to range over values. The output process $x!\langle v\rangle.P$ sends a value v on channel x and proceeds as process P; the input process $x?(y).P$ receives on channel x a value that is going to substitute the placeholder y in P. The process $\mathbf{0}$ is the standard inaction process. $(\nu xy)P$ is the scope restriction construct; it creates a session channel, more precisely its two endpoints x and y and binds them in P. The two endpoints should be distinguished to validate subject reduction, see [22]. The type system enforces that two endpoints specify dual behavior. The last two constructs represent the choices. The process $x \triangleleft l.P$ on channel x selects label l attached to process P. The process $x \triangleright \{l_1 : P_1, \ldots, l_n : P_n\}$ on channel x offers a range of alternatives each labelled with a different label taken from $l_1 \ldots l_n$. According to the label l_j that is selected the process P_j will be executed.

Duality Two processes willing to communicate, for example, a client and a server, must agree on a protocol. The protocol is abstracted as a structured type, namely a *session type*. Intuitively, client and server should perform dual operations: when one process sends, the other receives, when one offers, the other chooses. So, the dual of an input action is an output one, the dual of branch(offering) is select(choice), as formalized by the following definition:

$$\overline{end} = end$$
$$\overline{?T.S} = !T.\overline{S}$$
$$\overline{!T.S} = ?T.\overline{S}$$
$$\overline{\&\{l_1 : S_1, \ldots, l_n : S_n\}} = \oplus\{l_1 : \overline{S_1}, \ldots, l_n : \overline{S_n}\}$$
$$\overline{\oplus\{l_1 : S_1, \ldots, l_n : S_n\}} = \&\{l_1 : \overline{S_1}, \ldots, l_n : \overline{S_n}\}$$

In order to guarantee that communication is safe and proceeds without any mismatch, static checks are performed by the type system. Precisely, these checks consist in controlling that the opposite endpoints of the same session channel have dual types.

Typing Let us now consider the typing rules, listed in Figure 3. We have focused only on the most important ones. Typing derivations for processes are of the form $\Gamma \vdash P$. The typing rules handle context split ($\circ$) in order to deal with linearity of session channels [21] and context update ($+$) in order to deal with the continuation type to make sure they not discarded without being used or they are not used more than once session or duplicated [21]. Context split and context update are defined in Figure 2. These rules handle only the addition of session types S, as the standard types T can be added freely to the context without any particular treatment.

Some comments on the typing rules follow. The rule that better explains duality checks is the rule for restriction [*T-Res*]. Process $(\nu xy)P$ is well-typed in Γ if P is well-typed in Γ augmented with session channel endpoints having dual types ($x : T, y : \overline{T}$). Rule [*T-In*] splits in two the context in which the input process $x?(y).P$ is well-typed: one part type checks the variable x, the other part, augmented with $y : T$ and updated with $x : U$, type checks the continuation process P. The rule for output [*T-Out*] is similar. The context is split in three parts, one to type check x, another to type check v and the last part to type check the continuation P. Similarly to the rule for input, the continuation process uses channel x with its continuation type U. Let us now consider the typing rules for branch, [*T-Brch*], and select, [*T-Sel*].

$$\frac{\Gamma, x : T, y : \overline{T} \vdash P}{\Gamma \vdash (\nu xy)P}\ [T\text{-}Res] \qquad \frac{\Gamma_1 \vdash x : ?T.U \qquad (\Gamma_2, y : T) + x : U \vdash P}{\Gamma_1 \circ \Gamma_2 \vdash x?(y).P}\ [T\text{-}In]$$

$$\frac{\Gamma_1 \vdash x : !T.U \qquad \Gamma_2 \vdash v : T \qquad \Gamma_3 + x : U \vdash P}{\Gamma_1 \circ \Gamma_2 \circ \Gamma_3 \vdash x!\langle v \rangle.P}\ [T\text{-}Out]$$

$$\frac{\Gamma_1 \vdash x : \&\{l_1 : T_1, \ldots, l_n : T_n\} \qquad \Gamma_2 + x : T_i \vdash P_i \quad \forall i \in 1 \ldots n}{\Gamma_1 \circ \Gamma_2 \vdash x \rhd \{l_1 : P_1, \ldots, l_n : P_n\}}\ [T\text{-}Brch]$$

$$\frac{\Gamma_1 \vdash x : \oplus\{l_1 : T_1, \ldots, l_n : T_n\} \qquad \Gamma_2 + x : T_j \vdash P \quad j \in 1 \ldots n}{\Gamma_1 \circ \Gamma_2 \vdash x \lhd l_j.P}\ [T\text{-}Sel]$$

Figure 3. Some typing rules for session processes

As these constructs are a generalization of the input and output processes, respectively, the corresponding typing rules follow the intuitions above. The branching process $x \rhd \{l_1 : P_1, \ldots, l_n : P_n\}$ is well-typed if channel x is of branch type $\&\{l_1 : T_1, \ldots, l_n : T_n\}$ and every continuation process P_i is well-typed and uses x with type T_i. This rule introduces an external choice. Whilst, the rule for selection introduces an internal choice. To type check a process that selects label l_j on the channel x having type $\oplus\{l_1 : T_1, \ldots, l_n : T_n\}$, we have to type check that the continuation process P_j uses x with type T_j.

Operational Semantics The operational semantics is defined as a binary relation over processes $\longrightarrow$. We present in Figure 1 only two transition rules, *[R-Com]* and *[R-Case]*. For simplicity, we do not report the transition rules for the other cases as they are standard. In rule *[R-Com]*, two processes communicate on two co-variables, that are variables bound together: one sends a value v on x and the other receives it on y and substitutes the placeholder z with it. Rule *[R-Case]* follows the above rule, the communicating processes have prefixes that are co-variables. The selecting process continues as P and the offering one as Q_j, if the label l_j is selected. In order to complete the operational semantics rules, the standard structural congruence is needed.

2.2 π Types

Type Syntax We now consider the π- calculus [18]. The ordinary π-calculus types, ranged over by T, include various type constructs [18]. Here we focus on linear types and variant types, which will be used in the encoding. The syntax of the type constructs we want to discuss is presented in Figure 4. Linear types $\ell_i T$, $\ell_o T$ and $\ell_\sharp T$ are assigned to channels used *exactly once* in input to receive messages of type T, in output to send messages of type T and used once for sending and once for receiving messages of type T, respectively. The variant type $\langle l_1\_T_1 \ldots l_n\_T_n \rangle$ is a labelled form of disjoint union of types. The order of the components does not matter and labels are all distinct. Product types $(T_1 \times \ldots \times T_n)$ are needed to model the polyadic π-calculus. Other type constructs like ground types, recursive types etc. can be added to the syntax.

Language syntax The syntax of terms of the π-calculus is given in Figure 4. The output process $\overline{x}\langle \tilde{v} \rangle.P$ sends a tuple of values $\tilde{v}$ on channel x and proceeds as P; input process $x(\tilde{y}).P$ receives on x a tuple of values that is going to substitute $\tilde{y}$ in P; parallel composition and **0** inaction are standard; restriction creates a new name x and binds it with scope P (the same as in sessions for shared channels). Process $\texttt{case}\ v\ \texttt{of}\ [l_1\_(x_1) \rhd P_1 \ldots l_n\_(x_n) \rhd P_n]$ offers different behaviors depending on which variant value l_v it receives. Other values are boolean values and variables.

Typing Some typing rules for π processes are given in Figure 5. As in the previous section for session types, also here, there is a particular handling of typing environments in order to ensure linearity. The context is split following a split of linear types. which is defined as follows:

$$\ell_o T \uplus \ell_i T \triangleq \ell_\sharp T$$
$$T \uplus T \triangleq T$$
$$T \uplus S \triangleq (\texttt{error}) \text{ otherwise}$$

The context split is defined as follows:

$$(\Gamma_1 \uplus \Gamma_2)(x) \triangleq$$

$\Gamma_1(x) \uplus \Gamma_2(x)$	if both $\Gamma_1(x)$ and $\Gamma_2(x)$ are defined
$\Gamma_1(x)$	if $\Gamma_1(x)$, but not $\Gamma_2(x)$, is defined
$\Gamma_2(x)$	if $\Gamma_2(x)$, but not $\Gamma_1(x)$, is defined
$\texttt{undef}$	if both $\Gamma_1(x)$ and $\Gamma_2(x)$ are undefined

Some comments on the typing rules follow. Rules for input and output processes are straightforward: on a linear input, respectively output, channel x a value v of the correct type is received, respectively sent, with a continuation process P. Rule on restriction states asserts that process $(\nu x : \ell_\sharp T)P$ is well-typed provided P is well-typed in a context extended with $x : \ell_\sharp T$. Following the definition of context split above it means $x : \ell_o T, x : \ell_i T$ and this is a fundamental feature exploited in the encoding. It is important to notice that the standard rule for restriction assigns to x some general channel type T and not necessarily $: \ell_\sharp T$. We have adopted the rule in this simplified form as it used in our encoding, presented in the next section. A variant value l_v is of type $\langle l\_T \rangle$ if v is of type T. Notice that, by means of subtyping, we can also derive that l_v is of type $\langle l_1\_T_1 \ldots l\_T \ldots l_n\_T_n \rangle$. Process $\texttt{case}\ v\ \texttt{of}\ [l_1\_(x_1) \rhd P_1 \ldots l_n\_(x_n) \rhd P_n]$ is well-typed if value v has variant type and every process P_i is well-typed assuming x_i has type T_i.

Operational Semantics We present in Figure 4 two transition rules. Again, as for sessions, we do not present the other rules as they are standard. Rule *[Rπ-Com]* is very similar to the corresponding one in session processes. The only difference here is that we are considering the polyadic π-calculus. Rule *[Rπ-Case]* is also called a $\texttt{case}$ normalization. The $\texttt{case}$ process evolves to P_j substituting x_j with the value v, if the label l_j is chosen. Structural congruence and the corresponding rules are standard again.

3. Encoding

Session types guarantee that only the communicating parties know the corresponding endpoints of the session channel, thus providing

Types	$T ::= \ell_i T \mid \ell_o T \mid \ell_\sharp T$		linear input — linear output — linear connection
	$\langle l_1\_T \ldots l_n\_T \rangle$		variant type
	$(T \times \ldots \times T)$		product type
	$\ldots$		other constructs

Processes	$P ::= \overline{x}\langle \tilde{v} \rangle.P$	output	$(\nu x)P$	scope restriction
	$x(\tilde{y}).P$	input	$\texttt{case}\ v\ \texttt{of}\ [l_1\_(x_1) \triangleright P_1 \ldots l_n\_(x_n) \triangleright P_n]$	case
	$P \mid Q$	composition		
	$\mathbf{0}$	inaction		

Values	$v ::= x$	variable	$true \mid false$	boolean values
	l_v	variant value		

Transitions	$\overline{x}\langle \tilde{v} \rangle.P \mid x(\tilde{z}).Q \longrightarrow P \mid Q\{\tilde{v}/\tilde{z}\}$	[*Rπ-Com*]
	$\texttt{case}\ l_j\_v\ \texttt{of}\ [l_1\_(x_1) \triangleright P_1 \ldots l_n\_(x_n) \triangleright P_n] \longrightarrow P_j \quad j \in 1 \ldots n$	[*Rπ-Case*]

Figure 4. Syntax and Semantics for π-calculus

$$\frac{\Gamma_1 \vdash x : \ell_i T \qquad \Gamma_2, y : T \vdash P}{\Gamma_1 \uplus \Gamma_2 \vdash x(y).P}\ [T\pi\text{-}In]$$

$$\frac{\Gamma_1 \vdash x : \ell_o T \qquad \Gamma_2 \vdash v : T \qquad \Gamma_3 \vdash P}{\Gamma_1 \uplus \Gamma_2 \uplus \Gamma_3 \vdash \overline{x}v.P}\ [T\pi\text{-}Out]$$

$$\frac{\Gamma, x : \ell_\sharp T \vdash P}{\Gamma \vdash (\nu x : \ell_\sharp T)P}\ [T\pi\text{-}Res] \qquad \frac{\Gamma \vdash v : T}{\Gamma \vdash l\_v : \langle l\_T \rangle}\ [T\pi\text{-}Var]$$

$$\frac{\Gamma_1 \vdash v : \langle l_1\_T_1 \ldots l_n\_T_n \rangle \qquad \Gamma_2, x_i : T_i \vdash P_i \quad \forall i}{\Gamma_1 \circ \Gamma_2 \vdash \texttt{case}\ v\ \texttt{of}\ [l_1\_(x_1) \triangleright P_1 \ldots l_n\_(x_n) \triangleright P_n]}\ [T\pi\text{-}Case]$$

Figure 5. Some typing rules for π processes

privacy. Moreover, the opposite endpoints should have dual types, thus providing communication safety. The interpretation of session types should take into account these fundamental issues. In order to guarantee privacy and safety of communication we adopt linear channels that are used *exactly once*. Privacy is ensured since the linear channel is used *at most once* and so it is known only to the interacting parties. Communication safety is ensured since the linear channel is used *at least once* and so the input/output actions are necessarily performed. Obviously, values transmitted should be checked if they have the right type as specified by the protocol.

In the following we provide an encoding of session types into ordinary π types and of session processes into π-calculus ones. The intuition behind our encoding is that the continuation behavior of the session channel instead of being explicitly put into the type, as in session types, is sent along with the message at each output.

3.1 Type Encoding

First we present the encoding of session types into ordinary π types, which is defined in Figure 6.

The encoding of the terminated communication channel is a linear channel with no capabilities, meaning that it cannot be used neither for input nor for output. The session channel type $?T.S$ is interpreted as the linear input channel type carrying a pair of values of type the encoding of T and of the encoding of continuation S. The encoding of $!T.S$ is a linear type used in output to carry a pair of values of type the encoding of T and of type the encoding of the dual of S. Note that in this case it is the dual of S to be sent since it is the type of a channel as seen by the receiver. The branch and the select types are generalizations of input and output types, respectively. Consequently, they are interpreted as linear input and linear output channels carrying variant types having the same labels $l_1 \ldots l_n$ and the types encodings of $S_1 \ldots S_n$ and $\overline{S_1} \ldots \overline{S_n}$, respectively. Again, the reason for duality is the same as for the output type.

As mentioned above, in order to establish a communication, the opposite endpoints of the session channel should have dual types. Consider the following dual types: $S = ?Int.!Int.end$ and $\overline{S} = !Int.?Int.end$. Their encoding is the following: $[\![S]\!] = \ell_i\,[Int, \ell_o\,[Int, \ell_\emptyset[\,]]]$ and $[\![\overline{S}]\!] = \ell_o\,[Int, \ell_o\,[Int, \ell_\emptyset[\,]]]$. It turns out that the duality of session types boils down to opposite capabilities of linear channel types. The encodings above differ only in the outermost level, that corresponds to having ℓ_i or ℓ_o types. The π channels having these types carry exactly the same messages. This happens because duality is incorporated in the output typing, where the receiver's point of view of the output type is considered, which is therefore dual w.r.t. that of the sender. The encoding simplifies the structure of the pair of dual session types. So, it can render the process of abstracting protocols as structured types easier.

To conclude, let us recall the syntax of types in Vasconcelos [21], where the qualifiers are present. What we encode are the session types (given by the syntactic category S ::=), that correspond to the *linear* types in [21] while the standard π types (given by the syntactic category T ::=) that correspond to the *unrestricted* types in [21], remain as such, i.e. they are not encoded as they are already present in the π-calculus.

3.2 Process Encoding

The encoding of session processes into π-calculus processes is defined in Figure 6.

$$
\begin{array}{ll}
[\![end]\!] & = \ell_\varnothing[] \\
[\![?T.S]\!] & = \ell_i[[\![T]\!], [\![S]\!]] \\
[\![!T.S]\!] & = \ell_o[[\![T]\!], [\![\overline{S}]\!]] \\
[\![\{l_1 : S_1 \&, \ldots, \& l_n : S_n\}]\!] & = \ell_i[\langle l_1 : [\![S_1]\!], \ldots, l_n : [\![S_n]\!]\rangle] \\
[\![\{l_1 : S_1 \oplus, \ldots, \oplus l_n : S_n\}]\!] & = \ell_o[\langle l_1 : [\![\overline{S_1}]\!], \ldots, l_n : [\![\overline{S_n}]\!]\rangle]
\end{array}
$$

$$
\begin{array}{ll}
[\![P \mid Q]\!]_f & = [\![P]\!]_f \mid [\![Q]\!]_f \\
[\![x!\langle v\rangle.P]\!]_f & = (\nu c)\overline{f_x}\langle v, c\rangle.[\![P]\!]_{f,\{x\to c\}} \\
[\![x?(y).P]\!]_f & = f_x(y, c).[\![P]\!]_{f,\{x\to c\}} \\
[\![(\nu xy)P]\!]_f & = (\nu c)[\![P]\!]_{f,\{x\to c, y\to c\}} \\
[\![x \triangleleft l.P]\!]_f & = (\nu c)\overline{f_x}\langle l\_c\rangle.[\![P]\!]_{f,\{x\to c\}} \\
[\![x \triangleright \{l_1 : P_1, \ldots, l_n : P_n\}]\!]_f & = f_x(y).\ \texttt{case}\ y\ \texttt{of}\ [l_1\_c \Rightarrow [\![P_1]\!]_{f,\{x\to c\}} \ldots l_n\_c \Rightarrow [\![P_n]\!]_{f,\{x\to c\}}]
\end{array}
$$

Figure 6. Encoding of types and terms

The encoding of terms differs from the encoding of types as it is parametrized in a function f that renames the linear channels involved in the communication. The reason for f is the following: since we are using linear types, once a channel is used, it cannot be used again for transmission. To enable structured communications however, like session types do, the channel is renamed: a new channel is created and is sent to the partner in order to use it to continue the rest of the session. This procedure is repeated at every step of communication and the function f is updated to the new name created.

Some explanations on the encoding are provided. The encoding of the output process is as follows: a new channel name c is created and is sent together with the value v along channel x renamed by function f, we denote this by f_x; the encoding of the continuation process P is parametrized in f where name x is updated to c. Similarly, the input process listens on channel f_x and receives a value, that substitutes variable y and a fresh channel c that substitutes x in the continuation process encoded in f updated.

As shown in Section 2.1, the syntax of session processes we have adopted here has a particular treatment of the binding constructor: $(\nu xy)P$ creates two fresh names and binds them in P and together as being the opposite endpoints of the same session channel. Since there is no such binding in π-calculus, the encoding is given by the creation of a new name (νc) of linear channel type with both capabilities of input/output. This may lead the reader to think of subject reduction failure, as shown in [22], since two opposite endpoints are being encoded as a single name c . However, this name substitutes x and y in the encoding of P in such a way that the capability of c matches the encoding of the type of that name. Namely, each endpoint corresponds to channel c having only one of the capabilities, input or output, whereas the other one corresponds to the opposite endpoint. So, in session types we use two names x and y, whereas in π-calculus we introduce a single name c having two capabilities.This is a static check performed by the type system. We sometimes denote c_b and $c_{\overline{b}}$ to emphasize the capabilities of c.

The last two constructs correspond to selection and branching processes. The selection process $x \triangleleft l.P$ is encoded as the process that first creates a new channel c and then sends on f_x a variant value, l_c where l is the label it is selecting and c is the channel created to be used for the rest of the session. Afterwards it proceeds as process P encoded in f updated. The branching process is the most complicated one: it receives on f_x a value, typically being a variant value l_c, to substitute the placeholder y in the `case` process. The value l_c, as for the selection, is composed by the label l, that the partner has chosen and the channel c to be used in the continuation processes. According to the label received one of the corresponding processes $[\![P_1]\!]_{f,\{x\to c\}} \cdots [\![P_n]\!]_{f,\{x\to c\}}$ is chosen and again the encoding is parametrized in f updated by $\{x \to c\}$. Note that the name c is bound in any process $[\![P_i]\!]_{f,\{x\to c\}}$ The encoding of other process constructs, like inaction, standard scope restriction, parallel composition etc. is a homomorphism.

For a better understanding of the encoding, let us consider a simple example: the equality test. The server and client processes are the following.

$$server = x?(v_1).x?(v_2).x!\langle v_1 == v_2\rangle.\mathbf{0}$$
$$client = y!\langle 3\rangle.y!\langle 5\rangle.y?(eq).\mathbf{0}$$

They communicate on a session channel by owning two opposite endpoints x and y, respectively. The server accepts two integer values in sequence v_1 and v_2 and sends back true or false depending on whether these values are equal or not ($v_1 == v_2$). The client process behaves dually: it sends to the server two integer values 3 and 5 and waits for a boolean answer. After this communication, they both terminate. The encodings of server and client processes are:

$$[\![server]\!]_f = z(v_1, c).c(v_2, c').(\nu c'')\overline{c'}\langle v_1 == v_2, c''\rangle.\mathbf{0}$$
$$[\![client]\!]_f = (\nu c)\overline{z}\langle 3, c\rangle.(\nu c')\overline{c}\langle 5, c'\rangle.c'(eq, c'').\mathbf{0}$$

In the encoding, at the very first step, function f initializes x and y to a new name z, and after that, before every output action, a new channel c, c', c'' is created and sent to the partner together with the value.

Session types associated to channel endpoints x, y on which this interaction takes place, are as follows:

$$x : ?Int.?Int.!Bool.end \qquad y : !Int.!Int.?Bool.end$$

Following the encoding definition we have the following:

$$[\![x]\!] = \ell_i\,[Int, \ell_i\,[Int, \ell_o\,[Bool, unit]]]$$
$$[\![y]\!] = \ell_o\,[Int, \ell_i\,[Int, \ell_o\,[Bool, unit]]]$$

3.3 Properties

The encoding presented previously can be taken as the semantics of session types and session terms. The following results show that we can derive the typing judgments and Subject Reduction and Type Safety of the session calculus.

THEOREM 1 (Type Correctness). $\Gamma \vdash P$ *if and only if* $[\![\Gamma]\!]_f \vdash [\![P]\!]_f$.

PROOF 1. *($\Rightarrow$) It is proved by induction on the length of the derivation* $\Gamma \vdash P$. *Let us consider just one case of the proof.*

Case *[T-Res]:*

$$\frac{\Gamma, x : T, y : \overline{T} \vdash P}{\Gamma \vdash (\nu xy)P}\ \text{[T-Res]}$$

To prove $[\![\Gamma]\!]_f \vdash [\![(\nu xy)P]\!]_f$ *Following the encoding,* $[\![(\nu xy)P]\!]_f = (\nu z)[\![P]\!]_{f,\{x\to z, y\to z\}}$. *By IH* $[\![\Gamma]\!]_f, x : [\![T]\!], y : [\![\overline{T}]\!] \vdash [\![P]\!]_{f,\{x,y\}}$ *The encoding of dual types is as follows* $[\![T]\!] = \ell_c[[\cdot]]$ *and* $[\![\overline{T}]\!] = \ell_{\overline{c}}[[\cdot]]$ *where we leave unspecified the innermost level of the type as it is not important. We will introduce a fresh name z having type* $\ell_\sharp[[\cdot]]$ $\sharp = c + \overline{c}$ *i.e. a type having both the type capabilities of outermost capabilities of T and* $\overline{T}$ *maintaining the internal structure of the types. So, we can modify the IH as follows:* $[\![\Gamma]\!]_f, z : \ell_\sharp[[\cdot]] \vdash [\![P]\!]_{f,\{x\to z, y\to z\}}$, *where x is substituted by z having type* $\ell_c[[\cdot]]$ *whilst, y is substituted by z having type* $\ell_{\overline{c}}[[\cdot]]$. *Using rule* LIN-RES *in pi, we have:*

$$\frac{[\![\Gamma]\!]_f, z : \ell_\sharp[[\cdot]] \vdash [\![P]\!]_{f,\{x\to z,y\to z\}}}{[\![\Gamma]\!]_f \vdash (\nu z)[\![P]\!]_{f,\{x\to z,y\to z\}}}$$

($\Leftarrow$) *It is proved by induction on the structure of P. We consider again one case of the proof just to illustrate it.*
Case $P = x(y).P$. *Suppose* $[\![\Gamma]\!]_f \vdash [\![x(y).P]\!]_f \triangleq f_x(y,c).[\![P]\!]_{f,\{x\to c\}}$. *This is derived by using* LIN-INP *as the last rule:*

$$\frac{[\![\Gamma_1]\!]_f \vdash f_x : \ell_i[W_1, W_2] \qquad [\![\Gamma_2]\!]_f, y : W_1, c : W_2 \vdash [\![P]\!]_{f,\{x\to c\}}}{[\![\Gamma]\!]_f \vdash f_x(y,c).[\![P]\!]_{f,\{x\to c\}}}$$

Where $[\![\Gamma]\!]_f = [\![\Gamma_1]\!]_f \uplus [\![\Gamma_2]\!]_f$. *By IH* $\Gamma_1 \vdash x : ?T_1.T_2$ *and* $(\Gamma_2, y : T_1) + x : T_2 \vdash P$ *where* $W_1 = [\![T_1]\!]$ *and* $W_2 = [\![T_2]\!]$. *Using rule [T-In] we conclude the following:*

$$\frac{\Gamma_1 \vdash x : ?T_1.T_2 \qquad (\Gamma_2, y : T_1) + x : T_2 \vdash P}{\Gamma_1 \circ \Gamma_2 \vdash x?(y).P}\ \text{[T-In]}$$

Theorem 1, and more precisely its proof, shows that the encoding can be actually used to reconstruct the typing rules of session types.

THEOREM 2 (Operational Correspondence). *If* $P \to P'$ *then* $\exists Q$ *such that* $[\![P]\!]_f \to Q$ *and* $Q \hookrightarrow [\![P']\!]_f$ *where* $\hookrightarrow$ *is a structural congruence extended with* `case` *normalization.*

PROOF 2. *It is proved by induction on the length of the proof of the reduction* $P \to P'$. *We consider the following base cases:*
Case *(*R-Com*):*
$P = (\nu xy)(x!\langle v\rangle.P_1 \mid y?(z).P_2) \to (\nu xy)(P_1 \mid P_2\{v/z\}) = P'$.

$$\begin{aligned}
[\![P]\!]_f = {} & \\
& [\![(\nu xy)(x!\langle v\rangle.P_1 \mid y?(z).P_2)]\!]_f \\
& \triangleq (\nu t)[\![(x!\langle v\rangle.P_1 \mid y?(z).P_2)]\!]_{f,\{x\to t,y\to t\}} \\
& = (\nu t)\left([\![x!\langle v\rangle.P_1]\!]_{f,\{x\to t\}} \mid [\![y?(z).P_2]\!]_{f,\{y\to t\}}\right) \\
& \triangleq (\nu t)\left[\left((\nu c)\overline{t}\langle v,c\rangle.[\![P_1]\!]_{f,\{x\to t,t\to c\}}\right) \mid t(z,c).[\![P_2]\!]_{f,\{y\to t,t\to c\}}\right]
\end{aligned}$$

(an α*-conversion is performed in order to have c in the rhs)*

$$\begin{aligned}
& \to (\nu t)\left[(\nu c)\left([\![P_1]\!]_{f,\{x\to c\}} \mid [\![P_2]\!]_{f,\{y\to c\}}\{v/z\}\right)\right] = Q \\
& \equiv (\nu c)\left([\![P_1]\!]_{f,\{x\to c\}} \mid [\![P_2]\!]_{f,\{y\to c\}}\{v/z\}\right)
\end{aligned}$$

The following also holds:

$$\begin{aligned}
[\![P']\!]_f & \triangleq [\![(\nu xy)(P_1 \mid P_2\{v/z\})]\!]_f \\
& \triangleq (\nu c)[\![P_1 \mid P_2\{v/z\}]\!]_{f,\{x\to c,y\to c\}} \\
& \triangleq (\nu c)([\![P_1]\!]_{f,\{x\to c\}} \mid [\![P_2]\!]_{f,\{y\to c\}}\{v/z\})
\end{aligned}$$

Case *(*R-Case*):* $P = (\nu xy)(x \triangleleft l_j.R \mid y \triangleright \{l_1 : Q_1, \ldots, l_n : Q_n\}) \to (\nu xy)(R \mid Q_j) = P' j \in 1 \ldots n$.

$$\begin{aligned}
[\![P]\!]_f & \triangleq [\![(\nu xy)(x \triangleleft l_j.R \mid y \triangleright \{l_1 : Q_1, \ldots, l_n : Q_n\})]\!]_f \\
& \triangleq (\nu z)\left([\![x \triangleleft l_j.R \mid y \triangleright \{l_1 : Q_1, \ldots, l_n : Q_n\}]\!]_{f,\{x\to z,y\to z\}}\right) \\
& \triangleq (\nu z)\left([\![z \triangleleft l_j.R]\!]_{f,\{x\to z\}} \mid [\![z \triangleright \{l_1 : Q_1, \ldots, l_n : Q_n\}]\!]_{f,\{y\to z\}}\right) \\
& \triangleq (\nu z)\Big((\nu c)\overline{z}\langle l_j_c\rangle.[\![R]\!]_{f,\{x\to z,z\to c\}} \mid z(w).\ \texttt{case}\ w\ \texttt{of} \\
& \qquad [l_1_c : [\![Q_1]\!]_{f,\{y\to z,z\to c\}} \ldots l_n_c : [\![Q_n]\!]_{f,\{y\to z,z\to c\}}]\Big)
\end{aligned}$$

(an α*-conversion is performed in order to have c in the rhs)*

$$\begin{aligned}
& = (\nu c)\Big(\overline{z}\langle l_j_c\rangle.[\![R]\!]_{f,\{x\to c\}} \mid z(w).\ \texttt{case}\ w\ \texttt{of} \\
& \qquad [l_1_c : [\![Q_1]\!]_{f,\{y\to c\}} \ldots l_n_c : [\![Q_n]\!]_{f,\{y\to c\}}]\Big) \\
& \to (\nu c)\Big([\![R]\!]_{f,\{x\to c\}} \mid \texttt{case}\ l_j_c\ \texttt{of} \\
& \qquad [l_1_c : [\![Q_1]\!]_{f,\{y\to c\}} \ldots l_n_c : [\![Q_n]\!]_{f,\{y\to c\}}]\Big) = Q \\
& \hookrightarrow (\nu c)\left([\![R]\!]_{f,\{x\to c\}} \mid [\![Q_j]\!]_{f,\{y\to c\}}\right)
\end{aligned}$$

The following also holds:

$$\begin{aligned}
[\![P']\!]_f & \triangleq [\![(\nu xy)(R \mid Q_j)]\!]_f \\
& \triangleq (\nu c)[\![R \mid Q_j]\!]_{f,\{x\to c,y\to c\}} \\
& \triangleq (\nu c)([\![R]\!]_{f,\{x\to c\}} \mid [\![Q_j]\!]_{f,\{y\to c\}})
\end{aligned}$$

The inductive step is straightforward.

By exploiting Type Correctness and Operational Correspondence we derive for free the Subject Reduction and Type Safety (absence of run-time errors) in session types.

COROLLARY 1. *If* $\Gamma \vdash P$ *and* $P \to P'$ *then* $\Gamma \vdash P'$

PROOF 3. *The result follows from the subject reduction property in* π*-calculus and Theorems 1 and 2.*

After analyzing the effectiveness of the encoding on basic session types, in the following sections we show its robustness by examining three non-trivial extensions, namely subtyping, polymorphism and higher-order.

4. Subtyping

Subtyping is a relation among channel types based on a notion of substitutability, meaning that language constructs meant to act on channels of the supertype can also act on channels of the subtype. If T is a subtype of T', then any channel of type T can be safely used in a context where a channel of type T' is expected. The definition of subtyping must be done carefully in order for this substitutability property to hold.

Subtyping has been studied extensively in π-calculus [17, 18]. It has also been studied in session types [5]. In this section we show that the ordinary subtyping of the π-calculus is enough to derive subtyping in session types. Subtyping rules for both systems are presented in Figure 7. We use the symbol <: for session subtyping, and $\leq$ for standard π subtyping.

Rules *(S-inp)* and *(S-out)* define subtyping relation of input and output linear π channels. These rules assert that input channels are co-variant and output channels are contra-variant in the types of values they transmit. Rule *(S-variant)* presents subtyping of variant types. It is co-variant both in depth and in breadth. Rules *(S-?)* and *(S-!)* indicate subtyping in input and output session types, respectively. As before, input operation is co-variant whilst output

$$\frac{I = \{i, \sharp\} \qquad \forall i \in 1 \ldots n.\ \ T_i \leq S_i}{\ell_I[T_1, \ldots, T_n] \leq \ell_i[S_1, \ldots, S_n]}\ (S\text{-}inp) \qquad \frac{I = \{o, \sharp\} \qquad \forall i \in 1 \ldots n.\ \ S_i \leq T_i}{\ell_I[T_1, \ldots, T_n] \leq \ell_o[S_1, \ldots, S_n]}\ (S\text{-}out)$$

$$\frac{\forall i \in 1 \ldots n.\ \ T_i \leq S_i}{\langle l_1\_T_1 \ldots l_n\_T_n \rangle \leq \langle l_1\_S_1 \ldots l_{n+m}\_S_{n+m} \rangle}\ (S\text{-}variant)$$

$$\frac{T <: T' \qquad S <: S'}{?T.S <: ?T'.S'}\ (S\text{-}?) \qquad \frac{T' <: T \qquad S <: S'}{!T.S <: !T'.S'}\ (S\text{-}!)$$

$$\frac{I \subseteq J \qquad \forall i \in I.\ \ T_i <: S_i}{\&\{l_i : T_i\}_{i \in I} <: \&\{l_j : S_j\}_{j \in J}}\ (S\text{-}brch) \qquad \frac{I \supseteq J \qquad \forall j \in J.\ \ T_j <: S_j}{\oplus\{l_i : T_i\}_{i \in I} <: \oplus\{l_j : S_j\}_{j \in J}}\ (S\text{-}sel)$$

Figure 7. Subtyping rules for π types ($\leq$) and for session types ($<:$).

operation is contra-variant. The continuation type is co-variant in both cases. This is a difference w.r.t. the corresponding rules in π-calculus. There are two rules for labelled types, namely *(S-brch)* and *(S-sel)* being both co-variant in depth in the types of values they transmit and being co-variant and contra-variant in breadth, respectively.

In π-calculus with sessions and subtyping, one must deal both with ordinary subtyping on π types and subtyping on session types. This introduces a duplication of effort that grows as the type syntax and type system become richer. For example, this duplication is very heavy when recursive types are included. If the type system is structural, then subtyping on recursive types is established with coinductive techniques, e.g. simulation relations. These techniques must be defined and proved sound both on ordinary π types and on session types. In addition, on session types one also needs coinductive techniques to formalize type duality.

The encoding is used, as in the previous section, to derive basic properties of session types; in addition to Theorem 1 and 2 here we have to take into account the subtyping relation. Therefore, it is important to prove the validity of subtyping, which is necessary in order to extend Subject Reduction and Type Safety.

THEOREM 3 (Validity of Subtyping). *$T <: S$ if and only if $[\![T]\!] \leq [\![S]\!]$.*

PROOF 4. *($\Rightarrow$) The proof is by induction on the derivation of $T <: S$. To give an idea of the proof we consider the following case*
Case input*:*
Where $T = ?T_1.T_2$ and $S = ?S_1.S_2$. By induction hypothesis: $[\![T_1]\!] \leq [\![S_1]\!]$ and $[\![T_2]\!] \leq [\![S_2]\!]$. To prove $[\![?T_1.T_2]\!] \leq [\![?S_1.S_2]\!]$.

Since $[\![?T_1.T_2]\!] = \ell_i[[\![T_1]\!], [\![T_2]\!]]$ and $[\![?S_1.S_2]\!] = \ell_i[[\![S_1]\!], [\![S_2]\!]]$, using the IH and the rule (S-inp) *with $I = \{i\}$ we have:*

$$\frac{[\![T_1]\!] \leq [\![S_1]\!] \qquad [\![T_2]\!] \leq [\![S_2]\!]}{\ell_i[[\![T_1]\!], [\![T_2]\!]] \leq \ell_i[[\![S_1]\!], [\![S_2]\!]]}\ (\text{Sub-inp})$$

($\Leftarrow$) The proof is by induction on the structure of session types T, S. Again, let us consider as an example one case of the proof.
Case *$T = !T_1.T_2$ and $S = !S_1.S_2$. The encodings are $[\![!T_1.T_2]\!] = \ell_o[[\![T_1]\!], [\![\overline{T_2}]\!]]$ and $[\![!S_1.S_2]\!] = \ell_o[[\![S_1]\!], [\![\overline{S_2}]\!]]$ and we suppose $[\![T]\!] \leq [\![S]\!]$. To prove $T <: S$. Using the following rule in pi we have:*

$$\frac{[\![S_1]\!] \leq [\![T_1]\!] \qquad [\![\overline{S_2}]\!] \leq [\![\overline{T_2}]\!]}{\ell_o[[\![T_1]\!], [\![\overline{T_2}]\!]] \leq \ell_o[[\![S_1]\!], [\![\overline{S_2}]\!]]}\ (\text{Sub-out})$$

An auxiliary Lemma gives $[\![T_2]\!] \leq [\![S_2]\!]$ if and only if $[\![\overline{S_2}]\!] \leq [\![\overline{T_2}]\!]$ and by IH we have $S_1 <: T_1$ and $T_2 <: S_2$. We conclude using rule (S-!)*.*

The other cases of the proof follow in a similar way.

Subtyping in session types has been studied in details in [5, 21]: we can derive the main results in these papers as straightforward corollaries via the encoding along the lines of what we have shown for Subject Reduction and Validity of Subtyping. Examples are: reflexivity and transitivity of subtyping, and all the auxiliary lemmas (e.g. substitution).

The above results remain valid with the addition of recursive types; in this case we can also obtain for free all the coinductive techniques for subtyping and duality in session types.

5. Polymorphism

Polymorphism is a common and useful type abstraction in programming languages as it allows operations that are generic by using an expression with several types. Polymorphism is added both on session side and on the π side. In this section we show that this duplication is not necessary: all the theory of polymorphism in session types can be derived by the corresponding theory in the π-calculus. This holds for the standard parametric polymorphism as well as for bounded polymorphism.

5.1 Parametric Polymorphism

Let us first consider (existential) parametric polymorphism. This form of polymorphism has not been studied in session types. We need to extend the syntax of types T with type variable X and polymorphic type $\langle X; T \rangle$.

Types	$T ::= S$	session type
	$\sharp T$	channel type
	X	type variable
	$\langle X; T \rangle$	polymorphic type
	...	other π types constructs

The syntax of session types remains unchanged. Modifications in the syntax of types introduce modifications in the syntax of terms, as expected. So, we add *polymorphic value* $\langle T; v \rangle$ and *unpacking process* `open` v `as` $(X; x)$ `in` P, the same constructs as in π-calculus. Note that value v and hence name x, can be tuples of values, respectively names, in order to accommodate polyadicity.

Since we added polymorphic constructs in the syntax of standard types and we left the syntax of session types unchanged, the encoding of session types is the same as before, hence the encoding of types is a homomorphism. In particular, polymorphic constructs are encoded as

$$[\![X]\!] = X$$
$$[\![\langle X; T \rangle]\!] = \langle X; [\![T]\!] \rangle$$

The same holds for the terms of the calculus with or without sessions: we added the same value and process constructs on both sides and thus the encoding is again a homomorphism

$$[\![\langle T; v\rangle]\!]_f = \langle [\![T]\!]; [\![v]\!]_f\rangle$$
$$[\![\texttt{open } v \texttt{ as } (X;x) \texttt{ in } P]\!]_f = \texttt{open } [\![v]\!]_f \texttt{ as } [\![(X;x)]\!] \texttt{ in } [\![P]\!]_f$$

In the case of polymorphic calculi we prove the correctness of the typing derivation, by considering *only* the polymorphic types/terms constructs and the corresponding typing rules. We also prove the operational correspondence for the new process constructs added. The typing judgments are of the form $\Delta, \Gamma \vdash P$ where Δ is the set of type variables present in P. This is the only difference w.r.t. typings introduced before. The following theorem states the correctness result for polymorphic types.

THEOREM 4. $\Delta, \Gamma \vdash P$ *if and only if* $\Delta, [\![\Gamma]\!]_f \vdash [\![P]\!]_f$.

The operational correspondence for polymorphic calculi merely adds a case to Theorem 2 stated previously. Again, Subject Reduction and Type Safety and other basic properties are derived as in the previous sections.

5.2 Bounded Polymorphism

We now consider the bounded polymorphism, studied in [4], which is a form of parametric polymorphism. This kind of polymorphism has not been studied yet in π-calculus; we add it and show how we can derive bounded polymorphism in session types passing through the π types. Bounded polymorphism in session types [4] is added only to the labels in the branch and select constructs. The two type constructs have now the following shape:

$$\& \{l_1(X_1 \le B_1) : S_1, \ldots, l_n(X_n \le B_n) : S_n\}$$
$$\oplus \{l_1(X_1 \le B_1) : S_1, \ldots, l_n(X_n \le B_n) : S_n\},$$

where B stands for basic types (e.g. integer, boolean, $X, \ldots$) not channel types.

In order to have bounded polymorphism also in the π-calculus, we should add it to the syntax of types, precisely attached to the labels of variant types as follows:

$$\langle l_1(X_1 \le B_1) : T_1 \ldots l_n(X_n \le B_n) : T_n\rangle$$

So, on both π-calculi with or without sessions, we should take into account the condition $(X_i \le B_i)$ and X_i should be instantiated with a type that satisfies the condition. The syntax of processes should be modified accordingly, by adding the bound type to the labels. The typing rules are now similar on both calculi and the same holds for the operational semantics. The encoding is once again a homomorphism and is given in Figure 8.

By using the encoding and the bounded polymorphism in π-calculus, we can derive bounded polymorphism in session types. Furthermore, all the results presented in Section 4 and 5.1 are derivable for free.

6. Higher-Order

Higher-Order π-calculus (HOπ) models mobility of processes that can be sent and received and thus can be run locally [18]. Higher-order in sessions has the same benefits as that in π-calculus, in particular, it models code mobility in a distributed scenario. What we want to do is to use HOπ to provide sessions with higher-order capabilities by exploiting the encoding, as we did with subtyping and polymorphism.

Let us consider higher-order sessions [15].

The syntax of types is the following. We consider standard π channel types, session types and types taken from the simply-typed λ-calculus. The syntax T of types is extended with two functional type constructs: a standard one $T \to \diamond$, assigned to a functional term that can be used without any restriction and, a linear functional type $T \overset{1}{\to} \diamond$[1] assigned to a term that should be used *exactly once*. The reason for this is that a function may contain free session channels, hence it should necessarily be used at least once in order to complete the session and should not be used more than once, so not to violate session safety. Regarding terms, π-calculus with session primitives is augmented with call-by-value λ-calculus primitives, namely *abstraction* $(\lambda x : T.P)$ and *application* (PQ).

$T ::=$	$\sharp T$	standard channel type
	S	session type
	$T \to \diamond$	functional type
	$T \overset{1}{\to} \diamond$	linear functional type
$S ::=$	$\ldots$	Session Types

Figure 9. Higher-order session types

HOπ types, given in Figure 10, include the standard functional type and its terms include abstraction and application. The only type construct missing w.r.t. higher order session types is the linear functional type, which we add in order to properly define the encoding. The syntax of terms, on the contrary, is unchanged and remains the one of HOπ.

$T ::=$	$\ell_i T$	linear input
	$\ell_o T$	linear output
	$\ell_\sharp T$	linear connection
	$\langle l_1\_T_1 \ldots l_n\_T_n\rangle$	variant type
	$T \to \diamond$	functional type
	$T \overset{1}{\to} \diamond$	linear functional type

Figure 10. Higher-order π types

The encoding is a homomorphism on the higher-order constructs added to the syntax of types and terms on both calculi. It is presented in Figure 11.

$$[\![T \overset{1}{\to} \diamond]\!] = [\![T]\!] \overset{1}{\to} \diamond$$
$$[\![T \to \diamond]\!] = [\![T]\!] \to \diamond$$

$$[\![\lambda x : T.P]\!]_f = \lambda x : [\![T]\!].[\![P]\!]_f$$
$$[\![PQ]\!]_f = [\![P]\!]_f [\![Q]\!]_f$$

Figure 11. Encoding of higher-order types and terms

Typing judgements, in π-calculus with and without sessions are of the form $\Gamma; \Sigma; \mathcal{S} \vdash P$, where Σ denotes the set of session channels typed by session types, $\mathcal{S}$ is the set of linear functional variables and Γ contains the rest in order to type P.

Regarding the higher-order calculus, the assertion of type correctness becomes:

THEOREM 5. $\Gamma; \Sigma; \mathcal{S} \vdash P$ *if and only if* $[\![\Gamma]\!]_f; [\![\Sigma]\!]_f; [\![\mathcal{S}]\!]_f \vdash [\![P]\!]_f$

The result of the operational correspondence for the higher-order is as before. Again, we derive Subject Reduction, Type Safety and other Lemmas as corollaries.

7. Further Considerations

As explained in the previous sections, a session type is interpreted as a linear channel type, which in turn carries a linear channel. In

[1] In [15] they consider generic functional types $T \to T$. However, this does not add much to the calculi and as long as our goal for encoding is concerned $T \to \diamond$ is enough.

$$[\![\&\{l_i(X_i \leq T_i) : S_i\}_{i\in I}]\!] = \ell_i[\langle l_1(X_1 \leq T_1) : [\![S_1]\!], \ldots, l_n(X_n \leq T_n) : [\![S_n]\!]\rangle]$$
$$[\![\oplus\{l_i(X_i \leq T_i) : S_i\}_{i\in I}]\!] = \ell_o[\langle l_1(X_1 \leq T_1) : [\![\overline{S_1}]\!], \ldots, l_n(X_n \leq T_n) : [\![\overline{S_n}]\!]\rangle]$$

$$[\![x \lhd l(T).P]\!]_f = (\nu c)\overline{f_x}\langle l(T)\_c\rangle.[\![P]\!]_{f,\{x\to c\}}$$
$$[\![x \rhd \{l_1(X_1 \leq T_1) : P_1, \ldots, l_n(X_n \leq T_n) : P_n\}]\!]_f = f_x(y).\ \texttt{case}\ y\ \texttt{of}\ [l_1(X_1 \leq T_1)\_c \Rightarrow [\![P_1]\!]_{f,\{x\to c\}}\ \ldots\ l_n(X_n \leq T_n)\_c \Rightarrow [\![P_n]\!]_{f,\{x\to c\}}]$$

Figure 8. Encoding of polymorphic types and terms

order to satisfy this linearity, on behalf of terms, a fresh channel is created at any step of communication and is sent to the partner along with the message to be transmitted. The sent channel will be used to handle the rest of the communication. What we just said describes the encoding of the an output process transmitting some value v:

$$(\nu b)\overline{a}\langle v, b\rangle.[\![P]\!]_{\{a\to b\}} \tag{1}$$

One can argue that there is an overhead in doing so, and above all it is not necessary. Since the fresh names are assigned linear types, once they are used, we are guaranteed by the type system that those channels are not going to be used again. An optimized approach permits to reuse the same linear channel. For example, the above process would be as follows:

$$\overline{a}\langle v, a\rangle.[\![P]\!] \tag{2}$$

This leads to a typing problem, since the process is not well-typed, as it obviously violates linearity. In order to overcome this problem, we introduce the following typing rule:

$$\frac{\Gamma_1 \vdash v : \ell_o T \qquad \Gamma_2, v : \ell_c S \vdash w : T \qquad \Gamma_3, v : \ell_{\overline{c}} S \vdash P}{\Gamma_1, \Gamma_2, \Gamma_3 \vdash \overline{v}\langle w\rangle.P}$$

We have proved that (1) and (2) are typed strong barbed congruent. The modified rule may be seen as an optimization of linear types, allowing reuse of channel names. The optimization would make the encoding of session types simpler— a linear channel would be use like a session channel and therefore the function parameter f of the encoding would not be needed. In our presentation, we have preferred not to do so in order to relate ourselves to the standard π-calculus and its theory.

8. Conclusions, Related and Future Work

This paper proposes an interpretation of session types into ordinary π types, more precisely into *linear types* and *variant types*. Linear types [14] force a channel to be used exactly once. Variant types [18] are a labeled form of disjoint union of types.

The idea of the encoding of session types into π-calculus linear types is not new. Kobayashi [13] was the first to propose such an encoding, but he did not provide any formal study of it. Demangeon and Honda [2] provide a subtyping theory for a π-calculus augmented with branch and select constructs and show an encoding of the session calculus. They prove the soundness of the encoding and the full abstraction. The main differences w.r.t. our work are: (*i*) the target language is closer to the session calculus having branch and select constructs (instead of having just one variant construct), and a refined subtyping theory is provided, while we focus on encoding the session calculus in the standard π-calculus in order to exploit its rich and well-established theory; (*ii*) we study the encoding in a systematic way as a means to formally derive session types and all their properties, in order to provide a methodology for the treatment of session types and their extensions without the burden of establishing the underlying theory (specifically, [2] focuses on subtyping issues).

Other expressivity results regarding session types theory include the work by Caires and Pfenning [1]. They present a type system for the π-calculus that corresponds to the standard sequent calculus proof system for dual intuitionistic linear logic. They give an interpretation of intuitionistic linear logic formulas as a form of session types. These results are complemented and strengthened with a theory of logical relations [16]. Moreover an interpretation of the simply-typed λ-calculus in sessions π-calculus is given in [20].

Igarashi and Kobayashi [9] have developed a single generic type system (GTS) for the π-calculus from which numerous specific type systems can be obtained by varying certain parameters. A range of type systems are thus obtained as instances of the generic one. Gay, Gesbert and Ravara [6] define an interpretation from session types and terms into GTS by proving operational correspondence and correctness of the encoding. However, as the authors state, the encoding they present is very complex and deriving properties of sessions passing through GTS would be more difficult than proving them directly.

We develop Kobayashi's proposal of an encoding of session types into ordinary π types. We show that the encoding is faithful, in that it allows us to derive all the basic properties of session types, exploiting the analogous properties of π types. We then show that the encoding is robust, by analyzing a few non-trivial extensions to session types, namely subtyping, polymorphism and higher-order. Finally, we propose an optimization of linear channels permitting the reuse of the same channel for the continuation of the communication and prove a typed barbed congruence result. This optimization considerably simplifies Kobayashi's encoding, which on some terms (for example, input and output processes) becomes the identity relation (the encoding of session types, however is the same as before).

The benefits coming from the encoding include the elimination of the redundancy introduced both in the syntax of types and of terms, and the derivation of properties (Subject Reduction, Type Safety, ...) as straightforward corollaries (thus eliminating redundancy also in the proofs). Issues like opposite endpoints of a session channel and duality of types assigned to these endpoints are handled by the theory of π: there is just one channel we deal with (no need to distinguish endpoints) and duality boils down to having opposite outermost capabilities of linear channel types. Moreover, the robustness of the encoding allow us to easily obtain extensions of the session calculus, by exploiting the theory of the π-calculus. As we have shown in Section 5.2, where we presented the bounded polymorphism, our approach makes it easy even when the intended extension was not already present in the π-calculus. In these cases one can just provide the π-calculus with the intended capability and obtain the same capability in sessions. The whole process has shown to be much easier passing through π-calculus than doing it from scratch for sessions.

We conclude that session types theory is indeed derivable from the theory of π calculus. This does not mean that we believe session types are useless: on the contrary, due to their simple and intuitive structure they represent a fine tool for describing and reasoning about communication protocols in distributed scenarios. Our aim is to provide a methodology for facilitating the definition of session types and their extensions, hence encouraging their study.

We are planning to investigate whether our approach can be taken a step further, by modifying the encoding in order to accommodate notions of *causality* needed to capture multiparty communication behavior [8] and deadlock freedom [10, 12].

References

[1] L. Caires and F. Pfenning. Session types as intuitionistic linear propositions. In *CONCUR'10*, pages 222–236, 2010.

[2] R. Demangeon and K. Honda. Full abstraction in a subtyped pi-calculus with linear types. In *CONCUR'11*, pages 280–296, 2011.

[3] M. Dezani-Ciancaglini and U. de'Liguoro. Sessions and session types: An overview. In *WS-FM'09*, pages 1–28, 2009.

[4] S. J. Gay. Bounded polymorphism in session types. *Mathematical Structures in Computer Science*, 18(5):895–930, 2008.

[5] S. J. Gay and M. Hole. Subtyping for session types in the pi calculus. *Acta Inf.*, 42(2-3):191–225, 2005.

[6] S. J. Gay, N. Gesbert, and A. Ravara. Session types as generic process types. In *PLACES'08*, 2008.

[7] K. Honda, V. T. Vasconcelos, and M. Kubo. Language primitives and type discipline for structured communication-based programming. In *ESOP'98*, pages 122–138, 1998.

[8] K. Honda, N. Yoshida, and M. Carbone. Multiparty asynchronous session types. In *POPL'08*, pages 273–284, 2008.

[9] A. Igarashi, B. C. Pierce, and P. Wadler. Featherweight java: a minimal core calculus for java and gj. *ACM Trans. Program. Lang. Syst.*, 23 (3):396–450, 2001.

[10] N. Kobayashi. A partially deadlock-free typed process calculus. *ACM Trans. Program. Lang. Syst.*, 20(2):436–482, 1998. ISSN 0164-0925. doi: http://doi.acm.org/10.1145/276393.278524.

[11] N. Kobayashi. Type systems for concurrent programs. In *10th Anniversary Colloquium of UNU/IIST*, pages 439–453, 2002.

[12] N. Kobayashi. A new type system for deadlock-free processes. In *CONCUR'06*, pages 233–247, 2006.

[13] N. Kobayashi. Type systems for concurrent programs. Extended version of [11], Tohoku University, 2007.

[14] N. Kobayashi, B. C. Pierce, and D. N. Turner. Linearity and the pi-calculus. *ACM Trans. Program. Lang. Syst.*, 21(5):914–947, 1999.

[15] D. Mostrous and N. Yoshida. Two session typing systems for higher-order mobile processes. In *TLCA'07*, pages 321–335, 2007.

[16] J. A. Pérez, L. Caires, F. Pfenning, and B. Toninho. Linear logical relations for session-based concurrency. In *ESOP'12*, pages 539–558, 2012.

[17] B. C. Pierce and D. Sangiorgi. Typing and subtyping for mobile processes. In *LICS'93*, pages 376–385, 1993.

[18] D. Sangiorgi and D. Walker. *The Pi-Calculus - a theory of mobile processes*. Cambridge University Press, 2001. ISBN 978-0-521-78177-0.

[19] K. Takeuchi, K. Honda, and M. Kubo. An interaction-based language and its typing system. In *PARLE'94*, pages 398–413, 1994.

[20] B. Toninho, L. Caires, and F. Pfenning. Functions as session-typed processes. In *FoSSaCS'12*, pages 346–360, 2012.

[21] V. T. Vasconcelos. Fundamentals of session types. In *To appear in Information and Computation*, volume 217, pages 52–70, 2012.

[22] N. Yoshida and V. T. Vasconcelos. Language primitives and type discipline for structured communication-based programming revisited: Two systems for higher-order session communication. *Electr. Notes Theor. Comput. Sci.*, 171(4):73–93, 2007.

Exception Handling for Copyless Messaging

Svetlana Jakšić
Univerzitet u Novom Sadu, Fakultet tehničkih nauka
sjaksic@uns.ac.rs

Luca Padovani
Università di Torino, Dipartimento di Informatica
luca.padovani@unito.it

Abstract

Copyless messaging is a communication mechanism in which only pointers to messages are exchanged between sender and receiver processes. Because of its intrinsically low overhead, copyless messaging can be profitably adopted for the development of complex software systems where processes have access to a shared address space. However, the very same mechanism fosters the proliferation of programming errors due to the explicit use of pointers and to the sharing of data. In this paper we study a type discipline for copyless messaging that, together with some minimal support from the runtime system, is able to guarantee the absence of communication errors, memory faults, and memory leaks in presence of exceptions. To formalize the semantics of processes we draw inspiration from software transactional memories: in our case a transaction is a process that is meant to accomplish some exchange of messages and that should either be executed completely, or should have no observable effect if aborted by an exception.

Categories and Subject Descriptors F.3.3 [*Logics and Meanings of Programs*]: Studies of Program Constructs—Control primitives, Type structure; D.3.3 [*Programming Languages*]: Language Constructs and Features; F.1.2 [*Computation by Abstract Devices*]: Modes of Computation—Parallelism and concurrency

Keywords Session types, Copyless message passing, Exception handling, Memory leak prevention

1. Introduction

Communication has become a central aspect of all modern software systems, which range from distributed processes connected by wide area networks down to collections of threads running on different cores within the same processing unit. In all these scenarios, message passing is a flexible paradigm that allows autonomous entities to exchange information and to synchronize with each other. The term "message passing" seems to suggest a paradigm where messages *move* from one entity to another, although more often than not messages are in fact *copied* during communication. While this is inevitable in a distributed setting, the availability of a shared address space makes it possible to implement a *copyless* form of message passing, whereby only pointers to messages are exchanged.

The Singularity Operating System (Singularity OS) [10, 11] is a notable example of a system that heavily relies on the copyless paradigm. In Singularity OS, processes have access to a shared region called the *exchange heap* that is explicitly managed (for practical reasons, objects on the exchange heap cannot be garbage collected, but must be explicitly allocated and deallocated by processes). Inter-process communication solely occurs by means of message passing over channels allocated on the exchange heap and messages are themselves pointers to the exchange heap.

The copyless paradigm has obvious performance advantages over more conventional forms of message passing. At the same time, it fosters the proliferation of subtle programming errors arising from the explicit management of objects and the sharing of data. For this reason the designers of Singularity OS have equipped $\mathsf{Sing}^{\#}$, the programming language used for the development of Singularity OS, with explicit constructs, types, and static analysis techniques to assist programmers in writing code that is free from a number of programming errors, including: *memory faults* (the access to unallocated/deallocated objects in the heap); *memory leaks* (the accumulation of unreachable allocated objects in the heap); communication errors, which could cause the abnormal termination of processes and trigger the previous kinds of errors.

Earlier works [1, 5, 13, 14] have studied and formalized some aspects of $\mathsf{Sing}^{\#}$. In particular, in [1] it was shown that $\mathsf{Sing}^{\#}$ *channel contracts* can be conveniently represented as a variant of session types [8, 9], and that the information given by session types along with a linear type discipline can prevent memory leaks, memory faults, and communication errors. In the present paper we focus on *exception handling*. In particular, we contribute an extension of $\mathsf{Sing}^{\#}$ types together with an enhancement in the semantics of exception handling to prevent the aforementioned programming errors even in presence of exceptions, if suitable exception handlers are provided. Copyless messaging and exceptions are at odds with each other: on the one hand, copyless messaging requires a very disciplined and controlled access to memory; on the other hand, exceptions are in general unpredictable and disrupt the normal control flow of programs. Consequently, and perhaps not surprisingly, these two aspects can be reconciled only with some native support from the runtime system.

Structure of the paper. Section 2 illustrates the problem we are attacking and informally sketches our solution in terms of types and a revised exception handling construct. In Section 3 we formally define the syntax and the semantics of a language of processes to model $\mathsf{Sing}^{\#}$ programs. The section ends with the definition of *well-behaved processes*, namely of those processes in which memory faults, memory leaks, and communication errors do not occur. Section 4 develops a type system for the process language presented in Section 3 and shows its soundness (well-typed processes are well behaved). Section 5 discusses similarities and differences between the present work and related ones. Section 6 concludes with a brief summary of the work and hints at possible extensions of the type system, in light of the common pattern usage of exception handling mechanisms as found in the source code of Singularity OS. Proofs and additional definitions can be found in the technical report [12].

PPDP'12, September 19–21, 2012, Leuven, Belgium.

```
1  void GetNextDiskPath(out string! diskName,
2                       out SPContract.Exp! expService) {
3    DSContract.Imp:Ready ns = DS.NewClientEndpoint();
4    try {
5      while (true) {
6        SPContract.Imp! imp;
7        SPContract.Exp! exp;
8        SPContract.NewChannel(out imp, out exp);
9        diskName = pathPrefix + nextDiskNumber.ToString();
10       ns.SendRegister(Bitter.FromString2(diskName), imp);
11       switch receive {
12         case ns.AckRegister():
13           nextDiskNumber++;
14           expService = exp;
15           return;
16         case ns.NakRegister(nakImp, error):
17           if (error == ErrorCode.AlreadyExists)
18             nextDiskNumber++;
19           else
20             throw new Exception(error);
21           delete exp;
22           delete nakImp;
23           break;
24       }
25     }
26   } finally {
27     delete ns;
28   }
29 }
```

Figure 1. Example of Sing# function.

```
contract DSContract {
  out message Success();
  in  message Register(char[]! in ExHeap path,
                       SPContract.Imp:Start! imp);
  out message AckRegister();
  out message NakRegister(SPContract.Imp:Start imp,
                          ErrorCode error);

  // ...more message types

  state Start : one { Success! → Ready; }

  state Ready : one {
    Register? → DoRegister;
    CreateDirectory? → ...
    // ...more transitions
  }

  state DoRegister : one {
    AckRegister! → Ready;
    NakRegister! → Ready;
  }
}
```

Figure 2. Example of Sing# contract.

2. Motivating Example

To introduce the context in which we operate and the kind of problems we have to face let us take a look at a real fragment of Singularity OS. In the discussion that follows it is useful to keep in mind that Singularity channels consist of pairs of related *endpoints*, called the *peers* of the channel. Messages sent over one peer are received from the other peer, and vice versa. Each peer is associated with a FIFO buffer containing the messages sent to that peer that have not been received yet.

Figure 1 shows a Sing# function that computes the name for a newly allocated RAM disk.[1] The function has two output parameters, the computed disk name and the endpoint that links the disk to the `DirectoryService` (abbreviated `DS` in the code) which is part of the file system manager. The function begins by retrieving an endpoint `ns` for communicating with `DirectoryService` (line 3). Then the function repeatedly creates a new channel, represented as the peer endpoints `imp` and `exp` (lines 6–8), computes a new disk name (line 9), and tries to register the chosen name along with `imp` to `DirectoryService` through `ns` (line 10). The `switch receive` construct (lines 11–24) is used to receive messages and to dispatch the control flow to various cases depending on the kind of message that is received. Each `case` block specifies the endpoint from which a message is expected and the tag of the message. In this example, one of two kinds of messages are expected from the `ns` endpoint: either an `AckRegister`-tagged message (lines 12–15) or a `NakRegister`-tagged message (lines 16–23). In the first case the registration is successful (line 12), so the output parameter `expService` is properly initialized and the function terminates correctly (line 15). In the second case the registration is unsuccessful (line 16), hence a new registration is attempted if the error is recoverable (lines 17–18), otherwise an exception is thrown to abort the execution of the function (line 20). The main loop (lines 5–25) is protected within a `try` block with a `finally` clause that is executed regardless of whether the function terminates correctly or not. In the example, the clause deallocates the `ns` endpoint (line 27).

Sing# uses *channel contracts* to detect communication errors. Figure 2 shows (part of) the `DSContract` contract associated with endpoint `ns` in Figure 1. A contract is made of *message specifications* and of *states* connected by *transitions*. Each message specification begins with the `message` keyword and is followed by the *tag* of the message and the type of its arguments. In Figure 2, `DSContract` defines the `Register` message with two arguments (a string and another endpoint) and the `AckRegister` message with no arguments. The `in` and `out` qualifiers specify the direction of messages from the point of view of the process exporting the contract. The state of the contract gives information about which messages can be sent/received at every given point in time. In `DSContract` we have a `Ready` state from which `Register`, `CreateDirectory`, and other (here omitted) messages can be received. After receiving a `Register` message, the contract moves to state `DoRegister`, from which one of `AckRegister` or `NakRegister` messages can be sent, and then the contract goes back to the `Ready` state. In fact, each contract has two complementary views – called *exporting* and *importing* views – which are associated with the two peer endpoints of the channel. By convention, a contract declaration like that in Figure 2 specifies the exporting view of the contract: a provider of `DSContract` must adhere to its exporting view. On the contrary, the function `GetNextDiskPath` in Figure 1 acts as a consumer of `DSContract`, therefore the function performs complementary actions by sending a `Register` message and then waiting for either an `AckRegister` or a `NakRegister` message. In the code, the importing and exporting views correspond to the types obtained by appending `.Imp` and `.Exp` suffixes to the name of the contract. For example, the declaration on line 3 specifies that `ns` is an endpoint having as type the importing view of `DSContract` in state `Ready`. After line 10, the type associated with `ns` changes to `DSContract.Imp:DoRegister` and then it goes

[1] This function has been taken from `./Services/RamDisk/ClientManager/RamDiskClientManager.sg` in the Singularity OS source code available at `http://www.codeplex.com/singularity/`. Here we have shortened some identifiers to fit the available space.

back to `DSContract.Imp:Ready` after any of the receive operations on lines 12 and 16. Note that the changes in the state of the contract associated with `ns` (and therefore of the type of `ns`) are not explicit in the source code. They follow from the initial declaration that brings `ns` into scope (line 3) and from the way `ns` is used in the function. By keeping track of the contract state of `ns`, the compiler can statically check that the actions performed on `ns` (for sending and receiving messages) match corresponding co-actions (for receiving and sending) performed on its peer endpoint, which is in use by some other process in the system.

The code structure in Figure 1, involving channel allocation and deallocation, messaging, delegation (sending endpoints over other endpoints), and exception handling, is in fact typical throughout the whole Singularity OS and shows that these aspects are frequently mixed in non-trivial ways. We can identify two main problems caused by exceptions:

(1) Since communication errors are prevented by the complementarity of actions performed by processes accessing peer endpoints, a sudden jump in the control flow of one of these processes, like that caused by an exception, may disrupt the alignment of the two peers of a channel and compromise the correctness of subsequent interactions. Therefore, exceptions cannot be handled locally within a single `try` block, but must be propagated to all the processes affected so that they can move in a coordinated way to a new stage of the interaction.

(2) Messages that have been sent but not yet received and other objects allocated since the beginning of a `try` block cannot be simply forgotten if an exception is thrown, for they would immediately turn into memory leaks. In general, it is necessary to keep track of the allocated memory and of all the messages that have been circulating since the beginning of a `try` block so that these are properly deallocated or moved back to their original owner in case an exception is thrown.

Sing# provides limited and not fully satisfactory solutions for these problems. Regarding the first one, Sing# compensates the lack of a coordinated recovery for the processes affected by an exception by means of dynamic typing: endpoints have an `InState` method through which it is possible to query, at runtime, the actual state of an endpoint. This information can be used to attempt recovery from a possibly inconsistent state of the endpoints. The second problem seems to have been neglected. For example, the function in Figure 1 is prone to leak memory on line 20 in case the exception is thrown, since neither `exp` nor `nakImp` are properly deallocated. In this example it would suffice to move the `delete` instructions on lines 21 and 22 between lines 16 and 17 but, in general, it may be impossible to identify the exact point where an exception can be thrown and therefore when it is appropriate to deallocate resources. At the same time it is unreasonable to require the code in the exception handler to take care of deallocations, if only because the handler may not be in the scope of these resources: in the example, `exp` and `nakImp` are not visible in `finally` block so, by the time the exception has been thrown, it is too late to prevent the leak.

In the present paper we put forward an alternative solution that combines static analysis (inspired by existing works on exception handling for sessions [2, 3]) and a transaction-like, all-or-nothing semantics of `try` blocks: either a `try` block is executed completely by all processes affected, and then its effects are committed and become permanent, or its execution is aborted by an exception and the state of the affected processes is restored to the one they had at the beginning of the `try` block, except that control is passed to their exception handlers. To keep the cost of state restoration reasonable, we devise the following mechanisms:

(A) We decorate `try` blocks with the set of endpoints used in them and we synchronize the initiation of these blocks so that any message sent through one of these endpoints will be received from another endpoint from the same set. In this way, we identify a (small) portion of the heap that needs to be restored in case an exception is thrown.

(B) Inside `try` blocks, we "seal" the type of any endpoint that is not in the decoration of the block and we forbid processes to use endpoints with a sealed type. In this way, the type system can statically ensure that well-typed processes do not modify any portion of the heap outside the restorable one.

(C) We forbid the deallocation of endpoints inside `try` blocks, unless they have been allocated within the very same block. In this way, state restoration does not involve reallocations, which are difficult to implement correctly.

To prevent memory leaks, we need to dynamically keep track of the memory allocated within a `try` block so that this memory is properly reclaimed in case an exception is thrown. It is unsafe to deallocate an endpoint if its peer is not deallocated simultaneously: mechanism (A) guarantees that these deallocations are safe even if the type of these endpoints would not normally allow it.

P	$::=$		**Process**
		$\mathtt{done}$	(inaction)
	$\mid$	$\mathtt{open}(a,a).P$	(open channel)
	$\mid$	$\mathtt{close}(u).P$	(close endpoint)
	$\mid$	$u!\mathtt{m}(u).P$	(send)
	$\mid$	$\sum_{i\in I} u?\mathtt{m}_i(x_i).P_i$	(receive)
	$\mid$	$P \oplus P$	(conditional)
	$\mid$	$P \mid P$	(parallel)
	$\mid$	$\mathtt{try}(U)\ \{P\}P$	(initiate transaction)
	$\mid$	$\mathtt{throw}$	(exception)
	$\mid$	$\mathtt{commit}(U).P$	(commit transaction)
	$\mid$	$X\langle\tilde{u}\rangle$	(invocation)
D	$::=$		**Definition**
		$X(\tilde{u}) \stackrel{\text{def}}{=} P$	(rule)

Table 1. Syntax of processes and definitions.

3. Language

Syntax. We assume given an infinite set Pointers ranged over by $a, b, \ldots$ representing heap addresses and an infinite set Variables ranged over by $x, y, \ldots$. We let *names* $u, v, \ldots$ range over elements of Pointers $\cup$ Variables. We use $A, B, \ldots$ to denote sets of pointers, U to denote sets of names, and $\tilde{u}$, $\tilde{v}$ to denote sequences of names (we will sometimes use $\tilde{u}$ to denote also the set of names in $\tilde{u}$). Process variables are ranged over by $X, Y, \ldots$.

Processes are defined by the grammar in Table 1. The term $\mathtt{done}$ denotes the idle process that performs no action. The term $\mathtt{open}(a,b).P$ denotes a process that allocates a new channel, represented as the two peer endpoints a and b, in the heap and continues as P. The term $u!\mathtt{m}(v).P$ denotes a process that sends the message $\mathtt{m}(v)$ on the endpoint u and then continues as P. A *message* is made of a *tag* $\mathtt{m}$ and an argument v. The term $\sum_{i\in I} u?\mathtt{m}_i(x_i).P_i$ denotes a process that waits for a message from endpoint u. According to the tag $\mathtt{m}_i$ of the received message, the variable x_i is instantiated with the argument of the message in the continuation process P_i. We assume that the set I is always finite and non-empty. The term $P \oplus Q$ denotes a process that nondeterministically decides to behave as either P or Q, while the term $P \mid Q$ denotes the standard parallel composition of P and Q. The term $\mathtt{try}(U)\ \{Q\}P$ denotes a process willing to initiate a transaction involving the endpoints U. The process P is the *body* of the transaction and is executed when the transaction is initiated, while Q is the *handler* of the transaction

$$
\begin{array}{l}
\text{GetNextDiskPath}(DS, ret) \stackrel{\text{def}}{=} \\
\quad DS?\mathtt{NewClientEndpoint}(ns). \\
\quad \mathtt{try}(ns)\ \{\text{Finally}\langle ns, DS, ret\rangle\}\text{Loop}\langle ns, DS, ret\rangle \\
\\
\text{Loop}(ns, DS, ret) \stackrel{\text{def}}{=} \\
\quad \mathtt{open}(imp, exp).ns!\mathtt{Register}(imp). \\
\quad\quad ns?\mathtt{AckRegister}().\mathtt{commit}(ns). \\
\quad\quad\quad ret!\mathtt{SetService}(exp).\text{Finally}\langle ns, DS, ret\rangle \\
\quad\quad + ns?\mathtt{NakRegister}(nakImp). \\
\quad\quad\quad \mathtt{throw} \oplus \mathtt{close}(exp).\mathtt{close}(nakImp). \\
\quad\quad\quad\quad\quad \text{Loop}\langle ns, DS, ret\rangle \\
\\
\text{Finally}(ns, DS, ret) \stackrel{\text{def}}{=} \mathtt{close}(ns).ret!\mathtt{Result}(DS).\mathtt{close}(ret)
\end{array}
$$

Figure 3. Encoding of the function in Figure 1.

which is executed if the transaction is aborted during the execution of the body. The term `throw` denotes the throwing of an exception, whose effect is to abort the currently running transaction and to execute its handler. The term $\mathtt{commit}(U).P$ denotes a process willing to terminate the currently running transaction (involving the endpoints U). As soon as the transaction has ended, the process continues as P. The term $X\langle\tilde{u}\rangle$ denotes the invocation of the process associated with the process variable X. We assume to work with a global environment of process definitions of the form

$$X(\tilde{u}) \stackrel{\text{def}}{=} P$$

defining these associations.

The binders of the language are $\mathtt{open}(a,b).P$, which binds a and b in P, the input prefix $u?\mathtt{m}(x).P$, which binds x in P, and $X(\tilde{u}) \stackrel{\text{def}}{=} P$ which binds the names $\tilde{u}$ in P. The formal definitions of free and bound names of a process P, respectively denoted by $\mathsf{fn}(P)$ and $\mathsf{bn}(P)$, can be found in [12]. We identify processes modulo alpha renaming of bound names.

Syntactic conventions. We adopt some standard conventions regarding the syntax of processes: we sometimes use an infix form for receive operations and write, for example $u_1?\mathtt{m}_1(x_1).P_1 + \cdots + u_n?\mathtt{m}_n(x_n).P_n$ instead of $\sum_{i=1..n} u_i?\mathtt{m}_i(x_i).P_i$; we omit message arguments when they are not used; we sometimes use a prefix form for parallel compositions and write, for example, $\prod_{i=1..n} P_i$ instead of $P_1 \mid \cdots \mid P_n$; we identify `done` with $\prod_{i\in\emptyset} P_i$ and we omit trailing occurrences of `done`.

To ease the formalization, our process language sports a minimal set of critical features: we focus only on monadic messaging (messages have exactly one endpoint argument) and exception handling, disregarding other constructs and data types of Sing#; we assume that receive operations use the same endpoint in every branch, forbidding processes like $u?\mathtt{a}(x).P + v?\mathtt{b}(y).Q$ which are allowed by the `switch receive` construct in Sing#; we work with a purely prefix-based language without sequential composition, encoding `try-catch-finally` blocks in Sing# with transaction bodies and handlers and `commit` processes within bodies; we assume there is only one kind of exception which is implicitly thrown by a `throw` process, whereas Sing# supports multiple kinds. We claim that none of the choices we have made affects the results presented hereafter in a significant way.

Example 3.1. Figure 3 shows the encoding of the function in Figure 1 using the syntax of our process language. The structure of the process follows quite closely that of the function, except for some details which we explain here.

μ	::=		**Heap**
		$\emptyset$	(empty heap)
	|	$a \mapsto [a, \mathfrak{Q}]$	(endpoint structure)
	|	μ, μ	(heap composition)
$\mathfrak{Q}$	::=		**Queue**
		ε	(empty queue)
	|	$\mathtt{m}(a)$	(message)
	|	$\mathfrak{Q} :: \mathfrak{Q}$	(queue composition)
P	::=		**Runtime process**
		...	(as in Table 1)
	|	$\langle A, A, \{P\}P\rangle$	(running transaction)

Table 2. Syntax of heaps, queues, and runtime processes.

The loop on lines 5–25 is encoded as a recursive process Loop parameterized on its free names. The `finally` block on lines 26–28 is factored out as a named process Finally, since it must be executed regardless of whether the `try` block is terminated successfully (line 15) or not (line 20). Consequently, Finally is invoked twice in the encoding.

The main difference between the function Figure 1 and its encoding concerns parameter passing, which is encoded using explicit communication on the *ret* endpoint. In particular, the initialization of `expService` with `exp` on line 14 corresponds to the output operation $ret!\mathtt{SetService}(exp)$ in Figure 3.

Finally, note that in Figure 1 the function uses a free name `DS` for accessing a system service. In the encoding we explicitly mention *DS* as a parameter of the GetNextDiskPath process, implying that its ownership is transferred to GetNextDiskPath upon invocation. To preserve the linear usage of resources (of *DS* in this case), the Finally process sends *DS* back on *ret* before *ret* is closed (a more detailed example of ownership transfer can be found in [1]). ■

Operational semantics. In order to describe the operational semantics of processes, we need to represent the *heap* where channels are allocated and through which messages are exchanged. Indeed, channels are accessed through the pointers to their endpoints and message arguments are themselves pointers to heap objects. Intuitively, a heap μ is a finite map from pointers a to endpoint structures $[b, \mathfrak{Q}]$, where b is the *peer endpoint* of a and $\mathfrak{Q}$ is the queue of messages waiting to be received from a. In the model, we represent heaps and message queues as terms generated by the grammar in Table 2. The term $\emptyset$ denotes the empty heap, in which no endpoints are allocated. The term $a \mapsto [b, \mathfrak{Q}]$ denotes an endpoint allocated at a pointing to the endpoint structure $[b, \mathfrak{Q}]$. The term μ, μ' denotes the composition of the heaps μ and μ'. We write $\mathsf{dom}(\mu)$ for the *domain* of the heap μ, that is the set of pointers for which there is an allocated endpoint structure. The heap composition μ, μ' is well defined provided that $\mathsf{dom}(\mu) \cap \mathsf{dom}(\mu') = \emptyset$ (there cannot be two endpoint structures allocated at the same address). In the following, we work modulo commutativity and associativity of heap composition and assume that $\emptyset$ is neutral with respect to composition. We write $a \mapsto [b, \mathfrak{Q}] \in \mu$ to indicate that the endpoint structure $[b, \mathfrak{Q}]$ is allocated at location a in μ.

Message queues, ranged over by $\mathfrak{Q}$, are also represented as terms: ε denotes the empty queue, $\mathtt{m}(c)$ is a queue made of an m-tagged message with argument c, and $\mathfrak{Q} :: \mathfrak{Q}'$ is the queue composition of $\mathfrak{Q}$ and $\mathfrak{Q}'$. We identify queues modulo associativity of :: and we assume that ε is neutral for ::.

Before defining the operational semantics of processes we formalize two notions. The first one is that of peer endpoints:

Definition 3.1 (peer endpoints)**.** We say that a and b are *peer endpoints* in μ, written $a \overset{\mu}{\leftrightarrow} b$, if $a \mapsto [b, \Omega] \in \mu$ and $b \mapsto [a, \Omega'] \in \mu$.

The notion of "closed scope" that we mentioned in the introduction is formalized as a predicate on sets of pointers:

Definition 3.2 (balanced set of pointers)**.** We say that $A \subseteq \mathsf{dom}(\mu)$ is *balanced* in μ, written $\mu\text{-}\mathsf{balanced}(A)$, if, for every $a \in A$, $a \overset{\mu}{\leftrightarrow} b$ implies $b \in A$.

In words, A is balanced if for every a in A, the peer of a is also in A provided that it is still allocated. Since a message sent over a ends up in the queue of its peer, this means that any communication occurring on one of the endpoints in A remains within the scope identified by A.

In the operational semantics of processes, we need to distinguish between a transaction that has not started yet (and which is represented using the `try` construct of Table 1), and a *running transaction*. This need arises for two reasons: First, a running transaction generally involves more than one process, each with its own handler. Therefore, it is technically convenient to devise an explicit construct that defines the *scope* of the transaction. Second, it is necessary to keep track of the part of the heap that has been allocated since the initiation of the transaction. Table 2 extends the syntax of processes with the term $\langle A, B, \{Q\}P\rangle$ where A is the set of endpoints involved in the transaction, B is the set of endpoints that have been allocated since the transaction has started, and P and Q respectively represent the (residual) body and the handler of the transaction. In general, P and Q will be parallel compositions of the bodies and the handlers of the processes that have cooperatively initiated the transaction.

The operational semantics of processes is defined in terms of a structural congruence over processes (identifying structurally equivalent processes) and a reduction relation. Structural congruence is the least relation including alpha conversion and the laws in Table 3, stating that parallel composition is commutative, associative, and has `done` as neutral element. As process interaction mostly occurs through the heap, the reduction relation describes the evolution of *configurations* $\mu \fatsemi P$ rather than of processes alone, so that

$$\mu \fatsemi P \to \mu' \fatsemi P'$$

denotes the fact that process P evolves to P' and, in doing so, it changes the heap from μ to μ'.

We devote the following paragraphs to an informal description of the reduction rules of Table 3. Rule (R-OPEN) describes the creation of a new channel, which causes the allocation of two new endpoint structures in the heap. The endpoints are initialized with empty queues and are allocated at fresh locations, for otherwise the resulting heap would be ill formed. Since we have assumed that $\mathsf{Pointers}$ is infinite, it is always possible to alpha rename a and b to fresh pointers, so that an $\mathtt{open}(a,b).P$ is always able to reduce.

Rule (R-CLOSE) describes the closing of an endpoint, which deallocates its structure from the heap and discards its queue. Note that both endpoints of a channel are created simultaneously by (R-OPEN), but each is closed independently by (R-CLOSE).

Rule (R-CHOICE) (and its symmetric, omitted) states that a process $P \oplus Q$ nondeterministically reduces to P or Q.

Rule (R-SEND) describes the sending of a message $\mathtt{m}(c)$ on the endpoint a. The message is enqueued at the right end of the queue associated with the peer endpoint b of a. The operation may change the ownership of c, if b is owned by a process different from the sender. Note that, for this rule to be applicable, it is necessary for both endpoints of a channel to be allocated.

Rule (R-RECEIVE) describes the receiving of a message from endpoint a. In particular, the message at the left end of the queue associated with a is removed from the queue, its tag $\mathtt{m}_k$ is used to select one branch of the process, and its argument c instantiates the corresponding variable x_k.

Rule (R-PARALLEL) describes the independent evolution of parallel processes. Note how the heap is treated globally even when it is only one subprocess to reduce.

Rule (R-START TRANSACTION) describes the initiation of a transaction by a number of processes. The transaction is identified by a set of endpoints $\bigcup_{i\in I} A_i$ which are distributed among the processes. In order for the transaction to start, this set of endpoints must be balanced, so that for every endpoint in the set its peer is also in the set. The rule is nondeterministic, in the sense that there can be multiple combinations of processes that can initiate a transaction. We leave the choice of a particular strategy (for example, requiring $\bigcup_{i\in I} A_i$ to be non-empty, minimal, and μ-balanced) to the implementation. The residual process is the tuple

$$\langle \textstyle\bigcup_{i\in I} A_i, \emptyset, \{\prod_{i\in I} Q_i\} \prod_{i\in I} P_i\rangle$$

combining the bodies and the handlers of the processes involved in the transaction. The second component is $\emptyset$ indicating that at this stage no new endpoints have been allocated yet within the transaction.

Rule (R-END TRANSACTION) reduces a running transaction to its continuation when its body has terminated. The handler is discarded.

Rule (R-RUN TRANSACTION) allows the reduction of a transaction according to the reductions of its body. The rule keeps track of the memory (de)allocated by the body of the transaction by updating the B set according to the changes of the heap.

Rule (R-ABORT TRANSACTION) describes the abnormal termination of a running transaction when an exception is thrown within it. In this case, the queues of all the endpoints involved in the transactions are emptied, the memory allocated within the transaction is deallocated, and the handler is run.

Finally, rule (R-INVOKE) describe process invocations simply as the replacement of a process variable with the process it is associated with, modulo the substitution of its parameters. In this rule and in (R-RECEIVE), $P\{\tilde{u}/\tilde{v}\}$ denotes the capture-avoiding substitution of $\tilde{u}$ in place of $\tilde{v}$ in P.

We write $\mu \fatsemi P \to$ if $\mu \fatsemi P \to \mu' \fatsemi P'$ for some μ' and P' and $\mu \fatsemi P \not\to$ if not $\mu \fatsemi P \to$.

Well-behaved processes. We conclude this section providing a characterization of *well-behaved processes*, those that are free from memory leaks, memory faults, and communication errors. A *memory leak* occurs when no pointer to an allocated region of the heap is retained by any process. In this case, the allocated region has no owner, it occupies space, but it is no longer accessible. A *memory fault* occurs when a pointer is accessed and the endpoint it points to is not (or no longer) allocated. A *communication error* occurs when some process receives a message of unexpected type. To formalize well-behaved processes, we need to define the reachability of a heap object with respect to a set of *root* pointers. Intuitively, a process P may directly reach any object located at some pointer in the set $\mathsf{fn}(P)$ (we can think of the pointers in $\mathsf{fn}(P)$ as of the local variables of the process stored on its stack); from these pointers, the process may reach other heap objects by reading messages from the endpoints it can reach, and so forth.

Definition 3.3 (reachable pointers)**.** We say that c is *reachable* from a in μ, notation $c \prec_\mu a$, if $a \mapsto [b, \Omega :: \mathtt{m}(c) :: \Omega'] \in \mu$. We write $\preccurlyeq_\mu$ for the reflexive, transitive closure of $\prec_\mu$ and we define $\mu\text{-}\mathsf{reach}(A) = \{c \in \mathsf{Pointers} \mid \exists a \in A : c \preccurlyeq_\mu a\}$.

The last auxiliary notion we need provides a syntactic characterization of those configurations that cannot reduce but that do not represent any of the errors described above.

Structural congruence

$$\text{(S-PAR IDLE)}\quad P \mid \mathtt{done} \equiv P \qquad \text{(S-PAR COMM)}\quad P \mid Q \equiv Q \mid P \qquad \text{(S-PAR ASSOC)}\quad P \mid (Q \mid R) \equiv (P \mid Q) \mid R$$

Reduction relation

$$\text{(R-OPEN)}\quad \mu \,;\, \mathtt{open}(a,b).P \to \mu, a \mapsto [b,\varepsilon], b \mapsto [a,\varepsilon] \,;\, P$$

$$\text{(R-CLOSE)}\quad \mu, a \mapsto [b,\Omega] \,;\, \mathtt{close}(a).P \to \mu \,;\, P$$

$$\text{(R-CHOICE)}\quad \mu \,;\, P \oplus Q \to \mu \,;\, P$$

$$\text{(R-SEND)}\quad \mu, a \mapsto [b,\Omega], b \mapsto [a,\Omega'] \,;\, a!\mathtt{m}(c).P \to \mu, a \mapsto [b,\Omega], b \mapsto [a,\Omega' :: \mathtt{m}(c)] \,;\, P$$

$$\text{(R-END TRANSACTION)}\quad \mu \,;\, \langle A, B, \{Q\} \textstyle\prod_{i\in I} \mathtt{commit}(A_i).P_i\rangle \to \mu \,;\, \textstyle\prod_{i\in I} P_i$$

$$\text{(R-RECEIVE)}\quad \frac{k \in I}{\mu, a \mapsto [b, \mathtt{m}_k(c) :: \Omega] \,;\, \sum_{i\in I} a?\mathtt{m}_i(x_i).P_i \to \mu, a \mapsto [b,\Omega] \,;\, P_k\{c/x_k\}}$$

$$\text{(R-PARALLEL)}\quad \frac{\mu \,;\, P \to \mu' \,;\, P'}{\mu \,;\, P \mid Q \to \mu' \,;\, P' \mid Q}$$

$$\text{(R-START TRANSACTION)}\quad \frac{\mu\text{-balanced}(\bigcup_{i\in I} A_i)}{\mu \,;\, \prod_{i\in I} \mathtt{try}(A_i)\ \{Q_i\}P_i \to \mu \,;\, \langle \bigcup_{i\in I} A_i, \emptyset, \{\prod_{i\in I} Q_i\} \prod_{i\in I} P_i\rangle}$$

$$\text{(R-STRUCT)}\quad \frac{P \equiv P' \qquad \mu \,;\, P' \to \mu' \,;\, Q' \qquad Q' \equiv Q}{\mu \,;\, P \to \mu' \,;\, Q}$$

$$\text{(R-RUN TRANSACTION)}\quad \frac{\mu \,;\, P \to \mu' \,;\, P'}{\mu \,;\, \langle A, B, \{Q\}P\rangle \to \mu' \,;\, \langle A, (B \cup (\mathsf{dom}(\mu') \setminus \mathsf{dom}(\mu))) \setminus (\mathsf{dom}(\mu) \setminus \mathsf{dom}(\mu')), \{Q\}P'\rangle}$$

$$\text{(R-INVOKE)}\quad \frac{X(\tilde{u}) \stackrel{\text{def}}{=} P}{\mu \,;\, X\langle\tilde{a}\rangle \to \mu \,;\, P\{\tilde{a}/\tilde{u}\}}$$

$$\text{(R-ABORT TRANSACTION)}\quad \mu_1, \{a_i \mapsto [b_i,\Omega_i]\}_{i\in I}, \mu_2 \,;\, \langle \{a_i\}_{i\in I}, \mathsf{dom}(\mu_2), \{Q\}\mathtt{throw} \mid P\rangle \to \mu_1, \{a_i \mapsto [b_i,\varepsilon]\}_{i\in I}, \,;\, Q$$

Table 3. Operational semantics of processes.

Definition 3.4 (stuck configuration). We say that the configuration $\mu \,;\, P$ is *stuck* if the judgment $\mu \,;\, P \downarrow$ is inductively derivable by the rules:

$$\text{(ST-INPUT)}\quad \mu, a \mapsto [b,\varepsilon] \,;\, \textstyle\sum_{i\in I} a?\mathtt{m}_i(x_i).P_i \downarrow \qquad \text{(ST-COMMIT)}\quad \mu \,;\, \mathtt{commit}(A).P \downarrow$$

$$\text{(ST-TRY)}\quad \frac{\neg\mu\text{-balanced}(A)}{\mu \,;\, \mathtt{try}(A)\ \{Q\}P \downarrow} \qquad \text{(ST-PARALLEL)}\quad \frac{\mu \,;\, P \downarrow \qquad \mu \,;\, Q \downarrow}{\mu \,;\, P \mid Q \downarrow}$$

$$\text{(ST-IDLE)}\quad \mu \,;\, \mathtt{done} \downarrow \qquad \text{(ST-RUNNING TRANSACTION)}\quad \frac{\mu \,;\, P \downarrow \qquad P \not\equiv \prod_{i\in I} \mathtt{commit}(A_i).P_i}{\mu \,;\, \langle A, B, \{Q\}P\rangle \downarrow}$$

Rules (ST-IDLE) and (ST-PARALLEL) are obvious, while rules (ST-TRY) and (ST-COMMIT) state that transaction initiations and termination are stuck, if taken in isolation. In the former case, the set of involved endpoints must not be balanced, for otherwise the transaction could initiate. Rule (ST-RUNNING TRANSACTION) states that a running transaction is stuck if its body is stuck and different from a combination of processes willing to terminate the transaction, for otherwise the transaction could terminate. Finally, rule (ST-INPUT) states that a process waiting for a message from endpoint a is stuck only if the endpoint a is allocated and its queue is empty. Then, a configuration whose processes are all waiting for a message corresponds to a genuine deadlock. From these rules we deduce that a process willing to send a message on a is never stuck, and so is a process willing to receive a message from a if the queue associated with a is not empty.

Definition 3.5 (well-behaved process). We say that P is *well behaved* if $\emptyset \,;\, P \Rightarrow \mu \,;\, Q$ implies:

1. $\mathsf{dom}(\mu) = \mu\text{-}\mathsf{reach}(\mathsf{fn}(Q))$;
2. $Q \equiv Q_1 \mid Q_2$ and $\mu \,;\, Q_1 \not\to$ imply $\mu \,;\, Q_1 \downarrow$.

In words, a process P is well behaved if every residual Q of P is such that Q can reach every pointer in the heap and every subprocess Q_1 of Q that does not reduce is stuck. Here are a few examples of ill-behaved processes to illustrate the sort of errors we want to spot with our type system:

- The process $\mathtt{open}(a,b).\mathtt{done}$ violates condition (1), since it leaks endpoints a and b.
- The process $\mathtt{open}(a,b).(\mathtt{close}(a).\mathtt{close}(a) \mid \mathtt{close}(b))$ tries to deallocate the same endpoint a twice. This is an example of fault.
- The process $\mathtt{open}(a,b).(a!\mathtt{a}().\mathtt{close}(a) \mid b?\mathtt{b}().\mathtt{close}(b))$ violates condition (2) since it reduces to a parallel composition of subprocesses where one has sent an a-tagged message, but the other one was expecting a b-tagged message.
- The process

  $$\mathtt{open}(a,b).\mathtt{try}(\emptyset)\ \{\mathtt{done}\}\ \mathtt{throw} \oplus \mathtt{commit}(\emptyset).\mathtt{close}(a).\mathtt{close}(b)$$

  may leak a and b if the exception is thrown.

4. Type System

4.1 Syntax of Types

We assume given an infinite set of *type variables* ranged over by α; we use t, s, ... to range over types, and T, S, ... to range over endpoint types. The syntax of types and endpoint types is defined in Table 4. An endpoint type describes the behavior of a process with respect to a particular endpoint: the process may send messages over the endpoint, receive messages from the endpoint, deallocate the endpoint, initiate and terminate transactions involving the end-

t	$::=$		**Type**
		T	(endpoint type)
	$\mid$	$[t]$	(sealed type)
T	$::=$		**Endpoint type**
		$\mathtt{end}$	(termination)
	$\mid$	α	(type variable)
	$\mid$	$\{!\mathtt{m}_i(T_i).T_i\}_{i\in I}$	(internal choice)
	$\mid$	$\{?\mathtt{m}_i(T_i).T_i\}_{i\in I}$	(external choice)
	$\mid$	$\{T\}[\![T$	(initiate transaction)
	$\mid$	$]\!]T$	(commit transaction)
	$\mid$	$\mathtt{rec}\ \alpha : r.T$	(recursive type)
	$\mid$	$\{T\}T$	(running transaction)

Table 4. Syntax of types and endpoint types.

$$\text{(WF-END)}\quad \Theta \vdash \mathtt{end} : 0 \qquad \text{(WF-VAR)}\quad \Theta, \{\alpha : r\} \vdash \alpha : r \qquad \text{(WF-REC)}\quad \frac{\Theta, \{\alpha : r\} \vdash T : r}{\Theta \vdash \mathtt{rec}\ \alpha : r.T : r}$$

$$\text{(WF-PREFIX)}\quad \frac{\dagger \in \{?,!\} \qquad \Theta \vdash S_i : 0\ ^{(i\in I)} \qquad \Theta \vdash T_i : r\ ^{(i\in I)}}{\Theta \vdash \{\dagger\mathtt{m}_i(S_i).T_i\}_{i\in I} : r} \qquad \text{(WF-COMMIT)}\quad \frac{\Theta \vdash T : r}{\Theta \vdash]\!]T : r+1}$$

$$\text{(WF-INITIATE)}\quad \frac{\Theta \vdash S : r \qquad \Theta \vdash T : r+1}{\Theta \vdash \{S\}[\![T : r} \qquad \text{(WF-RUN)}\quad \frac{\Theta \vdash S : r \qquad \Theta \vdash T : r+1}{\Theta \vdash \{S\}T : r}$$

Table 5. Rank of endpoint types.

point. The endpoint type end denotes an endpoint that can only be deallocated. An internal choice $\{!\mathtt{m}_i(S_i).T_i\}_{i\in I}$ denotes an endpoint on which a process may send any message with tag $\mathtt{m}_i$ for $i \in I$. The message has an argument of type S_i and, depending on the tag $\mathtt{m}_i$ of the message, the endpoint can be used thereafter according to T_i. In a dual manner, an external choice $\{?\mathtt{m}_i(S_i).T_i\}_{i\in I}$ denotes an endpoint from which a process must be ready to receive any message with tag $\mathtt{m}_i$ for $i \in I$ and, depending on the tag $\mathtt{m}_i$ of the received message, the endpoint is to be used according to T_i. In endpoint types $\{!\mathtt{m}_i(S_i).T_i\}_{i\in I}$ and $\{?\mathtt{m}_i(S_i).T_i\}_{i\in I}$ we assume that $I \neq \emptyset$ and $\mathtt{m}_i = \mathtt{m}_j$ implies $i = j$ for every $i, j \in I$. That is, the tag $\mathtt{m}_i$ of the message that is sent or received identifies a unique continuation T_i. The endpoint type $\{S\}[\![T$ denotes an endpoint on which it is possible to initiate a transaction. The types T and S respectively specify how the endpoint is used within the transaction and if an exception aborts the transaction. The endpoint type $]\!]T$ denotes the termination of the transaction in which an endpoint with this type is involved. As soon as the transaction is properly terminated, the endpoint can be subsequently used according to T. Terms α and $\mathtt{rec}\ \alpha : r.T$ can be used to specify recursive behaviors, as usual. The annotation r associated with α represents the rank of α, which will be explained shortly. Finally, the endpoint type $\{S\}T$ is analogous to $\{S\}[\![T$, except that it specifies the type of an endpoint involved in a transaction which has already been initiated, but has not terminated yet. In fact, this type is needed for technical reasons only, and will be used in conjunction with running transaction processes $\langle A, B, \{Q\}P\rangle$. The programmer is in no case supposed to deal with endpoint types of this form.

Clearly, not every endpoint type written according to the syntax in Table 4 makes sense. For example, it is possible to write unbalanced terms such as $]\!]\mathtt{end}$ or $\{\mathtt{end}\}[\![\mathtt{end}$ or terms where recursions do not respect the intended nesting of transactions, like in $\mathtt{rec}\ \alpha.\{\mathtt{end}\}[\![\alpha$ or in $\{\mathtt{end}\}[\![\mathtt{rec}\ \alpha.]\!]\alpha$. As far as our analysis is concerned, the syntax does not even prevent end subterms from occurring within transactions, which as we have argued in Section 2 is undesirable since endpoints involved in transactions should not be closed. For all these reasons we define a subset of *well-formed* endpoint types based on a notion of *rank*. Intuitively, the rank of a term T is the number of transactions in which T is supposed to occur to make sense, with the proviso that end and, in general, well-formed endpoint types must have rank 0.

In general, we say that the endpoint type T is well formed and has rank r in Θ if $\Theta \vdash T : r$ is inductively derivable by the axioms and rules in Table 5, where Θ ranges over ranking contexts associating ranks to type variables. Then, a derivation of $\emptyset \vdash T : 0$ means that T is a closed endpoint type where transaction initiations and terminations are properly nested. Rules (WF-INITIATE), (WF-RUN), and (WF-COMMIT) count the number of nested transactions. Rule (WF-PREFIX) requires all branches of a choice to have the same rank, while rules (WF-REC) and (WF-VAR) deal with recursive types in a standard way, by respectively augmenting and accessing the ranking context. In the following we will omit Θ from judgments $\Theta \vdash T : r$ if Θ is empty.

As welcome side effects of well formedness, note that:

- message types have rank 0 (rule (WF-PREFIX)). Then, well-typed processes will not be able to send/receive endpoints involved in pending transactions;
- end cannot occur inside transactions (rule (WF-END)). Then, well-typed processes will not be able to close endpoints involved in pending transactions.

The rank annotation r in recursive terms $\mathtt{rec}\ \alpha : r.T$ guarantees that every well-formed endpoint type has a uniquely determined rank. Without this annotation a term like $\mathtt{rec}\ \alpha.!\mathtt{m}(\mathtt{end}).\alpha$ could be given any rank. The following proposition guarantees that the rank of well-formed endpoint types is unaffected by folding/unfolding of recursions:

Proposition 4.1. *If* $\vdash \mathtt{rec}\ \alpha : r.T : r$, *then* $\vdash T\{\mathtt{rec}\ \alpha : r.T/\alpha\} : r$.

In what follows, we will assume that all endpoint types are well formed and we will usually omit the rank annotation from recursive terms with the assumption that they can be properly annotated so that they are well formed; we will also write $\mathsf{rank}(T)$ for the rank of T. We will identify endpoint types modulo alpha renaming of bound type variables (the only binder being rec) and folding/unfolding of recursions knowing that this does not change their rank (Proposition 4.1). In particular, we have $\mathtt{rec}\ \alpha.T = T\{\mathtt{rec}\ \alpha.T/\alpha\}$. Finally, we will sometimes use an infix notation for internal and external choices and write $!\mathtt{m}_1(S_1).T_1 \oplus \cdots \oplus !\mathtt{m}_n(S_n).T_n$ instead of $\{!\mathtt{m}_i(S_i).T_i\}_{i\in\{1,\dots,n\}}$ and $?\mathtt{m}_1(S_1).T_1 + \cdots + ?\mathtt{m}_n(S_n).T_n$ instead of $\{?\mathtt{m}_i(S_i).T_i\}_{i\in\{1,\dots,n\}}$.

Types are possibly sealed endpoint types of the form $[\cdots[T]\cdots]$ for some arbitrary number of seals $[\cdots]$. Seals protect the endpoints not involved in a transaction: they are applied when the transaction is initiated (the try primitive is executed) and are stripped off when the transaction terminates (the commit primitive is executed). The type system prevents endpoints with a seal from being used, since any change to them would not be undoable in case the currently running transaction is aborted.

Example 4.1. According to the process definitions in Figure 3, the endpoint *ns* is involved in the transaction around the Loop process, it is used for sending a Register-tagged message and then for receiving either an AckRegister- or a NakRegister-tagged message. The same endpoint is then closed regardless of whether the transaction completes successfully or not. We can describe the overall behavior of GetNextDiskPath, Loop, and Finally on *ns* with the following endpoint type:

$$T_{ns} = \{\texttt{end}\}[\![\texttt{rec}\ \alpha.!\texttt{Register}(T_{imp}).\\ (?\texttt{AckRegister}().]\!]\texttt{end} + ?\texttt{NakRegister}(T_{imp}).\alpha)$$

where T_{imp} is the (unspecified) endpoint type associated with the *imp* and *nakImp* endpoints.

The endpoint *ret* is not used within the transaction, but its usage differs depending on whether or not the exception is thrown:

$$T_{ret} = \texttt{rec}\ \alpha.!\texttt{Result}(T_{DS}).\texttt{end} \oplus !\texttt{SetService}(T_{exp}).\alpha$$

If no exception is thrown, *ret* is used for sending a `SetRegister`-tagged message followed by a `Result`-tagged one; if an exception is thrown, only the `Result`-tagged message is sent. The above type T_{ret} takes into account both possibilities using conventional features of behavioral types (choices, sequentiality, and recursion). ■

In order to avoid communication errors, we associate peer endpoints with endpoint types describing complementary actions: if a process sends a message of some kind on one endpoint, another process is able to receive a message of that kind from the peer endpoint; if one process initiates a transaction involving one endpoint, the other process will do so as well on the peer endpoint; if one process has finished using an endpoint, the process owning the peer endpoint has finished too. We formalize this complementarity of actions by defining a function that, given an endpoint type, computes its dual:

Definition 4.1 (duality). *Duality* is the function $\overline{\cdot}$ on endpoint types defined coinductively by the equations:

$$\begin{array}{rcl}
\overline{\texttt{end}} & = & \texttt{end} \\
\overline{\{?\texttt{m}_i(S_i).T_i\}_{i\in I}} & = & \{!\texttt{m}_i(S_i).\overline{T_i}\}_{i\in I} \\
\overline{\{!\texttt{m}_i(S_i).T_i\}_{i\in I}} & = & \{?\texttt{m}_i(S_i).\overline{T_i}\}_{i\in I} \\
\overline{\{S\}[\![T} & = & \{S\}[\![\overline{T} \\
\overline{]\!]T} & = &]\!]\overline{T} \\
\overline{\{S\}T} & = & \{S\}\overline{T}
\end{array}$$

Roughly speaking, the dual of an endpoint type T is obtained from T by swapping internal and external choices. For example, the dual of the endpoint type T_{ret} defined in Example 4.1 is

$$\overline{T_{ret}} = \texttt{rec}\ \alpha.?\texttt{Result}(T_{DS}).\texttt{end} + ?\texttt{SetService}(T_{exp}).\alpha$$

Note that the dual $\overline{T}$ of T cannot be defined by a simple induction on the structure of T according to this intuition because the type of message arguments is *un*affected by duality. In particular we have

$$\begin{array}{rcl}
\overline{\texttt{rec}\ \alpha.?\texttt{m}(\alpha).\texttt{end}} & = & \overline{?\texttt{m}(\texttt{rec}\ \alpha.?\texttt{m}(\alpha).\texttt{end}).\texttt{end}} \\
& = & !\texttt{m}(\texttt{rec}\ \alpha.?\texttt{m}(\alpha).\texttt{end}).\texttt{end} \\
& \neq & \texttt{rec}\ \alpha.!\texttt{m}(\alpha).\texttt{end}.
\end{array}$$

The interested reader may refer to [1] for an equivalent inductive definition of duality.

We list here two important properties of duality, namely that it is an involution and it preserves ranks:

Proposition 4.2. *The following properties hold:*

1. $\overline{\overline{T}} = T$;
2. $\mathsf{rank}(\overline{T}) = \mathsf{rank}(T)$.

4.2 Type Weight

In previous work [1] it was observed that the delegation of endpoints having some particular type can generate memory leaks even if the delegating process appears to behave correctly with respect to the type of the endpoints it uses. For example, the process

$$P \stackrel{\text{def}}{=} \texttt{open}(a,b).a!\texttt{m}(b).\texttt{close}(a) \qquad (1)$$

uses a and b according to the endpoint types

$$T = !\texttt{m}(S).\texttt{end} \qquad \text{and} \qquad S = \texttt{rec}\ \alpha : 0.?\texttt{m}(\alpha).\texttt{end} \qquad (2)$$

respectively. Note that $\overline{T} = S$, therefore the complementarity of actions performed on the peer endpoints a and b is guaranteed. Now, the process P sends endpoint b over endpoint a. According to T, the process is indeed entitled to send an `m`-tagged message with argument of type S on a and b has precisely that type. After the output operation, the process no longer owns endpoint b and endpoint a is deallocated. Despite its apparent correctness, P generates a leak, as shown by the reduction:

$$\begin{array}{rl}
\emptyset \,\S\, P & \rightarrow\ \ a \mapsto [b,\varepsilon], b \mapsto [a,\varepsilon] \,\S\, a!\texttt{m}(b).\texttt{close}(a) \\
& \rightarrow\ \ b \mapsto [a,\texttt{m}(b)] \,\S\, \texttt{done}
\end{array}$$

In the final configuration we have $\mu\text{-}\mathsf{reach}(\mathsf{fn}(\texttt{done})) = \emptyset$ while $\mathsf{dom}(\mu) = \{b\}$. In particular, the endpoint b is no longer reachable and therefore this configuration violates condition (1) of Definition 3.5. A closer look at the heap in the reduction above reveals that the problem lies in the cycle involving b: it is as if the $b \mapsto [a,\texttt{m}(b)]$ region of the heap needs not be owned by any process because "it owns itself". To avoid these cycles we compute, for each endpoint type, a value in the set $\mathbb{N} \cup \{\infty\}$, that we call *weight*, estimating the length of any chain of pointers originating from the queue of the endpoints it denotes. A weight equal to ∞ means that this length can be infinite, in the sense that cycles such as the one shown above may be generated. Then, the type system makes sure that only endpoints having a finite-weight type can be sent as messages, and this has been shown to be enough for preventing these kinds of memory leaks.

We proceed by recalling here the definition of weight from [1], adapted to our context where we deal also with transaction types:

Definition 4.2 (weight). We say that $\mathscr{W}$ is a *coinductive weight bound* if $(T,n) \in \mathscr{W}$ implies either:

- $T = \texttt{end}$ or $T = \{S\}[\![T'$ or $T =]\!]T'$ or $T = \{!\texttt{m}_i(S_i).T_i\}_{i\in I}$, or
- $T = \{?\texttt{m}_i(S_i).T_i\}_{i\in I}$ and $n > 0$ and $(S_i, n-1) \in \mathscr{W}$ and $(T_i, n) \in \mathscr{W}$ for every $i \in I$, or
- $T = \{S\}T'$ and $(T',n) \in \mathscr{W}$.

We write $T :: n$ if $(T,n) \in \mathscr{W}$ for some coinductive weight bound $\mathscr{W}$. The *weight* of an endpoint type T, denoted by $\|T\|$, is defined by $\|T\| = \min\{n \in \mathbb{N} \mid T :: n\}$ where we let $\min\emptyset = \infty$. When comparing weights we extend the usual total orders $<$ and $\leq$ over natural numbers so that $n < \infty$ for every $n \in \mathbb{N}$ and $\infty \leq \infty$.

The weight of T is defined as the least of its weight bounds, or ∞ if there is no such weight bound. For example we have $\|\texttt{end}\| = \|\{!\texttt{m}_i(S_i).T_i\}_{i\in I}\| = 0$. Indeed, the queues of endpoints with type `end` and those in a send state are empty and therefore the chains of pointers originating from them have zero length. The same happens for endpoints whose type is $\{S\}[\![T$ and $]\!]T$, since we will enforce the invariant that when a transaction is initiated or successfully terminated, the endpoints involved in it have empty queues. Endpoint types in a receive state have a strictly positive weight. For instance we have $\|?\texttt{m}(\texttt{end}).\texttt{end}\| = 1$ and $\|?\texttt{m}(?\texttt{m}(\texttt{end}).\texttt{end}).\texttt{end}\| = 2$. If we go back to the endpoint types in (2) that we used to motivate this discussion, we have $\|T\| = 0$ and $\|S\| = \infty$, from which we deduce that endpoints with type S, like b in (1), are not safe to be used as messages.

4.3 Typing Processes

We can now proceed to defining a type system for processes. A *type environment* is a finite map $\Gamma = \{u_i : t_i\}_{i\in I}$ from names to types. We write $\mathsf{dom}(\Gamma)$ for the domain of Γ, namely the set $\{u_i\}_{i\in I}$; we write Γ, Γ' for the union of Γ and Γ' when $\mathsf{dom}(\Gamma) \cap \mathsf{dom}(\Gamma') = \emptyset$; finally, we write $\Gamma \vdash u : t$ if $\Gamma(u) = t$. We say that a type t is *local*, written

$$\text{(T-Inaction)}\quad \emptyset \vdash_n \texttt{done} \qquad \text{(T-Throw)}\quad \Gamma \vdash_{n+1} \texttt{throw} \qquad \text{(T-Close)}\quad \frac{\Gamma \vdash_n P}{\Gamma, u : \texttt{end} \vdash_n \texttt{close}(u).P}$$

$$\text{(T-Invoke)}\quad \frac{\Sigma(X) = (\tilde{t}, n)}{\tilde{u} : \tilde{t} \vdash_n X\langle\tilde{u}\rangle} \qquad \text{(T-Open)}\quad \frac{\vdash T : 0 \qquad \Gamma, a : T, b : \overline{T} \vdash_n P}{\Gamma \vdash_n \texttt{open}(a,b).P}$$

$$\text{(T-Send)}\quad \frac{k \in I \qquad \|S_k\| < \infty \qquad \Gamma, u : T_k \vdash_n P}{\Gamma, u : \{!\mathtt{m}_i(S_i).T_i\}_{i\in I}, v : S_k \vdash_n u!\mathtt{m}_k(v).P} \qquad \text{(T-Choice)}\quad \frac{\Gamma \vdash_n P \qquad \Gamma \vdash_n Q}{\Gamma \vdash_n P \oplus Q}$$

$$\text{(T-Receive)}\quad \frac{\Gamma, u : T_i, x_i : S_i \vdash_n P_i \ {}^{(i\in I)}}{\Gamma, u : \{?\mathtt{m}_i(S_i).T_i\}_{i\in I} \vdash_n \sum_{i\in I} u?\mathtt{m}_i(x_i).P_i} \qquad \text{(T-Parallel)}\quad \frac{\Gamma_1 \vdash_n P \qquad \Gamma_2 \vdash_n Q}{\Gamma_1, \Gamma_2 \vdash_n P \mid Q}$$

$$\text{(T-Try)}\quad \frac{[\Gamma], \{u_i : T_i\}_{i\in I} \vdash_{n+1} P \qquad \Gamma, \{u_i : S_i\}_{i\in I} \vdash_n Q}{\Gamma, \{u_i : \{S_i\}\llbracket T_i\}_{i\in I} \vdash_n \texttt{try}(\{u_i\}_{i\in I})\ \{Q\}P}$$

$$\text{(T-Commit)}\quad \frac{\mathsf{local}(\Gamma_2) \qquad \Gamma_1, \{u_i : T_i\}_{i\in I}, \Gamma_2 \vdash_n P}{[\Gamma_1], \{u_i : \rrbracket T_i\}_{i\in I}, \Gamma_2 \vdash_{n+1} \texttt{commit}(\{u_i\}_{i\in I}).P}$$

Table 6. Typing rules for processes.

$\mathsf{local}(t)$, if t is not sealed and has a null rank, namely $t = T$ for some T such that $\mathsf{rank}(T) = 0$. Intuitively, a local type denotes an endpoint that can be modified (its type is not sealed) and is not involved in any transaction. We extend the notion of local types to type environments so that $\mathsf{local}(\Gamma)$ holds if every type in the codomain of Γ is local.

The typing rules for processes are inductively defined in Table 6. Judgments have the form $\Gamma \vdash_n P$ and state that process P within n nested transactions is well typed in the type environment Γ. The type system makes use of a global process environment Σ associating process variables X with pairs $(\tilde{t}, n)$ containing the type of the parameters of X as well as the nesting level n at which X is supposed to be invoked. It is understood that the process environment Σ contains associations for all the global definitions D and that the judgment $\Sigma \vdash D$ defined by

$$\frac{\Sigma(X) = (\tilde{t}, n) \qquad \tilde{u} : \tilde{t} \vdash_n P}{\Sigma \vdash X(\tilde{u}) \stackrel{\text{def}}{=} P}$$

holds. In particular, *all* of the free names of P must occur in its binding variable X.

We describe the typing rules for processes in the following paragraphs. Rule (T-Idle) states that the idle process is well typed only in the empty type environment. This is a standard rule for linear type systems implying, in our case, that the terminated process has no leaks.

Rule (T-Close) states that a process $\texttt{close}(u).P$ is well typed provided that u corresponds to an endpoint with type $\texttt{end}$, on which no further interaction is possible, and P is well typed in the remaining type environment.

Rule (T-Open) deals with the creation of a new channel, which is visible in the continuation process as two peer endpoints typed by dual endpoint types. The premise $\vdash T : 0$ means that it is not possible to create endpoints with pending transactions on them.

Rule (T-Send) states that a process $u!\mathtt{m}(v).P$ is well typed if u is associated with an endpoint type T that permits the output of $\mathtt{m}$-tagged messages. The type S of the argument v must be unsealed, finite-weight, and has to match the expected type in the endpoint type. Finally, the continuation P must be well typed in a type environment where the endpoint u is typed according to the continuation T_k of T and the endpoint v is no longer visible.

Rule (T-Receive) deals with inputs: a process waiting for a message from an endpoint $u : \{?\mathtt{m}_i(S_i).T_i\}_{i\in I}$ is well typed if it can deal with all of the message tags $\mathtt{m}_i$. The continuation processes may use the endpoint u according to the endpoint type T_i and can access the message argument x_i of type S_i.

Rules (T-Choice) and (T-Parallel) are standard. In the latter, the type environment is linearly split into two environments to type the processes being composed.

Rule (T-Invoke) declares that a process invocation $X\langle\tilde{u}\rangle$ is well typed provided that the number and type of actual parameters $\tilde{u}$ match the number and type of formal parameters in $\Sigma(X)$ and that the process is invoked at the correct nesting level.

All the rules discussed so far can be applied at arbitrary nesting levels and do not change it. We now turn our attention to the constructs dealing with transactions and exceptions.

Rule (T-Throw) states that the process $\texttt{throw}$ is well typed in *any* type environment, provided that it occurs within a transaction (the nesting level must be strictly positive). For this reason, the violation of linearity for the assumptions in the type environment is only apparent, as control will be transferred at runtime to some appropriate exception handler.

Rule (T-Try) deals with transaction initiations. All the endpoints in the decoration U must have a type allowing them to be involved in a transaction, while the type of other names is sealed so that P is prevented from using them until the transaction is terminated. Seals are not applied in the type environment for the handler since Q executes only if and when the transaction is aborted and therefore acts outside of the transaction. Note that the nesting level is increased inside P but does not change in Q.

Rule (T-Commit) is almost the dual of rule (T-Try) and deals with transaction termination. Again, the endpoints in the decoration U must have a matching type in the context indicating the end of the transaction. Names with a sealed type must have been inherited from the context surrounding the transaction being terminated, so a seal is stripped off them in the continuation P. Names with a local type must have been created within the transaction being terminated, and can be used in the continuation as well. Note that the nesting level is decreased in P, since it executes after the transaction has terminated.

Example 4.2. Using the types defined in Example 4.1, the reader can verify that the bodies of the process definitions in Figure 3 for GetNextDiskPath, Loop, and Finally are respectively well typed according to the type environments

$$\begin{aligned}
\Gamma_1 &= DS : ?\texttt{NewClientEndpoint}(T_{ns}).T_{DS}, ret : T_{ret} \\
\Gamma_2 &= ns : T'_{ns}, DS : T_{DS}, ret : T_{ret} \\
\Gamma_3 &= ns : \texttt{end}, DS : T_{DS}, ret : T_{ret}
\end{aligned}$$

where

$$T'_{ns} = !\texttt{Register}(T_{imp}).(?\texttt{AckRegister}().\rrbracket\texttt{end} + ?\texttt{NakRegister}(T_{imp}).T_{ns})$$

is an appropriate residual of the unfolding of T_{ns}. ■

4.4 Typing the Heap

The typing rules in Table 6 are not sufficient for proving the soundness of the type system, because they are solely concerned with the static syntax of processes. At runtime, we must take care of running transaction processes (see Table 2) as well as of the heap. Indeed, since inter-process communication relies on heap-allocated structures, several properties of well-behaved processes depend on properties of the heap saying that its content is consistent with a given type environment. In this section and in the following one we develop a type system for the runtime components of our process language. We remark that the programmer is solely concerned with the typing rules for static processes presented in Section 4.3, while the technical material presented hereafter, which builds on and extends the previous one, is only required for proving that the type system is sound.

Just as we have type checked a process P against a type environment that associates types with the names occurring in P, we also need to check that the heap is consistent with respect to the same environment. This leads to a notion of well-typed heap that we develop in this section. More precisely, well-typedness of a heap μ is checked with respect to a pair $\Gamma_0;\Gamma$ of type environments: the context Γ_0,Γ must provide type information for *all* the allocated structures in μ (that is, $\mathsf{dom}(\Gamma_0,\Gamma) = \mathsf{dom}(\mu)$); the splitting $\Gamma_0;\Gamma$ distinguishes the pointers in $\mathsf{dom}(\Gamma)$ from the pointers in $\mathsf{dom}(\Gamma_0)$ so that Γ contains the *roots* of μ, namely the pointers that are not referenced from any endpoint structure in the heap, while Γ_0 contains pointers that are referenced from some endpoint structure.

Among the properties that a well-typed heap must enjoy is the complementarity between the endpoint types associated with peer endpoints. This notion of complementarity does not coincide with duality because the communication model is asynchronous: since messages can accumulate in the queue of an endpoint before they are received, the types of peer endpoints can be misaligned. The two peers are guaranteed to have dual types only when their queues are both empty. In general, we need to compute the actual endpoint type of an endpoint by taking into account the messages in its queue. To this aim we introduce a $\mathsf{tail}(\cdot,\cdot)$ function for endpoint types such that

$$\mathsf{tail}(T,\mathtt{m}_1(S_1)\cdots\mathtt{m}_n(S_n)) = T'$$

indicates that messages having tag $\mathtt{m}_i$ and an argument of type S_i can be received in the specified order from an endpoint with type T, which can be used according to type T' thereafter. The function is inductively defined by the following rules:

$$\mathsf{tail}(T,\varepsilon) = T$$

$$\frac{k \in I}{\mathsf{tail}(\{?\mathtt{m}_i(S_i).T_i\}_{i\in I},\mathtt{m}_k(S_k)) = T_k} \qquad \frac{\mathsf{tail}(T,\mathtt{m}(S)) = T'}{\mathsf{tail}(\{S'\}T,\mathtt{m}(S)) = T'}$$

$$\frac{\mathsf{tail}(T,\mathtt{m}_1(S_1)) = T' \qquad \mathsf{tail}(T',\mathtt{m}_2(S_2)\cdots\mathtt{m}_n(S_n)) = T''}{\mathsf{tail}(T,\mathtt{m}_1(S_1)\mathtt{m}_2(S_2)\cdots\mathtt{m}_n(S_n)) = T''}$$

Note that $\mathsf{tail}(T,\mathtt{m}(S))$ is undefined when $T = \mathsf{end}$ or T is an internal choice or T denotes the initiation or the termination of a transaction. This will enforce the property that the queue of endpoints having these types must be empty.

We now have all the notions to express the well-typedness of a heap μ with respect to a pair $\Gamma_0;\Gamma$ of type environments.

Definition 4.3 (well-typed heap). Let $\mathsf{dom}(\Gamma_0)\cap\mathsf{dom}(\Gamma) = \emptyset$. We write $\Gamma_0;\Gamma \Vdash \mu$ if all of the following conditions hold:

1. $a \mapsto [b,\Omega] \in \mu$ and $b \mapsto [a,\Omega'] \in \mu$ implies either $\Omega = \varepsilon$ or $\Omega' = \varepsilon$.
2. $a \mapsto [b,\mathtt{m}_1(c_1) :: \cdots :: \mathtt{m}_n(c_n)] \in \mu$ implies
$$\mathsf{tail}(T,\mathtt{m}_1(S_1)\cdots\mathtt{m}_n(S_n)) = S$$
where $\Gamma_0,\Gamma \vdash a : T$ and $\Gamma_0 \vdash c_i : S_i$ and $\|S_i\| < \infty$ and $\vdash S_i : 0$ for $1 \le i \le n$ and $b \mapsto [a,\varepsilon] \in \mu$ implies $\Gamma_0,\Gamma \vdash b : \overline{S}$ and $b \notin \mathsf{dom}(\mu)$ implies $S = \mathsf{end}$.
3. $\mathsf{dom}(\mu) = \mathsf{dom}(\Gamma_0,\Gamma) = \mu\text{-}\mathsf{reach}(\mathsf{dom}(\Gamma))$;
4. $A \cap B = \emptyset$ implies $\mu\text{-}\mathsf{reach}(A) \cap \mu\text{-}\mathsf{reach}(B) = \emptyset$ for every $A,B \subseteq \mathsf{dom}(\Gamma)$.

(T-RUNNING PROCESS)
$$\frac{\Gamma_0;\Gamma_R,\Gamma \Vdash \mu \qquad \Gamma \vdash_n P}{\Gamma_0;\Gamma_R;\Gamma \vdash_n \mu \fatsemi P}$$

(T-RUNNING PARALLEL)
$$\frac{\Gamma_0;\Gamma_R,\Gamma_2;\Gamma_1 \vdash_n \mu \fatsemi P \qquad \Gamma_0;\Gamma_R,\Gamma_1;\Gamma_2 \vdash_n \mu \fatsemi Q}{\Gamma_0;\Gamma_R;\Gamma_1,\Gamma_2 \vdash_n \mu \fatsemi P \mid Q}$$

(T-RUNNING TRANSACTION)
$$\frac{\begin{array}{c}\mu\text{-}\mathsf{balanced}(\{a_i : S_i\}_{i\in I}) \qquad \mu\text{-}\mathsf{balanced}(B) \qquad \mathsf{local}(\Gamma_2)\\ \{a_i\}_{i\in I}\cup B = \mu\text{-}\mathsf{reach}(\{a_i\}_{i\in I}\cup\mathsf{dom}(\Gamma_2))\\ \Gamma_0;\Gamma_R;[\Gamma_1],\{a_i : T_i\}_{i\in I},\Gamma_2 \vdash_{n+1} \mu \fatsemi P \qquad \Gamma_1,\{a_i : S_i\}_{i\in I} \vdash_n Q\end{array}}{\Gamma_0;\Gamma_R;\Gamma_1,\{a_i : \{S_i\}T_i\}_{i\in I},\Gamma_2 \vdash_n \mu \fatsemi \langle\{a_i\}_{i\in I},B,\{Q\}P\rangle}$$

Table 7. Typing rules for configurations.

Condition (1) requires that at least one of the queues of peer endpoints in a well-typed heap is empty. This invariant corresponds to half-duplex communication and is ensured by duality of endpoint types associated with peer endpoints, since a well-typed process cannot send messages on an endpoint until it has read all the pending messages from the corresponding queue. Condition (2) requires that the content of the queue of an endpoint must be consistent with the type of the endpoint, in the sense that the messages in the queue have the expected tag and an argument with the expected type. In addition, the endpoint types of message arguments must all have finite weight and null rank. Finally, the endpoint types of peer endpoints are dual of each other, modulo the content of the non-empty queue. Condition (3) states that the type environment Γ_0,Γ must specify a type for all of the allocated objects in the heap and, in addition, every object (located at) a in the heap must be reachable from a root $b \in \mathsf{dom}(\Gamma)$. Finally, condition (4) requires the uniqueness of the root for every allocated object. Overall, since the roots are distributed linearly among the processes of the system, conditions (3) and (4) guarantee that every allocated object belongs to one and only one process.

There are a few subtleties regarding conditions (1) and (2) and the fact that, in condition (2), the property $b \mapsto [a,\varepsilon] \in \mu$ is the head of an implication. First of all, condition (2) must hold for both peers of a channel, therefore if a is the peer with the empty queue ($n = 0$) while b has messages in its queue, then the type of a is not necessarily the dual of the type of b. The correct dual correspondence is checked when the symmetric pair of endpoints is considered. Second, it is possible that at some point only one endpoint of a channel is allocated. For example, the well-typed process $\mathtt{open}(a,b).\mathtt{close}(b).\mathtt{close}(a)$ reduces to $\mathtt{close}(a)$ in a configuration where the heap contains only $a \mapsto [b,\varepsilon]$. When this happens, the type of the remaining endpoint forbids any send operation (last property of condition (2)). Note that condition (1) is not implied by condition (2) and both conditions are necessary.

4.5 Typing Configurations

Table 7 defines typing rules for configurations $\mu \fatsemi P$ as an extension of the typing rules for processes. Judgments have the form

$$\Gamma_0;\Gamma_R;\Gamma \vdash_n \mu \fatsemi P$$

and state that the configuration $\mu \fatsemi P$ is well typed at nesting level n with respect to the triple $\Gamma_0;\Gamma_R;\Gamma$ of type environments. Intuitively, Γ is the type environment used to type check P, Γ_R is the type environment describing the type of root pointers owned by processes that are running in parallel with P, and Γ_0 describes the type of pointers that occur in some queue.

Rule (T-RUNNING PROCESS) lifts well-typed processes to well-typed configurations by requiring the heap to be well typed with respect to the pair of environments $\Gamma_0; \Gamma_R, \Gamma$ where Γ_R, Γ represents the whole set of roots obtained from those owned by the process being typed (in Γ) and those owned by processes in parallel with it (in Γ_R).

Rule (T-RUNNING PARALLEL) is similar to (T-PARALLEL), except that it deals with three type environments which are appropriately rearranged for keeping track of the roots of the heap.

Rule (T-RUNNING TRANSACTION) captures the basic properties regarding running transactions $\langle \{a_i\}_{i \in I}, B, \{Q\}P \rangle$, which we describe here. The rule makes use of a balancing predicate over type environments that generalizes the notion of balancing for sets of pointers (Definition 3.2):

Definition 4.4 (balanced context). We say that Γ is *balanced* in μ, written μ-balanced(Γ), if $a \in \mathsf{dom}(\Gamma)$ and $a \overset{\mu}{\leftrightarrow} b$ imply $b \in \mathsf{dom}(\Gamma)$ and $\Gamma(a) = \overline{\Gamma(b)}$.

First of all, it must be possible to partition the type environment in three parts Γ_1, $\{a_i : \{S_i\}T_i\}_{i \in I}$, and Γ_2 such that: the environment Γ_1 corresponds to the endpoints owned by P but which are not involved in the transaction. Consequently, the type of these endpoints are sealed in the judgment corresponding to the typing of P. The environment $\{a_i : \{S_i\}T_i\}_{i \in I}$ corresponds to the endpoints involved in the transaction (the first component of the running transaction process), and their type indicates that the transaction is in progress. The environment Γ_2 corresponds to the endpoints that have been allocated inside the transaction. Their type is not sealed in the judgment corresponding to the typing of P. The two premises μ-balanced$(\{a_i : S_i\}_{i \in I})$ and μ-balanced(B) indicate that the set of all the endpoints to which P has full access is balanced. Therefore, the transaction operates in a closed scope and cannot have "side effects" from the point of view of other processes. The first premise indicates, in addition, that the types S_i associated with peer endpoints are dual of each other (this property is a consequence of well-typedness of the heap before the transaction initiates, but it must be explicitly recovered in (T-RUNNING TRANSACTION) where the heap is checked against a type environment where the S_i's do not occur any more). The premise local(Γ_2) identifies the Γ_2 partition of the context corresponding to the endpoints that have been created inside the transaction. The premise $\{a_i\}_{i \in I} \cup B = \mu$-reach$(\{a_i\}_{i \in I} \cup \mathsf{dom}(\Gamma_2))$ states that all the endpoints allocated within the transaction have not escaped the scope of the transaction. The last two premises correspond to the premises of rule (T-TRY). In particular, note that the nesting level is increased by one when typing the body of the transaction.

Since running transaction processes appear only at runtime as the result of (R-START TRANSACTION) reductions, they can never occur behind a prefix and therefore the three rules in Table 7 are sufficient to cover all possible forms of runtime configurations.

4.6 Type Soundness

We conclude this section with the two main results about our framework: well-typedness is preserved by reduction, and well-typed processes are well behaved. Subject reduction takes into account the possibility that types in the environment may change as the process reduces, which is common in behavioral type theories.

Theorem 4.1 (subject reduction). *Let $\Gamma_0; \Gamma_R; \Gamma \vdash_n \mu \fatsemi P$ and $\mu \fatsemi P \to \mu' \fatsemi P'$. Then $\Gamma_0'; \Gamma_R; \Gamma' \vdash_n \mu' \fatsemi P'$ for some Γ_0' and Γ'.*

In fact, the proof of this theorem requires to specify a number of additional properties showing the precise relationship between Γ and Γ_0 (before the reduction) and Γ' and Γ_0' (after the reduction).

Theorem 4.2 (safety). *Let $\emptyset \vdash_0 P$. Then P is well behaved.*

5. Related Work

This work follows the type-based formalization of Singularity OS detailed in [1]. To simplify the formal development of the present paper we dropped polymorphism and non-linear types from the type system in [1]. These are orthogonal features that are independent of exception handling and can be added without affecting the results we have presented here. A radically different approach for the static analysis of Singularity processes is explored in [14, 15], where the authors develop a proof system based on a variant of *separation logic*. Exceptions are not taken into account in these works.

The works more closely related to ours, and which we used as starting points, are [3] and [2]. In [3], which was the first to investigate exceptions in calculi for session-oriented interactions and to propose type constructs to describe explicitly, at the type level, the handling of exceptional events, it is possible to associate an exception handler to a whole (dyadic) session; [2] generalizes this idea to multiparty sessions (those with multiple participants) and allows the same channel to be involved, at different times, in different `try` blocks, each with its own dedicated exception handler. In both [3] and [2] it is possible that messages already present in channel queues at the time an exception occurs are discarded. In our context, this would easily lead to undesired memory leaks, which we avoid by keeping track of the resources allocated during a transaction and by restoring the system to a consistent configuration in case an exception is thrown. Neither [3] nor [2] consider session delegation, namely the communication of channels. Also, in [2] the type system forces inner `try` blocks to use a subset of the channels involved in outer blocks. We relax this restriction and allow locally created channels to be involved in inner transactions. The most notable difference between [2] and the present work regards the semantics of exceptions in nested transactions: in [2], an exception thrown in one transaction is suspended as long as there are active handlers in the nested ones. This semantics is motivated by the observation that, in a distributed setting, it may be desirable to complete the execution of potentially critical handlers before outermost handlers take control. Our semantics allows handlers of outer transactions to take control at any time following the throwing of an exception. As a consequence, more constrained policies, such as the one adopted in [2], can be implemented without invalidating the results presented in our work.

The recent interest on Web services has spawned a number of works investigating (long running) transactions in a distributed setting; a detailed survey with lots of references is provided in [6]. In our context, the component Q of a process $\langle A, B, \{Q\}P \rangle$ is analogous to a *compensation handler*. The main difference between our handlers and compensations is that, in the latter case, it is usually made the assumption that it is not possible to restore the state of the system as it was at the beginning of the transaction. In our case, state restoration is made possible by the fact that the system is local and all the interactions occur through shared memory. In this context, we can rely on some native support from the runtime system to properly cleanup the state of the system and avoid memory leaks.

The operational semantics of exceptions and exception handling in the present paper has been loosely inspired by that of Haskell memory transactions described in [7]. In particular, our semantics describes *what* happens when an exception is thrown but not *how* exception notification and state restoration are implemented. In this sense our semantics is somewhat more abstract than the semantics given in similar works [2]. The semantics of [7] uses a clever combination of small- and big-step reduction rules and is even more abstract than ours, but we find it more appropriate in a functional setting since non-terminating functions have smaller practical interest than non-terminating processes.

The authors of [4] put forward a programming abstraction called *transactional events* for the modular composition of communication events into transactions with an all-or-nothing semantics. Their approach focuses on finding synchronization paths between threads communicating synchronously, while in our case transactions are required for preserving type consistency of endpoints and for undoing the effects of asynchronous communication.

Inadequacy of the standard error handling mechanisms provided by mainstream programming languages has already been recognized, even in sequential and communication-free scenarios. The authors of [16–18] develop a static analysis technique that spots error handling mistakes concerning proper resource release. Their technique is based on finite-state automata (in other words, a basic form of behavioral type) for keeping track of the state of resources along all possible execution paths. They also propose a more effective mechanism for preventing runtime errors. The basic idea is to accumulate compensation actions regarding resources on a *compensation stack* as resources are allocated. This technique closely resembles dynamic compensations in [6]. Because of their dynamic nature, compensation stacks do not provide any assistance as far as type consistency is concerned.

6. Conclusions and Future Work

We have formalized a core language for modeling Singularity processes that can throw exceptions and have studied a type system guaranteeing some safety properties, in particular that well-typed processes do no leak memory even in presence of (caught) exceptions. This property has fundamental importance in systems relying on copyless message passing, where the sharing of data and explicit memory allocation require controlled policies on the ownership of heap-allocated objects.

The choice of Sing# as our reference language has been motivated by the fact that the Singularity code base provides concrete programming patterns that the formal model is supposed to cover. In addition, Sing# already accommodates channel contracts, which play a crucial role in our formalization. However, we claim that our approach is abstract enough to be applicable to other programming languages and paradigms, provided that suitable type information (possibly in the form of code annotations) is attached to channel endpoints.

Future work. The one major theoretical aspect we are investigating is how to relax the type system and allow a wider set of messages to be exchanged within transactions. Currently, only local endpoints (those that are unsealed and have null rank) can be sent as messages inside transactions. This restriction results from the syntax of endpoint types (requiring that message arguments must have an unsealed type) and from rule (WF-PREFIX) regarding well-formed endpoint types (requiring that message argument types must have null rank). We claim that endpoints with a sealed type are also safe to be sent as messages, although the proof of this fact seems to require a non-trivial modification of rule (T-RUNNING TRANSACTION) which is already quite elaborate in the present state. There are two main reasons why we think this extension is interesting: first of all, because it would grant transactions the ability to change the ownership of *existing* heap-allocated objects, in addition to that of new ones as is currently the case; second, because endpoints with a sealed type can be safely sent regardless of the weight of their type. In other words, transactions provide an effective mechanism to safely circumvent the finite-weight restriction imposed by the typing rule (T-SEND).

On the practical side, we plan to work on prototype implementations of the exception handling mechanism in a few different programming languages so as to explore its practical costs.

Acknowledgments

This work has been supported by Cost Action IC0901, the Serbian Ministry of Education and Science (projects ON174026 and III44006). We are grateful to Sara Capecchi and Elena Giachino who were keen on discussing some aspects of the semantics of distributed exception handling. Mariangiola Dezani and the PPDP reviewers have provided useful feedback for improving both presentation and content of the paper.

References

[1] Viviana Bono and Luca Padovani. Typing Copyless Message Passing. *Logical Methods in Computer Science*, 8:1–50, 2012.

[2] Sara Capecchi, Elena Giachino, and Nobuko Yoshida. Global escape in multiparty sessions. In *Proceedings of FSTTCS'10*, pages 338–351, 2010.

[3] Marco Carbone, Kohei Honda, and Nobuko Yoshida. Structured interactional exceptions in session types. In *Proceedings of CONCUR'08*, LNCS 5201, pages 402–417. Springer, 2008.

[4] Kevin Donnelly and Matthew Fluet. Transactional events. In *Proceedings of ICFP'06*, pages 124–135. ACM, 2006.

[5] Manuel Fähndrich, Mark Aiken, Chris Hawblitzel, Orion Hodson, Galen Hunt, James R. Larus, and Steven Levi. Language Support for Fast and Reliable Message-based Communication in Singularity OS. In *Proceedings of EuroSys'06*, pages 177–190. ACM, 2006.

[6] Carla Ferreira, Ivan Lanese, Antonio Ravara, Hugo Torres Vieira, and Gianluigi Zavattaro. Advanced mechanisms for service combination and transactions. In *Rigorous Software Engineering for Service-Oriented Systems*, LNCS 6582, pages 302–325. Springer, 2011.

[7] Tim Harris, Simon Marlow, Simon Peyton-Jones, and Maurice Herlihy. Composable memory transactions. In *Proceedings of PPoPP'05*, pages 48–60. ACM, 2005.

[8] Kohei Honda. Types for Dyadic Interaction. In *Proceedings of CONCUR'93*, LNCS 715, pages 509–523. Springer, 1993.

[9] Kohei Honda, Vasco T. Vasconcelos, and Makoto Kubo. Language Primitives and Type Disciplines for Structured Communication-based Programming. In *Proceedings of ESOP'98*, LNCS 1381, pages 122–138. Springer, 1998.

[10] Galen Hunt, James Larus, Martín Abadi, Mark Aiken, Paul Barham, Manuel Fähndrich, Chris Hawblitzel, Orion Hodson, Steven Levi, Nick Murphy, Bjarne Steensgaard, David Tarditi, Ted Wobber, and Brian Zill. An Overview of the Singularity Project. Technical Report MSR-TR-2005-135, Microsoft Research, 2005.

[11] Galen C. Hunt and James R. Larus. Singularity: Rethinking the Software Stack. *SIGOPS Operating Systems Review*, 41:37–49, 2007.

[12] Svetlana Jakšić and Luca Padovani. Exception Handling for Copyless Messaging. Technical Report 3/2012, Università di Torino, Dipartimento di Informatica, 2012. Available at `http://www.di.unito.it/~padovani/Papers/JaksicPadovani12.pdf`.

[13] Zachary Stengel and Tevfik Bultan. Analyzing Singularity Channel Contracts. In *Proceedings of ISSTA'09*, pages 13–24. ACM, 2009.

[14] Jules Villard, Étienne Lozes, and Cristiano Calcagno. Proving Copyless Message Passing. In *Proceedings of APLAS'09*, LNCS 5904, pages 194–209. Springer, 2009.

[15] Jules Villard, Étienne Lozes, and Cristiano Calcagno. Tracking Heaps That Hop with Heap-Hop. In *Proceedings of TACAS'10*, LNCS 6015, pages 275–279. Springer, 2010.

[16] Westley Weimer. Exception-handling bugs in java and a language extension to avoid them. In *Advanced Topics in Exception Handling Techniques*, LNCS 4119, pages 22–41. Springer, 2006.

[17] Westley Weimer and George C. Necula. Finding and preventing run-time error handling mistakes. In *Proceedings of OOPSLA'04*, pages 419–431. ACM, 2004.

[18] Westley Weimer and George C. Necula. Exceptional situations and program reliability. *ACM Trans. Program. Lang. Syst.*, 30(2):8:1–8:51, 2008.

From the π-calculus to Flat GHC

Rubén Monjaraz * Julio Mariño

Facultad de Informática
Universidad Politécnica de Madrid
Campus de Montegancedo s/n
28660 Boadilla del Monte, Madrid, Spain
{rmonjaraz,jmarino}@fi.upm.es

Abstract

We formalize a translation of an asynchronous π-calculus into Flat GHC which does not disrupt too much the intuitive correspondence between them, specially in which regards *names* vs. *logical variables*. However, our approach depends on the introduction of some artifacts, namely *channel managers*. Contrasting other studies, here the communication between managers and other processes is asynchronous. Although this approach is justified by a relaxed notion of compositionality for process algebras, we still need some methodology that allows us to reason about programs in the presence of managers. We show how techniques from program transformation and a form of dynamic search strategy can cope with this. The encoding has been implemented in Haskell and executable programs are obtained from asynchronous π-calculus specifications by means of the KLIC compiler. Alternatively, we have developed in Prolog an interpreter for Flat GHC that has proven useful to analyze aspects of the translation.

Categories and Subject Descriptors D.3.3 [*Programming Languages*]: Language Constructs and Features—concurrent programming structures.

General Terms Languages, Theory.

Keywords concurrent logic programming, concurrent constraint programming, process algebra, encodability, program transformation.

1. Introduction

The π-calculus [16, 22] is a well-known mathematical model which allows the description and analysis of systems consisting of interacting, communicating agents. Primitive entities in the π-calculus are names and processes; the transfer of a name between a pair of processes is the basic computational step. Names identify many apparently different concepts: links, channels, variables, etc.

On the other hand, Flat Guarded Horn Clauses (*Flat GHC*) [31] is a concurrent logic programming language which has its roots in the so-called *process interpretation* of logic programs. Flat GHC provides a logical reading of programs and computations in which shared logical variables are used as communication channels; data-structures are embodied by logical terms and manipulated through unification; resolution is the underlying computation mechanism.

A fundamental question regarding programming languages is expressivity. In this respect, a number of papers have been devoted to the interpretation of concurrent logic programming languages or concurrent constraint programming languages[1] in a π-calculus framework, for example [10, 35]. In contrast, our aim here is to provide an expressivity result in the *other direction*. It is certainly true that studies like [4, 20] suggest already the impossibility of an encoding as we pretend to show here. This situation clearly arises as a consequence of the differences touching upon program constructs, communication semantics, but also encoding principles. It is precisely because the concurrency theory community, motivated by aspects of practical implementability among other concerns, is trying to establish a universally accepted notion of 'good' encoding [9, 18], that this work founds part of its motivation.

The relationship between the π-calculus and the concurrent logic/constraint programming frameworks has been observed elsewhere in the literature. In [32, 33] some similarities and differences between the π-calculus and Flat GHC are intuitively stressed. No formal treatment was given in those papers, so neither an expressivity nor an impossibility result was pronounced. In [25, Table 2], we find an encoding of an asynchronous π-calculus into a *linear* concurrent constraint language, *Linear Janus*. The qualifier linear here refers to the communication primitives of the language and is akin to Linear Logic [8]. In short, multiplicity of messages matters! More recently, [21] discusses aspects of linearity and its *dual*, persistence, in several formalisms including the π-calculus and concurrent constraint programming languages. The authors formalized a number of expressivity/impossibility results for fragments of an asynchronous π-calculus assuming certain conditions (i.e. uniformity). It is worth noticing that Flat GHC is neither linear nor fully persistent in the sense of [21, 25]. Trying to formalize Flat GHC's position in this picture is another source of motivation.

In this work, we formally investigate the relationship between an asynchronous π-calculus (π_a) [2, 11] and Flat GHC. We refer to the following questions: *(i)*. How to measure the expressiveness of two languages? *(ii)*. What are good encodability criteria? *(iii)*. How to correctly implement a certain specification given in terms of a process algebra?

* The work presented here was developed while the author completed his graduate studies at this institution.

[1] The framework of concurrent constraint programming [26] can be regarded as an elegant generalization of concurrent logic programming, see [5].

PPDP'12, September 19–21, 2012, Leuven, Belgium.

The standard technique to deal with *(i)* is to provide an encoding between the languages of interest.[2] This approach can be seen as *compiling* expressions of some source language S into some target language T. Thus we do not exhibit a π-calculus *interpreter*, based on Flat GHC in our case, as it has been done in [29, 36, 37]. As mentioned previously, there is no general consensus about *(ii)*. Furthermore, some proposals such as [9] delimit ideas around process algebras which may not be completely appropriate for concurrent declarative languages and even a number of process calculi. Point *(ii)* certainly has an impact on *(iii)*.

1.1 Two Different Views of Concurrency

We summarize in Table 1.*(a)* a number of differences between π_a and Flat GHC. Discrepancies on the notions of observation and the mathematical tools available to reason about processes are also notable. In process calculi, *observation* is understood as *interaction*, while in concurrent logic programming we focus our interest *on the answers a program may return* under each form of termination.[3]

In this note we explore until which extent these discrepancies can be reconciled.

1.2 Overview

Informally, the following are the main lines of our approach. *(1). We relate names to logical variables as both objects represent the notion of communication channel in their respective languages.* More precisely, we rely on *streams* in order to facilitate the exchange of more than one message. For each name on the source, we designate specific streams for sending and receiving messages on the target side. *(2). We recur to channel managers developing ideas from [12, 13].* Such a device collects send- and receive-requests from processes willing to communicate on a particular channel. The manager matches a pair of complementary requests when those are available in dedicated data-structures. The implementation is based on dynamic merge operators on streams [27, 28]. *(3). We show the treatment of π_a constructs Table 1.(b).*[4] Notice that restricted names are associated to *local* variables and fresh name generation corresponds to fresh variable generation, as required by the resolution principle.[5] Scope extrusion is achieved simply by sending a local variable to atoms outside its original scope. *(4). For a given π_a specification we are able to generate executable code.* The encoding has been implemented in the functional programming language Haskell. The Haskell output is passed to the KLIC compiler [3] in order to generate a C program and from this executable code. Alternatively, an experimental interpreter for Flat GHC has been implemented in Prolog that has been useful to anaylze properties of the translation. *(5). We prove the encoding correct by means of program transformation techniques and a form of dynamic search strategy.*

In this way we reconcile some notable differences underlying both approaches to concurrency. This work is derived from [17].

1.3 Organization

We recall the language of Flat GHC and the asynchronous π-calculus in §2 and §3, respectively. We present the details of the encoding in §4. We talk about correctness in §5. and our expressivity results are summarized in §6. Conclusions are given in §8. Due to lack of space, proofs have been moved to an appendix.[6]

[2] Thus we talk about *relative* expressiveness.

[3] Although other criteria exist, e.g. sequence based models [4].

[4] This refines Shapiro's analogy [27, Table 5] between CCS [15] and GHC [31].

[5] This implies that restriction is achieved when π_a processes are properly compiled. Here we do not address possible forms to circumvent this, such as access to and manipulation of the contents of the stack.

2. The Language of Flat Guarded Horn Clauses

Concepts such as terms, atoms, substitutions, unification, etc., are standard and can be found on several textbooks on logic programming, for instance [1, 14]. Here, due to space limitations, we restrict ourselves to setting the notation used through the rest of the paper.

2.1 Notation

We denote by $\mathcal{V}$ an infinite, non-empty set of *variables*. We speak about a set of *terms* $\mathcal{T}_{\mathcal{V},\Sigma}$ and a set of *atoms* $\mathcal{A}_{\mathcal{V},\Sigma,\Pi}$ defined inductively over $\mathcal{V}$, a *function symbol signature* Σ and a *predicate symbol signature* Π. We use the abbreviations $\mathcal{T}$ and $\mathcal{A}$, resp., for the set of terms and atoms when the signatures are obvious. By an *expression* E we mean a term t, an atom A, a collection of atoms $\overline{A}$, etc. By $var(E)$ we mean the set of variables occurring in E.

Substitutions are denoted by $\sigma, \theta, \eta, \rho$. We talk about the usual operations on substitutions: domain $dom(\theta)$, application $E\theta$, composition $\theta\eta$. The empty substitution is denoted by ϵ. We refer to a function mgu that takes as input two expressions and returns a *most general unifier* (MGU) for them if they are unifiable, or *fail* otherwise.

2.2 Syntax & Operational Semantics

DEFINITION 1 (Syntax: [30, 31]). *A flat guarded* ***Horn clause*** *is a formula of the form* $H \leftarrow G_1, \ldots, G_m \mid B_1, \ldots, B_n$, $m, n \geq 0$, *where the* ***head*** H *is an atom, the* ***guard*** $G_1, \ldots, G_m$ *and the* ***body*** $B_1, \ldots, B_n$ *are multisets of atoms. Further, the guard atoms* G_j, $1 \leq j \leq m$, *are restricted to* ***built-in*** *predicates including term unification* ($\approx$) *and not-unification* ($\not\approx$). *The symbol '*$|$*' stands here for the* ***commitment operator****. A goal* G *is a multiset of atoms* $A_1, \ldots, A_k$.

We denote an empty multiset of atoms as $true$. As a syntactic convention, we omit both the commitment operator and the guard when the latter is empty. A Flat GHC program, typically denoted by K, is a finite set of flat guarded Horn clauses.

The operational semantics of Flat GHC can be presented in the following way, which assumes a mechanism $eval$ evaluating a multiset of atoms either to $true$ or $false$ thereby producing a (possibly empty) substitution in the first case.

DEFINITION 2 (Operational Semantics:[4, 5]).
Consider a Flat GHC program K, *a goal* G *and an atom* A *in* G.

(OS-1)*If* A *is a* built-in body atom *then*

- *if* $eval(A) = true$ *with substitution* θ, *then* A ***succeeds****, that is, it is reduced to the empty goal. The remaining goal* $G' = G \setminus A$ *is instantiated by* θ, *i.e.* $G'\theta$.
- *if* $eval(A) = false$ *then* A ***fails****, as well as the entire goal.*

(OS-2) *If* A *is user-defined, then the computation proceeds as follows. Consider a clause* C *in* K *and a renamed apart copy* $\widehat{C} = H \leftarrow \overline{G} \mid \overline{B}$. *Then* $\widehat{C}$

- *is a* ***candidate clause*** *if*
  (CC1) $\exists\, \theta = mgu(H, A)$,
  (CC2) $\theta|_{var(A)} = \epsilon$,
  (CC3) $eval(\overline{G}\theta) = true$ *with substitution* η, *and*
  (CC4) $\eta|_{var(A)} = \epsilon$.
- ***suspends*** *when* (CC1) *holds but* (CC2) *does not; or* (CC1), (CC2), (CC3) *hold but* (CC4) *does not.*

[6] Available in the Digital Library version.

Table 1. Comparison of the asynchronous π-calculus and Flat GHC.

		Asynchronous π-calculus	Flat GHC
(a)	*Differences:*	binary communication	unbounded communication
		linear messages	persistent messages
		deadlock	success, suspension, failure
(b)	*Correspondence of constructs:*	nil	empty goal
		output particle	body unification
		input prefix	synchronization mechanism
		parallel	conjunction
		restriction	local variables
		replication	recursion

- ***fails*** *in all other cases.*

If there are candidate clauses, then the computation of A ***commits*** *to one of them, A is replaced by $\overline{B}(\theta\eta)$. If all clauses defining A fail, then A and the entire goal* ***fail****. If at least one clause suspends and there are no more candidate clauses, then A* ***suspends****. A can be* ***resumed*** *when its arguments get instantiated by other processes in the goal. If all the processes in the goal suspend, then the goal suspends.*

3. The Asynchronous Pi-calculus

We recall the asynchronous π-calculus, originally attributed to [2, 11], but presented for convenience as follows.

DEFINITION 3 (Syntax: [18, 19]). *We consider an infinite set of names $\mathcal{N}$ ranged over by $a, b, \ldots, z$. The set of process expressions (also denoted by) π_a, ranged over by P, Q, R, is generated by the syntax shown below.*

$$P \quad ::= \quad \mathbf{0} \mid \overline{a}\, x \mid (P \mid P) \mid (\nu\, y)\, P \mid a(y)\,.\,P \mid\, !a(y)\,.\,P$$

The last three constructs exhibit bounding capabilities on name occurrences: in each case, y is bounded in P. Therefore, in a process expression $P \in \pi_a$, a name that has no bounded occurrence is **free** in P. Free and bounded names in P are denoted, resp., by $\mathsf{fn}(P)$ and $\mathsf{bn}(P)$. The set of all names appearing in P will be denoted by $\mathsf{n}(P)$. A **substitution of names**, also denoted by σ, is written $\{x_1/y_1, \ldots, x_n/y_n\}$, where $y_1, \ldots, y_n$ are pairwise different names. The expression $P\,\{x/y\}$ means the agent obtained from P by replacing every free occurrence of y by x, avoiding capture by α-conversion.

DEFINITION 4 (Structural Congruence [18, 19]). *Structural congruence $\equiv$ satisfies the axioms of α-conversion, the commutative monoid laws for parallel with $\mathbf{0}$ as identity, as well as the restriction laws*

$$(\nu x)\mathbf{0} \equiv \mathbf{0}$$
$$(\nu x)(\nu y)P \equiv (\nu y)(\nu x)P$$
$$(\nu x)(P \mid Q) \equiv P \mid (\nu x)Q, \quad \text{if } x \notin \mathsf{fn}(P)$$

We show in Table 2 the reduction rules for π_a.

DEFINITION 5 (Normal Form: [18]). *A process*

$$\nu u_1 \ldots \nu u_k\ (P_1 \mid \cdots \mid P_n) \in \pi_a$$

is in ***normal form*** *if every P_j is an output, input, or replicated input.*

4. From the Async. Pi-calculus to FGHC

We describe formally the encoding of the asynchronous π-calculus into Flat GHC. First we introduce our implementation of channel manager, which has been formulated developing ideas from [12, 13]. We want to insist on the necessity of including channel managers, for possible ways to restrict π_a's expressions — with the purpose of ensuring a form of binary communication — based on type systems [24] or a *standard form* like [16, Definition 9.12] turn out to be either too restrictive or insufficient.

Table 2. Reduction rules: [18, 19].

COM: $\quad \overline{x}\, z \mid x(y)\,.\,P \quad \longrightarrow \quad P\,\{z/y\}$

RCOM: $\quad \overline{x}\, z \mid !x(y)\,.\,P \quad \longrightarrow \quad P\,\{z/y\} \mid !x(y)\,.\,P$

PAR: $$\frac{P \longrightarrow P'}{P \mid Q \longrightarrow P' \mid Q}$$

RES: $$\frac{P \longrightarrow P'}{(\nu x)\, P \longrightarrow (\nu x)\, P'}$$

STRUCT: $$\frac{P \equiv P' \longrightarrow Q' \equiv Q}{P \longrightarrow Q}$$

4.1 Channel Managers

A *channel manager* is a system of processes that coordinates the communication over a single determined channel corresponding to a π-calculus name. Intuitively, processes willing to communicate through some name must first send a request to the manager for that name. Naturally, we classify this kind of messages as **input**- or **output**-requests and handle requests of each kind through dedicated streams. The manager's ultimate task is to *non-deterministically* match complementary pairs of requests: an outgoing request is passed to one (and only one) of the processes that asked for an input. **It is at this level that communication becomes linear and one-to-one.** We introduce the following predicate and function symbols whose meaning will be explained below.

DEFINITION 6 (Signatures). *A predicate signature $\Sigma_{\mathcal{M}} = \{man/2, match/2, merge1/2, merge2/3, merge3/4\}$ for the channel manager implementation.*

A signature $\Sigma_{\mathcal{F}} = \{\ nil/0, cons/2, mrg/1, in/1, out/2, react/2\ \}$ of function symbols comprising the usual list constructors $nil/0$, $cons/2$ — which will be 'sugarized'.

More precisely, see Figure 1, the system consists of a procedure $match$ that keeps a pair of input streams: I and O. An input request is a term $in(X)$ and an output is a term $out(Z_i, Z_o)$ — in each case X, Z_i, Z_o are unbound variables. **Notice** that the variables Z_i and Z_o represent, resp., a pair of **input** and **output capabilities** on a particular channel: a process receiving them would be capable of sending or receiving messages through them, emulating its π−calculus counterpart.

```
1   match([],[]).
2   match([],[O|Os]) ← match(_,[O|Os]).
3   match(I,O) ←
4       I ≈ [in(X)|I1],O ≈ [out(Z1,Z2)|O1] |
5       X ≈ react(Z1,Z2), match(I1,O1).
6
7   man(Vi, Vo) ← merge1(Vi, I),
8       merge1(Vo, O), match(I,O).
```

Figure 1. Channel manager system.

Whenever $match$ finds some requests $in(X)$ and $out(Z_\text{i}, Z_\text{o})$ at the head of I and O, the unification $X \approx react(Z_\text{i}, Z_\text{o})$ in line 5 will be produced, thereby delivering the available input/output capabilities on a channel, i.e. the stream variables Z_i and Z_o resp., to the process that submitted the input request.[7] Each of the streams I, O is connected to the output of a *dynamic merge operator* in order for $match$ to safely — i.e. without interference — collect requests.

Listing 1 shows an outline of a Flat GHC implementation of this operator, which is inspired by the merge-tree solutions of [27, 28].

4.2 Name Environment

We relate names and logical variables as follows. We say that in a tuple (a, A_i, A_o) streams A_i and A_o are dedicated, resp., to transmit receive- and send-requests to the manager for name a. A name environment is an artifact which relates the names in a π-calculus agent to pairs of variables.

DEFINITION 7 (Name Environment). *A* ***name environment****, or simply environment, is a relation $\Gamma \subseteq_f \mathcal{N} \times \mathcal{V} \times \mathcal{V}$ which satisfies the following conditions: **(1)**. For any $(a, X, Y) \in \Gamma$: $X \neq Y$. **(2)**. For any $(a, V_1, V_2), (b, W_1, W_2) \in \Gamma$: $a \neq b$ implies $V_j \neq W_j$, $j = 1, 2$. **(3)**. For any $(a, V_1, V_2), (b, W_1, W_2) \in \Gamma$: $a = b$ implies $V_j = W_j$, $j = 1, 2$.*

Point *(1)* is clear. Condition *(2)* means that different names are related to pairwise different variables, while *(3)* means that any name is related to at most one pair of variables. In the following, the empty environment will be denoted by ϵ. The class of all name environments will be written as $\mathcal{E}$.

In the next definition, given a name a and two name environments Γ_1, Γ_2, we relate a to a pair of fresh variables if a has streams already dedicated in both environments. If a appears only in one of Γ_1, Γ_2, we *reuse* the variables dedicated.

DEFINITION 8 (Merge on Environments).
We define $\mu_0 \colon \mathcal{N} \to \mathcal{E} \times \mathcal{E} \rightharpoonup (\mathcal{N} \times \mathcal{V} \times \mathcal{V})$ as follows

$$\mu_0(a)(\Gamma_1, \Gamma_2) = \begin{cases} (a, X_0, Y_0) & \text{if } (a, X_i, Y_i) \in \Gamma_i, i = 1, 2, \\ & X_0, Y_0 \text{ are fresh variables} \\ (a, X_1, Y_1) & \text{if } (a, X_1, Y_1) \in \Gamma_1 \\ & \text{and } \forall\, X, Y : (a, X, Y) \notin \Gamma_2 \\ (a, X_2, Y_2) & \text{if } (a, X_2, Y_2) \in \Gamma_2 \\ & \text{and } \forall\, X, Y : (a, X, Y) \notin \Gamma_1 \\ \text{undefined} & \text{otherwise} \end{cases}$$

We extend μ_0 to sets of names, i.e. $\mu \colon \wp\mathcal{N} \to \mathcal{E} \times \mathcal{E} \rightharpoonup \mathcal{E}$, in the natural way.

[7] This technique is known as a *back-communication* protocol. Notice that the process sending the request $in(X)$ must keep a copy of the variable X in order to be able to receive a reply.

Intuitively, merging name environments allows us to keep separate streams for every name when composing the translation of π–calculus agents in parallel, thus preserving linearity and one-to-one communication. More specifically, if Γ_1, Γ_2 are name environments for $p_1, p_2 \in \pi_a$, resp., sharing a common name a then we need to merge the corresponding streams for a into new streams. Definition 8 realizes this at the level of environments while Definition 9 formalizes this idea at the level of FGHC atoms.

DEFINITION 9 (Merge request generation).
The function $\mu \colon \mathcal{E} \to \mathcal{E} \times \mathcal{E} \rightharpoonup \wp\mathcal{A}$ is given by

$$\mu(\Gamma_0)(\Gamma_1, \Gamma_2) = \{\, X_0 \approx [mrg(X_1)|X_2], Y_0 \approx [mrg(Y_1)|Y_2] \mid \exists\, a \in \mathcal{N}, X_i, Y_i \in \mathcal{V} : (a, X_i, Y_i) \in \Gamma_i, 0 \leq i \leq 2 \,\}$$

Very frequently, we will view the variables in an environment Γ as some unspecified, comma-separated sequence which will be denoted by $\overline{var}(\Gamma)$. The set of names occurring in an environment Γ will be denoted by $\mathsf{n}(\Gamma)$. Variable- and name-substitutions are applied to environments as expected.

4.3 Translation

We introduce the following signature:[8]

DEFINITION 10 (Signature for processes). *We define*

$$\Sigma_\mathcal{P} = \{input/k, inputWait/l, replication/k, replicationWait/l, restriction/m \mid k \geq 3,\ l = k + 1, m \geq 1\} \cup \{output/5\}.$$

In the rest of this note we will write $\mathcal{T}$ to mean the set of terms defined over $\mathcal{V}$ and $\Sigma_\mathcal{F}$, and write $\mathcal{A}$ to mean the set of atoms defined over $\mathcal{V}$, $\Sigma_\mathcal{F}$ and the predicate signature $\Sigma_\mathcal{M} \cup \Sigma_\mathcal{P} \cup \{\approx/2, \not\approx/2\}$, see Definition 6. By $\mathcal{K}$ we mean the class of all Flat GHC clauses defined over $\mathcal{A}$.

REMARK 1 (Intuition behind the translation). *In a first step, using a mapping $[\![\cdot]\!]$, we associate an arbitrary process P ($\in \pi_\text{a}$) with a system (G, K, Γ) consisting of a goal G, a program K, and a name environment Γ. The component K serves to provide with the necessary clause definitions for the atoms in G. In a second step, using a mapping $\{\![\cdot]\!\}$, the goal G is supplemented with channel managers, one for each name in Γ, and K is supplied with definitions for the managers and the clause below. To refer to an individual component in a triple (G, K, Γ), that is to project it, we will prefix each mapping with the letters $\mathscr{G}$, $\mathscr{K}$, $\mathscr{E}$ which are self explanatory.*

DEFINITION 11 (OUTPUT – Clause Definition).

$$output(\_, Yi, Yo, Zi, Zo) \leftarrow Yo \approx [out(Zi, Zo)],\ Yi \approx [\,].$$

The translation is based on a *global* identification system, which identifies each subcomponent of a process P. Here, for ease of presentation, we recur to identifiers taken from *tree addresses* as given in [7, §2.2], for instance $\{1, 11, 12, \ldots\}$. So, by $id \cdot n$ we mean the juxtaposition of id and n. A remark on notation: we will omit some brackets in our formulas, particularly when talking about singletons.

DEFINITION 12 (Inner Encoding). *Let $P \in \pi_\text{a}$. The function $[\![\cdot]\!]_{id} : \pi_\text{a} \to \wp\mathcal{A} \times \wp\mathcal{K} \times \mathcal{E}$ is defined according to the syntactical structure of P.*

<u>NIL</u> $P = \mathbf{0}$. *Then* $[\![P]\!]_{id} = (true, \emptyset, \epsilon)$.

[8] Although $\Sigma_\mathcal{P}$ is infinite by definition, the translation of any π_a expression is stated over a finite subset of this signature.

```
%%% merge1/2 ('root' of the tree)
merge1([X|Xs], Ys) ←                       % receive message X
    X ≉ mrg(_) |                           % not a merge request?
        Ys ≈ [X | Ys'],                    % forward X to the output
        merge1(Xs, Ys').                   % read more messages

merge1([mrg(Xs1) | Xs], Ys) ←              % receive merge request
    merge2(Xs1, Xs, Zs),                   % merge Xs1 with Xs and
    merge1(Zs, Ys).                        % forward the output to
                                           % the root (merge)
merge1([],Ys) ← Ys ≈ [].                   % close output

%%% merge2/3
merge2([X|Xs], Ys, Zs) ←                   % receive message X
    X ≉ mrg(_) |                           % not a merge request?
        Zs ≈ [X | Zs'],                    % forward X to the output
        merge2(Xs, Ys, Zs').               % read more messages

merge2([mrg(Ws) | Xs], Ys, Zs) ←           % receive merge request
    merge3(Ws, Xs, Ys, Zs).                % merge streams Ws, Xs, Ys

merge2([], Ys, Zs) ← Zs ≈ Ys.              % connect Ys to Zs
merge2(Xs, [], Zs) ← Zs ≈ Xs.              % connect Xs to Zs
merge2([], [], Zs) ← Zs ≈ [].              % close output

%%% merge3/4
merge3([W|Ws], Xs, Ys, Zs) ←               % receive message W
    W ≉ mrg(_) |                           % not a merge request?
        Zs ≈ [W | Zs'],                    % forward W to the output
        merge3(Ws, Xs, Ys, Zs').           % read more messages

merge3([mrg(Ws1)|Ws], Xs, Ys, Zs) ←        % receive merge request
    Zs ≈ [mrg(Zs1) | Zs'],                 % merge request to parent
    merge2(Ws1, Ws, Zs1),                  % merge Ws1, Ws to Zs1
    merge2(Xs, Ys, Zs').                   % merge Xs, Ys to Zs

merge3([], Xs, Ys, Zs) ←                   % merge remaining streams
    merge2(Xs, Ys, Zs).
merge3(Ws, [], Ys, Zs) ←
    merge2(Ws, Ys, Zs).
merge3(Ws, Xs, [], Zs) ←
    merge2(Ws, Xs, Zs).
```

Listing 1. A simple dynamic merge implementation.

OUTPUT $P = \overline{a}\, x$. *Then*

$$[\![P]\!]_{id} = (out(id, A_i, A_o, X_i, X_o),\ \emptyset,\ \{(a, A_i, A_o), (x, X_i, X_o)\})$$

PARALLEL $P = P_1 \mid P_2$. *Let* $[\![P_1]\!]_{id \cdot 1} = (G_1, K_1, \Gamma_1)$ *and* $[\![P_2]\!]_{id \cdot 2} = (G_2, K_2, \Gamma_2)$. *Further, let* $\Gamma = \mu(\mathsf{fn}(P))(\Gamma_1, \Gamma_2)$. *Then*

$$[\![P]\!]_{id} = (\mu(\Gamma)(\Gamma_1, \Gamma_2) \cup G_1 \cup G_2,\ K_1 \cup K_2,\ \Gamma)$$

RESTRICTION $P = (\nu\, y)\, Q$. *Let* $[\![Q]\!]_{id \cdot 1} = (G, K, \Gamma)$. *If* $(y, Y_i, Y_o) \in \Gamma$ *for some* $Y_i, Y_o \in \mathcal{V}$ *then let*

$$G' = \{man(Y_i, Y_o)\}\ ,$$

otherwise $G' = \emptyset$. *Let* $\overline{\mathcal{X}} = \overline{var}(\Gamma')$ *where* $\Gamma' = \Gamma \backslash (y, Y_i, Y_o)$. *Define* $K' = restriction(id, \overline{\mathcal{X}}) \leftarrow G', G$. *Then we have*

$$[\![P]\!]_{id} = (restriction(id, \overline{\mathcal{X}}),\ K \cup K',\ \Gamma')$$

INPUT $P = a(y) \,.\, Q$. *Let* $[\![Q]\!]_{id \cdot 1} = (G_1, K_1, \Gamma)$ *and consider fresh variables* A_i, Y. *If* $(a, A_1, A_2) \in \Gamma$ *for some* $A_1, A_2 \in \mathcal{V}$ *then let* $A'_i = A_1$, $A'_o = A_2$ *and* $G_2 = \emptyset$. *Otherwise let* A'_i, A'_o *be fresh variables and* $G_2 = \{A'_i \approx [\,], A'_o \approx [\,]\}$. *Similarly, if* $(y, Y_1, Y_2) \in \Gamma$ *for some* $Y_1, Y_2 \in \mathcal{V}$ *then let* $Y_i = Y_1$, $Y_o = Y_2$ *and* $G_3 = \emptyset$. *Otherwise let* Y_i, Y_o *be fresh variables and* $G_3 = \{Y_i \approx [\,], Y_o \approx [\,]\}$. *Now, let* $\overline{\mathcal{X}} = \overline{var}(\Gamma')$, *where* $\Gamma' = \Gamma \backslash \{(a, A_1, A_2), (y, Y_1, Y_2)\}$. *We define the set of clauses* K':

$$
\begin{array}{l}
input(id, \overline{\mathcal{X}}, A_i, A'_o) \ \leftarrow \\
\quad A_i \ \approx\ [in(Y) \mid A'_i]\,, \\
\quad inputWait(id, \overline{\mathcal{X}}, A'_i, A'_o, Y)\,. \\
inputWait(id, \overline{\mathcal{X}}, A'_i, A'_o, Y) \ \leftarrow \\
\quad Y \ \approx\ react(Y_i, Y_o) \mid G_1, G_2, G_3\,.
\end{array}
$$

Then,

$$[\![P]\!]_{id} = (input(id, \overline{\mathcal{X}}, A_i, A'_o),\ K_1 \cup K',\ \Gamma' \cup (a, A_i, A'_o))$$

REPLICATED INPUT $P = !a(y) . Q$. *Let* $[\![Q]\!]_{id \cdot 11} = (G_1, K, \Gamma)$ *and consider a couple of fresh variables* A''_i *and* Y. *If* $(a, A_1, A_2) \in \Gamma$ *for some* $A_1, A_2 \in \mathcal{V}$, *then let* $G_2 = \{\ A'_i \approx [mrg(A_1) \mid A_i],\ A'_o \approx [mrg(A_2) \mid A_o]\ \}$ *where* A_i, A_o, A'_i, A'_o *are fresh variables as well; otherwise let* A'_i, A'_o *be fresh and set* $A_i = A'_i$, $A_o = A'_o$, $G_2 = \emptyset$. *Similarly, if* $(y, Y_i, Y_o) \in \Gamma$ *for some* $Y_i, Y_o \in \mathcal{V}$ *then let* $G_3 = \emptyset$; *otherwise let* Y_i, Y_o *be fresh variables and* $G_3 = \{Y_i \approx [\,], Y_o \approx [\,]\}$.
Let $\Gamma' = \Gamma \setminus \{(a, A_1, A_2), (y, Y_i, Y_o)\}$ *and consider the environments* $\xi = \Gamma' \rho_1$, $\xi' = \Gamma' \rho_2$ *where* ρ_i, $i = 1, 2$, *are two different variable renamings introducing fresh variables. Let as well* $\overline{\mathcal{X}} = \overline{var}(\xi)$, $\overline{\mathcal{Z}} = \overline{var}(\xi')$ *and* $G_4 = \mu(\xi)(\xi', \Gamma')$.
We define K':

$$
\begin{array}{l}
replication(id, \overline{\mathcal{X}}, A''_i, A'_o) \ \leftarrow \\
\quad A''_i \ \approx\ [in(Y) \mid A'_i]\,, \\
\quad replicationWait(id, \overline{\mathcal{X}}, A'_i, A'_o, Y)\,. \\
replicationWait(id, \overline{\mathcal{X}}, A'_i, A'_o, Y) \ \leftarrow \\
\quad Y \ \approx\ react(Y_i, Y_o) \mid \\
\qquad G_1, G_2, G_3, G_4, \\
\qquad replication(id, \overline{\mathcal{Z}}, A_i, A_o)\,.
\end{array}
$$

Finally, we have

$$[\![P]\!]_{id} = (replication(id, \overline{\mathcal{X}}, A''_i, A'_o),\ K \cup K',\ \xi \cup \{(a, A''_i, A'_o)\})$$

Now we describe the so-called top encoding.

DEFINITION 13 (Top Encoding). *The function*

$$\{\![\cdot]\!\}_{id} : \pi_a \to \wp\mathcal{A}\ \times\ \wp\mathcal{K}\ \times\ \mathcal{E}$$

is defined as

$$\{\![P]\!\}_{id} \quad = \quad (\mathcal{M} \cup \mathscr{G}\,[\![P]\!]_{id}\ ,\ K_\Delta \cup \mathscr{K}\,[\![P]\!]_{id}\ ,\ \mathscr{E}\,[\![P]\!]_{id})$$

where $\mathcal{M}$ *is composed by goals of the form* $man(X_i, X_o)$ *for each* $(x, X_i, X_o) \in \Gamma$, K_Δ *provides the definitions of the channel manager (Figure 1) and the output predicate (Definition 11).*

The following is an auxiliary definition that will be helpful later on.

DEFINITION 14 (Networking Atoms). *For any goal* G *the set of* ***networking atoms*** $\mathfrak{Na}(G)$, *is defined as the subset of* G *containing atoms of the form* $V \approx [\,]$, $V \approx [t_1 \mid t_2]$, $merge1(t_1, V)$, $merge2(t_1, t_2, V)$, $merge3(t_1, t_2, t_3, V)$, *for any* $t_1, t_2, t_3 \in \mathcal{T}$ *and* $V \in \mathcal{V}$, *and nothing else.*

4.4 Transition System

Consider the translation $(G, K, \Gamma) = \{\![P]\!\}$ of some $P \in \pi_a$. We define a transition system tailored for K and G.[9]

DEFINITION 15 (Transition System).

State space $\mathcal{S}_{G,K}$**:** *Consists of pairs of the form*

- $\langle G'; \sigma \rangle$ *where* $G' \in \wp\mathcal{A}$ *and* σ *is a substitution, comprising an initial state* $\langle G; \epsilon \rangle$ *and success states* $\langle true; \sigma \rangle$,
- $\langle ff; \sigma \rangle$ *for failure states.*

Computation and Failure rules:

(TC0) $\langle G, V \approx react(V_1, V_2); \sigma \rangle \xrightarrow{\mathfrak{React}} \langle G\eta; \sigma\eta \rangle$, *with* $\eta = \{V \mapsto react(V_1, V_2)\}$

(TC1) $\langle G, V \approx t; \sigma \rangle \longrightarrow \langle G\eta; \sigma\eta \rangle$, *with* $\eta = \{V \mapsto t\} \wedge t \not\equiv react(\ldots, \ldots)$.

(TC2) $\langle G, A; \sigma \rangle \longrightarrow \langle G, \overline{B}(\theta\eta); \sigma \rangle$ *with* $A, \overline{B}, \theta, \eta$ *as in Def. 2* (OS-2).

(TF1) $\langle G, A; \sigma \rangle \longrightarrow \langle ff; \sigma \rangle$ *whenever* A *fails according to Def. 2* (OS-1) / (OS-2).

REMARK 2. *Rules* (TC0) *and* (TC1) *are a specialization of Definition 2* (OS-1). *The above rules reflect the view that in our construction all computations should be considered as internal. This occurs at two levels: 1.* (TC1) *and* (TC2) *capture computations in which: communication between processes-managers or components of the managers take place; atoms are expanded to their definitions. 2.* (TC0) *models a reaction — mediated by some manager — between two source* π_a *processes.*

DEFINITION 16 (Reaction Computation). *For any states* $s, r \in \mathcal{S}_{G,K}$ *we write* $s \overset{\mathfrak{React}}{\Longrightarrow} r$ *iff*

$$s \longrightarrow^* s' \xrightarrow{\mathfrak{React}} r' \longrightarrow^* r$$

for some $s', r' \in \mathcal{S}_{G,K}$.

[9] Failure states and rule (TF1) below are actually unnecessary for programs and goals generated by the translation as they do not fail. A deadlocked state $\langle G; \sigma \rangle$ is one in which every atom in G suspends, see Definition 2 (OS-2), and therefore has no outgoing transition and no rule to reflect this. Success states are not necessarily reachable.

```
1  %%% Clauses
2  input(1,Ai,Ao) ← Ai ≈ [in(X)|Ai'],
3      inputWait(1,Ai',Ao,X).
4
5  inputWait(1,Ai',Ao,X) ←
6     X ≈ react(Xi,Xo) |
7         Ai' ≈ [], Ao ≈ [],
8         Xi ≈ [], Xo ≈ [].
9
10 input(2,Ai,Ao) ← Ai ≈ [in(Y)|Ai'],
11     inputWait(2,Ai',Ao,Y).
12
13 inputWait(2,Ai',Ao,Y) ←
14     Y ≈ react(Yi,Yo) |
15         Ai' ≈ [], Ao ≈ [],
16         Yi ≈ [], Yo ≈ [].
17
18 output(3,Ai,Ao,Bi,Bo) ←
19     Ao ≈ [out(Bi,Bo)], Ai ≈ [].
20
21 %%% Goal
22 ←   man(Ai, Ao), man(Bi, Bo),
23     Ai ≈ [mrg(A1i) | A2i],
24     Ao ≈ [mrg(A1o) | A2o],
25     A2i ≈ [mrg(A3i) | A4i],
26     A2o ≈ [mrg(A3o) | A4o],
27     input(1, A1i, A1o),
28     output(3, A3i, A3o, Bi, Bo),
29     input(2, A4i, A4o).
```

Figure 2. Translation for $P = a(x) \,.\, \mathbf{0} \mid \overline{a}\, b \mid a(y) \,.\, \mathbf{0}$ (simplified).

4.5 One Example

Let $P = a(x) \,.\, \mathbf{0} \mid \overline{a}\, b \mid a(y) \,.\, \mathbf{0}$. The translation $\{\!\!\{P\}\!\!\}$ is shown in Figure 2. For the sake of simplicity, we omit the clauses for the managers.

Lines 2 and 10 show the clauses associated to the inputs $a(x) \,.\, \mathbf{0}$ and $a(y) \,.\, \mathbf{0}$, respectively. Both processes send an input-request and evolve to a process `inputWait` as they wait for a reply. Notice that both processes systematically keep a reference to the tail of the stream, A_i', which may be used to further transmit requests. In lines 5 and 13 the processes `inputWait` block until a reply arrives at the indicated variable. Since no further communication will take place, as we are translating $\mathbf{0}$, the streams get closed. Notice that in this case both translations are almost identical. Obvious differences will arise if we use different continuations.[10] Line 22 shows the managers for a and b, the only free names in P. Lines 23–29 show how the processes are interconnected.

[10] Notice that in this setting continuations are not part of the formal arguments.

The strategy given by

$$\Psi = \{output(3, V_1, V_2, V_3, V_4), input(2, V_5, V_6) \mid \forall\, V_j \in \mathcal{V},\ 1 \leq j \leq 6\}$$

$$\Lambda = \{A3_i, A3_o, B_i, B_o, A4_i, A4_o\}$$

$$\mathfrak{p}(C) = \begin{cases} \{Y, A_i'\} & \text{if } C \text{ is the clause in line 7} \\ \emptyset & \text{otherwise} \end{cases}$$

induces a computation that characterizes the reduction

$$a(x) \,.\, \mathbf{0} \mid \overline{a}\, b \mid a(y) \,.\, \mathbf{0} \longrightarrow a(x) \,.\, \mathbf{0} \mid \mathbf{0}$$

That is, reducing the goal in Figure 2 lines 15–18, we obtain the resolvent

$$merge1(A1_o, V_2), merge1(A1_i, V_1), match(V_1, V_2),$$
$$input(1, A1_i, A1_o), true$$

for some variables V_1, V_2. It can be seen that this resolvent is equivalent, by our transformation rules (Definition 17), to

$$man(A1_i, A1_o), input(1, A1_i, A1_o), true$$

which is the goal generated by encoding $a(x) \,.\, \mathbf{0} \mid \mathbf{0}$.

5. Correctness

We elaborate on the arguments for stating the correctness of the encoding. To this end we follow some of the criteria given in [9]. As a starter, the next result says that the translation of a π_a process does not change drastically under substitution of names [9, Property 2: Name Invariance].

PROPOSITION 1 (Name Invariance). *For any $P \in \pi_a$ and injective name substitution σ: $\{\!\!\{P\sigma\}\!\!\}$ and $\{\!\!\{P\}\!\!\}\sigma$ are variants of each other.*

5.1 Compositionality

The uniformity criteria [20, Remark 6.1] demand a compositional (homomorphical) mapping of the parallel operator, i.e. $[\![P \mid Q]\!] = [\![P]\!] \mid [\![Q]\!]$. Our encodings depend crucially on the introduction of channel managers and thus violate this principle, that is $[\![P \mid Q]\!] = [\![P]\!], G, [\![Q]\!]$ where G comprises managers and other atoms.

Some views in the literature suggest that the uniformity condition is perhaps too strong a requirement for practical purposes. A relaxed notion of compositionality is formulated by [9], requiring that $[\![P \mid Q]\!] = C[\, [\![P]\!], [\![Q]\!]\,]$ where $C[\cdot,\cdot]$ is a context depending on some program construct. This perception of compositionality allow us to justify the existence of managers. However, we still need some techniques to reason about processes in the presence of managers.

5.2 Structural Congruence & Program Transformation

We verify the structural congruence laws given in Table 2. Such a syntactic manipulation on processes corresponds in a certain sense to *program transformation* in (concurrent) logic programming. In order to talk about this correspondence in a precise fashion, we present a set of transformation rules which remind those found in [23, 34].

DEFINITION 17 (Transformation Rules). *Consider a Flat GHC program K. A sequence of programs $K = K^{(0)}, K^{(1)}, \ldots, K^{(k)}$, for some $k \geq 0$, may be obtained by application of the following rules.*

(UNFOLD) *Let $K^{(k)} = K' \cup C \cup D$ where $C = H \leftarrow \overline{G} \mid \overline{B} \uplus A$, and $D = H_D \leftarrow \overline{B_D}$, such that the guard $\overline{G}$ contain no unification atoms, A is a user-defined atom, and D is a candidate clause for A (see Definition 2 (OS-2)) with $\theta = mgu(H_D, A)$. We define a new clause $C' = H \leftarrow \overline{G} \mid$*

$\overline{B} \cup \overline{B_D}\theta$. *Thus, we obtain a transformed program* $K^{(k+1)} = K' \cup C' \cup D$.

(FOLD) *Let* $K^{(k)} = K' \uplus C \uplus D$ *such that* $C = H \leftarrow \overline{G} \mid \overline{F} \uplus \overline{B}$, *and* $D = H_D \leftarrow \overline{B_D}$, *such that the guard* $\overline{G}$ *contain no unification atoms and* $var(H_D) \subseteq var(B_D)$. *Assume the existence of an atom* A *and a substitution* θ *satisfying*
- (F-1) C *is a variant of* $H \leftarrow \overline{G} \mid \overline{F} \cup \overline{B_D}\theta$
- (F-2) $A = H_D\theta$,
- (F-3) *for any clause* $E = (H_E \leftarrow \overline{G_E} \mid \overline{B_E}) \in K' \uplus C$: $mgu(H_E, A) = fail$,
- (F-4) *for any variable* $X \in var(D) \setminus var(H_D)$:
  - $X\theta \in \mathcal{V}$ *and* $X\theta \notin var(H) \cup var(G) \cup var(F)$,
  - $X\theta \notin var(Y\theta)$, *for any* $Y \in \mathcal{V}$ *such that* $Y \in var(B_D)$ *and* $Y \neq X$.

We obtain a derived clause $C' = H \leftarrow \overline{G} \mid \overline{F} \cup A$, *and a new program of the form* $K^{(k+1)} = K' \cup C' \cup D$.

(INTRO) *A program* $K^{(k+1)}$ *is obtained from* $K^{(k)}$ *by adding to the latter a clause of the form* $p(\overline{t}) \leftarrow G \mid B$ *precisely when the predicate symbol* p *does not occur in* $K^{(k)}$ *and all predicate symbols occurring in* B *occur also in* $K^{(k)}$.

(ELIM) *A program* $K^{(k+1)}$ *is obtained from* $K^{(k)}$ *by removing from the latter a clause of the form* $p(\overline{t}) \leftarrow G \mid B$ *precisely when, for any user-defined atom* A *occurring in the body of any clause in* $K^{(k)}$, $mgu(p(\overline{t}), A) = fail$.

DEFINITION 18 (Extended Transformation Rules). *Consider a system* $(G, K, \Gamma) \in \wp\mathcal{A} \times \wp\mathcal{K} \times \mathcal{E}$. *A sequence of systems* $(G, K, \Gamma) = (G^{(0)}, K^{(0)}, \Gamma), (G^{(1)}, K^{(1)}, \Gamma), \ldots, (G^{(k)}, K^{(k)}, \Gamma)$, *for some* $k \geq 0$, *may be obtained by*[11]

- *Transforming* $K^{(k)}$ *through any rule in Def. 17 into* $K^{(k+1)}$, *with* $G^{(k+1)} = G^{(k)}$.
- *Unfolding/folding* $G^{(k)}$, *with respect to any clause in* $K^{(k)}$, *to get* $G^{(k+1)}$, *with* $K^{(k+1)} = K^{(k)}$.

However, since unfolding $G^{(k)}$ *may compromise the scope of some local variables we require a number of ensuing folding steps in order to restore the original scope. For* $S, S' \in \wp\mathcal{A} \times \wp\mathcal{K} \times \mathcal{E}$, *we will write* $S \equiv_{\mathfrak{T}} S'$ *when* S *can be transformed into* S', *and viceversa, using the above extended transformation rules and ensuring scope preservation.*

PROPOSITION 2 (Struct. Cong. Preservation). *For any* $P, Q \in \pi_a$: $P \equiv Q$ *implies* $\{\![P]\!\} \equiv_{\mathfrak{T}} \{\![Q]\!\}$.

5.3 Operational Correspondence

We demonstrate how our translation characterizes the π_a reduction relation, Table 2, through Flat GHC operational semantics, Def. 2. The approach revolves around the idea of a *search strategy* which is nothing more than a formal way to choose suitable atoms in a goal to be reduced according to some criteria. For instance we could reduce the atoms corresponding to a particular π_a sub-expression or give priority to atoms of a particular channel manager. Our motivation is two fold: on the one hand we set the stage to make and prove a statement, see Theorem 1; on the other hand this strategy serves us to materialize our enconding in an implementation, see Section 7.

The search strategy is based on the following selection rule. To keep the exposition simple, we assume some mechanism for establishing a set of *preferred atoms* Ψ and a set of *watch variables* Λ.

[11] Strictly speaking, this is considered in the literature as a *partial evaluation* technique [23].

DEFINITION 19 (Atom Selection Rule). *Let* G *be a goal,* Ψ *a set of atoms and* Λ *a set of variables. We define the function* $\mathsf{Sel} : \wp\mathcal{A} \times \wp\mathcal{A} \times \wp\mathcal{V} \rightarrow \wp\mathcal{A}$, *s.t.* $\mathsf{Sel}(G, \Psi, \Lambda) \subseteq G$, *as shown in algorithm 1.*

let $G' = \{A \in G \mid var(A) \cap \Lambda \neq \emptyset\}$;
if $G' \neq \emptyset$ **then**
  if $G' \cap \mathfrak{Na}(G) \neq \emptyset$ **then** $\mathsf{Sel}(G, \Psi, \Lambda) = G' \cap \mathfrak{Na}(G)$
  else $\mathsf{Sel}(G, \Psi, \Lambda) = G'$
else
  if $G \cap \Psi \neq \emptyset$ **then**
    $\mathsf{Sel}(G, \Psi, \Lambda) = G \cap \Psi$
  else
    $\mathsf{Sel}(G, \Psi, \Lambda) = G \cap \mathbb{M}$, where $\mathbb{M} =$;
    $\{\, match([\,],[\,]) \,\} \;\cup\; \{\, V \approx [\,],\, merge1([\,], V) \mid \forall V \in \mathcal{V} \,\} \;\cup$;
    $\{\, merge2(t_1, t_2, V) \mid \forall V \in \mathcal{V}, t_1, t_2 \in \mathcal{T} : \bigvee_{j=1}^{2} (t_j = [\,]) \,\} \;\cup$;
    $\{\, merge3(t_1, t_2, t_3, V) \mid \forall V \in \mathcal{V}, t_1, t_2, t_3 \in \mathcal{T} : \bigvee_{j=1}^{3} (t_j = [\,]) \,\}$
  end
end

Algorithm 1: Atom selection rule.

The following functions determine which variables and atoms should be tracked down during reduction.

DEFINITION 20 (Watch Policy). *Consider a program* K, *an atom* A *and sets* Ψ *and* Λ *as above. Further, consider a function* $\mathfrak{p} : K \rightarrow \wp\mathcal{V}$ *such that* $\mathfrak{p}(C) \subseteq var(C)$, *for any* $C \in K$. *The functions* $\mathsf{watch\_vars}(\cdot\,,\cdot)_{\Psi,\Lambda,\mathfrak{p}} : \mathcal{A} \times \wp\mathcal{K} \rightarrow \wp\mathcal{V}$ *and* $\mathsf{watch\_atoms}(\cdot\,,\cdot)_{\Psi,\Lambda,\mathfrak{p}} : \mathcal{A} \times \wp\mathcal{K} \rightarrow \wp\mathcal{A}$ *are defined as follows.*

(WP-1) *If* A *is a built-in atom and there exists* θ *as specified in Definition 2* (OS-1), *then* $\mathsf{watch\_atoms}(A, K)_{\Psi,\Lambda,\mathfrak{p}} = \Psi$ *and* $\mathsf{watch\_vars}(A, K)_{\Psi,\Lambda,\mathfrak{p}} = \{V \in \Lambda \mid V\theta = V\} \setminus \{V_1, V_2 \in \Lambda \mid \exists\, V \in dom(\theta) : V\theta = react(V_1, V_2)\}$.

(WP-2) *If* A *is a user-defined atom and* $C = H \leftarrow G \mid B$ *is the candidate clause chosen for reduction, with substitutions* θ *and* η *as specified in Definition 2* (OS-2), *then*

$$\mathsf{watch\_vars}(A, K)_{\Psi,\Lambda,\mathfrak{p}} = \Lambda \cup \mathfrak{p}(C)\theta\eta$$

and

$$\mathsf{watch\_atoms}(A, K)_{\Psi,\Lambda,\mathfrak{p}} = \{A' \in \Psi \mid mgu(A', A) = fail\}$$

We write $\mathsf{str}(\Psi, \Lambda, \mathfrak{p})$ to denote the search strategy induced by Ψ, Λ and $\mathfrak{p}$. Given a goal G and an initial strategy $\mathsf{str}(\Psi_0, \Lambda_0, \mathfrak{p})$ we obtain computations of the form

$$G = G_0 \underset{\mathsf{str}(\Psi_0,\Lambda_0,\mathfrak{p})}{\longrightarrow} G_1 \underset{\mathsf{str}(\Psi_1,\Lambda_1,\mathfrak{p})}{\longrightarrow} \cdots \underset{\mathsf{str}(\Psi_n,\Lambda_n,\mathfrak{p})}{\longrightarrow} G_{n+1}$$

such that for each goal or resolvent G_j: an atom $A \in \mathsf{Sel}(G_j, \Psi_j, \Lambda_j)$ is chosen for reduction; $\Psi_{j+1} = \mathsf{watch\_atoms}(A, K)_{\Psi_j,\Lambda_j,\mathfrak{p}}$ and $\Lambda_{j+1} = \mathsf{watch\_vars}(A, K)_{\Psi_j,\Lambda_j,\mathfrak{p}}$.

REMARK 3 (Intuition behind Theorem 1). *Any reduction* $P \longrightarrow P'$ *of* π_a *processes is justified by a proof according to the rules in Table 2 which finishes with an instance of* COM (RCOM). *In order to mimic such a proof, we exhibit a partial computation driven by a strategy in which we specify suitable atoms to be reduced, namely, those related to the output and input in* COM (RCOM), *or those having occurrences of variables of interest.*

THEOREM 1 (Op. Correspondence: Completeness). *Let* $P, P' \in \pi_a$. *A reduction* $P \longrightarrow P'$ *implies* $\langle \mathscr{G}\{\![P]\!\}; \sigma\rangle \xrightarrow{\mathfrak{React}} \langle G; \sigma'\rangle$

such that $(G, \mathscr{K}\{\![P]\!\}, \mathscr{E}\{\![P]\!\}) \equiv_{\mathfrak{T}} \{\![P']\!\}$ *for some strategy* $\mathsf{str}(\Psi, \Lambda, \mathfrak{p})$.

REMARK 4 (Corresponds relation). *The following relation captures the idea that the encoding of input or output particles is either contained in a given goal or it can be introduced by reducing a number of* $restriction(\ldots)$ *atoms, which establish an appropriate 'scoping', or the induced requests are being processed, i.e. forwarded to the manager.*

DEFINITION 21 (Correspondence). *Consider*

$$P = \nu\, u_1 \ldots \nu\, u_k\, (\Pi_{i \in I}\, \overline{w_i}\, z_i \mid \Pi_{j \in J}\, c_j(x_j).Q_j \mid \Pi_{l \in L}\, !d_l(y_l).R_l)$$

and a goal G *and a program* K. *Further, consider atoms* $A_i = output(i, \overline{\mathcal{W}}, Z_{i,1}, Z_{i,2})$, $A_j = input(j, \overline{\mathcal{X}_j}, C_{j,1}, C_{j,2})$, $A_l = replication(l, \overline{\mathcal{Y}_l}, D_{l,1}, D_{l,2})$ *which are instances of* $\mathscr{G}\,[\![\overline{w_i}\, z_i]\!]_i$, $\mathscr{G}\,[\![c_j(x_j) \,.\, Q_j]\!]_j$, *and* $\mathscr{G}\,[\![!d_l(y_l) \,.\, R_l]\!]_l$, *respectively. We relate* G *to each output, input and replicated input in* P *by means of the 'corresponds' relation* $\blacktriangleright_P \subseteq \wp\mathcal{A} \times \pi_{\mathrm{a}}$ *given as follows.*

- $G \blacktriangleright_P \overline{w_i}\, z_i$ *if (1).* $A_i \in G$, *or (2).* $\exists\, A : A \in \mathfrak{Na}(G) \vee A = man(t_1, t_2) \in G \vee A = match(t_1, t_2) \in G$ *such that* $out(Z_{i,1}, Z_{i,2})$ *is a subterm of* A.
- $G \blacktriangleright_P c_j(x_j) \,.\, Q_j$ *if (1).* $A_j \in G$, *or (2).* $\exists\, A : A \in \mathfrak{Na}(G) \vee A = man(t_1, t_2) \in G \vee A = match(t_1, t_2) \in G$ *such that* $in(X_j)$ *is a subterm of* A *and* G *contains the atom* $inputWait(j, \overline{\mathcal{X}_j}, \_, C_{j,2}, X_j)$. *(Similarly for replicated inputs)*
- $G \blacktriangleright_P R$, *where* R *is any of* $\overline{w_i}\, z_i$, $c_j(x_j) \,.\, Q_j$ *or* $!d_l(y_l) \,.\, R_l$, *if* $restriction(n, \overline{\mathcal{X}}) \in G$, $n \in \{1, \ldots, k\}$, *and there are clauses* $restriction(\ell, \overline{\mathcal{X}_\ell}) \leftarrow \overline{B}, restriction(\ell + 1, \overline{\mathcal{X}_{\ell+1}})$, $restriction(k, \overline{\mathcal{X}_k}) \leftarrow \overline{A}$ *in* K, *for* $1 \leq \ell < k$, *and the atom corresponding to* R, *that is* A_i, A_j *or* A_l, *appears in* $\overline{A}$.

THEOREM 2 (Op. Correspondence: Soundness). *Let* $P \in \pi_{\mathrm{a}}$ *be in normal form and* $(G, K, \Gamma) = \{\![P]\!\}$. *Let* $s_{i,j} = \langle G_{i,j}; \sigma_{i,j} \rangle \in \mathcal{S}_{G,K}$ *such that* $s_{0,0} = \langle G, \epsilon \rangle$ *and* $P_0 = P$. *For any (possibly infinite) computation*

$$s_{0,0} \longrightarrow^{*} s_{0,k_0} \xrightarrow{\mathfrak{React}} s_{1,0} \longrightarrow^{*} s_{1,k_1} \xrightarrow{\mathfrak{React}} s_{2,0} \longrightarrow^{*} s_{2,k_2} \xrightarrow{\mathfrak{React}} s_{3,0} \longrightarrow^{*} \cdots$$

there exists a (possibly infinite) sequence of reductions

$$P_0 \longrightarrow^{*} P_0 \longrightarrow P_1 \longrightarrow^{*} P_1 \longrightarrow P_2 \longrightarrow^{*} P_2 \longrightarrow P_3 \longrightarrow^{*} \cdots$$

where each P_i *is a normal form* $\nu\, u_1 \ldots \nu\, u_{k_i}\, (O_{1_i} \mid \cdots \mid O_{n_i})$ *and the following holds.*

(1). for $0 \leq j \leq k_0$, $1_0 \leq \ell \leq n_0$: $G_{0,j} \blacktriangleright O_\ell$.

(2). for $1 \leq i$, $0 \leq j \leq k_i$, $1_i \leq \ell \leq n_i$: *either* $G_{i,j} \blacktriangleright O_\ell$ *or* $\exists\, A \in G_{i,j}$ *s.t.* $A = p(id, \overline{\mathcal{X}}, react(V_1, V_2))$ *with* $p \in \{inputWait, replicationWait\}$ *and there is a clause* $p(id, \overline{\mathcal{Y}}, Y) \leftarrow Y \approx react(X_1, X_2) \mid \overline{A}$ *in* K *and* $\mathscr{G}\,[\![O_\ell]\!] \in \overline{A}$.

6. Expressivity

Figure 3 depicts some expressivity results involving π_{a}, Flat GHC, the languages: Linear Janus [25], ask-tell with *existentially* quantified asks $CC^{\exists}$ [26], ask-tell with *universally* quantified asks $CC^{\forall}$ [21], and an asynchronous, persistent π-calculus, $P\pi_{\mathrm{a}}$, with all inputs and outputs replicated [21].

Since we use the body predicate $\approx$ as a *single assignment*, i.e. $V := t$ where $V \in \mathcal{V}$, our translation is also valid for Strand [6]. Straightforward changes in Def. 12 and in the implementation of managers and merge operators allow for the elimination of any guard atoms. This suggests that the language constructs and semantics required to encode π_{a} are simpler than what was originally expected, see Table 1.*(b)*.

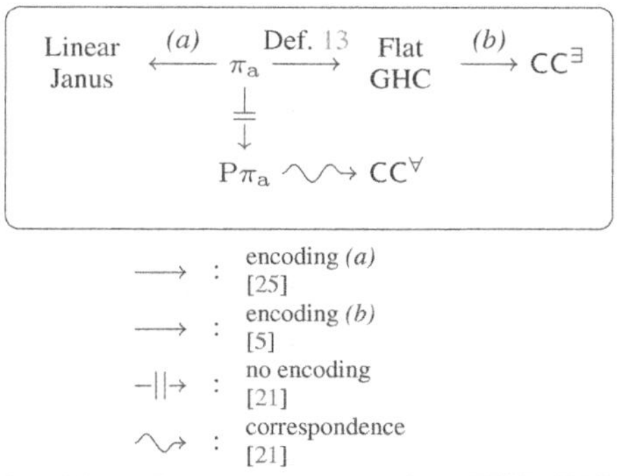

Figure 3. Expressivity hierarchy.

7. Implementation

We transform π_{a} specifications into executable programs by means of a Haskell implementation of the mappings given in Def. 12 and Def. 13. For a given π_{a} expression the Haskell output is fed to KLIC [3] to produce a C program from which we generate executable code. In order to have fine-grained control over the execution of the resulting Flat GHC programs, we have implemented in Prolog an experimental interpreter for a subset of Flat GHC. In this implementation a scheduler makes use of the atom selection rule in Def. 19 and the watch policy in Def. 20. We have observed experimentally how the translation of a π_{a} process p in both, the executable and interpreted frameworks, follows the behaviour of p.

8. Conclusions and future work

We present an encoding of the asynchronous π-calculus into Flat GHC. We show how program transformation techniques and an appropriate search strategy allow us to reason about the translation given that it does not adhere to the uniformity criteria. On the practical side we have developed some tools which, integrated with existent compilers, allow us to generate executable code from a π_{a} specification.

The expressiveness results shown in the previous section might suggest that an indirect way of achieving an analogous result could be to encode Flat GHC in some higher level language for which an encoding of π_{a} already exists (e.g. Linear Janus). However, that would shed no light on our initial motivation, i.e. to find the shortest connection between the two paradigms under study (process calculi and concurrent logic programming), exemplified by two of their simplest representatives.

The reasoning techniques presented here are at some extent non-standard. We believe that a statement showing that any computation of the translation reflects some computation of the source language — this is the essence of Theorem 2 — could be given by abstracting the state of the managers. In fact, Definition 21 goes in this direction. Our conjecture is that techniques from abstract interpretation could help in reasoning about our translation given that behavioral approaches are difficult to establish.

An open question that points to future work is the compositionality of our encoding. Our conjecture is that finding a minimal extension to Flat GHC that meets the uniformity criterion might produce a new concurrent logic language in which channel managers are nativelly supported.

Acknowledgements

The authors have been partially supported by grant S2009TIC-1465 *PROMETIDOS-CM* from Madrid Regional Government and grant TIN2009-14599-C03-03 *DESAFIOS10* from the Spanish Ministry of Science and Innovation. Rubén Monjaraz has also been supported by funds from Universidad Politécnica de Madrid.

The authors also want to thank James Gabbay and the anonymous referees for their useful comments on earlier versions of the paper.

References

[1] K. R. Apt. *From logic programming to Prolog*. Prentice-Hall, Inc., 1996. 2

[2] G. Boudol. Asynchrony and the π-calculus (note). Technical Report 1702, INRIA Sophia-Antipolis, May 1992. 1, 3

[3] T. Chikayama, T. Fujise, and D. Sekita. A portable and efficient implementation of kl1. In *PLILP '94: Proceedings of the 6th International Symposium on Programming Language Implementation and Logic Programming*, pages 25–39. Springer-Verlag, 1994. 2, 9

[4] F. S. de Boer and C. Palamidessi. On the asynchronous nature of communication in concurrent logic languages: A fully abstract model based on sequences. In J. Baeten and J. Klop, editors, *CONCUR 1990 Theories of Concurrency: Unification and Extension*, volume 458 of *LNCS*, pages 99–114. Springer-Verlag, 1990. 1, 2

[5] F. S. de Boer and C. Palamidessi. From concurrent logic programming to concurrent constraint programming. In *Advances in logic programming theory*, pages 55–113, NY, USA, 1994. Oxford University Press, Inc. 1, 2, 9

[6] I. Foster and S. Taylor. Strand: a practical parallel programming tool. In *Proc. North American Symp. on Logic Programming*, pages 497–512. MIT Press, 1989. 9

[7] J. H. Gallier. *Logic for Computer Science: Foundations of Automatic Theorem Proving*. Revised on-line version `http://www.cis.upenn.edu/~jean/gbooks/logic.html`, 2003. 4

[8] J.-Y. Girard. Linear logic. *Theoretical Computer Science*, 50(1):1–102, 1987. 1

[9] D. Gorla. Towards a unified approach to encodability and separation results for process calculi. In *CONCUR 2008 - Concurrency Theory*, volume 5201 of *LNCS*, pages 492–507. Springer-Verlag, 2008. 1, 2, 7

[10] K. Hirata. π-calculus semantics of Moded Flat GHC. Technical Report ISRL-95-3, NTT Basic Research Laboratories, 1995. 1

[11] K. Honda and M. Tokoro. An object calculus for asynchronous communication. In *ECOOP '91: Proc. of the European Conference on Object-Oriented Programming*, pages 133–147. Springer-Verlag, 1991. 1, 3

[12] F. Knabe. A distributed protocol for channel-based communication with choice. *Computers and Artificial Intelligence*, 12(5):475–490, 1993. 2, 3

[13] L. Leth and B. Thomsen. Some facile chemistry. *Formal Aspects of Computing*, 7(3):314–328, 1995. 2, 3

[14] J. W. Lloyd. *Foundations of logic programming*. Springer-Verlag New York, Inc., New York, NY, USA, 1984. 2

[15] R. Milner. *Communication and concurrency*. Prentice-Hall, 1989. 2

[16] R. Milner. *Communicating and Mobile Systems*. Cambridge University Press, 1999. 1, 3

[17] R. Monjaraz. From the π-calculus to Flat GHC. Master's thesis, Facultad de Informática, Universidad Politécnica de Madrid, Spain, 2010. 2

[18] U. Nestmann. What is a "good" encoding of guarded choice? *Inf. Comput.*, 156(1-2):287–319, 2000. 1, 3

[19] U. Nestmann and B. C. Pierce. Decoding choice encodings. In *CONCUR 1996: Concurrency Theory*, number 119 in LNCS, pages 179–194. Springer-Verlag, 1996. 3

[20] C. Palamidessi. Comparing the expressive power of the synchronous and asynchronous π-calculi. *Mathematical. Structures in Comp. Sci.*, 13(5):685–719, 2003. 1, 7

[21] C. Palamidessi, V. Saraswat, F. D. Valencia, and B. Victor. On the expressiveness of linearity vs persistence in the asynchronous π-calculus. In *LICS '06: Proceedings of the 21st Annual IEEE Symposium on Logic in Computer Science*, pages 59–68. IEEE Computer Society, 2006. 1, 9

[22] J. Parrow. An introduction to the π-calculus. In J. Bergstra, A. Ponse, and S. Smolka, editors, *Handbook of Process Algebra*, pages 479–543. Elsevier, 2001. 1

[23] A. Pettorossi and M. Proietti. Transformation of logic programs. In C. J. Hogger, D. M. Gabbay, and J. A. Robinson, editors, *Handbook of Logic in Artificial Intelligence and Logic Programming*, volume 5, pages 697–787. Oxford University Press, 1998. 7, 8

[24] D. Sangiorgi and D. Walker. *The π-calculus: A theory of mobile processes*. Cambridge University Press, 2001. 3

[25] V. Saraswat and P. Lincoln. Higher-order, linear, concurrent constraint programming. Technical report, Xerox PARC, 1992. 1, 9

[26] V. A. Saraswat. *Concurrent Constraint Programming*. The MIT Press, 1993. 1, 9

[27] E. Shapiro. The family of concurrent logic programming languages. *ACM Comput. Surv.*, 21(3):413–510, 1989. 2, 4

[28] E. Shapiro and C. Mierowsky. Fair, biased, and self-balancing merge operators: Their specification and implementation in Concurrent Prolog. In *Concurrent Prolog: collected papers*, volume 1, pages 392–413, Cambridge, MA, USA, 1987. MIT Press. 2, 4

[29] P. Thati, K. Sen, and N. Martí-Oliet. An executable specification of asynchronous pi-calculus semantics and may testing in Maude 2.0. *Electronic Notes in Theoretical Computer Science*, 71:261–281, 2004. WRLA 2002, Rewriting Logic and Its Applications. 2

[30] E. Tick. *Parallel logic programming*. MIT Press, Cambridge, MA, USA, 1991. 2

[31] K. Ueda. Guarded horn clauses. In E. Wada, editor, *Proc. Logic Programming '85*, volume 221 of *LNCS*, pages 168–179. Springer-Verlag, 1986. 1, 2

[32] K. Ueda. Resource-passing concurrent programming. In N. Kobayashi and B. C. Pierce, editors, *Theoretical Aspects of Computer Software 2001*, volume 2215 of *LNCS*, pages 95–126. Springer-Verlag, 2001. 1

[33] K. Ueda. Constraint-based concurrency and beyond. In L. Aceto and A. Gordon, editors, *Algebraic Process Calculi: The First Twenty Five Years and Beyond*, number NS–05–3 in BRICS Notes Series, pages 168–179. BRICS, Department of Computer Science, University of Aarhus, 2005. 1

[34] K. Ueda and K. Furukawa. Transformation rules for GHC programs. In *Proc. of the Int'l Conf. on Fifth Generation Computer Systems 1988, Tokyo, Japan*, pages 582–591. Springer-Verlag, 1988. 7

[35] B. Victor and J. Parrow. Constraints as processes. In U. Montanari and V. Sassone, editors, *Proc. of CONCUR 1996*, volume 1119 of *LNCS*, pages 389–405. Springer-Verlag, 1996. 1

[36] P. Viry. A rewriting implementation of pi-calculus. Technical report, University of Pisa, 1996. 2

[37] P. Yang, C. R. Ramakrishnan, and S. A. Smolka. A logical encoding of the π-calculus: Model checking mobile processes using tabled resolution. In *VMCAI 2003: Proceedings of the 4th International Conference on Verification, Model Checking, and Abstract Interpretation*, volume 2575 of *LNCS*, pages 116–131. Springer-Verlag, 2003. 2

Compiling CHR to Parallel Hardware

Andrea Triossi
DAIS, Università Ca' Foscari Venezia, Italy
triossi@unive.it

Salvatore Orlando
DAIS, Università Ca' Foscari Venezia, Italy
orlando@unive.it

Alessandra Raffaetà
DAIS, Università Ca' Foscari Venezia, Italy
raffaeta@unive.it

Thom Frühwirth
Inst. for Software Engineering and Compiler Construction, Ulm University, Germany
fruehwirth@uni-ulm.de

Abstract

This paper investigates the compilation of a committed-choice rule-based language, Constraint Handling Rules (CHR), to specialized hardware circuits. The developed hardware is able to turn the intrinsic concurrency of the language into parallelism. Rules are applied by a custom executor that handles constraints according to the best degree of parallelism the implemented CHR specification can offer. Our framework deploys the target digital circuits through the Field Programmable Gate Array (FPGA) technology, by first compiling the CHR code fragment into a low level hardware description language. We also discuss the realization of a hybrid CHR interpreter, consisting of a software component running on a general purpose processor, coupled with a hardware accelerator. The latter unburdens the processor by executing in parallel the most computational intensive CHR rules directly compiled in hardware. Finally the performance of a prototype system is evaluated by time efficiency measures.

Categories and Subject Descriptors F.4.1 [*Mathematical Logic*]: Logic and constraint programming

Keywords CHR, Parallelism, Hardware acceleration

1. Introduction

In this paper we focus on the hardware compilation of Constraint Handling Rules (CHR) [11] programs. CHR is a committed-choice rule-based language, first developed for writing constraint solvers [12, 14], and nowadays well-known as a general-purpose language [7, 16]. The plain and clear semantics of CHR makes it suitable for concurrent computation, thus allowing programs to be interpreted in a parallel computation model [10].

The hardware compilation technique presented in this paper takes advantage of these features of CHR. Given a program in a suitable subset of CHR, it generates a parallel hardware whose components are: (i) a set of parallel hardware blocks, realizing the rewriting procedures expressed by the CHR rules in the program, and (ii) a custom unit that interconnects the blocks, and concurrently enacts the rules embedded in the hardware blocks with the constraints in the store.

PPDP'12, September 19–21, 2012, Leuven, Belgium.

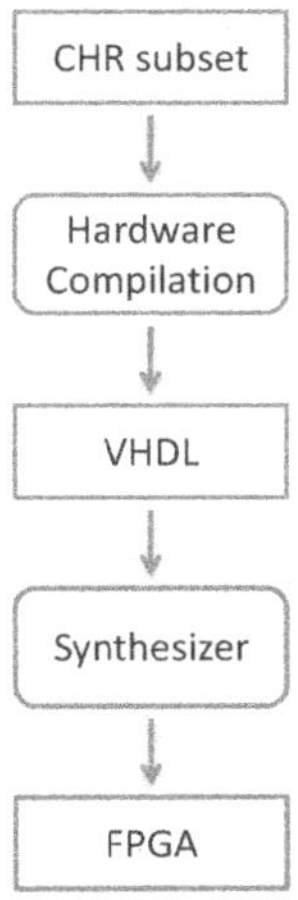

Figure 1. Hardware compilation diagram flow

More precisely, our technique to generate the final hardware digital circuit is based on an intermediate compilation phase, during which a CHR code fragment is first translated into a low level Hardware Description Language (HDL), namely VHDL [33]. From VHDL we can then easily generate synchronous digital circuits, by using automatic tools and the well known Field Programmable Gate Array (FPGA) [15] as deployment technology. Our methodology exploits the programmability features of FPGAs to generate specialized digital circuits for each specific code fragments occurring in a CHR program, in turn compiled in VHDL. The overall hardware compilation flow is depicted in Figure 1. As mentioned above the source language is a subset of CHR: this is due to the intrinsic limitations of hardware circuits, whose resources must be statically allocated. Still, the considered subset of CHR is Turing-complete [27] and it allows to provide natural solutions for several interesting problems.

Concerning the chosen hardware deployment technology, it is worth recalling that nowadays FPGAs take advantage of the growth in the number of transistors that can be integrated within a chip, and can also include more complex components, i.e., processors, memory blocks or special-purpose units. VHDL, the HDL target language of our compilation methodology, works at a very low level, i.e. very close to the Register Transfer Level (RTL). It models a synchronous digital circuit in terms of the flow of digital signals (data) between hardware registers, and the logical operations performed on those signals. The VHDL code can directly feed a vendor-specific design automation tool (the synthesizer) that through different steps produces a gate-level netlist to configure the FPGA. We could also adopt different behavioral HDLs (other than VHDL) as target languages of our hardware compilation methodology, provided that synthesizer tools to program the FPGA circuits are available for those HDLs. Finally, it is worth noting that a FPGA can be programmed multiple times, thus producing specialized circuits for different CHR code fragments at hand.

In order to overcome the limitations of a pure hardware compilation, which forces us to restrict to a subset of the CHR language, we also investigate a hybrid execution architecture for general CHR programs. It combines the custom hardware device described above with a CPU-based software interpreter. The idea is to move the heavier computational burden of a CHR program to this specialized parallel hardware (co-processor), by keeping the remaining part of the program on the main processor. Roughly, the CPU-based interpreter takes care of producing the constraints, while the custom hardware can efficiently consume or rewrite them.

In the current approach, the hardware-software partition for hybrid execution of a CHR program is established a priori by the programmer, who specifies the rules to deploy to the hardware accelerator. A wrapper function virtually encapsulates those rules. It is used as a call, which takes some constraints as input arguments. These are converted as a query for the hardware in a suitable format. The constraints resulting from the hardware execution are returned to the wrapper and made available to the software level.

We also evaluate our hardware compiling methodology in terms of performance. We prototyped the hardware specialized circuits for several significant CHR programs, and compared the execution times obtained. In most cases, we get an improvement of one (or many) order(s) of magnitude in the completion time over standard and optimized software-based CHR interpreters.

In summary, in this paper we provide the following original contributions:

- A novel technique for synthesizing behavioral hardware components starting from a subset of CHR;
- An implementation of an efficient and optimized parallel execution model of CHR by means of hardware blocks, implemented on FPGA (through an intermediate compilation into a low level VHDL language);
- The development of a custom reconfigurable hardware co-processor that significantly speeds up the execution of a CHR program.

The work is based on some preliminary results that appeared in informal workshop proceedings [30, 31].

The paper is organized as follows. An overview of the CHR language and of the FPGA architecture is presented respectively in Sections 2 and 3. In Section 4 we focus on the technique adopted for generating hardware blocks from CHR rules and in Section 5 we show how to efficiently accommodate in hardware parallel rules execution. In Section 6 we illustrate how the FPGA can fit into a complete computing architecture. Beyond a running example that drives the reader through the description of the parallelism between CHR and hardware, several complete practical examples of implementations are provided. Classical algorithms usually adopted for showing the expressiveness of CHR in multiset transformation or constraint solving, are chosen as case studies. Section 7 discusses related works and finally Section 8 draws the concluding remarks.

2. CHR overview

Constraint Handling Rules is a declarative multi-headed guarded rule-based programming language. It employs two kinds of constraints: built-in constraints, which are predefined by the host language, and CHR constraints, which are user-defined by program rules. Each constraint can have multiple arguments and its number is called arity. Null-arity built-in constraints are *true* (empty constraint) and *false* (inconsistent constraint). A CHR program is composed of a finite set of rules acting on constraints. We can distinguish two kinds of rules:

$$\text{Simplification:}\quad Name \ @\ H \Leftrightarrow G \mid B$$
$$\text{Propagation:}\quad Name \ @\ H \Rightarrow G \mid B$$

Where $Name$ is an optional unique identifier of the rule, H (*head*) is a non-empty conjunction of CHR constraints, G (*guard*) is an optional conjunction of built-in constraints, and B (*body*) is the goal, a conjunction of built-in and CHR constraints. These rules logically relate head and body provided that the guard is true. Simplification rules mean that the head is true if and only if the body is true and propagation rules mean that the body is true if the head is true. Rules are applied to an initial conjunction of constraints (*query*) until no more changes are possible. The intermediate goals of a computation are stored in the so called *constraint store*. During the computation if a simplification rule fires the head constraints are removed from the store and they are replaced by the body constraints. If the firing rule is a propagation rule the body constraints are added to the store keeping the head constraints. A third rule called simpagation permits to perform both a simplification and propagation rule:

$$\text{Simpagation:}\quad Name \ @\ H_1 \backslash H_2 \Leftrightarrow G \mid B$$

This rule means that the first part of the head (H_1) is kept while the second is removed from the constraint store. Simplification and propagation rules are special cases of simpagation when either H_1 or H_2, respectively, are empty.

EXAMPLE 1. *We use, as a running example, the program below which computes the greatest common divisor (gcd) of a set of integers using Euclid's algorithm.*

```
R0 @  gcd(N) <=> N = 0 | true.
R1 @  gcd(N) \ gcd(M) <=> M>=N | Z is M-N, gcd(Z).
```

Starting from a ground query `gcd(n1),...,gcd(nk)` *the program computes the gcd of* $n_1, \ldots, n_k$. *Rule* `R0` *states that the constraint* `gcd` *with the argument equal to zero can be removed from the store, while* `R1` *states that if two constraints* `gcd(N)` *and* `gcd(M)` *are present, the latter can be replaced with* `gcd(M-N)` *if* `M>=N`.

A central property of CHR is *monotonicity*: if a rule can fire in a given state then the same firing is possible in a state including some additional constraints. In symbols, for conjunctions of constraints A, B and E:

$$\frac{A \longmapsto B}{A \wedge E \longmapsto B \wedge E} \qquad (1)$$

A direct consequence is the *online* property, i.e., the fact that constraints can be added incrementally during the execution of a program. In fact, monotonicity implies that a final state reached after an execution with an incremental addition of constraints could have been equivalently obtained by having all constraints since the beginning.

Monotonicity is also at the basis of the parallelism of CHR [10]. In fact, it implies that rules operating on disjoint parts of the constraint store can be safely fired in parallel. This property is referred as *weak parallelism*. Formally, if A, B, C and D are conjunctions of constraints:

$$\frac{A \longmapsto B \quad C \longmapsto D}{A \wedge C \longmapsto B \wedge D} \tag{2}$$

Weak parallelism cannot be applied to rules that operate on non disjoint sets of constraints. *Strong parallelism*, instead, allows for the parallel execution of rules operating on some common constraints provided that they do not modify them. In symbols:

$$\frac{A \wedge E \longmapsto B \wedge E \qquad C \wedge E \longmapsto D \wedge E}{A \wedge E \wedge C \longmapsto B \wedge E \wedge D} \tag{3}$$

3. FPGA overview

FPGAs are instances of reconfigurable computing, i.e. computer architectures able to merge the flexibility of software with the performance of hardware, using as processing element high speed configurable hardware fabric [15].

FPGAs are devices containing programmable interconnections between logic components, called *logic blocks*, that can be programmed to perform complex combinational functions. In most FPGAs the logic blocks contain memory elements like simple flip-flops or complete blocks of memory. FPGAs can also host hardware components like embedded hard microprocessors or IP (Intellectual Property) cores that use the logic blocks themselves to realize predefined structures like soft microprocessor cores, i.e., real CPUs entirely implemented using logic synthesis.

The architecture of an FPGA is model and vendor dependent, but in most cases it consists of a bi-dimensional array of configuration logic blocks (CLBs), I/O pads, and routing channels. CLBs are made of few logic cells commonly called *slices*. Each of them consists of some n-bit lookup tables (LUT), full adders (FAs) and D-type flip-flops. The n-bit LUT realizes the combinatorial part of the circuit: it can encode any n-input Boolean function by a truth table model. The FA is used when there is the need to perform arithmetic functions, otherwise it can be bypassed by a multiplexer. Likewise the final D flip-flop can be skipped if we wish an asynchronous output.

The FPGA programmer usually begins the design flow by describing the behavior of the desired hardware in a HDL. The HDLs commonly adopted by the hardware engineers are VHDL [33] (used in all the implementations proposed in this paper) and Verilog [32]. HDL code can directly feed a vendor-specific design automation tool (called *synthesizer*) that through different steps generates a technology-mapped netlist used to configure each CLB. Since each FPGA differs from design architecture, a dedicated process, named place-and-route, takes care of choosing which CLBs need to be employed and how to physically connect them. Before the actual implementation in hardware, the programmer can validate the map via timing analysis, simulation, and other verification methodologies. The final result of the design flow is then a bitstream file that can be transferred via a serial interface to the FPGA or to an external memory device charged to deploy it at every boot of the FPGA.

The key factor that brought FPGAs to success is their programmability. Such a feature guarantees a very short time to production which can easily explain why they quickly emerged as a way for generating effective and low cost hardware prototypes. However, nowadays FPGAs are not only used for prototyping, but, due to the decreasing cost per gate, they are employed as a principal component in many digital hardware designs.

4. Compilation to hardware

Here we discuss the main ideas behind our CHR-based hardware specification approach. First, we investigate the features of CHR that could hamper the hardware synthesis, then we address the correspondence between CHR rules and hardware and finally we describe how to reproduce in hardware the execution from the query to the result. As depicted in Figure 1, the complete compilation flow starts from a subset of CHR and goes to an implementation on FPGA passing through the low level VHDL language. Part of the produced VHDL code from the running example is reported in Appendix A.

4.1 The CHR subset

Since the hardware resources can be allocated only at compile time (dynamic allocation is not allowed in hardware due to physical bounds), we need to know the largest number of constraints that must be kept in the constraint store during the computation. In order to establish an upper bound to the growth of constraints, we consider a subset of CHR, which does not include propagation rules. Programs are composed of simpagation rules of the form:

$$\begin{array}{ll} rule@ & c_1(\overline{X_1}), \ldots, c_p(\overline{X_p}) \backslash c_{p+1}(\overline{X_{p+1}}), \ldots, c_n(\overline{X_n}) \Leftrightarrow \\ & g(\overline{X_1}, \ldots, \overline{X_n}) \mid \\ & Z_1 \; is \; f_1(\overline{X_1}, \ldots, \overline{X_n}), \ldots, Z_m \; is \; f_m(\overline{X_1}, \ldots, \overline{X_n}), \\ & c_{i_1}(\overline{Z}), \ldots, c_{i_m}(\overline{Z}). \end{array} \tag{4}$$

where $\overline{X_i}$ $(i \in \{1, \ldots, n\})$ can be a set of variables, $\overline{Z} = Z_1, \ldots, Z_m$ and the number of body constraints is less than or equal to the number of constraints removed from the head $(m \leq n - p)$ and no new type of constraints is introduced: $\{i_1, \ldots, i_m\} \subseteq \{p + 1, \ldots, n\}$. In this way, the number of constraints cannot increase and the constraint store size is bounded by the width of the initial query.

Additionally, we will consider only computations starting from a ground goal. Note that, since the variables in the body of a rule are included in those occurring in the head, this implies that all constraints generated during the computations will be ground, a fact which will make possible the translation into hardware.

It is worth recalling that the CHR subset identified by the above conditions is still Turing-complete. This follows from [27], where several subclasses of CHR are shown to be Turing-complete. In particular it is shown that RAM machines can be simulated by CHR programs including only simpagation rules, without free variables and which do not increase the number of constraints (provided that the host language arithmetic is available).

4.2 Design of the hardware blocks

The framework we propose logically consists of two parts: (i) Several hardware blocks representing the rewriting procedure expressed by the program rules; (ii) an interconnection scheme among the blocks specific for a particular query. The first one is the hardware needed to implement the concurrent processes expressed by the CHR rules of the program, while the second one is intended for reproducing the query/solution mechanism typical of constraint programming.

The proposed hardware design scheme is outlined in Figure 2. A Program Hardware Block (PHB) is a collection of Rule Hardware Blocks (RHBs), each corresponding to a rule of the CHR program. Constraints are encoded as hardware signals and their arguments as the values that signals can assume. The initial query is directly placed in the constraint store from which several instances of the PHB concurrently retrieve the constraints, working on separate parts of the store. The newly computed constraints replace the input ones. A Combinatorial Switch (CS) sorts, partitions and assigns the constraints to the PHBs taking care of mixing the constraints in order to let the rules be executed on the entire store. The following paragraphs explain in detail the construction of the blocks.

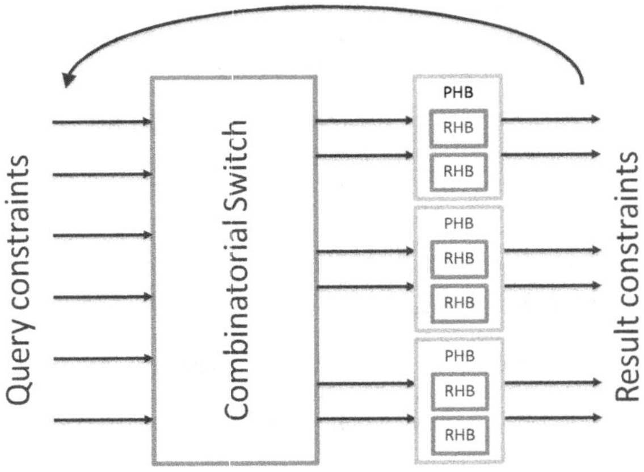

Figure 2. Hardware design scheme.

4.2.1 Rule Hardware Blocks

The RHB corresponding to the CHR rule in Eq. (4) inputs n signals that have the value of the variables $\overline{X_1} \dots \overline{X_n}$ (the arguments of the head constraints). If $\overline{X_1} \dots \overline{X_n}$ are sets of variables, we use vectors of signals (*records* in VHDL). The computational part of the RHB is given by the functions $f_1 \dots f_m$ that operate on the inputs. The resulting output signals have the value of the variables $\overline{X_1} \dots \overline{X_p}$ and $Z_1 \dots Z_m$.

We exploit *processes*, the basic VHDL concurrent statement, to translate the computational part of a rule to a sequential execution. Each rule is mapped into a single clocked *process* containing an *if* statement over the guard variables.

Since, due to constraint removals, the number of constraints can become smaller during the computation, each output signal for a given constraint is coupled with a *valid* signal. This tells to the other components whether the signal should be ignored.

EXAMPLE 2. *Figure 3 sketches the RHBs resulting from the two rules of the* `gcd` *program in Example 1. Notice that each constraint is associated with two signals: one contains the value of the variable of the constraint (solid line), and the other one models its validity (dashed line).*

The block in Figure 3(a) corresponds to Rule `R0`*. It has as input the value for variable* `N` *together with its* valid *signal. It performs a check over the guard and if the guard holds the* valid *signal is set to false whereas the value of the gcd signal is left unchanged. This simulates at the hardware level the removal of a constraint from the constraint store.*

The block in Figure 3(b) is the translation of Rule `R1`*. It has four input signals, corresponding to the values of the variables* `N` *and* `M`*, with their* valid *signals. According to the guard* `M>=N` *of* `R1`*, the inputs* `N` *and* `M` *feed a comparator that checks if the value of the second signal is greater than or equal to the first. If the condition is satisfied, the value of the second signal is replaced by* `Z = M-N`*, as computed by a subtractor, while the value of the first signal remains unchanged. If the guard does not hold, the outputs of the block coincide with the inputs. In both cases the* valid *signals remain unchanged. The computational part is carried out by the subtraction operator.*

4.2.2 Program Hardware Block

The PHB is the gluing hardware for the RHBs: it executes all the rules of the CHR program and hence it contains all the associated RHBs, with the corresponding input signals. Intuitively, for any

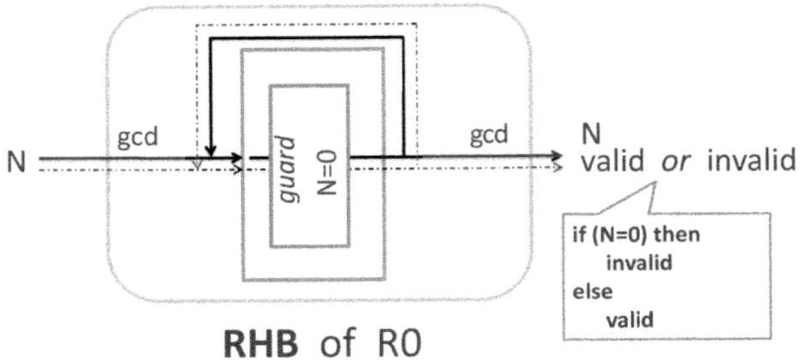

(a)

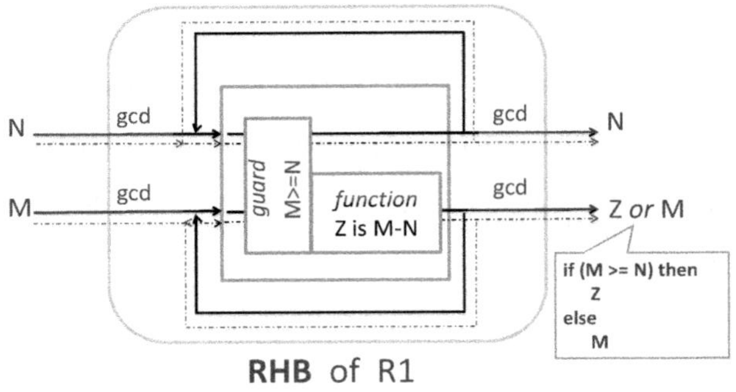

(b)

Figure 3. The Rule Hardware Blocks for the `gcd` rules.

constraint type, the PHB inputs the largest number of constraints of that type in input to the underlying RHBs. Additionally, the PHB takes as input the two global input signals *clk* and *reset* used for synchronization and initialization purposes. It provides for the *finish* control signal used to denote when the outputs are ready to be read by the following hardware blocks. The RHBs keep on applying the rules they implement until the output remains unchanged for two consecutive clock cycles.

Note that in the hardware each constraint is represented as a different signal. If the head of a rule contains more than one constraint of the same type, the corresponding signals must be considered as input in any possible order by a RHB encoding the rule. This is obtained by replicating the RHB a number of times equal to the possible permutations of the constraints of the same type.

More precisely, for the sake of simplicity, assume that there is a unique type of constraint and let k be the total number of input constraints to the PHB. For a rule whose head contains n constraints (as in the generic rule in Eq. (4)), the number of copies of RHBs needed is $k!/(k-n)!$, i.e., the number of sequences of length n over the set of k inputs. Finally there is a mechanism for ensuring that only one copy of the RHB can execute per clock cycle.

EXAMPLE 3. *Let us consider the PHB corresponding to the* `gcd` *program in Example 1. As depicted in Figure 4, it takes as input two signals corresponding to* `gcd` *constraints (the maximum between the number of inputs of* `R0` *and* `R1`*). According to the general argument above, the number of RHB instances for Rule* `R1` *is* $2 = 2!/(2-2)!$. *To see why these are required, note that when* `N` *is greater than* `M`*, the rule can fire only if fed with the constraint in reverse order, as it happens for the second copy RHB. Similarly the number of RHB instances needed for* `R0` *is* $2 = 2!/(2-1)!$.

A certain degree of parallelism for rules is set at the level of the PHB. Here, according to the notion of strong parallelism for

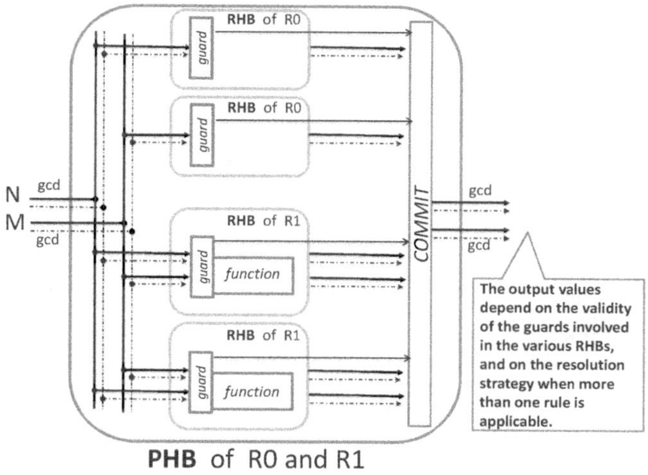

Figure 4. The Program Hardware Block for the gcd program

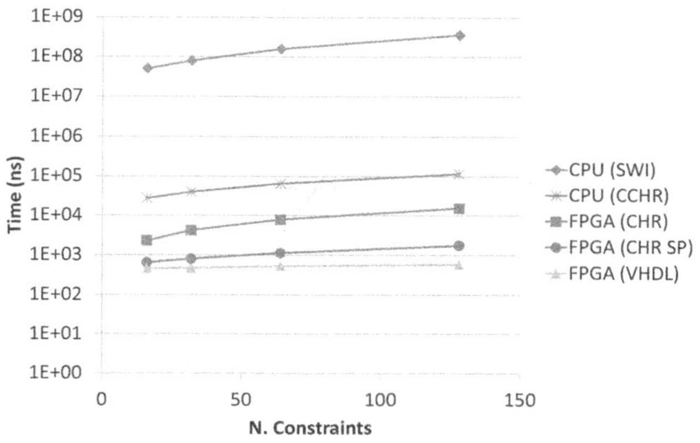

Figure 5. Gcd execution time (log scale)

CHR, introduced in Section 2, we allow for the parallel firing of rules sharing constraints which are not rewritten. Actually, all rule instances in the PHB are executed by one or more concurrent *processes* that fire synchronously at every clock cycle. Then, the commit block at the output stage selects only the outputs of a subset of rules which can fire in parallel, chosen according to some priority criteria. For instance in the PHB of the gcd example, Rule R0 cannot be executed in parallel with R1 because they could rewrite the same constraint.

4.2.3 Combinatorial Switch (CS)

A further level of parallelization is achieved by replicating the PHBs into several copies that operate on different parts of the global constraint store, according to weak parallelism as described in Section 2. PHBs can compute independently and concurrently because they operate on different constraints. Although they process data synchronously, since they share a common clock, it is not required that they terminate their computation at the same time. Indeed the CS acts as synchronization barrier letting the faster PHBs wait for the slower ones. It is also in charge to manage the communication among hardware blocks exchanging data: once all the PHBs have provided their results, it reassigns the output signals as input for other PHBs, applying first some permutation to guarantee that all the combinations will be considered.

In practice, the implementation of this interconnection element relies on a signal switch that sorts the n constraints in the query according to all the possible k-combinations on n (where k is the number of inputs to the single PHB) and connects them to the inputs of the PHBs. The maximum number of PHBs that can work in parallel on the constraint store is $\lfloor n/k \rfloor$, since, according to weak parallelism, the same signal (and hence the same constraint) cannot be fed to different PHBs at the same time.

Implementing CS as a finite state machine leads to a total number of states S equal to the number of possible combinations divided by the number of concurrent PHBs: $S = \frac{\binom{n}{k}}{\lfloor n/k \rfloor} \approx \frac{\prod_{i=1}^{k-1} n-i}{(k-1)!}$. Despite the good degree of parallelization achieved by the CS (it allows $\lfloor n/k \rfloor$ PHBs to execute in parallel), it needs a number of states $O(n^{k-1})$ in order to try all the possible combinations on the input signals. Since the time necessary for evaluating the query is proportional to the number of states, it is important to limit the number k of inputs for each PHB. This leak in performance is related to the complexity of the *search for matching problem*: a very well known issue in CHR [26] and in general in multi-headed constraint languages. An additional problem is that CS simply combines all the constraints (including the invalid ones) in all possible ways. In presence of algorithms that considerably reduce the number of constraints during computation this can be highly inefficient. In fact, constraints that have been removed by the PHBs still continue to be shuffled by the CS uselessly. In Section 5 we will discuss how to improve time complexity to space complexity's cost giving optimized structures for the CS.

4.2.4 Some experiments with gcd

Here we describe the hardware implementation of the algorithm presented in Example 1 tailored for finding the greatest common divisor of at most 128 integers. The resulting hardware design relies on 64 PHBs deriving in parallel the gcd. The CS pairs the constraints in a round robin tournament scheme where each constraint is coupled once with each other. For comparison purposes we implement the same algorithm directly in behavioral VHDL using a parallel reduction that exploits the associative property of the gcd operation. Both hardware specifications are then synthesized in a Xilinx Virtex4 FPGA (xc4vfx60) running at 100MHz. Figure 5 reports the execution times for 16, 32, 64 and 128 2-byte integers. The two FPGA implementations are labeled respectively as FPGA (CHR) and FPGA (VHDL). The curves labeled CPU (SWI) and CPU (CCHR) refer to the computational time of the CHR gcd program, compiled respectively with the K.U.Leuven CHR system of SWI Prolog [23] and the fast C-based system CCHR [35], and running on Intel Xeon 3.60GHz processor with 3GB of memory. Observe that the FPGA implementations are at least one order of magnitude faster than the software implementations (including CCHR which is claimed to be the fastest CHR implementation currently available). This is somehow expected, due to the completely different hardware nature, but still it provides an indication of the appropriateness of our approach.

Compared to the VHDL solution, the execution time can be more than an order of magnitude larger. This is primarily due to the fact that, as mentioned above, the CS does not take into account that the number of constraints can drastically decrease. An optimization addressing this issue will be discussed in Section 5.1 (the outcome of such an optimization is reported in Figure 5, labeled FPGA (CHR SP)).

The area needed for the largest gcd implementation we tried is about $2 \cdot 10^5$ LUTs corresponding to about 8% of occupation of a medium size FPGA. Finally we should notice that the resulting highest frequencies of operations are all above 250 MHz and up to 350 MHz, which is quite good for a non pipelined architecture.

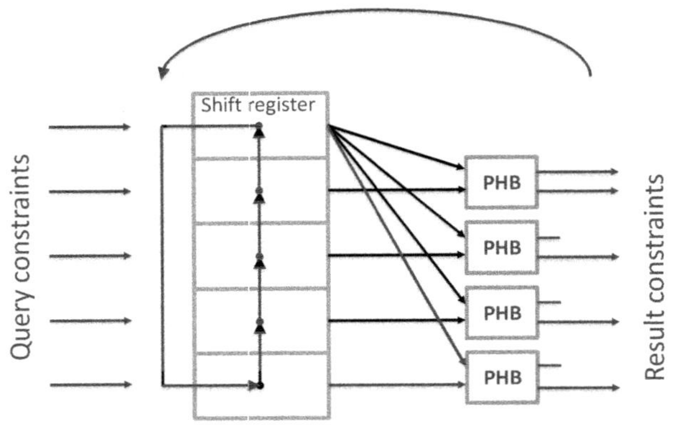

Figure 6. Optimization model for strong parallelism.

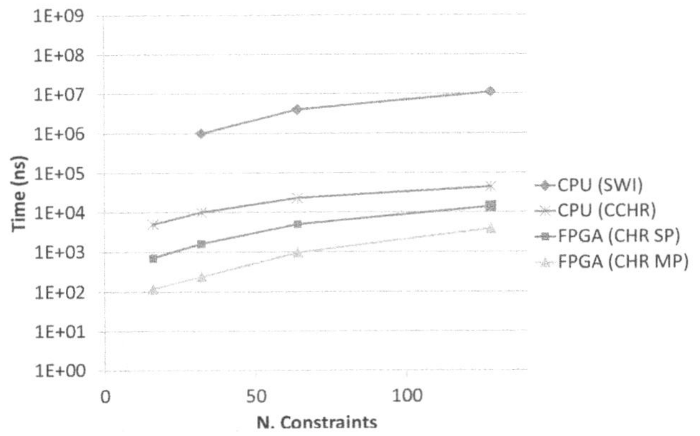

Figure 7. Prime execution time (log scale)

5. Optimizing hardware compilation

With the aim of facing the problem of time efficiency, three optimizations are proposed relying on different degrees of parallelization. In particular, in Section 5.1 we discuss how the property of strong parallelism can be further exploited with simple changes in the hardware framework. In Section 5.2 we show how the adoption of a set based semantics for CHR can enable a higher level of parallelism. Finally, in Section 5.3, the online property of CHR (see Section 2) is used for boosting the computation of a merge sort algorithm.

5.1 Strong parallelism

Here we propose an optimization which exploits the strong parallelism property of CHR also at the level of the CS. The idea consists of distinguishing between constraints that are read from those which are rewritten by the PHBs. Then, the same read constraints can be processed in parallel by all the PHBs. A hardware block, obtained as a modification of the CS used before, takes care of feeding the various PHBs instances with the same read constraints combined with different sets of rewritten constraints.

For instance, consider the `gcd` program. The PHB now contains a single instance of RHB for each Rule `R0` and `R1`. The PHB inputs a read constraint (the first input of `R1`) and a removed constraint (shared between the two rules). Note that in this case, since there is no rule duplication inside the PHB, the order of signals matters.

Figure 6 shows a possible refined CS for a five constraints query but the design can be easily adapted (with a linear growth) to a larger number of constraints. It relies on a circular shift register[1] preloaded with the query constraints and with one cell connected to all the first input (read constraint) and all the others connected to the second input (removed constraint) of each PHB. Each time the PHBs terminate their computation the new output constraints replace the old ones in the shift register and they shift until a *valid* constraint fills the first position of the register. Note that since the outputs carrying the read constraint refer to the same constraint for all PHBs, they are all left disconnected apart from the first one (see Figure 6).

Experimental results for the proposed strong parallel architecture are reported in Figure 5, labeled by FPGA (CHR SP). The reduction in execution time is relevant for all the experiments with different number of constraints, reaching up to one order of magnitude of speed up.

[1] A shift register is a cascade of registers in chain, with the data input of the first element connected to the output of the last one. An enable signal determines a circular shift of one position of the stored data.

5.2 Massive parallelism

The set-based semantics CHR^{mp} [21] relies on the idea that constraints can be considered as multiplicity independent objects so that additional copies of them can be freely used. In such a context, a duplicate removal of one constraint can be replaced by the removal of two copies of the same constraint. The degree of parallelism introduced by this change of perspective is extremely high since multiple rule instances removing or reading the same constraint can be applied concurrently (intuitively each one operates on a different copy of the constraint). The main drawback of CHR^{mp} is that it is not sound with respect to the sequential semantics when the program is not deletion-acyclic (i.e., when two distinct constraints are responsible for their mutual removal).

CHR^{mp} is particularly suited for algorithms that considerably reduce the number of constraints like the filtering ones. Consider as an example the program below that, starting from the query `prime(2), ..., prime(n)` extracts the prime numbers in the interval $[2, n]$:

```
Prime @ prime(X) \ prime(Y) <=> Y mod X = 0 | true.
```

Note that Rule `Prime` is in the CHR fragment defined by Eq. (4) as the number of `prime` constraints decreases every time the rule fires. The program is also deletion-acyclic since two integers cannot be one a proper multiple of the other. Moreover, the execution of the program can take advantage also from strong parallelism since multiple instances of the rule can use the same `prime` constraint for reading.

The idea for exploiting massive parallelism consists of providing all possible combinations of constraints (order matters) in input to distinct parallel PHB instances in a single step. This time the same constraint will be fed to several PHBs. Valid outputs are collected: a constraint is valid if no PHB has removed it. This is realized in hardware by suitable AND gates. Finally, valid outputs are used as input in the next round. The architecture thus ideally uses $\binom{n}{k}$ PHBs where n is the number of query constraints and k is the number of inputs of each PHB. In practice, physical bounds can impose to use a smaller number of PHBs, in a way that processing all possible combinations of constraints will require more than one step.

Figure 7 reports the execution time for the `Prime` program. The strong parallelism and massive parallelism optimizations are tagged as FPGA (CHR SP) and FPGA (CHR MP), respectively. The improvement determined by the massive parallelism is about an order of magnitude for queries with a low number of constraints, and it decreases with higher numbers of constraints. This is due to the fact that the physical bounds of the hardware are quickly

```
M0    @  arc(X,A) \ arc(X,B) <=> A<B | arc(A,B).
M1    @  seq(N,A), seq(N,B) <=>
                A<B | seq(N+N,A), arc(A,B).

                        ⇓

M0    @  c(0,X,A) \ c(0,X,B) <=> A<B | c(0,A,B).
M1    @  c(1,N,A), c(1,N,B) <=>
                A<B | c(1,N+N,A), c(0,A,B).
```

Figure 8. Merge sort algorithm

reached. The occupied area of the FPGA determined by a complete parallelization would increase as $\binom{n}{k}$. Even though in this case k is small ($k = 2$), we obtain a quadratic growth that is not sustainable and a partial serialization is needed.

5.3 Online optimization

In this section we illustrate the optimizations which can be allowed by the online property, working on a typical CHR program implementing the merge sort algorithm with optimal complexity [11].

The CHR program consists of the Rules `M0` and `M1` in the upper part of Figure 8. Given a ground query of the form `seq(1,n1)`, ..., `seq(1,nk)` the program returns the ordered sequence of the input numbers `n1`, ..., `nk`, represented as a chain of arcs using the constraint `arc/2`. For instance, starting from `seq(1,9)`, `seq(1,3)`, `seq(1,7)`, `seq(1,4)` the program returns the following `arc` constraints: `arc(3,4)`, `arc(4,7)`, `arc(7,9)`.

Rule `M0`, where two arcs `arc(X,A)` and `arc(X,B)` start from the same number `X`, performs their ordered merge into a chain. The arc with the smaller target is kept by the rule, while the other is replaced by an arc between `A` and `B`. The insertion in the store of such a constraint may cause a new branch in the sequence, and hence the rule keeps firing until all the branches have been removed. In order to reach the optimal complexity $O(n\ log(n))$, the chains which are merged should have the same length. Rule `M1` is responsible for the initialization of the `arc/2` constraints in order to meet such a requirement. In a constraint `seq(l,n)` the second argument `n` is one of the numbers to be ordered, while the first argument `l` represents the number of elements reachable from `n` via `arc` connections. In the initial query, since no `arc` connections exist, all constraints are of the kind `seq(1,ni)`.

The program, strictly speaking, does not belong to the CHR subset implementable in hardware. In fact, while Rule `M0` leaves unchanged the number of `arc/2` constraints, Rule `M1` reduces by one the number of `seq/2` constraints but introduces a *new* `arc/2` constraint. However, the program can be easily transformed into an equivalent one in the CHR subset of interest. Since in Rule `M1` the total number of constraints is left unchanged, it is sufficient to flatten the two types of constraints involved, i.e., `arc/2` and `seq/2`, into a single one `c/3`, with an additional argument used to encode the constraint type. The transformed program can be found in the bottom part of Figure 8.

Note that such constraint flattening is always possible using a new constraint with an arity equal to the greatest arity of the original constraints plus one.

Following the methodology described in Section 4.2, the transformed program for merge sort can be compiled into hardware. Each PHB has two inputs and two outputs and it includes four RHBs. In fact, since both Rules `M0` and `M1` have two constraints of the same type in the head, as in the running example (see in particular Example 3), two RHBs are needed for each rule. Note that the commit stage of a PHB selects the result of a single RHB since after the constraint flattening no parallelization is possible between

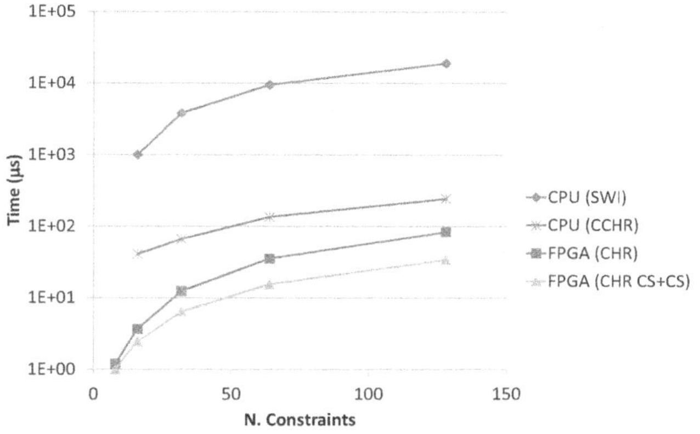

Figure 9. Merge sort execution time (log scale)

rules. The actual parallelization is performed by the CS that pairs the query constraints and assigns each couple to a different instance of the PHB. The number of instances of PHB which works in parallel on the constraint store is thus $\lfloor n/2 \rfloor$, where n is the total number of constraints in the store.

We next propose an alternative architecture, which further parallelizes rule executions by exploiting the online property of CHR. The key observation is that, relying on this property, the merging operation performed by Rule `M0` can be executed in parallel to the generation of the `arc` constraints as carried out by Rule `M1`. Hence the program can be naturally split into two parts corresponding to the two rules and some of the resulting constraints of one part can be used to populate runtime the constraint store of the second one. The `arc/2` constraints produced by Rule `M1` are consumed only by Rule `M0` while `seq/2` constraints are produced and consumed only by Rule `M1`. If we consider the two rules as separate programs joined by the `arc` production and consumption, we can design a hardware consisting of two executors linked by a one-way FIFO buffer.

The executor for each rule consists of a CS and $\lfloor n/2 \rfloor$ instances of the PHB described above, where n is the number of query constraints.

The `seq/2` query constraints are loaded in the CS of the first executor and, as new `arc/2` constraints are created (actually `c/3` constraint with the first argument equal to `0`), they are inserted in the FIFO that feeds the CS of the second executor. Such a CS at the beginning of the computation is empty, a fact which is concretely implemented by preloading the CS with constraints which are all non valid. Then, whenever a new constraint is received from the buffer it will replace one of the non valid constraints. The two CS and the FIFO should have the same dimension since, in a normal execution, all the `seq` constraints (except the last that always remains unpaired) are converted in `arc` constraints. The FIFO depth has to take into account the possibility that the second CS is not able to receive immediately the sent constraint because the receiving cell is occupied by a valid constraint.

Figure 9 shows a comparison between the execution time of the non optimized and optimized hardware implementations, labeled as FPGA(CHR) and FPGA(CHR CS + CS), respectively. The optimized implementation, when the number of elements to be ordered increases, outperforms the non-optimized one. This shows the advantage of exploiting the online property that gives the possibility of dividing the problem into two parts running in parallel. Also these experiments confirm that the FPGA implementations are much more efficient than the software ones, in SWI Prolog and CCHR.

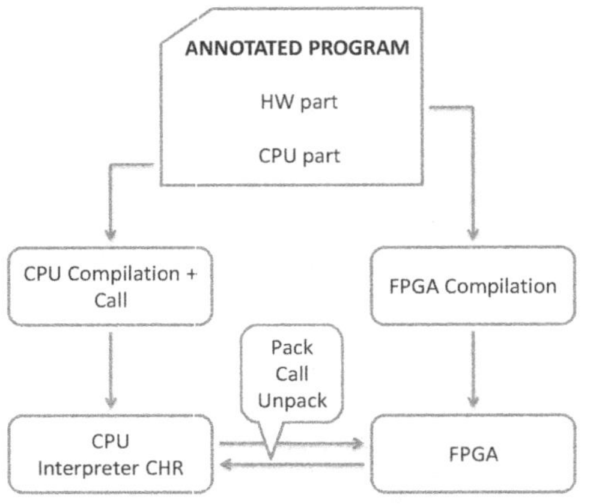

Figure 10. Hardware/software compilation diagram flow

Finally, we note that in the optimized FPGA architecture the CS of the second executor could be replaced by a shift register, like the one used in presence of strong parallelism (see Section 5.1). In fact, multiple instances of Rule `M0` can be strongly parallelized, because one constraint of the head is kept and hence can be shared among multiple rules. However experimental results shows that such a architecture does not speed up the execution at all. This is due to the fact that when the last `arc/2` constraint is generated by the first executor, the partial result of the second one approximates very closely the final result (which could be already the correct one). Thus when the last constraint is retrieved by the second executor, it has to apply just a single rule to reach the end of the execution. Hence the chosen parallelism for sorting the constraints does not matter.

6. An accelerator for CHR

In Section 4 it was shown how to synthesize hardware starting from a subset of CHR that does not allow constraint propagation. Since dynamic allocation is not permitted in hardware due to physical bounds, such a restriction might be expected for a hardware designer, but it turns out to be very restrictive for software programmer. In order to overcome this limitation, we propose a mixed (hardware/software) system where some rules, whose execution represents the heavier computational task, are executed by specialized hardware (synthesized through the aforementioned technique), while the remaining ones are executed by the main processor that can overcome the hardware limitations. The processor can easily take care of producing constraints, while the custom hardware can efficiently consume or rewrite them.

The issue of partitioning between hardware and software implementations is left to the programmer, who specifies which rules should be deployed to the hardware accelerator. A wrapper function virtually encapsulates those rules. It is used as a call, which takes some constraints as input arguments. These are converted to a query for the hardware in a suitable format. The constraints resulting from the hardware execution are given back to the wrapper and made available to the software level. The wrapper allows the programmer to access to lower level instructions (in this case a call to a hardware driver), which speed up the execution. This kind of modularity is known in the literature as hierarchical composition [8, 24] and an implementation similar to ours can be found for instance in [26].

The entire system compilation is split into two branches (see Figure 10) related to software and hardware parts. The source program is annotated by the programmer who specifies the rules that have to be executed by the hardware accelerator. The hardware compilation is performed according to the method in Section 4.2 which results in a bit stream directly deployable on an FPGA. On the other hand the standard software compilation will be necessarily altered to deal with the hardware realization of some rules of the program. Since our implementation relies on a CHR system that adopts Prolog as *host language*, the execution of the hardware implemented rules will be embedded in a custom made built-in foreign Prolog predicate (the wrapper). When it is called, all the constraints needed by the hardware are sent to the accelerator, which will return the resulting constraints back to the constraint store.

GCD matrix calculation. As a first case study, let us consider a program that, given a set of integers, computes the gcd of all the pairs of inputs. To this end it builds a bi-dimensional triangular upper matrix whose elements will contain the gcd of all pairs of integers belonging to the set. The query is formulated using the constraint `set/2`, where the second argument represents a number in the input set, while the first expresses its (arbitrary) order in the set, e.g., with the query `set(1,n1),...,set(k,nk)` the program will compute the gcd for the set $\{n_1, \ldots, n_k\}$. The matrix is built by using the constraint `gcd/3`. In the constraint `gcd(X,Y,M)` the first two arguments, `X,Y` denote the position of the element in the matrix whereas the third one will contain the gcd of `nX` and `nY`. The first and the last two rules reported in Figure 11 are the CHR implementation of the matrix computation. The computation of the gcd according to Euclid's algorithm is then expressed by Rules `GCD0` and `GCD1`. The propagation Rules `Matrix0` and `Matrix1` are employed to build the matrix from the initial set of inputs. Rule `Matrix0` produces the upper half of the matrix (due to the guard `X<Y`), creating the initial query `gcd(X,Y,N),gcd(X,Y,M)` for the computation of the `gcd` between the numbers `N` and `M`. Rule `Matrix1`, in contrast, generates the diagonal elements. In this case the `gcd` is trivially equal to the set element `N`. These two rules cannot be implemented in hardware because they are propagation rules that generate new `gcd` constraints.

In the hardware accelerator we deploy the functionality of rules `GCD0` and `GCD1` with the hardware blocks technique reported in Section 4.2. The remaining program running on the main processor consists of the two Rules `Matrix0` and `Matrix1`, with the addition of the rules reported in the central part of Figure 11. Rule `Pack` is intended to append all the constraints of type `gcd/3` to a *list* that has to be delivered to the hardware accelerator. `Call` is used to trigger the invocation of the custom Prolog predicate `hw_gcd/2` that is the actual responsible of the data transfer to and from the hardware accelerator. The constraint `call/0` is available to the programmer to make the rule fire at the preferred time. For instance, in our example we could use the query `set(1,n1),...,set(k,nk),call` if we wish that the `gcd` constraints were processed after the complete production of all of them. Finally the Rule `Unpack` transforms the output list returned by the hardware accelerator into constraints. In this particular example the application of such a rule would not be necessary because the output of the gcd computation is just one constraint, which could be returned by using the Rule `Call`. This rule is inserted for generality purpose.

The hardware setup of the test bench relies on a Xilinx Virtex4 FPGA (xc4vfx60) running at 100MHz and connected to a PCI-E root complex of an ASUS P7P550 motherboard hosting an Intel Core i7 CPU running at 2.8GHz. On the software side we use the CHR system [23] for SWI-Prolog which allows for an easy integration of memory mapping instructions thanks to the embedded interface to C [34]. We employed this feature for the wrapper implementation. In order to determine the total system execution time we used a single thread implementation in which the CPU is kept idle until the FPGA has performed its computation. Figure 12 com-

```
GCD0    @  gcd(_,_,0) <=> true.
GCD1    @  gcd(X,Y,N) \ gcd(X,Y,M) <=> M>=N | gcd(X,Y,M-N).

Pack    @  gcd(X,Y,N), list_in(L)#passive <=> list_in([(X,Y,N)|L]).
Call    @  call, list_in(L1) <=> hw_gcd(L1,L2), list_out(L2).
Unpack  @  list_out([(X,Y,N)|L]) <=> list_out(L), gcd(X,Y,N).

Matrix0 @  set(X,N), set(Y,M) ==> X<Y | gcd(X,Y,N), gcd(X,Y,M).
Matrix1 @  set(X,N) ==> gcd(X,X,N).
```

Figure 11. Gcd matrix program

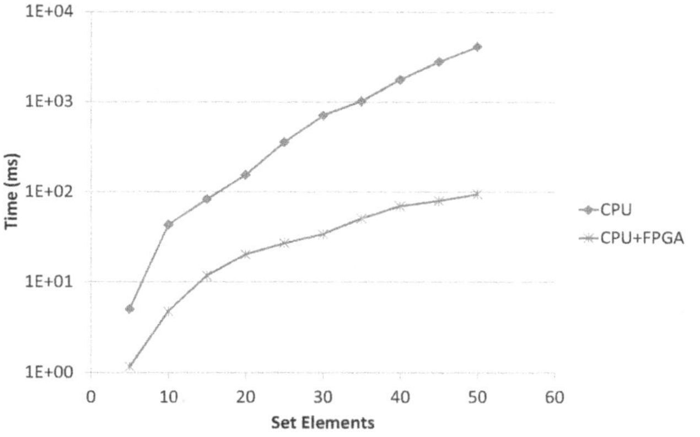

Figure 12. GCD matrix execution time (log scale)

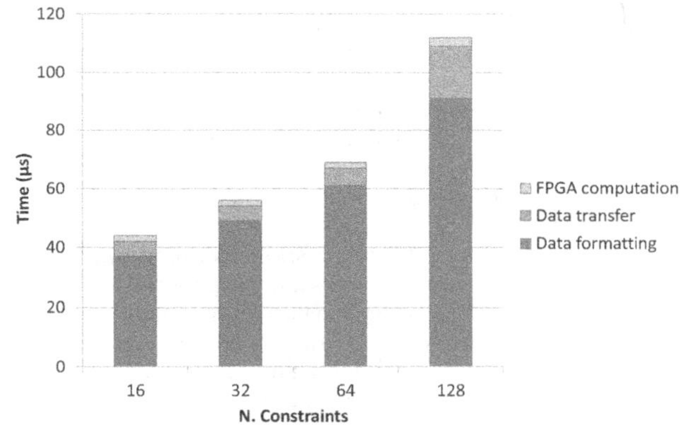

Figure 13. Additional time introduced by the hardware accelerator measured at different sizes of the query

pares the execution times of the gcd matrix running on the plain CPU and with the help of the FPGA (labeled CPU+FPGA in the plot). Even if the speed achieved is not comparable with the one obtained by the execution of the gcd algorithm entirely in FPGA (see Section 4.2.4), the execution time improvement with respect to the plain CPU is still in the range of one order of magnitude. This poorer speed up is rewarded by a higher flexibility.

A comparison of the extra time introduced with the addition of the hardware accelerator is presented in Figure 13, for 16, 32, 64, and 128 1-byte constraints. We measured the elapsed time as the sum of three different components: data formatting, data transfer and FPGA computation. The first one is the required time by a CHR rule for calling the foreign Prolog predicate that converts terms in basic C-type values, arranges the constraint values in data packets, decodes the incoming packets and unifies the C-type values with terms. The remaining two components are, respectively, the routing time to send data through the PCI-E bus and the time needed by the FPGA for packing/unpacking and processing data. The measures show that the most expensive phase is the data handling at the level of the CHR rule, responsible of the built-in execution that sets up the FPGA computation. Clearly such burden of few microseconds per constraint is fully rewarded by the speed up gained in the further concurrent execution of CHR rules in FPGA.

Interval domain solver. As a further case study we consider a classical problem for constraint programming, i.e., a finite domains system [1]. In the literature about CHR we can find several programs working on interval or enumeration constraints [13]. Here we implement a simple interval domains solver for bound consistency, whose CHR code can be found in Figure 15. The solver uses the CHR constraint `::/2` for stating that a given variable ranges on a finite set denoted by the custom operator `:`. For example, the constraint `X::a:b` means that the variable `X` can assume any integer value between `a` and `b`. Also `le/2`, `eq/2` and `ne/2` are CHR constraints, representing the less or equal, the equal and the not equal operators, while `min` and `max` are Prolog built-in operators. Rule `Redundant` eliminates an interval constraint for a variable when there exists another interval constraint for the same variable which is included in the first one. Rule `Intersect` replaces two intervals with their intersection which is obtained by calculating the maximum of the lower bounds and the minimum of the upper bounds. Rule `Inconsistent` identifies empty intervals (where lower bound is greater than the upper bound). Rules `LessEqual`, `Equal` and `NotEqual` represent the corresponding arithmetic relations. A sample query for the program can be: `X le Y, X::3:5, Y::2:4`. The program first produces the new constraints `X::3:4, Y::3:4`, and then it eliminates the redundant intervals giving as result `X le Y, X::3:4, Y::3:4`.

The first two Rules `Redundant` and `Intersect` are deployed on FPGA. Note that they are in the CHR fragment defined by Eq. (4): `Redundant` removes a constraint without introducing new ones while `Intersect` introduces a new constraint, but it removes two of them.

Observe that the typical queries include free logical variables as arguments for the constraints (e.g., `X` and `Y` occur free in the sample query above). This is not a problem for the hardware computation since during the whole program execution such variables are never bound. Hence they can be replaced by suitable indexes in the step of packing and formatting the constraints to be sent to the accelerator. When the output constraints from the accelerator are received the indexes can be replaced back with the corresponding logical variables.

The execution time of the interval domains solver is reported in Figure 14. The times correspond to queries of different length depending on the number of variables taken into account. More precisely, the queries contain 20 interval constraints (e.g. `X::3:15`) and one arithmetic relation (e.g. `X le Y`) for each variable. As

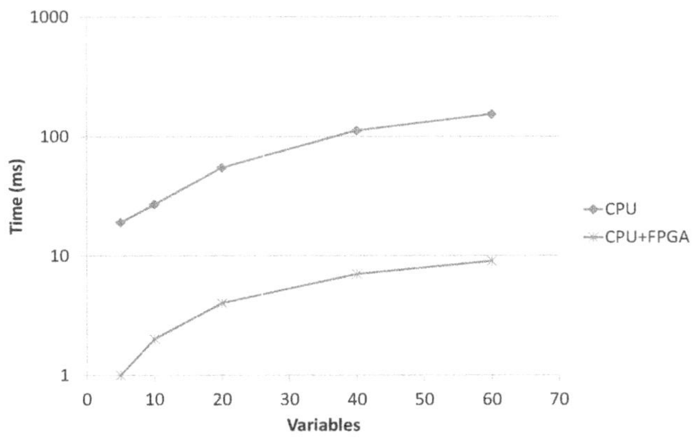

Figure 14. Interval domains solver execution time (log scale)

in the case of the computation of the gcd matrix, the speed up obtained with the support of the hardware accelerator is above one order of magnitude on all the queries we considered.

7. Related work

Our hardware compilation method, which starts from a subset of CHR to arrive at generating a synchronous digital circuit, can also be seen as an attempt to overcome the too low level feature of traditional HDLs, such as VHDL [33] and Verilog [32]. These are well proven and established standard languages for hardware design, but they force the hardware designer to think at the Register Transfer Level (RTL) level, thus modeling a synchronous digital circuit in terms of the flow of digital signals (data) between hardware registers, and the logical operations performed on those signals. From these low level language, is pretty easy to end in a gate-level netlist that can be directly mapped into hardware.

Many alternative environments have been proposed to unify the hardware engineers and the software developers through the use of a common high-level language, mainly based on imperative languages, but none of them has become a standard due to the inherent lack of concurrency and timing (essential elements for the hardware synthesis) of such languages [9]. On the other hand, extensions of commonly adopted HDLs like SystemVerilog [29] still require to the programmers to own a strong hardware background and are too specific to be used as general purpose languages.

We can count a large number of successful approaches to hardware description among the functional languages. Since the 80s one of the most popular domains in which functional languages have been extensively used is hardware design [25]. General purpose functional languages, like Haskell, have been widely used as host languages for embedding HDL (e.g. Hydra [20] or Lava [5]). More recent approaches like SAFL [19] move from a *structural* to a *behavioural* description of the hardware. They allow the programmer to directly describe the algorithm to be implemented rather than the interconnections among low-level hardware components.

Logic programming and especially Prolog have been used for many years as formalisms for hardware design specification and verification as well. We can mention some recent approaches [2, 3] that present a Prolog-based hardware design environment hinged on a high-level structural language called HIDE+. Such a language was developed with the purpose of filling the gap of the structural HDL languages that can only deal with small circuits. Indeed the HDL description tends to be very complex due to the need of making all the connections explicit. Another work on the track of the behavioural style was presented in [18]. It adopts the Byrd boxes model [6] of program execution originally developed as debugging tool for Prolog. The Byrd boxes are used to identify a statically allocable subset which can be executed by associating a single Byrd box with each predicate symbol.

CHR is deemed as a highly concurrent language and, indeed, in our hardware compilation framework we have largely exploited various forms of parallelism in CHR. However, it is broadly accepted that a parallel computation model for CHR is still *in fieri*. The first example of parallel implementation can be found in [10] where it is shown how to evaluate the degree of concurrency starting from the confluence analysis of a sequential program execution. Further works [17, 28] focus on the formal specification and the development of a parallel implementation of the CHR goal-based execution schema: multiple processor cores run multiple threads solving a single CHR goal. Other attempts to exploit concurrency in CHR were pursued in the last years, mainly driven by the CHR set-based operational semantics [22]. Although CHR programs usually adopt a multiset based semantics, it was shown how a large class of programs can benefit from a tabled rule execution schema that eliminates the need of a propagation history, and acquires a natural parallelism by the notion of set. The persistent constraint semantics presented in [4], which exploits the idea of a mixed store where the constraints can behave like a set or a multiset, achieves a higher degree of declarativity, keeping the potentiality of concurrency of the standard semantics. Finally, massive parallelism [21], used in Section 5.2, gives the possibility of applying multiple removals to the same constraint. Such semantics eliminates the conflicts in the constraint removals by allowing different rule instances to work concurrently on distinct copies of the constraints.

8. Conclusion

We described the general outline of an efficient hardware implementation of a CHR subset able to comply with the limitations imposed by hardware. The level of parallelization achieved provides a time efficiency comparable with that obtained with a design directly implemented in HDL. At the same time, the proposed solution offers a more general framework reusable for a wide range of tasks and easily integrable with existing low level HDLs. Different degrees of parallelization naturally embedded in CHR were pointed out and fully exploited thanks to the development of custom hardware structures. The proposed hardware compilation was validated on several case studies related to classical algorithms like Euclid's algorithm, a sieve for prime numbers and merge sort.

In order to cope with the static nature of hardware, which prevents a dynamic allocation, our translation has been restricted to a proper subset of CHR, not including propagation rules. For overcoming this limitation we proposed a classical CHR executor coupled with a hardware accelerator dedicated to simple tasks like the fast rewriting of some constraints. Such hybrid system can increase the performance of CHR, achieving a stronger coupling between algorithms and platforms. In case of data intensive algorithm, the burden of setting up the accelerator computation was fully paid off by the speed up gained in the concurrent execution of CHR rules in hardware.

Further improvements to the general framework, especially in terms of applicability to problems where the number of constraints does not necessarily decrease during the computation, will be subject to future research. A general treatment of rule dependencies at the PHB level is still missing and only appropriate considerations on rules interaction can lead to a hardware performing parallel execution, pipelining and balancing out circular dependencies. Regarding the hardware accelerator, we should mention the possibility of automating the process of rule selection for the hardware deployment. Results coming from a profiler could help a static analysis on the CHR program in order to identify the rules that are the most expensive to be executed. Moreover it would be interesting to test our

```
Redundant     @   X::A:B \ X::C:D <=> C=<A, B=<D | true.
Intersect     @   X::A:B, X::C:D <=> X::max(A,C):min(B,D).
--------------------------------------------------------------
Inconsistent  @   _::A:B <=> A>B | fail.
LessEqual     @   X le Y, X::A:_, Y::_:D ==> Y::A:D, X::A:D.
Equal         @   X eq Y, X::A:B, Y::C:D ==> Y::A:B, X::C:D.
NotEqual      @   X ne Y, X::A:A, Y::A:A <=> fail.
```

Figure 15. Interval domains solver algorithm

framework, which provided quite satisfactory preliminary result, to more complex applications.

References

[1] F. Benhamou. Interval Constraint Logic Programming. In *Constraint Programming: Basics and Trends*, volume 910 of *LNCS*, pages 1–21. Springer, 1995.

[2] A. Benkrid and K. Benkrid. HIDE+: A Logic Based Hardware Development Environment. *Engineering Letters*, 16(3):460–468, 2008.

[3] K. Benkrid and D. Crookes. From Application Description to Hardware in Seconds: A Logic-Based Approach to Bridging the Gap. *IEEE Transaction on VLSI System*, 12(4):420–436, 2004.

[4] H. Betz, F. Raiser, and T. W. Frühwirth. A complete and terminating execution model for constraint handling rules. *Theory and Practice of Logic Programming*, 10(4-6):597–610, 2010.

[5] P. Bjesse, K. L. Claessen, M. Sheeran, and S. Singh. Lava: Hardware design in Haskell. In *Proc. of the International Conference on Functional Programming*, pages 174–184. ACM Press, 1999.

[6] L. Byrd. Understanding the Control Flow of Prolog Programs. In *Workshop on Logic Programming*, pages 127–138. S.A. Tärnlund, 1980.

[7] H. Christiansen. CHR grammars. *Theory and Practice of Logic Programming*, 5(4-5):467–501, 2005.

[8] G. J. Duck, P. J. Stuckey, M. Garcia de la Banda, and C. Holzbaur. Extending arbitrary solvers with constraint handling rules. In *Proc. of PPDP'03*, pages 79–90. ACM, 2003.

[9] S. A. Edwards. The Challenges of Hardware Synthesis from C-Like Languages. In *Proc. of DATE'05*, pages 66–67. IEEE Computer Society, 2005.

[10] T. Frühwirth. Parallelizing Union-Find in Constraint Handling Rules Using Confluence Analysis. In *Proc. of ICLP'05*, volume 3668 of *LNCS*, pages 113–127. Springer, 2005.

[11] T. Frühwirth. *Constraint Handling Rules*. Cambridge University Press, 2009.

[12] T. Frühwirth and S. Abdennadher. The Munich rent advisor: A success for logic programming on the internet. *Theory and Practice of Logic Programming*, 1(3):303–319, 2001.

[13] T. Frühwirth and S. Abdennadher. *Essentials of constraint programming*. Springer, 2003.

[14] T. Frühwirth, P. Brisset, and J.-R. Molwitz. Planning cordless business communication systems. *Expert, IEEE [see also IEEE Intelligent Systems and Their Applications]*, 11(1):50–55, 1996.

[15] S. Hauck and A. DeHon. *Reconfigurable Computing: The Theory and Practice of FPGA-Based Computation*. Morgan Kaufmann Publishers Inc., 2007.

[16] Z. Hongwei, S. E. Madnick, and M. Siegel. Reasoning About Temporal Context Using Ontology and Abductive Constraint Logic Programming. In *Proc. of PPSWR'04*, volume 3208 of *LNCS*, pages 90–101. Springer, 2004.

[17] E. S. L. Lam and M. Sulzmann. Concurrent Goal-Based Execution of Constraint Handling Rules. *CoRR*, abs/1006.3039, 2010.

[18] A. Mycroft. Allocated Prolog—Hardware Byrd Boxes. 2002. Presented as part of 25th anniversary celebrations of the Computer Science Department of the Universidad Politécnica de Madrid.

[19] A. Mycroft and R. Sharp. Higher-level techniques for hardware description and synthesis. *International Journal on Software Tools for Technology Transfer (STTT)*, 4(3):271–297, 2003.

[20] J. O'Donnell. Hydra: hardware description in a functional language using recursion equations and high order combining forms. In *The Fusion of Hardware Design and Verifications*, pages 309–328. North Holland, 1988.

[21] F. Raiser and T. Frühwirth. Exhaustive parallel rewriting with multiple removals. In *Proc. of 24th Workshop on (Constraint) Logic Programming*, 2010.

[22] B. Sarna-Starosta and C. R. Ramakrishnan. Compiling Constraint Handling Rules for Efficient Tabled Evaluation. In *Proc. of PADL '07*, volume 4354 of *LNCS*, pages 170–184. Springer, 2007.

[23] T. Schrijvers and B. Demoen. The K.U.Leuven CHR System: Implementation and Application. In *First Workshop on Constraint Handling Rules: Selected Contributions*, pages 1–5, 2004.

[24] T. Schrijvers, B. Demoen, G. Duck, P. Stuckey, and T. Frühwirth. Automatic Implication Checking for CHR Constraints. In *Proc. of RULE'05*, volume 147 of *ENTCS*, pages 93–111. Elsevier, 2006.

[25] M. Sheeran. Hardware design and functional programming: a perfect match. *Journal of Universal Computer Science*, 11(7):1135–1158, 2005.

[26] J. Sneyers, T. Schrijvers, and B. Demoen. Dijkstra's Algorithm with Fibonacci Heaps: An Executable Description in CHR. In *Proc. of WLP'06*, pages 182–191, 2006.

[27] J. Sneyers, T. Schrijvers, and B. Demoen. The computational power and complexity of constraint handling rules. *ACM Trans. Program. Lang. Syst.*, 31(2):1–42, 2009.

[28] M. Sulzmann and E. S. L. Lam. Parallel Execution of Multi Set Constraint Rewrite Rules. In *Proc. of PPDP'08*, pages 20–31. ACM Press, 2008.

[29] Systemverilog. *SytemVerilog 3.1 - Accelleras Extensions to Verilog(R)*, 2003. Accellera Organization Inc.

[30] A. Triossi. Boosting CHR through Hardware Acceleration. In *Proc. of CHR'11*, pages 1–3, 2011. Invited talk.

[31] A. Triossi, S. Orlando, A. Raffaetà, F. Raiser, and T. Frühwirth. Constraint-based hardware synthesis. In *Proc. of Workshop on (Constraint) Logic Programming*, pages 119–130, 2010.

[32] Verilog. *IEEE Standard Hardware Description Language Based on the Verilog Hardware Description Language*, 1996. http://www.ieee.org/.

[33] Vhdl. *IEEE Standard VHDL Language Reference Manual*, 1994. http://www.ieee.org/.

[34] J. Wielemaker. An overview of the SWI-Prolog Programming Environment. In *Proceedings of the 13th International Workshop on Logic Programming Environments*, pages 1–16, 2003.

[35] P. Wuille, T. Schrijvers, and D. B. CCHR: the fastest CHR Implementation, in C. In *Proc. of CHR'07*, pages 123–137, 2007.

A. Generated VHDL code

This Appendix contains some program listings generated from the implementation of the running example presented in Section 4.

In the following we show the VHDL code that implements the hardware blocks needed to form the PHB of the gcd program reported in Example 3. The first part of the code shows the *entity* declaration of **gcd**, which contains the input and output signals of the PHB. Besides the signals related to the RHBs **gcdx**, **validx**, **gcd_outx** and **valid_outx**, the port listing contains the synchronization signals provided by the PHB: **clk**, **reset** and **finish**. The *architecture* of **gcd** has four *processes* executed in parallel, called **r0_1**, **r0_2**, **r1_1** and **r1_2**, which correspond to the four RHBs in Figure 4. In particular, they correspond to the two instances of Rule R0 and R1 presented in Figure 3. The committing part of the PHB is carried out by the *variable* **flag**, which gives a priority to the PHB outputs assignment. Finally, the *process* **finish_p** is charged to rise the finish signal, when the output signals cannot be further modified by the other *processes*.

```
entity gcd is
    Port ( clk : in  STD_LOGIC;
           reset : in STD_LOGIC;
           gcd1 : in  STD_LOGIC_VECTOR (7 downto 0);
           gcd2 : in  STD_LOGIC_VECTOR (7 downto 0);
           gcd_out1 : out  STD_LOGIC_VECTOR (7 downto 0)
                                                := X"00";
           gcd_out2 : out  STD_LOGIC_VECTOR (7 downto 0)
                                                := X"00";
           valid1 : out STD_LOGIC;
           valid2 : out STD_LOGIC;
           valid_out1 : out STD_LOGIC := '1';
           valid_out2 : out STD_LOGIC := '1';
           finish : out STD_LOGIC := '0');
end gcd;

architecture Behavioral of gcd is
  signal gcd1_sig : std_logic_vector (7 downto 0)
                                                := X"00";
  signal gcd2_sig : std_logic_vector (7 downto 0)
                                                := X"00";
  signal valid1_sig : std_logic := '1';
  signal valid2_sig : std_logic := '1';
  signal finish_sig : std_logic := '0';
  signal finish_sig_reg : std_logic := '0';
  signal gcd1_sig_reg : std_logic_vector (7 downto 0)
                                                := X"00";
  signal gcd2_sig_reg : std_logic_vector (7 downto 0)
                                                := X"00";
  shared variable flag : std_logic := '0';
  shared variable finish_flag : boolean := false;
begin
  r1_1: process (clk, reset, gcd1, gcd2, gcd1_sig,
                 gcd2_sig, valid1_sig, valid2_sig)
  begin  -- process r1_1
    if reset = '1' then
      gcd2_sig <= gcd2;
    elsif (clk'event and clk='1') then
      if (valid1_sig='1' and valid2_sig='1') then
        if gcd2_sig>=gcd1_sig then
          gcd2_sig <= gcd2_sig - gcd1_sig;
          flag := '1';
        else
          flag := '0';
        end if;
      end if;
    end if;
  end process r1_1;

  r1_2: process (clk, reset, gcd1, gcd2, gcd1_sig,
                 gcd2_sig, valid1_sig, valid2_sig)
  begin  -- process r1_2
    if reset='1' then
      gcd1_sig <= gcd1;
    elsif (clk'event and clk='1') then
      if (valid1_sig='1' and valid2_sig='1') then
        if flag='0' then
          if gcd1_sig>=gcd2_sig then
            gcd1_sig <= gcd1_sig - gcd2_sig;
          end if;
        end if;
      end if;
    end if;
  end process r1_2;

  r0_1: process (clk, reset, gcd1, gcd2, gcd1_sig,
                 gcd2_sig, valid1_sig, valid2_sig)
  begin  -- process r0_1
    if reset = '1' then
      valid1_sig <= valid1;
    elsif (clk'event and clk='1') then
      if gcd1_sig=X"00" then
        valid1_sig <= '0';
      else
        valid1_sig <= '1';
      end if;
    end if;
  end process r0_1;

  r0_2: process (clk, reset, gcd1, gcd2, gcd1_sig,
                 gcd2_sig, valid1_sig, valid2_sig)
  begin  -- process r0_2
    if reset='1' then
      valid2_sig <= valid2;
    elsif (clk'event and clk='1') then
      if gcd2_sig=X"00" then
        valid2_sig <= '0';
      else
        valid2_sig <= '1';
      end if;
    end if;
  end process r0_2;

  gcd_out1 <= gcd1_sig;
  gcd_out2 <= gcd2_sig;
  valid_out1 <= valid1_sig;
  valid_out2 <= valid2_sig;
  finish <= '1' when finish_sig='1' and finish_sig_reg='0'
                     and finish_flag else
            '0';

  finish_p: process (clk, reset, gcd1_sig, gcd2_sig,
                     finish_sig)
  begin  -- process finish_p
    if reset='1' then
      gcd1_sig_reg <= X"00";
      gcd2_sig_reg <= X"00";
      finish_sig_reg <= '0';
      finish_flag := true;
      finish_sig <= '0';
    elsif (clk'event and clk='1') then
      gcd1_sig_reg <= gcd1_sig;
      gcd2_sig_reg <= gcd2_sig;
      finish_sig_reg <= finish_sig;
      if gcd1_sig=gcd1_sig_reg and
           gcd2_sig=gcd2_sig_reg then
        finish_sig <= '1';
      else
        finish_sig <= '0';
      end if;
    end if;
    if finish_sig='1' then
      finish_flag := false;
    end if;
  end process finish_p;

end Behavioral;
```

Declarative Distributed Advertisement System for iDTV: an Industrial Experience

Macías López
MADS Research Group
University of A Coruña
A Coruña (SPAIN)
macias.lopez@madsgroup.org

Laura M. Castro
MADS Research Group
University of A Coruña
A Coruña (SPAIN)
laura.castro@madsgroup.org

David Cabrero
MADS Research Group
University of A Coruña
A Coruña (SPAIN)
david.cabrero@madsgroup.org

Abstract

When designing a distributed system, good practices like using modular architectures or applying design patterns are always desirable, but there are relevant aspects that may initially go unnoticed even if we carefully approach the task by the book. Among them, there are a number of decisions to be taken about the specifics of the communications between system nodes: the format of the messages to be sent, the desired/demanded features of the network (latency, bandwidth...), etc.

In particular, one of the most common problems in distributed systems design and implementation is the definition of a good approach to node failure or netsplits management. In fact, these are concerns that, in many cases, arise once the system is already at deployment stage. Different contingency mechanisms can be proposed to solve this kind of problems, and they vary greatly from one another: choosing which and how to implement them depends not only on the technology used, but also on the communications network reliability, or even the hardware where the system will be running on.

In this paper we present ADVERTISE, a distributed system for advertisement transmission to on-customer-home set-top boxes (STBs) over a Digital TV network (iDTV) of a cable operator. We use this system as a case study to explain how we addressed the aforementioned problems from a declarative point of view.

Categories and Subject Descriptors C2.4 [*Computer Systems Organization*]: Computer-Communication networks—Distributed systems, Distributed applications; D1.1 [*Software*]: Programming Techniques—Applicative (Functional) Programming.

General Terms Distributed systems, node failure, netsplit, reliability.

Keywords Declarative programming, fault-tolerance, distributed systems.

1. Introduction

The design and implementation of distributed systems is a very challenging software development activity [4, 12], which implies more than just thoroughly applying a certain concurrency model. To ensure the proper operation of these systems, we have to carefully consider the sort of issues which need to be solved in these kind of scenarios (i.e. establishing a communication protocol between nodes, deciding how the protocol messages are to be exchanged), and the common problems which usually appear (i.e. node failure or netsplits) [2, 18]. A good solution will allow us to ensure system and data integrity, minimising unexpected and undesired effects produced by a faulty communication between nodes.

Depending on the specific features or requirements for a given distributed system, when nodes cannot reach each other due to a netsplit, for instance, data re-synchronisation (either online or offline) may be very expensive, or even unaffordable [17]. At this point, the question becomes whether there is a way in which a distributed application can continue to be available and operating on consistent data during a netsplit, or if we have to choose between one of the two properties (availability vs. consistency), ensuring only one.

To study this problem, we have used an industrial case study: ADVERTISE, a distributed system for advertisement transmission to on-customer-home set-top boxes (STBs) over a Digital TV network (iDTV) of a cable operator. The system, built using the functional language Erlang [1, 5], must ensure the appropriate coordination of the advertisement mechanisms: compilation of events, emission of advertising signals to STBs during a period of time, recording the number of hits or displays of a specific piece of advertisement, etc. The major challenge in this case study was managing a communication network of this size, specifically the high –and growing– number of users (i.e. iDTV customers, which were about 100.000 at the time of writing this article). To meet its requirements, ADVERTISE was designed as a system composed of several nodes, and mechanisms for fault-tolerance were put in place to cope with the aforementioned problems.

In this paper, we will describe the general operation and architecture of ADVERTISE, along with the Erlang implementation of the mechanisms that were chosen to ensure system and data integrity. Today, ADVERTISE has been deployed and it is in operation 24/7, running on hardware with lower specifications than originally expected, which in our opinion would have been impossible had the aforementioned mechanisms, presented in this paper, not been implemented.

The rest of the paper is organised as follows: in Section 2, we describe the common challenges and problems we face when designing distributed systems, and some considerations about them from the point of view of Erlang as development and support platform. Section 3 presents detailed information about ADVERTISE, specifically its main functionalities and tasks, and the components

PPDP'12, September 19–21, 2012, Leuven, Belgium.

which carry them out. In Section 4, we show the Erlang-based distributed architecture we designed for ADVERTISE, and we explain the contingency mechanisms we have implemented. In Section 5 we discuss pros and cons of our implementation and we analyse other possible approaches. Finally, Section 6 presents our conclusions about this work.

2. Distributed software architectures

As software grows more and more complex, and tackles more and more demanding needs and tasks, software engineers have been forced to solve problems which go beyond the functionality of a given application, and have to do with non-functional user expectations and usability criteria such as execution and response times, security, reliability, robustness, fault-tolerance. One of the ways in which analysts and developers have dealt with these is by moving from a single process in a single piece of hardware, to a multi-process distributed ecosystem. Of course, distributed architectures and their great capabilities come at a cost, since they bring their own set of challenges [15, 21].

One of the main issues to consider when designing and implementing a distributed software architecture is node reachability [19]. When a node in a distributed system cannot be reached at a given time, it is usually very difficult to know the specific cause: it may be due to hardware failure, software failure, network congestion, netsplit, etc. In some of these cases the application is no longer running in the unreachable node, but if there are other nodes alive, it is likely that the application is still running on those. However, in other cases the unreachable node may still be running the application, and in those situations, it is all the remaining nodes which are down from its point of view. The desirable behaviour for the isolated node may differ not only in each of these situations, but also from one application to another.

2.1 The CAP theorem

In 2000, Professor Eric Brewer of U.C. Berkeley presented the CAP conjecture at the ACM Symposium of Principles of Distributed Computing [3]. The conjecture established that a distributed system that shared data could only present two of these three properties at the same time: **consistency**, **availability** and **network partition-tolerance**. In 2002, Seth Gilbert and Nancy Lynch from MIT proved the conjecture of Brewer [10], nowadays considered a theorem.

2.1.1 Consistency

The consistency property in a distributed system (that shares data, otherwise there are just no consistency concerns) implies that all operations over the data must be completed *atomically*, this is, in the same way as they would be if the data were an indivisible block shared by all nodes in the system. In other words, it is key that there are never two different operations using the same data and modifying it at the same time, otherwise different parts of the system (i.e. nodes) could be using different, inconsistent values for the same data.

This property is not concerned about the execution time of an operation, it plainly states that it should be possible to modify some available data without worrying about other processes/nodes/components using it simultaneously. Typically, this property is achieved by applying a transaction mechanism, where all nodes have to agree to make a modification, just like on a single node.

2.1.2 Availability

When we talk about system availability we mean that, anytime a client sends a request to the system, the system must always be able to return an answer. Originally, the type of response was not considered of utmost importance, only the fact that some sort of reply was sent for each and every incoming request. However, there are discussions about whether the response should actually contain useful information for considering this property true [10]. If the system gives no reply in return to a request, it does not possess the availability property.

2.1.3 Partition-tolerance

This is the key of the CAP theorem. Partition-tolerance is the resilience a network has to netsplits, and it implies that the system can continue running, preserving the two previous properties (consistency and availability) even when some of its components (i.e. nodes) cannot communicate (they are down or just unreachable). In other words, the system can still work seamlessly in the event of lost messages between nodes.

If a distributed system does not implement mechanisms for partition-tolerance, it means that if the network loses messages or nodes fail to send or receive them, then there can be no guarantee that the two previous properties are met either. Besides, the CAP theorem establishes that the three properties (consistency, availability, and partition-tolerance) cannot be met at once either.

Since a distributed system can, thus, only present two of these properties at a time, let us examine the combinations:

- **CA (Consistency + Availability)**. Actually, this combination is not possible. There is no hardware or network topology for which we can guarantee that communication failures will never happen, therefore, failure is always an option. Since we cannot assure that the network will never fail, the only way we can maintain consistency between nodes is by forcing them all to fail at once, if failure occurs, which makes the system unavailable.
- **CP (Consistency + Partitioned network)**. Those distributed systems in which data consistency is considered more important than availability in the presence of a netsplit, are expected to preserve the guarantee of atomicity in read and write requests in all circumstances. When the communications fail, the entire system can be stopped, or alternatively write requests can be rejected, allowing only read requests. This is a sound behaviour as long as there is no contradiction with the needs of customers who use the system.
- **AP (Availability + Partitioned network)**. Those distributed systems in which we want to guarantee availability to the detriment of consistency in the presence of a netsplit, will answer all requests, potentially returning old data in replies and accepting write requests that could cause conflicts. The system must then implement some inconsistency-resolution mechanism, such as the *last write wins* strategy [20] (the last update of the data prevails, which requires that time measurement is precise enough), or using *count-based clocks* (which track the number of updates on the data, rather than using absolute time to track the changes).

In practice, then, there are only two possible combinations of properties of distributed systems that are feasible according to the CAP theorem: CP or AP. A distributed system during a netsplit can remain available or consistent, but not both at once.

The AP approach, as seen, is more flexible than the CP one, but both are perfectly reasonable: there are many data models which resolve consistency conflicts and in which returning old data is an acceptable solution, since in many cases it is much more problematic (also economically) if the system is not available than if it is not consistent.

2.2 The distributed language Erlang

Erlang [13] is a distributed and concurrent functional programming language developed in the mid-eighties by Ericsson for telecommunication applications with strong demands for fault-tolerance. In Erlang terminology, a distributed system consists of nodes which communicate over a network. Each node can contain multiple lightweight processes that have their own memory space.

Processes use asynchronous message passing, which is implemented with a per-process mailbox. The process mailbox is always ready to receive messages. A process can use a powerful pattern matching syntax to retrieve messages from its mailbox in a different order to that of arrival.

Two or more Erlang processes can be linked, so if one of them crashes, the rest can receive a special message. This mechanism allows to create a hierarchy of supervising Erlang processes, where some of them do the 'real' work (workers), and others (supervisors) supervise workers and start/stop/restart them if needed.

The designers of Erlang made the decision of considering unreachable nodes as down, dead nodes, and therefore only nodes which can be contacted are considered active. This perspective makes sense when we need fast responses to system crashes, since it assumes that the network is less likely to fail than system software or system hardware. Indeed, this was the main concern in the vast majority of systems where Erlang was originally used. An opposite point of view, which assumes that unreachable nodes are still alive and tries to face such contingency, would delay fault-tolerance mechanisms, forcing the system to wait for and cope with the possible reintegration of allegedly dead nodes after network recovery.

However, nowadays most distributed systems, and amongst them those implemented using Erlang, make intensive use of relatively unreliable communication networks, and therefore, they face a significant number of failures due to unreachability problems. In Erlang distributed systems, we face the additional problem of reintegrating nodes that were considered dead but suddenly become available again, because they never really crashed due to software or hardware errors, but instead they were merely unreachable for a while due to network disruption, congestion, or netsplit. Failure to cope with this kind of contingency can lead to highly undesirable situations: if the re-connected node was operating normally while isolated from the cluster, this presents an important consistency problem, since the whole system may be handling outdated data.

2.2.1 Distributed architectures in Erlang

In Erlang semantics, a node is actually an instance of an Erlang Virtual Machine (EVM) which is up and running. There may be several Erlang nodes running on the same physical machine, and of course on different machines. When a node is started, a name is bound to it and it connects to an application daemon called EPMD (Erlang Port Mapper Daemon), which runs on each machine that is part of an Erlang cluster. The per-machine EPMD is started when the first EVM is launched on a given machine, and it acts like a node name server, managing possible name conflicts.

A node can establish a connection to another node. When this happens, the two nodes start monitoring each other and both can thus be aware whether the connection between them is interrupted. Whenever a new node joins one group, they are all linked in the same way. Although all nodes are connected, each one acts independently: each one manages its own set of registered processes, its own ETS (Erlang Term Storage), loaded modules, etc. Connected nodes can exchange messages; more precisely, processes running in connected nodes can send messages to each other. What is more important, the Erlang distribution model was designed so that from the process perspective, there is no difference between sending a message to a local process (i.e. a process in the same node) or to a remote process. Exchanged messages are automatically and

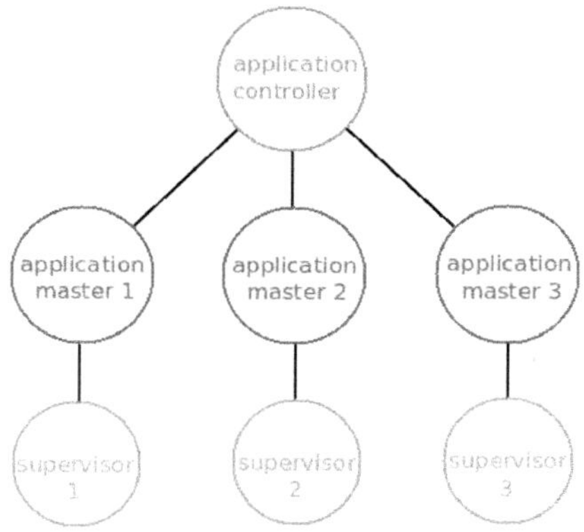

Figure 1. EVM: Application Controller

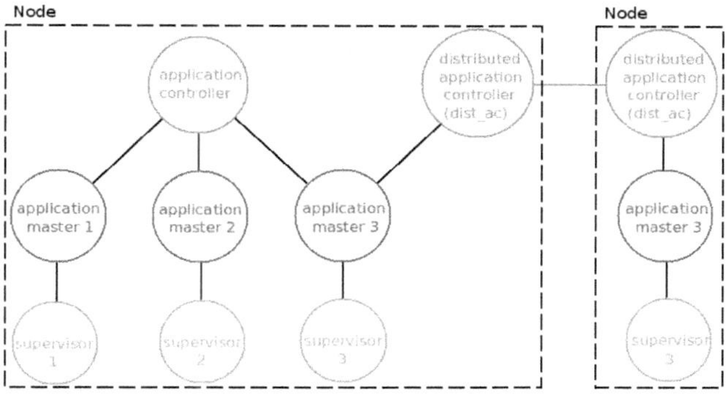

Figure 2. Several EVM: Distributed AC

transparently serialised and transmitted, including the data structures they may carry (even PIDs –process identifiers), which are equally valid at the local node or at remote one. This, for instance, allows to send PIDs over the network and use them to establish new links and monitors.

When a EVM is started, a process called Application Controller (AC) is also started. The AC acts like a supervisor of all applications which run on that node, provided that they comply with the Erlang/OTP *application behaviour*. A behaviour in Erlang is the implementation of a design principle, a common pattern, which is provided as a library and allows to give a component the corresponding behaviour by only implementing certain call-back functions. In particular, the application behaviour gives a set of components (i.e. modules or processes) the ability to be started and stopped as a unit. Thus, when this behaviour is used, the AC starts an application by simultaneously starting a process called Application Master (AM), which is an intermediate layer between the AC and the main supervisor of each specific application. According to this, Fig. 1 represents the process structure at an EVM running three applications.

In distributed applications, in addition to the scheme in Fig. 1, applications are controlled by a second AC called Distributed AC (Fig. 2). This allows that the nodes where a distributed application is to be run to contact each other and negotiate where to start the application using a list of node priorities. Each node starts an instance of the Distributed AC, and all DACs are in contact.

A distributed Erlang application can be in two different states at a given node: "started" or "running". The difference between the two is that an application can be started on all nodes of an Erlang cluster, but can only be running on one node at a time. In other words, what is distributed across multiple Erlang nodes is the management of the application. Nodes that are not running the application are on hold, in case the node where the application is running dies. At that moment, one of them takes over and continues running the application.

To better illustrate how Erlang distributed applications work, let us introduce two concepts: *failover* and *takeover*. A failover is the idea we have just described, the situation in which an application is restarted on a different node when the node that was originally running it goes down for whatever reason. A takeover, on the other hand, can occur when a node which died appears to be alive again. If the configuration of the distributed application indicates that the recovered node has higher priority (which would make sense if, for instance, it is running on better hardware), then the application must be transferred from the node that was running the application at that moment to the node with highest priority.

The next section describes our case study, an Erlang distributed application in which we have implemented two mechanisms to ensure the proper operation: the first of them checks periodically the integrity of the nodes (i.e. if the active nodes at a given time are the same as defined in configuration file); the second one launches contingency mechanisms that manage failovers and takeovers when a netsplit is detected. Both are explained in Sect. 4.

3. Case study: ADVERTISE

In the context of cable TV operators, the catalog of products they offer to their customers includes a range of services that provide a suitable scenario for advertisement transmission. Optimal use of the cable connection is thus a feasible and profitable source of revenue for the operator if there are minimal conditions for automation. Moreover, a complete system for advertisement transmission could potentially not only deliver advertising in a timely, efficient manner, but also do so taking into account customer's preferences and characteristics, allowing for powerful personalisation of the advertisements.

These requirements lead to the development of the ADVERTISE project, a system for advertisement transmission to on-customer-home set-top boxes (STBs) over a Digital TV network (iDTV) of a cable operator. ADVERTISE was designed as a distributed system, where the fault-tolerance and recovery mechanism from node failure or netsplits become essential.

3.1 Elements and definitions

To properly understand our case study, let us describe some core concepts:

- **Media:** Term that refers to any asset displayed by the STB. The system supports several media types: texts, images, and interactive medias.
- **Rule:** Each media to be shown by the system is handled by a rule. Rules set display parameters such as range of dates and times, targeted STBs, number of hits (i.e. times that a media is displayed), hit frequency, etc. Rules are organised in campaigns, but if both the campaign and the rule give a value to a certain parameter, the rule has a higher priority (i.e. a rule can *overwrite* a campaign parameter value).
- **Campaign:** Unit in which media and rules are organised, providing coherence and meaning. The campaign sets limits and default values for the medias included in it.
- **Action:** Each rule in a campaign is translated by ADVERTISE into an STB-readable, which is called action. Actions are, therefore, rules processed by ADVERTISE prior to be sent to the STBs.

3.2 General architecture

In Fig. 3 we show an overview of the ADVERTISE system, with its main modules. There are three main actors:

- **ADVERMAN Server**. Administration facade to ADVERTISE. Implemented in Java, it communicates with the ADVERTISE Server and manages all operations related to advertising: media upload, rule creation/update/removal, campaigns creation/activation/deactivation, etc. This subsystem can also generate graphics showing statistics on campaign data.
- **ADVERTISE Server**. The core of the advertisement system. Implemented using Erlang, it manages all campaigns, transforms rules into actions, and handles all details related to advertisement activation and submission to the STBs.
- **STBs**. The final receivers of the advertisement media.

3.2.1 ADVERTISE Server modules

The main modules of the ADVERTISE Server are:

- **Rule Engine**. Receives and organises campaigns, rules and medias. Among all campaigns and rules, this module determines, in each moment, which are active (checking validity dates and other constraints), verifies that the associated media is correctly stored in the system, and initiates the actions to be sent to the STBs, organising its distribution and keeping track of how many times each media was been shown. The time interval for campaign and rule check, after which actions are sent to STBs, is configurable. Naturally, this module is unique in the system and it runs only in the master node.
- **IDTV Adapter**. This module acts as an intermediate between the ADVERTISE Server and the STBs. It sends the actions and medias to the STBs, receives the accounting information, and manages system load among ADVERTISE physical nodes. The information received from the STBs is forwarded to the corresponding ADVERTISE modules, same as the decision to send the actions to the STBs comes from the Rule Engine. Since it is the closest component to the STBs and has state information about them (i.e. the kind of subscription of the customer), this module uses that information to decide whether an action is appropriate for an STB or not (i.e. it is relevant to a customer profile), preventing the delivery of invalid or irrelevant media. In addition, when a new STB arrives to the system, this module sends it the list of currently active actions, so it needs to store that list of valid actions in its state. Actual communication with the STBs is done through an adapter, in order to handle different types of requests and responses. Currently, ADVERTISE communicates with the STBs using permanent TCP connections through the return channel (i.e. long polling), exchanging asynchronous HTTP messages, encoding information using JSON [6] and XML.
- **Manager Adapter**. This module behaves like an interface adaptor between ADVERTISE and ADVERMAN. It handles the different requests that can arrive to the ADVERTISE Server from the ADVERMAN Server: adding a new campaign, updating a rule, uploading new media, etc. Information about campaigns, rules, and medias is encoded using JSON. The Manager Adapter supervises JSON REST [16], a module that handles a set of processes listening for TCP connections at specific ports. When an ADVERMAN request is received by any of those processes, the JSON REST module forwards it to the Manager Adapter, which in turn sends it to the Rule Engine after parsing the content and translating it into data structures that the Rule Engine can understand.

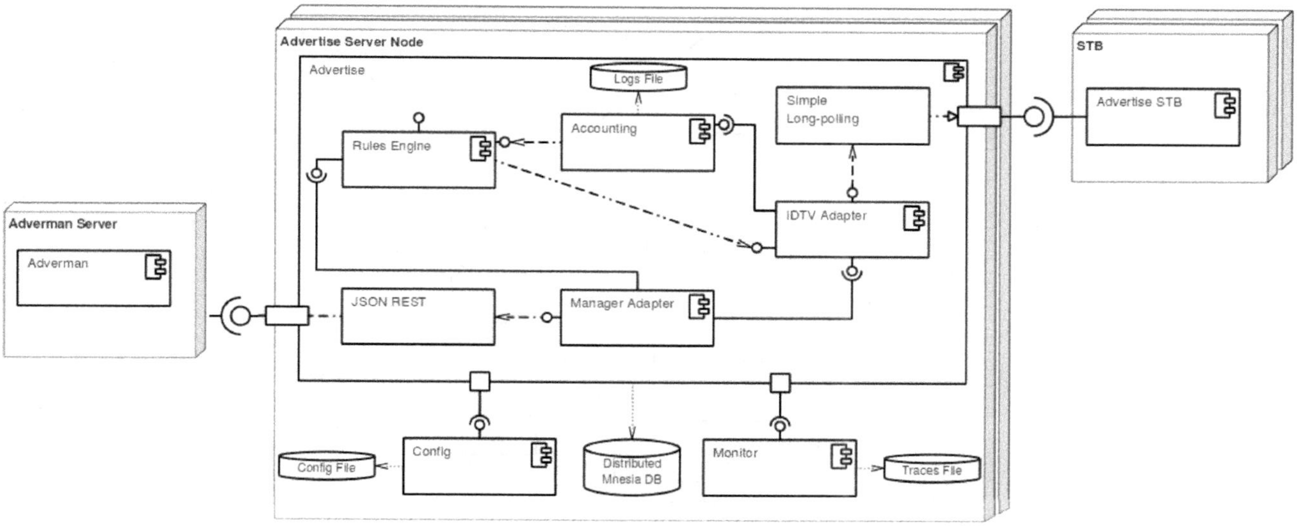

Figure 3. General architecture of ADVERTISE

- **Accounting**. This module stores all events related with the actions that the STB user can do: pressing keys, watching advertisements, etc. Other modules can ask for that accounting information (for example, ADVERMAN asks for it to display statistics).
- **Configuration and monitoring**. These are general purpose modules to get/set configuration information and write log traces to the file system, respectively.

3.2.2 Supervision tree

Fig. 4 shows the supervision tree designed for ADVERTISE. There are two Erlang applications: `supervisor` and `advertise`. The latter is the advertisement system which we have just described. The supervisor is a distributed Erlang application which handles master node selection, orchestrates coordinated booting, and executes the contingency mechanisms implemented in it.

4. ADVERTISE Erlang-based distributed architecture

As we explained before, a distributed Erlang application is started in all system nodes, but runs only on one of them. When this node goes down, the Erlang distribution mechanism selects another node of the cluster to continue running the application on (failover process).

To comply with the fault-tolerance requirements of the cable operator (as we will explain in Sect. 4.4), we designed our ADVERTISE case study to be deployed over at least three nodes, so at system installation the master node must be selected. This is the node where the supervisor application will be running.

Additionally, ADVERTISE uses Mnesia [14], the Erlang distributed database, to store all relevant information about campaigns, rules, and medias: when a write operation is performed in Mnesia, the modification is replicated to all system nodes. To start Mnesia properly on a cluster of Erlang nodes, all of them must be active, so we need a coordinated boot mechanism to effectively start all nodes to ensure that all of them have the newest copy of the data at all times.

We now explain the differences between the *initialisation* process and the *booting* process of ADVERTISE.

4.1 ADVERTISE initialisation process

The initialisation process of ADVERTISE is launched on the master node, and involves the following steps or tasks:

1. Initialisation of the `file_logger` process, which writes the traces of the initialisation procedure to a local file, thus registered with a local name.
2. Initialisation of `config` process, in this case to be globally available, thus registered with a global name.
3. Now the master node waits until the rest of the nodes of the cluster are up and running, sending a ping request every 2 seconds. The node list is specified as part of the configuration, as are other parameters such as IP addresses, ports, paths to write trace files, etc.
4. Once all nodes are connected:
   (a) Initialisation of the Mnesia database: schema and table creation, integrity check in all nodes.
   (b) Configuration of the distributed application.

The configuration we have used in ADVERTISE is:

```
[{distributed, [{supervisor, [ list_to_tuple(Nodes) ]}]},
 {sync_nodes_optional, [ Node || Node <- Nodes,
                                 Node /= node() ]},
 {start_dist_ac, true},
 {sync_nodes_timeout, 5000},
 {net_ticktime, 16}]}]
```

where:

- `supervisor` is the name of the distributed application (the global supervisor, we have previously referred to).
- `sync_nodes_optional` is the list of nodes where the supervisor can be executed (in our case, all nodes except the one executing this code).

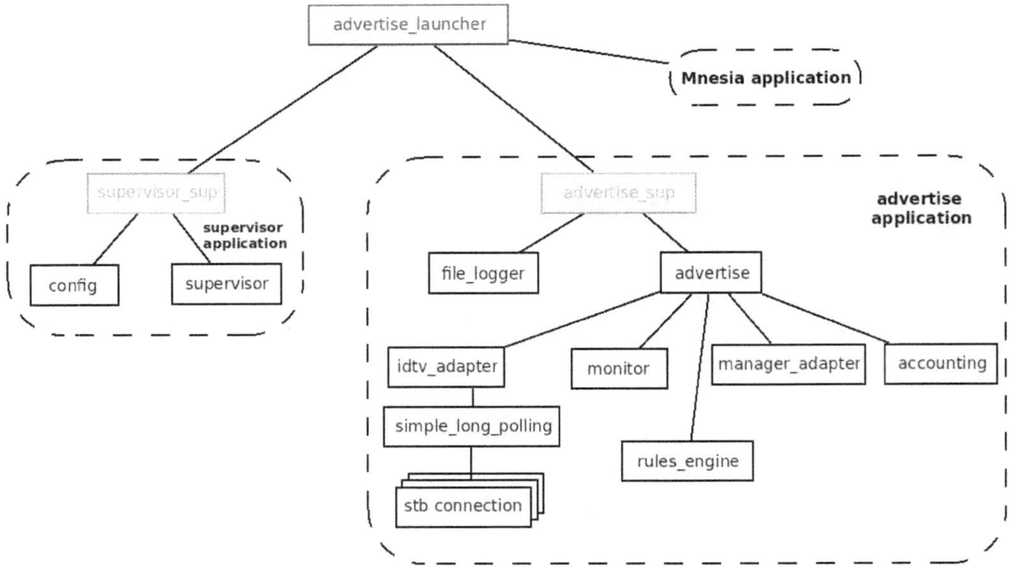

Figure 4. Supervision tree of ADVERTISE

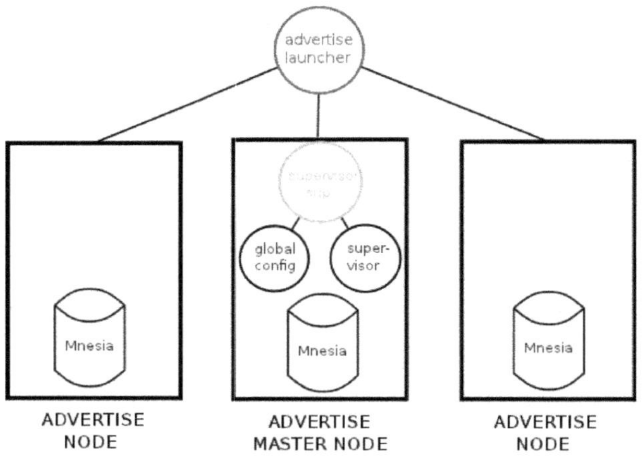

Figure 5. ADVERTISE nodes after init process

- `start_dist_ac` indicates we want to start the distributed application controller.
- `sync_nodes_timeout` is the maximum waiting time (in milliseconds) for the nodes, before booting; since we specify all nodes as optional, the system would boot after 5 seconds even with master node only.
- `net_ticktime` establishes the time lapse (in seconds) used to consider a node to be down; a node is deemed unreachable if it fails to send any messages in the last four tick times.

Summing up, in the configuration we are indicating that if the master node dies, any other node can take the control of the supervisor application. After the initialisation process, ADVERTISE nodes are in the situation shown in Fig. 5. This configuration is also used in the booting process of ADVERTISE (Sect. 4.2).

4.2 ADVERTISE booting process

The booting process of ADVERTISE, which can be launched on any node of the cluster, involves the following steps or tasks:

1. Initialisation of the `file_logger` process, which writes the traces of the booting procedure to a local file, thus registered with a local name.
2. Booting of the global supervisor application, which is registered with a global name. If the global name is already registered, we jump to 6.
3. All connected nodes are questioned to find out if the ADVERTISE application is running (this may be the case if the node is recovering from a failure). If it is already running in one of them, a monitor is created, linking the supervisor and the ADVERTISE application. This is the mechanism that will allow the node to run the advertise application if the node where the it is currently running happens to go down.
4. Initialisation of contingency mechanisms:
   (a) **Nodes integrity check** every 10 seconds (see Sect. 4.3.1).
   (b) **Distributed application controller check** every second (see Sect. 4.4.1).
5. Verification of Mnesia state.
6. Verification of aliveness of `file_logger` and global supervisor.
7. Verification of connectivity (ping requests to self node, `file_logger` and global supervisor).
8. Initialisation of the ADVERTISE application with a local supervisor (`advertise_sup`) and corresponding local services (`accounting`, `rule_engine`, `idtv_adapter` and `manager_adapter`).

Fig. 6 shows ADVERTISE running on three nodes as a result of the booting process.

As we saw on Sect. 4.1, after a (configurable) time, ADVERTISE starts with the nodes that have been able to complete the booting process. It is worth mentioning that, if there are nodes that have not been started at that moment and join the cluster later on, they will lose any information (regardless of it being older or newer) they may have (cfg. step 5 of the booting process). This situation could happen, for instance, if:

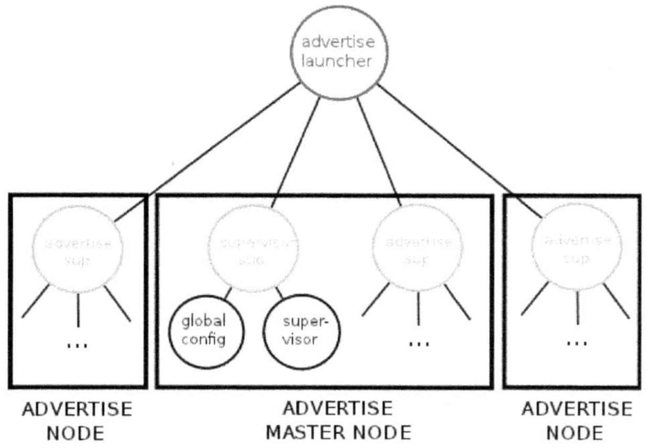

Figure 6. ADVERTISE nodes after boot process

- Node 1 (master) goes down due to a hardware failure.
- Node 2 takes control. After some time, node 3 stops.
- Node 1 is back alive and takes over node 2.
- Node 3 does not boot on time: its updates in Mnesia are lost.

Of course, this problem would not happen if the system runs without node crashes (which of course is non-realistic), or else if node 3 is booted before node 1. This is why we have introduced all the connectivity checks in the booting process, so that these situations can be detected and avoided. We detected this issue during ADVERTISE deployment, where we found ourselves in an environment which made netsplit events likely to happen. As we will explain in Sect. 4.3.1, the importance of a careful node recovery process led us to impose one constraint on the ADVERTISE cluster: we do not allow ADVERTISE to run on only one node.

4.3 Recovering from node failure

In order to implement contingency mechanisms to deal with node failure, we had to decide which property we wanted ADVERTISE to preserve in the presence of such contingencies: consistency or availability. In our case study, we decided that data consistency was more important, meaning that we could not afford that campaigns, rules, or medias information was ever corrupted or lost in situations of instability. Instead, it was acceptable that no advertisements were sent to STBs if at a specific moment the system was not available to analyse the campaigns and execute the active rules to produce the corresponding actions. After all, each STB is permanently connected to ADVERTISE with an unreliable long polling connection, so it was deemed not to be extremely important if an advertising campaign had a bit of delay, especially if the counterpart benefit is to prevent the corruption of data in ADVERTISE. Clearly, the consequences of the transmission of unsuitable data to the STBs would be much worse.

4.3.1 Nodes integrity check

Despite choosing consistency over availability, ADVERTISE is designed to be reasonably resistant to node failure: it will continue in operation, although degraded, until crashed nodes are recovered. There is one strict constraint, though: there must be at least two nodes running and connected to each other in order to keep the system running.

When a node goes down, the remaining nodes automatically take control. The contingency mechanism to handle these situations is implemented in the global supervisor application, checking the population of active nodes every 10 seconds. The algorithm is as follows:

1. Retrieve the last known population of active nodes.
2. Retrieve the list of all ADVERTISE nodes from the configuration.
3. Filter the list from step 2, removing nodes which are unreachable to ping.
   (a) If the resulting list has the same elements as the list from step 1, then no actions are taken and ADVERTISE continues in operation with the same population of active nodes.
   (b) Otherwise,
      i. If the resulting list is a one-element list (meaning there is only one active node in the system), ADVERTISE is rebooted.
      ii. Otherwise, no actions are taken and ADVERTISE continues in operation with the new population of active nodes.

4.4 Recovering from netsplits

If a node loses its connectivity to the network, and thus to the rest of the nodes in the ADVERTISE cluster, then we may face the situation in which that node without network believes that all the others went down and assumes all system functions, while at the same time the other nodes believe that indeed it is the isolated node who went down and they distribute the control amongst them. If and when the network recovers from this situation, there can be inconsistencies between the dataset handled by the formerly isolated node and the dataset handled by the rest of the nodes. There can also be other kinds of inconsistencies, such as duplicated responsibilities (like the global supervisor application). This is why we have chosen to, if a node loses its network connectivity and finds itself alone, immediately suspend the execution and wait, monitoring the network, until connectivity is restored. At that moment, automatic reboot is started.

This behaviour has the side effect that if all nodes in the system go down except one, the remaining node will still protect itself in the same way and it will stop working until at least one of the other nodes is restarted. This is the reason why, to ensure at least some basic fault-tolerance, it is recommended to run ADVERTISE in cluster of at least three nodes.

Admittedly, this version of the ADVERTISE contingency mechanisms does not detect network partitioning, i.e. a group of nodes that cannot connect to another group of nodes, but where nodes in the same group do connect to each other. However, when nodes are on the same network segment this situation should be extremely unlikely. All in all, if it happens, when the network is restored the system would need to be restarted manually, and the initialisation process would need to be run again to check the consistency of the database.

4.4.1 Distributed application controller check

The prevention mechanism that verifies the connectivity between nodes is implemented in the global supervisor application, and it operates as follows:

1. The distributed AC is queried on all ADVERTISE nodes, to get the PID of the ADVERTISE local supervisors.
2. If there are nodes for which the ADVERTISE local supervisor PID could not be retrieved, node failure is assumed and
   (a) If the node did not belong to the list of previously active nodes: no actions are taken and ADVERTISE continues in operation.

(b) If the node did belong to the list of active nodes, it means it replies to ping from the global supervisor but the node cannot reach other nodes. In this case, after a 10 seconds timeout:

   i. If the node is no longer in the list of active nodes: node failure is confirmed, no actions are taken and ADVERTISE continues in operation.

   ii. If the node is still in the list of active nodes: node is up and we reboot it so that it goes back to normal operation.

5. Discussion

When designing a distributed application, there is a number of decisions which are specific to the distributed world and need to be addressed properly [11]. When designing an Erlang-based distributed application, there are also some assumptions which are embedded in the Erlang built-in fault-tolerance mechanisms which need to be correctly understood and used. ADVERTISE, being built and deployed as a distributed system on multiple Erlang nodes, suffered from both these issues, but we demonstrated that careful thinking can successfully combine the strengths and elude the weaknesses.

5.1 Network reliability

When an application is running on multiple physical nodes on various locations, there will be many times when the network becomes unavailable, most of them for unknown reasons. Thus, when designing and implementing a distributed system, one must take into account that the nodes cannot be assumed to be always connected, and therefore, there will be times in which the nodes will not be able to establish any kind of communication amongst them. Although one possible solution is to add new nodes when this happens (so redundancy is increased if a failure is detected), applications must be prepared to lose requests and responses, and to cope with the fact that some system modules stop suddenly (especially if relying on third-party components).

When ADVERTISE was in its deployment stage, problems related with network reliability were the most common, especially netsplits. Their analysis and diagnosis lead to the implementation of specific monitoring mechanisms. We used Erlang monitors, a resource very similar to links between processes only they establish unidirectional links, to monitor local ADVERTISE supervisor instances on each node. Thus, if one of the local ADVERTISE supervisors went down, the global supervisor on the master node would be notified. In addition, we also established a ping-based mechanism for checking all nodes for aliveness from the node master.

The main advantage of using Erlang to address network reliability problems is its asynchronous communication model, intrinsic to the language. When using asynchronous messaging, the only way to notify that a message has been received at the other end, is to send a response back. The problem arises when a netsplit is mistaken for a node failure, and another node takes over the functions of the supposedly dead node as a consequence. When the node is available again shortly after, undesirable situations may occur (for instance, two nodes assuming the master node role). This problem was also detected in ADVERTISE and led us to the decision of not allowing to run the system in an isolated node, as we explained in Sect. 4.2 and Sect. 4.4.1.

5.2 Latency of requests

One of the most positive aspects of process communication in Erlang is that, from the implementation point of view, there is no difference whatsoever in the procedure to call a function in the same or in another process, in a local or a remote node. However, we should not forget that communications over a network are slower, even for small messages. Thus, communications may not produce the same results when we move from a limited and controlled development environment to a distributed production environment(i.e.messages can be dropped, arrive out of order, or too late for certain actions to be taken).

A good design for a distributed application should consider mechanisms to deal with situations in which operations show high latency. In ADVERTISE, several options were chosen and combined: execution of certain features in dedicated processes, use of asynchronous messages, timeouts, creation of links and monitors between processes, etc. The key is to think that there is always the possibility that any process can fail.

5.3 Bandwidth

Although the natural evolution of physical communication networks are allowing transfers over them to become faster, it is very risky to assume that sending large amounts of data over a network will present no problems. Small, short messages are generally better, but if we really need to send long messages, we should be aware of to what extent the underlying technology is sensitive to the size of the messages. For instance, Erlang nodes exchange messages using TCP connections, which means a large message will be fragmented and a number of TCP packets will be sent sequentially through the network. At the reception point, message order needs to be preserved, which can interfere and lead to delays in reception or sending of other messages.

Additionally, Erlang nodes use a keepalive mechanism to determine if the rest of the nodes they are linked to are up [9]. This keepalive mechanism is based on sending very short messages (heartbeats) at certain intervals of time: if a node does not answer these messages, it is assumed to be down. The time required to process a large message by a node can delay the heartbeats, which can even be interpreted as the node not being available when this is not true.

5.4 Network security

When designing distributed applications, it is often dangerous to rely on every message being received seamlessly, also from the security point of view. In a distributed environment, not only can messages be lost, but also unexpected messages can be received. If the sender of a message is not properly identified or can be easily impersonated, spurious processes may intercept and/or modify our messages and, in the worst-case scenario, they can provoke an application failure.

Erlang provides no special mechanism to deal with this security problem. The Erlang distributed model was initially designed for building fault-tolerant systems with high redundancy of components, but whose original ecosystem were telecommunication switches in particular, and applications deployed on a single piece of hardware in general. Several nodes deployed and executed on the same physical machine can assume a safer and more secure communication network than they have when they are in different locations. This means that for distributed systems with nodes deployed in different physical places, Erlang applications do not provide any specific mechanisms to ensure security of sent messages/data. Application designers and developers need, thus, to deal with the use of SSL [7] or else their own communication layer implementation, or consider tunneling over secure channels.

5.5 Network topology

In a distributed system, there are several factors that are generally not fixed and can be modified during the lifetime of the system. Examples of these include IP addresses, ports, hostnames, number of nodes on which the application runs, etc. Therefore, in order to increase the robustness of a system against changes on these parameters, it is important that they are part of the external configuration of the application. This will allow us to modify them when desired or needed.

In this sense, all Erlang nodes have a name and a hostname that should, then, be parameterised. With regard to processes, we can refer to them by PID or name, and we also need to know the node they are running on.

5.6 Heterogeneity of components

Applications or components which are integrated in a distributed system need not necessarily communicate in the same way. They may not use the same language or even the same formats.

Communication protocol with Erlang nodes is public [8], so any non-Erlang application could implement it and use it. Alternatively, both sides may agree to an ad-hoc format (i.e. XML or JSON) and implement a translation layer. The latter option was applied in certain ADVERTISE components (such as the `simple_long_polling` module, which communicates with the STBs, or the `manager_adapter`, that adapts the JSON-based REST API provided to external elements such as the ADVERMAN server).

6. Conclusions

The design of a distributed application requires a thorough analysis of requirements that must include all the aspects that are related to its distributed and concurrent nature. The specific purpose of the application will assign more or less importance to the CAP properties (consistency, availability, network partition) which need to be prioritised.

As a case study, in this paper we have presented a detailed description of the design decisions that were taken to provide the required fault-tolerance mechanisms for ADVERTISE, a distributed system built for a cable operator with a growing customer base (today, around 100.000). In building this system, we had to deal with common problems like node failure and netsplits. Here we have explained the approaches we took to minimise their impact on system performance.

The first time ADVERTISE was deployed in production, we detected that the deployment environment presented some particularities that had not been taken into account. Some nodes showed a tendency to failure more often than the others, and netsplits were very common during some time periods, specifically at noon and at night. In that situation, the fault tolerance requirements were not met, and thus contingency mechanisms to cope with them turned out essential to ensure the proper operation of the system. For ADVERTISE, consistency was the most important property to be preserved, so in the final configuration the system was not allowed to run on isolated nodes, in order to avoid conflict situations.

Had ADVERTISE requirements been substantially different, we would probably have favoured availability over consistency, for instance. In any case, Erlang has proved a great tool to deal with all particularities of distributed systems, adding to the power that it provides as implementation language thanks to its functional nature. We have no doubt that choosing Erlang and its OTP libraries as development platform has been a key factor in the eventual success of the ADVERTISE project.

The specific highlights and contributions of this paper are:

- Detailed description of the general architecture and operation of ADVERTISE, a distributed advertisement system for iDTV, implemented using Erlang/OTP with support for hundreds of thousands of customers, currently in operation.
- Description and discussion of the design decisions that were made to ensure proper operation of ADVERTISE after deployment, with careful consideration and study of the assumptions that Erlang makes about distributed systems.
- Problem abstraction and presentation of general guidelines to effectively protect a distributed system against node failure and netsplits.

To further increase our confidence in the proper operation of the system, our current work is focused on testing the most critical modules of ADVERTISE, such as the Rule Engine, using powerful and advanced techniques such as model-based and property-based testing.

7. Acknowledgments

This research has been partly sponsored by MICINN TIN-2010-20959 and FP7-ICT-2009-4 Ref. 248495.

We are forever thankful to Dr. Víctor M. Gulías, sadly deceased recently, for his unquestionable wisdom, unlimited support, reassuring guidance, and strong encouragement. His uncountable virtues most certainly outlive him, and will be always an inspiration for us.

We also want to thank Javier Mosquera for his remarkable work on the ADVERTISE project.

References

[1] J. Armstrong. *Programming Erlang: Software for a Concurrent World*. Pragmatic programmers. Pragmatic Bookshelf, 2007.

[2] M. Balazinska, H. Balakrishnan, S. Madden, and M. Stonebraker. Fault-tolerance in the borealis distributed stream processing system. *ACM Transactions on Database Systems*, 33(1):3:1–3:44, Mar. 2008.

[3] E. Brewer. Towards robust distributed systems. In *Proceedings of the Annual ACM Symposium on Principles of Distributed Computing*, pages 7–10, 2000.

[4] A. Carzaniga, G. Picco, and G. Vigna. Designing distributed applications with mobile code paradigms. pages 22–32, 1997.

[5] F. Cesarini and S. Thompson. *Erlang Programming*. O'Reilly Series. O'Reilly, 2009.

[6] D. Crockford. The application/json media type for javascript object notation (JSON). `http://www.ietf.org/rfc/rfc4627`, 2006.

[7] T. Dierks and E. Rescorla. The transport layer security (TLS) protocol. `http://tools.ietf.org/html/rfc5246`, 2008.

[8] Erlang. Distribution protocol. `http://www.erlang.org/doc/apps/erts/erl_dist_protocol.html`.

[9] Erlang. Heartbeat monitoring of an Erlang runtime system. `http://www.erlang.org/doc/man/heart.html`.

[10] S. Gilbert and N. Lynch. Brewer's conjecture and the feasibility of consistent, available, partition-tolerant web services. *SIGACT News*, 33(2):51–59, June 2002.

[11] M. Goff. *Network Distributed Computing: Fitscapes and Fallacies*. Prentice Hall Professional Technical Reference, 2003.

[12] H. Kopetz, A. Damm, C. Koza, M. Mulazzani, W. Schwabl, C. Senft, and R. Zainlinger. Distributed fault-tolerant real-time systems: The mars approach. *IEEE Micro*, 9(1):25–40, 1989.

[13] M. Logan, E. Merritt, and R. Carlsson. *Erlang and OTP in action*. Manning Publications Co., 2010.

[14] H. Mattsson, H. Nilsson, and C. Wikstrom. Mnesia a distributed robust DBMS for telecommunications applications. *Proceedings of the First International Workshop on Practical Aspects of Declarative Languages*, pages 152–163, 1999.

[15] M. Norman and P. Thanisch. Models of machines and computation for mapping in multicomputers. *ACM Computing Surveys*, 25(3):263–302, 1993.

[16] C. Pautasso, O. Zimmermann, and F. Leymann. Restful web services vs. "big" web services: Making the right architectural decision. pages 805–814, 2008.

[17] M. Shah, J. Hellerstein, and E. Brewer. Highly available, fault-tolerant, parallel dataflows. In *Proceedings of the 2004 ACM SIGMOD international conference on Management of data*, SIGMOD '04, pages 827–838. ACM, 2004.

[18] A. Srinivas and D. Janakiram. A model for characterizing the scalability of distributed systems. *SIGOPS Operating Systems Review*, 39(3):64–71, July 2005.

[19] L. Tang, J. Li, Y. L, and S. Shenker. An investigation of the internet's IP-layer connectivity. *Computer Communications*, 32(5):913–926, 2009.

[20] R. Thomas. A majority consensus approach to concurrency control for multiple copy databases. *ACM Transactions on Database Systems*, 4(2):180–209, 1979.

[21] M. Wooldridge and N. Jennings. Software engineering with agents: Pitfalls and pratfalls. *IEEE Internet Computing*, 3(3):p 6, 1999.

Task-Oriented Programming in a Pure Functional Language

Rinus Plasmeijer[1] Bas Lijnse[1,2] Steffen Michels[1]
Peter Achten[1] Pieter Koopman[1]

[1] Institute for Computing and Information Sciences, Radboud University Nijmegen
P.O. Box 9010, 6500 GL, Nijmegen, The Netherlands

[2] Faculty of Military Sciences, Netherlands Defense Academy
P.O. Box 10000, 1780 CA, Den Helder, The Netherlands

{rinus, b.lijnse, s.michels, p.achten, pieter}@cs.ru.nl

Abstract

Task-Oriented Programming (TOP) is a novel programming paradigm for the construction of distributed systems where users work together on the internet. When multiple users collaborate, they need to interact with each other frequently. TOP supports the definition of tasks that react to the progress made by others. With TOP, complex multi-user interactions can be programmed in a declarative style just by defining the tasks that have to be accomplished, thus eliminating the need to worry about the implementation detail that commonly frustrates the development of applications for this domain. TOP builds on four core concepts: *tasks* that represent computations or work to do which have an observable value that may change over time, *data sharing* enabling tasks to observe each other while the work is in progress, *generic* type driven generation of *user interaction*, and special combinators for *sequential* and *parallel* task composition. The semantics of these core concepts is defined in this paper. As an example we present the iTask**3** framework, which embeds TOP in the functional programming language Clean.

Categories and Subject Descriptors D.1.1 [*Programming Techniques*]: Applicative (Functional) Programming; D.2.11 [*Software Engineering*]: Software Architectures—Languages; D.2.11 [*Software Engineering*]: Software Architectures—Domain-specific architectures; D.3.2 [*Programming Languages*]: Language Classifications—Applicative (functional) languages; H.5.3 [*Information Interfaces And Presentation*]: Group and Organization Interfaces—Computer-supported cooperative work; H.5.3 [*Information Interfaces And Presentation*]: Group and Organization Interfaces—Web-based interaction

Keywords Task-Oriented Programming; Clean;

1. Introduction

When humans and software systems collaborate to achieve a certain goal they interact with each other frequently and in various ways. Constructing software systems that support human tasks in a flexible way is hard. In order to do their work properly human beings need to be well informed about the progress made by others. We lack a formalism in which this aspect of work is specified at a high level of abstraction.

In this paper we introduce *Task-Oriented Programming (TOP)*, a novel programming paradigm to define interactive systems using *tasks* as the main abstraction. TOP provides advanced features for task collaboration. We choose tasks as *unit of application logic* for three reasons. First, they cover many phenomena that have to be dealt with when constructing systems in a natural and intuitive way. In daily life we use this notion to describe activities that have to be done by persons to achieve a certain goal. In computer systems, running processes are also commonly called tasks. On a programming language scale, a function, a remote procedure, a method, or a web service, can all be seen as tasks that can be executed. Second, in daily life it is common practice to split work into parallel and sequential sub-tasks and at the same time, during execution, not to be very strict about their termination behavior and production of results. Progress of work can be guaranteed even though some, or all, sub-tasks produce partial results. This contrasts with the usual concept of computational tasks that are interpreted as well-defined units of work that take some arguments, take some time to complete, and terminate with a result. Third, tasks abstract from the operational details of the work that they describe, assuming that the processor of the task knows how to perform it. The processor must deal with a plethora of issues: generate and handle interactive web pages, communicate with browsers, interact with web services in the cloud, interface with databases, and so on. Application logic is polluted with the management of side effects, the handling of complicated I/O like communication over the web, and the sharing of information with all users and system components. In this pandemonium of technical details one needs to read between the lines to figure out what a program intends to accomplish. Using tasks as abstraction prevents this. For these reasons, we conjecture and show that in the TOP paradigm specifying what the task *is* that needs to be done, and *how* it can be divided into simpler tasks is sufficient to create the desired application.

We present a foundation for Task-Oriented Programming in a pure functional language. We formalize the notion of tasks as abstract descriptions of interactive persistent units of work. Tasks produce typed, observable, results but have an abstract implementation. When observed by other tasks, a task can either have no (meaningful) value, have a value that is a temporary result that may change, or have a stable final result. We show how to program using

PPDP'12, September 19–21, 2012, Leuven, Belgium.

this notion of tasks by defining a set of primitive tasks, a model for sharing data between tasks, and a set of operators for composing tasks. Because higher-order function composition provides powerful composition already, only a small set of operators is necessary. These are sequential composition, parallel composition, and the conversion of task results.

Most notably, we make the following contributions:

- We introduce *Task-Oriented Programming* as a paradigm for programming interactive multi-user systems composed of interacting tasks.
- We present *tasks* as abstract units of work with observable intermediate values and continuous access to shared information.
- We present combinators for composition and transformation of tasks and formally define their semantics.
- We demonstrate real-world TOP in Clean using the redesigned and extended iTask**3** framework.

The remainder of this paper is organized as follows: in Section 2 we informally explain the TOP paradigm by defining its concepts and a non-trivial example in Clean with the iTask**3** framework. In Section 3 we formalize the foundations of TOP component-wise: tasks and their evaluation, sharing information, user interaction, and sequential and parallel task composition. In Section 4 we reflect on the pragmatic issues that need to be dealt with in frameworks that facilitate real-world TOP programming. After a discussion of related work in Section 5, we conclude in Section 6 .

For readability, we use Clean$*$ (van Groningen et al., 2010) which is a dialect of Clean that adapts a number of Haskell language features. In this paper we deploy *curried function types* (Clean function types have arity), and the *unit type* ().

2. The TOP Paradigm

Task-Oriented Programming extends pure Functional Programming with a notion of *tasks* and operations for composing programs from tasks. Complex interactive multi-user systems are specified as decompositions of the tasks they aim to support.

2.1 TOP Concepts

Tasks: Tasks are abstract descriptions of interactive persistent units of work that have a typed value. When a task is *executed*, by a TOP framework, it has an opaque persistent state. Other tasks can observe the *current* value of a task in a carefully controlled way. When an executing task is observed, there are three possibilities:

1. **The task has no value observable for others:** This does not mean that no progress is made, but just means that no value of the right type can be produced that is ready for observation.
2. **The task has an unstable value:** When a task has an unstable value, it has a value of the correct type but this result may be different after handling an event. It is even possible that the next time the task is observed it has no value.
3. **The task has a stable value:** The task has a clear final result. This implies that if the task is observed again, it will always have the same value.

Tasks may be interactive. Such tasks process events and update their internal state. However, this event processing is abstracted from in Task-Oriented programs. The effects of events are only visible as changes in task results.

Many-to-many Communication with Shared Data: When multiple tasks are executed simultaneously, they may need to share data between them. How and where this data is stored however, is often completely irrelevant to the task. What matters is that the data is available and that it is shared. Thus, when one task modifies shared data, the other tasks can observe this change. In TOP we abstract from how and where data is stored and define *Shared Data Sources* (SDS) as typed abstract interfaces which can be read, written and updated atomically.

Generic Interaction: The smallest tasks into which an interactive system can be divided are single interactions, either between the system and its users or between the system and another system. Single interactions can be entering or updating some data, making a choice or just viewing some information. In TOP we abstract from how such interactions are realized unless it is essential to the task. A TOP framework *generates* user interfaces *generically* for any type of data used by tasks. This means that it is not necessary to design a user interface and program event handling just to enter or view some information. It is possible to specify interactions in more detail, but it is not needed to get a working program.

Task Composition: TOP introduces the notion of tasks as first-class values, but also leverages first-class functions from pure functional programming. This means that only a small carefully designed set of core combinator functions is needed from which complex patterns can be constructed.

1. **Sequential composition:** TOP uses *dynamic* sequential composition. Because task values are observable, sequential compositions are not defined by blindly executing one task after another. They are defined by composing an initial task with a set of functions that *compute* possible next steps from the observed value of the initial task.
2. **Parallel composition:** Parallel composition is defined as executing a set of tasks simultaneously. Tasks in a parallel set have read-only access to a shared data source that reflects the current values of all sibling tasks in the set. In this way tasks can monitor each other's progress and react accordingly.
3. **Value transformation:** Task domains can be converted by pure functions in order to combine tasks in a type consistent way.

2.2 An Example of TOP in Clean

To illustrate Task-Oriented Programming in practice, we present a non-trivial example that uses the novel iTask**3** framework. In the example, one specific user, the *coordinator*, has to collaborate with an arbitrary number of users to find a meeting date and time. Figure 1 displays that this task consists of three sub-tasks. This figure consists of actual screenshots of the user interfaces generated by the iTask**3** framework.

In sub-task *one*, the coordinator creates a number of date-time pairs. While doing so, he or she can rearrange their order, insert new date-time pairs, or remove them. Once satisfied, the coordinator confirms the work by pressing the *Continue* button, and *steps* into sub-task *two*.

This sub-task *two* consists of a number of tasks running in parallel. The users (Alice, Bob, and Carol in this example) are all asked to make a selection of the proposed date-time pairs (the *Enter preferences* windows). Meanwhile, the coordinator can monitor and follow the selections being made (the *Results so far* window). At any time, the coordinator can either choose to restart the entire task all over again, by pressing the *Try again* button. He or she can also select a date-time pair that is suitable for (the majority of) all users by pressing the *Make decision* button. In the first case, they *step* into the plan meeting task afresh, and in the latter case, they *step* into sub-task *three*.

In sub-task *three* the system provides the coordinator with an overview of available users per date-time pair, thus helping him or her to make a good decision. The coordinator can also decide not to pick any of the candidate date-time pairs and override them with a

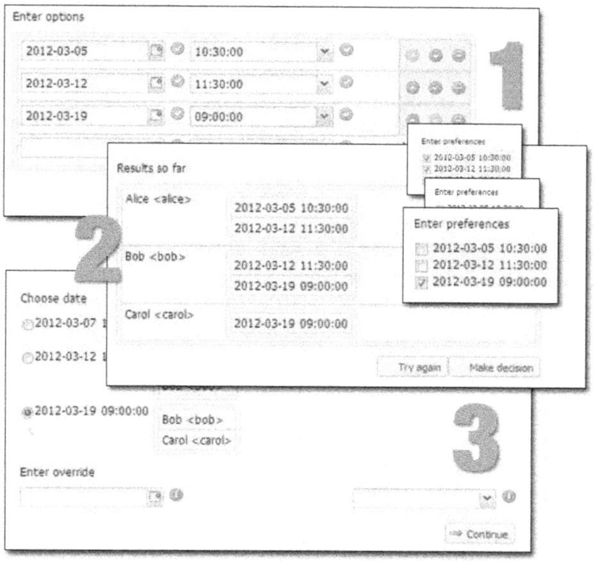

Figure 1. Selecting possible dates for a meeting

proposed alternative. Once satisfied with a choice, the coordinator terminates the entire task by pressing *Continue*, and returns a *stable* date-time value.

In the remainder of this section we show how to specify this example in a Task-Oriented way. Figure 2 displays the complete specification. It contains TOP-notions explained in detail further on in this paper. The key point of this example is to show how Task-Oriented Programming aids to create a specification that closely matches the description that is shown above. The semantics of the used concepts are defined in Section 3.

The entire task of the coordinator is described by `planMeeting`. Its type (line 1) expresses that given a list of users, it is a task that produces a date-time pair. `User` and `DateTime` are predefined data types. `User` represents a registered user. `DateTime` is just a pair of `Date` (day-month-year triplet) and `Time` (hours-minutes-seconds triplet) which also happen to be predefined.

As discussed, the main structure of `planMeeting` consists of three subsequent sub-tasks (lines 2-4), which are glued together by means of the *step* combinator `>>*`. The second argument of `>>*` enumerates the potential subsequent *task steps* that can be stepped into while the first argument task is in progress. Hence, the first sub-task, `enterDateTimeOptions`, is followed by `askPreferences`, which in turn is followed by *either* `tryAgain` *or* `decide`. Entering user information (performed by `enterDateTimeOptions`, `select`, and `pick`) is an example of a task that may or may not have a *task value*. This depends on the input provided by the user. The potential task steps which can follow can observe the task value and define whether or not sufficient information is provided to step into the next task. In case of the transition from the first sub-task to the second sub-task, this requires an *action* from the coordinator (line 12). This is only sensible if the previous task has a task value, which is tested by the predicate `hasValue`. In that case, the current task value is retrieved (`getValue`) and used to step into the next sub-task, which is to ask all users to choose preferred date-time pairs.

The *observable* task value is accessible in the step combinator to determine the next task steps chosen. The task value and its access functions are straightforward: `hasValue` tests for the `Val` data constructor, and `getValue` returns that value if present:

```
:: Value a    = NoVal    | Val a Stability
```

```
1  planMeeting :: [User] → Task DateTime
2  planMeeting users =  enterDateTimeOptions
3                       >>* [askPreferences users]
4                       >>* [tryAgain users, decide]
5
6  enterDateTimeOptions :: Task [DateTime]
7  enterDateTimeOptions = enterInformation "Enter options" []
8
9  askPreferences :: [User]
10        → TaskStep [DateTime] [(User,[DateTime])]
11 askPreferences users
12   = OnAction (Action "Continue") hasValue (ask users o getValue)
13
14 ask :: [User] → [DateTime] → Task [(User,[DateTime])]
15 ask users options
16   = parallel "Collect possibilities"
17     [ (Embedded, monitor)
18     :[(Detached (worker u),select u options) \\ u←users]
19     ]
20     @ λanswers → [a \\ (_,Val a _)←answers]
21
22 monitor :: ParallelTask a | iTask a
23 monitor all_results
24   = viewSharedInformation "Results so far" []
25       (mapRead tl (taskListState all_results))
26     @? λ_ → NoVal
27
28 select :: User → [DateTime] → ParallelTask (User,[DateTime])
29 select user options _
30   = enterMultipleChoice "Enter preferences" [] options
31     @ λchoice → (user,choice)
32
33 tryAgain :: [User] → TaskStep [(User,[DateTime])] DateTime
34 tryAgain users
35   = OnAction (Action "Try again") (const True)
36              (const (planMeeting users))
37
38 decide :: TaskStep [(User,[DateTime])] DateTime
39 decide
40   = OnAction (Action "Make decision") hasValue (pick o getValue)
41
42 pick :: [(User,[DateTime])] → Task DateTime
43 pick user_dates
44   =    (enterChoice "Choose date" [] (transpose user_dates) @ fst)
45        -||-
46        (enterInformation "Enter override" [])
47   >>* [OnAction (Action "Continue") hasValue (return o getValue)]
```

Figure 2. Complete task specification of the `planMeeting` example

```
:: Stability  = Unstable | Stable

hasValue :: Value a → Bool
hasValue (Val _ _) = True
hasValue _         = False

getValue :: Value a → a
getValue (Val a _) = a
```

Tasks with `Stable` values are terminated and can no longer produce a different task value. Hence *task values* are first-class citizens in Task-Oriented Programming. Two task transformer functions provide access: `@?` alters the task value of the preceding task, and `@` is similar, but only if a `Val` is present:

```
(@?) infixl 1 :: Task a → (Value a → Value b)
                                       → Task b | iTask a & iTask b
(@)  infixl 1 :: Task a → (a → b) → Task b | iTask a & iTask b
```

The second sub-task of the coordinator is to ask all users *in parallel* to make a selection of the created date-time pairs. In addition, the coordinator *constantly monitors* their progress. Parallel composition of tasks is defined with the `parallel` combinator. It is used explicitly in the `ask` task, and implicitly (by means of the derived parallel-or combinator -||- that provides a shorter notation for the common case of choice between two alternative tasks) in the `pick` task. Parallel composition is a core concept in Task-Oriented Programming. The second argument of `parallel` enumerates the sub-tasks that need to be evaluated in parallel. The progress is *shared* between all sub-tasks. Relevant to the example is the function `taskListState`, which transforms this shared state to share the current *task values*. This is used by the `monitor` task (lines 24-25) to create a view on the current task values of the users. The `monitor` task uses `@?` to explicitly state that its task value never contains a concrete value. These can be provided only by the `select` sub-tasks. They offer their user the means to make a multiple-choice of the provided date-time pairs, and use `@` to attach the user to identify who made that specific selection (lines 30-31).

Finally, the last sub-task can be stepped into when the coordinator either decides to start all over again (lines 34-36) or pick a value (lines 39-40). The first action step is always valid (`const True`, line 35) and the second action step only when the previous task actually has a value (line 40). The derived combinator -||- evaluates its two task arguments in parallel, and has a task value that is either stable (if one or both sub-tasks have one) or unstable (if one or both have one) or none. Hence, the action step can only occur when the coordinator has either selected one of the suggested date-time pairs or chosen to override them.

This example demonstrates how a TOP approach can lead to a concise specification in which tasks are glued together and overall progress can be achieved even though the tasks themselves might not terminate or consume too much time.

3. A Formal Foundation of TOP

In this section we introduce and semantically define the core concepts of Task-Oriented Programming. These are *task values*, *tasks* and their *evaluation* (Section 3.1), *many-to-many* communication (Section 3.2), *user-interaction* (Section 3.3), *sequential* task composition (Section 3.4), and *parallel* task composition (Section 3.5).

Except for Section 3.1, every section has the same structure: we first introduce the core concept and illustrate it by means of the iTask3 system, and then formally define the operational semantics using *rewrite semantics*. The rewrite rules are specified in Clean∗. Such a way of formal specification of semantics is somewhat unusual, but this approach has certain advantages over traditional ones (Koopman et al., 2009). The specification is well-defined, concise, compositional, executable, and can express even complicated language constructs as the ones introduced in this paper. Since we are dealing with constructs embedded in a functional language it is an advantage to describe their semantics as pure functions in a functional language as well. We have experimented with several alternative definitions which can easily introduce errors that remain overlooked. It is an advantage that the descriptions are checked by the compiler and that we have been able to test their correct working by applying it to concrete examples. Furthermore, the formal semantics is very suited and also used as blue print for the actual implementation and can serve as a reference implementation for implementations in other programming languages as well. In order to distinguish semantic definitions from **iTask3** API and code snippets, we display semantic definitions as *framed* verbatim text, and **iTask3** fragments as *unframed* verbatim text.

3.1 Tasks and their Evaluation

In this section we define *task results* and *task values* (Section 3.1.1), *tasks* (Section 3.1.2), their *evaluation* (Section 3.1.3), and a number of *task transformer functions* (Section 3.1.4).

3.1.1 Task Results and Task Values

A task of type `Task a` is a description of work which progress can be inspected by a *task value* of type `Value a` (Section 2.2). Tasks handle events. Events have a time stamp, for which we use an increasing counter, making it possible to determine the temporal order of events. The *task result* of handling an event may be a new task value. Semantically, we extend the task value with the time stamp of the event that caused the creation of that task value. Tasks that run into an exceptional situation have as task result an exception value instead of a task value. The domains of task results and task values capture these situations:

```
:: TaskResult a =   ValRes TimeStamp (Value a)
                |   ∃e: ExcRes e & iTask e
:: TimeStamp    :== Int
:: Value a      =   NoVal       | Val a Stability
:: Stability    =   Unstable | Stable
```

The task value of a task result can be in three different states: there can be no value at all (`NoVal`), there can be an `Unstable` value which may vary over time, or the value is `Stable` and fixed. To illustrate, consider the task of writing a paper p. At time t_0 you have no paper at all (`ValRes` t_0 `NoVal`). After a while, at time t_1 there may be a draft paper p_1, which is updated many times at subsequent time stamps $t_2 \ldots t_n$ with draft papers $p_2 \ldots p_n$ (`ValRes` t_i (`Val` p_i `Unstable`)). You may even start all over again (`ValRes` t_{n+1} `NoVal`). At a certain point in time, t_{n+k} say, when you decide that the paper is finished the task has result `ValRes` t_{n+k} (`Val` p_{n+k} `Stable`) meaning that the paper can no longer be altered.

Some tasks never produce a stable value. Examples are the interactive tasks (`enterInformation`, `viewSharedInformation`, `enterChoice`, `enterMultipleChoice`) that were used in Section 2.2: a user can create, change or delete a value as many times as wanted. Typical examples of tasks that produce a `Stable` value are ordinary functions, or system and web service calls. A task can raise an exception value (`ExcRes e`) in case it is known that it can no longer produce a meaningful value (for instance when a call to a web service turns out to be unavailable). Any value can be thrown as exception and inspected by an exception handler (Section 3.4), using existential quantification `∃e` and the type class context restriction `& iTask e`. Tasks with stable values or exception values have no visualization but memorize their task result forever. The other tasks require a visualization to support further interaction with the user.

3.1.2 Tasks

Semantically, we define a task to be a state transforming function that reacts to an event, rewrites itself to a reduct, and accumulates responses to users:

```
:: Task a      :== Event → *State → *(Reduct a, Reponses, *State)
:: Event        = RefreshEvent
                | EditEvent    TaskNo Dynamic   // Section 3.3.1
                | ActionEvent  TaskNo Action    // Section 3.4.1
:: *State       = { taskNo    :: TaskNo
                  , timeStamp :: TimeStamp       // Section 3.3.1
                  , mem       :: [Dynamic]       // Section 3.2.1
                  , world     :: *World
                  }
:: Reduct a     = Reduct (TaskResult a) (Task a)
:: TaskNo      :== Int
:: Responses   :== [(TaskNo, Response)]          // Section 3.3.1
```

We distinguish three sorts of events: a `RefreshEvent`, e.g. when an user wants to refresh a web page, an `EditEvent`, e.g. a new value that is committed intended for an interactive task (Section 3.3), and an `ActionEvent` which is used to tell the step combinator which task to do next (Section 3.4). The latter two cases identify the task that is required to handle the event. The interactive task and step task are provided with a fresh identification value and current time stamp, using the semantic function newTask:

```
newTask :: (TaskNo → TimeStamp → Task a) → Task a
newTask ta ev st=:{taskNo = no, timeStamp = t}
  = ta no t ev {st & taskNo = no+1}
```

Fresh task identification numbers are generated by keeping track of the latest assigned number in the State. The State extends the external environment of type *World with internal administration and is passed around in a single-threaded way which is enforced by the uniqueness attribute *.

The reduct contains both the *latest task result* and a *continuation* of type Task a, which is the remaining part of the work that still has to be done. This continuation can be further evaluated in the future when the next event arrives.

The responses collect all responses of all subtasks the task is composed of. They are used to update every client with the proper information about the latest state of affairs. A client can use this information to adjust the page in the browser or in an app.

In the remainder of this paper we define semantic task functions for the core basic tasks and task combinators, thus explaining how these elements rewrite to the next reduct.

3.1.3 Task Evaluation

A TOP application consists of one top level task, the main task, which has to be evaluated. The work continues until either an exception escapes handling, or the work at hand has obtained a stable task value.

```
1  evaluateTask :: Task a → *World → *(Maybe a, *World) | iTask a
2  evaluateTask ta world
3  # st      = {taskNo = 0, timeStamp = 0, mem = [], world = world}
4  # (ma,st) = rewrite ta st
5  = (ma,st.world )
6
7  rewrite :: Task a → *State → *(Maybe a, *State) | iTask a
8  rewrite ta st=:{world}
9  # (ev,world) = getNextEvent   world
10 # (t, world) = getCurrentTime world
11 # st         = {st & timeStamp = t, world = world}
12 # (Reduct res nta, rsp, st) = ta ev st
13 = case res of
14     ValRes _ (Val a Stable) → (Just a, st)
15     ExcRes _ → (Nothing, st)
16     _        → rewrite nta
17                  {st & world = informClients rsp st.world}
```

In Clean(*), passing around multiple unique environments explicitly, such as st (:: *State) and world (:: *World), is syntactically supported by means of the non-recursive #-let definitions. The main task is recursively rewritten by the function rewrite. Rewriting is triggered by an event. We abstract from the behaviour of clients and just assume that they send events and handle responses. We assume that all events are collected in a queue. In getNextEvent (line 9) the next event is fetched from this queue. If there are no events, the system waits until there is one. The current time is stored in the state (lines 10-11) to ensure that all tasks which update their value in this rewrite round, will get the same time stamp. Hereafter (line 12), the main task ta is evaluated given the event and current state. Any sub-task defined in the main task is a task as well, and can be evaluated in the same way: just apply the corresponding task function to the current event and the current state. Rewriting stops when the main task has delivered a stable value (line 14), or an uncaught exception is raised (line 15). Otherwise, the main task is not finished yet, and the continuation task returned in the reduct defines the remaining work which has to be done. First the accumulated responses are sent to the clients (informClients, line 17) to inform them about the latest state-of-affairs. We abstract in the semantics from the way this is done. Rewriting continues with the continuation nta and the updated state.

3.1.4 Utility Functions for Converting Tasks

The semantic function stable, when applied to a time stamp t and value va, defines a task that has reached a stable value:

```
stable :: TimeStamp → a → Task a
stable t va _ st
= (Reduct (ValRes t (Val va Stable)) (stable t va),[],st)
```

Notice that the continuation of the task stable t va in the reduct is exactly the same function stable t va. It is a kind of fixed point task, which, whenever it is evaluated in some future, always returns the same reduct (value and continuation). With this semantic function, we can define the semantic function of the core task return:

```
return :: a → Task a
return va ev st=:{timeStamp = t} = stable t va ev st
```

Here, return has a similar role as the return function in a monadic setting: it lifts an arbitrary value va of type a to the task domain.

Raising an exception is similar, except that the task result is always an exception value:

```
throw :: e → Task e | iTask e
throw e _ st = (Reduct (ExcRes e) (throw e),[],st)
```

With operator @? and a function f of type Value a → Value b a task ta of type Task a can be converted to a task of type Task b:

```
1  (@?) infixl 1 :: Task a → (Value a → Value b)
2                                → Task b | iTask a & iTask b
3  (@?) ta f ev st
4  = case ta ev st of
5      (Reduct (ValRes t aval) nta,rsp,nst)
6      → case f aval of
7          Val b Stable
8              → stable t b ev nst
9          bval → (Reduct (ValRes t bval) (nta @? f),rsp,nst)
10     (Reduct (ExcRes e) _,_,nst)
11     → throw e ev nst
12
13 (@) infixl 1 :: Task a → (a → b) → Task b | iTask a & iTask b
14 (@) ta f = t @? λaval → case aval of
15                          NoVal   = NoVal
16                          Val a s = Val (f a) s
```

First the task ta is evaluated (line 3). Exceptions raised by ta are simply propagated (lines 10-11). The resulting task value, if any, is converted by function f. If this results in a stable value, then the entire task becomes stable with the current time stamp (lines 7-8). Notice that this has as consequence that the original task ta is no longer needed. If the result is not stable, the original task may change its value over time, and we need to apply the conversion function to values produced in the future as well. Therefore, the current result bval of the conversion is stored in the reduct with the continuation nta @? f which takes care of the conversion of the new task values produced in the future (line 8). The derived operator @ uses @? to transform task values only when a concrete value is present.

3.2 Many-to-many Communication

For collaborating tasks it is important to keep each other up-to-date with the latest developments while the work is going on. Hence we need to be able to share information between tasks and support many-to-many communication.

How and where this data is stored, is completely irrelevant to the tasks. What matters is that the data is available and that it is shared. To achieve this abstraction we use the concept of multi-purpose Shared Data Sources (SDS) (Michels and Plasmeijer, 2012). SDSs are typed, abstract interfaces which can be read, written and updated atomically.

A SDS can represent a shared file, a shared structured database, reveal the current users of a system, or it can be a physical entity, like the current time or temperature. In general, a SDS abstracts from any shared entity that holds a value that varies over time.

```
:: RWShared r w

:: ROShared r :== RWShared r  ()
:: WOShared w :== RWShared () w
:: Shared a   :== RWShared a  a
```

A SDS has abstract type `RWShared r w`. *Reading* its current value returns a value of type `r`, and *writing* is done with a new value of type `w`. Read-only shared objects (`ROShared r`) only support reading as type `r`, write-only shared objects (`WOShared w`) only support writing as type `w`, and `Shared a` objects demand that the read and write values have the same type `a`.

As an example, we show a few shares that are offered by the iTask**3** system to create SDSs:

```
sharedFile   :: Path → a → Shared a | iTask a
currentTime  :: ROShared  Time
currentUsers :: ROShared [User]
```

With (`sharedFile fname content`) a task is described that associates a file identified by `fname` with an initial value of type `a`. A task gains access to the current time and registered users with the tasks `currentTime` and `currentUsers`.

SDSs provide many-to-many communication both between tasks and other applications. We make a difference between external and internal SDSs. External SDSs are abstractions of external objects such as files and databases and can be accessed anywhere in the application. For the internal communication between tasks only, one can create a shared memory SDS of type `Shared a` which has a limited scope. A task `ta` can be parameterized with a freshly created shared memory SDS `sa` of type `Shared a` that has some initial value `va` using the combinator `withShared va (λsa → ta)`:

```
withShared :: a → (Shared a → Task b) → Task b | iTask a
```

In this way, a shared memory is created which can only be accessed by the sub-tasks defined within `ta`. For an example of its use, see Section 4.

To write a value to a SDS, one can connect a task `ta` with a SDS `s` using a function `f` with the combinator `ta @> (f,s)`:

```
(@>) infixl 1 :: Task a
             → (Value a → r → Maybe w, RWShared r w)
             → Task a | iTask a
```

This enforces `f` to be repeatedly applied to the current task value of `ta` (if any) and the currently read value of `s`, the result of which is the new value (if any) that is written to `s`. The combinators `withShared` and `@>` are defined in Section 3.2.1.

SDSs integrate smoothly with interactive tasks. For every basic interactive task (such as `enterChoice` and `enterMultipleChoice`) a *shared* version (such as `enterSharedChoice` and `enterSharedMultipleChoice`) is provided that expects a SDS instead of a common value. This is discussed in Section 3.3 in more detail. In this way tasks can monitor and alter SDSs.

3.2.1 Semantics of Memory Shared between Tasks

To explain the semantics of SDSs, we restrict ourselves to their use for offering shared memory between (parallel) tasks. These SDSs cannot be accessed by external applications. Hence the semantic definition does not need to handle concurrency and atomicity issues: there is only one `rewrite` function (Section 3.1.3) that handles rewriting of all tasks defined in an application.

Shared memory cells are stored in the `State`, in record field `mem` of type `[Dynamic]`. Each SDS memory cell can be used to store a value of arbitrary type, hence `mem` is modeled as a heterogeneous list using Clean's built-in dynamic types (Vervoort and Plasmeijer, 2003; van Weelden, 2007). Any shared value of any type can be stored in a value of type `Dynamic`, together with a representation of its type (using the function `serialize :: a → Dynamic | iTask a`). It can be fetched from this store any time later, using a dynamic type pattern match that guarantees that no type errors can occur at run-time (using the function `de_serialize :: Dynamic → a | iTask a`). We define a SDS creation function, and two functions to update a SDS:

```
1  :: RWShared r w = { get :: *State → *(r,*State)
2                   , set :: w → *State → *State
3                   }
4
5  createShared :: a → *State → *(Shared a,*State) | iTask a
6  createShared a st=:{mem}
7  = ({get = get,set = set},{st & mem = mem ++ [serialize a]})
8  where
9    idx              = length mem
10   get   st=:{mem} = (de_serialize (mem!!idx),st)
11   set a st=:{mem} = {st & mem = updateAt idx (serialize a) mem}
12
13 updateShared :: (r → w) → RWShared r w → *State → *(w,*State)
14 updateShared f sh_a st
15 # (rv,st)     = sh_a.get st
16 # wv          = f rv
17 = (wv,sh_a.set wv st)
18
19 updateMaybeShared :: (r → Maybe w) → RWShared r w → *State
20                                              → *(Maybe w,*State)
21 updateMaybeShared f sh_rw st
22 # (readv,st) = sh_rw.get st
23 = case f readv of
24     Nothing  = (Nothing,st)
25     Just wv  = (Just wv,sh_rw.set wv st)
```

A SDS is represented by two access functions `get` and `set` that retrieve and store the required information from and to the state. Creating a shared value with `createShared` appends an initial serialized value to the list of memory locations (line 7), and returns two dedicated `get` and `set` functions that access this new memory location. The SDS update functions both obtain the current read value of the SDS argument (line 15 and 22). However, `updateShared` always updates the SDS with a new value, and `updateMaybeShared` does this only if the argument function actually produces a new value. With these internal functions, we can define `withShared` and `@>`:

```
withShared :: a → (Shared a → Task b) → Task b | iTask a
withShared va tfun ev st
# (sh_a,st) = createShared va st
= tfun sh_a ev st

(@>) infixl 1 :: Task a
             → (Value a → r → Maybe w, RWShared r w)
             → Task a | iTask a
(@>) ta (f,sh_rw) = update NoVal ta
where
 update otval ta ev st
 = case ta ev st of
   (Reduct (ExcRes e) nta, _, nst)
      → throw e ev nst
   (Reduct (ValRes ts ntval) nta,rsp,nst)
      → ( Reduct (ValRes ts ntval) (update ntval nta)
        , rsp
```

```
    , if (ntval==otval)                                                    18
        nst                                                                19
        (snd (updateMaybeShared (f ntval) sh_rw nst))                      20
    )                                                                      21
```

withShared creates a fresh SDS for its argument task function and applies it to obtain the proper task. The combinator ⓒ▷ memorizes the previous task value (initially NoVal) and the current task continuation (initially the task argument ta) (line 9 and 16). As usual, at each event the current task continuation is evaluated (line 12). Exceptions are propagated (lines 13-14). The only difference is that if the new task value ntval is different from the memorized task value otval, then the SDS is updated using the argument function of ⓒ▷ and the local function updateSDS (line 18). This function only updates the SDS if a new value is computed (lines 23 and 25). In this way unnecessary updates of shared data is avoided. Because ⓒ▷ keeps checking the SDS using the most recent task value, this leads to reactive behavior: every time the watched task is changing its value, the shared memory also gets updated conditionally, as described above.

3.3 User Interaction

In Task-Oriented Programming user-interactions are defined as tasks that allow a user to enter and modify a visualized value of some type. Such an interactive task is called an *editor*. The type of the value to be edited plays a central role. By using type indexed generic functions (Alimarine, 2005; Hinze, 2000) this visualization is generated fully automatically for any (first order) type. This way one can focus on defining tasks, without having to deal with the complexities of web protocols and formats.

Interaction tasks follow a model-view pattern where the value of the task is the model and the visualization is the view. Events in the view are processed by the TOP framework to update the model. Conversely, when the model changes the view is updated automatically by the TOP framework.

Interaction tasks are all alike, yet different. In this section we define the semantics of one core editor task (Section 3.3.1). However, to improve readability TOP frameworks can offer a range of predefined interaction tasks derived from this core editor. A few examples from the iTask3 framework are:

```
enterInformation       :: d → [EnterOpt m]
                          → Task m      | descr d & iTask m
updateInformation      :: d → [UpdateOpt m m] → m
                          → Task m      | descr d & iTask m
viewInformation        :: d → [ViewOpt m] → m
                          → Task m      | descr d & iTask m
updateSharedInformation :: d → [UpdateOpt r w] → RWShared r w
                          → Task w      | descr d
                                        & iTask r & iTask w
viewSharedInformation  :: d → [ViewOpt r] → RWShared r w
                          → Task r      | descr d & iTask r
```

With enterInformation an editor for type m is created, no initial value needs to be given. The update-editor variants allow editing of a given local, respectively shared, value. The view-editor variants only display the value of a given local, or shared, value. There are many more similar editor functions predefined in the library, with names like enterChoice, enterSharedChoice, updateChoice, updateSharedChoice, enterSharedMultipleChoice, and so on.

The overloaded argument d of class descr in these tasks is description of the task. This can be a simple string, or a more elaborate description. Although the generated view is certainly good enough for rapid prototyping, more fine-grained control is sometimes desirable. Therefore, the EnterOpt, UpdateOpt and ViewOpt arguments provide hooks for fine-tuning interactions.

```
:: ViewOpt a    =∃v: ViewWith  (a → v)              & iTask v
```

```
:: EnterOpt a    =∃v: EnterWith            (v → a)      & iTask v
:: UpdateOpt a b =∃v: UpdateWith (a → v) (a v → b) & iTask v
```

By defining a mapping, a different type v can be used to view, enter or update information. In Section 4 we discuss in more detail how this and other pragmatic issues are dealt with.

3.3.1 Semantics of a Task Editor

The iTask3 library provides many different editor task functions because this clarifies in the task descriptions what kind of interaction is required, and aids in creating the desired user interface. However, both in the implementation and the semantics all editor task variants can be created and handled by one single function. To understand how it works we restrict ourselves to a simplified version in which we omit the view list details because these are just trivial mapping functions. Before we discuss this function edit we first have a look at the use of Events and Responses. Due to the model-view nature of editor tasks, every user manipulation of an editor task of a value of type a can be expressed as sending a new value new of type a from the client to the server. If we wrap this value-type pair into a Dynamic and include the task identification number, no say, then this amounts to the (EditEvent no (**dynamic** new :: a)) event. The unique task number is used to map a task described in the code to the corresponding interactive view generated in the client, and is used to label the events and corresponding responses.

The responses of the server tell the client what interface should be rendered to the user.

```
:: Response        = EditorResponse EditorResponse
                   | ActionResponse ActionResponse // Section 3.4.1
:: EditorResponse  = { description :: String
                     , editValue   :: EditValue
                     , editing     :: EditMode
                     }
:: EditValue       :== (LocalVal, SharedVal)
:: LocalVal        :== Dynamic
:: SharedVal       :== Dynamic
:: EditMode        = Editing | Displaying
```

The response to an editor task executed on a client informs the client about the latest state of the editor (EditorResponse) and contains, in serialized form, the current local value to edit and a shared value to show. With these Events and Responses, we can define the semantics of the editor task combinator which updates a local value of type l while displaying the latest value r stored in an SDS of type RWShared r w.

```
edit :: String → l → RWShared r w → (l → r → Maybe a)      1
                                    → Task a | iTask l & iTask r   2
edit descr lv sh_rw cv = newTask (edit1 lv)                3
where                                                      4
  edit1 lv tn t ev st                                      5
  # (nt,nlv) = case ev of                                  6
                  EditEvent tid dyn                         7
                  → if (tid==tn)                            8
                      (st.timeStamp,de_serialize dyn)       9
                      (t,lv)                                10
                  _ → (t,lv)                                11
  # (sr,st)  = sh_rw.get st                                12
  = ( Reduct (ValRes nt (toValue (cv nlv sr))) (edit1 nlv tn nt)  13
    , [(tn,EditorResponse                                  14
          { description = descr                             15
          , editing     = Editing                           16
          , editValue   = (serialize nlv, serialize sr)     17
          }                                                 18
      )]                                                    19
    , st                                                   20
    )                                                      21
where                                                      22
  toValue :: Maybe a → Value a                             23
```

```
24 toValue (Just a) = Val a Unstable
25 toValue Nothing  = NoVal
```

The `edit` function, and its continuation in the reduct (line 13), is defined in terms of `edit1` that keeps track of the latest local value edited, the unique task number given to this interactive task, and the time the latest modification has been made.

Editor tasks always have an unstable value (if any). They return a response containing the latest information on the state of the editor (lines 14-19 and 23-25). It includes the latest value of the data stored in shared memory (line 12) which might have been changed by some other task (e.g. using the `@>` operator). Only when the received event is an edit event intended for this editor (the task numbers match), the local value is updated with the new value received from the client (line 9). The new task value is computed using the most recent local and shared value (line 13).

3.4 Sequential Tasks

Once a task is started, it stays alive until it is no longer needed. Its value, which might change over time, can be inspected while the work is going on in order to decide whether or not to step to a next task. The task *step* operator `>>*` does exactly this.

```
(>>*) infixl 1 :: Task a → [TaskStep a b] → Task b | iTask a
                                                   & iTask b
:: TaskStep a b
   = OnAction Action (Predicate a) (NextTask a b)
   | OnValue         (Predicate a) (NextTask a b)
   | ∃e: OnException (e → Task b) & iTask e

:: Predicate a  :==Value a → Bool
:: NextTask a b:==Value a → Task b

:: Action = Action String | ActionOk | ActionCancel | ...
```

The step operator is similar to an ordinary monadic "bind-operator" in the sense that it defines a sequence between two tasks. The first operand, a task of type `Task a`, is evaluated. Its current task value can be inspected to decide whether the next task can be stepped into. If so, the evaluation of the first task is abandoned and the application proceeds with the chosen task step. The step operator can offer several tasks to continue with in the list, but only one task step can be stepped into.

There are three categories of task steps: those that require the user to actively select an action (`OnAction`), those that inspect the current task value (if any) (`OnValue`), and those that handle exceptions (`OnException`). `OnAction` task steps are labeled with an `Action` that is presented to the user as a button or menu item. For frequently used action names such as `Ok` and `Cancel`, the `Action` data type enumerates a number of special combinators to enable the client to use special icons. The predicate determines which action steps are available at all. Selection of an action by the user causes the corresponding alternative to be continued with. `OnValue` task steps inspect the current task value to determine whether or not a task step can be performed. Finally, `OnException` task steps handle an exception only if their argument function matches the type of the exception. Uncaught exceptions are propagated by `>>*`.

It sometimes can be the case that none of the candidate task steps can be chosen. However, task values change over time, hence also the candidates that can be chosen change over time.

We illustrate the use of `>>*` with two examples.

```
palindrome :: Task (Maybe String)
palindrome =   enterInformation "Enter a palindrome" []
           >>* [ OnAction  ActionOk     ifPalindrome
                                 (return o Just o getValue)
               , OnAction  ActionCancel (const True)
                                 (const (return Nothing))
               ]
```

The `palindrome` task prompts the user to enter a palindrome. As usual, the user can enter a string and change it over time. With `>>*` two possible action task steps are added. The user can choose action `Ok`, but only when the entered string is indeed a palindrome. If `Ok` is chosen, `Just p` is returned, where `p` is the entered and checked palindrome. At any time, the user can choose `Cancel`, and the task returns `Nothing`.

In the second example we implement a traditional monadic bind operator `>>=` to demonstrate the general nature of `>>*`:

```
(>>=) infixl 1 :: Task a → (a → Task b) → Task b | iTask a
                                                 & iTask b
(>>=) ta atb = ta >>* [OnValue isStable (atb o getValue)]
```

Task evaluation starts with the first argument `ta`. *Only* when this task produces a *stable* value `a`, evaluation continues with `atb a`. For this reason, `>>=` is less suited in the domain of tasks that may not produce a stable result.

3.4.1 Semantics of the Step Combinator

First we finalize the details of `ActionResponses`. The client is informed by `>>*` about the current set of actions and whether they are enabled or disabled. This information is collected in the `ActionResponse` list and added to the response accumulator.

```
:: ActionResponse :== [(Action, Enabled)]
:: Enabled        :== Bool
```

The client may react by sending an action event `ActionEvent taskno action` telling which action is triggered by the user.

The complete semantic definition of `>>*` is given in Figure 3. It is rather long because it needs to handle all `TaskStep` cases and prioritize them properly. However, each of these cases is rather straightforward. The step combinator is handled by `step1` which memorizes the current task description in its first argument (initially task `ta`, line 3, and in the reduct `nta`, line 20). The semantic function

```
1  (>>*) infixl 1 :: Task a → [TaskStep a b] → Task b | iTask a
2                                                     & iTask b
3  (>>*) ta steps = newTask (step1 ta)
4  where
5    step1 ta tn t ev st
6    # (Reduct tval nta, rsp, st) = ta ev st
7    = hd (  findTriggers tval
8         ++ findActions  tval ev
9         ++ [step1‘ tval nta rsp]
10        ) ev st
11   where
12     findTriggers (ExcRes   e) = catchers e ++ [throw e]
13     findTriggers (ValRes _ v) = values v
14
15     findActions (ValRes _ v) (ActionEvent tid act)
16     | tid==tn                 = actions act v
17     findActions _ _           = []
18
19     step1‘ (ValRes _ v) nta rsp _ st
20       = (Reduct no_tval (step1 nta tn t), nrsp ++ rsp, st)
21     where
22       no_tval  = ValRes t NoVal
23       as       = [(a,p v) \\ OnAction a p _←steps]
24       nrsp     = if (isEmpty as) [] [(tn, ActionResponse as)]
25
26   catchers     e = [etb e \\ OnException  etb←steps       ]
27   values       v = [atb v \\ OnValue     p atb←steps | p v]
28   actions act  v = [atb v \\ OnAction a p atb←steps | act==a
29                                                   && p v]
```

Figure 3. The complete semantic definition of `>>*`.

newTask (Section 3.1.2) provides it with a unique task number for communication with the client and current time stamp t (line 3). The current task description is evaluated first (line 6), resulting in a new task value that is inspected to decide which task step can be stepped into. Triggers (line 7) take priority over actions (line 8). If no task step is applicable, then we proceed with step1 again, but now parameterized with the calculated reduced task (line 9).

A trigger is a task step that can continue without interference of the user. These are the OnException and OnValue task steps. In case of an exception, an exception handler is searched for (line 12 and 26). If none is defined, then the exception propagates (line 12). In case of a task value, all available OnValue task steps are searched for (line 13 and 27).

The actions are selected only if the event is an action event for this task (line 15 and 16). In that case all available OnAction task steps are searched for that match the received action and that are available, as determined by their predicate (lines 28-29).

Finally, when no task step can be selected a reduct is made by step1` that waits for a new event (line 20). All actions are collected in the response accumulator (line 23 and 24).

3.5 Parallel Tasks

Tasks can often be divided into parallel sub tasks if there is no specific predetermined order in which the sub tasks have to be done. It might not even be required that all sub tasks contribute sensibly to a stable result. All variants of parallel composition can be handled by a single parallel combinator:

```
parallel :: d → [(ParallelTaskType, ParallelTask a)]
            → Task [(TimeStamp, Value a)] | descr d & iTask a

:: ParallelTaskType = Embedded | Detached ManagementMeta
:: ManagementMeta   = { worker :: Maybe User
                      , role   :: Maybe Role
                      , ...
                      }
:: ParallelTask   a :== SharedTaskList a → Task a
:: SharedTaskList a :== ROShared (TaskList a)
:: TaskList       a = { state  :: [Value a]
                      , ...
                      }
```

We distinguish two sorts of parallel sub-tasks: Detached tasks get distributed to different users and and Embedded tasks are executed by the current user. The client may present these tasks in different ways. Detached tasks need a window of their own while embedded tasks may by visualized in an existing window. With the ManagementMeta structure properties can be set such as which worker must perform the sub-task, or which role he should have.

Whatever its sort, every parallel sub-task can inspect each others progress. Of each parallel sub-tasks its current task value and some other system information is collected in a shared task list. The parallel sub-tasks have *read-only* access to this task list. The parallel combinator also delivers all task values in a list of type [(TimeStamp,Value a)]. Hence, the progress of every parallel sub-task can also be monitored constantly from the "outside". For instance, a parallel task can be monitored with the step combinator >>* to decide if the parallel task as a whole can be terminated because its sub tasks have made sufficient progress for doing the next step. It is also possible to observe the task and convert its value to some other type using the conversion operator @? (Section 3.1.4).

For completeness, we remark that the shared task list is also used to allow dynamic creation and deletion of parallel sub-tasks. We do not discuss this further in this paper.

In the iTask3 library parallel is used to predefine several frequently used task patterns. In Section 2.2 the -||- combinator was used to start to tasks in parallel.

```
(-||-) infixr 3 :: Task a → Task a → Task a | iTask a
(-||-) a b
  = parallel () [(Embedded,const a),(Embedded,const b)] @? first
where
  first NoVal = NoVal
  first (Value vs _)
    = hd (   [v \\ (_,v=:(Val _ Stable)) ← vs]
          ++ [v \\ (_,v=:(Val _ _)) ← sortBy newer vs]
          ++ [NoVal]
         )
  newer (t1,_) (t2,_) = t1 > t2
```

The first function inspects the progress of both parallel sub-tasks to determine the task value of the composition. The first sub-task to produce a stable task value turns the composition into a stable task with that value. If no sub-task has produced a stable value, then the most recent unstable task value, if any, is the observable result, or no task value is observable at all.

3.5.1 Semantics of the Parallel Combinator

In the semantic description we ignore the meta information assigned to detached tasks and therefore do not distinguish embedded tasks from detached tasks. As another non-essential simplification, we define the shared task list as a *read-write* SDS instead of a *read-only* SDS. The shared task list is a finite map from process ids to task reducts:

```
:: SharedTaskList a :== RWShared (TaskList a)
:: TaskList       a :== [(Pid a, Reduct a)]
:: Pid            a :== Int
```

The complete semantic definition of parallel is given in Figure 4. The semantic function parallel` (lines 15-26) defines the purpose of the parallel combinator: to evaluate each and every sub-task (line 18) until either an exception has been thrown (line 19), or all sub-tasks have become stable (lines 23-24). While this is not the case, parallel` proceeds to rewrite to itself (line 25-26).

Both parallel` and its sub-tasks require access to their progress, which is stored in the shared task list which is created as the first step of the parallel combinator (line 4 and lines 7-13). Initially, the task list consists of all initial parallel sub-tasks that have access to the shared task list.

The semantic functions evalParTasks and evalParTask define the evaluation of the parallel sub tasks: evalParTasks collects the current list of sub-tasks (line 31) and applies evalParTask to each and every sub-task (line 32). Evaluation of a sub-task (line 39) might result in an exception (line 41), in which case the exception is propagated throughout the evaluation of all sub-tasks (lines 44-45). If a sub-task does not result in an exception, then its new reduct is stored in the shared task list (line 42), thus allowing the other sub-tasks to inspect its progress (updateFM (pid,newr) updates any existing element (pid,_) in the shared task list with (pid,newr)). The responses of the evaluated sub-task are collected and returned (line 43).

4. Practical TOP

Although the TOP paradigm adopts functional programming's emphasis of *what* over *how*, some pragmatic issues remain unavoidable in practical TOP programming. In this section we discuss pragmatics issues that we encountered in the implementation of the TOP concept in the iTask3 toolkit, and show examples of iTask3 programs to illustrate its use in real-world applications.

4.1 Pragmatic Issues

Custom Interaction: TOP programs focus on defining decompositions of tasks without worrying how interactions of basic tasks are implemented by the TOP framework. The underlying implementation has to take care of that. The iTask3 system follows the

```
parallel :: [ParallelTask a]
         → Task [(TimeStamp,Value a)] | iTask a
parallel ptas ev st
# (stt,st) = createTaskList ptas st
= parallel` stt ev st

createTaskList :: [ParallelTask a]
               → *State → *(SharedTaskList a,*State) | iTask a
createTaskList ptas st=:{timeStamp = t}
# (stt,st) = createShared [] st
= (stt,stt.set [  (pid,Reduct (ValRes t NoVal) (pta stt))
              \\ pta←ptas & pid←[0..]
              ] st)

parallel` :: SharedTaskList a
          → Task [(TimeStamp,Value a)] | iTask a
parallel` stt ev st
= case evalParTasks stt ev st of
    (Left (ExcRes e),st) = throw e ev st
    (Right rsp,st)
    # (values,st) = get_task_values stt st
    # maxt        = foldr max 0 (map fst values)
    | all (isStable o snd) values
                  = stable maxt values ev st
    | otherwise   = (Reduct (ValRes maxt (Val values Unstable))
                            (parallel` stt),rsp,st)

evalParTasks :: SharedTaskList a → Event → *State
  → *(Either (TaskResult a) Responses,*State) | iTask a
evalParTasks stt ev st
# (tt,st) = stt.get st
= foldl (evalParTask stt ev) (Right [],st) tt

evalParTask :: SharedTaskList a → Event
            → *(Either (TaskResult a) Responses,*State)
            → (Pid a,Reduct a)
            → *(Either (TaskResult a) Responses,*State)
evalParTask stt ev (Right rsp,st) (pid,Reduct _ ta)
# (newr,nrsp,st)     = ta ev st
# (Reduct ntval nta) = newr
| isExcRes ntval     = (Left ntval,st)
# (_,st)             = updateShared (updateFM (pid,newr)) stt st
= (Right (nrsp ++ rsp),st)
evalParTask _ _ (Left e,st) _
= (Left e,st)

get_task_values :: SharedTaskList a → *State
               → *([(TimeStamp, Value a)],*State)
get_task_values stt st
# (tt,st) = stt.get st
= ([(t,val) \\ (_,Reduct (ValRes t val) _)←tt],st)
```

Figure 4. The complete semantic definition of `parallel`.

semantic definitions, with additional support for customization for obtaining practical applicable applications. The interactive applications that are generated by default by the system suffice for rapid prototyping. However, aesthetic and ergonomic properties of these interactions affect the ease of use and attractiveness of a system. For example, the task of choosing a file from a file system is performed more easily by navigating a tree structure than by selecting an item from a long list of all files.

To allow for such task specific optimization, all interaction tasks in the iTask**3** framework have a *views* parameter, in which optional mappings between the task's domain and another arbitrary domain can be defined. The library provides types that represent abstract user interface controls with which customized interactions can be composed. Here is an example (see Figure 5):

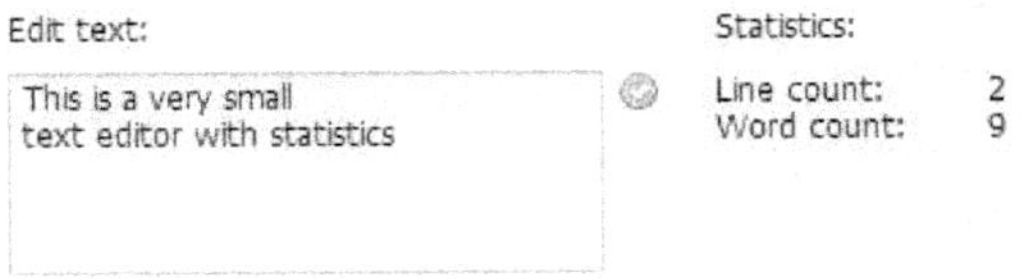

Figure 5. A very simple text editor

```
1  :: Statistics = { lineCount :: Int, wordCount :: Int }
2  derive class iTask Statistics
3  
4  simpleEdit :: Task Note
5  simpleEdit = withShared (Note "") edit
6  where
7   edit note
8   = updateSharedInformation "Enter text:" [] note
9     -||-
10    viewSharedInformation "Statistics:" [ViewWith stat] note
11                                              <<@ horizontal
12 
13   stat (Note txt) = { lineCount = length lines
14                     , wordCount = length words
15                     }
16   where lines     = split Newline txt
17         words     = split " " (replaceSubString Newline " " txt)
```

By default, if a value of the predefined type `Note` is used in an iTask**3** editor, a text box is presented to the user on the client to enter text. In `simpleEdit` we create a shared memory for a value of this type `Note` with initial value `Note ""` and we define two interactive tasks on this shared value. The first task allows the user to update the initial text (line 8), while the second gives a view on the shared text that is fine-tuned with `ViewWith` which, in this case, converts the text into a value of type `Statistics`. As a result, while entering text, the user sees the corresponding statistics.

Customized Layout: For task compositions a similar need for customization exist. Depending on the composition, it may be more appealing or easier to use when tasks are divided over tabs or windows than when tasks are shown side-by-side. To customize layout, the iTask**3** framework provides an annotation operator (`<<@`) that can be used to annotate tasks with custom layout functions or post-layout processing functions. Such functions combine a set of abstract GUI definitions into a single definition. By default a heuristic layout function is used to provide a sensible default. Post-processing functions modify a GUI definition after a task is layed out. Such modifications are for example changing its size, adding margins or changing to a horizontal layout as is done with the `<<@ horizontal` annotation in the simple editor. It is defined as:

```
horizontal = AfterLayout (tweakUI (setDirection Horizontal))
```

Localization: Another pragmatic aspect one may need to deal with is localization. Because task definitions contain many prompts, hints and other texts, one needs to deal with localization of such texts without compromizing the readability of task definitions. Furthermore, localization may also be required on the task level. To comply with local law and regulations, different task definitions may have to be used in different countries. The iTask**3** framework does not offer any special support for localization, but one can make use of the standard modular structure of Clean to create different local versions.

Third Party Formats and Protocols: To integrate TOP applications with other applications, the gap between the domain of tasks and the formats or protocols required to interact with these systems must be bridged. With TOP one does not escape writing the parsing, formatting and communication code that is necessary for such integrations, but it can be separated from the application code by moving it to task libraries.

4.2 Examples

A Generic Work List: A major leap in the development of TOP as a general paradigm was the insight that, from a user's point of view, interaction with a "Work List", in which users can work on tasks assigned to them, is actually part of the work that has to be done. Work list handling e.g. as offered by an email application or a workflow system is commonly hard coded in the systems used. In iTask**3** this functionality is defined in the system itself as "just" any other task. Figure 6 shows the generic work list task we offer as a

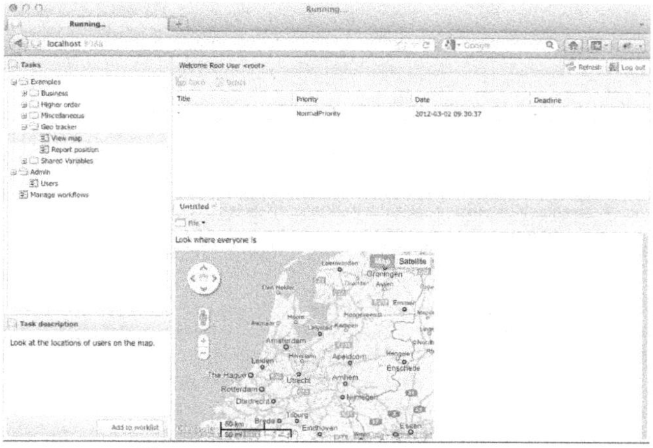

Figure 6. A generic WFMS Work List

standard example. In the left panel a tree of tasks that can be started is displayed. The tasks to do are displayed in the upper-right pane, similar to an inbox in a email application. The user can work on several tasks at the same time in the lower right pane, by opening them in separate tabs. This complete work list application is defined in less than 200 lines of TOP code.

The Incidone Incident Coordination Tool: The Coast Guard case study (Jansen et al., 2010; Lijnse et al., 2011) not only fueled the refinement of the task concept and the TOP paradigm, it also lead to the development of the Incidone tool (Lijnse et al., 2012). A preview of this tool for supporting Coast Guard operations is shown in Figure 7. It is being developed using the iTask**3**

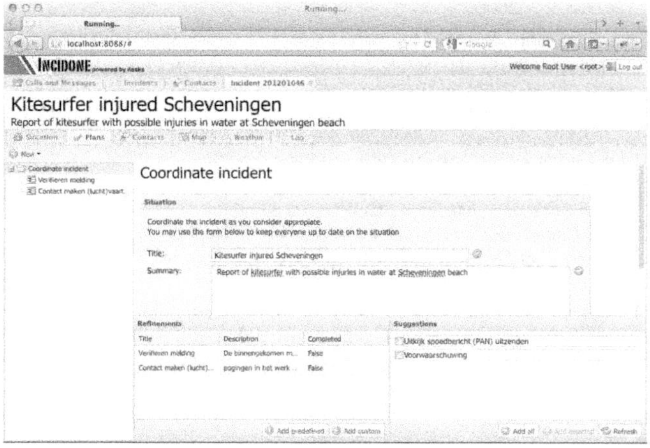

Figure 7. The Incidone Tool

framework to illustrate the use of TOP for crisis management applications. In this tool immediate information sharing between team members working together is crucial to handle incidents properly.

5. Related Work

The TOP paradigm emerged during continued work on the iTask system. In its first incarnation (Plasmeijer et al., 2007), iTask**1**, the notion of tasks was introduced for the specification of dedicated workflow management systems. In iTask**1** and its successor iTask**2** (Lijnse and Plasmeijer, 2010), a task is an opaque unit of work that, once completed, yields a result from which subsequent tasks can be computed. When deploying these systems for real-world applications, viz. in telecare (van der Heijden et al., 2011) and modeling the dynamic task of coordinating Coast Guard Search and Rescue operations (Jansen et al., 2010; Lijnse et al., 2011) we experienced that this concept of task is not adequate to express the coordination of tasks where teams constantly need to be informed about the progress made by others. The search for better abstraction has resulted in the TOP approach and task concept as introduced in this paper.

Task-Oriented programming touches on two broad areas of research. First the programming of interactive multi-user (web) applications, and second the specification of tasks.

There are many languages, libraries and frameworks for programming multi-user web applications. Some academic, and many more in the open-source and proprietary commercial software markets. Examples from the academic functional programming community include: the Haskell cgi library (Meijer, 2000); the Curry approach (Hanus, 2001); writing xml applications (Elsman and Friis Larsen, 2004) in *SMLserver* (Elsman and Hallenberg, 2003); WashCGI (Thiemann, 2002); the Hop (Loitsch and Serrano, 2007; Serrano et al., 2006) web programming language; Links (Cooper et al., 2006) and formlets (Cooper et al., 2007). All these solutions address the technical challenges of creating multi-user web applications. Naturally, these challenges also need to be addressed within the TOP approach. The principal difference between TOP and these web technologies is the emphasis on using tasks both as modeling and programming unit to abstract from these issues, including coordination of tasks that may or may not have a value.

Tasks are an ambiguous notion used in different fields, such as Workflow Management Systems (WFMS), human-computer interaction, and ergonomics. Although the iTask**1** system was influenced and partially motivated by the use of tasks in WFMSs (van der Aalst et al., 2002), iTask**3** has evolved to the more general TOP approach of structuring software systems. As such, it is more similar in spirit to the WebWorkFlow project (Hemel et al., 2008), which is an object oriented approach that breaks down the logic into separate clauses instead of functions. Cognitive Task Analysis methods (Crandall et al., 2006) seek to understand how people accomplish tasks. Their results are useful in the design of software systems, but they are not software development methods. In Robotics the notion of task and even the "Task-Oriented Programming" moniker are also used. In this field it is used to indicate a level of autonomy at which robots are programmed. To the best of our knowledge, TOP as a paradigm for interactive multi-user systems, rooted in functional programming is a novel approach, distinct from other uses of the notion of tasks in the fields mentioned above.

6. Conclusions and Future Work

In this paper we introduced Task-Oriented Programming, a paradigm for programming interactive multi-user applications in a pure functional language. The distinguishing feature of TOP is the ability to concisely describe and implement collaboration and complex interaction of tasks. This is achieved by four core concepts: 1) *Tasks observe intermediate values of other tasks* and react on these values before the other tasks are completely finished. 2) *Tasks* running in parallel *communicate via shared data sources*. Shared data sources enable useful lightweight communication between related tasks. By restricting the use of shared data sources we avoid an overly complex semantics. 3) *Tasks interact with users based on arbitrary typed data*, the interface required for this type is derived by type driven generic programming. 4) *Tasks are composed* to more complex tasks *using a small set of combinators*. The step combinator >>* subsumes the classic monad bind operator >>=. The presented operational semantics specifies the constructs unambiguously. The development of this semantics was an important anchor point during the design of TOP.

TOP is embedded in Clean by offering a newly developed iTask**3** library. We have used TOP successfully for the development of a prototype implementation of a Search and Rescue decision support system for the Dutch Coast Guard. The coordination of such rescue operations requires up-to-date information of subtasks, this is precisely the goal of TOP. In collaboration with Dutch industry we started to investigate and validate the suitability of the TOP paradigm to handle specific complex real world distributed application areas.

References

Wil van der Aalst, Arthur ter Hofstede, Bartek Kiepuszewski, and Ana Barros. Workflow patterns. Technical Report FIT-TR-2002-02, Queensland University of Technology, 2002.

Artem Alimarine. *Generic Functional Programming - Conceptual Design, Implementation and Applications*. PhD thesis, Radboud University Nijmegen, 2005. ISBN 3-540-67658-9.

Ezra Cooper, Sam Lindley, Philip Wadler, and Jeremy Yallop. Links: web programming without tiers. In *Proceedings of the 5th International Symposium on Formal Methods for Components and Objects, FMCO '06*, volume 4709, CWI, Amsterdam, The Netherlands, 7-10, November 2006. Springer-Verlag.

Ezra Cooper, Sam Lindley, Philip Wadler, and Jeremy Yallop. An idiom's guide to formlets. Technical report, The University of Edinburgh, UK, 2007. `http://groups.inf.ed.ac.uk/links/papers-/formlets-draft2007.pdf`.

Beth Crandall, Gary Klein, and Robert R Hoffman. *Working Minds: A practitioner's guide to cognitive task analysis*. MIT Press, 2006. ISBN 978-0-262-03351-0.

Martin Elsman and Ken Friis Larsen. Typing XHTML web applications in ML. In *Proceedings of the 6th International Symposium on the Practical Aspects of Declarative Programming, PADL '04*, volume 3057 of *Lecture Notes in Computer Science*, pages 224–238. Dallas, TX, USA, Springer-Verlag, June 2004.

Martin Elsman and Niels Hallenberg. Web programming with SMLserver. In *Proceedings of the 5th International Symposium on the Practical Aspects of Declarative Programming, PADL '03*. New Orleans, LA, USA, Springer-Verlag, January 2003.

John van Groningen, Thomas van Noort, Peter Achten, Pieter Koopman, and Rinus Plasmeijer. Exchanging sources between Clean and Haskell - A double-edged front end for the Clean compiler. In Jeremy Gibbons, editor, *Proceedings of the Haskell Symposium, Haskell '10, Baltimore, MD, USA*, pages 49–60. ACM Press, 2010.

Michael Hanus. High-level server side web scripting in Curry. In *Proceedings of the 3rd International Symposium on the Practical Aspects of Declarative Programming, PADL '01*, pages 76–92. Springer-Verlag, 2001.

Zef Hemel, Ruben Verhaaf, and Eelco Visser. WebWorkFlow: an object-oriented workflow modeling language for web applications. In K. Czarnecki, I. Ober, J.-M. Bruel, A. Uhl, and M. Völter, editors, *Proceedings of the 11th International Conference on Model Driven Engineering Languages and Systems, MoDELS '08*, volume 5301 of *Lecture Notes in Computer Science*, pages 113–127. Springer-Verlag, 2008.

Ralf Hinze. A new approach to generic functional programming. In Tom Reps, editor, *Proceedings of the 27th International Symposium on Principles of Programming Languages, POPL '00, Boston, MA, USA*, pages 119–132. ACM Press, 2000.

Jan Martin Jansen, Bas Lijnse, and Rinus Plasmeijer. Towards dynamic workflows for crisis management. In Simon French, Brian Tomaszewski, and Cristopher Zobel, editors, *Proceedings of the 7th International Conference on Information Systems for Crisis Response and Management, ISCRAM '10*, Seattle, WA, USA, May 2010.

Pieter Koopman, Rinus Plasmeijer, and Peter Achten. *An Effective Methodology for Defining Consistent Semantics of Complex Systems*, volume 6299 of *LNCS*, pages 224–267. Springer-Verlag, Komarno, Slovakia, 25-130, May 2009.

Bas Lijnse and Rinus Plasmeijer. iTasks 2: iTasks for End-users. In Marco Morazán and Sven-Bodo Scholz, editors, *Revised Selected Papers of the International Symposium on the Implementation and Application of Functional Languages, IFL '09, South Orange, NJ, USA*, volume 6041 of *LNCS*, pages 36–54. Springer-Verlag, 2010.

Bas Lijnse, Jan Martin Jansen, Ruud Nanne, and Rinus Plasmeijer. Capturing the netherlands coast guard's sar workflow with itasks. In David Mendonca and Julie Dugdale, editors, *Proceedings of the 8th International Conference on Information Systems for Crisis Response and Management, ISCRAM '11*, Lisbon, Portugal, May 2011. ISCRAM Association.

Bas Lijnse, Jan Martin Jansen, and Rinus Plasmeijer. Incidone: A task-oriented incident coordination tool. In Leon Rothkrantz, Jozef Ristvej, and Zeno Franco, editors, *Proceedings of the 9th International Conference on Information Systems for Crisis Response and Management, ISCRAM '12*, Vancouver, Canada, April 2012.

Florian Loitsch and Manuel Serrano. Hop client-side compilation. In *Proceedings of the 7th Symposium on Trends in Functional Programming, TFP '07*, pages 141–158, New York, NY, USA, 2-4, April 2007. Interact.

Erik Meijer. Server side web scripting in Haskell. *Journal of Functional Programming*, 10(1):1–18, 2000.

Steffen Michels and Rinus Plasmeijer. Uniform data sources in a functional language. Submitted for presentation at Symposium on Trends in Functional Programming, TFP '12, 2012. URL `https://wiki.clean.cs.ru.nl/File:Sharing_Data_Sources.pdf`.

Rinus Plasmeijer, Peter Achten, and Pieter Koopman. iTasks: executable specifications of interactive work flow systems for the web. In Ralf Hinze and Norman Ramsey, editors, *Proceedings of the International Conference on Functional Programming, ICFP '07*, pages 141–152, Freiburg, Germany, 2007. ACM Press.

Manuel Serrano, Erick Gallesio, and Florian Loitsch. Hop, a language for programming the web 2.0. In *Proceedings of the 11th International Conference on Object-Oriented Programming, Systems, Languages, and Applications, OOPSLA '06*, pages 975–985, Portland, Oregon, USA, 22-26, October 2006.

Peter Thiemann. WASH/CGI: server-side web scripting with sessions and typed, compositional forms. In Shriram Krishnamurthi and Raghu Ramakrishnan, editors, *Proceedings of the 4th International Symposium on the Practical Aspects of Declarative Programming, PADL '02*, volume 2257 of *Lecture Notes in Computer Science*, pages 192–208, Portland, OR, USA, 19-20, January 2002. Springer-Verlag.

Maarten van der Heijden, Bas Lijnse, Peter Lucas, Yvonne Heijdra, and Tjard Schermer. Managing COPD exacerbations with telemedicine. In *13th Conference on Artificial Intelligence in Medicine, AIME '11*, volume 6747 of *LNCS*, pages 169–178, Bled, Slovenia, July 2011. Springer-Verlag.

Martijn Vervoort and Rinus Plasmeijer. Lazy dynamic input/output in the lazy functional language Clean. In Ricardo Peña and Thomas Arts, editors, *Revised Selected Papers of the 14th International Workshop on the Implementation of Functional Languages, IFL '02, Madrid, Spain*, volume 2670 of *LNCS*, pages 101–117. Springer-Verlag, 2003.

Arjen van Weelden. *Putting types to good use*. PhD thesis, Radboud University Nijmegen, 17, October 2007. ISBN 978-90-9022041-3.

A Linear Concurrent Constraint Approach for the Automatic Verification of Access Permissions

Carlos Olarte, Camilo Rueda
Dept. de Electrónica y Ciencias de la Computación.
Pontificia Universidad Javeriana-Cali, Colombia
{caolarte, crueda}@cic.puj.edu.co

Elaine Pimentel
Universidad del Valle, Colombia.
Universidade Federal de Minas Gerais, Brasil
elaine @mat.ufmg.br

Néstor Cataño
The University of Madeira, Portugal
ncatano@uma.pt

Abstract

A recent trend in object oriented programming languages is the use Access Permissions (AP) as abstraction to control concurrent executions. AP define a protocol specifying how different references can access the mutable state of objects. Although AP simplify the task of writing concurrent code, an unsystematic use of permissions in the program can lead to subtle problems. This paper presents a Linear Concurrent Constraint (`lcc`) approach to verify AP annotated programs. We model AP as constraints (i.e., formulas in logic) in an underlying constraint system, and we use entailment of constraints to faithfully model the flow of AP in the program. We verify relevant properties about programs by taking advantage of the declarative interpretation of `lcc` agents as formulas in linear logic. Properties include deadlock detection, program correctness (whether programs adhere to their AP specifications or not), and the ability of methods to run concurrently. We show that those properties are decidable and we present a complexity analysis of finding such proofs. We implemented our verification and analysis approach as the Alcove tool, which is available on-line.

Categories and Subject Descriptors F.3.1 [*Specifying and Verifying and Reasoning about Programs*]: Logics of programs; D.3.2 [*Language Classifications*]: Constraint and logic languages. Concurrent, distributed, and parallel languages.

General Terms Theory, Verification, Concurrency

Keywords Concurrent Constraint Programming, Access Permissions, Linear Logic, Verification

1. Introduction

Reasoning about concurrent programs is much harder than reasoning about sequential ones. Programmers often find themselves overwhelmed by the many subtle cases of thread interaction they must be aware of so as to decide whether a concurrent program is correct or not. Also, the need of finding the right level of thread atomicity, avoiding race conditions, coping with mutual exclusion requirements, guaranteeing deadlock freeness, make it very hard to design reliable concurrent software. Furthermore, the attempt to find errors through testing is doomed to failure because of the non-determinism caused by thread scheduling.

This complexity of concurrent software is aggravated when software designers, wishing to take advantage of object oriented (OO) design strategies, use OO languages to write concurrent programs. The distribution of state in objects that might have multiple references (aliases), probing or modifying concurrently their *local* contents, contributes significantly to the complexity of sound concurrent program design. This potential data race situation occurs when a reading and a writing trace both access a shared memory location. This should be considered a program error since it gives rise to inconsistent executions paths. To cope with this problem, a simple strategy is to wrap each object access up in an atomic block. However, this negatively affects program performance. A better strategy would be for the programmer to lock just those objects that are actually shared among threads. It is very hard, however, to figure out which objects are to be shared and what locations are really protected by the locks simply by looking at the program text.

Languages like Æminium [18] and Plaid [19] propose a different strategy to concurrency based on *access permissions* (AP) [5] to objects. AP are descriptions about how various references to an object can coexist. They permit a direct control about the access to the mutable state of an object. Making the access to a shared mutable state explicit facilitates verification and it also permits parallelization of code. For instance, a *unique* AP, which describes the case when only one reference to a given object exists, enforces absence of interference and simplifies verification. On the other hand, a *shared* AP, which describes the case when an object may be accessed and modified by multiple references, allows for concurrent executions and makes verification trickier.

Although AP greatly help to devise static strategies for correct concurrent sharing of objects, the interactions resulting from dynamic bindings (e.g., aliasing of variables) might still lead to subtle difficulties. Indeed, it may happen that apparently correct permissions assignments in simple programs lead to deadlocks.

We propose a Linear Concurrent Constraint (`lcc`) [7] programming approach to the verification of AP annotated programs. In our approach, programs are interpreted as `lcc` agents that use constraints to keep information about AP, object references, object fields, and method calls. We use constraint entailment to verify compliance of methods and arguments to their AP based signatures. Furthermore, by exploiting the declarative view of `lcc` agents as logical formulas, we are able to analyze and verify programs. The proposed program verification includes (1) deadlock detection; (2) whether it is possible for methods to be executed concurrently

PPDP'12, September 19–21, 2012, Leuven, Belgium.

```
1  class stats {...}
2  class collection {
3    collection() none(this) ⇒ unq(this) {...}
4    sort() unq(this) ⇒ unq(this) {...}
5    print() imm(this) ⇒ imm(this) {...}
6    compStats(stats s) imm(this), unq(s) ⇒
                          imm(this), unq(s) {...}
7    removeDuplicates() unq(this) ⇒ unq(this){...}}
8  main() {
9    let collection c, stats s in
10     c := new collection()
11     s := new stats()
12     c.sort()
13     c.print()
14     c.compStats(s)
15     c.removeDuplicates()
16   end }
```

Figure 1. Example of an Æminium program.

or not; and (3) whether annotations adhere to the intended semantics associated with AP or not.

The contributions of the this paper are four-fold (1) the definition of an elegant `lcc` semantics of AP for an object oriented concurrent programming language; (2) the definition of a decidable efficient verification procedure of non-recursive programs; (3) a complexity analysis of the effort required to verify a program; and (4) the implementation of the Alcove tool that automates our verification approach.

The rest of the paper is organized as follows. Section 2 presents the syntax of the AP based language used here and recalls `lcc`. Section 3 presents the model of AP as `lcc` agents. We also show how the proposed model is a runnable specification that allows users to observe the flow of program permissions. We implemented this models as the Alcove LCC Animator. Section 4 describes our approach to verify programs and its implementation as the Alcove LL prover. It also presents a complexity analysis about the proposed verification. Section 5 concludes the paper.

2. Preliminaries

2.1 Programs Syntax

Access permissions (AP) are abstractions describing how objects are accessed. Assume a variable x that points to the object o. The unique permission `unq` states that x is the sole reference to object o. The shared permission `shr` provides x with reading and modifying access to object o, which allows other references to o (called aliases) to exist and to read from it or to modify it. The immutable permission `imm` provides x with read-only access to o, and allows any other reference to object o to exist and to read from it. If x points to null, the permission `none` represents the fact that x is a null reference and it has no permission to access any object.

Figure 1 shows a program (taken and slightly modified from [18]) that operates over a collection of elements. Starting at line 8, the program creates an object of type *collection* at Line 10 and an object of type *stats* at line 11. The program sorts the collection c at line 12, and prints it at line 13. It computes some statistics at line 14, and removes duplicates from the collection at line 15. Lines 3-7 declare the signatures for the methods. The signature of class *collection* constructor returns a unique reference to a new collection at line 3. Methods *sort* and *removeDuplicates* require a unique reference to the collection to exist and to return a unique permission to it. Method *compStats* requires and returns an immutable (read-only) AP to the collection c and a unique AP to the parameter s.

Given these method signatures, the AP flow for the program is computed. Permissions can be produced and consumed. Hence, the unique permission returned by the constructor of class *collection* is consumed by the call of *sort*. Once this method terminates, the unique permission is restored and split into two immutable permissions, and methods *print* and *compStats* can be executed concurrently. Once both methods have finished their execution, the immutable access permissions are joined back into a unique access permission, and the method *removeDuplicates* can be executed.

The analyses presented in this paper considers a subset of Æminium [18], a concurrent-by-default object oriented programming language based on the above idea of AP (see Figure 2). Methods specify the required permissions for the caller ($p(\texttt{this})$) and for each argument ($\overline{p(y)}$) as well as the permissions restored to the environment when the method terminates ($p'(\texttt{this})$ and $\overline{p'(y)}$). Similarly for class constructors (CTR). We assume that in a call to a method (or constructor), the actual parameters are *references* (i.e., variables, object fields or `this`) and not arbitrary expressions. Since we have parameters by reference, we assume that the returned type is `void` and we omit it in the signature. For assignments we allow only statements of the form $r_l := r_r$, where the right and left hand side are references. Notice that we do not lose generality by imposing these syntactic restrictions since it is possible to unfold more general expressions by using local variables.

2.2 Linear `ccp`

Concurrent Constraint Programming (`ccp`) [17] is a model for concurrency that combines the traditional operational view of process calculi with a declarative view based on logic. This allows `ccp` to benefit from the large set of reasoning techniques of both process calculi and logic. Agents in `ccp` *interact* with each other by *telling* and *asking* information represented as *constraints* to a global store.

The basic constructs (processes) in `ccp` are: (1) the *tell* agent c, which adds the constraint c to the store, thus making it available to the other processes. Once a constraint is added, it cannot be removed from the store (i.e., the store grows monotonically). And (2), the *ask* process $c \rightarrow P$, which queries if c can be deduced from the information in the current store; if so, the agent behaves like P, otherwise, it remains blocked until more information is added to the store. In this way, ask processes define a simple and powerful synchronization mechanism based on entailment of constraints.

Linear Concurrent Constraint (`lcc`) [7] is a `ccp`-based calculus that considers constraint systems built from a fragment of Girard's intuitionistic linear logic (ILL) [8]. The move to a *linear discipline* permits ask agents to *consume* information (i.e., constraints) from the store.

Definition 1 (Linear Constraint Systems [7]). *A linear constraint system is a pair $(\mathcal{C}, \vdash)$ where $\mathcal{C}$ is a set of formulas (linear constraints) built from a signature Σ (a set of function and relation symbols), a denumerable set of variables $\mathcal{V}$ and the following ILL operators:* multiplicative *conjunction ($\otimes$) and its neutral element (1), the existential quantifier ($\exists$), the exponential bang ($!$) and the constant top ($\top$). Let Δ be a (possibly empty) subset of $\mathcal{C} \times \mathcal{C}$ defining the non-logical axioms of the constraint system (i.e, a theory). Then the entailment relation $\vdash$ is the least set containing Δ and closed by the rules of ILL (see Figure 3).*

We shall use $c, c', d, d' \ldots$ to denote elements in $\mathcal{C}$. We recall that $!\,c$ represents the arbitrary duplication of the resource c. The entailment $d \vdash c$ means that the information c can be deduced from the information represented by d.

(programs)	P	::=	$\langle \overline{CL}\ main \rangle$
(class decl.)	CL	::=	$\texttt{class}\ cname\ \{\ \overline{F}\ \overline{M}\ \}$
(field decl.)	F	::=	$cname\ fname$
(method decl.)	M	::=	$meth(\overline{cname\ y})\ p(\texttt{this}), \overline{p(y)} \Rightarrow p'(\texttt{this}), \overline{p'(y)}\ \{s\}$
	CTR	::=	$cname(\overline{cname\ y})\ \texttt{none}(\texttt{this}), \overline{p(y)} \Rightarrow p'(\texttt{this}), \overline{p'(y)}\ \{s\}$
(main)	$main$	::=	$\texttt{main}()\ \{s\}$
(references)	r	::=	$x \mid x.fname \mid \texttt{this}$
(statements)	s	::=	$\texttt{let}\ \overline{cname\ x}\ \texttt{in}\ s\ \texttt{end} \mid r_l := r_r \mid x.meth(\overline{r}) \mid x := \texttt{new}\ cname(\overline{r}) \mid s_1\ s_2\ ...\ s_n$
(permissions)	p	::=	$\texttt{unq} \mid \texttt{shr} \mid \texttt{imm}$

Figure 2. Reduced Syntax of Æminium programs. $\overline{x}$ denotes a sequence of variables $x_1, ..., x_n$. This notation is similarly used for other syntactic categories.

$$c \vdash c \qquad \vdash 1 \qquad \Gamma \vdash \top$$

$$\frac{\Gamma \vdash c}{\Gamma, 1 \vdash c} \qquad \frac{\Gamma, c_1, c_2 \vdash c}{\Gamma, c_1 \otimes c_2 \vdash c} \qquad \frac{\Gamma \vdash c_1 \quad \Delta \vdash c_2}{\Gamma, \Delta \vdash c_1 \otimes c_2}$$

$$\frac{\Gamma \vdash c[t/x]}{\Gamma \vdash \exists x.c} \qquad \frac{\Gamma, c \vdash d \quad x \notin fv(\Gamma, d)}{\Gamma, \exists x.c \vdash d} \qquad \frac{\Gamma, c \vdash d}{\Gamma, !c \vdash d}$$

$$\frac{\Gamma \vdash d}{\Gamma, !c \vdash d} \qquad \frac{\Gamma, !c, !c \vdash d}{\Gamma, !c \vdash d} \qquad \frac{!\Gamma \vdash d}{!\Gamma \vdash !d}$$

Figure 3. Rules for the $1, \otimes, \exists, !$ fragment of the Intuitionistic Linear Logic (ILL). $fv(A)$ denotes the set of free variables of formula A. Γ, Δ denote set of formulas.

The Language of Processes. Similar to other ccp-based calculi, lcc, in addition to tell and ask agents, provides constructs for parallel composition, hidden of variables, non-deterministic choices and process definitions and calls.

Definition 2 (lcc agents [7]). *Agents in lcc are built from constraints in the underlying linear constraint system, following the syntax below.*

$$P, Q, ... ::= c \mid \forall \overline{x}(c \to P) \mid P \parallel Q \mid \exists x(P) \mid P + Q \mid p(\overline{x})$$

Tell Agent. Given a store d, the *tell* agent c adds c to d producing the new store $d \otimes c$.

Linear ask agent. Let d be the current store and θ be the substitution $[\overline{t}/\overline{x}]$ for some list of terms $\overline{t}$. If d entails $d' \otimes c\theta$ for some d' (i.e., $d \vdash d' \otimes c\theta$), the ask agent $\forall \overline{x}(c \to P)$ *consumes* $c\theta$ and executes $P\theta$ under the new store d'. If c (the *guard*) cannot be deduced from d, the ask agent blocks until more information is added to the store. If the sequence of variables $\overline{x}$ is empty then $\forall \overline{x}(c \to P)$ is written as $c \to P$.

Parallel Composition. $P \parallel Q$ stands for the interleaved parallel execution of agents P and Q, possibly communicating through shared variables in the store. Given a finite set of indexes $I = \{1, 2, ..., n\}$, instead of $P_1 \parallel P_2 \parallel ... \parallel P_n$, we write $\prod_{i \in I} P_i$.

Locality. The agent $\exists x(P)$ behaves like P and binds the variable x to be local to it.

Non-deterministic choice. The process $P_1 + ... + P_n$ non-deterministically chooses one P_i for execution whenever P_i can evolve (one-step guarded choice). The chosen alternative precludes the others. We assume here that each P_i is an ask agent. Hence, the agent $\sum_{i \in I} \forall \overline{x_i}(c_i \to P_i)$ evolves into $P_j[\overline{t_j}/\overline{x_j}]$ whenever the store entails $c_j[\overline{t_j}/\overline{x_j}]$ for some $j \in I$. Otherwise, the agent blocks until more information is added to the store.

Procedure Calls. Assume a process declaration:

$$p(\overline{x}) \stackrel{\Delta}{=} P$$

where all free variables of P are in the set of pairwise distinct variables $\overline{x}$. The agent $p(\overline{y})$ evolves into $P[\overline{y}/\overline{x}]$.

We assume that "$\otimes$" has a higher precedence than "$\to$", hence $c_1 \otimes c_2 \to c_1' \otimes c_2'$ should be read as $(c_1 \otimes c_2) \to (c_1' \otimes c_2')$. Furthermore, "!" has a tighter binding than $\otimes$ so we understand $!c_1 \otimes c_2$ as $(!c_1) \otimes c_2$. For the rest of the operators we shall explicitly use parenthesis to avoid confusions.

In the following example we show how lcc agents evolve. We shall use $\langle P, c\rangle \to \langle P', c'\rangle$ to denote that the agent P under store c evolves into the agent P' producing the store c'. The reader may refer to [7] for a complete account of the lcc operational semantics.

Example 2.1 (Consuming Permissions). *Let's assume that we have a constraint system with a ternary predicate* $\mathit{ref}(\cdot)$, *constant symbols* unq *and* shr *and equipped with the axiom:* $\Delta = \mathit{ref}(x, o, \mathit{unq}) \vdash \mathit{ref}(x, o, \mathit{shr})$. *Let's assume also a process* $R = P \parallel Q$ *such that*

$$P = \mathit{ref}(x, o, \mathit{unq})$$
$$Q = \forall y(\mathit{ref}(x, y, \mathit{shr}) \to Q')$$

From the initial store $\top$ *(true),* Q *cannot deduce its guard and it remains blocked. Hence,* P *evolves by executing the tell agents* $\mathit{ref}(x, o, \mathit{unq})$:

$$\langle R, \top\rangle \to \langle Q, \top \otimes \mathit{ref}(x, o, \mathit{unq})\rangle$$

Afterwards, the store $\top \otimes \mathit{ref}(x, o, \mathit{unq})$ *is strong enough to entail the guard of* Q *by using the axiom* Δ. *We thus observe the following transition:*

$$\langle Q, \top \otimes \mathit{ref}(x, o, \mathit{unq})\rangle \to \langle Q'[o/y], \top\rangle$$

Roughly speaking, P *adds to the store the information required to state that* x *points to* o *and has a unique permission to* o *(i.e.,* $\mathit{ref}(x, o, \mathit{unq})$*). By using* Δ*, from* $\mathit{ref}(x, o, \mathit{unq})$ *we can deduce* $\mathit{ref}(x, o, \mathit{shr})$*, i.e., the unique permission of* x *can be downgraded to a share permission on* o*. Thereafter,* Q consumes *this information, leading to the store* $\top$ *where the agent* $Q'[o/y]$ *is executed.* □

We finish this section by introducing the derived operator $P; Q$ that delays the execution of Q until the "end" of the execution of P. This will be useful for the model we present in the forthcoming sections. Let z, w, w' be variables that do not occur either in P or in Q and $\texttt{sync}(\cdot)$ be an uninterpreted predicate symbol. The process $P; Q$ can be defined as $\exists z(\mathcal{C}[\![P]\!]_z \parallel \mathtt{sync}(z) \rightarrow Q)$ where

$$\begin{array}{lcl}
\mathcal{C}[\![c]\!]_z & = & c \otimes \mathtt{sync}(z) \\
\mathcal{C}[\![\forall y(c \rightarrow P)]\!]_z & = & \forall y(c \rightarrow \mathcal{C}[\![P]\!]_z) \\
\mathcal{C}[\![P \parallel R]\!]_z & = & \exists w, w'(\mathcal{C}[\![P]\!]_w \parallel \mathcal{C}[\![R]\!]_{w'} \parallel \\
 & & \mathtt{sync}(w) \otimes \mathtt{sync}(w') \rightarrow \mathtt{sync}(z)) \\
\mathcal{C}[\![P + R]\!]_z & = & \mathcal{C}[\![P]\!]_z + \mathcal{C}[\![R]\!]_z \\
\mathcal{C}[\![\exists y(P)]\!]_z & = & \exists y(\mathcal{C}[\![P]\!]_z) \\
\mathcal{C}[\![p(\overline{x})]\!]_z & = & p(\overline{x}, z)
\end{array}$$

Intuitively $\mathcal{C}[\![P]\!]_z$ adds the constraint $\mathtt{sync}(z)$ when it terminates. Then, the ask agent $\mathtt{sync}(z) \rightarrow Q$ reduces to Q. Notice for example that in a parallel composition $P \parallel R$, we wait for both P and R to finish and then, the constraint $\mathtt{sync}(z)$ is emitted. As we shall see, we only use calls and process definitions when modeling aliasing of variables and Æminium constructs and methods declarations. Hence, in Section 3.2 we shall rewrite the signature of a process definition $p(\overline{y})$ as $p(\overline{y}, w) \stackrel{\Delta}{=} P$. Then, the call $p(\overline{x}, z)$ evolves into $P[\overline{x}/\overline{y}, z/w]$ that later adds the constraint $\mathtt{sync}(z)$ when needed to synchronize with the rest of the processes.

3. A LCC Interpretation of AP

Our `lcc` interpretation of access permissions in Æminium programs assumes a constraint system with the following axioms, predicate and constant symbols:

Permissions: We assume the set of constant symbols $\mathtt{PER} = \{\mathtt{unq}, \mathtt{shr}, \mathtt{imm}, \mathtt{none}\}$ in order to represent the permissions introduced in Section 2.1.

References and Fields: We use the predicate symbol $\mathtt{ref}(x, o, p)$ (x points to object o with permission $p \in \mathtt{PER}$), $\mathtt{field}(x, o, \mathit{field})$ (x points to $o.\mathit{field}$), $\mathtt{sync}(z)$ (synchronizing on variable z) and $\mathtt{ct}(o, n)$ (there are n references pointing to o). For the last constraint, we also assume the constant $\mathbf{0}$ (zero) and the successor function $s(\cdot)$. Furthermore, we assume the constants nil (null reference) and $\mathit{cname\_fname}$ for each field "fname" of class "cname".

Non-logical axioms: We assume the following axioms:

$$\begin{array}{lcl}
\mathtt{downgrade}_1 & : & \mathtt{ref}(x, o, \mathtt{unq}) \vdash \mathtt{ref}(x, o, \mathtt{shr}) \\
\mathtt{downgrade}_2 & : & \mathtt{ref}(x, o, \mathtt{unq}) \vdash \mathtt{ref}(x, o, \mathtt{imm}) \\
\mathtt{upgrade}_1 & : & \mathtt{ref}(x, o, \mathtt{shr}) \otimes \mathtt{ct}(o, s(\mathbf{0})) \\
 & & \vdash \mathtt{ref}(x, o, \mathtt{unq}) \otimes \mathtt{ct}(o, s(\mathbf{0})) \\
\mathtt{upgrade}_2 & : & \mathtt{ref}(x, o, \mathtt{imm}) \otimes \mathtt{ct}(o, s(\mathbf{0})) \\
 & & \vdash \mathtt{ref}(x, o, \mathtt{unq}) \otimes \mathtt{ct}(o, s(\mathbf{0}))
\end{array}$$

The axiom $\mathtt{downgrade}_1$ (resp. $\mathtt{downgrade}_2$) transforms a unique permission into a share (resp. immutable) permission. The axiom $\mathtt{upgrade}_1$ (resp. $\mathtt{upgrade}_2$) builds a unique permission from a share (resp. immutable) permission. Hence, to be able to upgrade a permission to unique, the reference x needs to be the unique reference with share or immutable permission to the pointed object o. Conversions from share permissions into immutable and vice versa require first to upgrade the permission to unique and then, apply the appropriate downgrade axiom.

3.1 Modeling Statements.

We interpret Æminium statements through the function $\mathcal{S}[\![s]\!]_z$ that given a statement s returns an `lcc` agent that synchronizes with the rest of the program by adding the constraint $\mathtt{sync}(z)$ to the store. We assume (by renaming variables if necessary) that z does not occur in s. In the following we define $\mathcal{S}[\![s]\!]_z$ for each type of statement in Figure 2.

Local variables in Æminium are defined as local agents in `lcc`. The local variable x points to nil with no permissions.

$$(\mathrm{R_{LOC}}) \quad \mathcal{S}[\![\mathtt{let}\ x\ \mathtt{in}\ s\ \mathtt{end}]\!]_z = \exists x(\mathtt{ref}(x, \mathit{nil}, \mathtt{none}); \mathcal{S}[\![s]\!]_z)$$

For the **assignment** $x := y$, we define the rule:

$$(\mathrm{R_{ALIAS}}) \quad \mathcal{S}[\![x := y]\!]_z = \mathtt{assg}(x, y, z)$$

where

$$\begin{array}{ll}
\mathtt{assg}(x, y, z) \stackrel{\Delta}{=} & \mathtt{drop}(x); \mathtt{gain}(x, y); \mathtt{sync}(z) \\
\mathtt{drop}(x) \quad \stackrel{\mathrm{def}}{=} & \forall o, n((\mathtt{ref}(x, \mathit{nil}, \mathtt{none}) \rightarrow \top) + \\
 & \sum_{p \in \mathtt{PER} \setminus \{\mathtt{none}\}} \mathtt{ref}(x, o, p) \otimes \mathtt{ct}(o, s(n)) \rightarrow \mathtt{ct}(o, n)) \\
\mathtt{gain}(x, y) \quad \stackrel{\mathrm{def}}{=} & \\
\multicolumn{2}{l}{\quad \mathtt{ref}(y, \mathit{nil}, \mathtt{none}) \rightarrow \mathtt{ref}(x, \mathit{nil}, \mathtt{none}) \otimes \mathtt{ref}(y, \mathit{nil}, \mathtt{none})} \\
\multicolumn{2}{l}{\quad + \ \forall o, n((\mathtt{ref}(y, o, \mathtt{unq}) \otimes \mathtt{ct}(o, s(\mathbf{0})) \rightarrow} \\
\multicolumn{2}{l}{\qquad \mathtt{ref}(y, o, \mathtt{shr}) \otimes \mathtt{ref}(x, o, \mathtt{shr}) \otimes \mathtt{ct}(o, s(s(\mathbf{0}))))} \\
\multicolumn{2}{l}{\qquad + (\mathtt{ref}(y, o, \mathtt{shr}) \otimes \mathtt{ct}(o, n) \rightarrow} \\
\multicolumn{2}{l}{\qquad \mathtt{ref}(y, o, \mathtt{shr}) \otimes \mathtt{ref}(x, o, \mathtt{shr}) \otimes \mathtt{ct}(o, s(n)))} \\
\multicolumn{2}{l}{\qquad + (\mathtt{ref}(y, o, \mathtt{imm}) \otimes \mathtt{ct}(o, n) \rightarrow} \\
\multicolumn{2}{l}{\qquad \mathtt{ref}(y, o, \mathtt{imm}) \otimes \mathtt{ref}(x, o, \mathtt{imm}) \otimes \mathtt{ct}(o, s(n)))}
\end{array}$$

Here, the variable x loses its permission to the pointed object o, and the object o has one less reference pointing to it (Definition $\mathtt{drop}$[1]). Thereafter, x and y point to the same object and the permission of y is split between x and y (Definition $\mathtt{gain}$) as follows: if y has a unique permission to o, this permission is split into two share permissions, one for x and one for y. If y has a share (resp. immutable) permission to o, then both x and y will have a share (resp. immutable) permission to o after the assignment. Recall that ask agents consume their guard when evolving. Therefore, we add back the permission for y in the right-hand side of the rule. Finally, once the permission to y is split, the constraint $\mathtt{sync}(z)$ is added to the store to synchronize with the rest of the program.

If the variable x points to the object o of class cname, then the field fname of o can be accessed by the variable u whenever $\mathtt{field}(u, o, \mathit{cname\_fname})$ holds. Intuitively, u points to $o.\mathit{fname}$ and then a constraint $\mathtt{ref}(u, o', p)$ enforces $o.\mathit{fname}$ to point to o' with permission p. As we shall show later, the model of constructors adds the constraint $!\mathtt{field}(u, o, \mathit{cname\_fname})$ to establish the connection between objects and their fields. The model of the assignment $\mathcal{S}[\![x.\mathit{fname} := y]\!]$ is thus obtained from that of $\mathcal{S}[\![u := y]\!]$:

$$\begin{array}{l}
(\mathrm{R_{ALIAS_F}}) \\
\mathcal{S}[\![x.f := y]\!]_z = \forall u, o, p(\ \mathtt{ref}(x, o, p) \otimes \mathtt{field}(u, o, \mathit{cname_f}) \\
\qquad \rightarrow (\mathtt{ref}(x, o, p); \mathcal{S}[\![u := y]\!]_z))
\end{array}$$

The models for the statements $\mathcal{S}[\![x.\mathit{fname} := y.\mathit{fname}]\!]_z$ and $\mathcal{S}[\![x := y.\mathit{fname}]\!]_z$ are similar and thus omitted.

For the **composition of statements** $\{s_1\ s_2\ ...\ s_n\}$, the agent modeling s_i runs in parallel with the other agents once the agent modeling the statement s_{i-1} adds the constraint $\mathtt{sync}(z_{i-1})$. After the execution of the statement s_n, the constraint $\mathtt{sync}(z)$ is added to the store to synchronize with the rest of the program.

$$\begin{array}{lcl}
\multicolumn{3}{l}{(\mathrm{R_{COMP}})} \\
\mathcal{S}[\![\{s_1\ ...\ s_i\ ...\ s_n\}]\!]_z & = & \exists z_1, ... z_n(\mathcal{S}[\![s_1]\!]_{z_1} \parallel \\
 & & \mathtt{sync}(z_1) \rightarrow \mathcal{S}[\![s_2]\!]_{z_2} \parallel ... \parallel \\
 & & \mathtt{sync}(z_{n-1}) \rightarrow \mathcal{S}[\![s_n]\!]_{z_n} \parallel \\
 & & \mathtt{sync}(z_n) \rightarrow \mathtt{sync}(z))
\end{array}$$

Method calls and **Object instantiation**. For the sake of simplicity, we write methods and constructors using functional nota-

[1] Definitions ($\stackrel{\mathrm{def}}{=}$) must be understood as shorthands.

tion rather than object-oriented notation. For instance, $x.meth(\overline{y})$ is written as $cname\_meth(x, \overline{y})$ when x is an object of type $cname$. Similarly, the expression x := new $cname(\overline{y})$ is written as $cname\_cname(x, \overline{y})$. As we shall see, for each method of the form $meth(x, \overline{y})$ in class $cname$, we shall generate a process definition $cname\_meth(x, \overline{y}, z) \triangleq P$. The Æminium statement $cname\_meth(x, \overline{y})$ is then modeled as the lcc call $cname\_meth(x, \overline{y}, z)$. This thus triggers the execution of the body of the method. Notice that we add the variable z as last parameter to be able to synchronize with the rest of the program.

$$(\text{R}_{\text{CALL}}) \quad \mathcal{S}[\![x.meth(\overline{y})]\!]_z \quad = \quad cname\_meth(x, y_1, .., y_n, z) \text{ if } x \text{ is of type } cname$$

The model of an object initialization is defined similarly:

$$(\text{R}_{\text{NEW}})\ \mathcal{S}[\![x := \texttt{new}\ cname(\overline{y})]\!]_z = cname\_cname(x, \overline{y}, z)$$

3.2 Modeling Class Definitions.

The model of method declarations and constructors is given by the function $\mathcal{D}[\![\cdot]\!]$. Hence, a **method definition** M_D of the class $cname$ of the form

$$meth(cname\ x, \overline{class_y\ y})\ p(x), \overline{p(y)} \Rightarrow p'(x), \overline{p'(y)}\ \{s\}$$

is modeled as a process definition:

$$(\text{R}_{\text{MDEF}})\ \mathcal{D}[\![M_D]\!] = cname\_meth(x, \overline{y}, z) \triangleq P_M$$

Recall that the first parameter x of the method represents the object caller this and the last parameter z is used for synchronization. The body of the definition P_M models the behavior of the method as follows:

$$P_M \stackrel{\text{def}}{=} \forall \overline{o}, o_t, \overline{n}, n_t(\texttt{consume}; \exists \overline{y'}, x'(\texttt{params}\ ; \texttt{sync}(z); P_B))$$

where $m = |\overline{y}|$ is the number of parameters of the method and $|\overline{o}| = |\overline{n}| = m$. The process P_M first consumes the required permissions from the parameters $\overline{y}$ and from the caller x. If the required permission is share or immutable, those permissions are restored to allow concurrent executions in the environment that called the method. Unique and none permissions are consumed to later be *transferred* to the body of the method:

$$\begin{array}{lll} \texttt{consume} & \stackrel{\text{def}}{=} & \prod_{i \in 1..m} \texttt{consume}_{y_i}; \texttt{consume}_x \\ \texttt{consume}_{y_i} & \stackrel{\text{def}}{=} & \texttt{ref}(y_i, o_i, p_i) \otimes \texttt{ct}(o_i, n_i) \rightarrow \\ & & \texttt{ref}(y_i, o_i, p_i) \otimes \texttt{ct}(o_i, s(n_i)) \text{ if } p_i \in \{\texttt{shr}, \texttt{imm}\} \\ \texttt{consume}_{y_i} & \stackrel{\text{def}}{=} & \texttt{ref}(y_i, o_i, p_i) \rightarrow \top \text{ if } p_i \in \{\texttt{unq}, \texttt{none}\} \end{array}$$

Definition $\texttt{consume}_x$ is similar to that of $\texttt{consume}_{y_i}$ but it considers the variable x, the object o_t and the permission p.

Once the permissions are consumed according to the signature of the method, the agent P_M creates local variables $\overline{y'}$ and x' to replace the formal parameters ($\overline{y}$) and the caller (x) by the actual parameters:

$$\texttt{params} \stackrel{\text{def}}{=} \texttt{ref}(x', o_t, p) \otimes \bigotimes_{i \in 1..m} \texttt{ref}(y'_i, o_i, p_i)$$

At this point, P_M adds $\texttt{sync}(z)$ to release the program control. Thereafter the body of the method can be executed. This is done by modeling the statement s as the agent P_B where $\widehat{s}$ denotes s after replacing y_i by y'_i and x by x':

$$P_B \stackrel{\text{def}}{=} \exists z'(\mathcal{S}[\![\widehat{s}]\!]_{z'}; \texttt{sync}(z') \rightarrow (\texttt{r\_env}(x : p, x' : p') \parallel \prod_{i \in 1..m} \texttt{r\_env}(y_i : p_i, y'_i : p'_i)))$$

Once the execution of s releases the control (i.e., it adds $\texttt{sync}(z')$ to the store), the references and permissions of the local variables created to handle the parameters are consumed and restored to the environment according to:

$$\begin{array}{l} \texttt{r\_env}(x : p, x' : p') \stackrel{\text{def}}{=} \forall o', n(\texttt{ref}(x', o', p') \otimes \texttt{ct}(o', s(n)) \rightarrow \\ \qquad\qquad \texttt{ct}(o', n)) \quad \text{if } p, p' \in \{\texttt{imm}, \texttt{shr}\} \\ \texttt{r\_env}(x : p, x' : p') \stackrel{\text{def}}{=} \forall o'(\texttt{ref}(x', o', p') \rightarrow \\ \qquad\qquad \texttt{ref}(x, o', p')) \quad \text{if } p \in \{\texttt{unq}, \texttt{none}\} \\ \texttt{r\_env}(x : p, x' : p') \stackrel{\text{def}}{=} \forall o, n, o'((\texttt{ref}(x, o, p) \otimes \texttt{ct}(o, s(n)) \rightarrow \\ \qquad\qquad \texttt{ct}(o, n)); \\ \qquad\qquad \texttt{ref}(x', o', p') \rightarrow \texttt{ref}(x, o', p')) \\ \qquad\qquad \text{if } p \in \{\texttt{shr}, \texttt{imm}\}, p' \in \{\texttt{unq}, \texttt{none}\} \end{array}$$

Let us give some intuition about the cases considered in the definitions above. Recall that consume *duplicates* the shr and imm permissions for the variables internal to the method. Then, we only need to consume such permissions and decrease the number of references pointing to object o'. As for unq and none as input permissions, consume *transfers* such permissions to the local variables and *consumes* the external references. Then, r_env needs to restore the external reference and consume the local one (the number of references pointing to o' remains the same). When the method changes the input permission from share or immutable into a unique or none, we need to *consume* first the external reference. Then, we *transfer* the internal permission and reference to the external variable.

A **constructor** C_D of the form

$$cname(cname\ x, \overline{class_y\ y})\ \texttt{none}(x), \overline{p(y)} \Rightarrow p'(x), \overline{p'(y)}\ \{s\}$$

is modeled similarly as a method definition:

$$(\text{R}_{\text{CDEF}})\mathcal{D}[\![\text{C}_\text{D}]\!] = cname(x, \overline{y}, z) \triangleq P_C$$

$$\begin{array}{l} P_C \stackrel{\text{def}}{=} \forall \overline{o}(\texttt{consume}'; \\ \quad \exists \overline{y'}, x', o_{new}(\texttt{params}'; \\ \quad\quad \exists \overline{u}(\texttt{fields-init}\ ; \\ \quad\quad\quad \exists z'(\mathcal{S}[\![\overline{s}]\!]_{z'}; \texttt{sync}(z') \rightarrow (\texttt{r\_env}(x : p, x' : p') \parallel \\ \quad\quad\quad\quad \prod_{i \in 1..m} \texttt{r\_env}(y_i : p_i, y'_i : p'_i))))) \\ \quad ; \texttt{sync}(z)) \end{array}$$

Here $\texttt{consume}'$ is similar to consume but with $o_t = nil$, i.e., x in x := new $cname(\overline{y})$ is restricted to be a null reference. Definition $\texttt{params}'$ is similar to params except that it considers $p = \texttt{unq}$, i.e. x' has a unique permission to o_{new}. Furthermore, $\texttt{params}'$ adds $\texttt{ct}(o_{new}, s(\mathbf{0}))$ to the store. Class fields are initialized to nil and the link between the variable u_i and the field $o_{new}.f_i$ is established:

$$\begin{array}{l} \texttt{fields-init} \stackrel{\text{def}}{=} \\ \quad !\texttt{field}(u_1, o_{new}, cname\_f_1) \otimes \texttt{ref}(u1, nil, \texttt{none}) \otimes ... \otimes \\ \quad !\texttt{field}(u_k, o_{new}, cname\_f_k) \otimes \texttt{ref}(u_k, nil, \texttt{none}) \end{array}$$

Finally, notice that the synchronization constraint $\texttt{sync}(z)$ is added only in the end of the rule since the constructor needs to be fully executed before returning the new reference.

The following example shows how the proposed model works.

Example 3.1 (Access Permission Flow)**.** *Assume the class definitions stats and collection in Figure 1 and the following main body written in functional notation.*

```
1  let collection c, stats s in
2    collection_collection(c);  //c := new collection()
3    stats_stats(s);  //s := new stats()
4    collection_compStats(c, s);  //c.compStats(s)
5    collection_removeDuplicates(c);  //c.rDup() end
```

The lcc *agent modeling the statement in line 2 performs the call* $collection\_collection(c, z_1)$*, which triggers the execution of the* *body of the constructor collection (see Rules* $\mathrm{R}_{\mathrm{CDEF}}$ *and* $\mathrm{R}_{\mathrm{CALL}}$ *). Variable* z_1 *is the local variable used to synchronize with the rest of the program (see Rule* $\mathrm{R}_{\mathrm{COMP}}$*). Once the agents modeling the statements in lines* 2 *and* 3 *are executed, the store below is observed.*

$$\exists c, s, o_c, o_s(\mathit{ref}(c, o_c, \mathit{unq}) \otimes \mathit{ref}(s, o_s, \mathit{unq}) \otimes \\ \mathtt{ct}(o_c, s(\mathbf{0})) \otimes \mathtt{ct}(o_s, s(\mathbf{0})))$$

Hence, c (resp. s) points to o_c *(resp.* o_s*) with a unique permission. Since collection_compStats*(c, s) *requires c to have an immutable permission to* o_c*, the axiom downgrade*$_1$ *is used to entail the guard of* **consume** *in the definition of the method (see Rule* $\mathrm{R}_{\mathrm{MDEF}}$*). Let* c' *be the representation of c inside the method (see* **params** *in Rule* $\mathrm{R}_{\mathrm{MDEF}}$*). We notice that when the body of the method is being executed, both c and* c' *have an immutable permission to* o_c*. Before executing the body of method compStats, the constraint* $\mathit{sync}(z_1)$ *is added so as to allow possibly concurrent executions in the main body. The agent modeling the statement in line* 5 *can be then executed. However, this call requires c to have a unique permission to* o_c *which is not possible since the axiom upgrade*$_1$ *requires that c is the sole reference to* o_c*. Hence, the guard* **consume** *for this call is delayed (synchronized) until the permission on* c' *is consumed and restored to the environment (see definition* **r_env***). We then observe that statements in lines* 4 *and* 5 *are executed sequentially due to the way permissions evolve.* □

3.3 The Model as a Runnable Specification

`ccp`-based models can be regarded as runnable specifications, and so we can observe how permissions evolve during program execution by running the underlying `lcc` model. We implemented an interpreter of `lcc` on top of the Mozart system (`http://www.mozart-oz.org/`). This interpreter uses records (Mozart data structures) to represent `lcc` linear constraints. The store was modeled as a multiset of records, and the entailment of constraints for universally quantified asks was implemented via record unification. On top of this interpreter, we implemented a parser that takes an Æminium program and generates the corresponding `lcc` agents. The `lcc` agent is then executed and a program trace is generated. The interpreter and the parser have been integrated into Alcove (Æminium Linear COnstraints VErifier) LCC Animator, a PHP application freely available at `http://escher.puj.edu.co/~caolarte/alcove/`. The URL further includes the examples presented in this section.

Example 3.2 (Trace of Access Permissions). *The program in Example 3.1 generates the following trace:*

```
[init(collection_collection [c1 z9])]
[running(collection_collection [c1 z9])]
[init(stats_stats [s2 z10])]
[running(stats_stats [s2 z10])]
[init(collection_compstats [c1 s2 z11])]
[running(collection_compstats [c1 s2 z11])]
[init(collection_removeduplicates [c1 z13])
 running(collection_compstats [c1 s2 z11])]
[running(collection_removeduplicates [c1 z13])]

c1(obj:ot16 objfields:none per:unq)
s2(obj:ot27 objfields:none per:unq)
```

Output `init(collection_collection [c1 z9])` *represents the call to a method (recall that parameter z is used for synchronization purposes). If a method is currently being executed, the constraint* `running(collection_collection [c1 z9])` *is present in the store. Notice that the execution of the method collection_removeduplicates is delayed until the end of the execution of collection_compstats (i.e., the store does not contain simultaneously both* `running(collection_compstats)` *and* `running(collection_removeduplicates))` *as explained in Example 3.1. The last two lines of the trace show that both c and s ends with a unique permission to objects* `ot16` *and* `ot27` *respectively* [2] □

Example 3.3 (Deadlock Detection). *Let us assume now the class definitions in Figure 1 and the following* `main`*:*

```
let collection c, stats s, stats svar in
  collection_collection(c); //c := new collection()
  stats_stats(s); //s := new stats()
  svar := s;
  collection_compStats(c, s); //c.compStats(s)
end
```

This code aliases svar and s after the assignment svar := s, so that they share the same permission afterwards. Therefore, s cannot recover the unique permission to execute the statement collection_compStats(c, s)*, thus leading to a permission deadlock. This bug is detected by Alcove:*

```
[init(collection_collection [c1 z10])]
[running(collection_collection [c1 z10])]
[init(stats_stats [s2 z11])]
[running(stats_stats [s2 z11])]
[init(collection_compstats [c1 s2 z14])]
c1(obj:ot17 objfields:none per:imm)
svar9(obj:ot28 objfields:none per:shr)
s2(obj:ot28 objfields:none per:shr)
Error: Permissions for collection_compstats(c1 s2 z14)
       could not be obtained.
```

We notice that in the trace above, the call to the method compstats is invoked (`init`*) but the method was not executed (*`running`*). Furthermore, both s and svar have a share permission on the pointed object.* □

4. Verification Techniques

Besides playing the role of executable specifications, `ccp`-based models can be declaratively interpreted as formulas in logic (see e.g., [17]). This section provides additional mechanisms and tools for verifying properties of access-permission based programs. More concretely, we take the `lcc` agents generated by the Alcove LCC Animator and translate them into a linear logic (LL) formula. Then, a property specified in LL is verified with the Alcove LL Prover, a bespoken theorem prover implemented on top of λ-Prolog [14] based on the prover described in [9].

4.1 Agents as Formulas

In `lcc`, processes are not only agents that evolve according to the rules of the underlying operational semantics, but also are formulas in linear logic [8]. The logical interpretation of `lcc` is defined with the aid of a function $\mathcal{L}[\![\cdot]\!]$ defined as [7]:

$$\begin{array}{lcl} \mathcal{L}[\![c]\!] & = & c \\ \mathcal{L}[\![p(\overline{x})]\!] & = & p(\overline{x}) \\ \mathcal{L}[\![P \parallel Q]\!] & = & \mathcal{L}[\![Q]\!] \otimes \mathcal{L}[\![P]\!] \\ \mathcal{L}[\![P + Q]\!] & = & \mathcal{L}[\![Q]\!] \& \mathcal{L}[\![P]\!] \\ \mathcal{L}[\![\forall \overline{x}(c \to P)]\!] & = & \forall \overline{x}(c \multimap \mathcal{L}[\![P]\!]) \\ \mathcal{L}[\![\exists x(P)]\!] & = & \exists x(\mathcal{L}[\![P]\!]). \end{array}$$

where $\&$ is the linear additive conjunction and $\multimap$ is the linear implication. The first step of our approach for the verification of programs consists in interpreting the `lcc` model in Section 3 as a LL formula according to function $\mathcal{L}[\![\cdot]\!]$. Furthermore, process definitions of the form $p(\overline{x}) \stackrel{\Delta}{=} P$ (i.e., assignment and constructor and method definitions) are transformed into a LL clause

[2] The numbers that follow the variable names are generated each time a local variable is created to avoid clash of names.

$\forall \overline{x}.p(\overline{x}) \multimap P$. We shall call these clauses *definition clauses* and they are stored together with the axioms of the constraint system (upgrade and downgrade):

$$
\begin{array}{l}
\mathtt{ref}(x, o, \mathtt{unq}) \multimap \mathtt{ref}(x, o, \mathtt{shr}).\\
\mathtt{ref}(x, o, \mathtt{unq}) \multimap \mathtt{ref}(x, o, \mathtt{imm}).\\
\mathtt{ref}(x, o, \mathtt{shr}) \otimes \mathtt{ct}(o, s(\mathbf{0})) \multimap \mathtt{ref}(x, o, \mathtt{unq}) \otimes \mathtt{ct}(o, s(\mathbf{0})).\\
\mathtt{ref}(x, o, \mathtt{imm}) \otimes \mathtt{ct}(o, s(\mathbf{0})) \multimap \mathtt{ref}(x, o, \mathtt{unq}) \otimes \mathtt{ct}(o, s(\mathbf{0})).
\end{array}
$$

into a theory Δ. Example 4.1 illustrates this translation. Observe that, in what follows, we present a simplified version of the translation where the empty synchronizations were omitted.

Example 4.1 (Agents as formulas). *Assume the program in Example 3.3. The predicate collection_collection(x, z) for the constructor is built from Rule* $\mathrm{R}_{\mathrm{CDEF}}$*, giving rise to the following (universally quantified) definition clause:*

$$
\begin{array}{l}
col\_collection(x,z) \multimap \exists w_1(ref(x, nil, none) \multimap sync(w_1)\otimes\\
\quad sync(w_1) \multimap \exists x', o_{new}, w_2(ref(x', o_{new}, unq) \otimes ct(o_{new}, s(\mathbf{0}))\otimes\\
\qquad\qquad sync(w_2) \quad \otimes\\
\qquad sync(w_2) \multimap \exists w_3 \forall o'(ref(x', o', unq) \multimap ref(x, o', unq)\otimes\\
\qquad\qquad sync(w_3) \quad \otimes\\
\qquad sync(w_3) \multimap sync(z))))).
\end{array}
$$

The interpretation for methods is obtained similarly by following the rule $\mathrm{R}_{\mathrm{MDEF}}$.

The assignment of variables is encoded by the predicate $assg(x, y, z)$ resulting from the translation of the Rule $\mathrm{R}_{\mathrm{ALIAS}}$*:*

$$
\begin{array}{l}
assg(x,y,z) \multimap\\
\exists z_1, z_2(\forall o, n((ref(x, o, none) \multimap \top \otimes sync(z_1)\&\\
\qquad ref(x, o, unq) \otimes ct(o, s(n)) \multimap ct(o, n) \otimes sync(z_1)\&\\
\qquad ref(x, o, shr) \otimes ct(o, s(n)) \multimap ct(o, n) \otimes sync(z_1)\&\\
\qquad ref(x, o, imm) \otimes ct(o, s(n)) \multimap ct(o, n) \otimes sync(z_1))\otimes\\
\\
\quad sync(z_1) \multimap ref(y, nil, none) \multimap\\
\qquad ref(x, nil, none) \otimes ref(y, nil, none) \otimes sync(z_2))\&\\
\qquad (\forall o, n(ref(y, o, unq) \otimes ct(o, s(\mathbf{0})) \multimap ref(y, o, shr)\otimes\\
\qquad ref(x, o, shr) \otimes ct(o, s(s(\mathbf{0}))) \otimes sync(z_2)\&\\
\qquad ref(y, o, shr) \otimes ct(o, n) \multimap ref(y, o, shr)\otimes\\
\qquad ref(x, o, shr) \otimes ct(o, s(n)) \otimes sync(z_2)\&\\
\qquad ref(y, o, imm) \otimes ct(o, n) \multimap ref(y, o, imm)\otimes\\
\qquad ref(x, o, imm) \otimes ct(o, s(n)) \otimes sync(z_2)))\otimes\\
\qquad sync(z_2) \multimap sync(z)).
\end{array}
$$

Hence, for this example, the theory Δ would contain the definition clauses for collection_collection, stats_stats, assig and collection_compStats, together with axioms for upgrading and downgrading permissions.

Let A be the `lcc` *agent related to the main program. Then,*

$$
\begin{array}{rl}
F = & \exists c, s, svar, z, z_1, z_2, z_3, z_4, z_5(ref(c, nil, none)\otimes\\
& ref(s, nil, none) \otimes ref(svar, nil, none) \otimes sync(z_1)\otimes\\
& \quad sync(z_1) \multimap collection\_collection(c, z_2)\otimes\\
& \quad sync(z_2) \multimap stats\_stats(s, z_3)\otimes\\
& \quad sync(z_3) \multimap assig(svar, s, z_4)\otimes\\
& \quad sync(z_4) \multimap collection\_compStats(c, s, z_5)\otimes\\
& sync(z_5) \multimap sync(z)).
\end{array}
$$

corresponds to $\mathcal{L}[\![A]\!]$ (see Rules $\mathrm{R}_{\mathrm{COMP}}$, $\mathrm{R}_{\mathrm{NEW}}$, $\mathrm{R}_{\mathrm{CALL}}$ *and* $\mathrm{R}_{\mathrm{ALIAS}}$ *in Section 3).* □

4.2 Linear Logic as a Framework for Verifying Access Permission Properties

Assume the translation $\mathcal{L}[\![A]\!]$ as described in Example 4.1, producing a theory Δ and a formula F. In order to verify a certain property $\mathcal{T}$, specified by a LL formula T, we test if the sequent $!\Delta, F \vdash T$ is provable. In this section, we will give an estimate of the complexity of finding such a proof.

First of all, observe that the fragment of ILL needed for encoding access permissions is given by the following grammar for guards G, processes P and properties T:

$$
\begin{array}{rcl}
G & := & A \mid G \otimes G\\
P & := & \forall x.G \multimap P \mid P \otimes P \mid \exists x.P \mid P \& P \mid\\
& & !(\forall \overline{x}.p(\overline{x}) \multimap P) \mid 1 \mid \top \mid !A \mid A\\
T & := & \exists x.T \mid G.
\end{array}
$$

where A is an atomic formula. Notice that this grammar is well defined, since the left context in the sequent $!\Delta, F \vdash T$ will be formed by P formulas, the right context will have only T formulas. Besides, implications on the left can only introduce guards on the right side of a sequent and $G \subset T$[3].

We note that classical and intuitionistic provability coincide for this fragment, since the right side of sequents are composed by existentially quantified Horn clauses.

The fragment described above is undecidable in general, due to the presence of processes declarations [13]. It turns out that Æminium applications dealt in the present paper are such that process declarations $p(\overline{x})$ do not have circular recursive calls. More precisely, in an Æminium program, there is no a sequence of methods or constructs of the form $m_1, m_2, \cdots m_n$ such that m_i calls m_{i+1} and m_n calls m_1. Hence, if a method m_1 calls m_2, we can syntactically expand the body of m_2 into the body of m_1. Therefore, it is straightforward to see that provability in the resulting LL translation is decidable (see Theorem 4.1). It is worth mentioning that the analyses presented here could be enhanced in order to deal with mutual recursive calls and some types of controlled recursion, as in [16] (see more in Section 5).

Complexity Analysis. We will show now how to measure the complexity of proofs in our system. It is worth noticing that Alcove LL Prover actually uses the proposed measure as a limit on the proof search.

For reasoning about complexity of proofs in LL we need to use a proof system for it where proof search can be controlled and measured. We thus move from ILL to the *focused classical* linear logic system in *one sided* sequent style (LLF) [12][4]. In a nutshell, moving into the *classical* setting means adding the connectives ? (exponential dual to !) and $\oplus, \parr$ (additive and multiplicative versions of the disjunction) together with their neutral elements, 0 and $\perp$ respectively. *One sided* means moving from sequents of the shape $!\Delta, F \vdash T$ into sequents of the form $\vdash ?\Delta^{\perp}, P^{\perp}, T$, where negation is a logical connective that has only atomic scope: if B is a general formula then $B^{\perp}$ denotes the result of moving negations inward until it has only atomic scope. We shall call *literal* an atomic formula or its negation. For convenience, the clause $B \multimap C$ will be represented by the formula $B^{\perp} \parr C$.

Intuitively, the *focusing* discipline organizes proofs into two alternating phases, called *negative* and *positive* phases. In the negative phase, all (invertible) rules over the connectives of *negative polarity* $(\forall, \parr, \&, ?, \perp, \top)$ are applied eagerly, while in the positive phase a formula of *positive* polarity $(\exists, \otimes, \oplus, !, 0, 1)$ is focused on and its positive subformulas are eagerly introduced.

Thus, on searching for proofs in focused systems, the only nondeterministic step is the one choosing the *positive formula* to focus on from the context. This determines completely the complexity of a proof in LLF and justifies the next definitions.

[3] On examining a proof bottom-up, decomposing the implication on the sequent $\Gamma_1, \Gamma_2, B \multimap C \vdash D$ will produce the premises $\Gamma_1, C \vdash D$ and $\Gamma_2 \vdash B$. Hence it is important to guarantee that B is a T formula.

[4] As already noted, provability in the fragment used here is the same in intuitionistic and classical settings.

Definition 3 (Proof Depth). *Let Π be a proof in LLF. The* depth *of Π is the maximum number of decisions over focused formulas along any path in Π from the root.*

Definition 4 (Degree of a positive formula). *The* degree *of a positive formula is the maximum number of nested alternating polarities in it.*

The next lemma shows the relation between depth of derivations in LLF and degree of a formula. The proof is discharged by structural induction.

Lemma 4.1. *Decomposing a focused positive formula F of degree n into its literal or purely positive subformulas gives rise to a derivation of depth $\lceil \frac{n}{2} \rceil$.*

Example 4.2 (Degree of a formula). *Consider the negation of the definition clause for $collection\_collection(x, z)$ in Example 4.1:*

$$col\_collection(x, z) \otimes \forall w_1(\texttt{ref}(x, nil, \texttt{none}) \otimes \texttt{sync}(w_1)^{\perp} \parr \texttt{sync}(w_1) \otimes \forall x', o_{new}, w_2(\texttt{ref}(x', o_{new}, \texttt{unq})^{\perp} \parr \texttt{ct}(o_{new}, s(\mathbf{0}))^{\perp} \parr \texttt{sync}(w_2)^{\perp} \parr \texttt{sync}(w_2) \otimes \forall w_3 \exists o'(\texttt{ref}(x', o', \texttt{unq}) \otimes \texttt{ref}(x, o', \texttt{unq})^{\perp} \parr \texttt{sync}(w_3)^{\perp} \parr \texttt{sync}(w_3) \otimes \texttt{sync}(z)^{\perp})))).$$

The degree of such a formula is 10. *Hence the depth of decomposing the formula above into its literal or purely positive subformulas is* $10/2 = 5$. □

We will now proceed with a careful complexity analysis of all the formulas produced by the specification of Æminium programs. The calculation of the complexity is done by counting the changes of nested polarities, which are produced mostly by synchronizations.

- If $cname\_method(x, \overline{y}, z) \multimap P$ is a definition clause (DC) in Δ, its negation $cname\_method(x, \overline{y}, z) \otimes P^{\perp}$ is a positive formula of degree at most $11 + n + m$ where m is the length of $\overline{y}$ and n is the degree of the formula encoding the body of the constructor, i.e., $\mathcal{S}[\![\widehat{s}]\!]_{z'}^{\perp}$.
- If $cname(x, \overline{y}, z) \multimap P$ is a DC in Δ, its negation is a positive formula of degree at most $12 + n + m$ where m is the length of $\overline{y}$ and n is the degree of $\mathcal{S}[\![\widehat{s}]\!]_{z'}^{\perp}$.
- If $\texttt{assig}(y, x, z) \multimap P$ is a DC in Δ, its negation is a positive formula of degree at most 5.
- For any formula F interpreting an Æminium main program with n statement calls, $F^{\perp}$ is a negative formula whose biggest positive subformula has degree at most $(2n + 1) + m$ where m is the sum of the degrees of all negated definition clauses corresponding to the statement calls in F.
- The negated upgrade (resp. downgrade) axiom is a positive formula of degree 1 (resp. degree 0).

The next theorem determines the complexity of the provability of sequents given by specification of Æminium programs.

Theorem 4.1 (Complexity). *Let Δ be a theory containing the definition clauses for method and constructor definitions, the definition of* $\texttt{assig}$ *and the upgrade and downgrade axioms. Let F be the formula interpreting the main program and T a formula interpreting a property to be proven. It is decidable whether or not the sequent $\vdash\ ?\Delta^{\perp}, F^{\perp}, T$ is provable. In fact, if such a sequent is provable, then its proof is bounded in LLF by the depth $\lceil \frac{k}{2} \rceil$ where $k =$ degree $F^{\perp}$.*

Proof. As noted before, as there are no circular recursive definitions, we may assume that the heads of definition clauses in Δ do not contain calls for other statements, i.e., the code of such calls can be directly written as part of the head. Hence, focusing over definition clauses is completely determined by the calls in $F^{\perp}$. Due to the synchronization procedure, proving a sequent in Æminium is equivalent to decompose its formulas completely. Therefore, the complexity of the proof of the sequent $\vdash\ ?\Delta^{\perp}, F^{\perp}, T$ is completely determined by the degree of $F^{\perp}$ since T is a purely positive formula, hence having degree 0. □

In the following, we explain our verification technique for three properties.

Deadlock Detection. Consider Example 3.3. We already showed that this code leads to a deadlock since the variable s cannot upgrade its unique permission to execute $collection\_compStats(c, s)$. We are then interested in providing a proof to the programmer showing that the code leads to a deadlock. For doing this, let Def be the definition of the method $collection\_compStats$ and the constructor $collection\_collection$, st be the statement in the `main` program and A be the `lcc` agent $A = \exists z(\mathcal{D}[\![Def]\!] \parallel (\mathcal{S}[\![st]\!]_z \parallel \texttt{sync}(z) \rightarrow \texttt{ok}))$. This agent adds the constraint `ok` only when the process $\mathcal{S}[\![st]\!]_z$ adds $\texttt{sync}(z)$. According to the definition of $\mathcal{S}[\![\cdot]\!]$ and $\mathcal{D}[\![\cdot]\!]$, this happens only when the call $collection\_compStats(c, s)$ is able to successfully consume the permissions required for the method (see Rule R_{MDEF}). The translation $\mathcal{L}[\![A]\!]$ will give rise to the theory Δ and the formula F described in Example 4.1. Let $F' = F \otimes \texttt{sync}(z) \multimap \texttt{ok}$. The verification technique consists in showing that the sequent $!\Delta, F' \vdash \texttt{ok}$ is not provable. This verification is done automatically by using Alcove-Prover, a theorem prover for LLF developed in λ-Prolog and integrated to the tool described in Section 3.3. Basically, we look for proofs with depth less or equal to 19, given by the depth of F'. If the prover fails, that means there is no proof for the sequent above.

The URL of the Alcove tool includes the output of the theorem prover and the `lcc` interpreter for this example. It is worth noticing that the `lcc` interpreter only computes a possible trace of the program while the theorem prover gives a guarantee that a certain property is verified or not by the program. The use of "animators" and provers is complementary. Existing formal models for system construction, such as the *Rodin* ([1]) tool for the event B modeling language, usually include both. The idea is that by using the animator the user gain a global understanding of the behavior of the program before attempting the proof of more precise desirable properties. This usually avoids frustrations in trying to figure out corrections of the model to discharge unproved properties.

Concurrency Analysis. Assume now the Example in Figure 1. For the method $collection\_print$ assume that we define $\mathcal{D}'[\![\cdot]\!]$ as $\mathcal{D}[\![\cdot]\!]$ but replacing $\texttt{sync}(z)$ with "$\texttt{sync}(z); \texttt{begin}_{print}(z)$" and adding "$; \texttt{begin}_{print}(z) \rightarrow \texttt{end}_{print}(z)$" in Rule R_{MDEF}. Similarly for method $collection\_compStats$. This will allow us to specify when a method starts its execution and when it terminates.

Let $A = \exists z(\mathcal{D}'[\![Def]\!] \parallel \mathcal{S}[\![st]\!]_z)$ where st corresponds to the main method. One can prove the linear logic sequent

$$\mathcal{L}[\![A]\!] \vdash \exists z_1, z_2(\texttt{begin}_{print}(z_1) \otimes \texttt{begin}_{compStats}(z_2)) \otimes \top$$

The provability of such a sequent means that the statements $collection\_print(c)$ and $collection\_compStats(c, s)$ may be executed in parallel.

Verifying a Method Specification Finally, assume that we add the field "a" in class $collection$ and the method:

$$m1()\ \texttt{unq(this)} \Rightarrow \texttt{unq(this)}\ \{\texttt{this}.a := \texttt{this}\}$$

Assume also that $m1$ is called in the main body. The signature of $m1$ requires that the unique permission to the caller must be restored to the environment. Nevertheless, the implementation of the method splits the unique permission into a share permissions for the field a and another for the caller (Rule $\mathrm{R_{ALIAS}}$). Then, the axiom $upgrade_1$ cannot be used to recover the unique permission and the ask agent in definition `r_env` remains blocked. An analysis similar to that of deadlocks will warn the programmer about this.

5. Concluding Remarks

We presented an approach to verify programs annotated with access-permissions. We use `lcc` to verify properties related to concurrency. Hence, program statements are modeled as `lcc` agents that faithfully represent statement permissions flow. The declarative reading of `lcc` agents as formulae in Linear Logic permits the use of theorem provers to verify properties such as deadlocks, the ability to run in parallel, and whether programs are correct with respect to access permission specifications. Central to our verification approach is the synchronization mechanism based on constraints and the logical interpretation of `lcc`. Ours is certainly a novel application for `ccp` that opens a new window for the automatic verification of (object-oriented) concurrent programs.

We automated our verification approach as the Alcove tool that implements a simulator and a prover. The simulator serves to *animate* a program by observing the evolution of its permissions. The simulator issues a message if a program blocks. It is therefore a useful companion for a verifier. A good strategy for understanding the behavior of a concurrent program is to run the simulator first to observe the global program behavior and then to run the prover to verify additional properties. We used the Alcove tool to verify the examples presented in this paper and also to verify properties about ordering of method invocations for a critical zone management system (see Appendix A). The reader can find these and other examples at the Alcove tool web-site.

Related and Future work. `ccp`-based calculi have been extensively used to reason about concurrent systems. The work in [10] proposes a timed-`ccp` model for role-based access control in distributed systems. The authors combine constraint reasoning and temporal logic model-checking to reason about when a resource (e.g. a directory in a file system) can be accessed.

Languages like Æminium [18] and Plaid [19] offer a series of guarantees such as (1) absence of AP usage protocol violation at run time; (2) when a program has deterministic results and (3) whether programs are free of race conditions on the abstract state of the objects [3, 4]. Our verification technique is complementary to those works since we have shown that well-typed programs (i.e., they follow the usage protocol of AP) can lead to a blockage.

The constraint system we propose to model the downgrade and upgrade of axioms was inspired by the work of *fractional* permissions in [4] (see also [3]). *Fractional* in this setting means that an AP can be split into several more *relaxed* permissions and then joined back to form a more *restrictive* permission. For instance, a unique permission can be split into two share permissions of weight $k/2$. Therefore, to recover a unique permission, it is necessary to have two $k/2$-share permissions. The constraint system described in this paper keeps explicitly the information about the fractions by means of the predicate $\mathtt{ct}(\cdot)$.

Chalice [11] is a program verifier for OO concurrent programs that uses permissions to control memory accesses. Unlike Æminium and Plaid, concurrency in Chalice is explicitly stated by the user by means of execution threads.

AP annotations in concurrent-by-default OO languages can be enhanced with the notion of *typestates* [2, 3]. Typestates describe abstract states in the form of state-machines, thus defining a usage protocol (or *contract*) of objects. For instance, consider the class *File* with states `opened` and `closed`. The signature of the method *open* can be specified as the agent $\mathtt{unq(this)} \otimes \mathtt{closed(this)} \rightarrow \mathtt{unq(this)} \otimes \mathtt{opened(this)}$. The general idea is to verify whether a program follows correctly the usage protocol defined by the class. For example, calling the method $read$ on a `closed` file leads to an error. Typestates then impose certain order in which methods can be called. The approach our paper defines can be straightforwardly extended to deal with typestates annotations, thus widening its applicability.

The work in [18] and [15] define more specific systems and rules for access permissions to deal respectively with *group permissions* and *borrowing permissions*. A group permission represents an abstract collection of objects and allows programmers to define containers that share the same permissions to an object. The approach of borrowing permissions aims at dealing more effectively with local variable aliasing, and how permissions flow from the environment to method formal parameters. Considering these systems in Alcove amounts to refine our model of permissions in Section 3. Verification techniques should remain the same.

We intend to relax the restriction about recursion imposed on Æminium programs for obtaining a decidable analysis. More precisely, we plan to translate more involving AP based programs with controlled recursion. This can be done by finding systems with a stratified set of definition clauses, hence allowing well formed recursion in the processes declarations. This shall allow us to take into account constructors like *iterators* in the source program.

Finally, we plan to undertake a case study on the verification of a commercial multi-task threaded application that has been used for massively parallelising computational tasks [6].

Acknowledgments

This work has been partially supported by grant 1251-521-28471 from Colciencias. The work of E. Pimentel and C. Olarte has been partially carried out during their visit to the Equipe Comète, at LIX (Ecole Polytechnique). Their visits have been supported resp. by Digiteo and DGAR funds for visitors. The work of N. Cataño has been supported by the Portuguese Research Agency FCT through the CMU-Portugal program, R&D Project Aeminium, CMU-PT/SE/0038/2008.

References

[1] J.-R. Abrial, M. J. Butler, S. Hallerstede, T. S. Hoang, F. Mehta, and L. Voisin. Rodin: an open toolset for modelling and reasoning in event-b. *STTT*, 12(6):447–466, 2010.

[2] N. E. Beckman, K. Bierhoff, and J. Aldrich. Verifying correct usage of atomic blocks and typestate. In G. E. Harris, editor, *OOPSLA*, pages 227–244. ACM, 2008.

[3] K. Bierhoff and J. Aldrich. Modular typestate checking of aliased objects. In R. P. Gabriel, D. F. Bacon, C. V. Lopes, and G. L. S. Jr., editors, *OOPSLA*, pages 301–320. ACM, 2007.

[4] J. Boyland. Checking interference with fractional permissions. In R. Cousot, editor, *SAS*, volume 2694 of *Lecture Notes in Computer Science*, pages 55–72. Springer, 2003.

[5] J. Boyland, J. Noble, and W. Retert. Capabilities for sharing: A generalisation of uniqueness and read-only. In J. L. Knudsen, editor, *ECOOP*, volume 2072 of *Lecture Notes in Computer Science*, pages 2–27. Springer, 2001.

[6] N. Cataño and I. Ahmed. Lightweight verification of a multi-task threaded server: A case study with the plural tool. In G. Salaün and B. Schätz, editors, *FMICS*, volume 6959 of *Lecture Notes in Computer Science*, pages 6–20. Springer, 2011.

[7] F. Fages, P. Ruet, and S. Soliman. Linear concurrent constraint programming: Operational and phase semantics. *Inf. Comput.*, 165(1): 14–41, 2001.

[8] J.-Y. Girard. Linear logic. *Theor. Comput. Sci.*, 50:1–102, 1987.

[9] J. S. Hodas and D. Miller. Logic programming in a fragment of intuitionistic linear logic. *Inf. Comput.*, 110(2):327–365, 1994.

[10] R. Jagadeesan, W. Marrero, C. Pitcher, and V. A. Saraswat. Timed constraint programming: a declarative approach to usage control. In P. Barahona and A. P. Felty, editors, *PPDP*, pages 164–175. ACM, 2005.

[11] K. R. M. Leino. Verifying concurrent programs with Chalice. In G. Barthe and M. V. Hermenegildo, editors, *VMCAI*, volume 5944 of *Lecture Notes in Computer Science*, page 2. Springer, 2010.

[12] C. Liang and D. Miller. A focused approach to combining logics. *Ann. Pure Appl. Logic*, 162(9):679–697, 2011.

[13] P. Lincoln, J. C. Mitchell, A. Scedrov, and N. Shankar. Decision problems for propositional linear logic. *Ann. Pure Appl. Logic*, 56 (1-3):239–311, 1992.

[14] D. Miller and G. Nadathur. *Programming with Higher-Order Logic*. Cambridge University Press, 2012.

[15] K. Naden, R. Bocchino, J. Aldrich, and K. Bierhoff. A type system for borrowing permissions. In J. Field and M. Hicks, editors, *POPL*, pages 557–570. ACM, 2012.

[16] E. Pimentel and D. Miller. On the specification of sequent systems. In G. Sutcliffe and A. Voronkov, editors, *LPAR*, volume 3835 of *Lecture Notes in Computer Science*, pages 352–366. Springer, 2005.

[17] V. A. Saraswat, M. C. Rinard, and P. Panangaden. Semantic foundations of concurrent constraint programming. In D. S. Wise, editor, *POPL*, pages 333–352. ACM Press, 1991.

[18] S. Stork, P. Marques, and J. Aldrich. Concurrency by default: using permissions to express dataflow in stateful programs. In S. Arora and G. T. Leavens, editors, *OOPSLA Companion*, pages 933–940. ACM, 2009.

[19] J. Sunshine, K. Naden, S. Stork, J. Aldrich, and É. Tanter. First-class state change in plaid. In C. V. Lopes and K. Fisher, editors, *OOPSLA*, pages 713–732. ACM, 2011.

A. Critical Zone Management System

Assume the class definitions for a critical zone management system in Figure 4. There are three classes, `lock`, `process` and `cs`. Each critical section has a private lock managed by an object of the class `cs`. When a process wants to enter a critical section, it tries first to invoke method `acq` of the `cs` manager. If successful, the process obtains a lock (i.e. an object of class `lock`) that it uses then to enter the critical zone. When the process wants to leave the critical zone, it invokes the method `release`. This releases ownership of the critical section lock.

Method `acq` has three parameters: `this`, the `cs` manager, `b` the process wanting to enter the critical zone and `l`, a field of `b` that will hold the lock of the `cs` supplied by the manager. Since `this` has unique permission, only one reference to the manager object can exist for `acq` to be invoked. The body of method `acq` stores the lock in `l` and a reference to the manager in field `s1` or `s2` of `b`, depending on whether the lock for `cs1` or for `cs2` is requested. Storing this reference to the manager implies that it can no longer have unique permission, so the output permission for `this` becomes shared. Moreover, `l` holds now the only reference to the private lock of the manager, so its output permission becomes unique. The effect is that field `lock1` or `lock2` of object `b` uniquely acquires the section lock. The method `enter` requires a unique permission on the lock. This ensures that only one process has a reference to the lock at any given time when entering the critical section. Method `release` restores conditions as they were before invocation to `acq`, i.e. the manager regains the unique permission and stores a unique reference to its private lock. Process fields loose the lock and the reference to the manager.

Assume now the following main code:

```
class lock {
  lock() none(this) => unq(this) {};
  enter(b) unq(this), shr(b) => unq(this), shr(b){} }
class process{
  attrs  lock lock1,  lock lock2, cs cs1, cs cs2;
  process() none(this) => unq(this) {} }
class cs {
  attrs  lock mylock;
  cs() none(this) => unq(this) {
     this.mylock := new lock()};
     acq1(process b, lock l) unq(this), shr(b), none(l)
                    => shr(this),shr(b),unq(l) {
        l := this.mylock;
        b.cs1 := this;
        this.mylock := null };
  acq2(process b, lock l) unq(this), shr(b), none(l)
                    => shr(this),shr(b),unq(l){
        l := this.mylock;
        b.cs2 := this;
        this.mylock := null  };
  release1(lock a, process b) shr(this),unq(a),shr(b)
              =>unq(this),none(a),shr(b){
        this.mylock := a;
        b.cs1 := null;
        a := null };
 release2(lock a, process b) shr(this),unq(a),shr(b)
                 => unq(this),none(a),shr(b)   {
        this.mylock := a;
        b.cs2 := null;
        a := null } }
```

Figure 4. Class definitions for a critical zone management system.

```
main () {   let cs x, cs w, process y, process z in
     x:= new cs(); w := new cs();
     y := new process(); z := new process();
     x.acq1(y, y.lock1); y.lock1.enter(y);
     w.acq2(z, z.lock2); z.lock2.enter(z) ;
     x.acq1(z, z.lock1); z.lock1.enter(z);
     w.acq2(y, y.lock2); y.lock2.enter(y); }
```

where there are two section manager objects, `x` for `cs1` and `w` for `cs2`. There are also two processes, `y` and `z`. Consider the situation where `y` acquires the lock from `x` (i.e. for `cs1`) by invoking the method `acq1(x, y, y.lock1)` and enters `cs1`. Then `z` acquires the lock from `w` (i.e. for `cs2`) by invoking `acq2(w, z, z.lock2)` and enters `cs2`. Now, `z` tries to acquire the lock from `x` by invoking `acq1(x,z, z.lock1)`, but this is not possible because `x` has no longer unique permission and execution blocks. The output of Alcove for this program is:

```
Error: The end of the program could not be reached.
Error: The perm. for cs_acq1( x1 z12 __f__lock1121 z24 )
    could not be obtained.
```

Consider now the program where processes leave the critical section before attempting to acquire another lock:

```
main () {   let cs x, cs w, process y, process z in
     x:= new cs(); w := new cs();
     y := new process(); z := new process();
     x.acq1(y, y.lock1); y.lock1.enter(y);
     w.acq2(z, z.lock2); z.lock2.enter(z) ;
     x.release1(y.lock1, y);
     x.acq1(z, z.lock1); z.lock1.enter(z);
     w.release2(z.lock2, z);
     w.acq2(y, y.lock2); y.lock2.enter(y);
     x.release1(z.lock1, z);  w.release2(y.lock2, y); }
```

In this case, all invocations run without blockage and Alcove successfully finishes the analysis.

Author Index

www.ingramcontent.com/pod-product-compliance
Lightning Source LLC
Chambersburg PA
CBHW061415210326
41598CB00035B/6220
* 9 7 8 1 4 5 0 3 1 5 2 2 7 *